New Perspectives on

MICROSOFT OFFICE 2000

Brief

JUNE JAMRICH PARSONS

DAN OJA

ROY AGELOFF
University of Rhode Island

BEVERLY B. ZIMMERMAN
Brigham Young University

S. SCOTT ZIMMERMAN
Brigham Young University

JOSEPH J. ADAMSKI
Grand Valley State University

KATHLEEN T. FINNEGAN

ANN SHAFFER

ROBIN ROMER

25 THOMSON PLACE, BOSTON, MA 02210

Australia • Canada • Mexico • Singapore • Spain • United Kingdom • United States

New Perspectives on Microsoft® Office 2000—Brief is published by Course Technology.

Managing Editor	Greg Donald
Senior Editor	Donna Gridley
Senior Product Manager	Rachel A. Crapser
Product Manager	Catherine V. Donaldson
Associate Product Manager	Melissa Dezotell
Editorial Assistant	Jill M. Kirn
Developmental Editors	Ann Shaffer, Jessica Evans, Terry Ann Kremer, Joan Kalkut, Mary Kemper, Dan Seiter
Production Editor	Jennifer Goguen
Cover Designer	Meral Dabcovich
Text Designer	Douglas Goodman

© 2001 by Course Technology, a division of Thomson Learning

For more information contact:

Course Technology
25 Thomson Place
Boston, MA 02210
Or find us on the World Wide Web at: http://www.course.com

For permission to use material from this text or product, contact us by

- Web: www.thomsonrights.com
- WebPhone: 1-800-730-2214
- WebFax: 1-800-730-2215

All rights reserved. This publication is protected by federal copyright law. No part of this publication may be reproduced, stored in a retrieval system, or transmitted in any form or by any means, electronic, mechanical, photocopying, recording, or otherwise, or be used to make a derivative work (such as translation or adaptation), without prior permission in writing from Course Technology.

Trademarks

Course Technology and the Open Book logo are registered trademarks and CourseKits is a trademark of Course Technology. Custom Edition is a registered trademark of Thomson Learning.

The Thomson Learning logo is a registered trademark used herein under license.

Some of the product names and company names used in this book have been used for identification purposes only and may be trademarks or registered trademarks of their respective manufacturers and sellers.

Disclaimer

Course Technology reserves the right to revise this publication and make changes from time to time in its content without notice.

ISBN 0-619-02000-8

Printed in the United States of America

1 2 3 4 5 6 7 8 9 10 BM 05 04 03 02 01

PREFACE
The New Perspectives Series

About New Perspectives
Course Technology's **New Perspectives Series** is an integrated system of instruction that combines text and technology products to teach computer concepts, the Internet, and microcomputer applications. Users consistently praise this series for innovative pedagogy, use of interactive technology, creativity, accuracy, and supportive and engaging style.

How is the New Perspectives Series different from other series?
The New Perspectives Series distinguishes itself by **innovative technology**, from the renowned Course Labs to the state-of-the-art multimedia that is integrated with our Concepts texts. Other distinguishing features include **sound instructional design**, **proven pedagogy**, and **consistent quality**. Each tutorial has students learn features in the context of solving a realistic case problem rather than simply learning a laundry list of features. With the **New Perspectives Series**, instructors report that students have a complete, integrative learning experience that stays with them. They credit this high retention and competency to the fact that this series incorporates critical thinking and problem-solving with computer skills mastery. In addition, we work hard to ensure accuracy by using a multi-step quality assurance process during all stages of development. Instructors focus on teaching and students spend more time learning.

Choose the coverage that's right for you
New Perspectives applications books are available in the following categories:

Brief
2-4 tutorials

Brief: approximately 150 pages long, two to four "Level I" tutorials, teaches basic application skills.

Introductory
6 or 7 tutorials, or Brief + 2 or 3 more tutorials

Introductory: approximately 300 pages long, four to seven tutorials, goes beyond the basic skills. These books often build out of the Brief book, adding two or three additional "Level II" tutorials.

Comprehensive
Introductory + 4 or 5 more tutorials. Includes Brief Windows tutorials and Additional Cases

Comprehensive: approximately 600 pages long, eight to twelve tutorials, all tutorials included in the Introductory text plus higher-level "Level III" topics. Also includes two Windows tutorials and three or four fully developed Additional Cases.

Advanced
Quick Review of basics + in-depth, high-level coverage

Advanced: approximately 600 pages long, cover topics similar to those in the Comprehensive books, but offer the highest-level coverage in the series. Advanced books assume students already know the basics, and therefore go into more depth at a more accelerated rate than the Comprehensive titles. Advanced books are ideal for a second, more technical course.

Office: approximately 800 pages long, covers all components of the Office suite as well as integrating the individual software packages with one another and the Internet.

Custom Books The New Perspectives Series offers you two ways to customize a New Perspectives text to fit your course exactly: *CourseKits*™ are two or more texts shrink-wrapped together, and offer significant price discounts. *Custom Editions*® offer you flexibility in designing your concepts, Internet, and applications courses. You can build your own book by ordering a combination of topics bound together to cover only the subjects you want. There is no minimum order, and books are spiral bound. Contact your Course Technology sales representative for more information.

What course is this book appropriate for?

New Perspectives on Microsoft Office 2000—Brief can be used in any course in which you want students to learn some of the most important topics of Office 2000, including Word, Excel, Access, PowerPoint, Windows 98, and Outlook. This book is recommended for a course in which you want students to learn the basics of all the core Office 2000 applications, as well as the e-mail capabilities of Outlook 2000. This book assumes no prior computer experience.

Proven Pedagogy

Tutorial Case Each tutorial begins with a problem presented in a case that is meaningful to students. The case turns the task of learning how to use an application into a problem-solving process.

45-minute Sessions. Each tutorial is divided into sessions that can be completed in about 45 minutes to an hour. Sessions allow instructors to more accurately allocate time in their syllabus, and students to better manage their own study time.

Step-by-Step Methodology We make sure students can differentiate between what they are to *do* and what they are to *read*. Through numbered steps – clearly identified by a gray shaded background – students are constantly guided in solving the case problem. In addition, the numerous screen shots with callouts direct students' attention to what they should look at on the screen.

TROUBLE? Paragraphs These paragraphs anticipate the mistakes or problems that students may have and help them continue with the tutorial.

"Read This Before You Begin" Page Located opposite the first tutorial's opening page for each level of the text, the Read This Before You Begin Page helps introduce technology into the classroom. Technical considerations and assumptions about software are listed to save time and eliminate unnecessary aggravation. Notes about the Student Disks help instructors and students get the right files in the right places, so students get started on the right foot.

Quick Check Questions Each session concludes with meaningful, conceptual Quick Check questions that test students' understanding of what they learned in the session. Answers to the Quick Check questions are provided at the end of each tutorial.

Reference Windows Reference Windows are succinct summaries of the most important tasks covered in a tutorial and they preview actions students will perform in the steps to follow.

Task Reference Located as a table at the end of the book, the Task Reference contains a summary of how to perform common tasks using the most efficient method, as well as references to pages where the task is discussed in more detail.

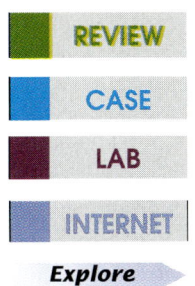

End-of-Tutorial Review Assignments, Case Problems, and Lab Assignments Review Assignments provide students with additional hands-on practice of the skills they learned in the tutorial using the same case presented in the tutorial. These Assignments are followed by three to four Case Problems that have approximately the same scope as the tutorial case but use a different scenario. In addition, some of the Review Assignments or Case Problems may include Exploration Exercises that challenge students encourage them to explore the capabilities of the program they are using, and/or further extend their knowledge. Finally, if a Course Lab accompanies a tutorial, Lab Assignments are included after the Case Problems.

File Finder Chart This chart, located in the back of the book, visually explains how a student should set up their data disk, what files should go in what folders, and what they'll be saving the files as in the course of their work.

The New Perspectives Supplements Package

Electronic Instructor's Manual. Our Instructor's Manuals include tutorial overviews and outlines, technical notes, lecture notes, solutions, and Extra Case Problems. Many instructors use the Extra Case Problems for performance-based exams or extra credit projects. The Instructor's Manual is available as an electronic file, which you can get from the Instructor Resource Kit (IRK) CD-ROM or download it from www.course.com.

Data Files Data Files contain all of the data that students will use to complete the tutorials, Review Assignments, and Case Problems. A Readme file includes instructions for using the files. See the "Read This Before You Begin" page/pages for more information on Student Files.

Solution Files Solution Files contain every file students are asked to create or modify in the tutorials, Tutorial Assignments, Case Problems, and Extra Case Problems. A Help file on the Instructor's Resource Kit includes information for using the Solution files.

Course Labs: Concepts Come to Life These highly interactive computer-based learning activities bring concepts to life with illustrations, animations, digital images, and simulations. The Labs guide students step-by-step, present them with Quick Check questions, let them explore on their own, test their comprehension, and provide printed feedback. Lab icons at the beginning of the tutorial and in the tutorial margins indicate when a topic has a corresponding Lab. Lab Assignments are included at the end of each relevant tutorial. The Labs available with this book and the tutorials in which they appear are:

TUTORIAL 1
Windows 98

TUTORIAL 1
Windows 98

TUTORIAL 2
Windows 98

TUTORIAL 1
Word 2000

TUTORIAL 1
Excel 2000

TUTORIAL 1
Access 2000

TUTORIAL 1
Outlook 2000

Figure Files Many figures in the text are provided on the IRK CD-ROM to help illustrate key topics or concepts. Instructors can create traditional overhead transparencies by printing the figure files. Or they can create electronic slide shows by using the figures in a presentation program such as PowerPoint.

Course Test Manager: Testing and Practice at the Computer or on Paper Course Test Manager is cutting-edge, Windows-based testing software that helps instructors design and administer practice tests and actual examinations. Course Test Manager can automatically grade the tests students take at the computer and can generate statistical information on individual as well as group performance.

Online Companions: Dedicated to Keeping You and Your Students Up-To-Date Visit our faculty sites and student sites on the World Wide Web at www.course.com. Here instructors can browse this text's password-protected Faculty Online Companion to obtain an online Instructor's Manual, Solution Files, Student Files, and more. Students can also access this text's Student Online Companion, which contains Student files and all the links that the students will need to complete their tutorial assignments.

More innovative technology

Course CBT Enhance your students' Office 2000 classroom learning experience with self-paced computer-based training on CD-ROM. Course CBT engages students with interactive multimedia and hands-on simulations that reinforce and complement the concepts and skills covered in the textbook. All the content is aligned with the MOUS (Microsoft Office User Specialist) program, making it a great preparation tool for the certification exams. Course CBT also includes extensive pre- and post-assessments that test students' mastery of skills. These pre- and post-assessments automatically generate a "custom learning path" through the course that highlights only the topics students need help with.

Course Assessment How well do your students *really* know Microsoft Office? Course Assessment is a performance-based testing program that measures students' proficiency in Microsoft Office 2000. Previously known as SAM, Course Assessment is available for Office 2000 in either a live or simulated environment. You can use Course Assessment to place students into or out of courses, monitor their performance throughout a course, and help prepare them for the MOUS certification exams.

WebCT WebCT is a tool used to create Web-based educational environments and also uses WWW browsers as the interface for the course-building environment. The site is hosted on your school campus, allowing complete control over the information. WebCT has its own internal communication system, offering internal e-mail, a Bulletin Board, and a Chat room.

Course Technology offers pre-existing supplemental information to help in your WebCT class creation, such as a suggested Syllabus, Lecture Notes, Figures in the Book/Course Presenter, Student Downloads, and Test Banks in which you can schedule an exam, create reports, and more.

BRIEF CONTENTS

Preface   iii
Tutorial Tips   xvi

Microsoft Windows 98—Level I Tutorials   WIN 98 1.01

Tutorial 1   WIN 98 1.03
Exploring the Basics
Investigating the Windows 98 Operating System

Tutorial 2   WIN 98 2.01
Working with Files
Creating, Saving, and Managing Files

Microsoft Word 2000—Level I Tutorials   WD 1.01

Tutorial 1   WD 1.03
Creating a Document
Writing a Business Letter for Crossroads

Tutorial 2   WD 2.01
Editing and Formatting a Document
Preparing an Annuity Plan Description for Right-Hand Solutions

Microsoft Excel 2000—Level I Tutorials   EX 1.01

Tutorial 1   EX 1.03
Using Worksheets to Make Business Decisions
Evaluating Sites for an Inwood Design Group Golf Course

Tutorial 2   EX 2.01
Creating a Worksheet
Producing a Sales Comparison Report for MSI

Tutorial 3   EX 3.01
Developing a Professional-Looking Worksheet
Producing a Projected Sales Report for the Pronto Salsa Company

Microsoft Access 2000—Level I Tutorials — AC 1.01

Tutorial 1 — AC 1.03
Introduction to Microsoft Access 2000
Viewing and Working with a Table Containing Customer Data

Tutorial 2 — AC 2.01
Maintaining a Database
Creating, Modifying, and Updating an Order Table

Tutorial 3 — AC 3.01
Querying a Database
Retrieving Information About Restaurant Customers and Their Orders

Microsoft PowerPoint 2000—Level I Tutorials — PPT 1.01

Tutorial 1 — PPT 1.03
Using PowerPoint to Create Presentations
Presentation to Reach Potential Customers of Inca Imports International

Microsoft Outlook 2000—Level I Tutorials — OUT 1.01

Tutorial 1 — OUT 1.03
Communicating with Outlook 2000
Sending and Receiving E-mail Messages for The Express Lane

Index	1
Task Reference	15
File Finder	26

TABLE OF CONTENTS

Preface	iii
Tutorial Tips	xvi

Microsoft Windows 2000—
Level I Tutorials	WIN 98 1.01
Read This Before You Begin	WIN 98 1.02

Tutorial 1 — WIN 98 1.03

Exploring the Basics
Investigating the Windows 98 Operating System

SESSION 1.1	WIN 98 1.04
Starting Windows 98	WIN 98 1.04
The Windows 98 Desktop	WIN 98 1.04
Using a Pointing Device	WIN 98 1.05
Pointing	WIN 98 1.06
Clicking	WIN 98 1.07
Selecting	WIN 98 1.08
Right-Clicking	WIN 98 1.09
Starting and Closing a Program	WIN 98 1.11
Running Multiple Programs	WIN 98 1.12
Switching Between Programs	WIN 98 1.13
Accessing the Desktop from the Quick Launch Toolbar	WIN 98 1.14
Closing Inactive Programs from the Taskbar	WIN 98 1.14
Shutting Down Windows 98	WIN 98 1.15
Quick Check	WIN 98 1.16
SESSION 1.2	WIN 98 1.17
Anatomy of a Window	WIN 98 1.17
Manipulating a Window	WIN 98 1.18
Minimizing a Window	WIN 98 1.18
Redisplaying a Window	WIN 98 1.20
Maximizing a Window	WIN 98 1.20
Restoring a Window	WIN 98 1.20
Moving a Window	WIN 98 1.20
Changing the Size of a Window	WIN 98 1.21
Using Program Menus	WIN 98 1.21
Selecting Commands from a Menu	WIN 98 1.21
Using Toolbars	WIN 98 1.23
Using List Boxes and Scroll Bars	WIN 98 1.24
Using Dialog Box Controls	WIN 98 1.25
Using Help	WIN 98 1.27
Viewing Topics from the Contents Tab	WIN 98 1.27
Selecting a Topic from the Index	WIN 98 1.28
Returning to a Previous Help Topic	WIN 98 1.30
Quick Check	WIN 98 1.30
Tutorial Assignments	WIN 98 1.31
Projects	WIN 98 1.32
Lab Assignments	WIN 98 1.33
Quick Check Answers	WIN 98 1.34

Tutorial 2 — WIN 98 2.01

Working with Files
Creating, Saving, and Managing Files

SESSION 2.1	WIN 98 2.02
Formatting a Disk	WIN 98 2.02
Working with Text	WIN 98 2.04
The Insertion Point Versus the Pointer	WIN 98 2.04
Selecting Text	WIN 98 2.05
Inserting a Character	WIN 98 2.06
Saving a File	WIN 98 2.07
Opening a File	WIN 98 2.08
Printing a File	WIN 98 2.10
Quick Check	WIN 98 2.11
SESSION 2.2	WIN 98 2.12
Changing Desktop Style Settings	WIN 98 2.12
Switching to Web Style	WIN 98 2.12
Selecting an Icon in Web Style	WIN 98 2.13
Opening a File in Web Style	WIN 98 2.14
Creating Your Student Disk	WIN 98 2.15
My Computer	WIN 98 2.15
Changing My Computer View Options	WIN 98 2.17
Controlling the Toolbar Display	WIN 98 2.17
Web View	WIN 98 2.18
Changing the Icon Display	WIN 98 2.19
Hiding File Extensions	WIN 98 2.20
Folders and Directories	WIN 98 2.20
Moving and Copying a File	WIN 98 2.21
Navigating Explorer Windows	WIN 98 2.23
Deleting a File	WIN 98 2.24
Renaming a File	WIN 98 2.24
Copying an Entire Floppy Disk	WIN 98 2.25
Quick Check	WIN 98 2.26
Tutorial Assignments	WIN 98 2.26
Projects	WIN 98 2.28
Lab Assignments	WIN 98 2.29
Quick Check Answers	WIN 98 2.30

Microsoft Word 2000—
Level I Tutorials   WD 1.01
Read This Before You Begin   WD 1.02

Tutorial 1   WD 1.03

Creating a Document
Writing a Business Letter for Crossroads

SESSION 1.1	WD 1.04
Four Steps to a Professional Document	WD 1.04
Starting Word	WD 1.05
Viewing the Word Screen	WD 1.06
Checking the Screen Before You Begin Each Tutorial	WD 1.07
Setting the Document View to Normal	WD 1.07
Displaying the Toolbars and Ruler	WD 1.08
Setting the Font and Font Size	WD 1.09
Displaying Nonprinting Characters	WD 1.10
Session 1.1 Quick Check	WD 1.11
SESSION 1.2	WD 1.12
Typing A Letter	WD 1.12
Using AutoComplete Tips	WD 1.14
Entering Text	WD 1.15
Saving a Document for the First Time	WD 1.16
Adding Properties to a Document	WD 1.18
Word Wrap	WD 1.20
Scrolling a Document	WD 1.20
Correcting Errors	WD 1.21
Finishing the Letter	WD 1.23
Saving a Completed Document	WD 1.24
Previewing and Printing a Document	WD 1.25
Getting Help	WD 1.27
Exiting Word	WD 1.29
Session 1.2 Quick Check	WD 1.30
Review Assignments	WD 1.31
Case Problems	WD 1.33
Lab Assignments	WD 1.36
Internet Assignments	WD 1.37
Quick Check Answers	WD 1.38

Tutorial 2   WD 2.01

Editing and Formatting a Document
Preparing an Annuity Plan Description for Right-Hand Solutions

SESSION 2.1	WD 2.02
Opening the Document	WD 2.02
Renaming the Document	WD 2.05
Using the Spelling and Grammar Checker	WD 2.05
Moving the Insertion Point Around a Document	WD 2.07
Using Select, Then Do	WD 2.09
Deleting Text	WD 2.09
Using the Undo and Redo Commands	WD 2.10
Moving Text Within a Document	WD 2.12
Dragging and Dropping Text	WD 2.12
Cutting or Copying and Pasting Text	WD 2.13
Finding and Replacing Text	WD 2.15
Session 2.1 Quick Check	WD 2.18
SESSION 2.2	WD 2.18
Changing the Margins	WD 2.18
Changing Line Spacing	WD 2.20
Aligning Text	WD 2.22
Indenting a Paragraph	WD 2.23
Using Format Painter	WD 2.24
Adding Bullets and Numbers	WD 2.25
Changing the Font and Font Size	WD 2.27
Emphasizing Text with Boldface, Underlining, and Italics	WD 2.29
Bolding Text	WD 2.29
Underlining Text	WD 2.30
Italicizing Text	WD 2.30
Saving and Printing	WD 2.31
Session 2.2 Quick Check	WD 2.32
Review Assignments	WD 2.33
Case Problems	WD 2.35
Quick Check Answers	WD 2.38

NEW PERSPECTIVES SERIES | XI | CONTENTS

Microsoft Excel 2000—
Level I Tutorials   EX 1.01
Read This Before You Begin   EX 1.02

Tutorial 1   EX 1.03

Using Worksheets to Make Business Decisions

Evaluating Sites for an Inwood Design Group Golf Course

SESSION 1.1	EX 1.03
What is Excel?	EX 1.04
Starting Excel	EX 1.04
The Excel Window	EX 1.06
Toolbars	EX 1.06
Formula Bar	EX 1.06
Workbook Window	EX 1.07
Pointer	EX 1.07
Sheet Tabs	EX 1.07
Moving Around a Worksheet	EX 1.07
Using the Mouse	EX 1.07
Using the Keyboard	EX 1.07
Navigating in a Workbook	EX 1.10
Opening a Workbook	EX 1.10
Layout of the Inwood Workbook	EX 1.12
Session 1.1 Quick Check	EX 1.14
SESSION 1.2	EX 1.14
Text, Values, Formulas, and Functions	EX 1.14
Text	EX 1.14
Values	EX 1.15
Formulas	EX 1.16
Functions	EX 1.18
Saving the Workbook	EX 1.21
What-if Analysis	EX 1.23
Correcting Mistakes	EX 1.25
Getting Help	EX 1.26
Clearing Cell Contents	EX 1.29
Printing the Worksheet	EX 1.31
Closing the Workbook	EX 1.33
Exiting Excel	EX 1.34
Session 1.2 Quick Check	EX 1.34
Review Assignments	EX 1.35
Case Problems	EX 1.35
Lab Assignments	EX 1.38
Internet Assignments	EX 1.40
Quick Check Answers	EX 1.40

Tutorial 2   EX 2.01

Creating a Worksheet

Producing a Sales Comparison Report for MSI

SESSION 2.1	EX 2.02
Developing Worksheets	EX 2.02
Planning the Worksheet	EX 2.02
Building the Worksheet	EX 2.03
Entering Labels	EX 2.03
Entering Data	EX 2.05
Using the AutoSum Button	EX 2.06
Entering Formulas	EX 2.07
Copying a Formula Using the Fill Handle	EX 2.08
Copying a Formula Using Relative References	EX 2.10
Copying a Formula Using an Absolute Reference	EX 2.10
Absolute Versus Relative References	EX 2.12
Copying Cell Contents Using the Copy-and-Paste Method	EX 2.13
Renaming the Worksheet	EX 2.14
Saving the New Workbook	EX 2.14
Session 2.1 Quick Check	EX 2.15
SESSION 2.2	EX 2.15
Excel Functions	EX 2.15
Average Function	EX 2.16
MAX Function	EX 2.19
MIN Function	EX 2.19
Building Formulas by Pointing	EX 2.19
Testing the Worksheet	EX 2.20
Spell Checking the Worksheet	EX 2.20
Improving the Worksheet Layout	EX 2.21
Changing Column Width	EX 2.21
Inserting a Row into a Worksheet	EX 2.22
Using the Undo Button	EX 2.24
Moving a Range Using the Mouse	EX 2.25
Using AutoFormat	EX 2.26
Previewing the Worksheet Using Print Preview	EX 2.28
Centering the Printout	EX 2.29
Adding Headers and Footers	EX 2.30
Setting the Print Area	EX 2.33
Documenting the Workbook	EX 2.33

Adding Cell Comments	EX 2.34
Displaying and Printing Worksheet Formulas	EX 2.35
Session 2.2 Quick Check	EX 2.37
Review Assignments	EX 2.37
Case Problems	EX 2.38
Quick Check Answers	EX 2.44

Tutorial 3 — EX 3.01

Developing a Professional-Looking Worksheet

Producing a Projected Sales Report for the Pronto Salsa Company

SESSION 3.1	EX 3.02
Opening the Workbook	EX 3.02
Formatting Worksheet Data	EX 3.04
Changing the Appearance of Numbers	EX 3.05
Currency and Accounting Formats	EX 3.05
The Format Painter Button	EX 3.08
Number Symbol (###) Replacement	EX 3.08
Number Formats	EX 3.09
Percentage Format	EX 3.10
Aligning Cell Contents	EX 3.11
Wrapping Text in a Cell	EX 3.11
Centering Text Across Cells	EX 3.12
Indenting Text Within a Cell	EX 3.13
Changing the Font, Font Style, and Font Size	EX 3.14
Using Styles	EX 3.17
Clearing Formats from Cells	EX 3.17
Deleting Cells from a Worksheet	EX 3.18
Session 3.1 Quick Check	EX 3.19
SESSION 3.2	EX 3.19
Adding and Removing Borders	EX 3.19
Using Color for Emphasis	EX 3.22
Using the Drawing Toolbar for Emphasis	EX 3.24
Activating the Drawing Toolbar	EX 3.24
Adding a Text Box	EX 3.25
Adding an Arrow	EX 3.28
Controlling the Display of Gridlines	EX 3.30
Printing the Worksheet	EX 3.31
Portrait and Landscape Orientations	EX 3.32
Hiding and Unhiding Rows and Columns	EX 3.34
Session 3.2 Quick Check	EX 3.36
Review Assignments	EX 3.36
Case Problems	EX 3.37

Internet Assignments	EX 3.41
Quick Check Answers	EX 3.42

Microsoft Access 2000—Level I Tutorials — AC 1.01

Read This Before You Begin — AC 1.02

Tutorial 1 — AC 1.03

Introduction to Microsoft Access 2000

Viewing and Working with a Table Containing Customer Data

SESSION 1.1	AC 1.04
Introduction to Database Concepts	AC 1.04
Organizing Data	AC 1.04
Databases and Relationships	AC 1.05
Relational Database Management Systems	AC 1.06
Starting Access	AC 1.07
Opening an Existing Database	AC 1.09
The Access and Database Windows	AC 1.10
Opening an Access Table	AC 1.11
Navigating an Access Datasheet	AC 1.12
Printing a Table	AC 1.13
Exiting Access	AC 1.13
Session 1.1 Quick Check	AC 1.13
SESSION 1.2	AC 1.14
Creating and Printing a Query	AC 1.14
Creating and Printing a Form	AC 1.17
Getting Help	AC 1.19
Finding Information with the Office Assistant	AC 1.19
Creating, Previewing, and Printing a Report	AC 1.23
Compacting a Database	AC 1.25
Compacting and Repairing a Database	AC 1.25
Compacting a Database Automatically	AC 1.26
Backing Up and Restoring a Database	AC 1.27
Session 1.2 Quick Check	AC 1.27
Review Assignments	AC 1.27
Case Problems	AC 1.28
Internet Assignments	AC 1.31
Lab Assignments	AC 1.31
Quick Check Answers	AC 1.32

NEW PERSPECTIVES SERIES | XIII | CONTENTS

Tutorial 2 — AC 2.01
Maintaining a Database
Creating, Modifying, and Updating an Order Table

SESSION 2.1	AC 2.02
Guidelines for Designing Databases	AC 2.02
Guidelines for Designing Access Tables	AC 2.04
Naming Fields and Objects	AC 2.04
Assigning Field Data Types	AC 2.04
Assigning Field Sizes	AC 2.05
Creating a Table	AC 2.06
Defining Fields	AC 2.08
Specifying the Primary Key	AC 2.14
Saving the Table Structure	AC 2.16
Adding Records to a Table	AC 2.17
Saving a Database	AC 2.20
Session 2.1 Quick Check	AC 2.20
SESSION 2.2	AC 2.21
Modifying the Structure of an Access Table	AC 2.21
Deleting a Field	AC 2.21
Moving a Field	AC 2.22
Adding a Field	AC 2.23
Changing Field Properties	AC 2.24
Copying Records from Another Access Database	AC 2.27
Using the Office Clipboard	AC 2.29
Updating a Database	AC 2.30
Deleting Records	AC 2.30
Changing Records	AC 2.31
Session 2.2 Quick Check	AC 2.33
Review Assignments	AC 2.34
Case Problems	AC 2.36
Internet Assignments	AC 2.40
Quick Check Answers	AC 2.40

Tutorial 3 — AC 3.01
Querying a Database
Retrieving Information About Restaurant Customers and Their Orders

SESSION 3.1	AC 3.02
Introduction to Queries	AC 3.02
Query Window	AC 3.02
Creating and Running a Query	AC 3.04
Defining Table Relationships	AC 3.06
One-to-Many Relationships	AC 3.07
Referential Integrity	AC 3.08
Defining a Relationship Between Two Tables	AC 3.08
Sorting Data in a Query	AC 3.12
Using a Toolbar Button to Sort Data	AC 3.13
Sorting Multiple Fields in Design View	AC 3.14
Filtering Data	AC 3.17
Session 3.1 Quick Check	AC 3.19
SESSION 3.2	AC 3.19
Defining Record Selection Criteria for Queries	AC 3.20
Specifying an Exact Match	AC 3.20
Changing a Datasheet's Appearance	AC 3.23
Using a Comparison Operator to Match a Range of Values	AC 3.24
Defining Multiple Selection Criteria for Queries	AC 3.26
The And Logical Operator	AC 3.27
The Or Logical Operator	AC 3.28
Performing Calculations	AC 3.30
Creating a Calculated Field	AC 3.30
Using Aggregate Functions	AC 3.34
Using Record Group Calculations	AC 3.36
Session 3.2 Quick Check	AC 3.37
Review Assignments	AC 3.38
Case Problems	AC 3.39
Internet Assignments	AC 3.42
Quick Check Answers	AC 3.42

Microsoft PowerPoint 2000—
Level I Tutorials — PPT 1.01
Read This Before You Begin — PPT 1.02

Tutorial 1 — PPT 1.03
Using PowerPoint to Create Presentations
Presentation to Reach Potential Customers of Inca Imports International

Session 1.1	PPT 1.04
What is PowerPoint?	PPT 1.04
Starting PowerPoint	PPT 1.04
Opening an Existing PowerPoint Presentation	PPT 1.06

Understanding the PowerPoint Window	PPT 1.07
Common Windows Elements	PPT 1.07
The Toolbars	PPT 1.08
The PowerPoint Panes	PPT 1.08
Viewing a Presentation in a Slide Show View	PPT 1.08
Closing a Presentation and Exiting PowerPoint	PPT 1.12
Planning a Presentation	PPT 1.13
Using the AutoContent Wizard	PPT 1.13
Editing AutoContent Slides	PPT 1.16
Saving a Presentation	PPT 1.18
Session 1.1 Quick Check	PPT 1.19
SESSION 1.2	**PPT 1.19**
Modifying a Presentation	PPT 1.19
Deleting Slides	PPT 1.19
Moving Slides and Text in the Outline Pane	PPT 1.21
Promoting and Demoting Outline Text	PPT 1.23
Adding a New Slide and Choosing a Layout	PPT 1.27
Using the Style Checker	PPT 1.28
Using Help	PPT 1.30
Getting Help with the Office Assistant	PPT 1.30
Creating Notes for Slides	PPT 1.31
Previewing and Printing the Presentation	PPT 1.31
Session 1.2 Quick Check	PPT 1.35
Review Assignments	PPT 1.35
Case Problems	PPT 1.35
Quick Check Answers	PPT 1.43

Microsoft Outlook 2000—
Level I Tutorials   OUT 1.01
Read This Before You Begin   OUT 1.02

Tutorial 1   OUT 1.03

Communicating with Outlook 2000
Sending and Receiving E-mail Messages for The Express Lane

SESSION 1.1	**OUT 1.04**
Exploring Outlook	OUT 1.04
Starting Outlook	OUT 1.04
Navigating Between Outlook Components	OUT 1.07
Creating and Sending E-mail Messages	OUT 1.07
Choosing a Message Format	OUT 1.08
Adding a Signature	OUT 1.09
Using Stationery	OUT 1.10
Creating an E-mail Message	OUT 1.11
Sending E-mail	OUT 1.12
Organizing Contact Information	OUT 1.14
Creating Contacts	OUT 1.14
Editing Contacts	OUT 1.17
Session 1.1 Quick Check	OUT 1.17
SESSION 1.2	**OUT 1.17**
Receiving E-mail	OUT 1.17
Reading Messages	OUT 1.18
Replying to and Forwarding Mail	OUT 1.19
Printing Messages	OUT 1.20
Working with Attachments	OUT 1.21
Managing Messages	OUT 1.23
Creating a Folder	OUT 1.23
Filing Messages	OUT 1.24
Archiving Mail Messages	OUT 1.24
Finding Messages	OUT 1.25
Sorting Messages	OUT 1.26
Filtering a View	OUT 1.27
Getting Help	OUT 1.27
Exiting Outlook	OUT 1.29
Session 1.2 Quick Check	OUT 1.29
Review Assignments	OUT 1.30
Case Problems	OUT 1.31
Quick Check Answers	OUT 1.34

Index	**1**
Task Reference	**15**
File Finder	**26**

Reference Window List

Starting a Program	WIN 98 1.11	Moving a Range Using the Mouse	EX 2.25
Moving a File	WIN 98 2.21	Using AutoFormat	EX 2.26
Copying a File	WIN 98 2.22	Inserting a Comment	EX 2.34
Copying a Disk	WIN 98 2.25	Formatting Numbers	EX 3.05
Saving a Document for the First Time	WD 1.17	Changing Font, Font Style, and Font Size	EX 3.14
Getting Help from the Office Assistant	WD 1.27	Creating a Style by Example	EX 3.17
Exiting Word	WD 1.30	Clearing Formats from Cells, Rows, and Columns	EX 3.17
Checking a Document for Spelling and Grammatical Errors	WD 2.05	Deleting Cells, Rows, or Columns	EX 3.18
Using Undo and Redo	WD 2.11	Adding a Border	EX 3.20
Dragging and Dropping Text	WD 2.12	Applying Patterns and Color	EX 3.22
Cutting or Copying and Pasting Text	WD 2.14	Activating and Removing Toolbars	EX 3.24
Finding and Replacing Text	WD 2.16	Adding a Text Box	EX 3.26
Changing Margins for the Entire Document	WD 2.19	To Hide Rows and Columns	EX 3.34
Changing Line Spacing in a Document	WD 2.21	Opening an Access Object	AC 1.11
Changing the Font and Font Size	WD 2.27	Using the Office Assistant	AC 1.20
Opening a Workbook	EX 1.10	Compacting a Database Automatically	AC 1.26
Entering a Formula	EX 1.17	Defining a Field in a Table	AC 2.08
Entering the SUM Function	EX 1.19	Specifying a Primary Key for a Table	AC 2.15
Saving a Workbook with a New Filename	EX 1.22	Saving a Table Structure	AC 2.16
Correcting Mistakes Using Edit Mode	EX 1.26	Deleting a Field from a Table Structure	AC 2.21
Using the Office Assistant	EX 1.27	Adding a Field Between Two Existing Fields	AC 2.23
Clearing Cell Contents	EX 1.30	Deleting a Record	AC 2.30
Printing a Worksheet	EX 1.31	Sorting a Query Datasheet	AC 3.15
Copying Cell Contents with the Fill Handle	EX 2.09	Using Filter By Selection	AC 3.18
Changing Absolute, Mixed, and Relative References	EX 2.12	Using Expression Builder	AC 3.31
Copying and Pasting a Cell or Range of Cells	EX 2.13	Creating Effective Text Presentations	PPT 1.17
Using the Paste Function Button	EX 2.17	Using the Office Assistant	PPT 1.30
Checking the Spelling in a Worksheet	EX 2.21		
Changing Column Width	EX 2.22		
Inserting a Row	EX 2.23		
Inserting a Column	EX 2.23		

Tutorial Tips

These tutorials will help you learn about Microsoft Office 2000. The tutorials are designed to be worked through at a computer. Each tutorial is divided into sessions. Watch for the session headings, such as Session 1.1 and Session 1.2. Each session is designed to be completed in about 45 minutes, but take as much time as you need. It's also a good idea to take a break between sessions.

To use the tutorials effectively, you read the following questions and answers before you begin.

Where do I start?
Each tutorial begins with a case, which sets the scene for the tutorial and gives you background information to help you understand what you will be doing. Read the case before you go to the lab. In the lab, begin with the first session of a tutorial.

How do I know what to do on the computer?
Each session contains steps that you will perform on the computer to learn how to use Microsoft Office 2000. Read the text that introduces each series of steps. The steps you need to do at a computer are numbered and are set against a shaded background. Read each step carefully and completely before you try it.

How do I know if I did the step correctly?
As you work, compare your computer screen with the corresponding figure in the tutorial. Don't worry if your screen display is somewhat different from the figure. The important parts of the screen display are labeled in each figure. Check to make sure these parts are on your screen.

What if I make a mistake?
Don't worry about making mistakes—they are part of the learning process. Paragraphs labeled "TROUBLE?" identify common problems and explain how to get back on track. Follow the steps in a TROUBLE? paragraph only if you are having the problem described. If you run into other problems:

- Carefully consider the current state of your system, the position of the pointer, and any messages on the screen.
- Complete the sentence, "Now I want to…" Be specific, because identifying your goal will help you rethink the steps you need to take to reach that goal.
- If you are working on a particular piece of software, consult the Help system.
- If the suggestions above don't solve your problem, consult your technical support person for assistance.

How do I use the Reference Windows?
Reference Windows summarize the procedures you will learn in the tutorial steps. Do not complete the actions in the Reference Windows when you are working through the tutorial. Instead, refer to the Reference Windows while you are working on the assignments at the end of the tutorial.

How can I test my understanding of the material I learned in the tutorial?
At the end of each session, you can answer the Quick Check questions. The answers for the Quick Checks are at the end of that tutorial.

After you have completed the entire tutorial, you should complete the Review Assignments and Case Problems. They are carefully structured so that you will review what you have learned and then apply your knowledge to new situations.

What if I can't remember how to do something?
You should refer to the Task Reference at the end of the book; it summarizes how to accomplish tasks using the most efficient method.

Before you begin the tutorials, you should know the basics about your computer's operating system. You should also know how to use the menus, dialog boxes, Help system, and My Computer.

Now that you've read Tutorial Tips, you are ready to begin.

LEVEL I

New Perspectives on

MICROSOFT® WINDOWS® 98

TUTORIAL 1   WIN 98 1.3
Exploring the Basics
Investigating the Windows 98 Operating System

TUTORIAL 2   WIN 98 2.1
Working with Files
Creating, Saving, and Managing Files

Read This Before You Begin

To the Student

Make Student Disk Program

To complete the Level I tutorials, Tutorial Assignments, and Projects, you need 2 Student Disks. Your instructor will either provide you with Student Disks or ask you to make your own.

If you are making your own Student Disks you will need 2 blank, formatted high-density disks and access to the Make Student Disk program. If you wish to install the Make Student Disk program to your home computer, you can obtain it from your instructor or from the Web. To download the Make Student Disk program from the Web, go to **www.course.com**, click Data Disks, and follow the instructions on the screen.

To install the Make Student Disk program, select and click the file you just downloaded from **www.course.com**, 5446-0.exe. Follow the on-screen instructions to complete the installation. If you have any trouble installing or obtaining the Make Student Disk program, ask your instructor or technical support person for assistance.

Once you have obtained and installed the Make Student Disk program, you can use it to create your student disks according to the steps in the tutorials.

Course Labs

The Level I tutorials in this book feature 3 interactive Course Labs to help you understand selected computer concepts. There are Lab Assignments at the end of Tutorials 1 and 2 that relate to these Labs. To start a Lab, click the **Start** button on the Windows 98 Taskbar, point to **Programs**, point to **Course Labs**, point to **New Perspectives Course Labs**, and click the name of the Lab you want to use.

Using Your Own Computer

If you are going to work through this book using your own computer, you need:

Computer System Microsoft Windows 98 must be installed on a local hard drive or on a network drive.

Student Disks You will not be able to complete the tutorials or exercises in this book using your own computer until you have your Student Disks. See "Make Student Disk Program" above for details on obtaining your student disks.

Course Labs See your instructor or technical support person to obtain the Course Lab software for use on your own computer.

Visit Our World Wide Web Site

Additional materials designed especially for you are available on the World Wide Web. Go to **http://www.course.com**.

To the Instructor

The Make Student Disk Program and Course Labs for this title are available on the Instructor's Resource Kit for this title. Follow the instructions in the Help file on the CD-ROM to install the programs to your network or standalone computer. For information on using the Make Student Disk Program or the Course Labs, see the "To the Student" section above. Students will be switching the default installation settings to Web style in Tutorial 2. You are granted a license to copy the Student Files and Course Labs to any computer or computer network used by students who have purchased this book.

TUTORIAL 1

OBJECTIVES

In this tutorial you will:

- Start and shut down Windows 98
- Identify the objects on the Windows 98 desktop
- Practice mouse functions
- Run software programs and switch between them
- Identify and use the controls in a window
- Use Windows 98 controls such as menus, toolbars, list boxes, scroll bars, option buttons, tabs, and check boxes
- Explore the Windows 98 Help system

LABS

Using a Keyboard

Using a Mouse

EXPLORING THE BASICS

Investigating the Windows 98 Operating System

CASE

Your First Day on the Computer

You walk into the computer lab and sit down at a desk. There's a computer in front of you, and you find yourself staring dubiously at the screen. Where to start? As if in answer to your question, your friend Steve Laslow appears.

"You start with the operating system," says Steve. Noticing your puzzled look, Steve explains that the **operating system** is software that helps the computer carry out operating tasks such as displaying information on the computer screen and saving data on your disks. Your computer uses the **Microsoft Windows 98** operating system—Windows 98, for short.

Steve tells you that Windows 98 has a "gooey" or **graphical user interface (GUI)**, which uses pictures of familiar objects, such as file folders and documents, to represent a desktop on your screen. Microsoft Windows 98 gets its name from the rectangular work areas, called "windows," that appear on your screen.

Steve explains that much of the software available for Windows 98 has a standard graphical user interface. This means that once you have learned how to use one Windows software package, such as word-processing software, you are well on your way to understanding how to use other Windows software. Windows 98 lets you use more than one software package at a time, so you can easily switch between your word-processing software and your appointment book software, for example. Finally, Windows 98 makes it very easy to access the **Internet**, the worldwide collection of computers connected to one another to enable communication. All in all, Windows 98 makes your computer an effective and easy-to-use productivity tool.

Steve recommends that you get started right away by using some tutorials that will teach you the skills essential for using Microsoft Windows 98. He hands you a book and assures you that everything on your computer system is set up and ready to go.

SESSION 1.1

In this session, in addition to learning basic Windows terminology, you will learn how to use a pointing device, how to start and stop a program, and how to use more than one program at a time.

Starting Windows 98

Windows 98 automatically starts when you turn on the computer. Depending on the way your computer is set up, you might be asked to enter your username and password.

To start Windows 98:

1. Turn on your computer.

   TROUBLE? If prompted to do so, type your assigned username and press the Tab key. Then type your password and press the Enter key to continue.

   TROUBLE? If this is the first time you have started your computer with Windows 98, messages might appear on your screen informing you that Windows is setting up components of your computer. If the Welcome to Windows 98 box appears, press and hold down the Alt key on your keyboard and then, while you hold down the Alt key, press the F4 key. The box closes.

After a moment, Windows 98 starts.

The Windows 98 Desktop

In Windows terminology, the area displayed on your screen represents a **desktop**—a workspace for projects and the tools needed to manipulate those projects. When you first start a computer, it uses **default** settings, those preset by the operating system. The default desktop, for example, has a plain teal background. However, Microsoft designed Windows 98 so that you can easily change the appearance of the desktop. You can, for example, add color, patterns, images, and text to the desktop background.

Many institutions design customized desktops for their computers. Figure 1-1 shows the default Windows 98 desktop and two other examples of desktops, one designed for a business, North Pole Novelties, and one designed for a school, the University of Colorado. Although your desktop might not look exactly like any of the examples in Figure 1-1, you should be able to locate objects on your screen similar to those in Figure 1-1. Look at your screen display and locate the objects labeled in Figure 1-1. The objects on your screen might appear larger or smaller than those in Figure 1-1, depending on your monitor's settings.

Figure 1-1 — THE WINDOWS 98 DESKTOP

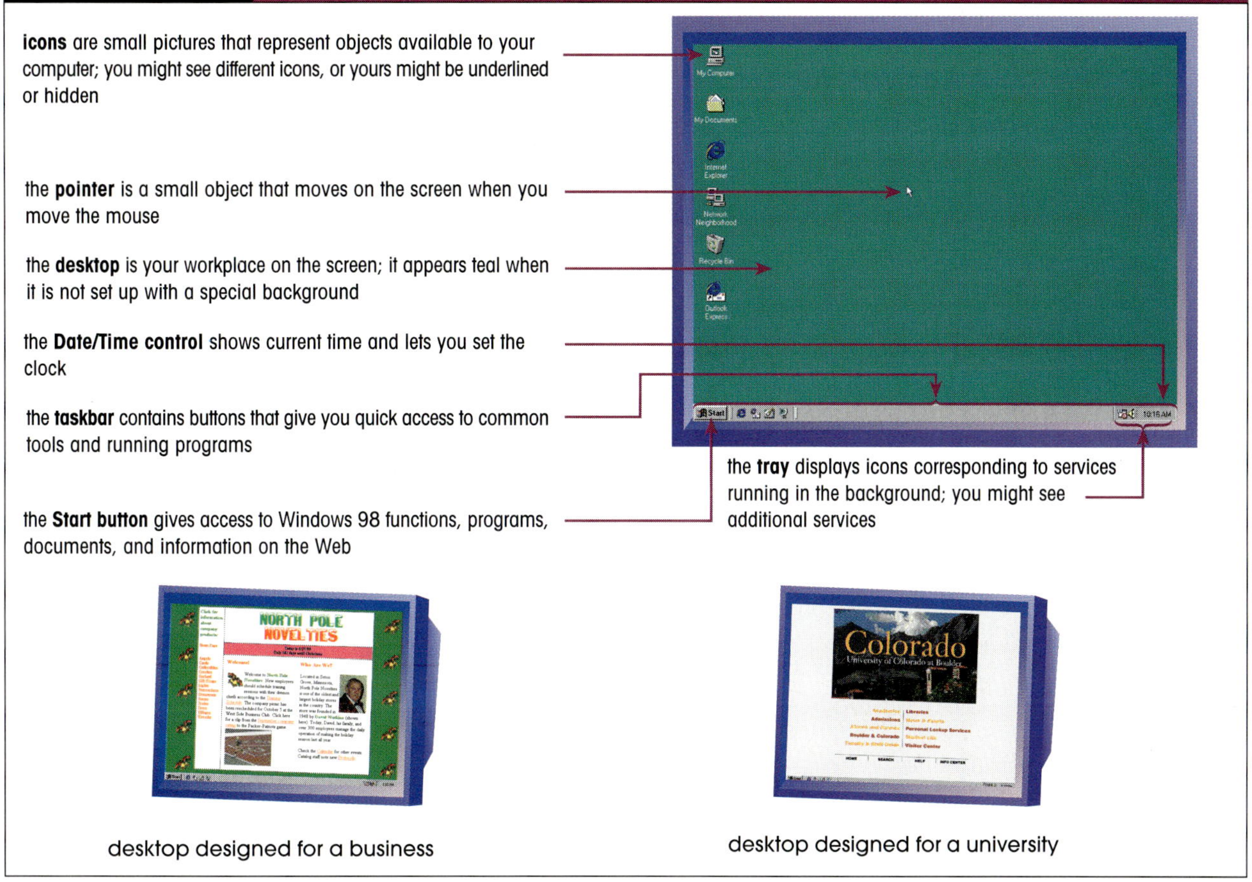

icons are small pictures that represent objects available to your computer; you might see different icons, or yours might be underlined or hidden

the **pointer** is a small object that moves on the screen when you move the mouse

the **desktop** is your workplace on the screen; it appears teal when it is not set up with a special background

the **Date/Time control** shows current time and lets you set the clock

the **taskbar** contains buttons that give you quick access to common tools and running programs

the **Start button** gives access to Windows 98 functions, programs, documents, and information on the Web

the **tray** displays icons corresponding to services running in the background; you might see additional services

desktop designed for a business

desktop designed for a university

If the screen goes blank or starts to display a moving design, press any key to restore the Windows 98 desktop.

Using a Pointing Device

A **pointing device** helps you interact with objects on the screen. Pointing devices come in many shapes and sizes; some are designed to ensure that your hand won't suffer fatigue while using them. Some are directly attached to your computer via a cable, whereas others function like a TV remote control and allow you to access your computer without being right next to it. Figure 1-2 shows examples of common pointing devices.

The most common pointing device is called a **mouse**, so this book uses that term. If you are using a different pointing device, such as a trackball, substitute that device whenever you see the term "mouse." In Windows 98 you need to know how to use the mouse to manipulate the objects on the screen. In this session you will learn about pointing and clicking. In Session 1.2 you will learn how to use the mouse to drag objects.

You can also interact with objects by using the keyboard; however, the mouse is more convenient for most tasks, so the tutorials in this book assume you are using one.

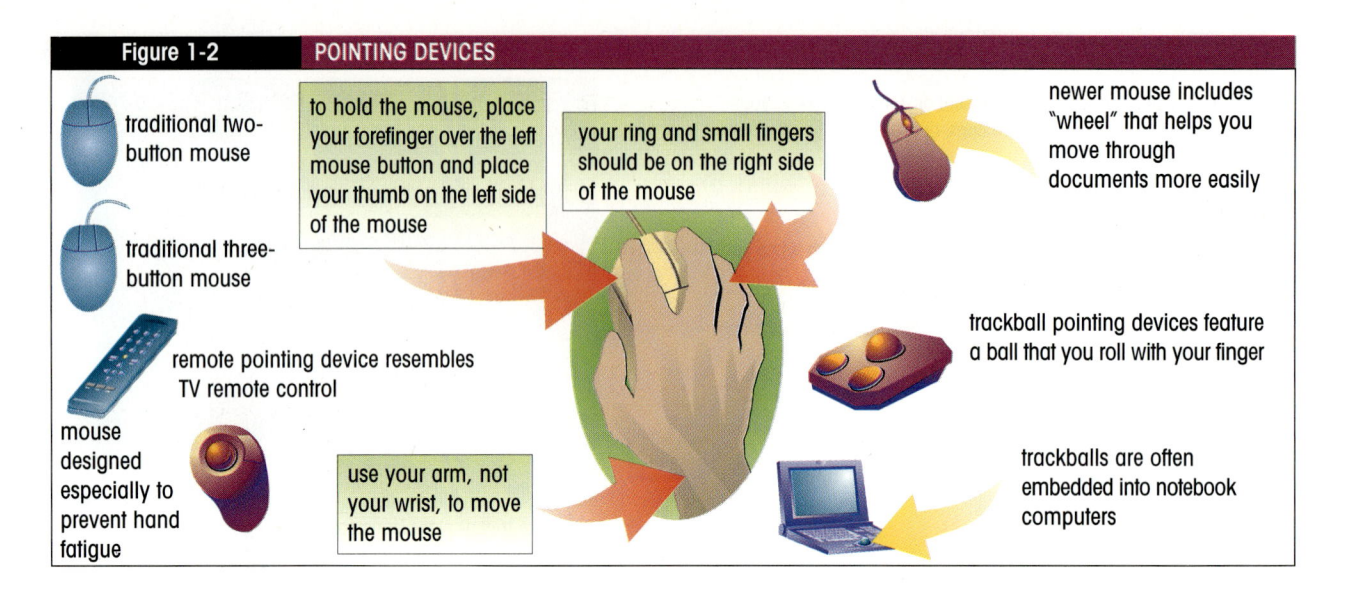

Figure 1-2: POINTING DEVICES

- traditional two-button mouse
- traditional three-button mouse
- remote pointing device resembles TV remote control
- mouse designed especially to prevent hand fatigue
- to hold the mouse, place your forefinger over the left mouse button and place your thumb on the left side of the mouse
- use your arm, not your wrist, to move the mouse
- your ring and small fingers should be on the right side of the mouse
- newer mouse includes "wheel" that helps you move through documents more easily
- trackball pointing devices feature a ball that you roll with your finger
- trackballs are often embedded into notebook computers

Pointing

You use a pointing device to move the pointer, in order to manipulate objects on the desktop. The pointer is usually shaped like an arrow, although it can change shape depending on where it is on the screen. How skilled you are in using a mouse depends on your ability to position the pointer. Most computer users place the mouse on a **mouse pad**, a flat piece of rubber that helps the mouse move smoothly. As you move the mouse on the mouse pad, the pointer on the screen moves in a corresponding direction.

You begin most Windows operations by positioning the pointer over a specific part of the screen. This is called **pointing**.

To move the pointer:

1. Position your right index finger over the left mouse button, as shown in Figure 1-2. Lightly grasp the sides of the mouse with your thumb and little fingers.

   TROUBLE? If you want to use the mouse with your left hand, ask your instructor or technical support person to help you use the Control Panel to swap the functions of the left and right mouse buttons. Be sure to find out how to change back to the right-handed mouse setting, so that you can reset the mouse each time you are finished in the lab.

2. Place the mouse on the mouse pad and then move the mouse. Watch the movement of the pointer.

   TROUBLE? If you run out of room to move your mouse, lift the mouse and place it in the middle of the mouse pad. Notice that the pointer does not move when the mouse is not in contact with the mouse pad.

When you position the mouse pointer over certain objects, such as the objects on the taskbar, a "tip" appears. These "tips" are called **ToolTips**, and they tell you the purpose or function of an object.

TUTORIAL 1 EXPLORING THE BASICS WIN 98 1.7 WINDOWS

To view ToolTips:

1. Use the mouse to point to the **Start** button . After a few seconds, you see the tip "Click here to begin," as shown in Figure 1-3.

Figure 1-3 **VIEWING TOOLTIPS**

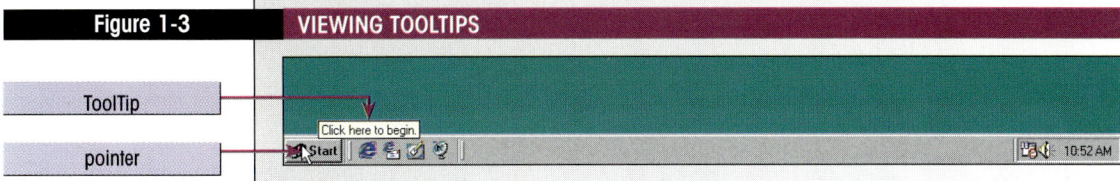

- ToolTip
- pointer

2. Point to the time on the right end of the taskbar. Notice that today's date (or the date to which your computer's time clock is set) appears.

Clicking

Clicking is when you press a mouse button and immediately release it. Clicking sends a signal to your computer that you want to perform an action on the object you click. In Windows 98 you can click using both the left and right mouse buttons, but most actions are performed using the left mouse button. If you are told to click an object, click it with the left mouse button, unless instructed otherwise.

When you click the Start button, the Start menu appears. A **menu** is a list of options that helps you work with software. The **Start menu** provides you with access to programs, documents, and much more. Try clicking the Start button to open the Start menu.

To open the Start menu:

1. Point to the **Start** button .

2. Click the left mouse button. An arrow ▶ following an option on the Start menu indicates that you can view additional choices by navigating a **submenu**, a menu extending from the main menu. See Figure 1-4.

Figure 1-4 **START MENU**

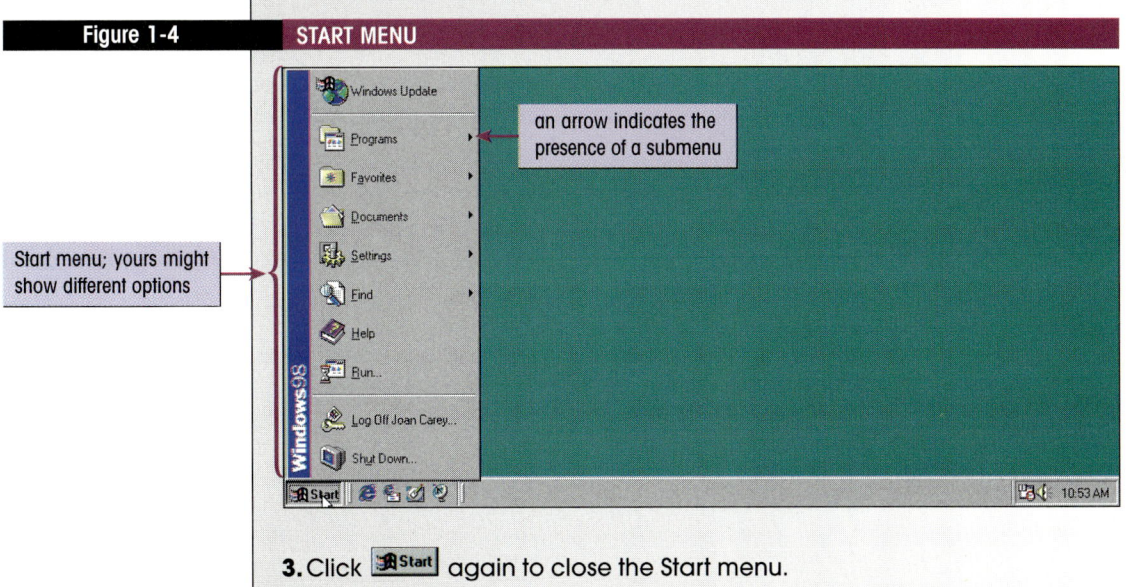

- Start menu; yours might show different options
- an arrow indicates the presence of a submenu

3. Click again to close the Start menu.

Next you'll learn how to open a submenu by selecting it.

Selecting

In Windows 98, pointing and clicking are often used to **select** an object, in other words, to choose it as the object you want to work with. Windows 98 shows you which object is selected by highlighting it, usually by changing the object's color, putting a box around it, or making the object appear to be pushed in, as shown in Figure 1-5.

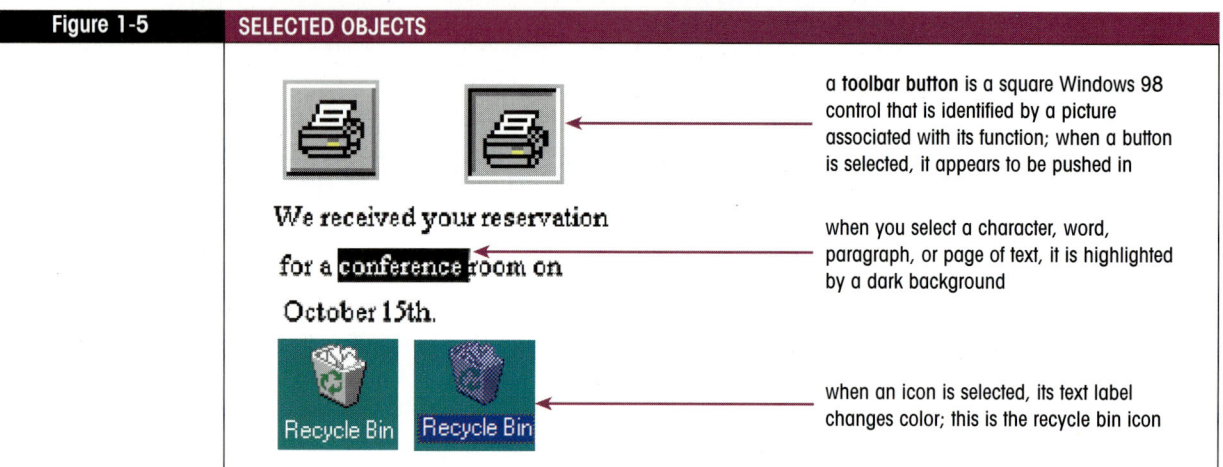

Figure 1-5 SELECTED OBJECTS

a **toolbar button** is a square Windows 98 control that is identified by a picture associated with its function; when a button is selected, it appears to be pushed in

when you select a character, word, paragraph, or page of text, it is highlighted by a dark background

when an icon is selected, its text label changes color; this is the recycle bin icon

In Windows 98, depending on your computer's settings, some objects are selected when you simply point to them, others when you click them. Practice selecting the Programs option on the Start menu to open the Programs submenu.

To select an option on a menu:

1. Click the **Start** button and notice how it appears to be pushed in, indicating it is selected.

2. Point to the **Programs** option. After a short pause, the Programs submenu opens, and the Programs option is highlighted to indicate it is selected. See Figure 1-6.

   TROUBLE? If a submenu other than the Programs menu opens, you selected the wrong option. Move the mouse so that the pointer points to Programs.

   TROUBLE? If the Programs option doesn't appear, your Start menu might have too many options to fit on the screen. If that is the case, a small arrow appears at the top or bottom of the Start menu. Click first the top and then the bottom arrow to view additional Start menu options until you locate the Programs menu option, and then point to it.

TUTORIAL 1 EXPLORING THE BASICS   WIN 98   1.9   WINDOWS

Figure 1-6   **PROGRAMS SUBMENU**

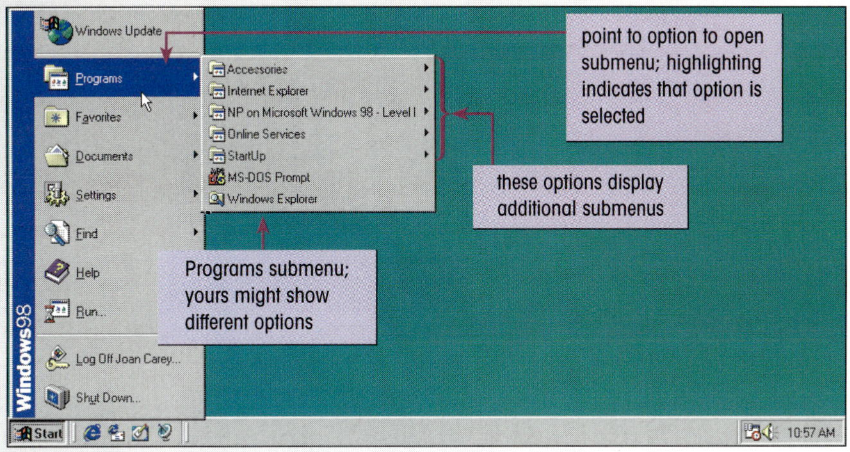

[Screenshot of Windows 98 Start menu with Programs submenu open, showing callouts: "point to option to open submenu; highlighting indicates that option is selected", "these options display additional submenus", and "Programs submenu; yours might show different options"]

3. Now close the Start menu by clicking **Start** again.

You return to the desktop.

Right-Clicking

Pointing devices were originally designed with a single button, so the term "clicking" had only one meaning: you pressed that button. Innovations in technology, however, led to the addition of a second and even a third button (and more recently, options such as a wheel) that expanded the pointing device's capability. More recent software—especially that designed for Windows 98—takes advantage of additional buttons, especially the right button. However, the term "clicking" continues to refer to the left button; clicking an object with the *right* button is called **right-clicking**.

In Windows 98, right-clicking both selects an object and opens its **shortcut menu**, a list of options directly related to the object you right-clicked. You can right-click practically any object—the Start button, a desktop icon, the taskbar, and even the desktop itself—to view options associated with that object. For example, the first desktop shown in Figure 1-7 illustrates what happens when you click the Start button with the left mouse button to open the Start menu. Clicking the Start button with the right button, however, opens the Start button's shortcut menu, as shown in the second desktop.

Figure 1-7 CLICKING WITH THE LEFT AND RIGHT MOUSE BUTTONS

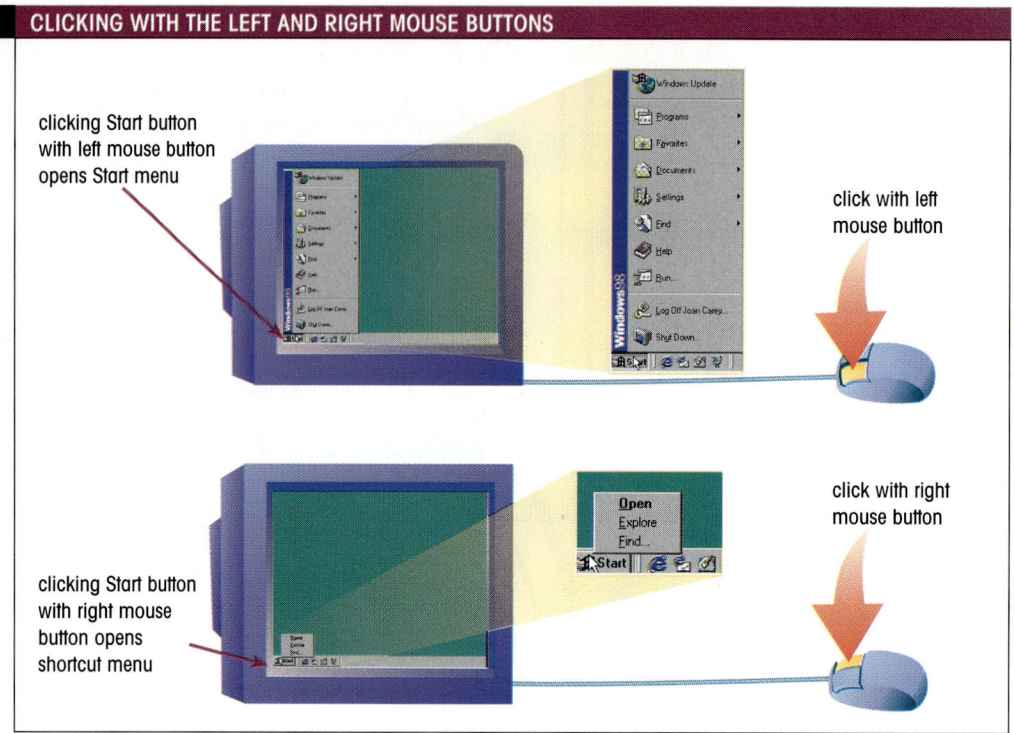

Try using right-clicking to open the shortcut menu for the Start button.

To right-click an object:

1. Position the pointer over the Start button.

2. Right-click the **Start** button. The shortcut menu that opens offers a list of options available to the Start button.

   TROUBLE? If you are using a trackball or a mouse with three buttons or a wheel, make sure you click the button on the far right, not the one in the middle.

   TROUBLE? If your menu looks slightly different from the one in Figure 1-8, don't worry. Computers with different software often have different options.

Figure 1-8 START BUTTON SHORTCUT MENU

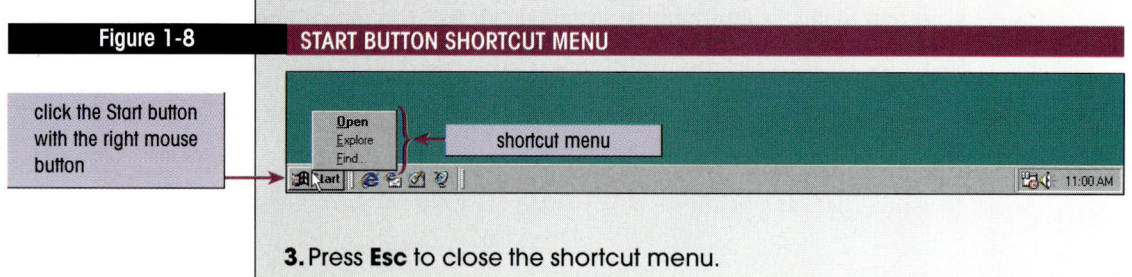

click the Start button with the right mouse button

3. Press **Esc** to close the shortcut menu.

You again return to the desktop.

TUTORIAL 1 EXPLORING THE BASICS   WIN 98   1.11   WINDOWS

Starting and Closing a Program

The software you use is sometimes referred to as a **program** or an **application**. To use a program, such as a word-processing program, you must first start it. With Windows 98 you start a program by clicking the Start button.

The Reference Window below explains how to start a program. Don't do the steps in the Reference Window now; they are for your later reference.

REFERENCE WINDOW — RW

Starting a Program
- Click the Start button, and point to Programs.
- If necessary, point to the submenu option that contains your program, then click the name of the program you want to run.

Windows 98 includes an easy-to-use word-processing program called WordPad. Suppose you want to start the WordPad program and use it to write a letter or report. You open Windows 98 programs from the Start menu. Programs are usually located on the Programs submenu or on one of its submenus. To start WordPad, for example, you navigate the Programs and Accessories submenus.

To start the WordPad program from the Start menu:

1. Click the **Start** button 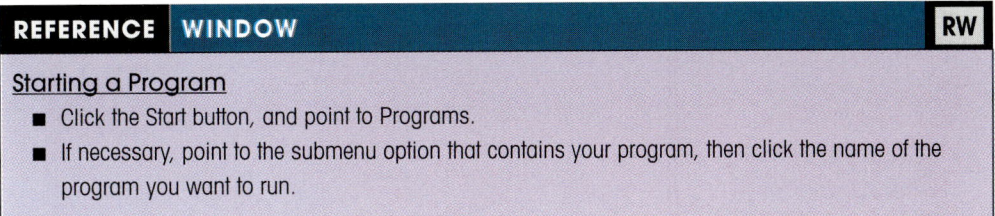 to open the Start menu.

2. Point to **Programs**. The Programs submenu appears.

3. Point to **Accessories**. Another submenu appears. Figure 1-9 shows the open menus.

   TROUBLE? If a different menu opens, you might have moved the mouse diagonally so that a different submenu opened. Move the pointer to the right across the Programs option, and then move it up or down to point to Accessories. Once you're more comfortable moving the mouse, you'll find that you can eliminate this problem by moving the mouse quickly.

Figure 1-9 START MENU

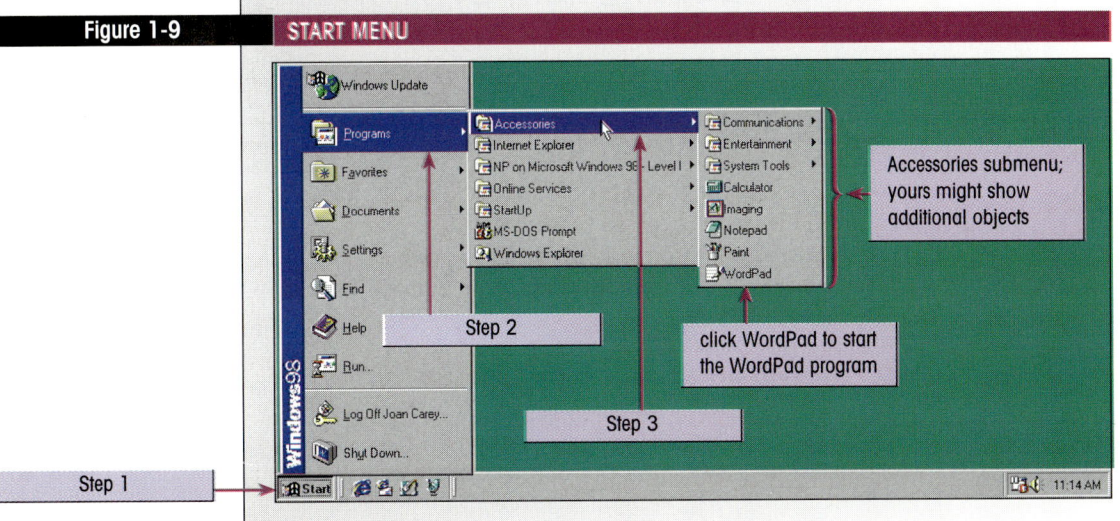

4. Click **WordPad**. The WordPad program opens, as shown in Figure 1-10. If the WordPad window does not fill the entire screen, don't worry. You will learn how to manipulate windows in Session 1.2.

Figure 1-10   THE WORDPAD PROGRAM

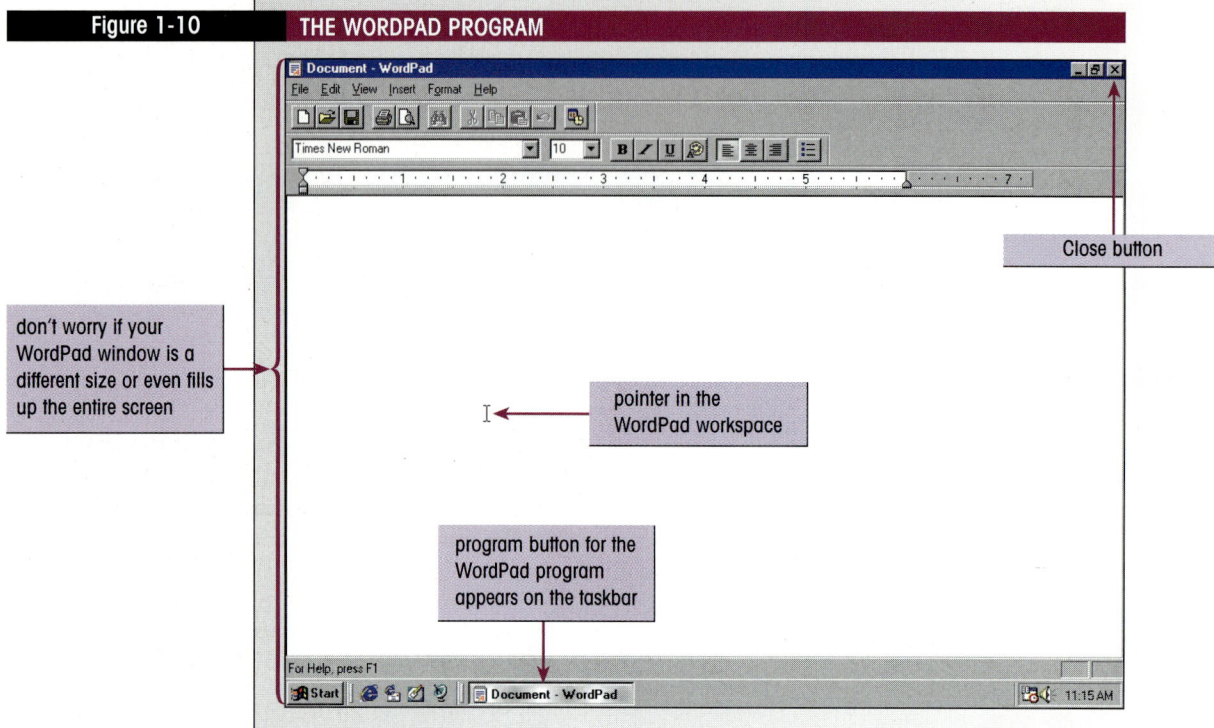

don't worry if your WordPad window is a different size or even fills up the entire screen

When a program is started, it is said to be **running**. A program button appears on the taskbar. **Program buttons** give you access to the programs running on the desktop.

When you are finished using a program, the easiest way to close it is to click the Close button ⊠.

To exit the WordPad program:

1. Click the **Close** button ⊠. See Figure 1-10. You return to the Windows 98 desktop.

Running Multiple Programs

One of the most useful features of Windows 98 is its ability to run multiple programs at the same time. This feature, known as **multitasking**, allows you to work on more than one project at a time and to switch quickly between projects. For example, you can start WordPad and leave it running while you then start the Paint program.

To run WordPad and Paint at the same time:

1. Start WordPad, then click the **Start** button again.
2. Point to **Programs**, then point to **Accessories**.

3. Click **Paint**. The Paint program appears, as shown in Figure 1-11. Now two programs are running at the same time.

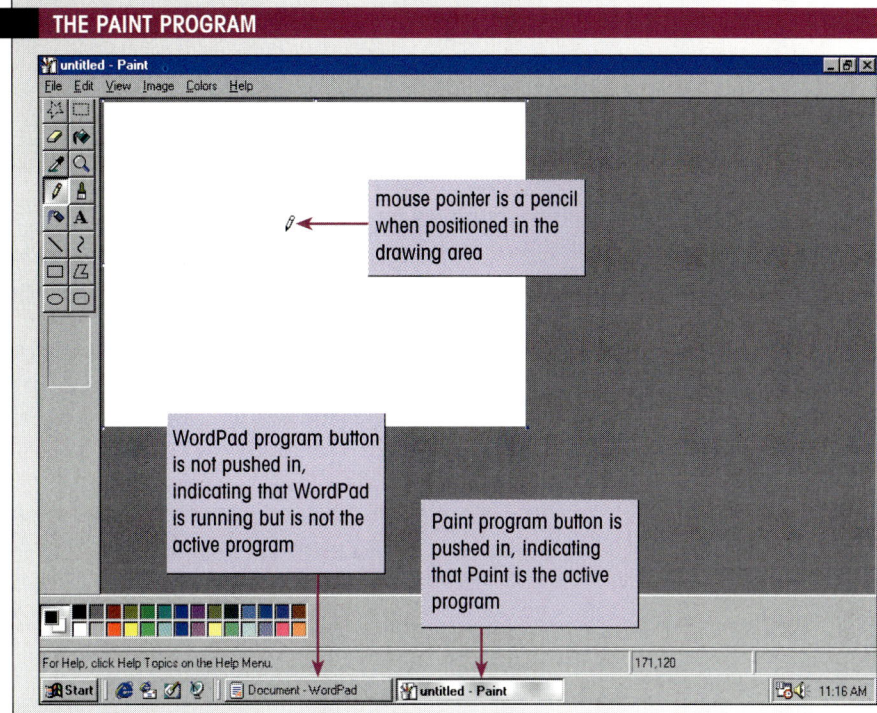

Figure 1-11 **THE PAINT PROGRAM**

TROUBLE? If the Paint program does not fill the entire screen, don't worry. You will learn how to manipulate windows in Session 1.2.

What happened to WordPad? The WordPad program button is still on the taskbar, so even if you can't see it, WordPad is still running. You can imagine that it is stacked behind the Paint program, as shown in Figure 1-12.

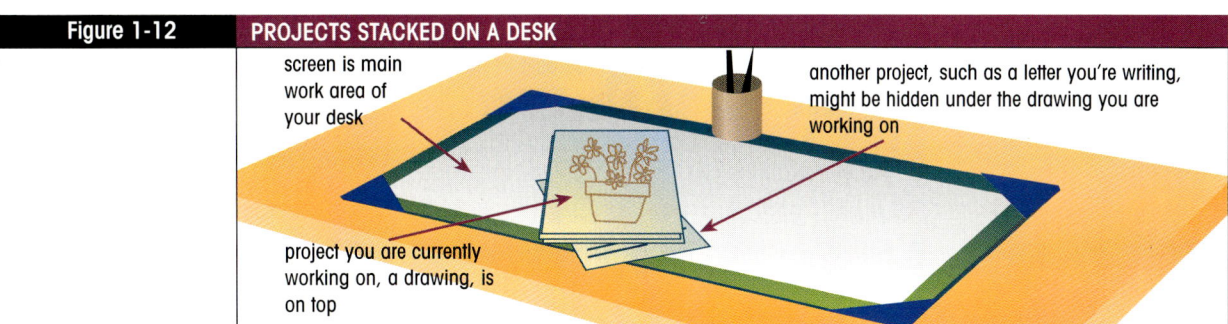

Figure 1-12 **PROJECTS STACKED ON A DESK**

Switching Between Programs

Although Windows 98 allows you to run more than one program, only one program at a time is active. The **active** program is the program with which you are currently working. The easiest way to switch between programs is to use the buttons on the taskbar.

To switch between WordPad and Paint:

1. Click the button labeled **Document - WordPad** on the taskbar. The Document - WordPad button now looks as if it has been pushed in, to indicate that it is the active program, and WordPad moves to the front.

2. Next, click the button labeled **untitled - Paint** on the taskbar to switch to the Paint program.

The Paint program is again the active program.

Accessing the Desktop from the Quick Launch Toolbar

The Windows 98 taskbar, as you've seen, displays buttons for programs currently running. It also can contain **toolbars**, sets of buttons that give single-click access to programs or documents. In its default state, the Windows 98 taskbar displays the **Quick Launch toolbar**, which gives quick access to Web programs and to the desktop. Your taskbar might contain additional toolbars, or none at all.

When you are running more than one program but you want to return to the desktop, perhaps to use one of the desktop icons such as My Computer, you can do so by using one of the Quick Launch toolbar buttons. Clicking the Show Desktop button returns you to the desktop. The open programs are not closed; they are simply inactive.

To return to the desktop:

1. Click the **Show Desktop** button on the Quick Launch toolbar. The desktop appears, and both the Paint and WordPad programs are temporarily inactive. See Figure 1-13.

   TROUBLE? If the Quick Launch toolbar doesn't appear on your taskbar, right-click the taskbar, point to Toolbars, and then click Quick Launch and try Step 1 again.

Figure 1-13 ACCESSING THE DESKTOP

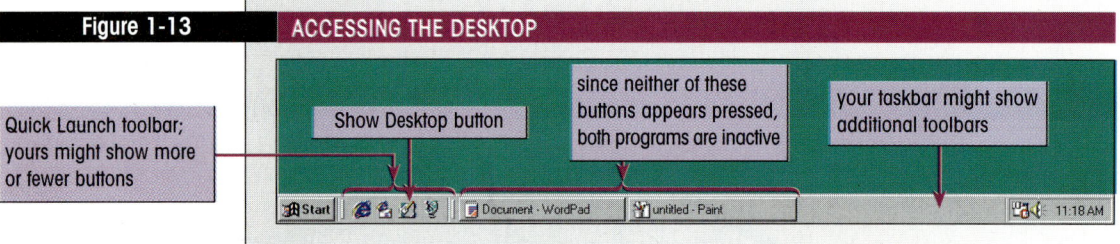

Closing Inactive Programs from the Taskbar

It is good practice to close each program when you are finished using it. Each program uses computer resources, such as memory, so Windows 98 works more efficiently when only the programs you need are open. You've already seen how to close an open program using the Close button. You can also close a program, whether active or inactive, by using the shortcut menu associated with the program button on the taskbar.

TUTORIAL 1 EXPLORING THE BASICS   WIN 98 1.15   WINDOWS

To close WordPad and Paint using the program button shortcut menus:

1. Right-click the **untitled - Paint** button on the taskbar. To right-click something, remember that you click it with the right mouse button. The shortcut menu for that program button opens. See Figure 1-14.

Figure 1-14   PROGRAM BUTTON SHORTCUT MENU

- shortcut menu opens when you right-click program button
- click to close inactive program

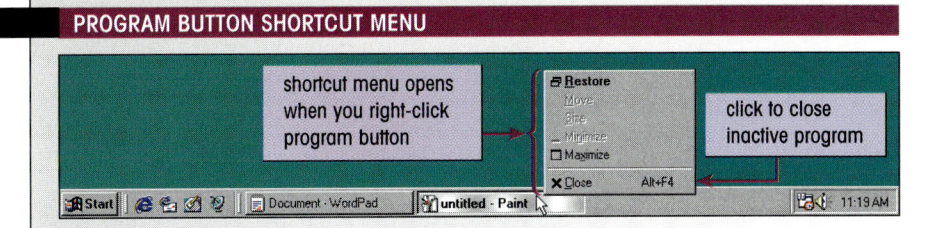

2. Click **Close**. The button labeled "untitled – Paint" disappears from the taskbar, and the Paint program closes.

3. Right-click the **Document - WordPad** button on the taskbar, and then click **Close**. The WordPad button disappears from the taskbar.

Shutting Down Windows 98

It is very important to shut down Windows 98 before you turn off the computer. If you turn off your computer without correctly shutting down, you might lose data and damage your files.

You should typically use the "Shut down" option when you want to turn off your computer. However, your school might prefer that you select the Log Off option on the Start menu. This option logs you out of Windows 98, leaves the computer turned on, and allows another user to log on without restarting the computer. Check with your instructor or technical support person for the preferred method at your school's computer lab.

To shut down Windows 98:

1. Click the **Start** button on the taskbar to display the Start menu.

2. Click the **Shut Down** menu option. A box titled "Shut Down Windows" opens.

   TROUBLE? If you can't see the Shut Down menu option, your Start menu has more options than your screen can display. A small arrow appears at the bottom of the Start menu. Click this button until the Shut Down menu option appears, and then click Shut Down.

   TROUBLE? If you are supposed to log off rather than shut down, click the Log Off option instead and follow your school's logoff procedure.

3. Make sure the **Shut down** option is preceded by a small black bullet. See Figure 1-15.

   TROUBLE? If your Shut down option is not preceded by a small black bullet, point to the circle preceding the Shut down option and click it. A small black bullet appears in the circle, indicating that Windows 98 will perform the Shut down option. Your Shut Down Windows dialog box might show additional options, such as Stand by.

Figure 1-15 | **SHUTTING DOWN**

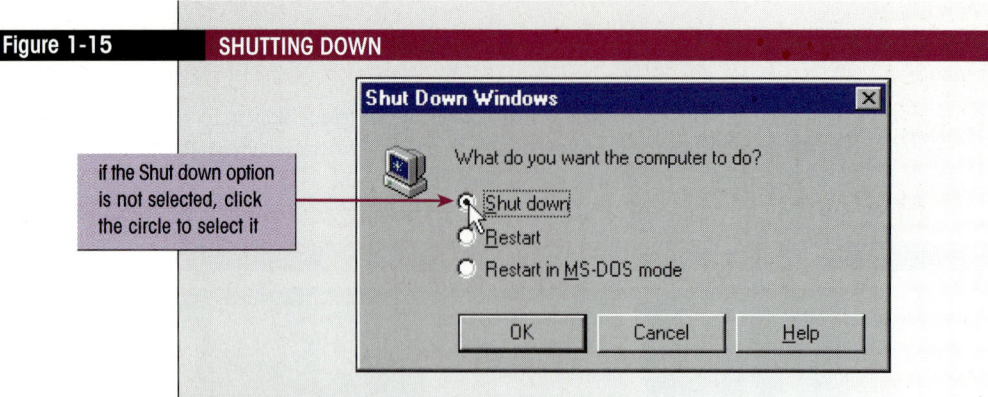

if the Shut down option is not selected, click the circle to select it

4. Click the **OK** button.

5. Click the **Yes** button if you are asked if you are sure you want to shut down.

6. Wait until you see a message indicating it is safe to turn off your computer. If your lab staff has requested you to switch off your computer after shutting down, do so now. Otherwise leave the computer running. Some computers turn themselves off automatically.

Quick Check

1. What is the purpose of the taskbar?

2. The _____ feature of Windows 98 allows you to run more than one program at a time.

3. The _____ is a list of options that provides you with access to programs, documents, submenus, and more.

4. What should you do if you are trying to move the pointer to the left edge of your screen, but your mouse bumps into the keyboard?

5. Even if you can't see an open program on your desktop, the program might be running. How can you tell if a program is running?

6. Why is it good practice to close each program when you are finished using it?

7. Why should you shut down Windows 98 before you turn off your computer?

SESSION 1.2

In this session you will learn how to use many of the Windows 98 controls to manipulate windows and programs. You will also learn how to change the size and shape of a window; how to move a window; and how to use menus, dialog boxes, tabs, buttons, and lists to specify how you want a program to carry out a task.

Anatomy of a Window

When you run a program in Windows 98, it appears in a window. A **window** is a rectangular area of the screen that contains a program or data. Windows, spelled with an uppercase "W," is the name of the Microsoft operating system. The word "window" with a lowercase "w" refers to one of the rectangular areas on the screen. A window also contains controls for manipulating the window and for using the program. Figure 1-16 describes the controls you are likely to see in most windows.

Figure 1-16	WINDOW CONTROLS
CONTROL	DESCRIPTION
Menu bar	Contains the titles of menus, such as File, Edit, and Help
Pointer	Lets you manipulate window objects
Program button	Appears on the taskbar to indicate that a program is running on the desktop; appears pressed when program is active and not pressed when program is inactive
Sizing buttons	Let you enlarge, shrink, or close a window
Status bar	Provides you with messages relevant to the task you are performing
Title bar	Contains the window title and basic window control buttons
Toolbar	Contains buttons that provide you with shortcuts to common menu commands
Window title	Identifies the program and document contained in the window
Workspace	Part of the window you use to enter your work—to enter text, draw pictures, set up calculations, and so on

WordPad is a good example of a typical window, so try starting WordPad and identifying these controls in the WordPad window.

To look at window controls:

1. Make sure Windows 98 is running and you are at the Windows 98 desktop.
2. Start WordPad.

   TROUBLE? To start WordPad, click the Start button, point to Programs, point to Accessories, and then click WordPad.

3. On your screen, identify the controls labeled in Figure 1-17. Don't worry if your window fills the entire screen or is a different size. You'll learn to change window size shortly.

WINDOWS WIN 98 1.18 TUTORIAL 1 EXPLORING THE BASICS

Figure 1-17 **WORDPAD WINDOW CONTROLS**

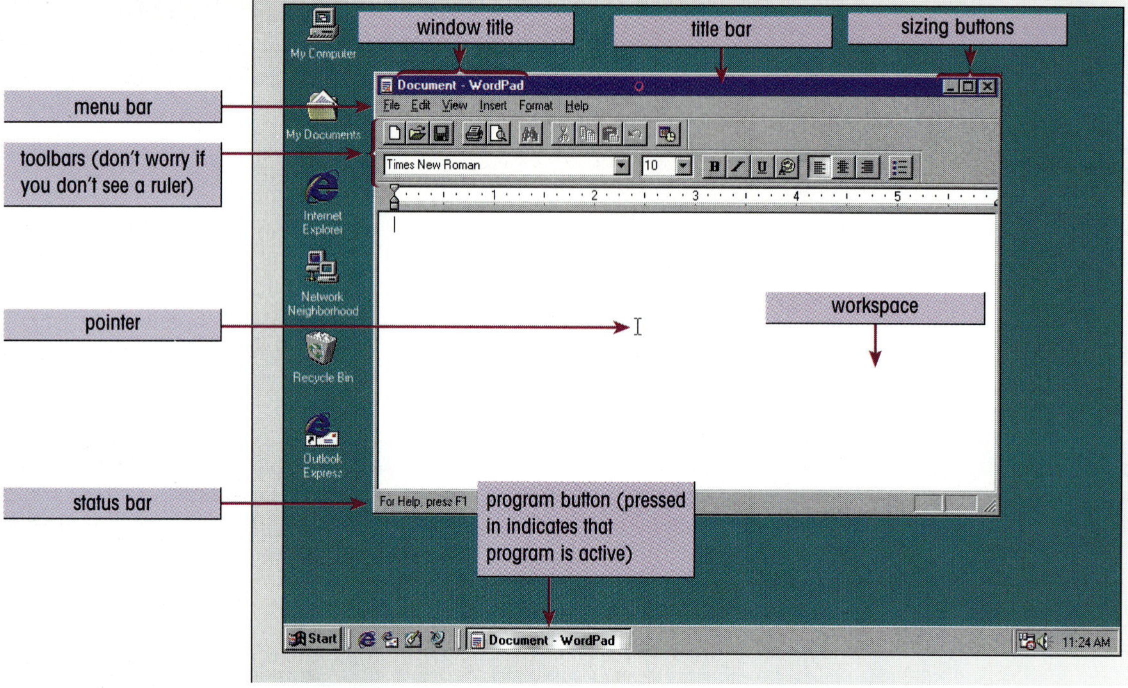

- menu bar
- toolbars (don't worry if you don't see a ruler)
- pointer
- status bar
- window title
- title bar
- sizing buttons
- workspace
- program button (pressed in indicates that program is active)

Manipulating a Window

There are three buttons located on the right side of the title bar. You are already familiar with the Close button. The Minimize button hides the window so that only its program button is visible on the taskbar. The other button either maximizes the window or restores it to a predefined size. Figure 1-18 shows how these buttons work.

Minimizing a Window

The Minimize button hides a window so that only the button on the taskbar remains visible. You can use the Minimize button when you want to temporarily hide a window but keep the program running.

To minimize the WordPad window:

1. Click the **Minimize** button. The WordPad window shrinks so that only the Document - WordPad button on the taskbar is visible.

   TROUBLE? If you accidentally clicked the Close button and closed the window, use the Start button to start WordPad again.

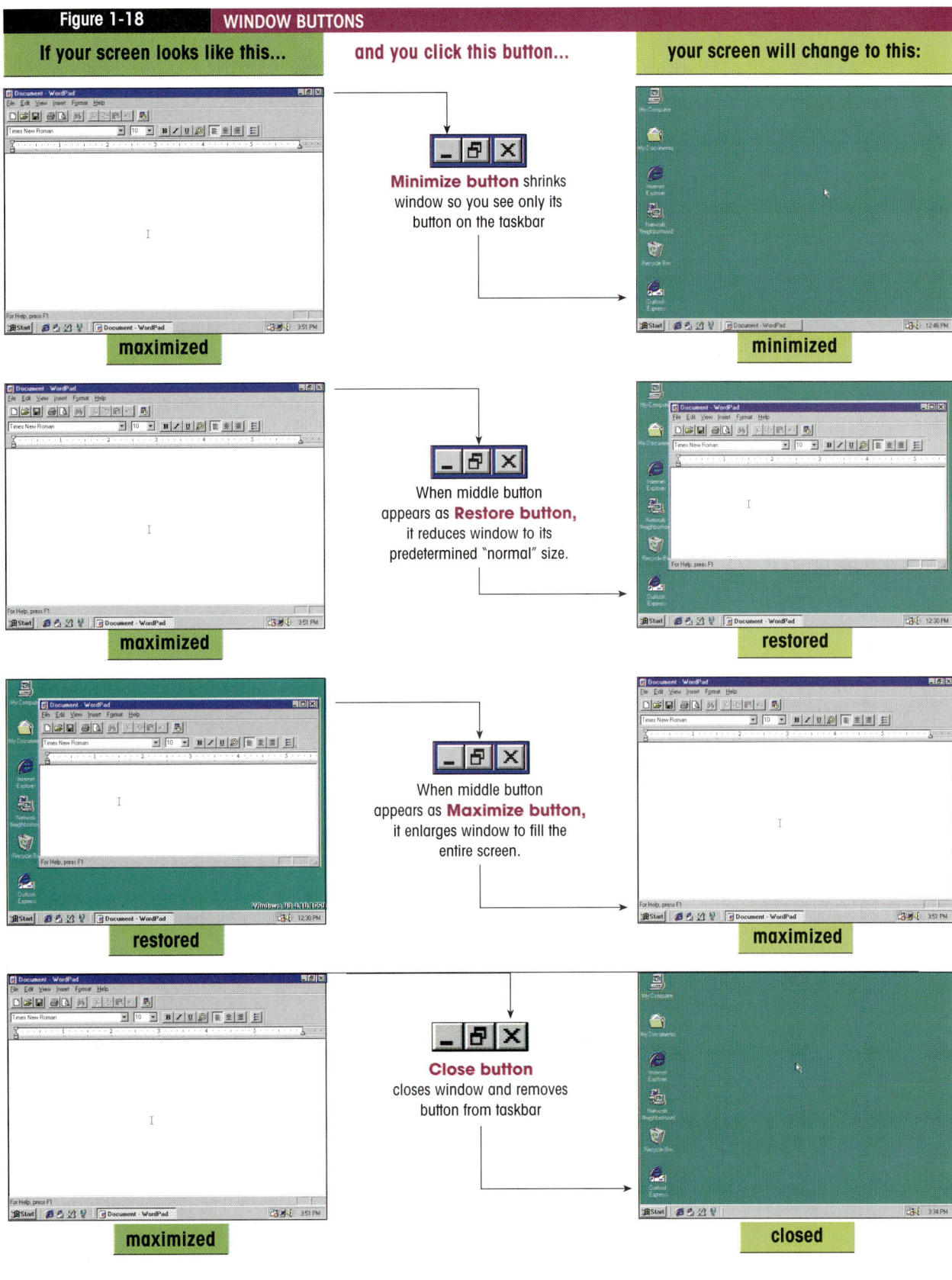

Redisplaying a Window

You can redisplay a minimized window by clicking the program's button on the taskbar. When you redisplay a window, it becomes the active window.

> #### To redisplay the WordPad window:
> 1. Click the **Document - WordPad** button on the taskbar. The WordPad window is restored to its previous size. The Document - WordPad button looks pushed in as a visual clue that WordPad is now the active window.
> 2. The taskbar button provides another means of switching a window between its minimized and active state: click the **Document - WordPad** button on the taskbar again to minimize the window.
> 3. Click the **Document - WordPad** button once more to redisplay the window.

Maximizing a Window

The Maximize button enlarges a window so that it fills the entire screen. You will probably do most of your work using maximized windows because they allow you to see more of your program and data.

> #### To maximize the WordPad window:
> 1. Click the **Maximize** button on the WordPad title bar.
>
> **TROUBLE?** If the window is already maximized, it will fill the entire screen, and the Maximize button won't appear. Instead, you'll see the Restore button. Skip Step 1.

Restoring a Window

The Restore button reduces the window so it is smaller than the entire screen. This is useful if you want to see more than one window at a time. Also, because of its smaller size, you can drag the window to another location on the screen or change its dimensions.

> #### To restore a window:
> 1. Click the **Restore** button on the WordPad title bar. Notice that once a window is restored, changes to the Maximize button.

Moving a Window

You can use the mouse to move a window to a new position on the screen. When you hold down the mouse button while moving the mouse, you are said to be **dragging**. You can move objects on the screen by dragging them to a new location. If you want to move a window, you drag its title bar. You cannot move a maximized window.

To drag the WordPad window to a new location:

1. Position the mouse pointer on the WordPad window title bar.
2. While you hold down the left mouse button, move the mouse to drag the window. A rectangle representing the window moves as you move the mouse.
3. Position the rectangle anywhere on the screen, then release the left mouse button. The WordPad window appears in the new location.
4. Now drag the WordPad window to the upper-left corner of the screen.

Changing the Size of a Window

You can also use the mouse to change the size of a window. Notice the sizing handle at the lower-right corner of the window. The **sizing handle** provides a visible control for changing the size of a window.

To change the size of the WordPad window:

1. Position the pointer over the sizing handle. The pointer changes to a diagonal arrow.
2. While holding down the mouse button, drag the sizing handle down and to the right.
3. Release the mouse button. Now the window is larger.
4. Practice using the sizing handle to make the WordPad window larger or smaller, and then maximize the WordPad window.

You can also drag the window borders left, right, up, or down to change a window's size.

Using Program Menus

Most Windows programs use menus to provide an easy way for you to select program commands. The menu bar is typically located at the top of the program window and shows the titles of menus such as File, Edit, and Help.

Windows menus are relatively standardized—most Windows programs include similar menu options. It's easy to learn new programs, because you can make a pretty good guess about which menu contains the command you want.

Selecting Commands from a Menu

When you click any menu title, choices for that menu appear below the menu bar. These choices are referred to as **menu options** or **commands**. To select a menu option, you click it. For example, the File menu is a standard feature in most Windows programs and contains the options typically related to working with a file: creating, opening, saving, and printing a file or document.

WINDOWS | WIN 98 | 1.22 | TUTORIAL 1　EXPLORING THE BASICS

To select the Print Preview menu option from the File menu:

1. Click **File** in the WordPad menu bar to display the File menu. See Figure 1-19.

   TROUBLE? If you open a menu but decide not to select any of the menu options, you can close the menu by clicking its title again.

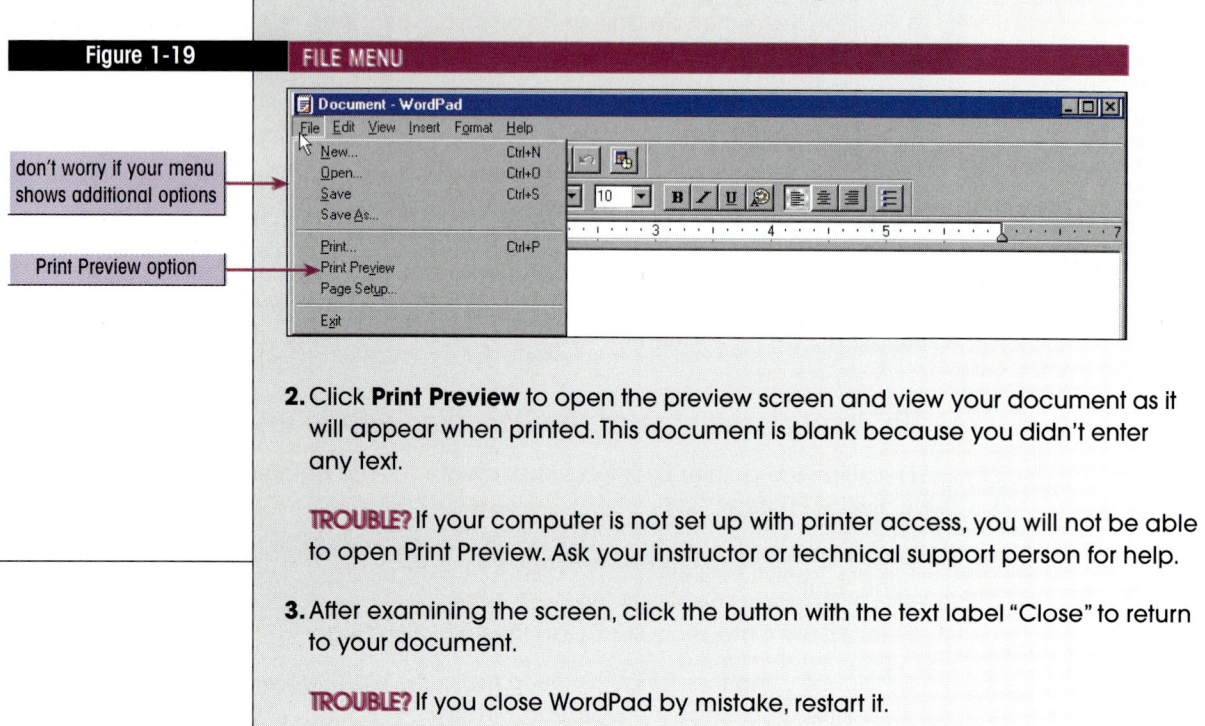

Figure 1-19　　FILE MENU

don't worry if your menu shows additional options

Print Preview option

2. Click **Print Preview** to open the preview screen and view your document as it will appear when printed. This document is blank because you didn't enter any text.

   TROUBLE? If your computer is not set up with printer access, you will not be able to open Print Preview. Ask your instructor or technical support person for help.

3. After examining the screen, click the button with the text label "Close" to return to your document.

   TROUBLE? If you close WordPad by mistake, restart it.

Not all menu options immediately carry out an action—some show submenus or ask you for more information about what you want to do. The menu gives you hints about what to expect when you select an option. These hints are sometimes referred to as **menu conventions**. Figure 1-20 describes the Windows 98 menu conventions.

Figure 1-20　　MENU CONVENTIONS

CONVENTION	DESCRIPTION
Check mark	Indicates a toggle, or "on-off" switch (like a light switch) that is either checked (turned on) or not checked (turned off)
Ellipsis	Three dots that indicate you must make additional selections after you select that option. Options without dots do not require additional choices—they take effect as soon as you click them. If an option is followed by an ellipsis, a dialog box opens that allows you to enter specifications for how you want a task carried out
Triangular arrow	Indicates presence of a submenu. When you point at a menu option that has a triangular arrow, a submenu automatically appears
Grayed-out option	Option that is not available. For example, a graphics program might display the Text Toolbar option in gray if there is no text in the graphic to work with
Keyboard shortcut	A key or combination of keys that you can press to activate the menu option without actually opening the menu

Figure 1-21 shows examples of these menu conventions.

Figure 1-21 EXAMPLES OF MENU CONVENTIONS

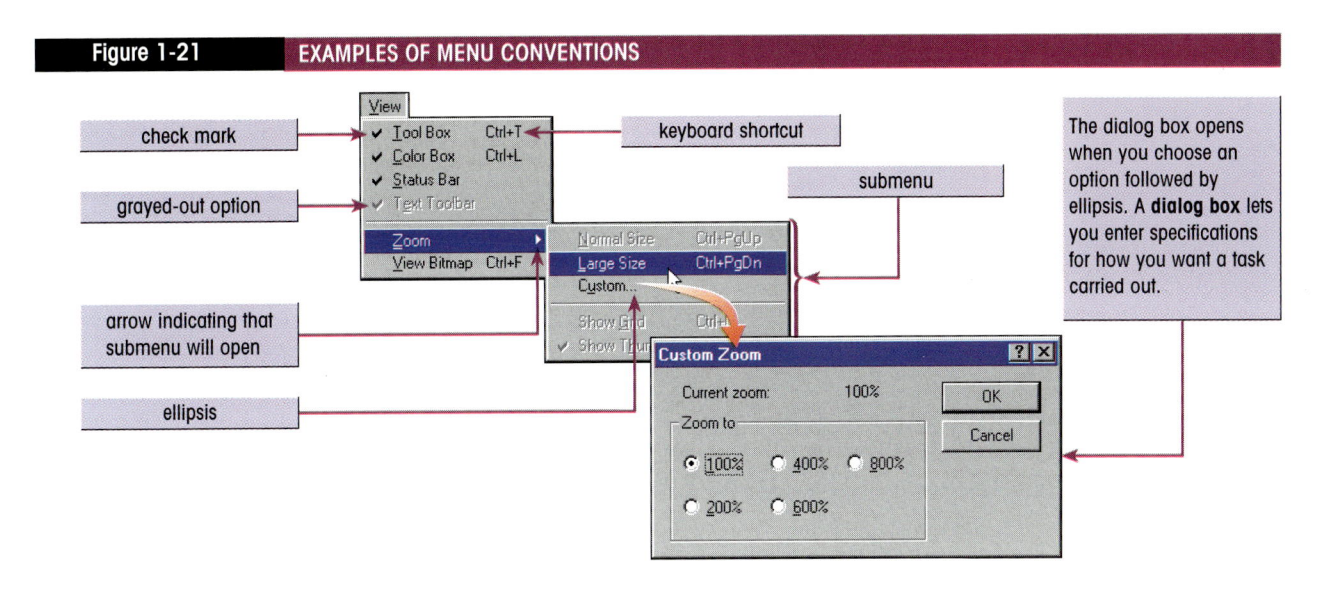

- check mark
- grayed-out option
- arrow indicating that submenu will open
- ellipsis
- keyboard shortcut
- submenu
- The dialog box opens when you choose an option followed by ellipsis. A **dialog box** lets you enter specifications for how you want a task carried out.

Using Toolbars

A toolbar, as you've seen, contains buttons that provide quick access to important commands. Although you can usually perform all program commands using menus, the toolbar provides convenient one-click access to frequently used commands. For most Windows 98 functions, there is usually more than one way to accomplish a task. To simplify your introduction to Windows 98 in this tutorial, we will usually show you only one method for performing a task. As you become more accomplished at using Windows 98, you can explore alternate methods.

In Session 1.1 you learned that Windows 98 programs include ToolTips, which indicate the purpose and function of a tool. Now is a good time to explore the WordPad toolbar buttons by looking at their ToolTips.

To find out a toolbar button's function:

1. Position the pointer over any button on the toolbar, such as the Print Preview button. After a short pause, the name of the button appears in a box near the button, and a description of the button appears in the status bar just above the Start button. See Figure 1-22.

Figure 1-22 TOOLBAR BUTTON AIDS

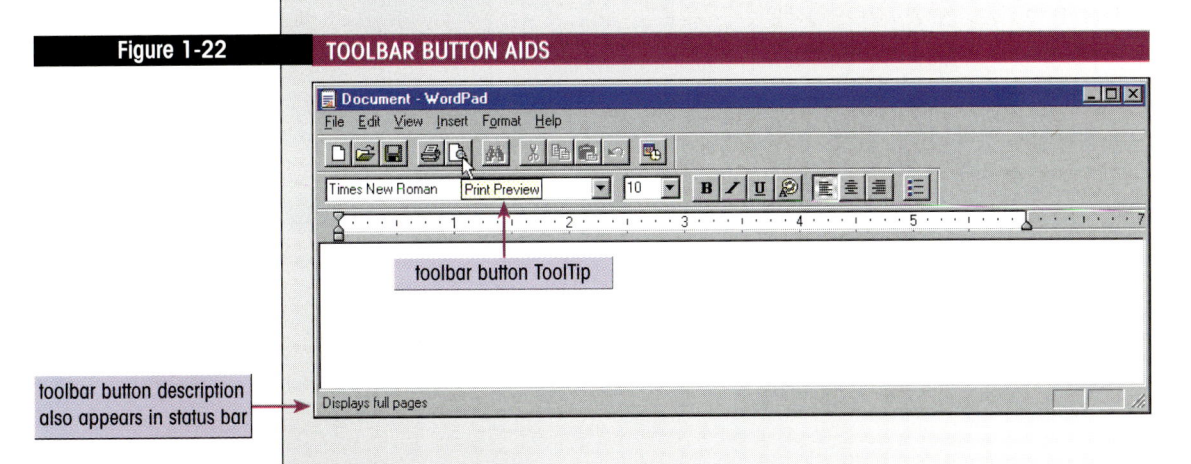

- toolbar button ToolTip
- toolbar button description also appears in status bar

2. Move the pointer to each button on the toolbar to see its name and purpose.

You select a toolbar button by clicking it.

To select the Print Preview toolbar button:

1. Click the **Print Preview** button 🔍. The Print Preview screen appears. This is the same screen that appeared when you selected Print Preview from the File menu.

2. After examining the screen, click the button with the text label "Close" to return to your document.

Using List Boxes and Scroll Bars

As you might guess from the name, a **list box** displays a list of choices. In WordPad, date and time formats are shown in the Date/Time list box. List box controls usually include arrow buttons, a scroll bar, and a scroll box, as shown in Figure 1-23.

To use the Date/Time list box:

1. Click the **Date/Time** button 📅 to display the Date and Time dialog box. See Figure 1-23.

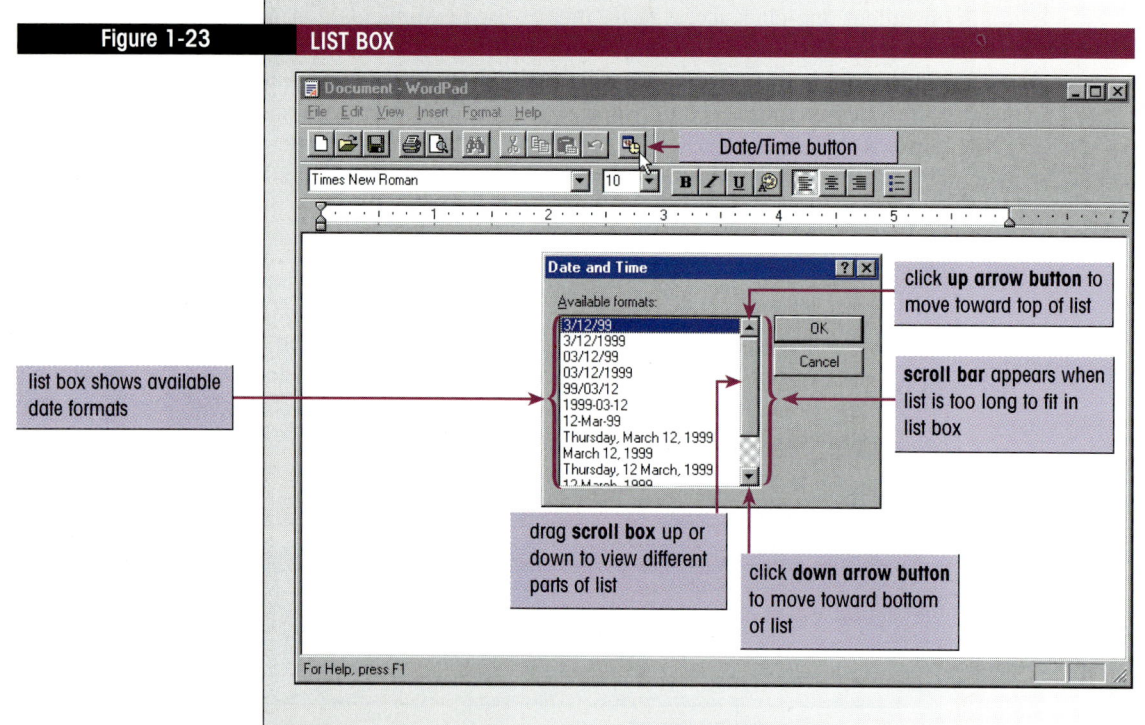

Figure 1-23   **LIST BOX**

- Date/Time button
- list box shows available date formats
- click **up arrow button** to move toward top of list
- **scroll bar** appears when list is too long to fit in list box
- drag **scroll box** up or down to view different parts of list
- click **down arrow button** to move toward bottom of list

2. To scroll down the list, click the **down arrow** button ▼. See Figure 1-23.

3. Find the scroll box on your screen. See Figure 1-23.

4. Drag the **scroll box** to the top of the scroll bar. Notice how the list scrolls back to the beginning.

TUTORIAL 1 EXPLORING THE BASICS   WIN 98 1.25   WINDOWS

> **TROUBLE?** You learned how to drag when you learned to move a window. To drag the scroll box up, point to the scroll box, press and hold down the mouse button, and then move the mouse up.
>
> 5. Find a date format similar to "March 12, 1999." Click that date format to select it.
>
> 6. Click the **OK** button to close the Date and Time dialog box. This inserts the current date in your document.

You can access some list boxes directly from the toolbar. When a list box is on the toolbar, only the current option appears in the list box. A **list arrow** appears on the right of the box that you can click to view additional options.

To use the Font Size list box:

1. Click the **list arrow** shown in Figure 1-24.

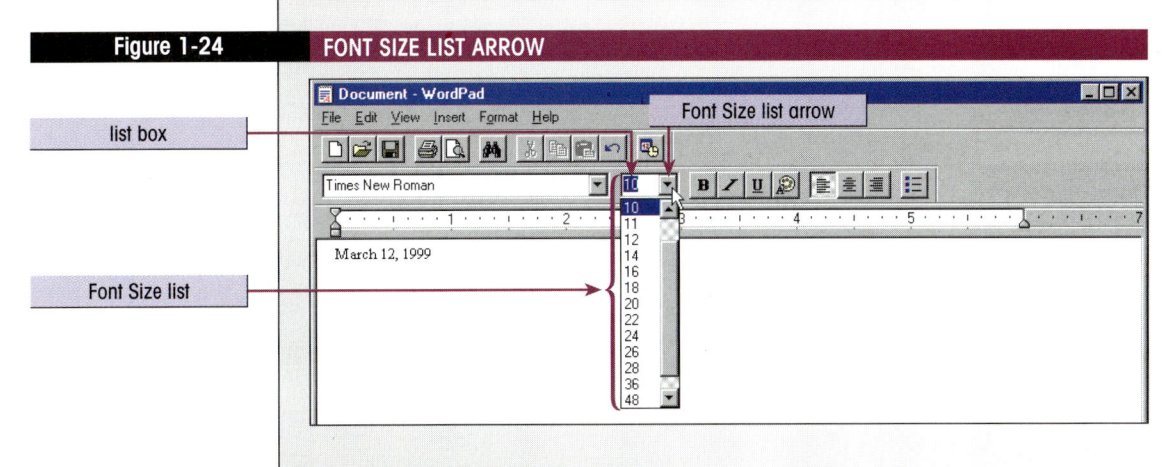

Figure 1-24 **FONT SIZE LIST ARROW**

list box

Font Size list

2. Click **18**. The list disappears, and the font size you selected appears in the list box.

3. Type a few characters to test the new font size.

4. Click the **Font Size** list arrow again.

5. Click **12**.

6. Type a few characters to test this type size.

7. Click the **Close** button ⊠ to close WordPad.

8. When you see the message "Save changes to Document?" click the **No** button.

Using Dialog Box Controls

Recall that when you select a menu option or button followed by an ellipsis, a dialog box opens that allows you to provide more information about how a program should carry out a task. Some dialog boxes group different kinds of information into bordered rectangular areas called **panes**. Within these panes, you will usually find tabs, option buttons, check boxes, and other controls that the program uses to collect information about how you want it to perform a task. Figure 1-25 describes common dialog box controls.

Figure 1-25   DIALOG BOX CONTROLS

CONTROL	DESCRIPTION
Tabs	Modeled after the tabs on file folders, tab controls are often used as containers for other Windows 98 controls such as list boxes, radio buttons, and check boxes. Click the appropriate tab to view different pages of information or choices.
Option buttons	Also called **radio buttons**, option buttons allow you to select a single option from among one or more options.
Check boxes	Click a check box to select or deselect it; when it is selected, a check mark appears, indicating that the option is turned on; when deselected, the check box is blank and the option is off. When check boxes appear in groups, you can select or deselect as many as you want; they are not mutually exclusive, as option buttons are.
Spin boxes	Allow you to scroll easily through a set of numbers to choose the setting you want
Text boxes	Boxes into which you type additional information

Figure 1-26 displays examples of these controls.

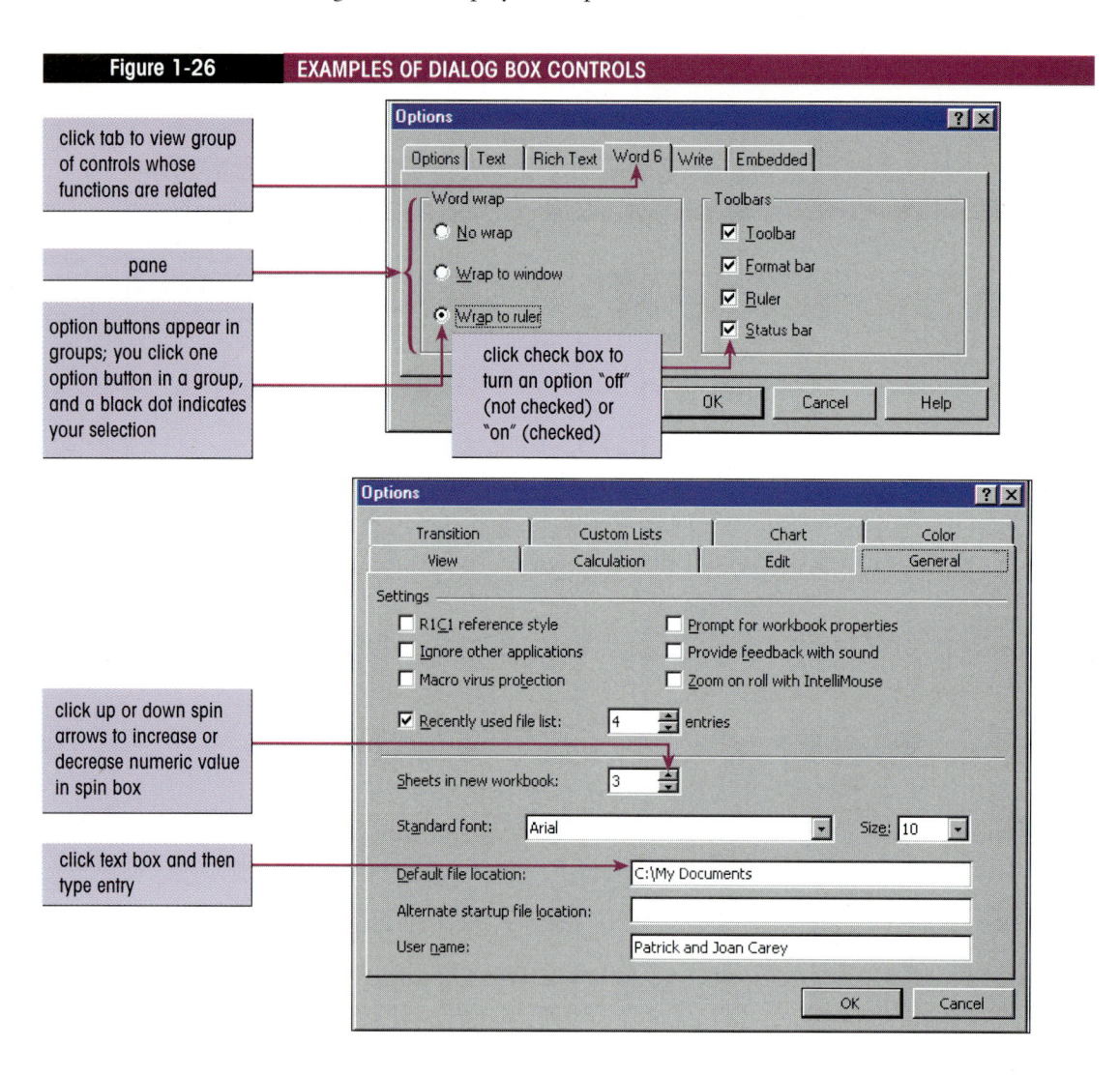

Figure 1-26   EXAMPLES OF DIALOG BOX CONTROLS

- click tab to view group of controls whose functions are related
- pane
- option buttons appear in groups; you click one option button in a group, and a black dot indicates your selection
- click check box to turn an option "off" (not checked) or "on" (checked)
- click up or down spin arrows to increase or decrease numeric value in spin box
- click text box and then type entry

Using Help

Windows 98 **Help** provides on-screen information about the program you are using. Help for the Windows 98 operating system is available by clicking the Start button on the taskbar, then selecting Help from the Start menu. If you want Help for a program, such as WordPad, you must first start the program, then click Help on the menu bar.

When you start Help, a Windows Help window opens, which gives you access to help files stored on your computer as well as help information stored on Microsoft's Web site. If you are not connected to the Web, you only have access to the help files stored on your computer.

To start Windows 98 Help:

1. Click the **Start** button.
2. Click **Help**. The Windows Help window opens to the Contents tab. See Figure 1-27.

   TROUBLE? If the Contents tab is not in front, click the Contents tab to view Help contents.

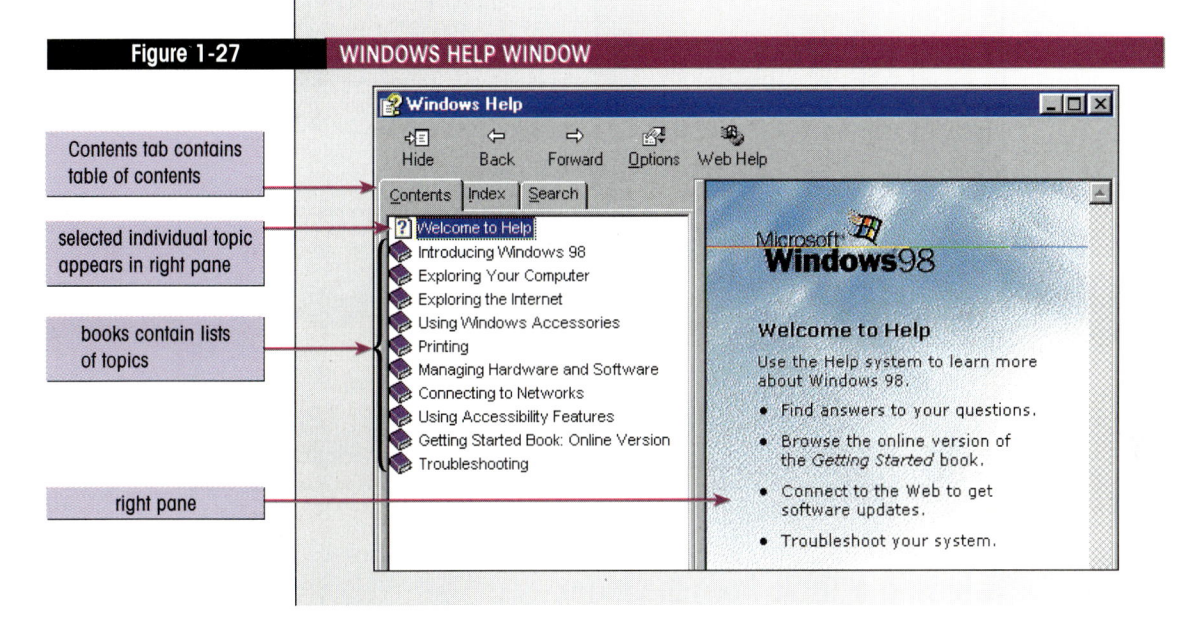

Figure 1-27   WINDOWS HELP WINDOW

- Contents tab contains table of contents
- selected individual topic appears in right pane
- books contain lists of topics
- right pane

Help uses tabs for the three sections of Help: Contents, Index, and Search. The **Contents tab** groups Help topics into a series of books. You select a book by clicking it. The book opens, and a list of related topics appears from which you can choose. Individual topics are designated with the icon.

The **Index tab** displays an alphabetical list of all the Help topics from which you can choose. The **Search tab** allows you to search the entire set of Help topics for all topics that contain a word or words you specify.

Viewing Topics from the Contents Tab

You've already opened two of the Windows accessories, Paint and WordPad. Suppose you're wondering about the other accessory programs. You can use the Contents tab to find more information on a specific topic.

To use the Contents tab:

1. Click the **Using Windows Accessories** book icon . A list of topics and related books appears below the book title. You decide to explore entertainment accessories.

2. Click the **Entertainment** book icon .

3. Click the **CD Player** topic icon . Information about the CD Player accessory appears in the right pane, explaining how you can use the CD-ROM drive (if you have one) on your computer to play your favorite music CDs. See Figure 1-28.

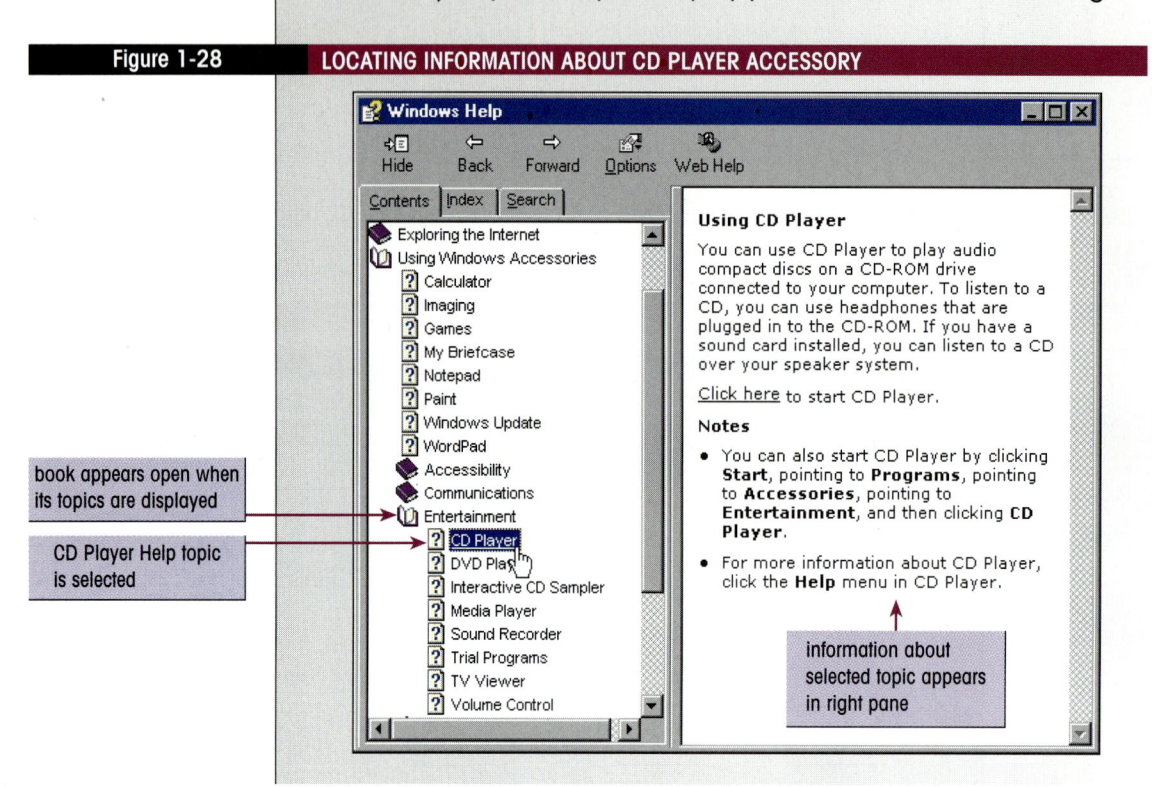

Figure 1-28   **LOCATING INFORMATION ABOUT CD PLAYER ACCESSORY**

- book appears open when its topics are displayed
- CD Player Help topic is selected
- information about selected topic appears in right pane

Selecting a Topic from the Index

The Index tab allows you to jump to a Help topic by selecting a topic from an indexed list. For example, you can use the Index tab to learn how to arrange the open windows on your desktop.

To find a Help topic using the Index tab:

1. Click the **Index** tab. A long list of indexed Help topics appears.

   TROUBLE? If this is the first time you've used Help on your computer, Windows 98 needs to set up the Index. This takes just a few moments. Wait until you see the list of index entries in the left pane, and then proceed to Step 2.

2. Drag the scroll box down to view additional topics.

3. You can quickly jump to any part of the list by typing the first few characters of a word or phrase in the box above the Index list. Click the box and then type **desktop** to display topics related to the Windows 98 desktop.

TUTORIAL 1 EXPLORING THE BASICS   WIN 98   1.29

4. Click the topic **arranging windows on** and then click the **Display** button. When there is just one topic, it appears immediately in the right pane; otherwise, the Topics Found window opens, listing all topics indexed under the entry you're interested in. In this case, there are two choices.

5. Click **To minimize all open windows**, and then click the **Display** button. The information you requested appears in the right pane. See Figure 1-29. Notice in this topic that there is an underlined word: taskbar. You can click underlined words to view definitions or additional information.

Figure 1-29   USING THE INDEX TO LOCATE INFORMATION

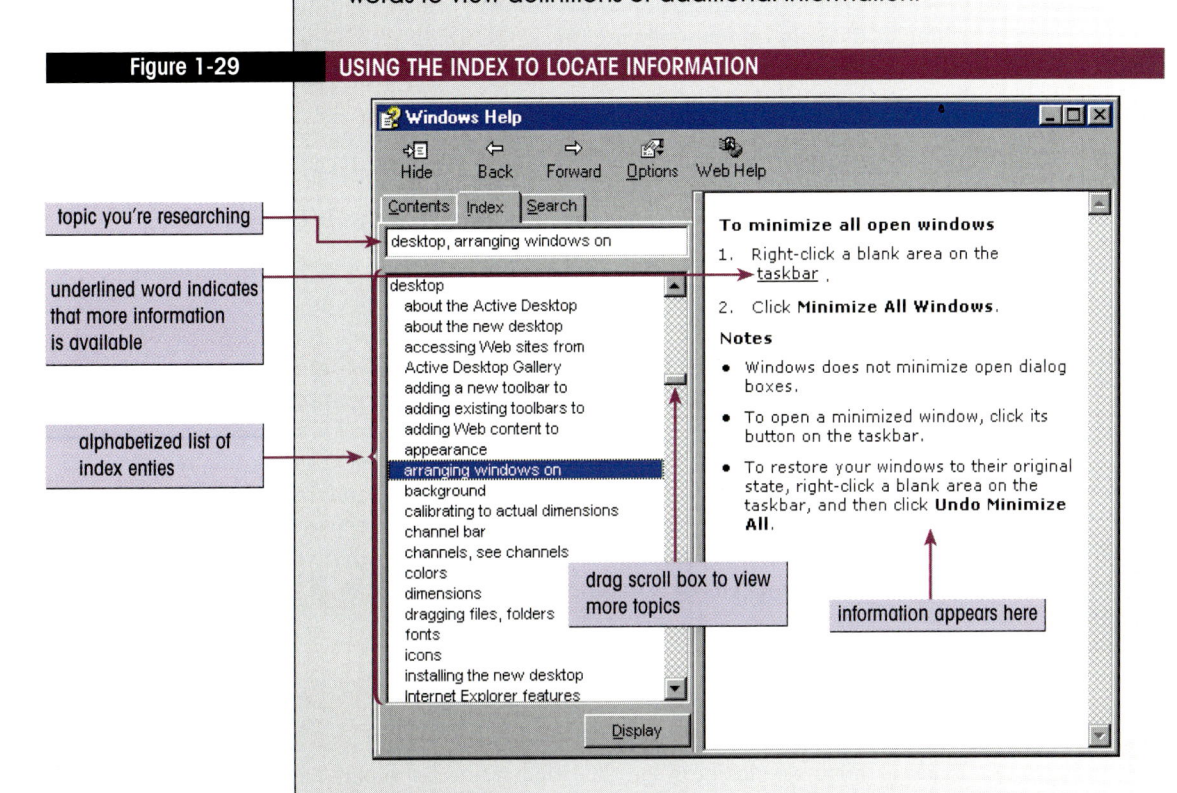

- topic you're researching
- underlined word indicates that more information is available
- alphabetized list of index entries
- drag scroll box to view more topics
- information appears here

6. Click **taskbar**. A small box appears that defines the term "taskbar." See Figure 1-30.

Figure 1-30   VIEWING ADDITIONAL INFORMATION

- clicking underlined word opens small box with more information

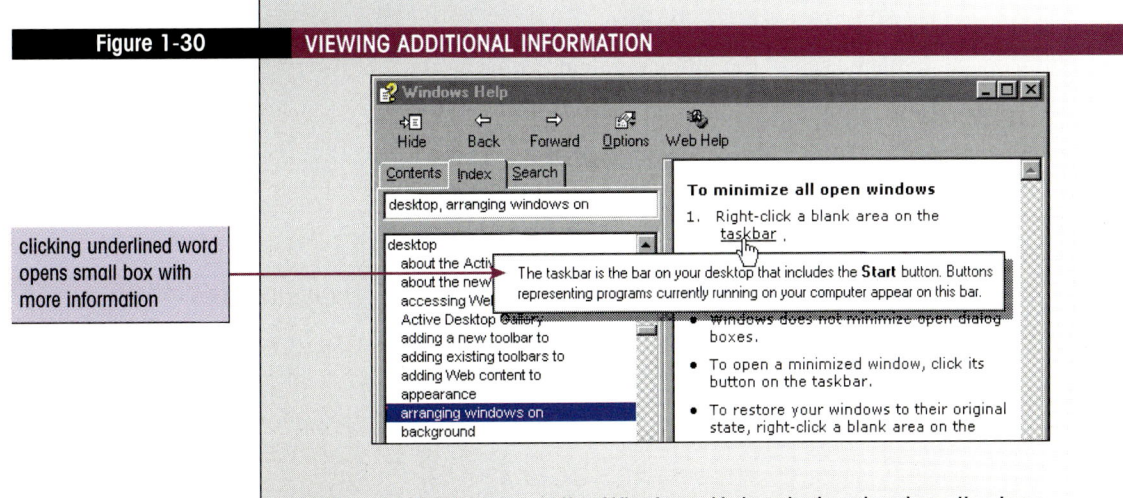

7. Click a blank area of the Windows Help window to close the box.

The third tab, the Search tab, works similarly to the Index tab, except that you type a word, and then the Help system searches for topics containing that word. You'll get a chance to experiment with the Search tab in the Tutorial Assignments.

Returning to a Previous Help Topic

You've looked at a few topics now. Suppose you want to return to the one you just saw. The Help window includes a toolbar of buttons that help you navigate the Help system. One of these buttons is the **Back** button, which returns you to topics you've already viewed. Try returning to the help topic on playing music CDs on your CD-ROM drive.

To return to a help topic:

1. Click the **Back** button. The Using CD Player topic appears.
2. Click the **Close** button ⊠ to close the Windows Help window.
3. Log off or shut down Windows 98, depending on your lab's requirements.

Now that you know how Windows 98 Help works, don't forget to use it! Use Help when you need to perform a new task or when you forget how to complete a procedure.

You've finished the tutorial, and as you shut down Windows 98, Steve Laslow returns from class. You take a moment to tell him all you've learned: you know how to start and close programs and how to use multiple programs at the same time. You have learned how to work with windows and the controls they employ. Finally, you've learned how to get help when you need it. Steve congratulates you and comments that you are well on your way to mastering the fundamentals of using the Windows 98 operating system.

QUICK CHECK

1. What is the difference between the title bar and a toolbar?
2. Provide the name and purpose of each button:
   a. ▭   b. ▭   c. ▭   d. ⊠
3. Explain each of the following menu conventions:
   a. Ellipsis...   b. Grayed-out   c. ▶   d. ✔
4. A(n) _____ consists of a group of buttons, each of which provides one-click access to important program functions.
5. What is the purpose of the scrollbar?
6. Option buttons allow you to select _____ option(s) at a time.
7. It is a good idea to use _____ when you need to learn how to perform new tasks.

TUTORIAL ASSIGNMENT

1. **Running Two Programs and Switching Between Them** In this tutorial you learned how to run more than one program at a time, using WordPad and Paint. You can run other programs at the same time, too. Complete the following steps and write out your answers to questions b through f:

   a. Start the computer. Enter your username and password if prompted to do so.
   b. Click the Start button. How many menu options are on the Start menu?
   c. Run the Calculator program located on the Accessories menu. How many program buttons are now on the taskbar (don't count toolbar buttons or items in the tray)?
   d. Run the Paint program and maximize the Paint window. How many programs are running now?
   e. Switch to Calculator. What are two visual clues that tell you that Calculator is the active program?
   f. Multiply 576 by 1457 using the Calculator accessory. What is the result?
   g. Close Calculator, then close Paint.

Explore

2. **WordPad Help** In Tutorial 1 you learned how to use Windows 98 Help. Just about every Windows 98 program has a help feature. Many computer users can learn to use a program just by using Help. To use Help, you start the program, then click the Help menu at the top of the screen. Try using WordPad Help:

   a. Start WordPad.
   b. Click Help on the WordPad menu bar, and then click Help Topics.
   c. Using WordPad Help, write out your answers to questions 1 through 4.
      1. How do you create a bulleted list?
      2. How do you set the margins in a document?
      3. How do you undo a mistake?
      4. How do you change the font style of a block of text?
   d. Close WordPad.

Explore

3. **The Search Tab** In addition to the Contents and Index tabs you worked with in this tutorial, Windows 98 Help also includes a Search tab. You may have heard that Windows 98 makes it possible to view television programs on your computer. You could browse through the Contents tab, although you might not know where to look to find information about television. You could also use the Index tab to search through the indexed entry. Or you could use the Search tab to find all Help topics that mention television.

   a. Start Windows 98 Help and use the Index tab to find information about television. How many topics are listed? What is their primary subject matter?
   b. Now use the Search tab to find information about television. Type "television" into the box on the Search tab, and then click the List Topics button.
   c. Write a paragraph comparing the two lists of topics. You don't have to view them all, but in your paragraph, indicate which tab seems to yield more information, and why. Close Help.

4. **Discover Windows 98** Windows 98 includes an online tour that helps you discover more about your computer and the Windows 98 operating system. You can use this tour to review what you learned in this tutorial and to pick up some new tips for using Windows 98. Complete the following steps and write out your answers to questions d–j.

   a. Click the Start button, point to Programs, point to Accessories, point to System Tools, and then click Welcome to Windows. If an error message appears at any point or if you can't locate this menu option, Welcome to Windows is probably not loaded on your computer. You will not be able to complete this assignment unless you have the Windows 98 CD. Check with your instructor.
   b. Click Discover Windows 98.
   c. Click Computer Essentials and follow the instructions on the screen to step through the tour.
   d. What is the "brain" of your computer, according to the tour information?
   e. What two devices do you use to communicate with your computer?

f. What is the purpose of the ESC key?
g. What is double-clicking?
h. What is the purpose of the top section of the Start menu?
i. What is another term for "submenu"?
j. What function key opens the Help feature in most software?

PROJECTS

1. There are many types of pointing devices on the market today. Go to the library and research the types of devices that are available. Consider what devices are appropriate for these situations: desktop or laptop computers, connected or remote devices, and ergonomic or standard designs (look up the word "ergonomic").

   Use up-to-date computer books, trade computer magazines such as *PC Computing* and *PC Magazine*, or the Internet (if you know how) to locate information. Your instructor might suggest specific resources you can use. Write a one-page report describing the types of devices available, the differing needs of users, special features that make pointing devices more useful, price comparisons, and finally, an indication of what you would choose if you needed to buy a pointing device.

2. Using the resources available to you, either through your library or the Internet (if you know how), locate information about the release of Windows 98. Computing trade magazines are an excellent source of information about software. Read several articles about Windows 98 and then write a one-page essay that discusses the features that seem most important to the people who have evaluated the software. If you find reviews of the software, mention the features that reviewers had the strongest reaction to, pro or con.

3. **Upgrading** is the process of placing a more recent version of a product onto your computer. When Windows 98 first came out, people had to decide whether or not they wanted to upgrade their computers to Windows 98. Interview several people you know (at least three) who are well-informed Windows computer users. Ask them whether they are using Windows 98 or an older version of Windows. If they are using an older version, ask why they have chosen not to upgrade. If they are using Windows 98, ask them why they chose to upgrade. Ask such questions as:

   a. What features convinced you to upgrade or made you decide to wait?
   b. What role did the price of the upgrade play?
   c. Would you have had (or did you have) to purchase new hardware to make the upgrade? How did this affect your decision?
   d. If you did upgrade, are you happy with that decision? If you didn't, do you intend to upgrade in the near future? Why, or why not?

   Write a single-page essay summarizing what you learned from these interviews about making the decision to upgrade.

4. Choose a topic you'd like to research using the Windows 98 online Help system. Look for information on your topic using all three tabs: the Contents tab, the Index tab, and the Search tab. Once you've found all the information you can, compare the three methods (Contents, Index, Search) of looking for information. Write a paragraph that discusses which tab proved the most useful. Did you reach the same information topics using all three methods? In a second paragraph, summarize what you learned about your topic. Finally, in a third paragraph, indicate under what circumstances you'd use which tab.

LAB ASSIGNMENTS

Using a Keyboard To become an effective computer user, you must be familiar with your primary input device—the keyboard. See the Read This Before You Begin page for information on installing and starting the lab.

1. The Steps for the Using a Keyboard Lab provide you with a structured introduction to the keyboard layout and the function of special computer keys. Click the Steps button and begin the Steps. As you work through the Steps, answer all of the Quick Check questions that appear. When you complete the Steps, you will see a Summary Report that summarizes your performance on the Quick Checks. Follow the directions on the screen to print the Summary Report.

2. In Explore, start the typing tutor. You can develop your typing skills using the typing tutor in Explore. Take the typing test and print out your results.

3. In Explore, try to improve your typing speed by 10 words per minute. For example, if you currently type 20 words per minute, your goal will be 30 words per minute. Practice each typing lesson until you see a message that indicates that you can proceed to the next lesson. Create a Practice Record, as shown here, to keep track of how much you practice. When you have reached your goal, print out the results of a typing test to verify your results.

Practice Record

Name:

Section:

Start Date: Start Typing Speed: wpm

End Date: End Typing Speed: wpm

Lesson #:   Date Practiced/Time Practiced

Using a Mouse A mouse is a standard input device on most of today's computers. You need to know how to use a mouse to manipulate graphical user interfaces and to use the rest of the Labs. See the Read This Before You Begin page for information on installing and starting the lab.

1. The Steps for the Using a Mouse Lab show you how to click, double-click, and drag objects using the mouse. Click the Steps button and begin the Steps. As you work through the Steps, answer all of the Quick Check questions that appear. When you complete the Steps, you will see a Summary Report that summarizes your performance on the Quick Checks. Follow the directions on the screen to print the Summary Report.

2. In Explore, create a poster, to demonstrate your ability to use a mouse and to control a Windows program. To create a poster for an upcoming sports event, select a graphic, type the caption for the poster, then select a font, font styles, and a border. Print your completed poster.

Quick Check Answers

Session 1.1

1. The taskbar contains buttons that give you access to tools and programs.
2. multitasking
3. Start menu
4. Lift the mouse up and move it to the right.
5. Its button appears on the taskbar.
6. To conserve computer resources such as memory.
7. To ensure you don't lose data and damage your files.

Session 1.2

1. The title bar identifies the window and contains window controls; toolbars contain buttons that provide you with shortcuts to common menu commands.
2. a. Minimize button shrinks window so you see button on taskbar
   b. Maximize button enlarges window to fill entire screen
   c. Restore button reduces window to predetermined size
   d. Close button closes window and removes button from taskbar
3. a. ellipsis indicates a dialog box will open
   b. grayed-out indicates option is not currently available
   c. arrow indicates a submenu will open
   d. check mark indicates a toggle option
4. toolbar
5. Scrollbars appear when the contents of a box or window are too long to fit; you drag the scroll box to view different parts of the contents.
6. one
7. online Help

TUTORIAL 2

OBJECTIVES

In this tutorial you will:

- Format a disk
- Enter, select, insert, and delete text
- Create and save a file
- Open, edit, and print a file
- Switch to Web style
- Create a Student Disk
- View the list of files on your disk and change view options
- Move, copy, delete, and rename a file
- Navigate Explorer windows
- Make a copy of your Student Disk

LABS

Using Files

WORKING WITH FILES

Creating, Saving, and Managing Files

CASE

Distance Education

You recently purchased a computer in order to gain new skills and stay competitive in the job market. Your friend Shannon suggests that you broaden your horizons by enrolling in a few distance education courses. **Distance education**, Shannon explains, is formalized learning that typically takes place using a computer, replacing normal classroom interaction with modern communications technology. Many distance education courses take advantage of the **Internet**, a vast structure of millions of computers located all over the world that are connected together so that they are able to share information. The **World Wide Web**, usually called the **Web**, is a popular service on the Internet that makes information readily accesssible. Educators can make their course material available on the Web.

Windows 98 makes it possible for your computer to display content in a way that is similar to the way it appears on the Web, and Shannon is eager to show you how. She suggests, however, that first you should get more comfortable with your computer—especially using programs and files. Shannon points out that most of the software installed on your computer was created especially for the Windows 98 operating system. This software is referred to as **Windows 98 applications** or **Windows 98 programs**. You can use software designed for older operating systems, but Windows 98 applications take better advantage of the features of the Windows 98 operating system.

You typically use Windows 98 applications to create files. A **file**, often referred to as a **document**, is a collection of data that has a name and is stored in a computer. Once you create a file, you can open it, edit its contents, print it, and save it again—usually using the same application program you used to create it.

Shannon suggests that you become familiar with how to perform these tasks in Windows 98 applications. Then she'll show you how to set up your computer so it incorporates the look and feel of the Web. Finally, you'll spend time learning how to organize your files.

SESSION 2.1

In Session 2.1 you will learn how to format a disk so it can store files. You will create, save, open, and print a file. You will find out how the insertion point differs from the mouse pointer, and you will learn the basic skills for Windows 98 text entry, such as inserting, deleting, and selecting. *For the steps of this tutorial you will need two blank 3½-inch disks.*

Formatting a Disk

Before you can save files on a disk, the disk must be formatted. When the computer **formats** a disk, the magnetic particles on the disk surface are arranged so data can be stored on the disk. Today, many disks are sold preformatted and can be used right out of the box. However, if you purchase an unformatted disk, or if you have an old disk you want to completely erase and reuse, you can format the disk using the Windows 98 Format command. This command is available through the **My Computer window**, a window that gives you access to the objects on your computer. You open My Computer by using its icon on the desktop. You'll learn more about the My Computer window later in this tutorial.

The following steps tell you how to format a 3½-inch high-density disk using drive A. Your instructor will tell you how to revise the instructions given in these steps if the procedure is different for your lab equipment.

Make sure you are using a blank disk before you perform these steps.

To format a disk:

1. Start Windows 98, if necessary.

2. Write your name on the label of a 3½-inch disk and insert your disk in drive A. See Figure 2-1.

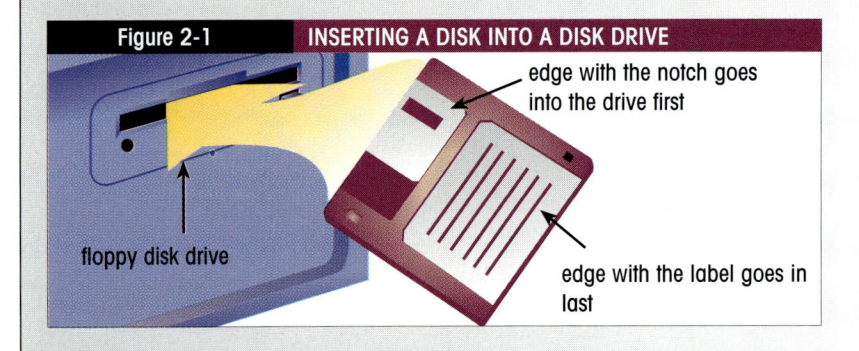

Figure 2-1 INSERTING A DISK INTO A DISK DRIVE

- edge with the notch goes into the drive first
- floppy disk drive
- edge with the label goes in last

TROUBLE? If your disk does not fit in drive A, put it in drive B and substitute drive B for drive A in all of the steps for the rest of the tutorial.

3. Click the **My Computer** icon on the desktop. The icon is selected. Figure 2-2 shows the location of this icon on your desktop.

TROUBLE? If the My Computer window opens, skip Step 4. Your computer is using different settings, which you'll learn to change in Session 2.2.

4. Press **Enter** to open the My Computer window. See Figure 2-2 (don't worry if your window opens maximized).

TROUBLE? If you see a list instead of icons like those in Figure 2-2, click View, then click Large Icons. Don't worry if your toolbars don't exactly match those in Figure 2-2.

TUTORIAL 2 WORKING WITH FILES   WIN 98   2.3   WINDOWS

TROUBLE? If you see additional information or a graphic image on the left side of the My Computer window, Web view is enabled on your computer. Don't worry. You will learn how to enable and disable Web view in Session 2.2.

Figure 2-2   MY COMPUTER WINDOW

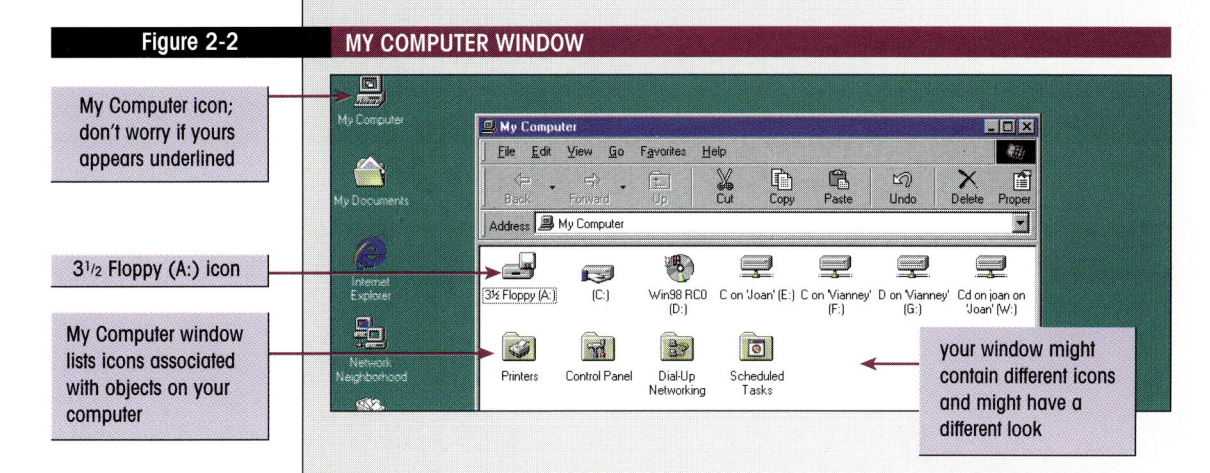

- My Computer icon; don't worry if yours appears underlined
- 3½ Floppy (A:) icon
- My Computer window lists icons associated with objects on your computer
- your window might contain different icons and might have a different look

5. Right-click the **3½ Floppy (A:)** icon to open its shortcut menu.

6. Click **Format** on the shortcut menu. The Format dialog box opens.

7. Click the **Full** option button to perform a full format. Make sure the other dialog box settings on your screen match those in Figure 2-3.

Figure 2-3   FORMAT DIALOG BOX

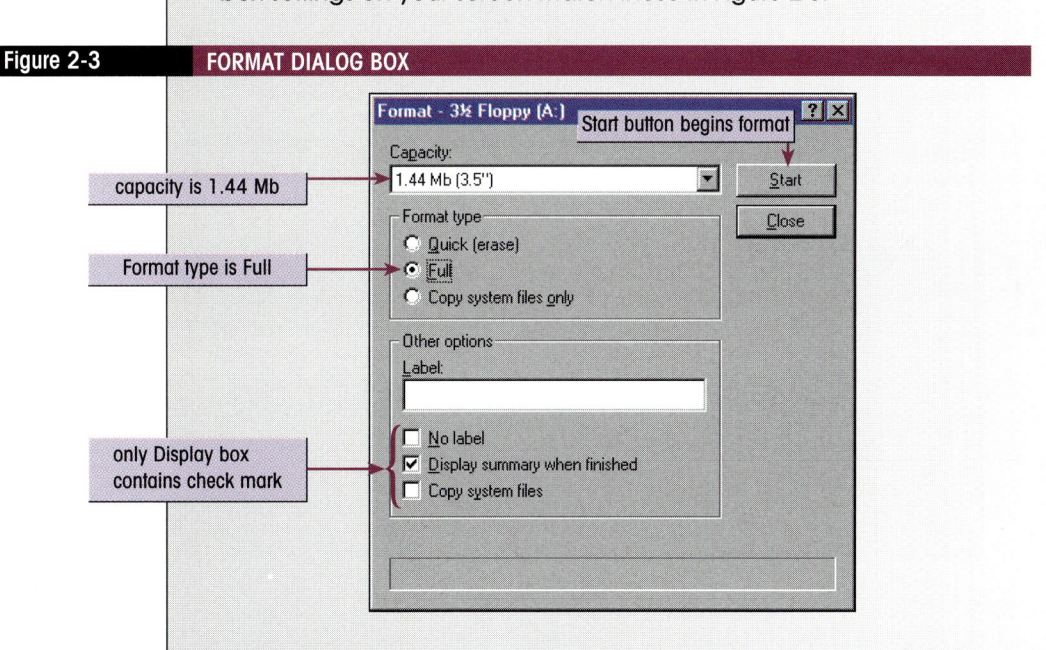

- capacity is 1.44 Mb
- Format type is Full
- only Display box contains check mark
- Start button begins format

8. On the right side of the dialog box is a Start button. Click this **Start** button to begin formatting the disk. A series of blue boxes at the bottom of the Format window shows you how the format is progressing. When the format is complete, the Format Results dialog box appears.

9. Click the **Close** button, and then close any open windows on the desktop.

TROUBLE? To close the windows, click each Close button ⊠.

Working with Text

To accomplish many computing tasks, you need to type text in documents and text boxes. Windows 98 facilitates basic text entry by providing a text-entry area, by showing you where your text will appear on the screen, by helping you move around on the screen, and by providing insert and delete functions.

When you type sentences of text, do not press the Enter key when you reach the right margin of the page. Most software contains a feature called **word wrap**, which automatically continues your text on the next line. Therefore, you should press Enter only when you have completed a paragraph.

If you type the wrong character, press the Backspace key to back up and delete the character. You can also use the Delete key. What's the difference between the Backspace and the Delete keys? The Backspace key deletes the character to the left, while the Delete key deletes the character to the right.

Now you will type some text using WordPad, to practice what you've learned about text entry. When you first start WordPad, notice the flashing vertical bar, called the **insertion point**, in the upper-left corner of the document window. The insertion point indicates where the characters you type will appear.

To type text in WordPad:

1. Start WordPad and locate the insertion point.

   TROUBLE? If the WordPad window does not fill the screen, click the Maximize button.

   TROUBLE? If you can't find the insertion point, click in the WordPad workspace area.

2. Type your name, using the Shift key to type uppercase letters and using the Spacebar to type spaces, just as on a typewriter.

3. Press the **Enter** key to end the current paragraph and move the insertion point down to the next line.

4. As you type the following sentences, watch what happens when the insertion point reaches the right edge of the page:

   This is a sample typed in WordPad. See what happens when the insertion point reaches the right edge of the page.

   TROUBLE? If you make a mistake, delete the incorrect character(s) by pressing the Backspace key on your keyboard. Then type the correct character(s).

   TROUBLE? If your text doesn't wrap, your screen might be set up to display more information than the screen used for the figures in this tutorial. Type the sentences again until text wraps automatically.

The Insertion Point Versus the Pointer

The insertion point is not the same as the mouse pointer. When the mouse pointer is in the text-entry area, it is called the **I-beam pointer** and looks like I. Figure 2-4 explains the difference between the insertion point and the I-beam pointer.

Figure 2-4   THE INSERTION POINT VS. THE POINTER

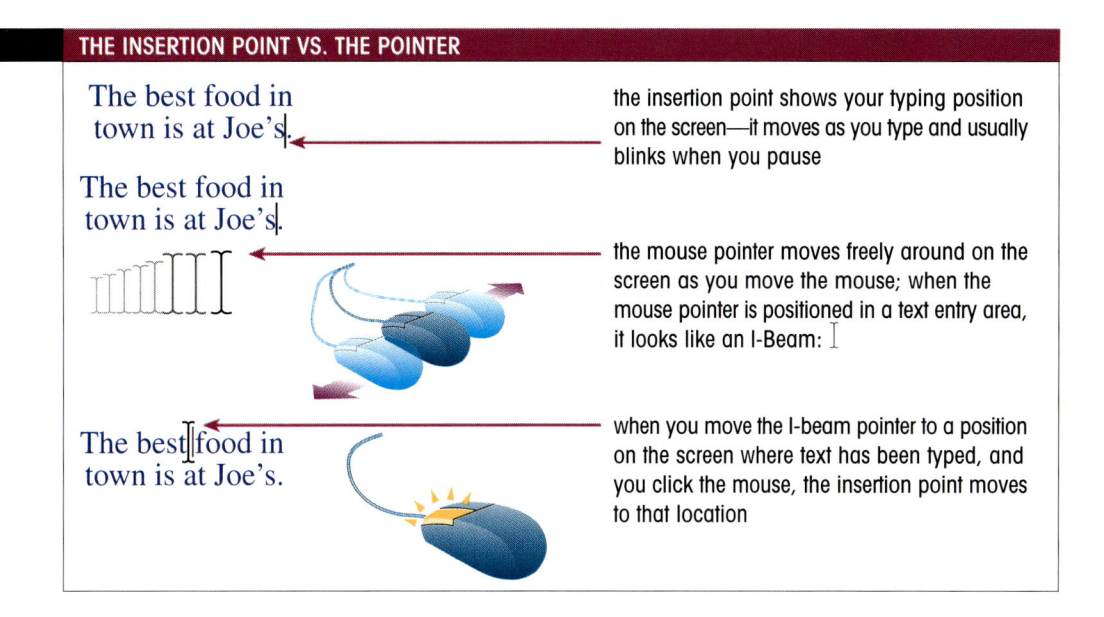

The best food in town is at Joe's. — the insertion point shows your typing position on the screen—it moves as you type and usually blinks when you pause

The best food in town is at Joe's. — the mouse pointer moves freely around on the screen as you move the mouse; when the mouse pointer is positioned in a text entry area, it looks like an I-Beam: I

The best food in town is at Joe's. — when you move the I-beam pointer to a position on the screen where text has been typed, and you click the mouse, the insertion point moves to that location

To enter text, you move the I-beam pointer to the location where you want to type, and then click. The insertion point jumps to the location you clicked and, depending on the program you are using, may blink to indicate the program is ready for you to type. When you enter text, the insertion point moves as you type.

To move the insertion point:

1. Check the locations of the insertion point and the I-beam pointer. The insertion point should be at the end of the sentence you typed in the last set of steps.

   TROUBLE? If you don't see the I-beam pointer, move your mouse until you see it.

2. Use the mouse to move the I-beam pointer to the word "sample," then click the mouse button. The insertion point jumps to the location of the I-beam pointer.

3. Move the I-beam pointer to a blank area near the bottom of the workspace, and click. Notice the insertion point does not jump to the location of the I-beam pointer. Instead the insertion point jumps to the end of the last sentence. The insertion point can move only within existing text. It cannot be moved out of the existing text area.

Selecting Text

Many text operations are performed on a **block** of text, which is one or more consecutive characters, words, sentences, or paragraphs. Once you select a block of text, you can delete it, move it, replace it, underline it, and so on. As you select a block of text, the computer highlights it. If you want to remove the highlighting, just click in the margin of your document.

If you want to delete the phrase "See what happens" in the text you just typed and replace it with the phrase "You can watch word wrap in action," you do not have to delete the first phrase one character at a time. Instead, you can highlight the entire phrase and then type the replacement phrase.

To select and replace a block of text:

1. Move the I-beam pointer just to the left of the word "See."
2. While holding down the mouse button, drag the I-beam pointer over the text to the end of the word "happens." The phrase "See what happens" should now be highlighted. See Figure 2-5.

   TROUBLE? If the space to the right of the word "happens" is also selected, don't worry. Your computer is set up to select spaces in addition to words. After completing Step 4, simply press the Spacebar to type an extra space if required.

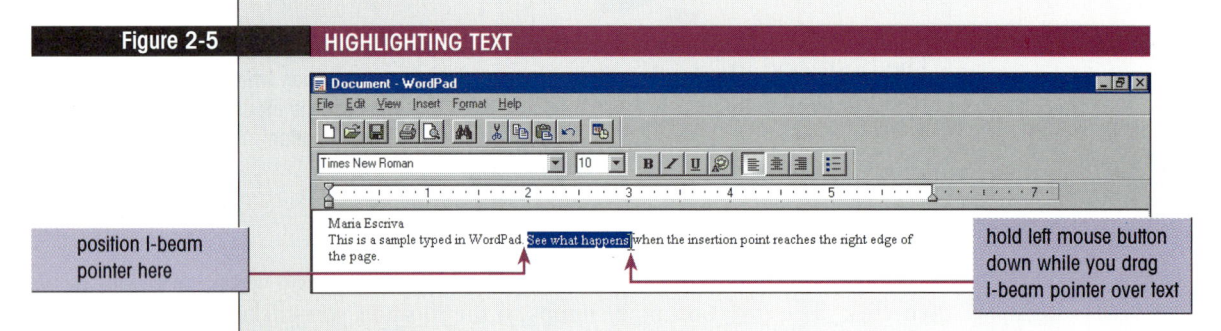

Figure 2-5   HIGHLIGHTING TEXT

position I-beam pointer here

hold left mouse button down while you drag I-beam pointer over text

3. Release the mouse button.

   TROUBLE? If the phrase is not highlighted correctly, repeat Steps 1 through 3.

4. Type **You can watch word wrap in action**

The text you typed replaces the highlighted text. Notice you did not need to delete the highlighted text before you typed the replacement text.

Inserting a Character

Windows 98 programs usually operate in **insert mode**—when you type a new character, all characters to the right of the insertion point are pushed over to make room.

Suppose you want to insert the word "sentence" before the word "typed" in your practice sentences.

To insert text:

1. Move the I-beam pointer just before the word "typed," then click to position the insertion point.
2. Type **sentence**
3. Press the **Spacebar**.

Notice how the letters in the first line are pushed to the right to make room for the new characters. When a word gets pushed past the right margin, the **word-wrap** feature moves it down to the beginning of the next line.

Saving a File

As you type text, it is held temporarily in the computer's memory. For permanent storage, you need to save your work on a disk. In the computer lab, you will probably save your work on a floppy disk in drive A.

When you save a file, you must give it a name. Windows 98 allows you to use up to 255 characters in a filename, although usually the operating system requires some of those characters for designating file location and file type. So, while it is unlikely you would need that many characters, you should be aware that the full 255 characters might not always be available. You may use spaces and certain punctuation symbols in your filenames. You cannot use the symbols \ / ? : * " < > | in a filename, but other symbols such as & ; - and $ are allowed. Furthermore, filenames for files used by older Windows 3.1 or DOS applications (pre-1995 operating systems) must be eight characters or less. Thus when you save a file with a long filename in Windows 98, Windows 98 also creates an eight-character filename that can be used by older applications. The eight-character filename is created from the first six nonspace characters in the long filename, with the addition of a tilde (~) and a number. For example, the filename Car Sales for 1999 would be converted to Carsal~1.

Most filenames have an extension. An **extension** is a suffix, usually of three characters, separated from the filename by a period. In the filename Car Sales for 1999.doc, a period separates the filename from the file extension. The file extension "doc" helps categorize the file by type or by the software that created it. Files created with Microsoft Word software have a .doc extension, such as Resume.doc (pronounced "Resume dot doc"). In general you will not add an extension to your filenames, because the application software automatically does this for you.

Windows 98 keeps track of file extensions, but does not always display them. The steps in these tutorials refer to files using the filename, but not its extension. So if you see the filename Practice Text in the steps, but "Practice Text.doc" on your screen, don't worry—these refer to the same file. Also don't worry if you don't use consistent lowercase and uppercase letters when saving files. Usually the operating system doesn't distinguish between them. Be aware, however, that some programs are "case-sensitive"—they check for case in filenames.

Now you can save the document you typed.

To save a document:

1. Click the **Save** button on the toolbar. Figure 2-6 shows the location of this button and the Save As dialog box that appears after you click it.

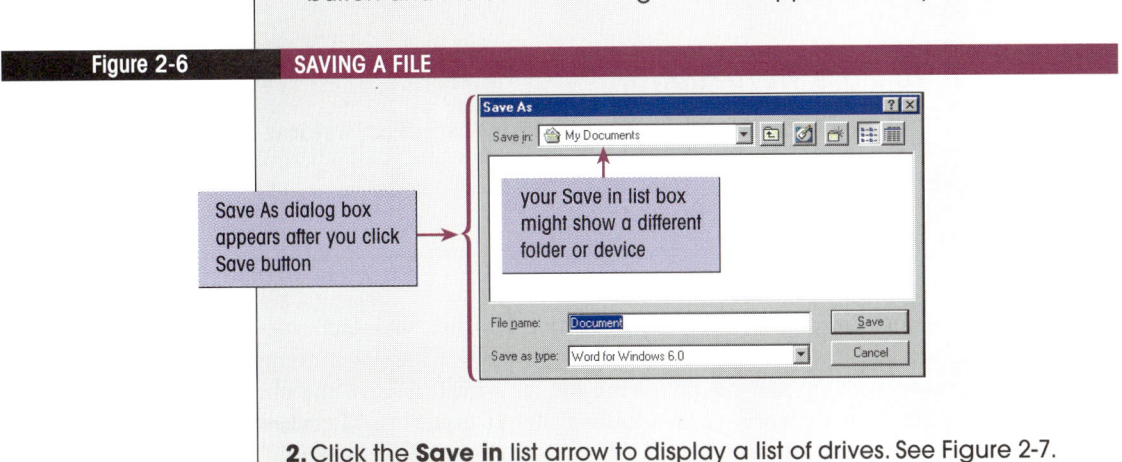

Figure 2-6 SAVING A FILE

Save As dialog box appears after you click Save button

your Save in list box might show a different folder or device

2. Click the **Save in** list arrow to display a list of drives. See Figure 2-7.

Figure 2-7   **SELECTING THE DRIVE**

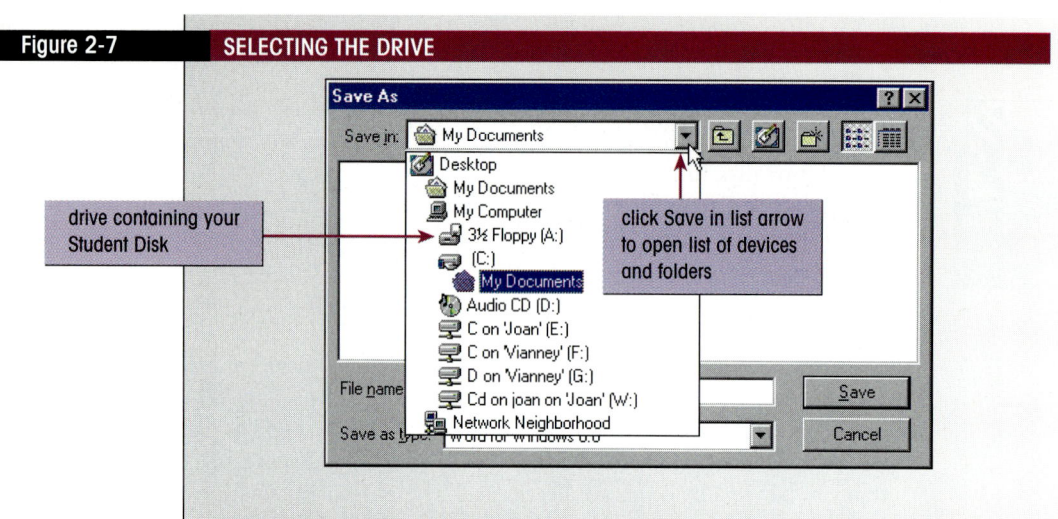

drive containing your Student Disk → 3½ Floppy (A:)

click Save in list arrow to open list of devices and folders

3. Click **3½ Floppy (A:)**, and select the text in the File name box.

   TROUBLE? To select the text, move the I-beam pointer to the beginning of the word "Document." While you hold down the mouse button, drag the I-beam pointer to the end of the word.

4. Type **Practice Text** in the File name box.

5. Click the **Save** button in the lower-right corner of the dialog box. Your file is saved on your Student Disk, and the document title, "Practice Text," appears on the WordPad title bar.

What if you try to close WordPad before you save your file? Windows 98 will display a message—"Save changes to Document?" If you answer "Yes," Windows will display the Save As dialog box so you can give the document a name. If you answer "No," Windows 98 will close WordPad without saving the document. Any changes you made to the document would be lost, so when you are asked if you want to save a file, answer Yes, unless you are absolutely sure you don't need to keep the work you just did.

After you save a file, you can work on another document or close WordPad. Since you have already saved your Practice Text document, you'll continue this tutorial by closing WordPad.

To close WordPad:

1. Click the **Close** button ☒ to close the WordPad window.

Opening a File

Suppose you save and close the Practice Text file, then later you want to revise it. To revise a file you must first open it. When you **open** a file, its contents are copied into the computer's memory. If you revise the file, you need to save the changes before you close the application or work on a different file. If you close a revised file without saving your changes, you will lose them.

Typically, you use one of two methods to open a file. You could select the file from the Documents list or the My Computer window, or you could start an application program and then use the Open button to open the file. Each method has advantages and disadvantages.

The first method for opening the Practice Text file simply requires you to select the file from the Documents list or from the My Computer window. With this method the document, not the application program, is central to the task; hence, this method is sometimes referred to as **document-centric**. You only need to remember the name of your document or file—you do not need to remember which application you used to create the document.

The Documents list contains the names of the last 15 documents used. You access this list from the Start menu. When you have your own computer, the Documents list is very handy. In a computer lab, however, the files other students use quickly replace yours on the list.

If your file is not in the Documents list, you can open the file by selecting it from the My Computer window. Windows 98 starts an application program you can use to revise the file, then automatically opens the file. The advantage of this method is its simplicity. The disadvantage is Windows 98 might not start the application you expect. For example, when you select Practice Text, you might expect Windows 98 to start WordPad because you used WordPad to create it. Depending on the software installed on your computer system, however, Windows 98 might start the Microsoft Word application instead. Usually this is not a problem. Although the application might not be the one you expect, you can still use it to revise your file.

To open the Practice Text file by selecting it from My Computer:

1. From the desktop, open the **My Computer** window.

2. Click the **3½ Floppy (A:)** icon in the My Computer window.

    TROUBLE? If the 3½ Floppy (A:) window opens, skip Step 3.

3. Press **Enter**. The 3½ Floppy (A:) window opens.

4. Click the **Practice Text** file icon.

    TROUBLE? If the Practice Text document appears in a word-processing window, skip Step 5.

5. Press **Enter**. Windows 98 starts an application program, then automatically opens the Practice Text file. You could make revisions to the document at this point, but instead, you'll close all the windows on your desktop so you can try the other method for opening files.

    TROUBLE? If Windows 98 starts Microsoft Word or another word-processing program instead of WordPad, don't worry. You can use Microsoft Word to revise the Practice Text document.

6. Close all open windows on the desktop.

The second method for opening the Practice Text file requires you to open WordPad, then use the Open button to select the Practice Text file. The advantage of this method is you can specify the application program you want to use—WordPad, in this case. This method, however, involves more steps than the method you tried previously.

To start WordPad and open the Practice Text file using the Open button:

1. Start WordPad and maximize the WordPad window.

2. Click the **Open** button on the toolbar.

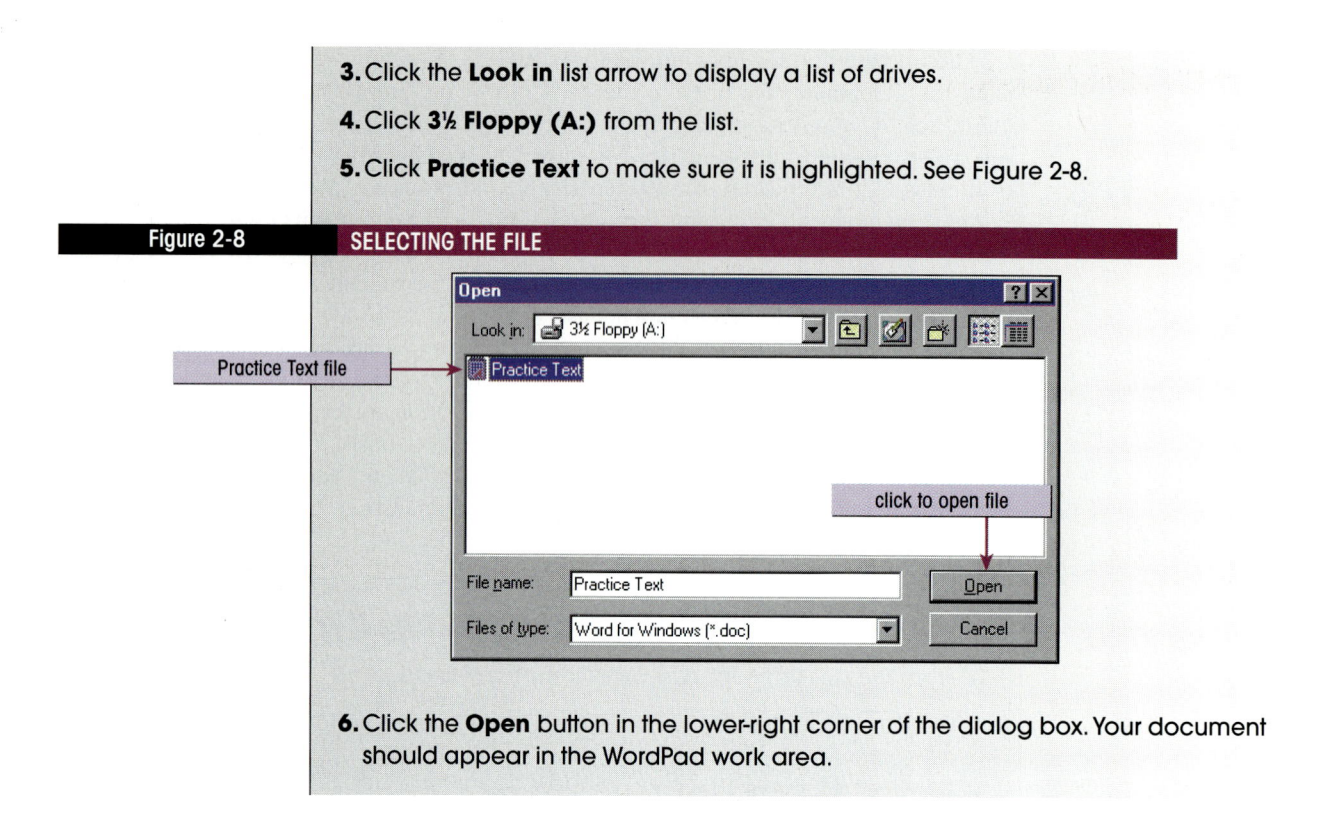

3. Click the **Look in** list arrow to display a list of drives.
4. Click **3½ Floppy (A:)** from the list.
5. Click **Practice Text** to make sure it is highlighted. See Figure 2-8.

Figure 2-8 SELECTING THE FILE

Practice Text file → *(Open dialog box showing Practice Text file selected, with Look in: 3½ Floppy (A:), File name: Practice Text, Files of type: Word for Windows (*.doc))*

click to open file → Open button

6. Click the **Open** button in the lower-right corner of the dialog box. Your document should appear in the WordPad work area.

Printing a File

Now that the Practice Text file is open, you can print it. It is a good idea to use Print Preview before you send your document to the printer. **Print Preview** shows on the screen exactly how your document will appear on paper. You can check your page layout so you don't waste paper printing a document that is not quite the way you want it. Your instructor might supply you with additional instructions for printing in your school's computer lab.

To preview, then print, the Practice Text file:

1. Click the **Print Preview** button 🔍 on the toolbar.

   TROUBLE? If an error message appears, printing capabilities might not be set up on your computer. Ask your instructor or lab assistant for help, or skip this set of steps.

2. Look at your print preview. Before you print the document and use paper, you should make sure the font, margins, and other document features look the way you want them to.

   TROUBLE? If you can't read the document text on screen, click the Zoom In button.

3. Click the **Print** button. A Print dialog box appears. Study Figure 2-9 to familiarize yourself with the controls in the Print dialog box.

TUTORIAL 2 WORKING WITH FILES **WIN 98** 2.11 **WINDOWS**

Figure 2-9 | **PRINTING A FILE**

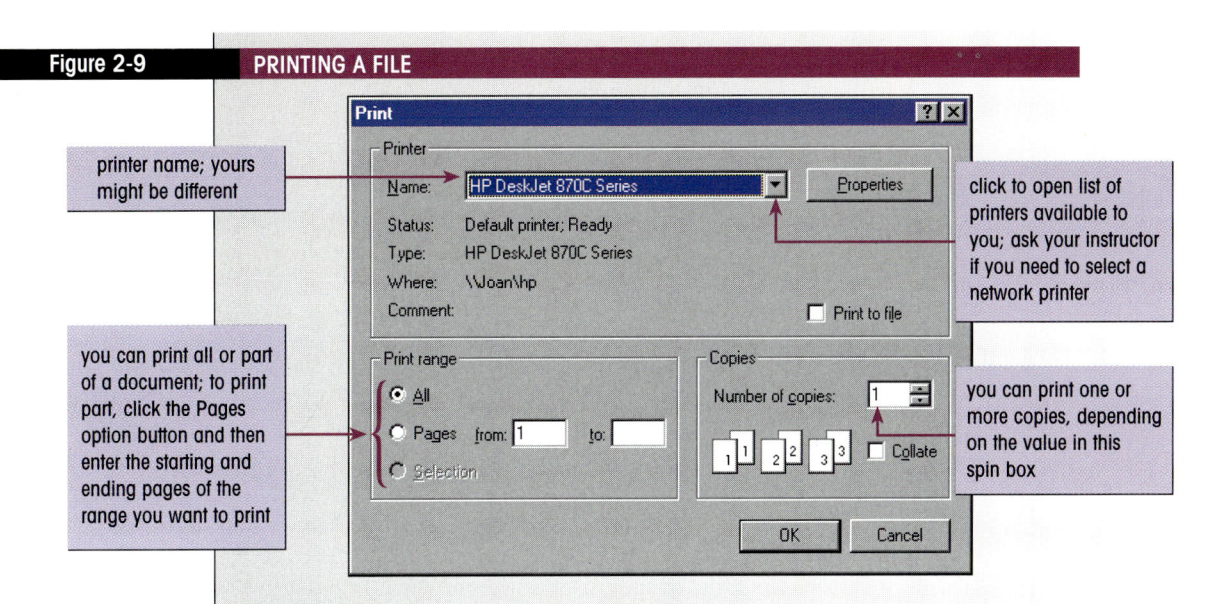

- printer name; yours might be different
- click to open list of printers available to you; ask your instructor if you need to select a network printer
- you can print all or part of a document; to print part, click the Pages option button and then enter the starting and ending pages of the range you want to print
- you can print one or more copies, depending on the value in this spin box

4. Make sure your screen shows the Print range set to "All" and the number of copies set to "1."

5. Click the **OK** button to print your document.

   TROUBLE? If your document does not print, make sure the printer has paper and the printer online light is on. If your document still doesn't print, ask your instructor or lab assistant for help.

6. Close WordPad.

   TROUBLE? If you see the message "Save changes to Document?" click the No button.

You've now learned how to create, save, open, and print word-processed files—essential skills for students in distance education courses that rely on word-processed reports transmitted across the Internet. Shannon assures you that the techniques you've just learned apply to most Windows 98 programs.

QUICK CHECK

1. A(n) _____ is a collection of data that has a name and is stored on a disk or other storage medium.

2. _____ erases all the data on a disk and arranges the magnetic particles on the disk surface so the disk can store data.

3. True or False: When you move the mouse pointer over a text entry area, the pointer shape changes to an I-bar.

4. What shows you where each character you type will appear?

5. _____ automatically moves text down to the beginning of the next line when you reach the right margin.

6. How do you select a block of text?

7. In the filename New Equipment.doc, doc is a(n) _____.

SESSION 2.2

In this session you will learn how to change settings in the My Computer window to control its appearance and the appearance of desktop objects. You will then learn how to use My Computer to manage the files on your disk; view information about the files on your disk; organize the files into folders; and move, delete, copy, and rename files.
For this session you will use a second blank 3½-inch disk.

Changing Desktop Style Settings

Shannon tells you that in Windows 98 you work with files by manipulating icons that represent them. These icons appear in many places: the desktop, the My Computer windows, the 3½ Floppy (A:) window, and other similar windows. The techniques you use to manipulate these icons depend on whether your computer is using Classic-style or Web-style settings or a customized hybrid. **Classic style** allows you to use the same techniques in Windows 98 that are used in Windows 95, the previous version of the Windows operating system. **Web style**, on the other hand, allows you to access files on your computer's hard drives just as you access files on the Web. In Classic style, to select an item you click it, and to open an item you click it and then press Enter. In Web style, to select an item you point to it, and to open an item you click it.

Thus, if you wanted to open your Practice Text document from the My Computer window, in Classic style you would click its icon and press Enter, but in Web style you would simply click its icon.

Switching to Web Style

By default, Windows 98 starts using a combination of Classic and Web style settings, but it uses Classic click settings. Your computer might have been set differently. If you have your own computer, you can choose which style you want to use. If you want to minimize the number of mouse actions for a given task, or if you want to explore your computer in the same way you explore the Web, you'll probably want to use Web style. On the other hand, if you are used to Classic style settings, you might want to continue using them. Shannon suggests that you use Web style because you'll be able to use the same techniques on the Web, and you'll be more at ease with your distance learning courses. The next set of steps shows you how to switch to Web style, and the rest of the tutorial assumes that you're using Web-style settings.

To switch styles:

1. Click the **Start** button [Start] and then point to **Settings**.

2. Click **Folder Options**. The Folder Options dialog box opens.

   TROUBLE? If you can't open the Folder Options dialog box, or you can't make any changes to it, you probably don't have permission to change these settings. If your computer is set to use Classic style and you can't change this setting, you will notice a few differences in subsequent steps in this tutorial. The **TROUBLE?** paragraphs will help to ensure that you learn the proper techniques for the settings you are using.

3. On the General tab, click the **Web style** option button. See Figure 2-10.

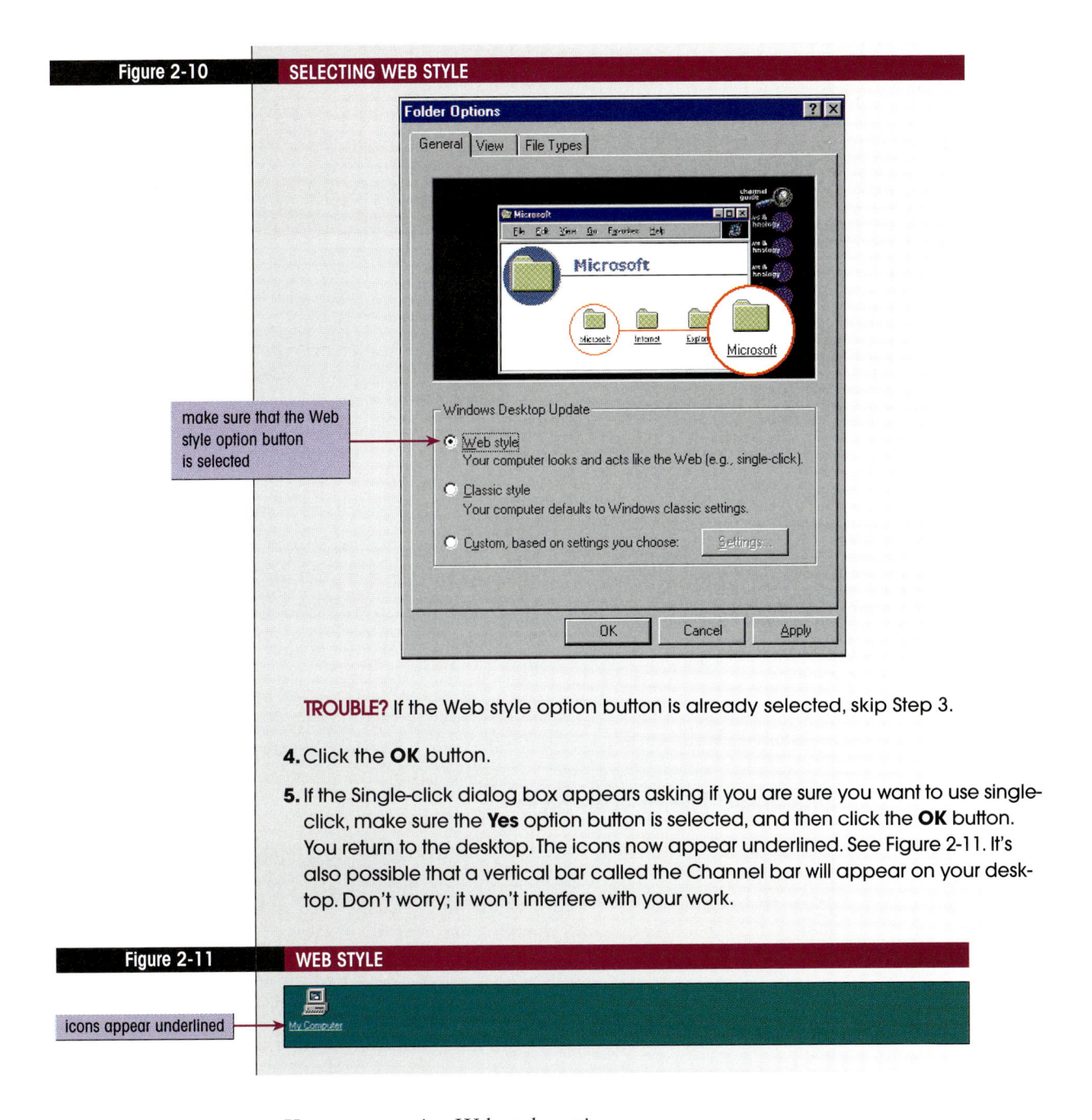

TUTORIAL 2 WORKING WITH FILES   WIN 98   2.13   WINDOWS

Figure 2-10   SELECTING WEB STYLE

make sure that the Web style option button is selected

TROUBLE? If the Web style option button is already selected, skip Step 3.

4. Click the **OK** button.

5. If the Single-click dialog box appears asking if you are sure you want to use single-click, make sure the **Yes** option button is selected, and then click the **OK** button. You return to the desktop. The icons now appear underlined. See Figure 2-11. It's also possible that a vertical bar called the Channel bar will appear on your desktop. Don't worry; it won't interfere with your work.

Figure 2-11   WEB STYLE

icons appear underlined

You are now using Web-style settings.

Selecting an Icon in Web Style

In Web style, you select an icon representing a device, folder, or file by pointing to the icon long enough for it to become highlighted. This technique is sometimes called **hovering**. The pointer changes from ◦ to ◦ when you point to the icon. Try selecting the My Computer icon in Web style.

To select the My Computer icon in Web style:

1. Position the pointer over the My Computer icon on the desktop and notice how the pointer changes from ⇖ to 👆 and the color of the text label changes to show it is selected. See Figure 2-12.

Figure 2-12 SELECTING AN ICON IN WEB STYLE

pointer when you point at icon in Web style

TROUBLE? If the My Computer icon is not selected when you point to it, you might not be holding the mouse steadily. You need to steadily "hover" the pointer over the object long enough for the object to become highlighted. Simply passing the mouse over an object will not select it.

TROUBLE? If in Web style you click the My Computer icon instead of simply pointing at it, the My Computer window will open. Close the window and repeat Step 1.

TROUBLE? If you were unable to switch to Web style because you didn't have permission, you'll need to click the My Computer icon to select it.

Note that the Web style selection technique only applies to icons on the desktop and icons in windows such as My Computer.

Opening a File in Web Style

You saw in Session 2.1 that you can open the Practice Text document directly from the 3½ Floppy (A:) window. The steps in Session 2.1 assumed you were using Classic style. Now you'll try opening the Practice Text document using Web style. You open an object by simply clicking it. Try opening your Practice Text file in Web style.

To open the Practice Text file in Web style:

1. Click the **My Computer** icon. The My Computer window opens.

   TROUBLE? If you were unable to switch to Web style, you'll need to press Enter after Steps 1, 2, and 3.

2. Click the **3½ Floppy (A:)** icon. The 3½ Floppy (A:) window opens.

3. Click the **Practice Text** icon. Your word-processing software starts and the Practice Text file opens.

4. Close all open windows.

Now that you've practiced working with icons in Web style, you'll learn other tasks you can perform with these icons to manage your files.

Creating Your Student Disk

For the rest of this session, you must create a Student Disk that contains some practice files. *You can use the disk you formatted in the previous session.*

If you are using your own computer, the NP on Microsoft Windows 98 menu selection will not be available. Before you proceed, you must go to your school's computer lab and find a computer that has the NP on Microsoft Windows 98 program installed. If you cannot get the files from the lab, ask your instructor or lab assistant for help. Once you have made your own Student Disk, you can use it to complete this tutorial on any computer you choose.

To add the practice files to your Student Disk:

1. Write "Disk 1 - Windows 98 Tutorial 2 Student Disk" on the label of your formatted disk (the same disk you used to save your Practice Text file).

2. Place the disk in drive A.

3. Click the **Start** button [Start].

4. Point to **Programs**.

5. Point to **NP on Microsoft Windows 98 - Level I**.

    TROUBLE? If NP on Microsoft Windows 98 - Level I is not listed ask your instructor or lab assistant for help.

6. Click **Disk 1 (Tutorial 2)**. A message box opens, asking you to place your disk in drive A.

7. Click the **OK** button. Wait while the program copies the practice files to your formatted disk. When all the files have been copied, the program closes.

Your Student Disk now contains practice files you will use throughout the rest of this tutorial.

My Computer

The My Computer icon, as you have seen, represents your computer, its storage devices, printers, and other objects. The My Computer icon opens into the My Computer window, which contains an icon for each of the storage devices on your computer. On most computer systems, the My Computer window also contains the Control Panel and Printers folders, which help you add printers, control peripheral devices, and customize your Windows 98 work environment. Depending on the services your computer is running, you might see additional folders such as Dial-Up Networking (for some Internet connections) or Scheduled Tasks (for scheduling programs provided with Windows 98) that help you keep your computer running smoothly). Figure 2-13 shows how the My Computer window relates to your computer's hardware.

Figure 2-13 RELATIONSHIP BETWEEN COMPUTER AND MY COMPUTER WINDOW

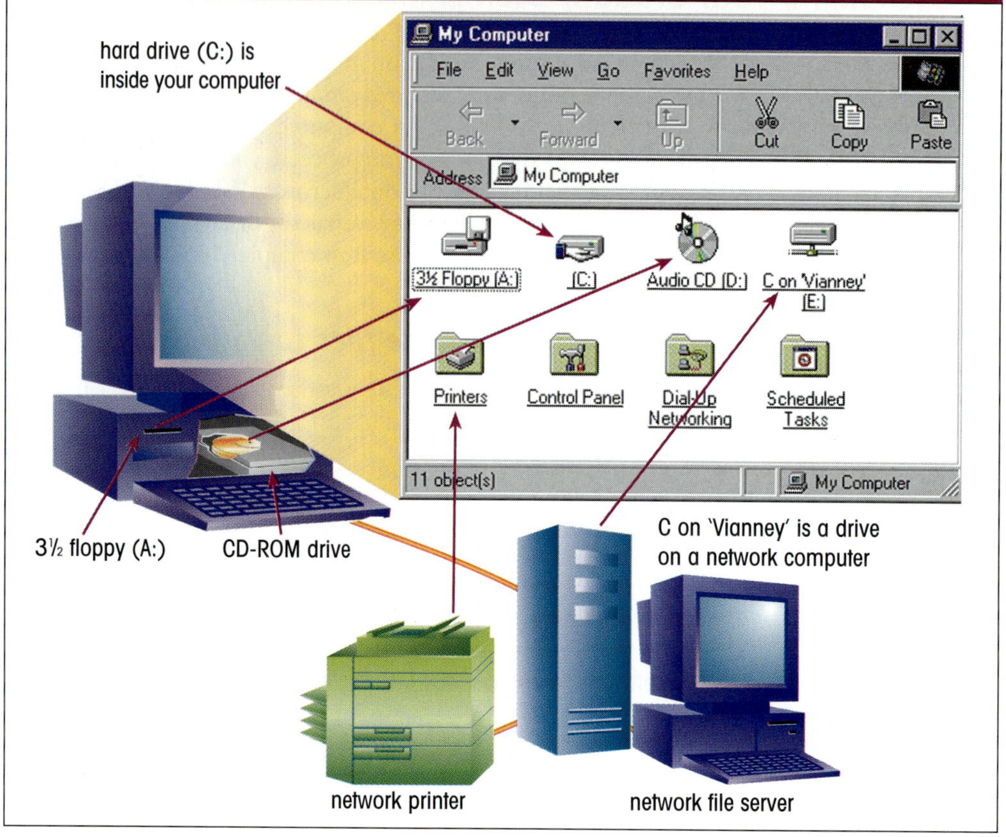

The first floppy drive on a computer is designated as drive A (if you add a second drive it is usually designated as drive B), and the first hard drive is designated drive C (if you add additional hard drives they are usually designated D, E, and so on).

You can use the My Computer window to keep track of where your files are stored and to organize your files. In this section of the tutorial you will move and delete files on your Student Disk in drive A. If you use your own computer at home or work, you will probably store your files on drive C instead of drive A. However, in a school lab environment you usually don't know which computer you will use, so you need to carry your files with you on a floppy disk that you use in drive A. In this session, therefore, you will learn how to work with the files on drive A. Most of what you learn will also work on your home or work computer when you use drive C (or other drives).

Now you'll open the My Computer window.

To open the My Computer window and explore the contents of your Student Disk:

1. Open the My Computer window.

2. Click the **3½ Floppy (A:)** icon. A window appears showing the contents of drive A; maximize this window if necessary. See Figure 2-14.

   TROUBLE? If you are using Classic style, click Settings, click the 3½ Floppy (A:) icon and then press Enter. Your window might look different from Figure 2-14; for example, you might see only files, and not the additional information on the left side of the window.

TUTORIAL 2 WORKING WITH FILES   WIN 98   2.17   WINDOWS

> **TROUBLE?** If you see a list of filenames instead of icons, click View, then click Large Icons.

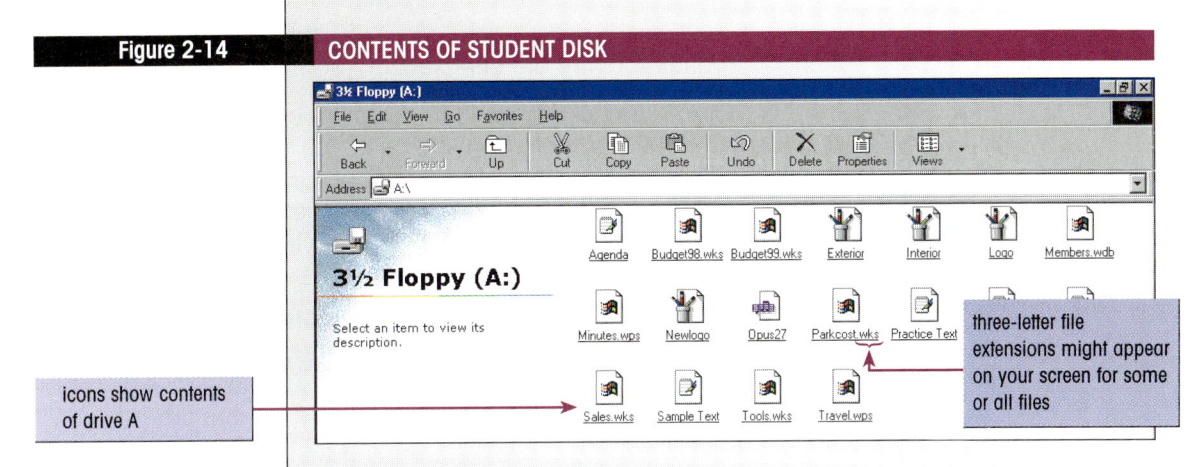

Figure 2-14 CONTENTS OF STUDENT DISK

[Screenshot of 3½ Floppy (A:) window showing files: Agenda, Budget98.wks, Budget99.wks, Exterior, Interior, Logo, Members.wdb, Minutes.wps, Newlogo, Opus27, Parkcost.wks, Practice Text, Sales.wks, Sample Text, Tools.wks, Travel.wps]

- icons show contents of drive A
- three-letter file extensions might appear on your screen for some or all files

Changing My Computer View Options

Windows 98 offers several different options that control how toolbars, icons, and buttons appear in the My Computer window. You can choose to hide or display these options, depending on the task you are performing. To make the My Computer window on your computer look the same as it does in the figures in this book, you need to ensure four things: that only the Address and Standard toolbars are visible and Text Labels is enabled, that Web view is disabled, that Large Icons view is enabled, and that file extensions are hidden.

Controlling the Toolbar Display

The My Computer window, in addition to featuring a Standard toolbar, allows you to display the same toolbars that can appear on the Windows 98 taskbar, such as the Address toolbar or the Links toolbar. These toolbars make it easy to access the Web from the My Computer window. In this tutorial, however, you need to see only the Address and Standard toolbars. You can hide one or all of the My Computer toolbars, and you can determine how they are displayed, with or without text labels. Displaying the toolbars without text labels takes up less room on your screen, but it is not as easy to identify the button's function.

> **To display only the Address and Standard toolbars and to hide text labels:**
>
> 1. Click **View**, point to **Toolbars**, and then examine the Toolbars submenu. The Standard Buttons, Address Bar, and Text Labels options should be preceded by a check mark. The Links option should not be checked.
>
> 2. If the Standard Buttons option *is not checked*, click it.
>
> 3. If necessary, reopen the Toolbars submenu, and then repeat Step 2 with the Address Bar and Text Labels options.
>
> 4. Open the Toolbars submenu once again, and if the Links option *is checked*, click it to disable it.

5. Click **View** and then point to **Toolbars** one last time and verify that your Toolbars submenu and the toolbar display look like Figure 2-15.

TROUBLE? If the checkmarks are distributed differently than in Figure 2-15, repeat Steps 1–5 until the correct options are checked.

TROUBLE? If your toolbars are not displayed as shown in Figure 2-15 (for example, both the Standard and Address toolbars might be on the same line, or the Standard toolbar might be above the Address toolbar), you can easily rearrange them. To move a toolbar, drag the vertical bar at the far left of the toolbar. By dragging that vertical bar, you can drag the toolbar left, right, up, or down.

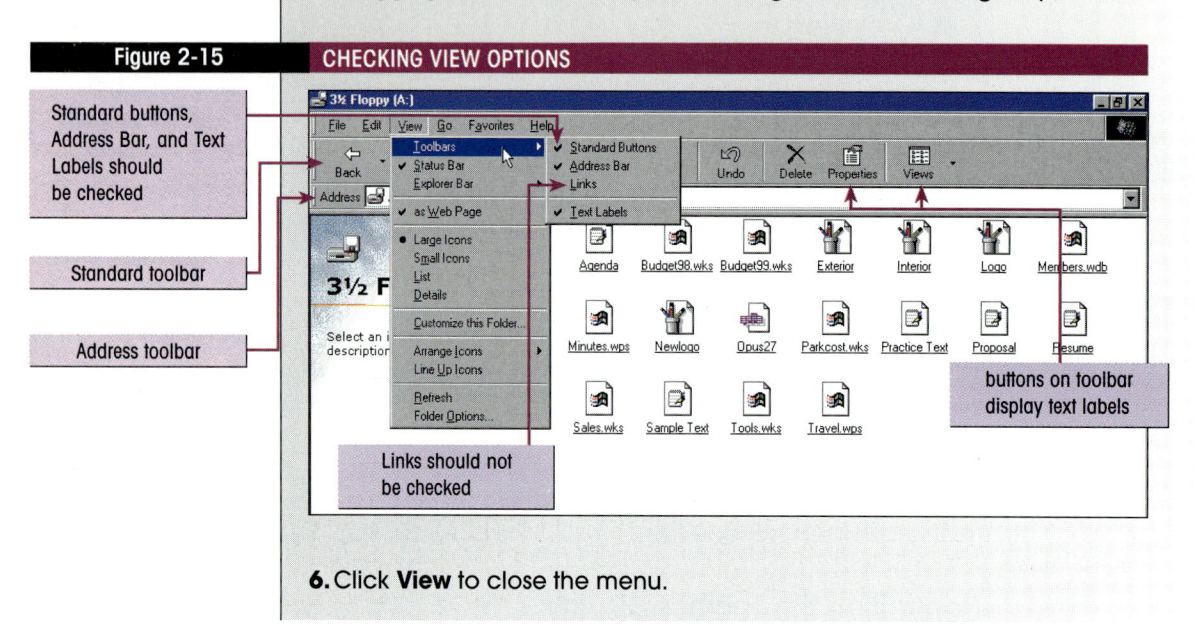

Figure 2-15 **CHECKING VIEW OPTIONS**

- Standard buttons, Address Bar, and Text Labels should be checked
- Standard toolbar
- Address toolbar
- Links should not be checked
- buttons on toolbar display text labels

6. Click **View** to close the menu.

Web View

The My Computer window also can be viewed in **Web view**, which allows you to display and customize the My Computer window as a document you would see on the Web. Web view is automatically enabled when you switch to Web style; in its default appearance Web view shows information about the open folder or selected file, along with a decorated background. There are many advantages to Web view, including the ability to place information, graphics, and Web content in a folder window. Shannon says you'll find this feature useful once you've started your distance education courses. For now, however, you don't need to customize Web view, so you'll disable it.

To disable Web view:

1. Click **View**.

2. If the option "as Web Page" is preceded by a check mark, click **as Web Page** to disable Web view.

3. Click **View** again and ensure that as Web Page is not checked.

> **TROUBLE?** If as Web Page is checked, repeat Steps 1 and 2.
>
> 4. Click **View** again to close the View menu.

Changing the Icon Display

Windows 98 provides four ways to view the contents of a disk—large icons, small icons, list, or details. The default view, Large Icons view, displays a large icon and title for each file. The icon provides a visual cue to the type and contents of the file, as Figure 2-16 illustrates.

Figure 2-16	TYPICAL ICONS AS THEY APPEAR IN MY COMPUTER
FILE AND FOLDER ICONS	
	Text documents that you can open using the Notepad accessory are represented by notepad icons.
	Graphic image documents that you can open using the Paint accessory are represented by drawing instruments.
	Word-processed documents that you can open using the WordPad accessory are represented by a formatted notepad icon, unless your computer designates a different word-processing program to open files created with WordPad.
	Word-processed documents that you can open using a program such as Microsoft Word are represented by formatted document icons.
	Files created by programs that Windows does not recognize are represented by the Windows logo.
	A folder icon represents folders.
	Certain folders created by Windows 98 have a special icon design related to the folder's purpose.
PROGRAM ICONS	
	Icons for programs usually depict an object related to the function of the program. For example, an icon that looks like a calculator represents the Calculator accessory.
	Non-windows programs are represented by the icon of a blank window.

Large Icons view helps you quickly identify a file and its type, but what if you want more information about a set of files? Details view shows more information than the large icon, small icon, and list views. Details view shows the file icon, the filename, the file size, the application you used to create the file, and the date/time the file was created or last modified.

> ### To view a detailed list of files:
>
> 1. Click **View** and then click **Details** to display details for the files on your disk, as shown in Figure 2-17. Your files might be in a different order.
> 2. Look at the file sizes. Do you see that Exterior and Interior are the largest files?
> 3. Look at the dates and times the files were modified. Which is the oldest file?

Figure 2-17 DETAILS VIEW

- file icon
- filename
- total number of objects in window
- file size (1 KB is equal to about 1,000 characters)
- date and time the file was created or last modified; yours might differ
- file type or application used to create the file; yours might be different, depending on the software installed on your computer

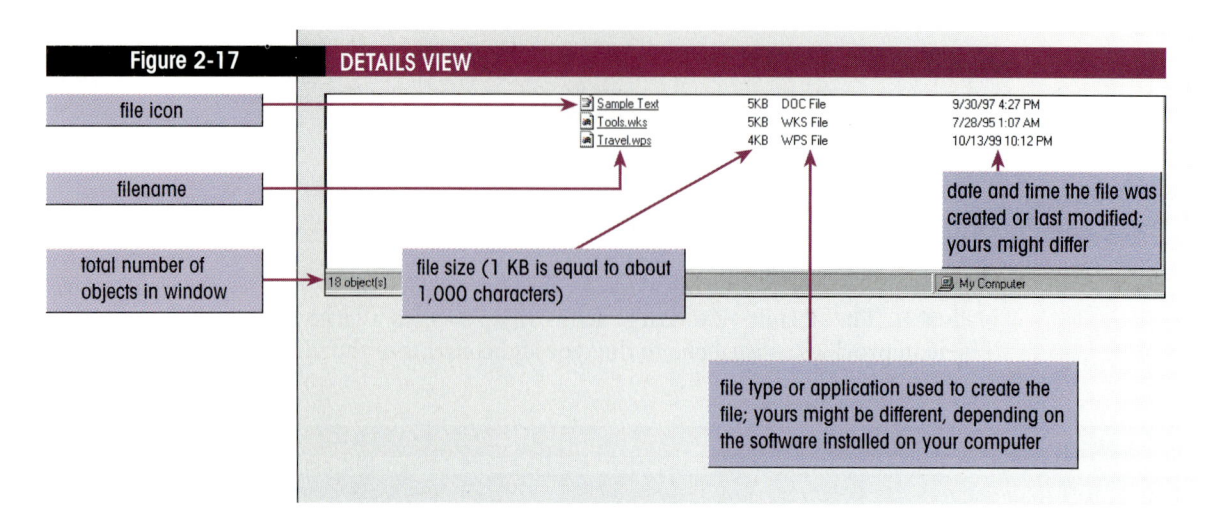

Now that you have looked at the file details, switch back to Large Icon view.

To switch to Large Icon view:

1. Click **View** and then click **Large Icons** to return to the large icon display.

Hiding File Extensions

You have the option to show or hide file extensions for file types that Windows recognizes. Showing them takes up more room but gives more information about the file. In this tutorial, however, you don't need to see file extensions, so you'll hide them. They might already be hidden on your computer.

To hide file extensions:

1. Click **View** and then click **Folder Options**. Note this is the same dialog box you saw when switching to Web style. It is accessible from the Start menu and the My Computer window.
2. Click the **View** tab.
3. Make sure the **Hide file extensions for known file types** check box is checked. If it is not, click it to insert a check mark.
4. Click the **OK** button.

The only file extensions that now appear are those whose file type Windows doesn't recognize.

Folders and Directories

A list of related files located in the same place is referred to as a **directory**. The main directory of a disk is sometimes called the **root directory**, or the **top-level directory**. The root directory is created when you format a disk, and it is designated by a letter—usually A for your floppy disk and C for your hard disk. All of the files on your Student Disk are currently in the root directory of your floppy disk.

TUTORIAL 2 WORKING WITH FILES   WIN 98 2.21   **WINDOWS**

If too many files are stored in a directory, the directory list becomes very long and difficult to manage. You can divide a directory into **folders**, into which you group similar files. The directory of files for each folder then becomes much shorter and easier to manage. A folder within a folder is called a **subfolder**. Now, you'll create a folder called Practice to hold your documents.

To create a Practice folder:

1. Click **File**, and then point to **New** to display the submenu.
2. Click **Folder**. A folder icon with the label "New Folder" appears.
3. Type **Practice** as the name of the folder.

   TROUBLE? If nothing happens when you type the folder name, it's possible that the folder name is no longer selected. Right-click the Practice folder, click Rename, and then repeat Step 3.

4. Press the **Enter** key.

When you first create a folder, it doesn't contain any files. In the next set of steps, you will move a file from the root directory to the Practice folder.

Moving and Copying a File

You can move a file from one directory to another, or from one disk to another. When you move a file, it is copied to the new location you specify, and then the version in the old location is erased. The move feature is handy for organizing or reorganizing the files on your disk by moving them into appropriate folders. The easiest way to move a file is to hold down the right mouse button and drag the file from the old location to the new location. A menu appears and you select Move Here.

REFERENCE WINDOW	RW
Moving a File	
■ Locate the file in the My Compuuter window.	
■ Hold down the right mouse button while you drag the file icon to its new folder or disk location.	
■ Click Move Here.	

Suppose you want to move the Minutes file from the root directory to the Practice folder. Depending on your computer's settings, this file appears either as Minutes or Minutes.wps. In the following steps, the file is referred to as Minutes.

To move the Minutes file to the Practice folder:

1. Point to the **Minutes** icon.
2. Press and hold the right mouse button while you drag the Minutes icon to the Practice folder. See Figure 2-18.

TROUBLE? If you release the mouse button by mistake before dragging the Minutes icon to the Practice folder, the Minutes shortcut menu opens. Press Esc and then repeat Steps 1 and 2.

Figure 2-18 **MOVING A FILE**

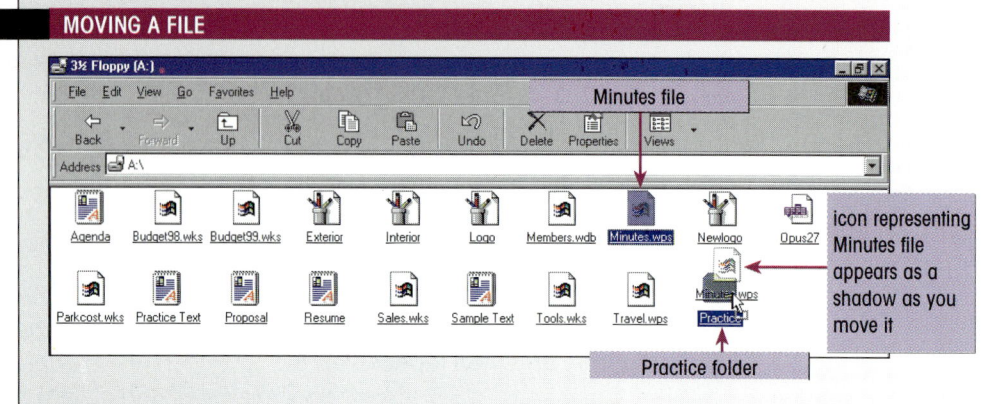

[Screenshot of 3½ Floppy (A:) window showing file icons including Agenda, Budget98.wks, Budget99.wks, Exterior, Interior, Logo, Members.wdb, Minutes.wps, Newlogo, Opus27, Parkcost.wks, Practice Text, Proposal, Resume, Sales.wks, Sample Text, Tools.wks, Travel.wps, and Practice folder. Labels indicate: "Minutes file", "icon representing Minutes file appears as a shadow as you move it", and "Practice folder".]

3. Release the right mouse button. A menu appears.

4. Click **Move Here**. The Minutes icon disappears from the window showing the files in the root directory.

Anything you do to an icon in the My Computer window is actually done to the file represented by that icon. If you move an icon, the file is moved; if you delete an icon, the file is deleted.

You can also copy a file from one folder to another, or from one disk to another. When you copy a file, you create an exact duplicate of an existing file in whatever disk or folder you specify. To copy a file from one folder to another on your floppy disk, you use the same procedure as for moving a file, except that you select Copy Here from the menu.

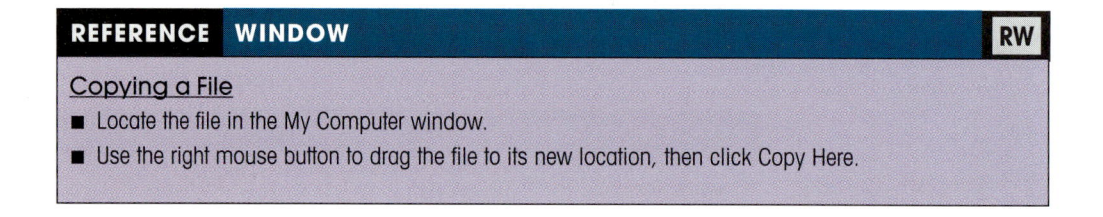

REFERENCE WINDOW RW

Copying a File
- Locate the file in the My Computer window.
- Use the right mouse button to drag the file to its new location, then click Copy Here.

Try copying the Resume file into the Practice folder.

To copy the Resume file into the Practice folder:

1. Using the right mouse button, drag the Resume file into the Practice folder.

2. Click **Copy Here**. Notice this time the file icon does not disappear, because you didn't actually move it, you only copied it.

After you move or copy a file, it is a good idea to make sure it was moved to the correct location. You can easily verify that a file is in its new folder by displaying the folder contents.

To verify that the Minutes file was moved and the Resume file was copied to the Practice folder:

1. Click the **Practice** folder icon. The Practice window appears, and it contains two files—Minutes, which you moved, and Resume, which you copied.

   TROUBLE? If you are using Classic style, click Settings, click the Practice folder icon and then press Enter to open the Practice window.

Navigating Explorer Windows

The title bar of the open window on your computer, "Practice," identifies the name of the folder you just opened. Before you opened the Practice folder, you were viewing the contents of your floppy disk, so the window's title bar, 3½ Floppy (A:) (or possibly just A:/, depending on how your computer is set up), identified the drive containing your disk, drive A. Before you opened that window you were viewing the My Computer window. Windows that show the objects on your computer are called **Explorer windows** because they allow you to explore the contents of your computer's devices and folders.

You've seen that to navigate through the devices and folders on your computer, you open My Computer and then click the icons representing the objects you want to explore. But what if you want to move back to a previous Explorer window? The Standard toolbar, which stays the same regardless of which Explorer window is open, includes buttons that help you navigate through your Explorer windows. Figure 2-19 summarizes the navigation buttons on the Standard toolbar.

Figure 2-19		NAVIGATIONAL BUTTONS
BUTTON	**ICON**	**DESCRIPTION**
Back	⇦	Returns you to the Explorer window you were most recently viewing. This button is active only when you have viewed more than one Explorer window in the current session.
Forward	⇨	Reverses the effect of the Back button.
Up	🗁	Moves you up one level on the hierarchy of your computer's objects; for example, moves you from a folder Explorer window to the drive containing the folder.

Try returning to the 3½ Floppy (A:) window using the Back button.

To navigate Explorer windows:

1. Click the **Back** button ⇦ to return to the 3½ Floppy (A:) window.

2. Click the **Forward** button ⇨ to reverse the effect of the Back button and return to the Practice window.

3. Click the **Up** button 🗁 to move up one level. You again return to the 3½ Floppy (A:) window because the Practice folder is contained within the 3½ Floppy (A:) drive.

Deleting a File

You delete a file or folder by deleting its icon. However, be careful when you delete a folder, because you also delete all the files it contains! When you delete a file from a *hard drive* on your computer, the filename is deleted from the directory but the file contents are held in the Recycle Bin. The **Recycle Bin** is an area on your hard drive that holds deleted files until you remove them permanently; an icon on the desktop allows you easy access to the Recycle Bin. If you change your mind and want to retrieve a file deleted from your hard drive, you can recover it by using the Recycle Bin.

When you delete a file from a *floppy disk*, it does not go into the Recycle Bin. Instead, it is deleted as soon as its icon disappears.

Try deleting the file named Agenda from your Student Disk. Because this file is on the floppy disk and not on the hard disk, it will not go into the Recycle Bin, and if you change your mind you won't be able to recover it.

To delete the file Agenda:

1. Right-click the icon for the file Agenda.
2. Click **Delete**.
3. If a message appears asking, "Are you sure you want to delete Agenda?", click **Yes**. The file is deleted and the Agenda icon no longer appears.

Renaming a File

Sometimes you decide to give a file a different name to clarify the file's contents. You can easily rename a file by using the Rename option on the file's shortcut menu or by using the file's label. The same rules apply for renaming a file as applied for naming a file, and you are limited in the number and type of characters you can use.

When you rename a file when file extensions are showing, make sure to include the extension in the new name. If you don't, Windows warns you it might not be able to identify the file type with the new name. Since you set up View options to hide file extensions, this should not be an issue unless you are trying to rename a file whose type Windows doesn't recognize.

Practice using this feature by renaming the Logo file to give it a more descriptive filename.

To rename Logo:

1. Right-click the **Logo** icon.
2. Click **Rename**. After a moment, a box appears around the label.
3. Type **Corporate Logo Draft** as the new filename.
4. Press the **Enter** key. The file now appears with the new name.
5. Click the **Up** button to move up one level to the My Computer window.

You can also edit an existing filename when you use the Rename command. Click to place the cursor at the location you want to edit, and then use the text-editing skills you learned with WordPad to edit the filename.

Copying an Entire Floppy Disk

You can have trouble accessing the data on your floppy disk if the disk is damaged, is exposed to magnetic fields, or picks up a computer virus. To avoid losing all your data, it is a good idea to make a copy of your floppy disk.

If you wanted to make a copy of an audio cassette, your cassette player would need two cassette drives. You might wonder, therefore, how your computer can make a copy of your disk if you have only one disk drive. Figure 2-20 illustrates how the computer uses only one disk drive to make a copy of a disk.

REFERENCE WINDOW

Copying a Disk
- Insert the disk you want to copy in drive A.
- In My Computer, right-click the 3½ Floppy (A:) icon, and then click Copy Disk.
- Click Start to begin the copy process.
- When prompted, remove the disk you want to copy, place your second disk in drive A, then click OK.

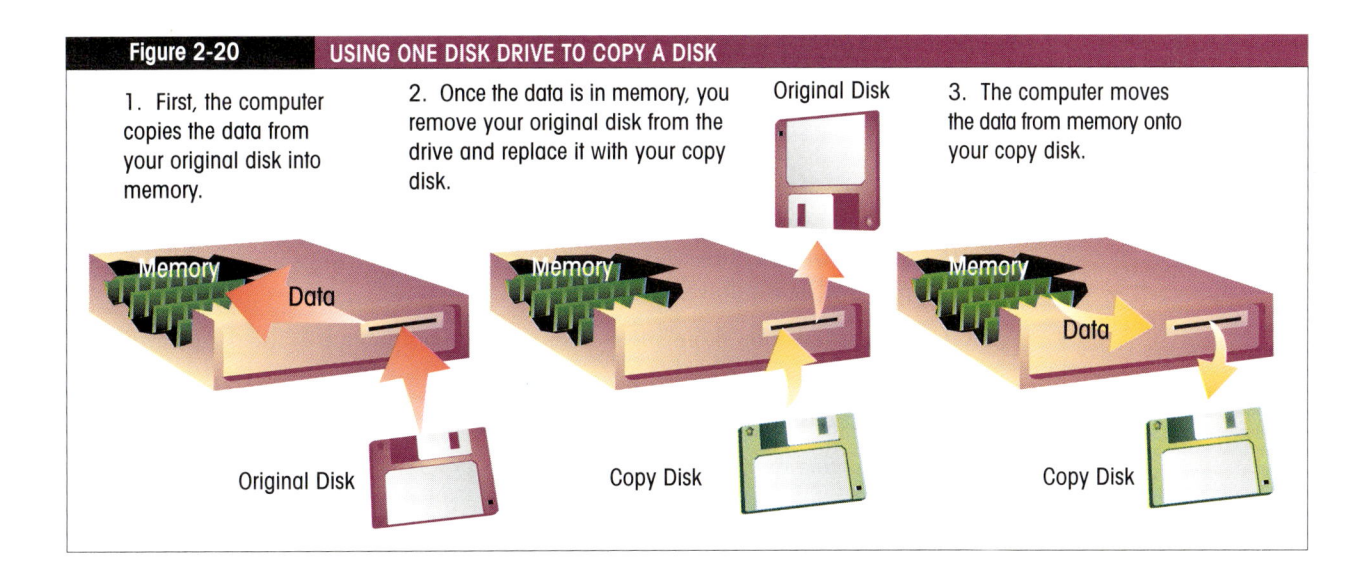

Figure 2-20 USING ONE DISK DRIVE TO COPY A DISK

1. First, the computer copies the data from your original disk into memory.
2. Once the data is in memory, you remove your original disk from the drive and replace it with your copy disk.
3. The computer moves the data from memory onto your copy disk.

If you have an extra floppy disk, you can make a copy of your Student Disk now. If you change the files on your disk, make sure you copy the disk regularly to keep it updated.

To copy your Student Disk:

1. Write your name and "Windows 98 Disk 1 Student Disk Copy" on the label of your second disk. Make sure the disk is blank and formatted.

    TROUBLE? If you aren't sure the disk is blank, place it in the disk drive and open the 3½ Floppy (A:) window to view its contents. If the disk contains files you need, get a different disk. If it contains files you don't need, you could format the disk now, using the steps you learned at the beginning of this tutorial.

2. Make sure your Student Disk is in drive A and the My Computer window is open.

3. Right-click the **3½ Floppy (A:)** icon, and then click **Copy Disk**. The Copy Disk dialog box opens.

4. Click the **Start** button to begin the copy process.

5. When the message "Insert the disk you want to copy to (destination disk)..." appears, remove your Student Disk and insert your Windows 98 Disk 1 Student Disk Copy in drive A.

6. Click the **OK** button. When the copy is complete, you will see the message "Copy completed successfully." Click the **Close** button.

7. Close the My Computer window.

8. Remove your disk from the drive.

As you finish copying your disk, Shannon emphasizes the importance of making copies of your files frequently, so you won't risk losing important documents for your distance learning course. If your original Student Disk were damaged, you could use the copy you just made to access the files.

Keeping copies of your files is so important that Windows 98 includes with it a program called **Backup** that automates the process of duplicating and storing data. In the Projects at the end of the tutorial you'll have an opportunity to explore the difference between what you just did in copying a disk and the way in which a program such as the Windows 98 Backup program helps you safeguard data.

Quick Check

1. If you want to find out about the storage devices and printers connected to your computer, what window can you open?

2. If you have only one floppy disk drive on your computer, it is usually identified by the letter _____.

3. The letter C is typically used for the _____ drive of a computer.

4. What information does Details view supply about a list of folders and files?

5. The main directory of a disk is referred to as the _____ directory.

6. True or False: You can divide a directory into folders.

7. If you have one floppy disk drive, but you have two disks, can you copy the files on one floppy disk to the other?

Tutorial Assignment

1. **Opening, Editing, and Printing a Document** In this tutorial you learned how to create a document using WordPad. You also learned how to save, open, and print a document. Practice these skills by opening the document called Resume in the Practice folder of your Student Disk. This document is a resume for Jamie Woods. Make the changes shown in Figure 2-21, and then save the document in the Pratice folder with the name "Resume 2" using the Save As command. After you save your revisions, preview and then print the document. Close WordPad.

Figure 2-21

change to your name, address, and phone number; delete office number if you don't have one →

JAMIE WOODS

The Envoy
1694 Columbia Rd. N.W.
Washington, D.C. 20009

Home (202) 328-1615
Office (301) 723-0345

OBJECTIVE: A challenging public relations position in the travel and tourism industry.

EDUCATION: B.A., Journalism (to be awarded June 1999)
change to the name of your university or college → Georgetown University
Major: Public Relations
Minor: Psychology
Major G.P.A.: 3.6/4.0

Core Courses:
Writing for public relations
Magazine production and design
News writing and editing

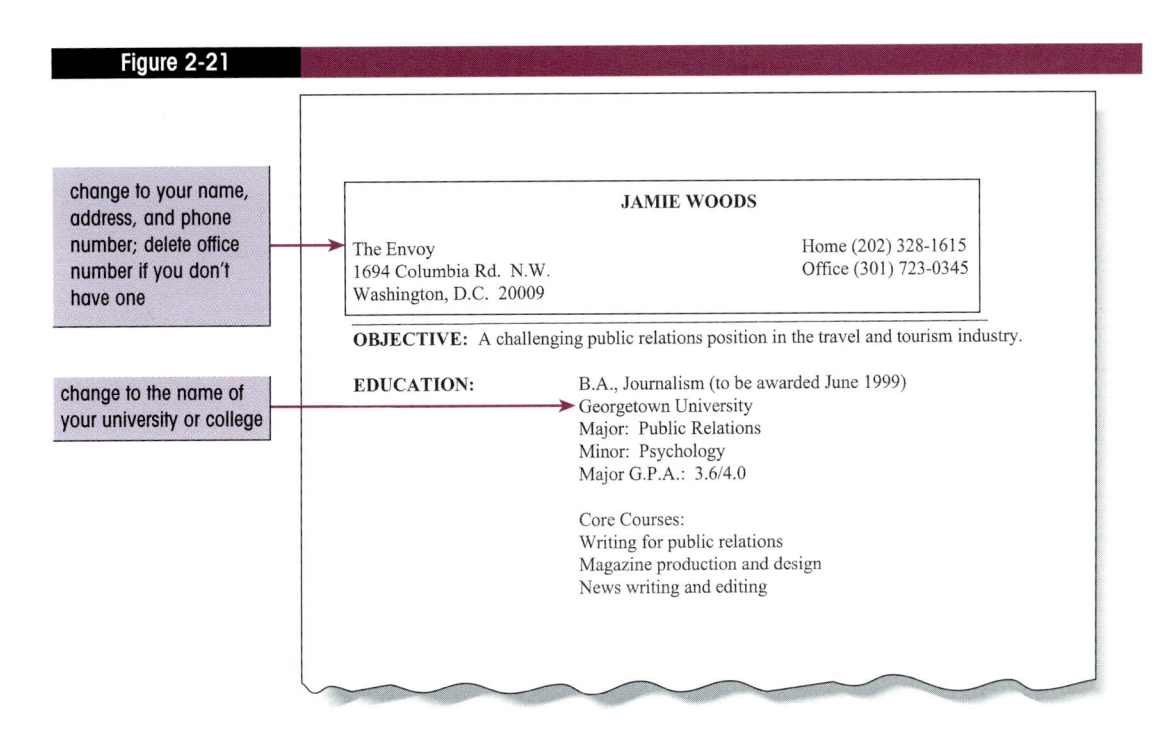

2. **Creating, Saving, and Printing a Letter** Use WordPad to write a one-page letter to a relative or a friend. Save the document in the Practice folder on your Student Disk with the name "Letter." Use the Print Preview feature to look at the format of your finished letter, then print it, and be sure to sign it. Close WordPad.

3. **Managing Files and Folders** Using the copy of the disk you made at the end of the tutorial, complete parts a through f below to practice your file management skills.
    a. Create a folder called Spreadsheets on your Student Disk.
    b. Move the files Parkcost, Budget98, Budget99, and Sales into the Spreadsheets folder.
    c. Create a folder called Park Project.
    d. Move the files Proposal, Members, Tools, Corporate Logo Draft, and Newlogo into the Park Project folder.
    e. Delete the file called Travel.
    f. Switch to the Details view and write out your answers to questions 1 through 5:
        1. What is the largest file or files in the Park Project folder?
        2. What is the newest file or files in the Spreadsheets folder?
        3. How many files (don't include folders) are in the root directory of your Student Disk?
        4. How are the Opus and Exterior icons different? Judging from the appearance of the icons, what would you guess these two files contain?
        5. Which file in the root directory has the most recent date?

4. **More Practice with Files and Folders** For this assignment, you need a third blank disk. Complete parts a through g below to practice your file management skills.
    a. Write "Windows 98 Tutorial 2 Assignment 4" on the label of the blank disk, and then format the disk if necessary.
    b. Create a new Student Disk, using the Assignment 4 disk. Refer to the section "Creating Your Student Disk" in Session 2.2.
    c. Create three folders on the Assignment 4 Student Disk you just created: Documents, Budgets, and Graphics.
    d. Move the files Interior, Exterior, Logo, and Newlogo to the Graphics folder.
    e. Move the files Travel, Members, and Minutes to the Documents folder.

f. Move Budget98 and Budget99 to the Budgets folder.
g. Switch to the Details view and write out your answers to questions 1 through 5:
   1. What is the largest file or files in the Graphics folder?
   2. How many word-processed documents are in the root directory? *Hint*: These documents will appear with the WordPad, Microsoft Word, or some other word-processing icon, depending on what software you have installed.
   3. What is the newest file or files in the root directory (don't include folders)?
   4. How many files in all folders are 5 KB in size?
   5. How many files in the root directory are WKS files? *Hint*: Look in the Type column to identify WKS files.
   6. Do all the files in the Graphics folder have the same icon? What type are they?

5. **Finding a File**   The Help system includes a topic that discusses how to find files on a disk without looking through all the folders. Start Windows Help, then locate this topic, and answer questions a through c:
   a. To display the Find dialog box, you must click the _____ button, then point to _____ from the menu, and finally click _____ from the submenu.
   b. Do you need to type in the entire filename to find the file?
   c. How do you perform a case-sensitive search?

6. **Help with Files and Folders**   In Tutorial 2 you learned how to work with Windows 98 files and folders. What additional information on this topic does Windows 98 Help provide? Use the Start button to access Help. Use the Index tab to locate topics related to files and folders. Find at least two tips or procedures for working with files and folders that were not covered in the tutorial. Write out the tip in your own words and include the title of the Help screen that contains the information.

Explore

7. **Formatting Text**   You can use a word processor such as WordPad to **format** text, that is, to give it a specific look and feel by using bold, italics, and different fonts, and by applying other features. Using WordPad, type the title and words to one of your favorite songs and then save the document on your Student Disk (make sure you use your original Student Disk) with the name Song.
   a. Select the title, and then click the Center, Bold, and Italic buttons on the toolbar.
   b. Click the Font list arrow and select a different font. Repeat this step several times with different fonts until you locate a font that matches the song.
   c. Experiment with formatting options until you find a look you like for your document. Save and print the final version.

PROJECTS

1. Formatting a floppy disk removes all the data on a disk. Answer the following questions using full sentences:
   a. What other method did you learn in this tutorial to remove data from a disk?
   b. If you wanted to remove all data from a disk, which method would you use? Why?
   c. What method would you use if you wanted to remove only one file? Why?

2. A friend who is new to computers is trying to learn how to enter text into WordPad. She has just finished typing her first paragraph when she notices a mistake in the first sentence. She can't remember how to fix a mistake, so she asks you for help. Write the set of steps she should try.

3. Computer users usually develop habits about how they access their files and programs. Take a minute to practice methods of opening a file, and then evaluate which method you would be likely to use and why.

   a. Using WordPad, create a document containing the words to a favorite poem, and save it on your Student Disk with the name Poem.
   b. Close WordPad and return to the desktop.
   c. Open the document using a *document-centric* approach.
   d. After a successful completion of part c, close the program and reopen the same document using another approach.
   e. Write the steps you used to complete parts c and d of this assignment. Then write a paragraph discussing which approach is most convenient when you are starting from the desktop, and indicate what habits you would develop if you owned your own computer and used it regularly.

Explore

4. The My Computer window gives you access to the objects on your computer. In this tutorial you used My Computer to access your floppy drive so you could view the contents of your Student Disk. The My Computer window gives you access to other objects too. Open My Computer and write a list of the objects you see, including folders. Then click each icon and write a two-sentence description of the contents of each window that opens.

Explore

5. In this tutorial you learned how to copy a disk to protect yourself in the event of data loss. If you had your own computer with an 80 MB hard drive that was being used to capacity, it would take many 1.44 MB floppy disks to copy the contents of the entire hard drive. Is copying a reasonable method to use for protecting the data on your hard disk? Why, or why not?

   a. As mentioned at the end of the tutorial, Windows 98 also includes an accessory called Backup that helps you safeguard your data. Backup doesn't just copy the data—it organizes it so that it takes up much less space than if you simply copied it. This program might not be installed on your computer, but if it is, try starting it (click the Start button, point to Programs, point to Accessories, point to System Tools, and then click Backup) and opening the Help files to learn what you can about how it functions. If it is not installed, skip part a.
   b. Look up the topic of backups in a computer concepts textbook or in computer trade magazines. You could also interview experienced computer owners to find out which method they use to protect their data. When you have finished researching the concept of the backup, write a single-page essay that explains the difference between copying and backing up files, and evaluates which method is preferable for backing up large amounts of data, and why.

LAB ASSIGNMENTS

Using Files In this Lab you manipulate a simulated computer to view what happens in memory and on disk when you create, save, open, revise, and delete files. Understanding what goes on "inside the box" will help you quickly grasp how to perform basic file operations with most application software. See the Read This Before You Begin page for instructions on starting the Using Files Course Lab.

1. Click the Steps button to learn how to use the simulated computer to view the contents of memory and disk when you perform basic file operations. As you proceed through the Steps, answer all of the Quick Check questions that appear. After you complete the Steps, you will see a Quick Check Summary Report. Follow the instructions on the screen to print this report.

2. Click the Explore button and use the simulated computer to perform the following tasks:
   a. Create a document containing your name and the city in which you were born. Save this document as NAME.
   b. Create another document containing two of your favorite foods. Save this document as FOODS.
   c. Create another file containing your two favorite classes. Call this file CLASSES.
   d. Open the FOOD file and add another one of your favorite foods. Save this file without changing its name.
   e. Open the NAME file. Change this document so it contains your name and the name of your school. Save this as a new document called SCHOOL.
   f. Write down how many files are on the simulated disk and the exact contents of each file.
   g. Delete all the files.

3. In Explore, use the simulated computer to perform the following tasks.
   a. Create a file called MUSIC that contains the name of your favorite CD.
   b. Create another document that contains eight numbers and call this file LOTTERY.
   c. You didn't win the lottery this week. Revise the contents of the LOTTERY file, but save the revision as LOTTERY2.
   d. Revise the MUSIC file so it also contains the name of your favorite musician or composer, and save this file as MUSIC2.
   e. Delete the MUSIC file.
   f. Write down how many files are on the simulated disk and the exact contents of each file.

QUICK CHECK ANSWERS

Session 2.1

1. file
2. Formatting
3. True
4. insertion point
5. Word wrap
6. Move the I-beam pointer to the left of the first word you want to select, then drag the I-beam pointer over the text to the end of the last word you want to select.
7. file extension

Session 2.2

1. My Computer
2. A
3. hard
4. file name, size, type, and date modified
5. root or top-level
6. True
7. yes

LEVEL 1

New Perspectives on

MICROSOFT® WORD 2000

TUTORIAL 1 WD 1.03

Creating a Document
Writing a Business Letter for Crossroads

TUTORIAL 2 WD 2.01

Editing and Formatting a Document
Preparing an Annuity Plan Description for Right-Hand Solutions

Read This Before You Begin

To the Student

Data Disks
To complete the Level I tutorials, Review Assignments, and Case Problems, you need 1 Data Disk. Your instructor will either provide you with this Data Disk or ask you to make your own.

If you are making your own Data Disk, you will need 1 blank, formatted high-density disk. You will need to copy a set of folders from a file server or standalone computer or the Web onto your disks. Your instructor will tell you which computer, drive letter, and folders contain the files you need. You could also download the files by going to **www.course.com**, clicking Data Disk Files, and following the instructions on the screen.

The following shows you which folders go on your disk, so that you will have enough disk space to complete all the tutorials, Review Assignments, and Case Problems:

Data Disk 1
Write this on the disk label:

Data Disk 1: Word 2000 Tutorials 1-2

Put these folders on the disk:

Tutorial.01, Tutorial.02

When you begin each tutorial, be sure you are using the correct Data Disk. Refer to the "File Finder" Chart at the back of this text for more detailed information on which files are used in which tutorials. See the inside front cover of this book for more information on Student Disk files, or ask your instructor or technical support person for assistance.

Course Labs
The Word Level I tutorials feature an interactive Course Lab to help you understand word processing concepts. There are Lab Assignments at the end of Tutorial 1 that relate to this Lab.

To start a Lab, click the **Start** button on the Windows taskbar, point to **Programs**, point to **Course Labs**, point to **New Perspectives Course Labs**, and click the name of the Lab you want to use.

Using Your Own Computer
If you are going to work through this book using your own computer, you need:

- **Computer System** Microsoft Windows 95, 98, NT, or higher must be installed on your computer. This book assumes a typical installation of Microsoft Word.

- **Data Disk** You will not be able to complete the tutorials or exercises in this book using your own computer until you have your Data Disk.

- **Course Labs** See your instructor or technical support person to obtain the Course Lab software for use on your own computer.

Visit Our World Wide Web Site
Additional materials designed especially for you are available on the World Wide Web. Go to **http://www.course.com**.

To the Instructor

The Data Files and Course Labs are available on the Instructor's Resource Kit for this title. Follow the instructions in the Help file on the CD-ROM to install the programs to your network or standalone computer. For information on creating Data Disks or the Course Labs, see the "To the Student" section above.

You are granted a license to copy the Data Files and Course Labs to any computer or computer network used by students who have purchased this book.

TUTORIAL 1

OBJECTIVES

In this tutorial you will:

- Start and exit Word
- Identify the components of the Word window
- Choose commands using the toolbars and menus
- Create and edit a document
- Enter the date with AutoComplete
- Correct spelling errors with AutoCorrect
- Scroll through a document
- Save, preview, and print a document
- Record properties for a document
- Use the Word Help system to get help

LAB

CREATING A DOCUMENT

Writing a Business Letter for Crossroads

CASE

Crossroads

Karen Liu is executive director of Crossroads, a small, nonprofit organization in Tacoma, Washington. Crossroads distributes business clothing to low-income clients who are returning to the job market or starting new careers. To make potential clients in the community more aware of their services, Crossroads reserves an exhibit booth each year at a local job fair sponsored by the Tacoma Chamber of Commerce. Crossroads needs to find out the date and location of this year's fair, as well as some other logistical information, before reserving a booth. Karen asks you to write a letter requesting this information from the Tacoma Chamber of Commerce.

In this tutorial you will create Karen's letter using Microsoft Word 2000, a popular word-processing program. Before you begin typing the letter, you will learn to start the Word program, identify and use the elements of the Word screen, and adjust some Word settings. Next you will create a new Word document, type the text of the Crossroads letter, save the letter, and then print the letter for Karen. In the process of entering the text, you'll learn several ways of correcting typing errors. You'll also find out how to use the Word Help system, which allows you to quickly find answers to your questions about the program.

SESSION 1.1

In this session you will learn how to start Word, how to identify and use the parts of the Word screen, and how to adjust some Word settings. With the skills you learn in this session, you'll be prepared to use Word to create a variety of documents, such as letters, reports, and memos.

Four Steps to a Professional Document

Word helps you produce quality work in minimal time. Not only can you type a document in Word, you can quickly make revisions and corrections, adjust margins and spacing, create columns and tables, and add graphics to your documents. The most efficient way to produce a document is to follow these four steps: (1) planning and creating, (2) editing, (3) formatting, and (4) printing.

In the long run, *planning* saves time and effort. First, you should determine what you want to say. State your purpose clearly and include enough information to achieve that purpose without overwhelming or boring your reader. Be sure to *organize* your ideas logically. Also, decide how you want your document to look. In this case, your letter to the Tacoma Chamber of Commerce will take the form of a standard business letter. Karen has given you a handwritten note with all her questions for the Tacoma Chamber of Commerce, as shown in Figure 1-1.

Figure 1-1   **KAREN'S QUESTIONS ABOUT THE JOB FAIR**

> Please write the Tacoma Chamber of Commerce and find out the following:
>
> What are the location and dates for this year's job fair?
>
> Is a map of the exhibit area available? What size booths are available and how can we reserve a booth?
>
> Who do we contact about what physical facilities are available at each booth?
>
> Send the letter to the Chamber's president. The address is 210 Shoreline Vista, Suite 1103, Tacoma WA 98402.

After you've planned your document, you can go ahead and *create* it using Word. The next step, *editing*, consists of reading the document you've created, then correcting your errors, and, finally, adding or deleting text to make the document easy to read.

Once your document is error-free, you can *format* it to make it visually appealing. Formatting features, such as white space (blank areas of a page), line spacing, boldface, and italics can help make your document easier to read. *Printing* is the final phase in creating an effective document. In this tutorial, you will preview your document before you spend time and resources to print it.

TUTORIAL 1 CREATING A DOCUMENT   WD 1.05   WORD

Starting Word

Before you can apply these four steps to produce a letter in Word, you need to start Word and learn about the general organization of the Word screen. You'll do that now.

To start Microsoft Word:

1. Make sure Windows is running on your computer and the Windows desktop appears on your screen.

2. Click the **Start** button on the taskbar to display the Start menu, and then point to **Programs** to display the Programs menu.

3. Point to **Microsoft Word** on the Programs menu. See Figure 1-2.

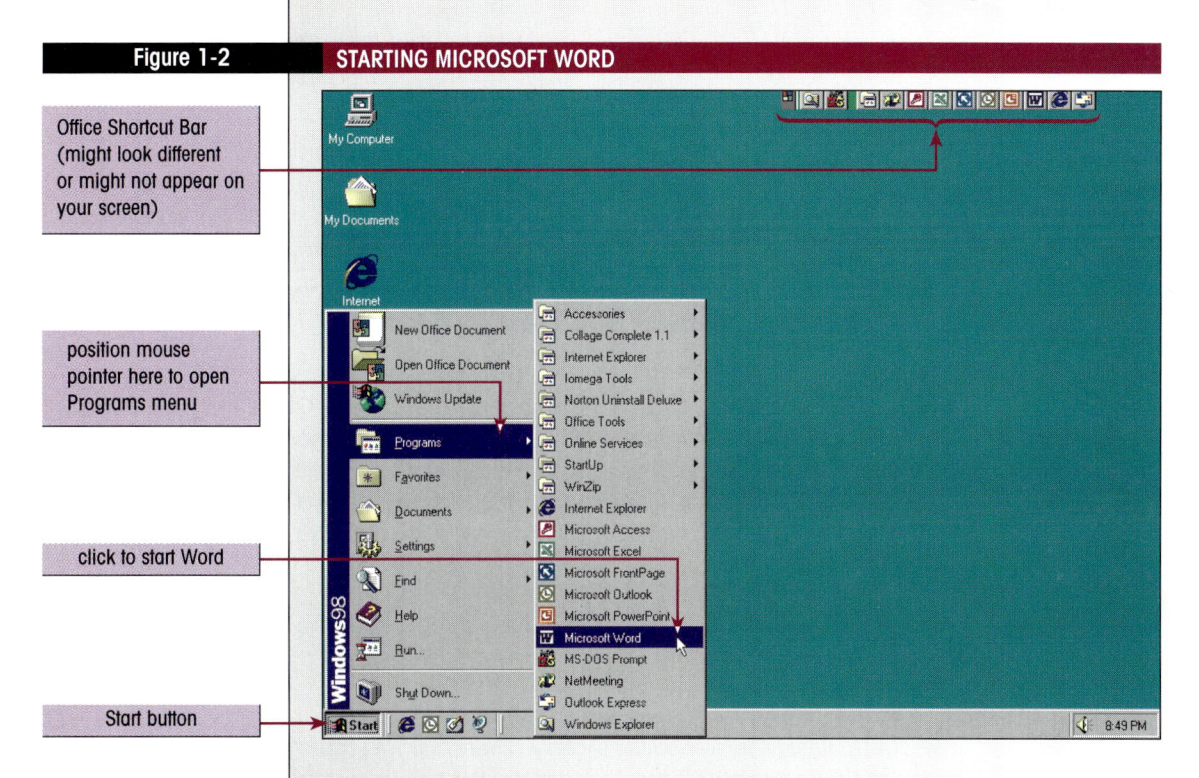

Figure 1-2   **STARTING MICROSOFT WORD**

- Office Shortcut Bar (might look different or might not appear on your screen)
- position mouse pointer here to open Programs menu
- click to start Word
- Start button

TROUBLE? Don't worry if your screen differs slightly from Figure 1-2. Although the figures in this book were created while running Windows 98 in its default settings, these operating systems share the same basic user interface. Microsoft Word should run equally well using Windows 95, Windows 98 in Web style, Windows NT, or Windows 2000.

TROUBLE? If you don't see the Microsoft Word option on the Programs menu, ask your instructor or technical support person for help.

TROUBLE? If the Office Shortcut Bar appears on your screen, your system is set up to display it. Because the Office Shortcut Bar is not required to complete these tutorials, it has been omitted from the remaining figures in this text. You can close it or simply ignore it.

4. Click **Microsoft Word**. After a short pause, the Microsoft Word copyright information appears in a message box and remains on the screen until the Word program window, containing a blank Word document, is displayed. See Figure 1-3.

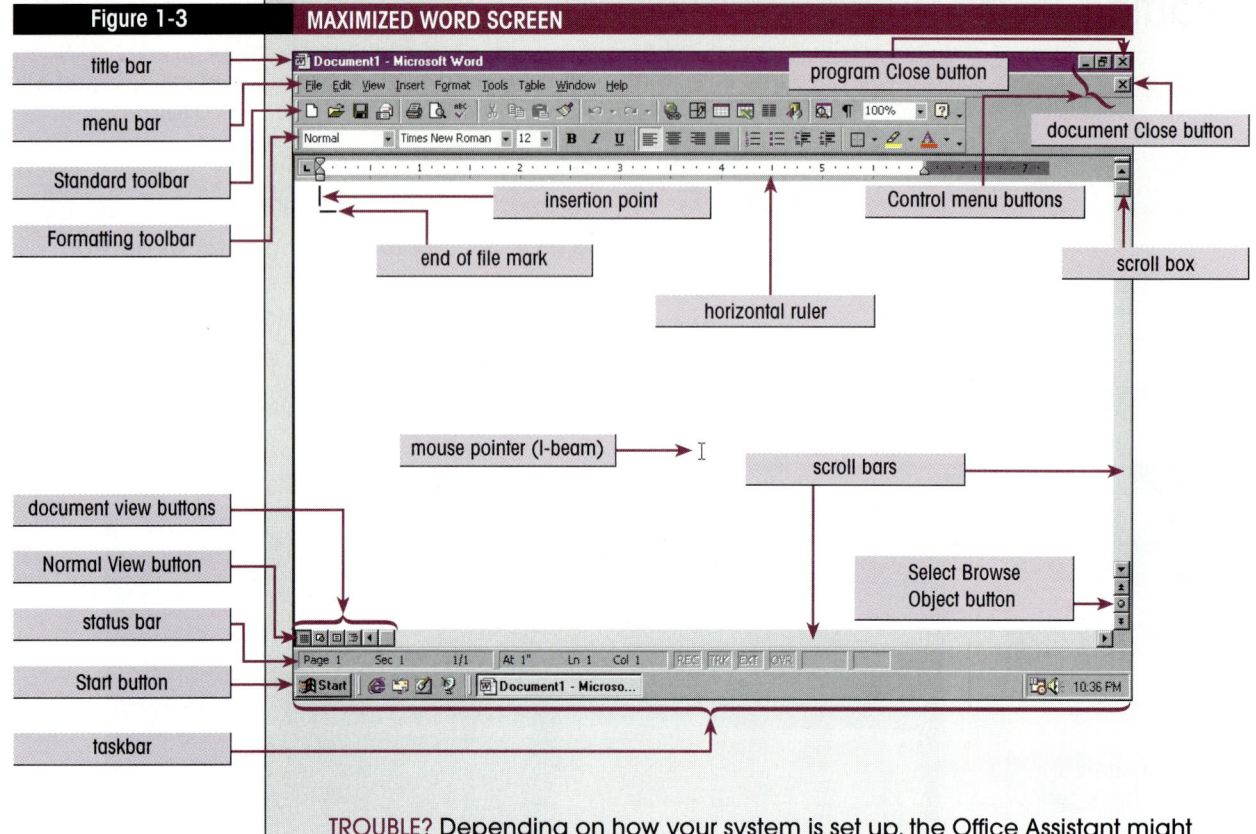

Figure 1-3   MAXIMIZED WORD SCREEN

Labels identifying parts of the Word screen: title bar, menu bar, Standard toolbar, Formatting toolbar, insertion point, end of file mark, horizontal ruler, program Close button, document Close button, Control menu buttons, scroll box, mouse pointer (I-beam), scroll bars, Select Browse Object button, document view buttons, Normal View button, status bar, Start button, taskbar.

> **TROUBLE?** Depending on how your system is set up, the Office Assistant might open when you start Word. For now, click Help on the menu bar, and then click Hide the Office Assistant. You'll learn more about the Office Assistant later in this tutorial. If you've just installed Microsoft Word, you'll need to click the Start Using Microsoft Word button, which the Office Assistant displays, before closing the Office Assistant window.

5. If the Word window does not fill the entire screen, click the **Maximize** button ☐ in the upper-right corner of the Word window. Your screen should now resemble Figure 1-3.

> **TROUBLE?** If your screen looks slightly different from Figure 1-3 (for example, if you see the paragraph mark character ¶ on your screen, the Standard and Formatting toolbars appear on one row, or an additional toolbar is displayed), just continue with the steps. You will learn how to make some adjustments to the Word screen shortly.

Word is now running and ready to use.

Viewing the Word Screen

The Word screen is made up of a number of elements, each of which is described in Figure 1-4. You are already familiar with some of these elements, such as the menu bar, title bar, and status bar, because they are common to all Windows screens.

If at any time you would like to check the name of a Word toolbar button, just position the mouse pointer over the button without clicking. A **ScreenTip**, a small yellow box with the name of the button, will appear.

TUTORIAL 1 CREATING A DOCUMENT   WD 1.07   WORD

Figure 1-4	DESCRIPTION OF WORD SCREEN ELEMENTS
SCREEN ELEMENT	DESCRIPTION
Control menu buttons	Size and close the Word window and the document
Document Close button	Closes the open document when only one document is open
Document view buttons	Switch the document between four different views: normal view, Web layout view, print layout view, and outline view
Document window	Area where you enter text and graphics
End-of-file mark	Indicates the end of the document
Formatting toolbar	Contains buttons to activate common font and paragraph formatting commands
Horizontal ruler	Adjusts margins, tabs, and column widths; vertical ruler appears in print layout view
Insertion point	Indicates location where characters will be inserted or deleted
Menu bar	Contains lists or menus of all the Word commands. When you first display a menu, you see a short list of the most frequently used commands. To see the full list of commands in the menu, you can either click the menu and then wait a few seconds for the remaining commands to appear or click the menu and then click or point to the downward-facing double-arrow at the bottom of the menu.
Mouse pointer	Changes shape depending on its location on the screen (i.e., I-beam pointer in text area; arrow in nontext areas)
Program Close button	Closes the current document if more than one document is open. Closes Word if one or no document is open.
Scroll bars	Shifts text vertically and horizontally on the screen so you can see different parts of the document
Scroll box	Helps you move quickly to other pages of your document
Select Browse Object button	Displays buttons that allow you to move quickly through the document
Standard toolbar	Contains buttons to activate frequently used commands
Start button	Starts a program, opens a document, provides quick access to Windows Help
Status bar	Provides information regarding the location of the insertion point
Taskbar	Shows programs that are running and allows you to switch quickly from one program to another
Title bar	Identifies the current application (i.e., Microsoft Word); shows the filename of the current document

Keep in mind that the commands on the menu bars initially display the commands that are used most frequently on your particular computer. When you leave the menu displayed for a few seconds or point to the double-arrow, a more complete list of commands appears. Throughout these tutorials, point to the double-arrow if you do not see the command you need.

Checking the Screen Before You Begin Each Tutorial

Word provides a set of standard settings, called **default settings**, that are appropriate for most documents. However, the setup of your Word document might have different default settings from those shown in the figures. This often happens when you share a computer and another user changes the appearance of the Word screen. The rest of this section explains what your screen should look like and how to make it match those in the tutorials.

Setting the Document View to Normal

You can view your document in one of four ways—normal, Web layout, print layout, or outline. **Web layout view** and **outline view** are designed for special situations that you don't need to worry about now. You will, however, learn more about **print layout view**—which allows you to see a page's design and format—in later tutorials. You will use **normal view,** which allows you to see more of the document, for this tutorial. Depending on the document view selected by the last person who used Word, you might need to change the document back to normal view.

To make sure the document window is in normal view:

1. Click the **Normal View** button to the left of the horizontal scroll bar. See Figure 1-5. If your document window was not in normal view, it changes to normal view now. The Normal View button looks pressed in to indicate that it is selected.

Figure 1-5 CHANGING TO NORMAL VIEW

- Web Layout button
- Print Layout button
- Outline View button
- Normal View button
- status bar

Displaying the Toolbars and Ruler

These tutorials frequently use the Standard toolbar and the Formatting toolbar to help you work more efficiently. Each time you start Word, check to make sure both toolbars appear on your screen, with the Standard toolbar on top of the Formatting toolbar. Depending on the settings specified by the last person to use your computer, you may not see both toolbars, or your toolbars may appear all on one row, rather than one on top of another. You also may see additional toolbars, such as the Drawing toolbar.

If either toolbar is missing, or if other toolbars are displayed, perform the next steps.

To display or hide a toolbar:

1. Position the pointer over any visible toolbar and click the right mouse button. A shortcut menu appears. The menu lists all available toolbars and displays a check mark next to those currently displayed.

2. If the Standard or Formatting toolbar is not visible, click its name on the shortcut menu to place a check mark next to it. If any toolbars besides the Formatting and Standard toolbars have check marks, click each one to remove the check mark and hide the toolbar. Only the Standard and Formatting toolbars should be visible, as shown in Figure 1-6.

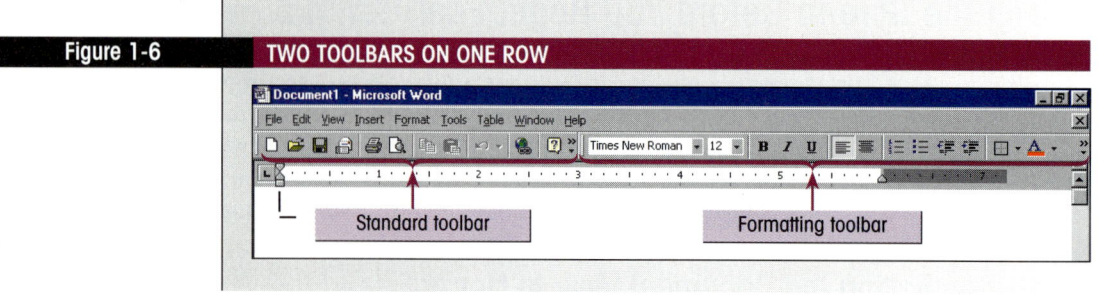

Figure 1-6 TWO TOOLBARS ON ONE ROW

- Standard toolbar
- Formatting toolbar

If the toolbars appear on one row, as in Figure 1-6, perform the next steps to move the Formatting toolbar below the Standard toolbar.

To move the Formatting toolbar:

1. Click **Tools** on the menu bar, and then click **Customize**. The Customize dialog box opens.

   TROUBLE? If you don't see the Customize command on the Tools menu, point to the double-arrow, as explained earlier in this tutorial, to display the full list of commands.

2. Click the **Options** tab, and then click the **Standard and Formatting toolbars share one row** check box to remove the check.

3. Click **Close**. The Customize dialog box closes. The toolbars on your screen should now match those in Figure 1-3.

As you complete these tutorials, the ruler also should be visible to help you place items precisely.

To display the ruler:

1. Click **View** on the menu bar, and then point to the double-arrow at the bottom of the menu to display the hidden menu commands.

2. If "Ruler" does not have a check mark next to it, then click **Ruler**.

Setting the Font and Font Size

A **font** is a set of characters that has a certain design, shape, and appearance. Each font has a name, such as Courier, Times New Roman, or Arial. The **font size** is the actual height of a character, measured in points, where one point equals 1/72 of an inch in height. You'll learn more about fonts and font sizes later, but for now simply keep in mind that most of the documents you create will use the Times New Roman font in a font size of 12 points. Word usually uses a default (or predefined) setting of Times New Roman 12 point in new documents, but someone else might have changed the setting after Word was installed on your computer. You can see your computer's current settings in the Font list box, and the Font Size list box, in the Formatting toolbar, as shown in Figure 1-7.

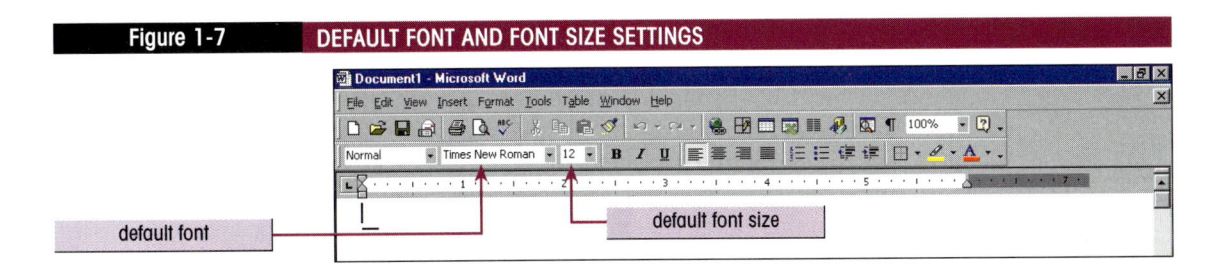

| Figure 1-7 | DEFAULT FONT AND FONT SIZE SETTINGS |

If your font setting is not Times New Roman 12 point, you should change the default setting now. You'll use the menu bar to choose the desired commands.

To change the default font and font size:

1. Click **Format** on the menu bar, and then click **Font** to open the Font dialog box. If necessary, click the Font tab. See Figure 1-8.

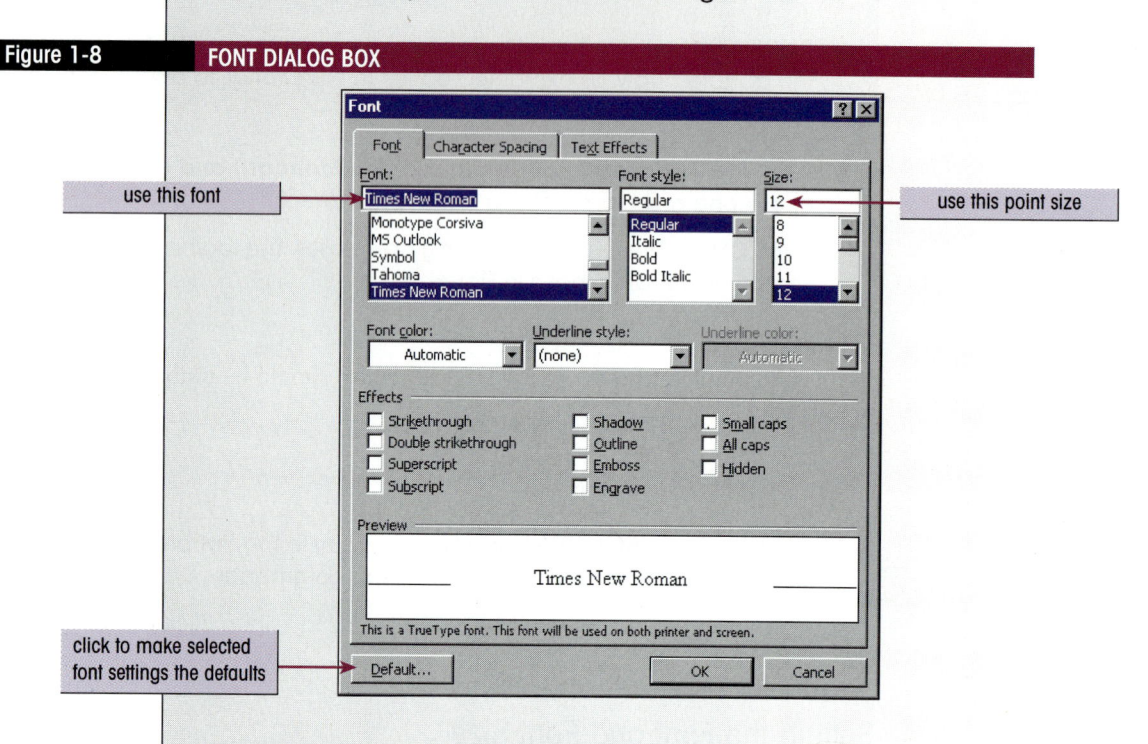

Figure 1-8   **FONT DIALOG BOX**

use this font → Times New Roman

use this point size → 12

click to make selected font settings the defaults → Default...

2. In the Font text box, click **Times New Roman**.
3. In the Size list box, click **12** to change the font to 12 point.
4. Click the **Default** button to make Times New Roman and 12 point the default settings. Word displays a message asking you to verify that you want to make 12-point Times New Roman the default font.
5. Click the **Yes** button.

Displaying Nonprinting Characters

Nonprinting characters are symbols that can be displayed on the screen but that do not show up when you print your document. You can display them when you are working on the appearance, or **format**, of your document. For example, one nonprinting character marks the end of a paragraph (¶), and another marks the space between words (•). It's sometimes helpful to display nonprinting characters so you can see whether you've typed an extra space, ended a paragraph, typed spaces instead of tabs, and so on. Generally, in these tutorials, you will display nonprinting characters only when you are formatting a document. You'll display them now, though, so you can use them as guides when typing your first letter.

To display nonprinting characters:

1. Click the Show/Hide ¶ button ¶ on the Standard toolbar. A paragraph mark (¶) appears at the top of the document window. See Figure 1-9.

TUTORIAL 1 CREATING A DOCUMENT   WD 1.11   WORD

| Figure 1-9 | NONPRINTING CHARACTERS ACTIVATED |

hide paragraph mark

Show/Hide ¶ button is activated

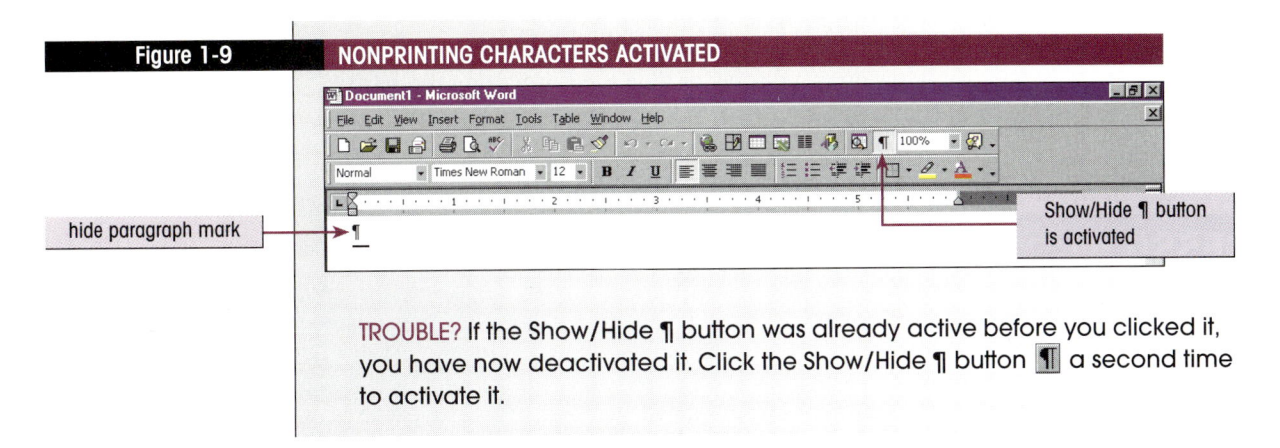

TROUBLE? If the Show/Hide ¶ button was already active before you clicked it, you have now deactivated it. Click the Show/Hide ¶ button ¶ a second time to activate it.

To make sure your screen always matches the figures in these tutorials, remember to complete the checklist in Figure 1-10 each time you sit down at the computer.

| Figure 1-10 | WORD SCREEN SESSION CHECKLIST |

SCREEN ELEMENT	SETTING	CHECK
Document view	Normal view	☐
Word window	Maximized	☐
Standard toolbar	Displayed, below the menu bar	☐
Formatting toolbar	Displayed, below the Standard toolbar	☐
Other toolbars	Hidden	☐
Nonprinting characters	Hidden	☐
Font	Times New Roman	☐
Point size	12 point	☐
Ruler	Displayed	☐

Now that you have planned a document, opened the Word program, identified screen elements, and adjusted settings, you are ready to create a new document. In the next session, you will create Karen's letter to the Tacoma Chamber of Commerce.

Session 1.1 QUICK CHECK

1. In your own words, list and describe the steps in creating a document.
2. How do you start Word from the Windows desktop?
3. Define each of the following in your own words:
   a. nonprinting characters
   b. document view buttons
   c. font size
   d. default settings

4. How do you change the default font size?

5. How do you display or hide the Formatting toolbar?

6. How do you change the document view to normal view?

SESSION 1.2

In this session you will create a one-page document using Word. You'll correct errors and scroll through your document. You'll also name, save, preview, and print the document, and learn how to use the Word Help system.

Typing a Letter

You're ready to type Karen's letter to the Tacoma Chamber of Commerce. Figure 1-11 shows the completed letter printed on the company letterhead. You'll begin by opening a new blank page (in case you accidentally typed something in the current page). Then you'll move the insertion point to about 2½ inches from the top margin of the paper to allow space for the Crossroads letterhead.

Figure 1-11   JOB FAIR LETTER

crossroads
1414 East Bellingham S.W.
Suite 318
Tacoma, WA 98402

February 21, 2001

Deborah Brown, President
Tacoma Chamber of Commerce
210 Shoreline Vista, Suite 1103
Tacoma, WA 98402

Dear Deborah:

Recently, you contacted our staff about the Chamber's decision to sponsor a job fair again this year. We are interested in participating as we have done in the past.

Please send us information about the dates and location for this year's fair. If a map of the exhibit area is available, we would appreciate receiving a copy of it. Also, please send us the name and address of someone we can contact regarding the on-site physical facilities. Specifically, we need to know what size the exhibit booths are and how we can reserve one.

Thank you for your help in this matter. We look forward to participating in the job fair and hope to hear from you soon.

Sincerely yours,

Karen Liu
Executive Director

TUTORIAL 1 CREATING A DOCUMENT   WD 1.13   WORD

To open a new document:

1. If you took a break after the last session, make sure the Word program is running, that nonprinting characters are displayed, and that the font settings in the Formatting toolbar are set to 12-point Times New Roman. Also verify that the toolbars and the ruler are properly displayed.

2. Click the **New Blank Document** button on the Standard toolbar to open a fresh document.

   If you have the taskbar displayed at the bottom of your screen, you see an additional button for the new document. If you wanted to switch back to Document1, you could simply click its button on the taskbar. Notice that the new document has only one set of Control menu buttons. When two or more documents are open, you click the Close button in the upper-right corner of the title bar to close that document. When only one document is open, you can click the Close Window button in the upper-right corner of the menu bar to close the document and leave Word open, or you can click the Close button in the upper-right corner of the title bar to close the document and exit Word.

3. Press the **Enter** key eight times. Each time you press the Enter key, a nonprinting paragraph mark appears. In the status bar (at the bottom of the document window), you should see the setting "At 2.5"," indicating that the insertion point is approximately 2½ inches from the top of the page. Another setting in the status bar should read "Ln 9," indicating the insertion point is in line 9 of the document. Note that your settings may be slightly different. See Figure 1-12.

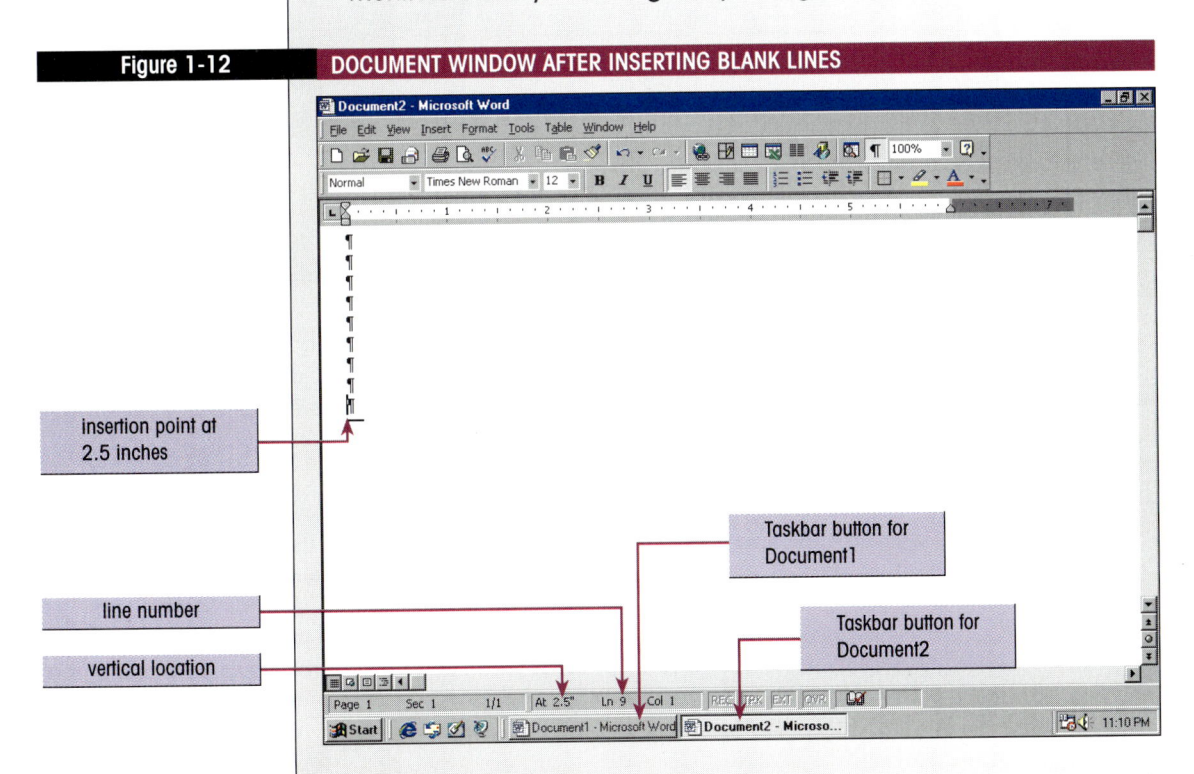

Figure 1-12   **DOCUMENT WINDOW AFTER INSERTING BLANK LINES**

- insertion point at 2.5 inches
- line number
- vertical location
- Taskbar button for Document1
- Taskbar button for Document2

TROUBLE? If the paragraph mark doesn't appear each time you press the Enter key, the nonprinting characters might be hidden. To show the nonprinting characters, click the Show/Hide ¶ button on the Standard toolbar, as described earlier in this tutorial.

> TROUBLE? If you pressed the Enter key too many times, press the Backspace key to delete each extra line and paragraph mark. If you're on line 9 but the "At" number is not 2.5", don't worry. Different monitors produce slightly different measurements when you press the Enter key.

Using AutoCompleteTips

Now you're ready to type the date. You'll take advantage of Word's **AutoComplete** feature, which automatically types dates and other regularly used words and text for you.

To insert the date using an AutoComplete tip:

1. Type **Febr** (the first four letters of February). An AutoComplete tip appears above the line, as shown in Figure 1-13. If you wanted to type something other than February, you would simply continue typing to complete the word. In this case, though, you want to accept the AutoComplete tip, so you will press the Enter key in the next step.

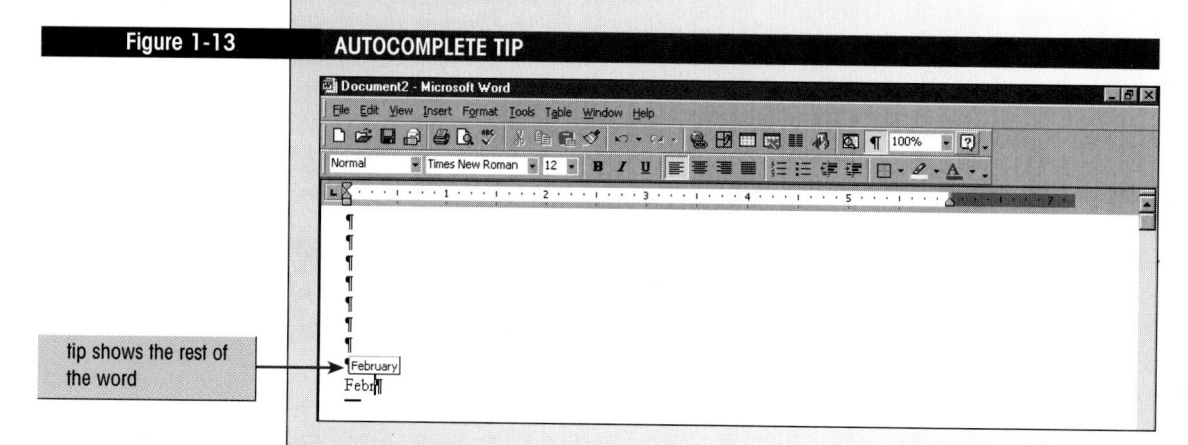

Figure 1-13 AUTOCOMPLETE TIP

tip shows the rest of the word

> TROUBLE? If the AutoComplete tip doesn't appear, this feature may not be active. Click Tools on the menu bar, click AutoCorrect, click the AutoText tab, click the Show AutoComplete tip for AutoText and dates check box to insert a check, and then click OK.

2. Press the **Enter** key to insert the rest of the word "February."

3. Press the **spacebar** and then type **21, 2001** to complete the date. See Figure 1-14.

> TROUBLE? If February happens to be the current month, you will see an AutoComplete tip displaying the current date after you press the spacebar. To accept that AutoComplete tip, press Enter. Otherwise, simply type the rest of the date as instructed in Step 3.

Figure 1-14 | **DATE ENTERED IN THE DOCUMENT**

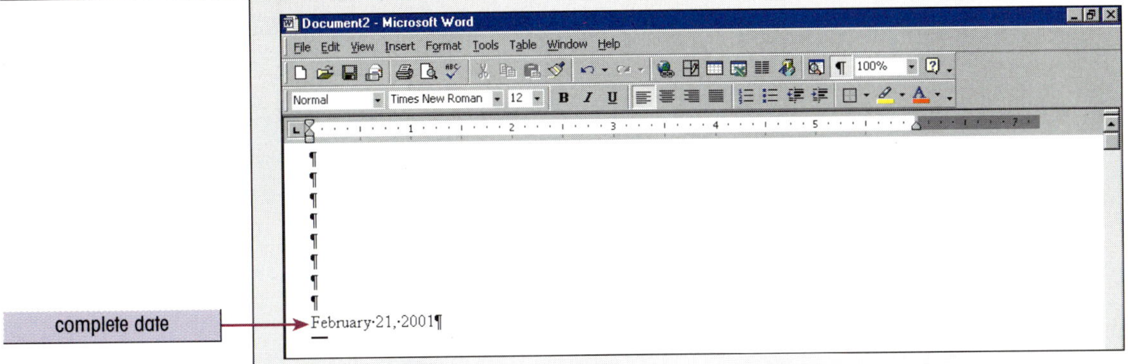

complete date → February 21, 2001

4. Press the **Enter** key four times to insert three blank lines between the date and the inside address. The status bar now should display "Ln13."

Next, you'll enter the inside address shown on Karen's note.

Entering Text

You'll enter the inside address by typing it. If you type a wrong character, simply press the Backspace key to delete the mistake and then retype it.

To type the inside address:

1. Type **Deborah Brown, President** and then press the **Enter** key. As you type, the nonprinting character (•) appears between words to indicate a space.

   TROUBLE? If a wavy red or green line appears beneath a word, check to make sure you typed the text correctly. If you did not, use the Backspace key to remove the error, and then retype the text correctly.

2. Type the following text, pressing the **Enter** key after each line to enter the inside address:

   Tacoma Chamber of Commerce
   210 Shoreline Vista, Suite 1103
   Tacoma, WA 98402

3. Press the **Enter** key again to add a blank line between the inside address and the salutation.

4. Type **Dear Deborah:** and press the **Enter** key twice to double space between the salutation and the body of the letter. When you press the Enter key the first time, the Office Assistant might appear, asking if you would like help writing your letter. Depending on the settings on your computer, you might see a different Office Assistant than the one shown in Figure 1-15.

Figure 1-15   **OFFICE ASSISTANT**

[Screenshot of Microsoft Word showing the Office Assistant dialog with "It looks like you're writing a letter. Would you like help?" options: "Get help with writing the letter", "Just type the letter without help", Cancel. Callouts point to:]

- your Office Assistant may differ
- inside address
- extra blank line
- salutation

The letter content visible:
February 21, 2001

Deborah Brown, President
Tacoma Chamber of Commerce
210 Shoreline Vista, Suite 1103
Tacoma, WA 98402

Dear Deborah:

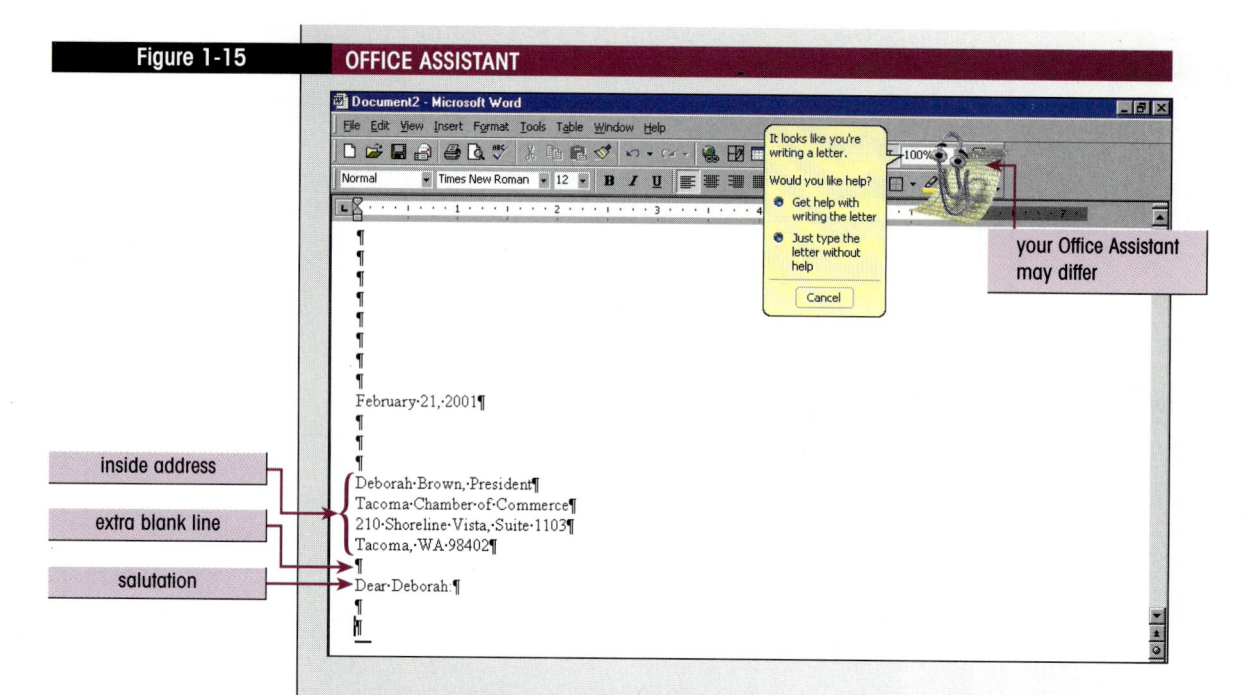

The Office Assistant is an interactive feature that sometimes appears to offer help on routine tasks. In this case, you could click the "Get help with writing the letter" button and have the Office Assistant lead you through a series of dialog boxes designed to set up the basic elements of your letter. You'll learn more about the Office Assistant later in this tutorial. For now, though, you'll close the Office Assistant and continue writing your letter.

5. Click the **Just type the letter without help** button to close the Office Assistant.

   TROUBLE? If the Office Assistant remains open, right-click the Office Assistant, and then click Hide to close it.

You have completed the date, the inside address, and the salutation of Karen's letter, using a standard business letter format. You're ready to complete the letter. Before you do, however, you should save what you have typed so far.

Saving a Document for the First Time

The letter on which you are working is stored only in the computer's memory, not on a disk. If you were to exit Word, turn off your computer, or experience an accidental power failure, the part of Karen's letter that you just typed would be lost. You should get in the habit of frequently saving your document to a disk.

The first time you save a document, you need to name it. The name you use is usually referred to as the **filename**. To make it easy for you to keep track of the various documents stored on your computer, or 3½-inch disk, or Zip disk, it's important to use names that accurately describe their contents. For example, if you use a generic name such as "Letter" for this particular document, you won't be able to differentiate it from other letters in the future. Instead, you should use a more descriptive name, such as Tacoma Job Fair Letter.

TUTORIAL 1 CREATING A DOCUMENT WD 1.17 WORD

> **REFERENCE WINDOW**
>
> **Saving a Document for the First Time**
> - Click the Save button on the Standard toolbar (or click File on the menu bar, and then click Save).
> - If necessary, change the folder and drive information.
> - In the File name text box, type the filename.
> - Click the Save button (or press the Enter key).

After you name your document, Word automatically appends the .doc filename extension to identify the file as a Microsoft Word document. However, depending on how Windows is set up on your computer, you might not actually see the .doc extension. These tutorials assume that filename extensions are hidden.

To save the document:

1. Place your Data Disk in the appropriate disk drive.

   TROUBLE? If you don't have a Data Disk, you need to get one before you can proceed. Your instructor or technical support person will either give you one or ask you to make your own by following the instructions on the "Read This Before You Begin" page at the beginning of this tutorial. See your instructor or technical support person for more information.

2. Click the **Save** button on the Standard toolbar. The Save As dialog box opens. See Figure 1-16. Note that Word suggests using the first few characters of the letter ("February 21") as the filename. You will replace the suggested filename with something more descriptive.

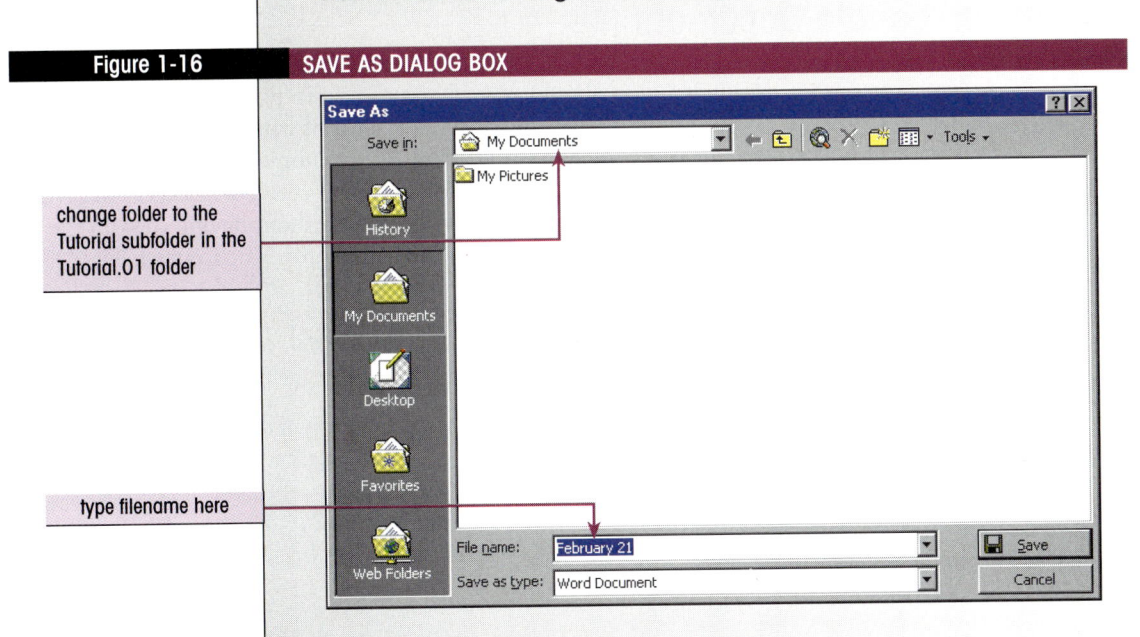

Figure 1-16   SAVE AS DIALOG BOX

- change folder to the Tutorial subfolder in the Tutorial.01 folder
- type filename here

3. Type **Tacoma Job Fair Letter** in the File name text box.

4. Click the **Save in** list arrow, click the drive containing your Data Disk, double-click the **Tutorial.01** folder, then double-click the **Tutorial** folder. The Tutorial folder is now open and ready for you to save the document. See Figure 1-17.

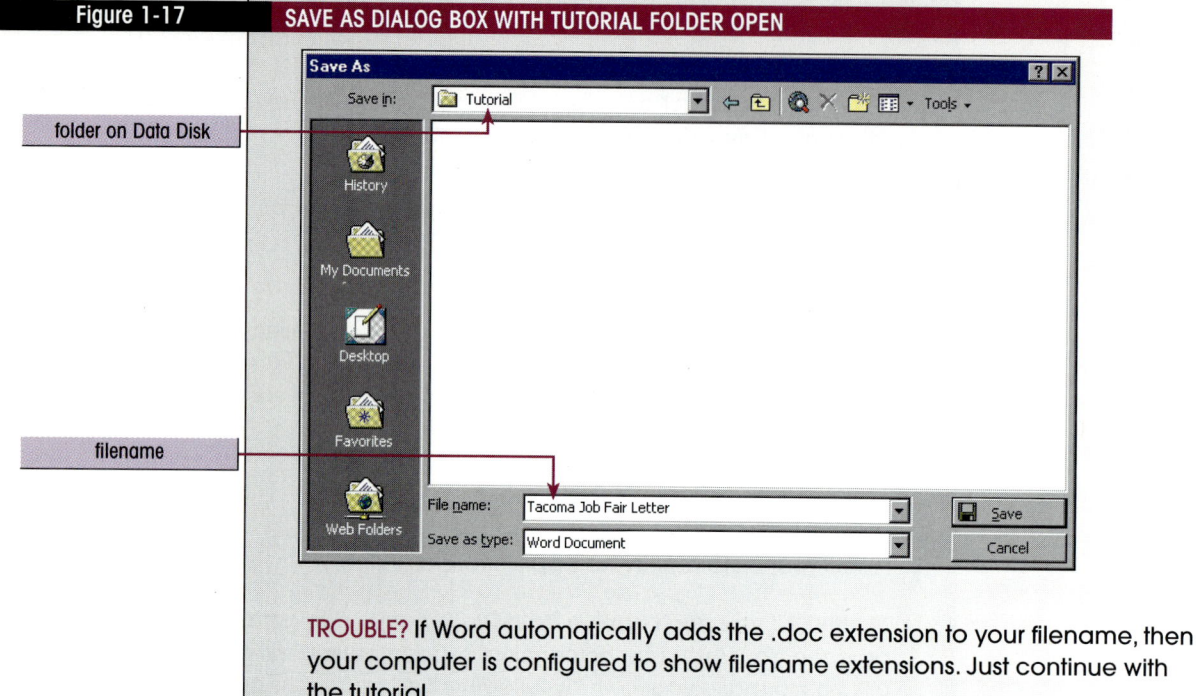

Figure 1-17 SAVE AS DIALOG BOX WITH TUTORIAL FOLDER OPEN

folder on Data Disk → (Save in: Tutorial)

filename → (File name: Tacoma Job Fair Letter)

TROUBLE? If Word automatically adds the .doc extension to your filename, then your computer is configured to show filename extensions. Just continue with the tutorial.

5. Click the **Save** button in the Save As dialog box. The dialog box closes, and you return to the document window. The name of your file appears in the title bar.

Adding Properties to a Document

After you save a document, you should record some descriptive information in a special dialog box known as the document's **properties page**. The information that you record here is known, collectively, as a document's **properties**. For example, you might include your name and a description of the document. Later, you or one of your co-workers can review the document's properties for a quick summary of its purpose, without having to skim the entire document. You'll look at the properties page for the Tacoma Job Fair Letter next.

To view the properties page for the Tacoma Job Fair Letter document:

1. Click **File** on the menu bar, click **Properties**, and then, if necessary, click the **Summary** tab. The Tacoma Job Fair Letter Properties dialog box opens, as shown in Figure 1-18.

TUTORIAL 1 CREATING A DOCUMENT   WD 1.19

Figure 1-18   PROPERTIES PAGE FOR THE ACTIVE DOCUMENT

your name may appear here automatically → Author: Evan Brillstein

(Tacoma Job Fair Letter Properties dialog box, Summary tab; Title: February 21, 2001; Template: Normal)

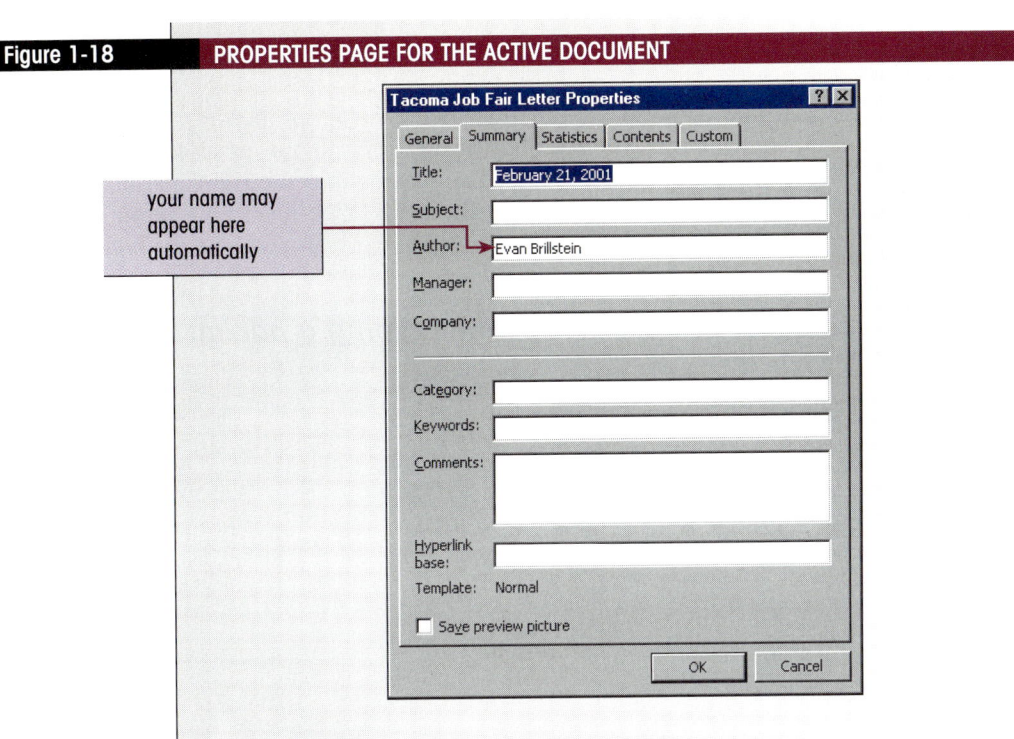

TROUBLE? If you don't see the Properties command on the File menu, point to the double-arrow to display the hidden menu commands.

This dialog box takes its name from the active document (in this case, "Tacoma Job Fair Letter"). Depending on how your computer is set up, the Author text box already may contain your name or the name of the registered owner of your copy of Word. In addition, the Title text box may contain the document's first line of text, "February 21, 2001." Because you already have assigned a descriptive name to this file ("Tacoma Job Fair Letter"), there's no reason to include a title here. You can delete this title and then enter relevant information in the appropriate text boxes. The Comments text box is a good place to record useful notes about the document, such as its purpose.

To edit the contents of the properties page:

1. Verify that the text in the Title text box is highlighted, and then press the **Delete** key.

2. Press the **Tab** key twice. The insertion point moves to the Author text box.

3. If necessary, type your name in the Author text box.

4. Click the Comments text box, and then type **A letter requesting information on the job fair.**

5. Click **OK**. The Tacoma Job Fair Letter dialog box closes, and the document's new properties are saved.

It's good practice to add information to a document's properties page right after you save the document for the first time. You will find such information useful once you have accumulated a number of Word documents and want to organize them. You can use the properties to find documents quickly. As you will see in the Review Assignments at the end of this tutorial, you can view a document's properties page without actually opening the document.

Word Wrap

Now that you have saved your document and its properties, you're ready to complete Karen's letter. As you type the body of the letter, do not press the Enter key at the end of each line. When you type a word that extends into the right margin, both the insertion point and the word move automatically to the next line. This automatic line breaking is called **word wrap**. You'll see how word wrap works as you type the body of Karen's letter.

To observe word wrap while typing a paragraph:

1. Make sure the insertion point is at Ln 20 Col 1 (according to the settings in the status bar). If it's not, move it to that location by pressing the arrow keys.

2. Type the following sentence slowly and watch when the insertion point jumps to the next line: **Recently, you contacted our staff about the Chamber's decision to sponsor a job fair again this year.** Notice how Word moves the last few words to a new line when the previous one is full. See Figure 1-19.

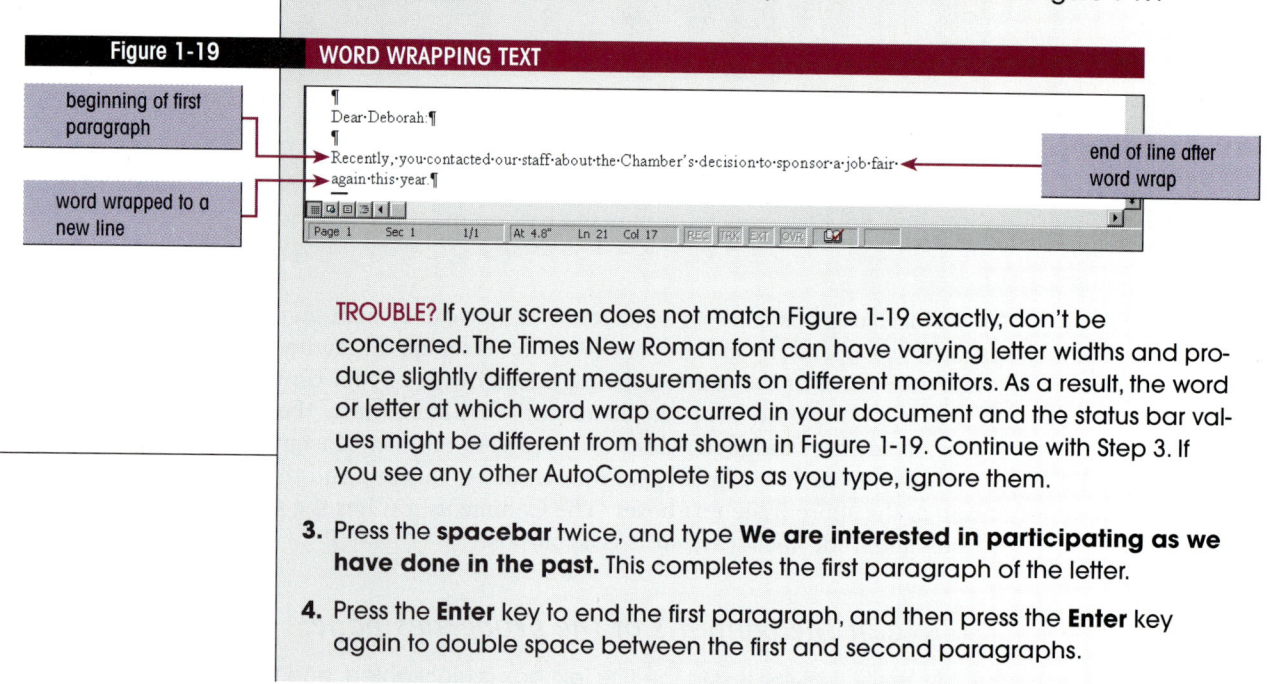

Figure 1-19   WORD WRAPPING TEXT

- beginning of first paragraph
- word wrapped to a new line
- end of line after word wrap

¶
Dear Deborah:¶
¶
Recently, you contacted our staff about the Chamber's decision to sponsor a job fair again this year.¶

Page 1   Sec 1   1/1   At 4.8"   Ln 21   Col 17

TROUBLE? If your screen does not match Figure 1-19 exactly, don't be concerned. The Times New Roman font can have varying letter widths and produce slightly different measurements on different monitors. As a result, the word or letter at which word wrap occurred in your document and the status bar values might be different from that shown in Figure 1-19. Continue with Step 3. If you see any other AutoComplete tips as you type, ignore them.

3. Press the **spacebar** twice, and type **We are interested in participating as we have done in the past.** This completes the first paragraph of the letter.

4. Press the **Enter** key to end the first paragraph, and then press the **Enter** key again to double space between the first and second paragraphs.

Scrolling a Document

After you finish the last set of steps, the insertion point will be at or near the bottom of your document window. It might seem that no room is left in the document window to type the rest of Karen's letter. However, as you continue to add text at the end of your document, the text that you typed earlier will **scroll** (or shift up) and disappear from the top of the document window. You'll see how scrolling works as you enter the final text of Karen's letter.

To observe scrolling while you're entering text:

1. Make sure the insertion point is at the bottom of the screen, to the left of the second paragraph mark in the body of the letter.

TUTORIAL 1 CREATING A DOCUMENT   WD 1.21   WORD

TROUBLE? If you are using a very large monitor, your insertion point may still be some distance from the bottom of the screen. In that case, you may not be able to perform the scrolling steps that follow. Simply read the steps to familiarize yourself with the process of scrolling. You'll scroll longer documents later.

2. Type the second paragraph, as shown in Figure 1-20, and then press the **Enter** key twice to insert a blank line. Notice that as you type the paragraph, the top of the letter scrolls off the top of the document window. Don't worry if you make a mistake in your typing. You'll learn a number of ways to correct errors in the next section.

TROUBLE? If you have difficulty reading the text in Figure 1-20, refer back to Figure 1-11.

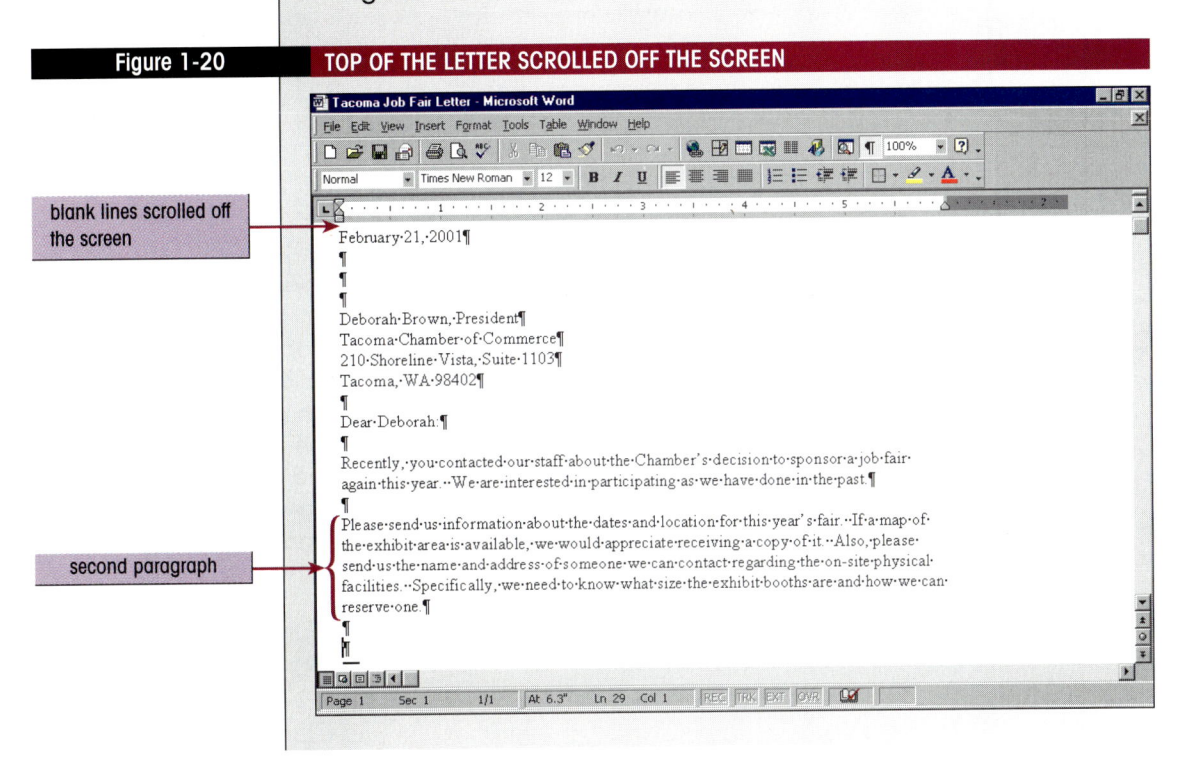

Figure 1-20   TOP OF THE LETTER SCROLLED OFF THE SCREEN

- blank lines scrolled off the screen
- second paragraph

Correcting Errors

Have you made any typing mistakes yet? If so, don't worry. The advantage of using a word processor is that you can correct mistakes quickly and efficiently. Word provides several ways to correct errors when you're entering text.

If you discover a typing error as soon as you make it, you can press the Backspace key to erase the characters and spaces to the left of the insertion point one at a time. Backspacing will erase both printing and nonprinting characters. After you erase the error, you can type the correct characters.

Word also provides a feature, called **AutoCorrect**, that checks for errors in your document as you type and automatically corrects common typing errors, such as "adn" for "and." If the spelling of a particular word differs from its spelling in the Word electronic dictionary, or if a word isn't in the dictionary at all (for example, a person's name), a wavy *red* line appears beneath the word. A wavy red line also appears if you type duplicate words (such as "the the"). If you accidentally type an extra space between words or make a grammatical error (such as typing "He walk to the store." instead of "He walks to the store."), a wavy *green* line appears beneath the error. You'll see how AutoCorrect works when you intentionally make typing errors.

To correct common typing errors:

1. Carefully and slowly type the following sentence exactly as it is shown, including the spelling errors and the extra space between the last two words: **Word corects teh commen typing misTakes you make.** Press the **Enter** key when you are finished typing. Notice that as you press the spacebar after the word "commen," a wavy red line appears beneath it, indicating that the word might be misspelled. Notice also that when you pressed the spacebar after the words "corects," "teh," and "misTakes," Word automatically corrected the spelling. After you pressed the Enter key, a wavy green line appeared under the last two words, alerting you to the extra space. See Figure 1-21.

Figure 1-21   DOCUMENT WINDOW SHOWING TYPING ERRORS

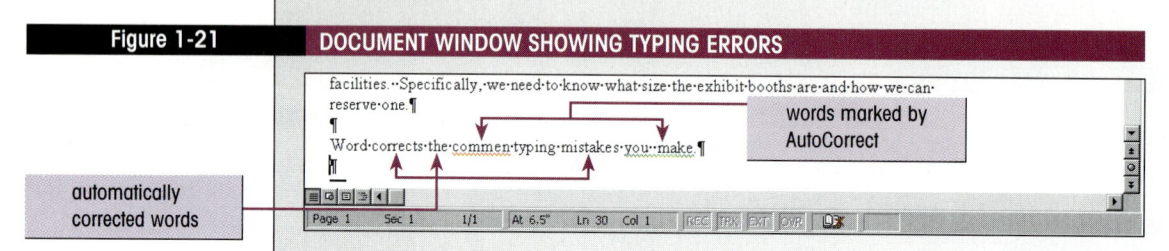

automatically corrected words

words marked by AutoCorrect

TROUBLE? If red and green wavy lines do not appear beneath mistakes, Word is probably not set to automatically check spelling and grammar as you type. Click Tools on the menu bar, and then click Options to open the Options dialog box. Click the Spelling & Grammar tab. Make sure there are check marks in the Check spelling as you type and the Check grammar as you type check boxes, and click OK. If Word does not automatically correct the incorrect spelling of "the," click Tools on the menu bar, click AutoCorrect, and make sure that all five boxes at the top of the AutoCorrect tab have check marks. Then scroll down the AutoCorrect list to make sure that there is an entry that changes "teh" to "the," and click OK.

2. Position the I-Beam pointer I over the word "commen" and click the right mouse button. A list box appears with suggested spellings. See Figure 1-22.

Figure 1-22   LIST BOX SHOWING AUTOCORRECT SUGGESTED SPELLINGS

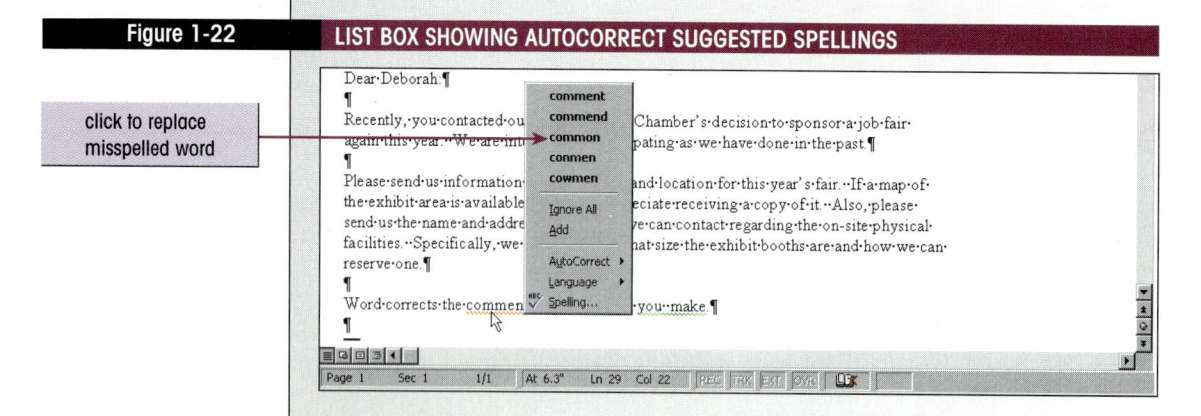

click to replace misspelled word

TROUBLE? If the list box doesn't appear, repeat Step 2, making sure you click the right mouse button, not the left one.

3. Click **common** in the list box. The list box disappears, and the correct spelling appears in your document. Notice that the wavy red line disappears after you correct the error.

4. Click to the right of the letter "u" in the word "you." Press the **Delete** key to delete the extra space.

You can see how quick and easy it is to correct common typing errors with AutoCorrect. Remember, however, that there is no substitute for your own eyes. You should thoroughly proofread each document you create, keeping in mind that AutoCorrect will not catch words that are spelled correctly, but used improperly (such as "your" for "you're"). Proofread your document now, and use AutoCorrect or the Backspace or Delete keys to correct any mistakes.

Before you continue typing Karen's letter, you'll need to delete your practice sentence.

To delete the practice sentence:

1. Click between the period and the paragraph mark at the end of the sentence.

2. Press and hold the **Backspace** key until the entire sentence is deleted. Then press the **Delete** key to delete the extra paragraph mark.

3. Make sure the insertion point is in line 29. There should be one nonprinting paragraph mark between the second paragraph and the paragraph you will type next.

Finishing the Letter

You're ready to complete the rest of the letter. As you type, you can use any of the techniques you learned in the previous section to correct mistakes.

To complete the letter:

1. Type the final paragraph of the body of the letter, as shown in Figure 1-23, and then press the **Enter** key twice. Accept or ignore AutoComplete tips as necessary. Unless you have a very large monitor, the date and, possibly, part of the inside address scroll off the top of the document window completely.

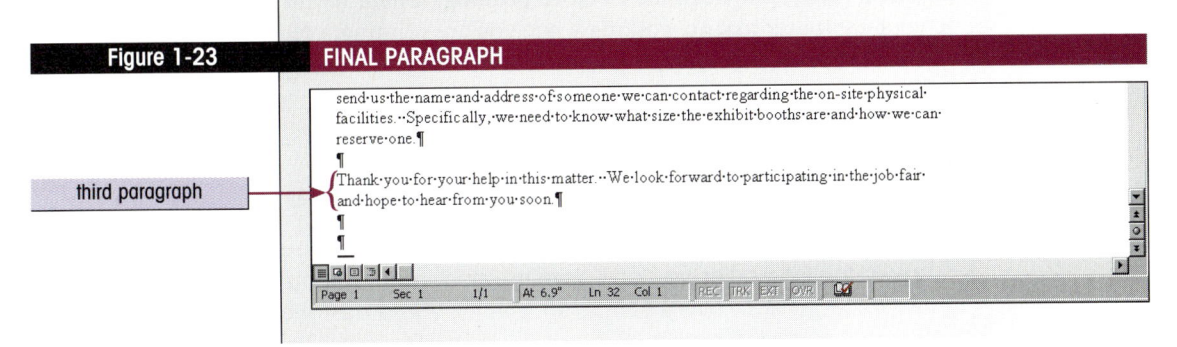

Figure 1-23   FINAL PARAGRAPH

send·us·the·name·and·address·of·someone·we·can·contact·regarding·the·on-site·physical·
facilities.··Specifically,·we·need·to·know·what·size·the·exhibit·booths·are·and·how·we·can·
reserve·one.¶
¶
third paragraph → Thank·you·for·your·help·in·this·matter.··We·look·forward·to·participating·in·the·job·fair·
and·hope·to·hear·from·you·soon.¶
¶
¶

Page 1   Sec 1   1/1   At 6.9"   Ln 32   Col 1

2. Type **Sincerely yours,** (including the comma) to enter the complimentary close.

3. Press the **Enter** key four times to allow space for your signature.

4. Type your name. See Figure 1-24.

Figure 1-24 **COMPLIMENTARY CLOSING OF LETTER**

```
reserve one.¶
¶
Thank you for your help in this matter.  We look forward to participating in the job fair
and hope to hear from you soon.¶
¶
Sincerely Yours,¶
¶
¶
¶
Evan Brillstein¶
```

In the last set of steps, you watched the text at the top of your document move off your screen. You can scroll this hidden text back into view so you can read the beginning of the letter. When you do, the text at the bottom of the screen will scroll out of view.

To scroll the text using the scroll bar:

1. Position the mouse pointer on the up arrow at the top of the vertical scroll bar. Press and hold the mouse button to scroll the text. When the text stops scrolling, you have reached the top of the document and can see the beginning of the letter. Note that scrolling does not change the location of the insertion point in the document.

If you wanted to view the end of the letter, you would use the down arrow at the bottom of the vertical scroll bar. Because you have completed the letter, you'll save the document.

Saving a Completed Document

Although you saved the letter earlier, the text that you typed since then exists only in the computer's memory. That means you need to save your document again. It's especially important to save your document before printing. Then, if you experience problems that cause your computer to stop working while you are printing, you will still have on your disk a copy of the document containing your most recent additions and changes.

To save the completed letter:

1. Make sure your Data Disk is still in the appropriate disk drive.

2. Click the **Save** button on the Standard toolbar. Because you named and saved this file earlier, you can save the document without being prompted for information. Word saves your letter with the same name and to the same location you specified earlier.

TUTORIAL 1 CREATING A DOCUMENT   WD 1.25   WORD

Previewing and Printing a Document

The current document window displays the text, but you cannot see an entire page without scrolling. To see how the page will look when printed, you need to use the Print Preview window.

To preview the document:

1. Click the **Print Preview** button on the Standard toolbar. The Print Preview window opens and displays a full-page version of your letter, as shown in Figure 1-25. This shows how the letter will fit on the printed page.

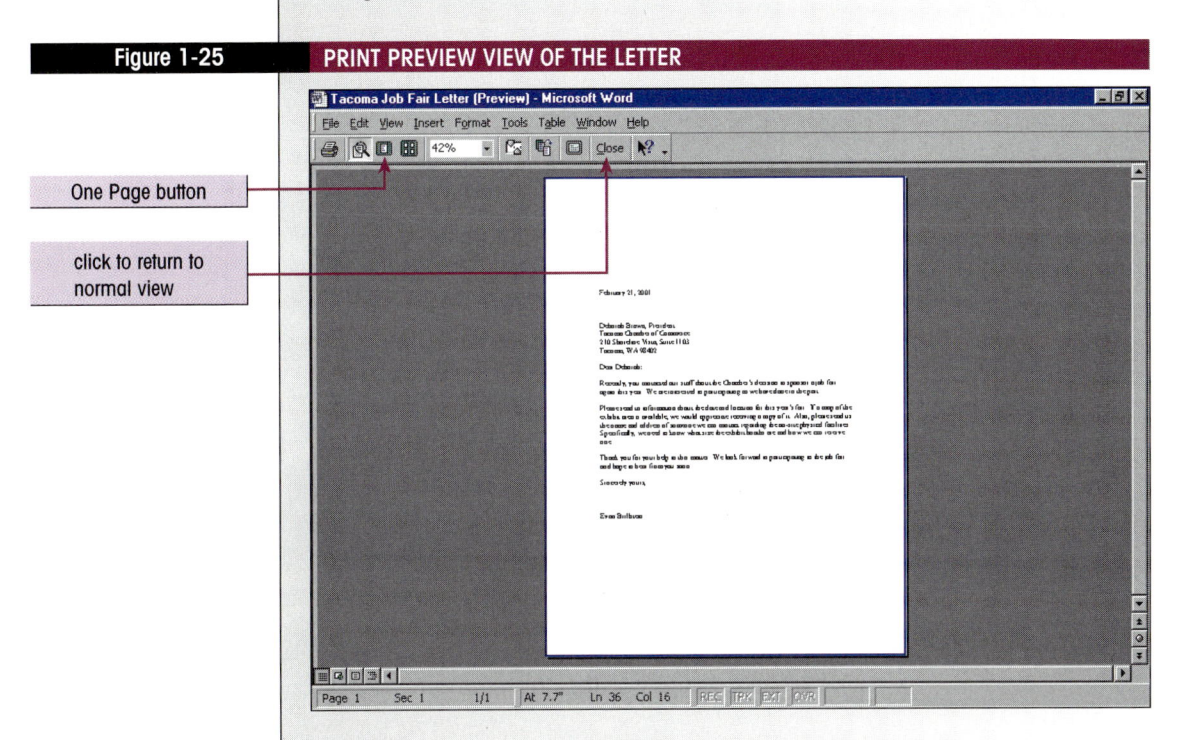

Figure 1-25   PRINT PREVIEW VIEW OF THE LETTER

- One Page button
- click to return to normal view

TROUBLE? If your letter in the Print Preview window is smaller and off to the left rather than centered in the window, click the One Page button on the Print Preview toolbar.

TROUBLE? If you see rulers above and to the left of the document, your rulers are displayed. You can hide the rulers in Print Preview by clicking the View Rulers button on the Print Preview toolbar.

2. Click the **Close** button on the Print Preview toolbar to return to normal view.

Note that you should always preview a document before printing. That way, you can correct problems without wasting paper on an imperfect document. It's especially important to preview documents if your computer is connected to a network so that you don't keep a shared printer tied up with unnecessary printing. In this case, the text looks well-spaced and the letterhead will fit at the top of the page. You're ready to print the letter.

When printing a document, you have two choices. You can use the Print command on the File menu, which opens the Print dialog box in which you can adjust some printer settings. Also, you can use the Print button on the Standard toolbar, which simply prints the document using default settings, without displaying a dialog box. In each session of these tutorials, the first time you print from a shared computer, you should check the settings in the Print dialog box and make sure the number of copies is set to one. After that, you can use the Print button.

To print a document:

1. Make sure your printer is turned on and contains paper.

2. Click **File** on the menu bar, and then click **Print**. The Print dialog box opens. See Figure 1-26.

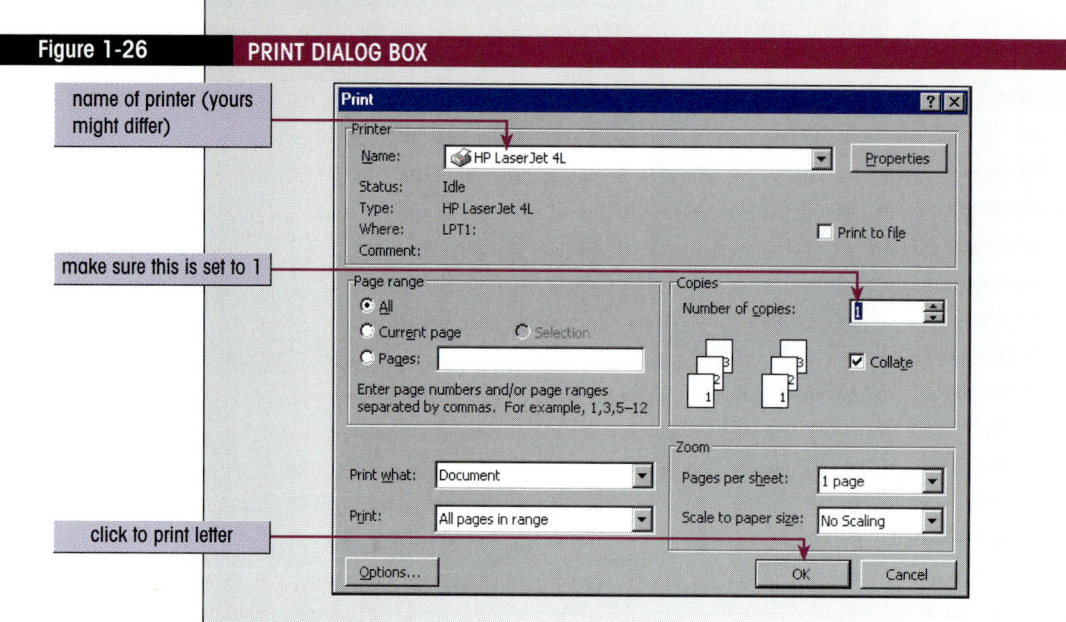

Figure 1-26 PRINT DIALOG BOX

- name of printer (yours might differ)
- make sure this is set to 1
- click to print letter

3. Verify that your settings match those in Figure 1-26. In particular, make sure the number of copies is set to 1. Also make sure the Printer section of the dialog box shows the correct printer. If you're not sure what the correct printer is, check with your instructor or technical support person.

   TROUBLE? If the Print dialog box shows the wrong printer, click the Printer Name list arrow, and then select the correct printer from the list of available printers.

4. Click the **OK** button to print Karen's letter. A printer icon appears at the far right of the taskbar to indicate that your document is being sent to the printer.

Your printed letter should look similar to Figure 1-11 but without the Crossroads letterhead. The word wraps, or line breaks, might not appear in the same places on your letter because the size and spacing of characters vary slightly from one printer to the next.

Karen also needs an envelope to mail her letter in. Printing an envelope is easy in Word. You'll have a chance to try it in the Review Assignments at the end of this tutorial. If you wanted to find out how to print an envelope yourself, you could use the Word Help system.

Getting Help

The Word Help system provides quick access to information about commands, features, and screen elements.

The **What's This?** command on the Help menu provides context-sensitive Help information. When you choose this command, the pointer changes to the Help pointer, which you can then use to click any object or option on the screen, including menu commands, to see a description of the item.

You've already encountered another form of help, the animated Office Assistant. The **Office Assistant** is an interactive guide to finding information on Microsoft Word. As you learned earlier in this tutorial, the Office Assistant sometimes opens automatically to help you with routine tasks. You also can ask the Office Assistant a direction question, and it will search the Help system to find an answer in plain English. The Office Assistant is a context-sensitive tool, which means that it is designed to offer information related to your current task. If you simply want to look up some information in Word's Help system, as you would in an Encyclopedia, you can use the Index and Contents tabs. You will learn how to use the Office Assistant as well as to display the Index and Contents tabs in the following steps.

REFERENCE WINDOW

Getting Help from the Office Assistant
- Click the Microsoft Word Help button on the Standard toolbar (or click Help on the menu bar and then click Microsoft Word Help).
- Type your question, and then click the Search button.
- Click a topic from the list of topics displayed.
- Read the information in the Microsoft Word Help window. For more information, click the relevant underlined text.
- To display the Index or Contents tab, click the Show button in the Microsoft Word Help window. Click the Hide button to hide these tabs.
- To close the Microsoft Word Help window, click its Close button.
- To hide the Office Assistant, click Help on the menu bar, and then click Hide the Office Assistant.

You'll use the Office Assistant now to learn how to print an envelope.

To use the Office Assistant to learn how to print an envelope:

1. Click the **Microsoft Word Help** button on the Standard toolbar. The Office Assistant opens, offering help on topics related to the task you most recently performed (if any), and asking what you'd like to do. The Office Assistant shown in Figure 1-27 takes the form of an animated paperclip, but your Office Assistant may differ.

WORD   WD 1.28   TUTORIAL 1   CREATING A DOCUMENT

Figure 1-27   OFFICE ASSISTANT

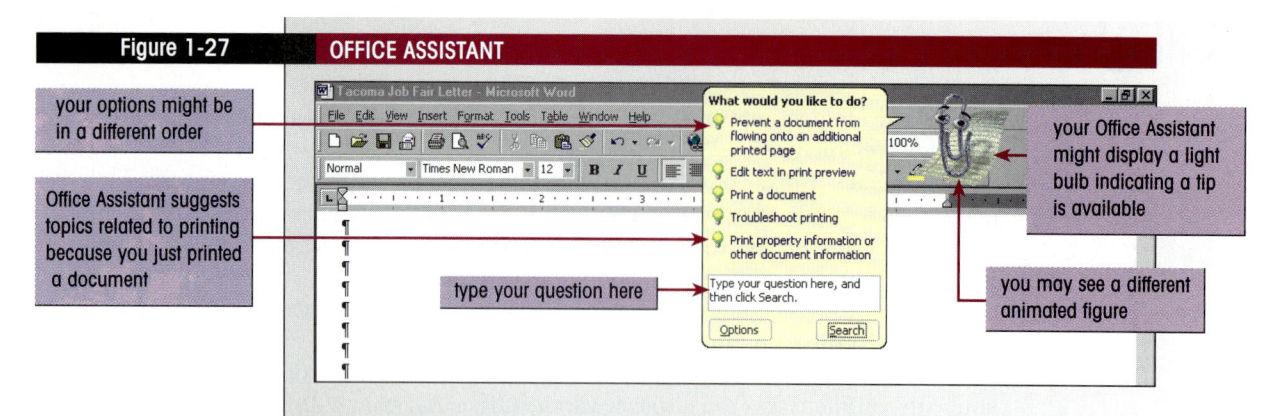

- your options might be in a different order
- Office Assistant suggests topics related to printing because you just printed a document
- type your question here
- your Office Assistant might display a light bulb indicating a tip is available
- you may see a different animated figure

2. Type **How do I print an envelope?** and then click the **Search** button. The Office Assistant window shows topics related to envelopes.

   TROUBLE? If you do not see a space to type a question, click the Help with something else option button, and then continue with Step 2.

3. Click **Create and print envelopes.** The Microsoft Word Help window opens next to or on top of the Word window, with even more specific topics related to printing envelopes.

4. Click **Create and print an envelope.** The Microsoft Word Help window displays the precise steps involved in printing an envelope. See Figure 1-28. To scroll through the steps, drag the vertical scroll bar. Note that within a Help window, you can click on underlined text to display more information.

Figure 1-28   STEPS FOR PRINTING AN ENVELOPE

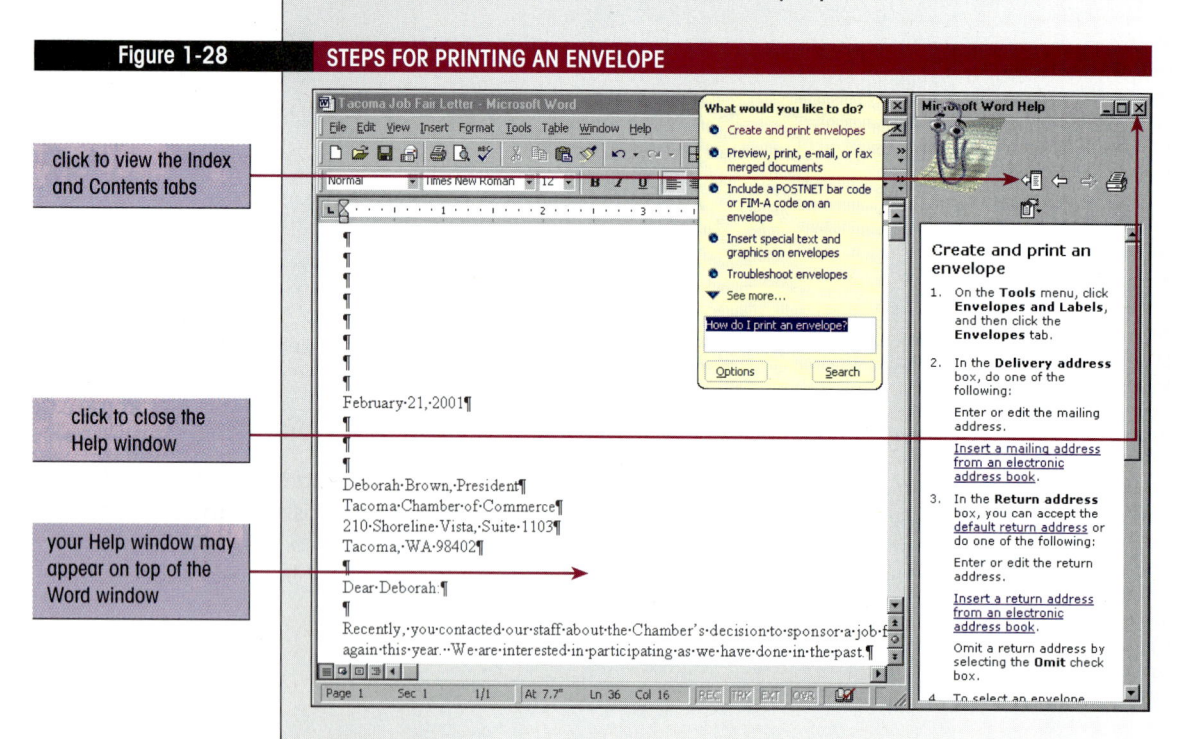

- click to view the Index and Contents tabs
- click to close the Help window
- your Help window may appear on top of the Word window

TROUBLE? If your Help window doesn't exactly match the one in Figure 1-28, just continue with these steps. You will learn how to display and hide additional tabs of the Help Window shortly.

5. Click the **Show** button . Additional Help window tabs appear, as in Figure 1-29. The most useful of these are the Contents tab (where you can search by general topics) and the Index tab (where you can look up a specific entry). You will have a chance to practice using these tabs in the Review Assignments at the end of this tutorial.

Figure 1-29 ADDITIONAL HELP TABS

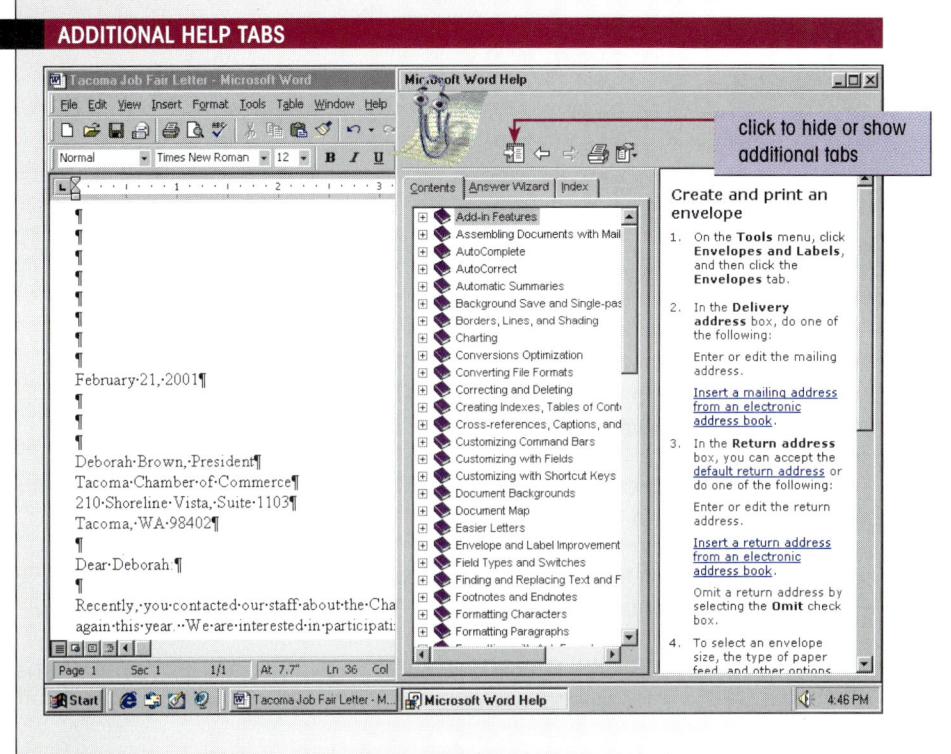

6. Click the **Hide** button to return the Help window to its original size.

7. Click the **Close** button on the Microsoft Word Help window. The Microsoft Word Help window closes, and the Word program window fills the screen again.

8. Click **Help** on the menu bar, and then click **Hide the Office Assistant**. The animated Office Assistant disappears.

   TROUBLE? If the Office Assistant asks if you want to hide it permanently, choose the "No just hide me" option.

Some Help windows have different formats than those you've just seen. However, they all provide the information you need to complete any task in Word.

Exiting Word

You have now finished typing and printing the letter to the Tacoma Chamber of Commerce, and you are ready to **exit**, or quit, Word. When you exit Word, you close both the document and the program window.

> **REFERENCE WINDOW**
>
> **Exiting Word**
> - Click the Close button for each open document (or click File on the menu bar, and then click Exit).
> - If you're prompted to save changes to the document, click the Yes button; then, if necessary, type a document name and click the Save button.

Because you've completed the first draft of Karen's letter, you can close the document window and exit Word now.

To close documents and exit Word:

1. Click the **Close** button ⊠ in the title bar to close the letter.

   TROUBLE? If you see a dialog box with the message "Do you want to save the changes you made to Tacoma Job Fair Letter?," you have made changes to the document since the last time you saved it. Click the Yes button to save the current version and close it.

2. Click the **Close Window** button ⊠ on the right side of the menu bar to close the blank Document1.

   TROUBLE? If you see a dialog box with the message "Do you want to save the changes you made to Document1?," click the No button.

3. Click the **Close** button ⊠ in the upper-right corner of the Word window. Word closes, and you return to the Windows desktop.

You give the letter for the Tacoma Chamber of Commerce to Karen for her to review. Now that you have created and saved your letter, you are ready to learn about editing and formatting a document in the next tutorial.

Session 1.2 QUICK CHECK

1. Explain how to save a document for the first time.
2. What is the advantage of recording information about a document in its Properties dialog box?
3. Explain how word wrap works in a Word document.
4. What is the Office Assistant, and how do you use it?
5. In your own words, define each of the following:
   a. scrolling
   b. AutoComplete
   c. AutoCorrect
   d. print preview
6. Describe two methods for exiting Word.

REVIEW ASSIGNMENTS

Karen received a response from the Tacoma Chamber of Commerce containing the information she requested about the job fair, and Crossroads has firmed up its plans to participate as an exhibitor. Karen must now staff the booth with Crossroads employees for each day of the five-day fair. She sends a memo to employees asking them to commit to two dates. Create the memo shown in Figure 1-30 by completing the following:

1. If necessary, start Word and make sure your Data Disk is in the appropriate disk drive, and then check your screen to make sure your settings match those in the tutorials.

2. If the Office Assistant is open, hide it by using the appropriate command on the Help menu.

3. Click the New Blank Document button on the Standard toolbar to display a new document.

4. Press the Enter key six times to insert approximately 2 inches of space before the memo headings.

5. Press the Caps Lock key, and then type "MEMORANDUM" (without the quotation marks) in capital letters.

6. Press the Enter key twice, type "TO:" (without the quotation marks), press the Caps Lock key to turn off capitalization, press the Tab key three times, and then type "Crossroads Staff Members" (without the quotation marks).

7. Press the Enter key twice, type "FROM:" (without the quotation marks), press the Tab key twice, and then type your name. Throughout the rest of this exercise, use the Caps Lock Key as necessary to turn capitalization on and off.

Explore

8. Press the Enter key twice, type "DATE:" (without the quotation marks), press the Tab key three times. Insert today's date from your computer clock by clicking Insert on the menu bar, clicking Date and Time, clicking the date format that corresponds to June 16, 2001, and then clicking OK.

9. Continue typing the rest of the memo exactly as shown in Figure 1-30, including any misspellings and extra words. Notice how Word automatically corrects some misspellings. (You will have a chance to practice correcting the remaining errors later.) Press the Tab key twice after "SUBJECT:" to align the memo heading evenly. Include two blank lines between the Subject line and the body of the memo.

Figure 1-30 SAMPLE MEMO

MEMORANDUM

TO: Crossroads Staff Members

FROM: Karen Liu

DATE: June 16, 2001

SUBJECT: Dates for 2001 Job Fair

The the 2001 Job Fair sponsored by the Tacoma Chamber of Commerce will be held October 20-25, 2001,from 11:00 a.m. to 5:00 p.m.. This fiar provvides us with an oportunity to inform Tacoma residents about our services. Previously, we have each spent two days helping at the exhibet. Please let me know which days you would prefer this year. I would like this information by tomorrow.

Thanks for your help.

10. Save your work as **Job Fair Reminder Memo** in the Review folder for Tutorial 1.

11. Click File on the menu bar, and then click Properties. Delete the existing title for the document, verify that your name appears in the Author text box, and type a brief description of the document in the Comments text box. Click OK to close the document's properties page.

12. Correct the misspelled words, indicated by the wavy red lines. If the correct version of a word does not appear in the list box, press the Escape key to close the list, and then make the correction yourself. To ignore an AutoCorrect suggestion, click Ignore All. Then correct any grammatical or other errors indicated by wavy green lines. Use the Backspace key to delete any extra words or spaces.

13. Scroll to the beginning of the memo. Click at the beginning of the first line and insert room for the letterhead by pressing the Enter key until MEMORANDUM is at line 12.

14. Save your most recent changes.

Explore 15. Use the What's This? feature to learn about the Word Count command on the Tools menu. Click Help on the menu bar, and then click What's This? Click Tools on the menu bar, click Word Count, and then read the text box. When you are finished, click the text box to close it.

16. Preview and print the memo.

17. Use the Office Assistant to open a Microsoft Word Help menu with the steps necessary for printing an address on an envelope.

Explore 18. With the Help window open on one side of the screen, and the Word window open on the other, follow the instructions for printing an envelope. (Check with your instructor or technical support person to make sure you can print envelopes. If not, print on an 8½ x 11-inch sheet of paper.) To place the Help and Word windows side by side, right-click the taskbar and then click Tile Windows Vertically. When you are done, right-click the taskbar and then click Undo Tile.

Explore 19. With the Help window open, click the Show button, if necessary, to display the additional Help tabs. Click the Index tab, type "Help" (without the quotation marks) and then click the Search button. View the topics related to Word's Help system in the Choose a topic list box. Click any topic in the right-hand window to read more about it. Next, click the Contents tab, review the main topics on that tab, and then click any plus sign to display subtopics. Click a subtopic to display additional topics in the right-hand window, then click one of those topics to display even more information. Continue to explore the Contents and Index tabs. When you are finished, close the Microsoft Word Help window. Hide the Office Assistant.

20. Close the document without saving your most recent changes.

21. Click the Open button on the Standard toolbar.

Explore 22. Verify that the Review folder for Tutorial 1 is displayed in the Look in list box, right-click the Job Fair Reminder Memo, and then click Properties in the shortcut menu. Review the document's properties page. You can use this technique to find out about the contents of a document quickly, without opening the document. Click OK to close the document's properties page, and then click Cancel to close the Open dialog box.

23. Close any open documents.

CASE PROBLEMS

Case 1. Letter to Confirm a Conference Date As catering director for the Madison Convention and Visitors Bureau, you are responsible for managing food service at the convention center. The Southern Wisconsin chapter of the National Purchasing Management Association has requested a written confirmation of a daily breakfast buffet during its annual convention scheduled for July 6-10, 2001.

Create the letter using the skills you learned in the tutorial. Remember to include today's date, the inside address, the salutation, the date of the reservation, the complimentary close, and your name and title. If the instructions show quotation marks around text you type, do not include the quotation marks in your letter. To complete the letter, do the following:

1. If necessary, start Word, make sure your Data Disk is in the appropriate disk drive, and check your screen to make sure your settings match those in the tutorials.

2. Open a new, blank document and press the Enter key until the insertion point is positioned about 2 inches from the top of the page. (Remember that you can see the exact position of the insertion point, in inches, in the status bar.)

Explore 3. Begin typing today's date. If an AutoComplete tip appears to finish the month, press Enter to accept it. Press the spacebar. If another AutoComplete tip appears with the rest of the date, press Enter to accept it. Otherwise, continue typing the date.

4. Press the Enter key six times after the date, and, using the proper business letter format, type the inside address: "Charles Quade, 222 Sydney Street, Whitewater, WI 57332."

5. Double space after the inside address (that is, press the Enter key twice), type the salutation "Dear Mr. Quade:," and then double space again. If the Office Assistant opens, click Cancel to close it.

6. Write one paragraph confirming the daily breakfast buffets for July 6-10, 2001.

7. Double space and type the complimentary close "Sincerely," (include the comma).

8. Press the Enter key four times to leave room for the signature, and then type your name and title.

9. Save the letter as **Confirmation Letter** in the Cases folder for Tutorial 1.

10. Use the document's properties page to record your name and a brief summary of the document.

11. Reread your letter carefully, and correct any errors.

12. Save any new changes.

13. Preview and print the letter.

14. Close the document.

Case 2. Letter to Request Information about a "Climbing High" Franchise You are the manager of the UpTown Sports Mall and are interested in obtaining a franchise for "Climbing High," an indoor rock-climbing venture marketed by Ultimate Sports, Inc. After reading an advertisement for the franchise, you decide to write for more information.

Create the letter by doing the following:

1. If necessary, start Word, make sure your Data Disk is in the appropriate disk drive, and check your screen to make sure your settings match those in the tutorials.

2. Open a new blank document, and press the Enter key until the insertion point is positioned about 2 inches from the top of the page. (Remember that you can see the exact position of the insertion point, in inches, in the status bar.)

3. Use AutoComplete (as described in Step 3 of the previous case project) to type today's date at the insertion point.

4. Press the Enter key six times after the date, and, using the proper business letter format, type the inside address: "Ultimate Sports, Inc., 2124 Martin Luther King Jr. Avenue, Rockton, CO 80911."

5. Insert a blank line after the inside address, type the salutation "Dear Franchise Manager:," and then insert another blank line.

6. Type the first paragraph as follows: "I'd like some information about the Climbing High indoor rock-climbing franchise. As manager of UpTown Sports Mall, a large sporting goods store, I've had success with similar programs, including both bungee jumping and snowboarding franchises."(Do not include the quotation marks.)

7. Save your work as **Rock Climbing Request Letter** in the Cases folder for Tutorial 1.

8. Use the document's properties page to record your name and a brief summary of the document.

Explore

9. Insert one blank line, and type the following: "Please answer the following questions:". Then press the Enter key, and type these questions on separate lines: "How much does your franchise cost?" "Does the price include the cost for installing the 30-foot simulated rock wall illustrated in your advertisement?" "Does the price include the cost for purchasing the ropes and harnesses?" Open the Office Assistant, type the question, "How can I add bullets to lists?," click the Search button, and then click the "Add bullets to lists" topic. In the Microsoft Word Help window, click the "Add bullets or numbering" subtopic, and then follow the instructions to insert a bullet in front of each question in the document. Close the Office Assistant and the Microsoft Word Help window when you are finished.

10. Correct any typing errors indicated by wavy lines. (*Hint:* Because "UpTown" is spelled correctly, click Ignore All on the shortcut menu to remove the wavy red line under the word "UpTown" and prevent Word from marking the word as a misspelling.)

11. Insert another blank line at the end of the letter, and type the complimentary close "Sincerely," (include the comma).

12. Press the Enter key four times to leave room for the signature, and type your full name and title. Then press the Enter key and type "UpTown Sports Mall." Notice that UpTown is not marked as a spelling error this time.

13. Save the letter with changes.

14. Preview the letter using the Print Preview button.

15. Print the letter.

16. Close the document.

Case 3. Memo of Congratulations Judy Davidoff is owner, founder, and president of Blossoms Unlimited, a chain of garden stores. She was recently honored by the Southern Council of Organic Gardeners for her series of free public seminars on organic vegetable gardening. Also, she was named businesswoman of the year by the Georgia Women's Business Network. Do the following:

1. If necessary, start Word, make sure your Data Disk is in the appropriate disk drive, and check your screen to make sure your settings match those in the tutorials.

2. Write a brief memo congratulating Judy on receiving these awards. Remember to use the four-part planning process. You should plan the content, organization, and style of the memo, and use a standard memo format similar to the one shown in Figure 1-30.

3. Save the document as **Awards Memo** in the Cases folder for Tutorial 1.

4. Use the document's properties page to record your name and a brief summary of the document.

5. Preview and print the memo.

6. Close the document.

Case 4. Writing a Personal Letter with the Letter Template Word provides templates—that is, models with predefined formatting—to help you create documents quickly and effectively. For example, the Letter template helps you create letters with professional-looking letterheads and with various letter formats. Do the following:

Explore

1. If necessary, start Word, make sure your Data Disk is in the appropriate disk drive, and check your screen to make sure your settings match those in the tutorials.

2. Click File on the menu bar, and then click New. The New dialog box opens.

3. Click the Letters & Faxes tab, click Elegant Letter, and then click the OK button. A letter template opens, as shown in Figure 1-31, containing generic, placeholder text that you can replace with your own information.

Figure 1-31   ELEGANT LETTER TEMPLATE

placeholder text

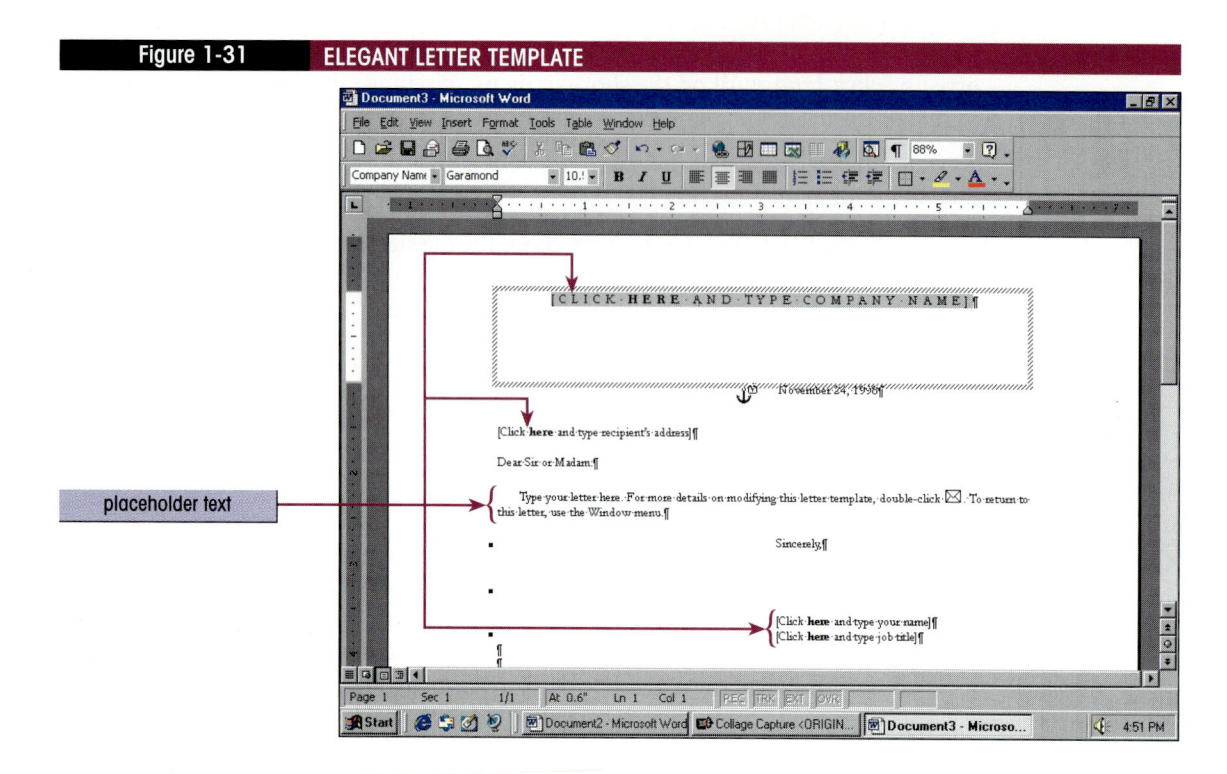

4. Click the line "CLICK HERE AND TYPE COMPANY NAME" (at the top of the document), and type the name of your school or company.

5. Click the line "Click here and type recipient's address," and type a real or fictitious name and address.

6. Delete the placeholder text in the body of the letter, and replace it with a sentence or two explaining that you're using the Word letter template to create this letter.

7. At the end of the letter, replace the placeholder text with your name and job title.

8. At the bottom of the page, replace the placeholder text with your address, phone number, and fax number. (Use fictious information if you prefer.)

9. Save the letter as **My Template Letter** (in the Cases folder for Tutorial 1), and then print it.

10. Use the document's properties page to record your name and a brief summary of the document.

11. Close the document.

LAB ASSIGNMENTS

The New Perspectives Labs are designed to help you master some of the key computer concepts and skills presented in each chapter of the text. If you are using your school's lab computers, your instructor or technical support person should have installed the Labs software for you. If you want to use the Labs on your home computer, ask your instructor for the appropriate software. See the Read This Before You Begin page for more information on installing and starting the Lab.

Each Lab has two parts: Steps and Explore. Use Steps first to learn and review concepts. Read the information on each page and do the numbered steps. As you work through the Lab, you will be asked to answer Quick Check questions about what you have learned. At the end of the Lab, you will see a Summary Report of your answers to the Quick Checks. If your instructor wants you to turn in this Summary Report, click the Print button on the Summary Report screen.

When you have completed the Steps, you can click the Explore button to complete the Lab Assignments. You also can use Explore to practice the skills you learned and to explore concepts on your own.

Word Processing Word-processing software is the most popular computerized productivity tool. In this Lab, you will learn how word-processing software works. When you have completed this Lab, you should be able to apply the general concepts you learned to any word-processing package you use at home, at work, or in your school lab.

1. Click the Steps button to learn how word-processing software works. As you proceed through the Steps, answer all of the Quick Check questions that appear. After you complete the Steps, you will see a Quick Check Summary Report. Follow the instructions on the screen to print this report.

2. Click the Explore button to begin. Click File, then click Open to display the Open dialog box. Click the file **Timber.tex**, then press the Enter key to open the letter to Northern Timber Company. Make the following modifications to the letter, then print it. You do not need to save the letter.

    a. In the first and last lines of the letter, change "Jason Kidder" to your name.
    b. Change the date to today's date.
    c. The second paragraph begins "Your proposal did not include…". Move this paragraph so it is the last paragraph in the text of the letter.
    d. Change the cost of a permanent bridge to $20,000.
    e. Spell check the letter.

3. In Explore, open the file **Stars.tex**. Make the following modifications to the document, then print it. You do not need to save the document.

    a. Center and boldface the title.
    b. Change the title font to size-16 Arial.
    c. Boldface the DATE, SHOWER, and LOCATION.
    d. Move the January 2-3 line to the top of the list.
    e. Double space the entire document.

4. In Explore, compose a one-page double-spaced letter to your parents or to a friend. Make sure you date the letter and check your spelling. Print the letter and sign it. You do not need to save your letter.

INTERNET ASSIGNMENTS

The purpose of the Internet Assignments is to challenge you to find information on the Internet that you can use to create effective documents. The actual assignments are updated and maintained on the Course Technology Web site. Log on to the Internet and use your Web browser to go to the Student Online Companion to accompany this text at **www.course.com/NewPerspectives/office2000**. Click the Word link, and then click the link for Tutorial 1.

QUICK CHECK ANSWERS

Session 1.1

1. (1) Plan the content, purpose, organization, and look of your document. (2) Create and then edit the document. (3) Format the document to make it visually appealing. (4) Preview and then print the document.
2. Click the Start button, point to Programs, and then click Microsoft Word.
3. a. symbols you can display on-screen but that don't print
   b. buttons to the left of the horizontal status bar that switch the document to normal view, Web layout view, print layout view, or outline view
   c. actual height of a character measured in points
   d. standard settings
4. Click Format on the menu bar, click Font, select the font size in the Size list box, click the Default button, and then click Yes.
5. Right-click a toolbar, and then click Formatting on the shortcut menu.
6. Click the Normal View button.

Session 1.2

1. Click the Save button on the Standard toolbar, switch to the drive and folder where you want to save the document, enter a filename in the File name text box, and then click the Save button.
2. Anyone can determine the document's purpose without having to open the document and skim it.
3. When you type a word that extends into the right margin, Word moves that word and the insertion point to the next line.
4. An interactive guide to finding information about Word; click the Microsoft Word Help button on the Standard toolbar, type your question and click Search, click the help topic you want to read.
5. a. as you type, text shifts out of view
   b. typing dates and other regularly used words and text for you
   c. checks for spelling and grammar errors as you type and fixes common typing errors automatically
   d. shows how the document will look when printed
6. Click the Close button in the upper-right corner of the screen; click File on the menu bar and then click Exit.

TUTORIAL 2

OBJECTIVES

In this tutorial you will:

- Open, rename, and save a previously saved document
- Check spelling and grammar
- Move the insertion point around the document
- Select and delete text
- Reverse edits using the Undo and Redo commands
- Move text within the document
- Find and replace text
- Change margins, line spacing, alignment, and paragraph indents
- Copy formatting with the Format Painter
- Emphasize points with bullets, numbering, boldface, underlining, and italics
- Change fonts and adjust font sizes

EDITING AND FORMATTING A DOCUMENT

Preparing an Annuity Plan Description for Right-Hand Solutions

CASE

Right-Hand Solutions

Reginald Thomson is a contract specialist for Right-Hand Solutions, a company that provides small businesses with financial and administrative services. Right-Hand Solutions contracts with independent insurance companies to prepare insurance plans and investment opportunities for these small businesses. Brandi Paxman, vice president of administrative services, asked Reginald to plan and write a document that describes the tax-deferred annuity plan for their clients' employee handbooks. Now that Brandi has commented on and corrected the draft, Reginald asks you to make the necessary changes and print the document.

In this tutorial, you will edit the annuity plan description according to Brandi's comments. You will open a draft of the annuity plan, resave it, and delete a phrase. You will check the plan's grammar and spelling, and then move text using two different methods. Also, you will find and replace one version of the company name with another.

Next, you will change the overall look of the document by changing margins and line spacing, indenting and justifying paragraphs, and copying formatting from one paragraph to another. You'll create a bulleted list to emphasize the types of financial needs the annuity plan will cover and a numbered list for the conditions under which employees can receive funds. Then you'll make the title more prominent by centering it, changing its font, and enlarging it. You'll italicize the questions within the plan to set them off from the rest of the text and underline an added note about how to get further information to give it emphasis. Finally, you will print a copy of the plan.

WORD | WD 2.02 | TUTORIAL 2 EDITING AND FORMATTING A DOCUMENT

SESSION 2.1

In In this session you will learn how to use the Spelling and Grammar checker to correct any errors in your document. Then you will edit Reginald's document by deleting words and moving text. Finally, you'll find and replace text throughout the document.

Opening the Document

Brandi's editing marks and notes on the first draft are shown in Figure 2-1. You'll begin by opening the first draft of the description, which has the filename Annuity.

Figure 2-1 — DRAFT OF ANNUITY PLAN SHOWING BRANDI'S EDITS (PAGE 1)

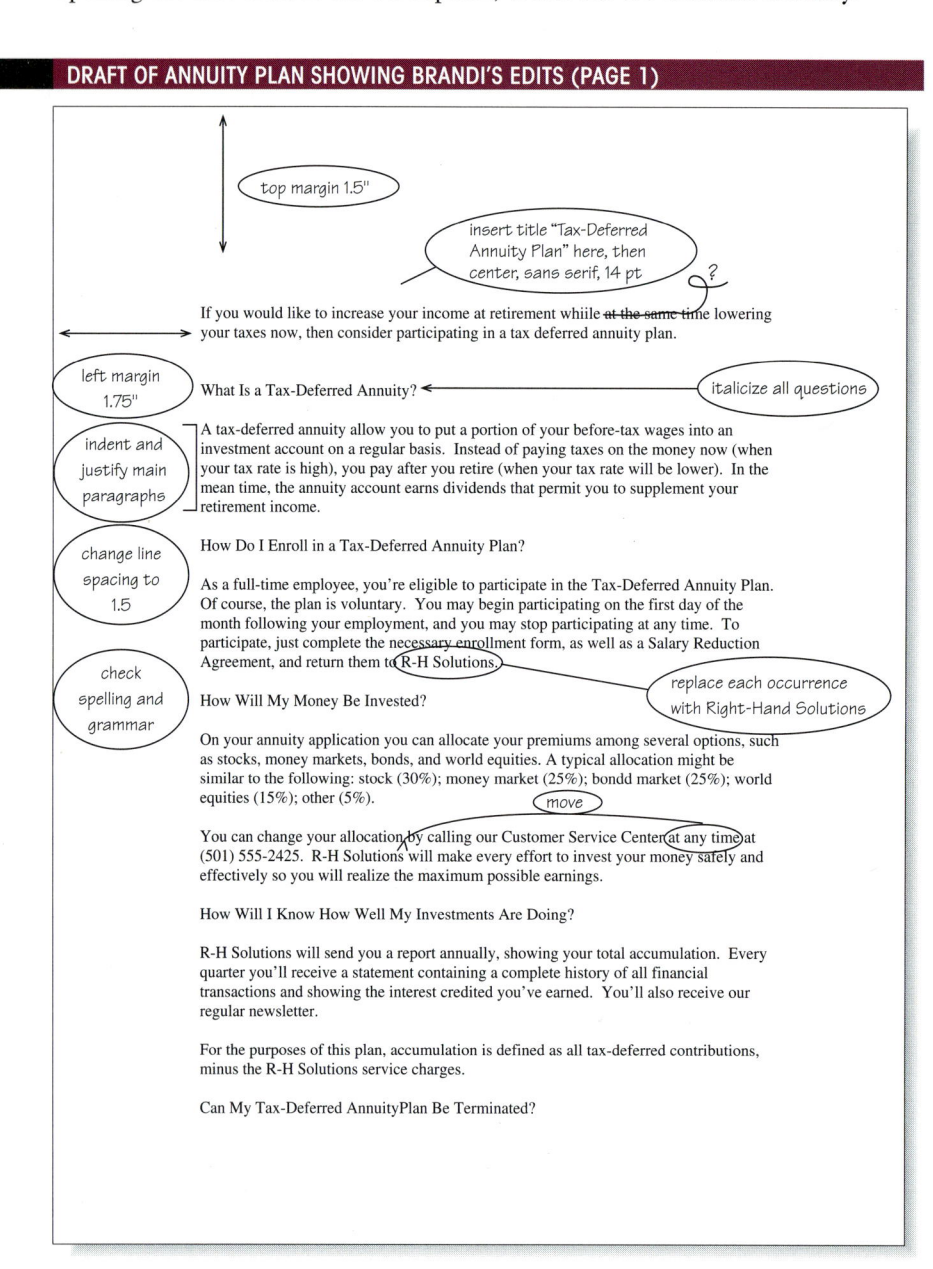

top margin 1.5"

insert title "Tax-Deferred Annuity Plan" here, then center, sans serif, 14 pt

If you would like to increase your income at retirement whiile ~~at the same time~~ lowering your taxes now, then consider participating in a tax deferred annuity plan.

left margin 1.75"

What Is a Tax-Deferred Annuity?   *italicize all questions*

indent and justify main paragraphs

A tax-deferred annuity allow you to put a portion of your before-tax wages into an investment account on a regular basis. Instead of paying taxes on the money now (when your tax rate is high), you pay after you retire (when your tax rate will be lower). In the mean time, the annuity account earns dividends that permit you to supplement your retirement income.

change line spacing to 1.5

How Do I Enroll in a Tax-Deferred Annuity Plan?

As a full-time employee, you're eligible to participate in the Tax-Deferred Annuity Plan. Of course, the plan is voluntary. You may begin participating on the first day of the month following your employment, and you may stop participating at any time. To participate, just complete the necessary enrollment form, as well as a Salary Reduction Agreement, and return them to R-H Solutions.

check spelling and grammar

How Will My Money Be Invested?   *replace each occurrence with Right-Hand Solutions*

On your annuity application you can allocate your premiums among several options, such as stocks, money markets, bonds, and world equities. A typical allocation might be similar to the following: stock (30%); money market (25%); bondd market (25%); world equities (15%); other (5%).

move

You can change your allocation by calling our Customer Service Center at any time at (501) 555-2425. R-H Solutions will make every effort to invest your money safely and effectively so you will realize the maximum possible earnings.

How Will I Know How Well My Investments Are Doing?

R-H Solutions will send you a report annually, showing your total accumulation. Every quarter you'll receive a statement containing a complete history of all financial transactions and showing the interest credited you've earned. You'll also receive our regular newsletter.

For the purposes of this plan, accumulation is defined as all tax-deferred contributions, minus the R-H Solutions service charges.

Can My Tax-Deferred AnnuityPlan Be Terminated?

TUTORIAL 2 EDITING AND FORMATTING A DOCUMENT   WD 2.03   WORD

Figure 2-1   DRAFT OF ANNUITY PLAN SHOWING BRANDI'S EDITS (PAGE 2)

Your Tax-Deferred Annuity Plan can be terminated only if you're no longer an eligible employee, you stop contributing to the plan, or your employer discontinues the contract with R-H Solutions. *(bold: only)*

Can I Withdraw Money from My Tax-Deferred Annuity Plan?

Normally, if you make an early withdrawal from your tax-deferred annuity plan, you will incur substantial financial penalties. However, you can withdraw money without penalty if you have an immediate and severe financial need (as defined below) and the money from your plan is necessary to meet those needs. Under current law, these withdrawals are subject to ordinary income taxes.

The following are considered to be immediate and severe financial needs:

(indent, add bullets)
- tuition for post-secondary education for you or your dependents
- medical expenses that exceed 7.5% of your annual salary
- purchase (excluding mortgage payments) of a principal residence *(move)*
- other circumstances as regulated by the Internal Revenue Service

When Can I Begin to Receive Funds from My Tax-Deferred Annuity Plan?

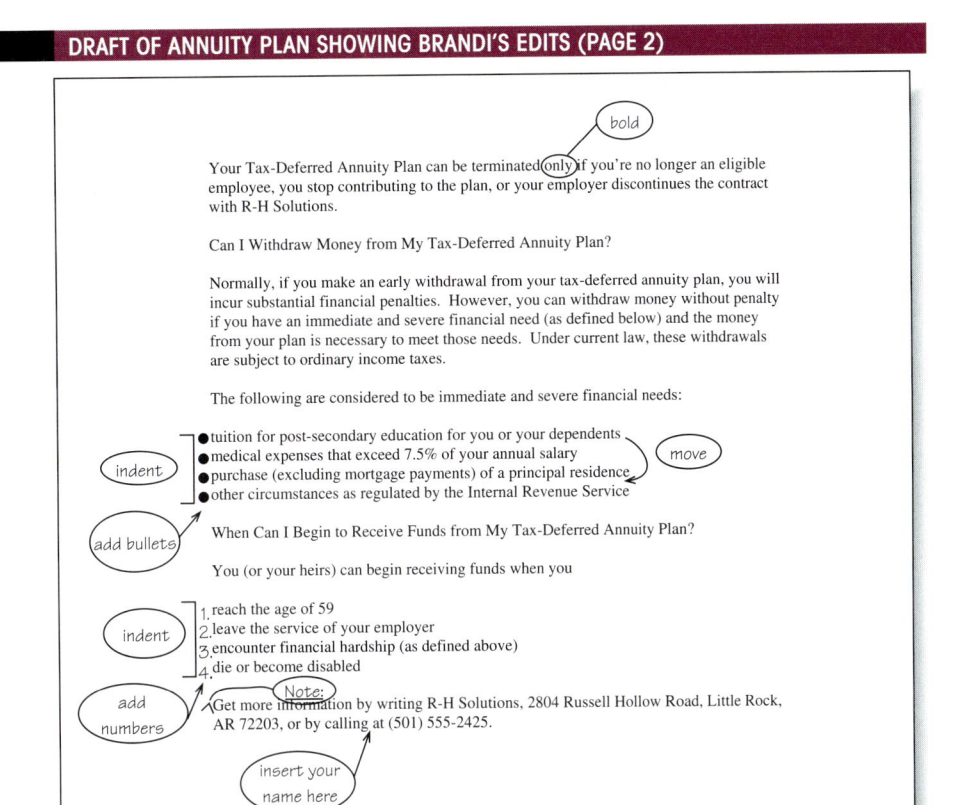

You (or your heirs) can begin receiving funds when you

(indent, add numbers)
1. reach the age of 59
2. leave the service of your employer
3. encounter financial hardship (as defined above)
4. die or become disabled

Note: Get more information by writing R-H Solutions, 2804 Russell Hollow Road, Little Rock, AR 72203, or by calling at (501) 555-2425.

(insert your name here)

To open the document:

1. Place your Data Disk into the appropriate disk drive.
2. Start Word as usual.
3. Click the **Open** button on the Standard toolbar to display the Open dialog box, shown in Figure 2-2.

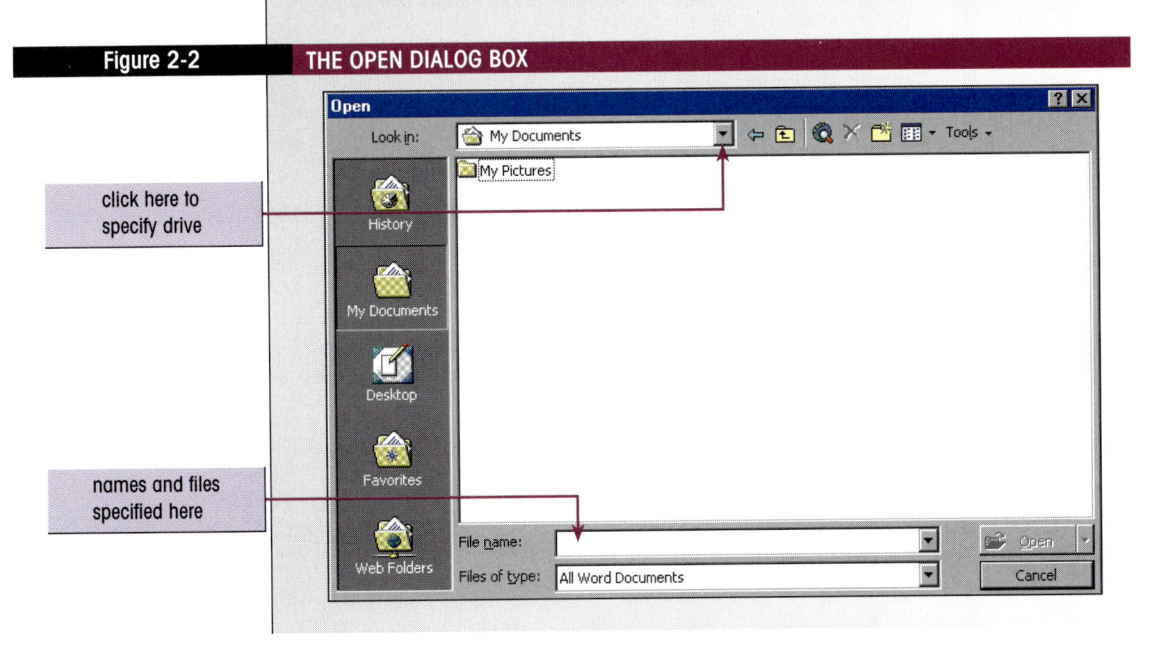

Figure 2-2   THE OPEN DIALOG BOX

click here to specify drive

names and files specified here

4. Click the **Look in** list arrow. The list of drives and files appears.

5. Click the drive that contains your Data Disk.

6. Double-click the **Tutorial.02** folder, then double-click the **Tutorial** folder.

7. Click **Annuity** to select the file, if necessary.

   TROUBLE? If you see "Annuity.doc" in the folder, Windows might be configured to display filename extensions. Click Annuity.doc and continue with Step 8. If you can't find the file with or without the filename extension, make sure you're looking in the Tutorial subfolder within the Tutorial.02 folder on the drive that contains your Data Disk, and check to make sure the Files of type text box displays All Word Documents or All Files. If you still can't locate the file, ask your instructor or technical support person for help.

8. Click the **Open** button. The document opens, with the insertion point at the beginning of the document. See Figure 2-3.

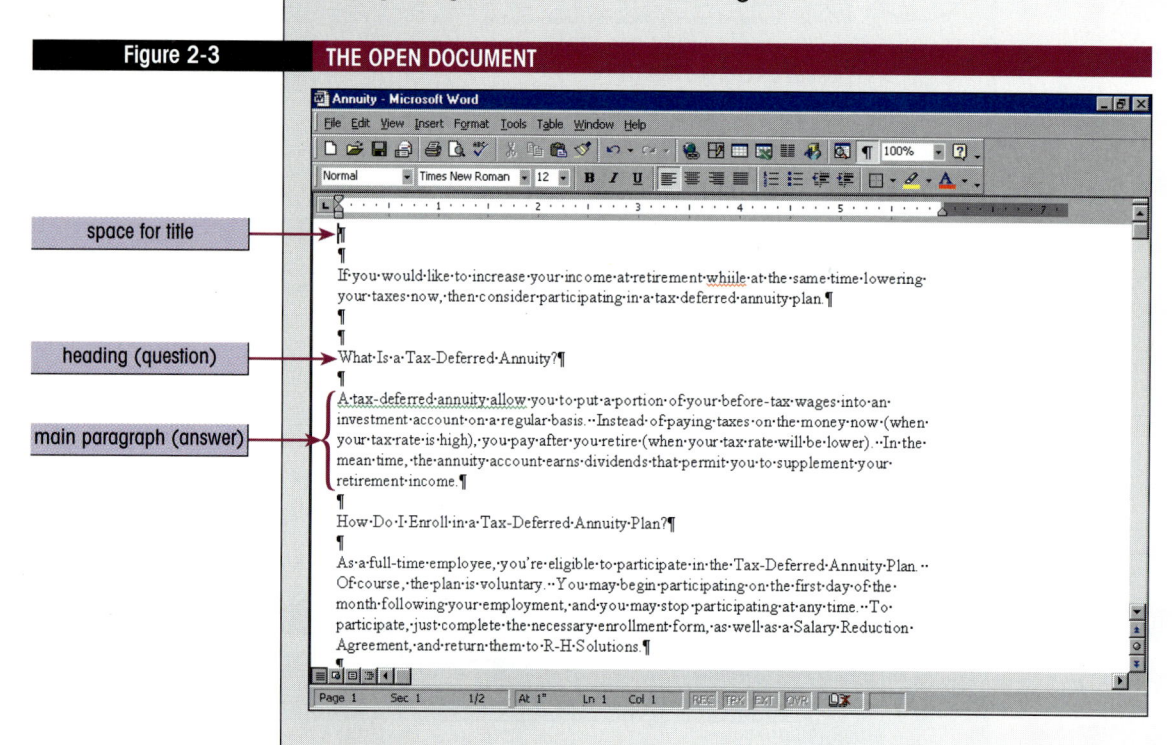

| Figure 2-3 | THE OPEN DOCUMENT |

9. Check that your screen matches Figure 2-3. For this tutorial, display the non-printing characters so that the formatting elements (tabs, paragraph marks, and so forth) are visible and easier to change.

Now that you've opened the document, you can save it with a new name.

Renaming the Document

To avoid altering the original file, Annuity, you will save the document using the filename RHS Annuity Plan. Saving the document with another filename creates a copy of the file and leaves the original file unchanged in case you want to work through the tutorial again.

> ### To save the document with a new name:
>
> 1. Click **File** on the menu bar, and then click **Save As**. The Save As dialog box opens with the current filename highlighted in the File name text box. You could type an entirely new filename, or you could edit the current one. In the next step, practice editing a filename.
>
> 2. Click to the left of "Annuity" in the File name text box, type **RHS**, and then press the **spacebar**. Press the → key to move the insertion point to the right of the letter "y" in "Annuity," press the **spacebar**, and then type **Plan**. The filename changes to RHS Annuity Plan.
>
> 3. Click the **Save** button to save the document with the new filename.

Now you're ready to begin working with the document. First, you will check it for spelling and grammatical errors.

Using the Spelling and Grammar Checker

When typing a document, you can check for spelling and grammatical errors simply by looking for words underlined in red (for spelling errors) or green (for grammatical errors). But when you're working on a document that someone else typed, it's a good idea to start by using the Spelling and Grammar checker. This feature checks a document word by word for a variety of spelling and grammatical errors. Among other things, the Spelling and Grammar checker can sometimes find words that, though spelled correctly, are not used properly. For example, the word "their" instead of the word "there" or "form" instead of "from."

> **REFERENCE WINDOW** | **RW**
>
> ### Checking a Document for Spelling and Grammatical Errors
>
> - Click at the beginning of the document, then click the Spelling and Grammar button on the Standard toolbar.
> - In the Spelling and Grammar dialog box, review any errors highlighted in color. Grammatical errors appear in green; spelling errors appear in red. Review the possible corrections in the Suggestions list box.
> - To accept a suggested correction, click it in the Suggestions list box. Then click Change to make the correction and continue searching the document for errors.
> - Click Ignore to skip this instance of the highlighted text and continue searching the document for errors.
> - Click Ignore All to skip all instances of the highlighted text and continue searching the document for errors. Click Ignore Rule to skip all instances of a particular grammatical error.
> - To type your correction directly in the document, click outside the Spelling and Grammar dialog box, make the desired correction, and then click Resume in the Spelling and Grammar dialog box.

You'll see how the Spelling and Grammar checker works as you check the annuity plan document for mistakes.

To check the annuity plan document for spelling and grammatical errors:

1. Verify that the insertion point is located at the beginning of the document, to the left of the first paragraph mark.

2. Click the **Spelling and Grammar** button on the Standard toolbar. The Spelling and Grammar dialog box opens with the word "whiile" highlighted in red. The word "while" is suggested as a possible replacement. The line immediately under the title bar indicates the type of problem, in this case, "Not in Dictionary." See Figure 2-4.

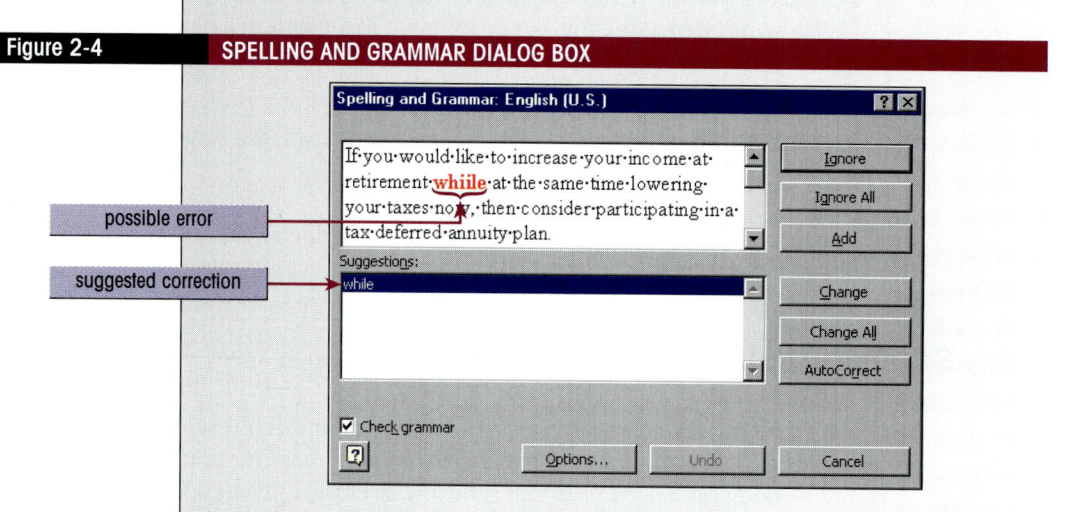

Figure 2-4   SPELLING AND GRAMMAR DIALOG BOX

[Dialog box showing:
- Spelling and Grammar: English (U.S.)
- Text area with: "If you would like to increase your income at retirement whiile at the same time lowering your taxes now, then consider participating in a tax-deferred annuity plan."
- possible error → whiile
- Suggestions: while ← suggested correction
- Buttons: Ignore, Ignore All, Add, Change, Change All, AutoCorrect
- Check grammar checkbox
- Options..., Undo, Cancel]

3. Verify that "while" is highlighted in the Suggestions list box, and then click **Change**. "While" is inserted into the document. Next, the grammatical error "A tax-deferred annuity allow" is highlighted in green, with two possible corrections listed in the Suggestions box. The dialog box indicates that the problem concerns subject-verb agreement.

   TROUBLE? If you see the word "bondd" selected instead of "a tax-deferred annuity allow," your computer is not set up to check grammar. Click the Check grammar check box to insert a check, and then click Cancel to close the Spelling and Grammar dialog box. Next, click at the beginning of the document, and then repeat Step 2.

4. Click **A tax-deferred annuity allows** in the Suggestions box, if necessary, and then click **Change**. The misspelled word "bondd" is highlighted in red, with two possible replacements listed in the Suggestions list box.

5. Click **bond**, if necessary, to highlight it, and then click **Change**.

6. Click the **Ignore Rule** button to prevent the Spelling and Grammar checker from stopping at each of the remaining seven bullets in the document. You see a message indicating that the spelling and grammar check is complete. The Spelling and Grammar checker next selects the word "tuition," with the capitalized version

TUTORIAL 2 EDITING AND FORMATTING A DOCUMENT   WD 2.07

> of the same word, "Tuition," listed in the Suggestions box. You do not want to accept the change because the highlighted word is the beginning of a bulleted list, not a sentence, and doesn't have to be capitalized.
>
> **7.** Click **OK**. You return to the annuity plan document.

Although the Spelling and Grammar checker is a useful tool, remember that there is no substitute for careful proofreading. Always take the time to read through your document to check for errors the Spelling and Grammar checker might have missed. Keep in mind that Spelling and Grammar checker probably won't catch *all* instances of words that are spelled correctly but used improperly. And of course, the Spelling and Grammar checker cannot pinpoint phrases that are simply confusing or inaccurate. To produce a professional document, you must read it carefully several times, and, if necessary, ask a co-worker to read it, too.

> ### To proofread the annuity plan document:
>
> **1.** Scroll to the beginning of the document and begin proofreading.
>
> The first error is a missing hyphen in the phrase "tax deferred annuity plan" at the end of the first paragraph.
>
> **2.** Click after the "x" in "tax," type - (a hyphen), and then press the **Delete** key to remove the space. Now the phrase is hyphenated correctly.
>
> The next error is the word "mean time" in the paragraph below the "What Is a Tax-Deferred Annuity?" heading. You need to delete the space.
>
> **3.** Click after the letter "n" in "mean" and then press the **Delete** key.
>
> **4.** Continue proofreading the document.

Once you are certain the document is free from errors, you are ready to make some more editing changes. To make all of Brandi's editing changes, you'll need to learn how to quickly move the insertion point to any location in the document.

Moving the Insertion Point Around a Document

The arrow keys on your keyboard, ↑, ↓, →, and ←, allow you to move the insertion point one character at a time to the left or right, or one line at a time up or down. If you want to move more than one character or one line at a time, you can point and click in other parts of a line or the document. You also can press a combination of keys to move the insertion point. As you become more experienced with Word, you'll decide which method you prefer.

To see how quickly you can move through the document, you'll use keystrokes to move the insertion point to the beginning of the second page and to the end of the document.

> ### To move the insertion point with keystrokes:
>
> **1.** Press the **Ctrl** key and hold it down while you press the **Home** key. The insertion point moves to the beginning of the document.
>
> **2.** Press the **Page Down** key to move the insertion point down to the next screen.

3. Press the **Page Down** key again to move the insertion point down to the next screen.

4. Notice that the status bar indicates the location of the insertion point.

5. Press the ↓ or ↑ key to move the insertion point to the paragraph that begins "Your Tax-deferred Annuity Plan can be terminated…." The insertion point is now at the beginning of page 2. Notice the **automatic page break**, a dotted line that Word inserts automatically to mark the beginning of the new page. See Figure 2-5. As you insert and delete text or change formatting in a document, the location of the automatic page breaks in your document continually adjusts to account for the edits.

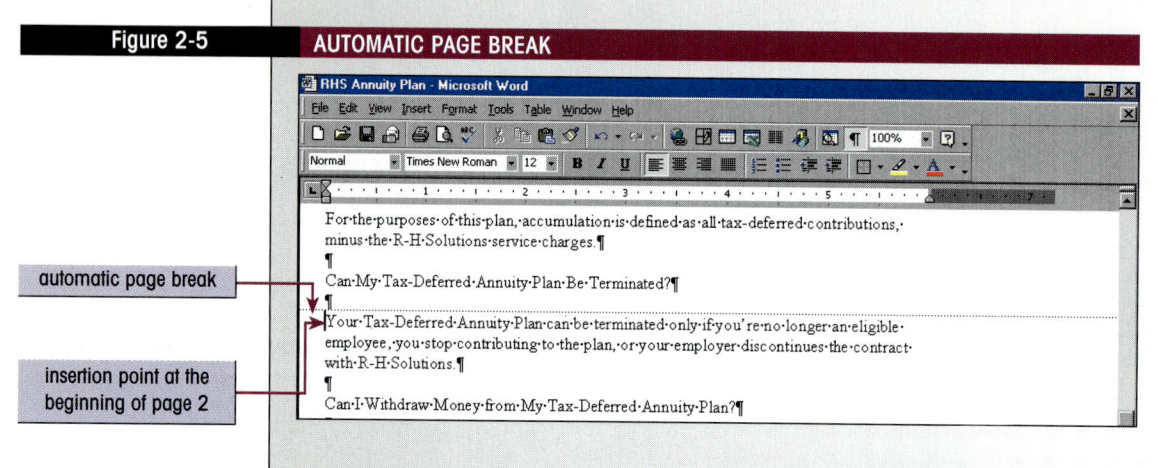

Figure 2-5   AUTOMATIC PAGE BREAK

- automatic page break
- insertion point at the beginning of page 2

6. Press **Ctrl+End**. (That is, press and hold down the **Ctrl** key while you press the **End** key.) The insertion point moves to the end of the document.

7. Use the ← key to move the insertion point immediately before the phrase "at (501) 555-2425," and then type your name and a space.

8. Move the insertion point back to the beginning of the document.

Figure 2-6 summarizes the keystrokes you can use to move the insertion point around the document.

Figure 2-6   KEYSTROKES FOR MOVING THE INSERTION POINT

PRESS	TO MOVE INSERTION POINT
← or →	Left or right one character at a time
↑ or ↓	Up or down one line at a time
Ctrl+← or Ctrl+→	Left or right one word at a time
Ctrl+↑ or Ctrl+↓	Up or down one paragraph at a time
Home or End	To the beginning or to the end of the current line
Ctrl+Home or Ctrl+End	To the beginning or to the end of the document
PageUp or PageDown	To the previous screen or to the next screen
Alt+Ctrl+PageUp or Alt+Ctrl+PageDown	To the top or to the bottom of the document window

Using Select, Then Do

One of the most powerful editing features in Word is the "select, then do" feature. It allows you to select (or highlight) a block of text and then do something to that text, such as deleting, moving, or formatting it. You can select text using either the mouse or the keyboard; however, the mouse is usually the easier and more efficient way. With the mouse, you can quickly select a line or paragraph by clicking the **selection bar**, which is the blank space in the left margin area of the document window. Also, you can select text using various combinations of keys. Figure 2-7 summarizes methods for selecting text with the mouse and the keyboard. The notation "Ctrl+Shift" indicates that you should press and hold two keys (the Ctrl key and the Shift key) at the same time.

Figure 2-7	METHODS FOR SELECTING TEXT WITH THE MOUSE AND KEYBOARD		
TO SELECT	**MOUSE**	**KEYBOARD**	**MOUSE AND KEYBOARD**
A word	Double-click the word.	Move the insertion point to the beginning of the next word, hold down Ctrl+Shift, and then press → once.	
A line	Click in the selection bar next to the line.	Move the insertion point to the beginning of the line, hold down Ctrl+Shift, and then press → until the line is selected.	
A sentence			Press and hold down the Ctrl key, and click within the sentence.
Multiple lines	Click and drag in the selection bar next to the lines.	Move the insertion point to the beginning of the first line, hold down Ctrl+Shift, and then press → until all the lines are selected.	
A paragraph	Double-click in the selection bar next to the paragraph, or triple-click within the paragraph.	Move the insertion point to the beginning of the paragraph, hold down Ctrl+Shift, and then press ▼.	
Multiple paragraphs	Click and drag in the selection bar next to the paragraphs, or triple-click within the first paragraph and drag.	Move the insertion point to the beginning of the first paragraph, hold down Ctrl+Shift, and then press ▼ until all the paragraphs are selected.	
Entire document	Triple-click in the selection bar.	Press Ctrl+A.	Press and hold down the Ctrl key and click in the selection bar.
A block of text			Click at the beginning of the block, press and hold down the Shift key, and then click at the end of the block.

Deleting Text

Brandi wants you to delete the phrase "at the same time" in the first paragraph of the document. You'll use the "select, then do" feature to delete the phrase now.

To select and delete a phrase from the text:

1. Click and drag over the phrase **at the same time** located in the first line of the first paragraph. The phrase and the space following it are highlighted, as shown in Figure 2-8. Notice that dragging the pointer over the second and successive words automatically selects the entire words and the spaces following them. This makes it much easier to select words and phrases than selecting them one character at a time.

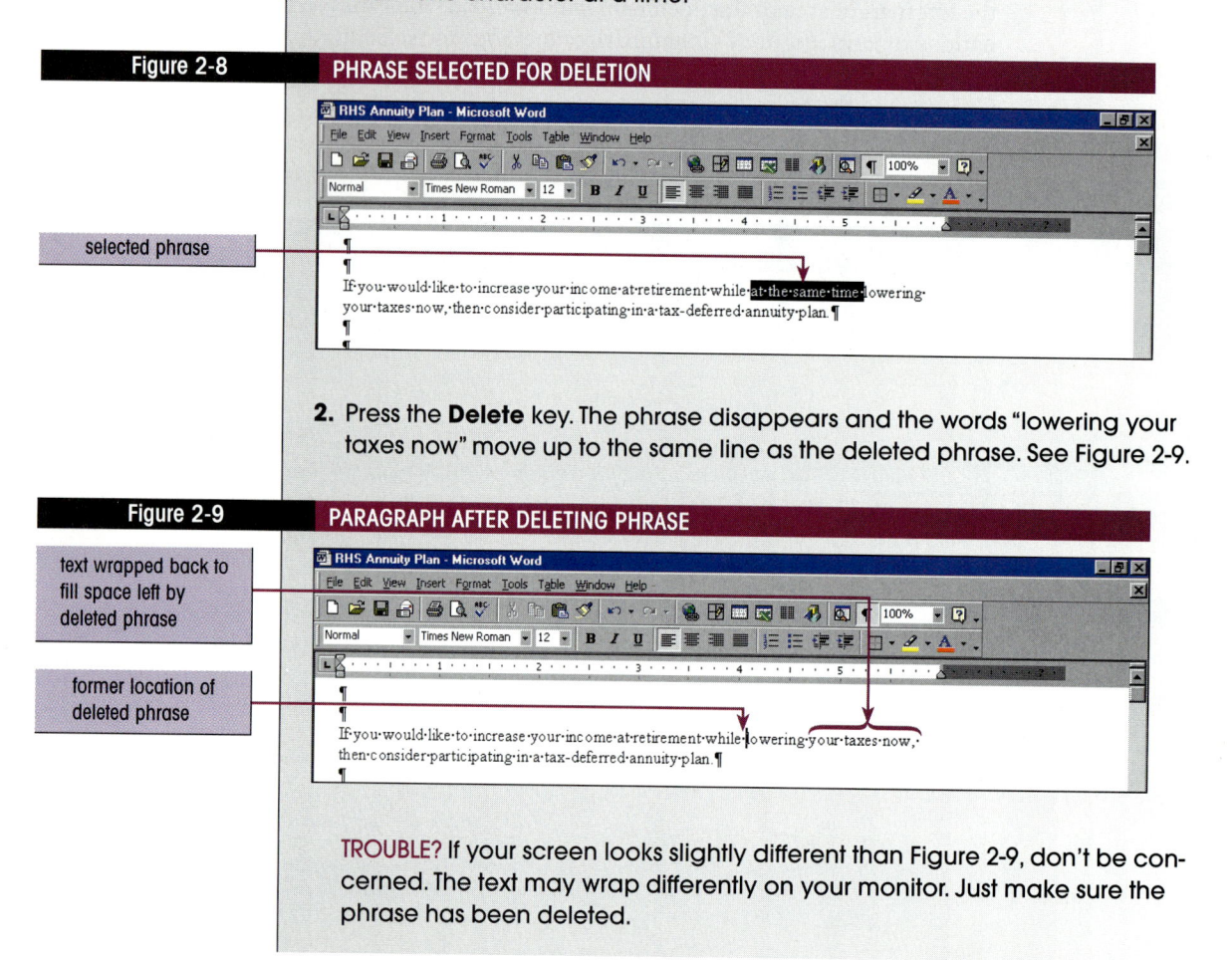

Figure 2-8   **PHRASE SELECTED FOR DELETION**

selected phrase

2. Press the **Delete** key. The phrase disappears and the words "lowering your taxes now" move up to the same line as the deleted phrase. See Figure 2-9.

Figure 2-9   **PARAGRAPH AFTER DELETING PHRASE**

text wrapped back to fill space left by deleted phrase

former location of deleted phrase

TROUBLE? If your screen looks slightly different than Figure 2-9, don't be concerned. The text may wrap differently on your monitor. Just make sure the phrase has been deleted.

After rereading the paragraph, Reginald decides the phrase shouldn't have been deleted after all. He checks with Brandi, and she agrees. You could retype the text, but there's an easier way to restore the phrase.

Using the Undo and Redo Commands

To undo (or reverse) the very last thing you did, simply click the **Undo button** on the Standard toolbar. If you want to reinstate your original change, the **Redo button** reverses the action of the Undo button (or redoes the undo). To undo anything more than your last action, you can click the Undo list arrow on the Standard toolbar. This list shows your most recent actions. Undo reverses the action only at its original location. You can't delete a word or phrase and then undo it at a different location.

> **REFERENCE WINDOW**
>
> **Using Undo and Redo**
> - Click the Undo button on the Standard toolbar to reverse your last action. Or click Edit on the menu bar, and then click Undo. Note that the exact command you see on the Edit menu will reflect your most recent action, such as "Undo Typing."
> - To reverse several previous actions, click the Undo list arrow on the Standard toolbar. Click an action on the list to reverse all actions up to and including the one you click.
> - To display a ScreenTip reminder of your last action, place the mouse pointer over the Undo button.
> - To undo your previous actions one-by-one, in the reverse order in which you performed them, click the Undo button once for every action you want to reverse.
> - If you undo an action by mistake, click the Redo button on the Standard toolbar (or click Edit on the menu bar, and then click Redo) to reverse the undo.

You decide to undo the deletion to see how the sentence reads. Rather than retyping the phrase, you will reverse the edit using the Undo button.

To undo the deletion:

1. Place the mouse pointer over the Undo button on the Standard toolbar. The label "Undo Clear" appears in a ScreenTip, indicating that your most recent action involved deleting (or clearing) text.

2. Click the **Undo** button. The phrase "at the same time" reappears in your document and is highlighted.

   TROUBLE? If the phrase doesn't reappear and something else changes in your document, you probably made another edit or change to the document (such as pressing the Backspace key) between the deletion and the undo. Click the Undo button on the Standard toolbar until the phrase reappears in your document. If a list of possible changes appears under the Undo button, you clicked the list arrow next to the Undo button rather than the Undo button itself. Click the Undo button to restore the deleted phrase and close the list box.

3. Click within the paragraph to deselect the phrase.

   As you read the sentence, you decide that it reads better without the phrase. Instead of deleting it again, you'll redo the undo. As you place the pointer over the Redo button, notice that its ScreenTip indicates the action you want to redo.

4. Place the mouse pointer over the Redo button on the Standard toolbar and observe the "Redo Clear" label.

5. Click the **Redo** button. The phrase "at the same time" disappears from your document again.

6. Click the **Save** button on the Standard toolbar to save your changes to the document.

You have edited the document by deleting the text that Brandi marked for deletion. Now, you are ready to make the rest of the edits she suggested.

Moving Text Within a Document

One of the most important uses of "select, then do" is moving text. For example, Brandi wants to reorder the four points Reginald made in the section "Can I Withdraw Money from My Tax-Deferred Annuity Plan?" on page 2 of his draft. You could reorder the list by deleting the sentence and then retyping it at the new location, but a much more efficient approach is to select and then move the sentence. Word provides several ways to move text: drag and drop, cut and paste, and copy and paste.

Dragging and Dropping Text

One way to move text within a document is called drag and drop. With **drag and drop**, you select the text you want to move, press and hold down the mouse button while you drag the selected text to a new location, and then release the mouse button.

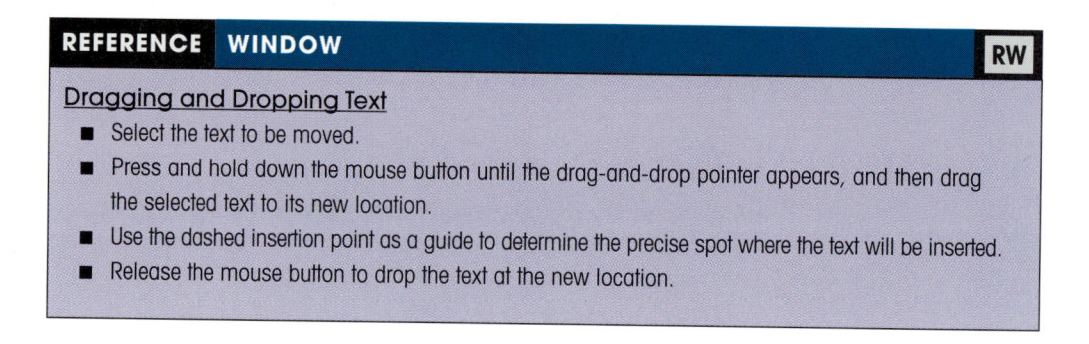

REFERENCE WINDOW

Dragging and Dropping Text
- Select the text to be moved.
- Press and hold down the mouse button until the drag-and-drop pointer appears, and then drag the selected text to its new location.
- Use the dashed insertion point as a guide to determine the precise spot where the text will be inserted.
- Release the mouse button to drop the text at the new location.

Brandi requested a change in the order of the items in the bulleted list on page 2 of the document, so you'll use the drag-and-drop method to reorder the items. At the same time, you'll practice using the selection bar to highlight a line of text.

To move text using drag and drop:

1. Scroll through the document until you see "tuition for post-secondary education...," the first item in the list of "immediate and severe financial needs:" that begins in the middle of page 2.

2. Click in the selection bar to the left of the line beginning "tuition..." to select that line of text, including the return character. See Figure 2-10.

Figure 2-10 SELECTED TEXT TO DRAG AND DROP

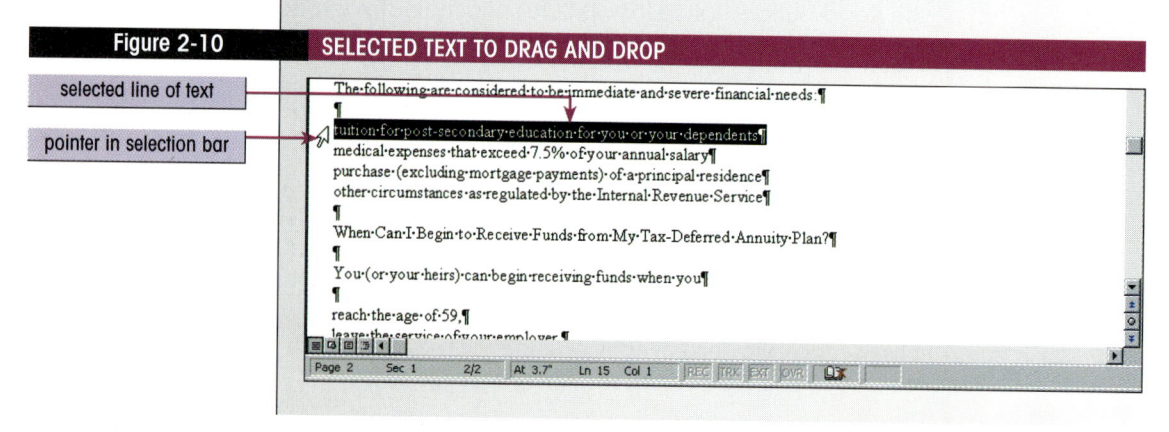

- selected line of text
- pointer in selection bar

3. Position the pointer over the selected text. The pointer changes from a right-facing arrow to a left-facing arrow.

4. Press and hold down the mouse button until the drag-and-drop pointer, which has a dashed insertion point, an arrow, and a small square called a move box, appears.

5. Drag the selected text down three lines until the dashed insertion point appears to the left of the word "other." Make sure you use the dashed insertion point to guide the text to its new location rather than the mouse pointer or the move box; the dashed insertion point marks the precise location of the drop. See Figure 2-11.

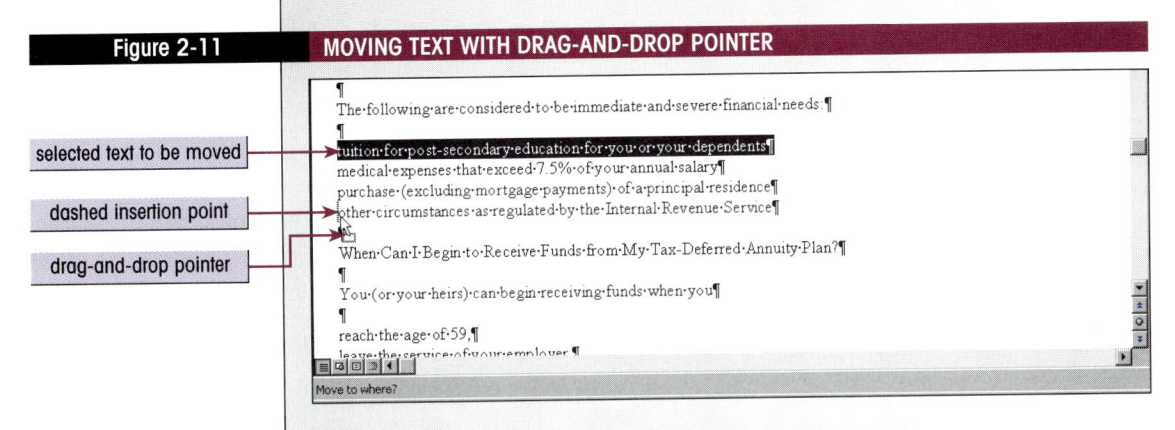

Figure 2-11 | **MOVING TEXT WITH DRAG-AND-DROP POINTER**

- selected text to be moved
- dashed insertion point
- drag-and-drop pointer

```
¶
The·following·are·considered·to·be·immediate·and·severe·financial·needs:¶
¶
tuition·for·post-secondary·education·for·you·or·your·dependents¶
medical·expenses·that·exceed·7.5%·of·your·annual·salary¶
purchase·(excluding·mortgage·payments)·of·a·principal·residence¶
other·circumstances·as·regulated·by·the·Internal·Revenue·Service¶
¶
When·Can·I·Begin·to·Receive·Funds·from·My·Tax-Deferred·Annuity·Plan?¶
¶
You·(or·your·heirs)·can·begin·receiving·funds·when·you¶
¶
reach·the·age·of·59,¶
leave·the·service·of·your·employer¶
```
Move to where?

6. Release the mouse button. The selected text moves to its new location, as the third item in the list.

   TROUBLE? If the selected text moves to the wrong location, click the Undo button on the Standard toolbar, and then repeat Steps 3 through 6, making sure you hold the mouse button until the dashed insertion point appears in front of the word "other."

7. Deselect the highlighted text by clicking anywhere in the document window.

Dragging and dropping works well if you're moving text a short distance in a document; however, Word provides another method, called cut and paste, that works well for moving text either a short distance or beyond the current screen.

Cutting or Copying and Pasting Text

To **cut** means to remove text from the document and place it on the **Office Clipboard**, which stores up to 12 items at a time. To **paste** means to transfer a copy of the text from the Clipboard into the document at the insertion point. To perform a cut-and-paste action, you select the text you want to move, cut (or remove) it from the document, and then paste (or restore) it into the document in a new location. If you don't want to remove the text from its original location, you can copy it (rather than cutting it) and then paste the copy in a new location. This procedure is known as "copy and paste."

If you cut or copy more than one item, the Clipboard toolbar opens, making it easier for you to select which items you want to paste into the document.

> **REFERENCE WINDOW**
>
> **Cutting or Copying and Pasting Text**
> - Select the text you want to move.
> - Click the Cut button on the Standard toolbar. (If you want to make a copy, click the Copy button instead.)
> - Move the insertion point to the target location in the document.
> - Click the Paste button on the Standard toolbar.
> - If you have cut or copied more than one block of text, the Clipboard toolbar will open, containing one icon for each item stored on the Clipboard. To paste an item from the Clipboard toolbar into the document, click where you want the item to be inserted, and then click its icon on the Clipboard toolbar. To paste the entire contents of the Clipboard at the insertion point, click the Paste All button in the Clipboard toolbar. To erase the contents of the Clipboard, click the Clear Clipboard button on the Clipboard toolbar.

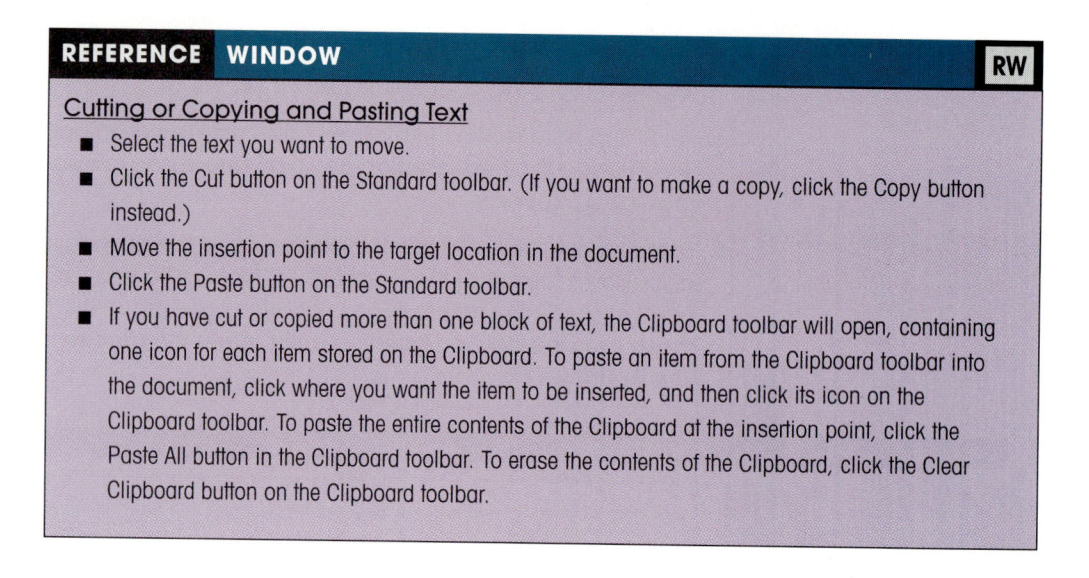

Brandi suggested moving the phrase "at any time" (in the paragraph beginning "You can change your allocation...") to a new location. You'll use cut and paste to move this phrase.

To move text using cut and paste:

1. Scroll the document up until you can see the paragraph just above the heading "How Will I Know...." on page 1.

2. Click and drag the mouse to highlight the complete phrase **at any time**. See Figure 2-12.

Figure 2-12 TEXT TO MOVE USING CUT AND PASTE

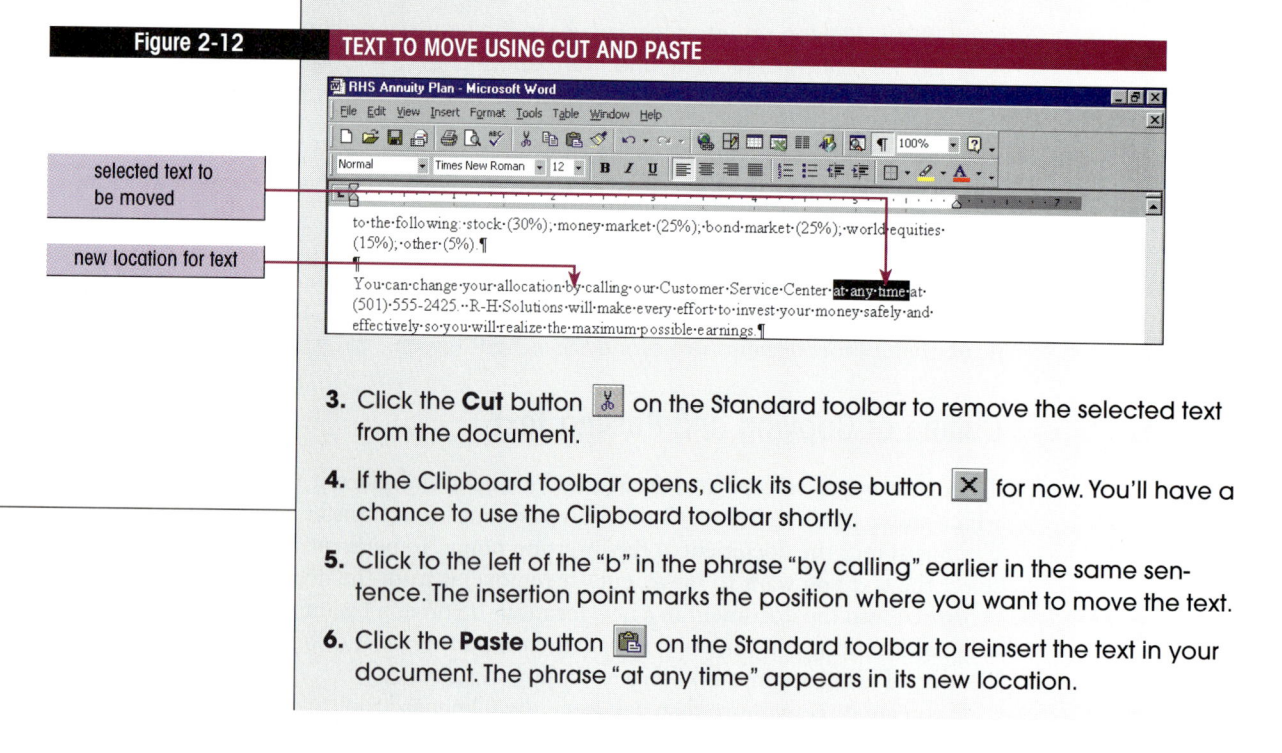

selected text to be moved

new location for text

3. Click the **Cut** button on the Standard toolbar to remove the selected text from the document.

4. If the Clipboard toolbar opens, click its Close button for now. You'll have a chance to use the Clipboard toolbar shortly.

5. Click to the left of the "b" in the phrase "by calling" earlier in the same sentence. The insertion point marks the position where you want to move the text.

6. Click the **Paste** button on the Standard toolbar to reinsert the text in your document. The phrase "at any time" appears in its new location.

The copy and paste feature works much the same way as cut and paste. You can try using this technique now, as you copy the phrase "Tax-Deferred Annuity Plan" from the middle of the document and then paste it at the top of the document.

1. Scroll the document up until you can see the heading "How Do I Enroll in a Tax-Deferred Annuity Plan?" on page 1.

2. In the headings, click and drag the mouse to highlight the complete phrase "Tax-Deferred Annuity Plan."

3. Click the **Copy** button on the Standard toolbar. The Clipboard toolbar opens, containing icons for each item currently stored on the Clipboard, as shown in Figure 2-13. The "W" on the icons indicates that the copied items contain Word text. Note that your Clipboard toolbar might contain more than two icons, depending on whether you (or another user) cut or copy text before completing this tutorial. You also may see icons for other Office programs, such as Excel.

Figure 2-13   CLIPBOARD TOOLBAR WITH CUT AND COPIED ITEMS

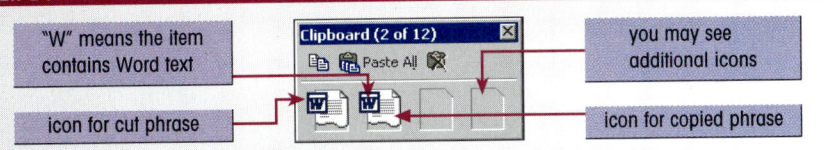

- "W" means the item contains Word text
- you may see additional icons
- icon for cut phrase
- icon for copied phrase

TROUBLE? If the Office Assistant opens, hide it and continue with Step 4.

4. Place the mouse pointer over each of the icons, one at a time, until the ScreenTip "at any time" appears, indicating that this is the icon for the text you cut in the previous set of steps.

5. Place the mouse pointer over each of the icons, one at a time, until the ScreenTip "Tax-Deferred Annuity Plan" appears, indicating that this is the icon for the text you just copied.

6. Scroll up and click at the beginning of the document to move the insertion point there.

7. Click the **Tax-Deferred Annuity Plan** icon in the Clipboard toolbar. The phrase is inserted at the top of the document. Now that you are finished using the Clipboard toolbar, you will delete its contents.

8. Click the **Clear Clipboard** button button on the Clipboard toolbar. All of the icons disappear from the Clipboard toolbar.

9. Click the **Close** button on the Clipboard toolbar. The Clipboard toolbar disappears.

Finding and Replacing Text

When you're working with a longer document, the quickest and easiest way to locate a particular word or phrase is to use the Find command. If you want to replace characters or a phrase with something else, you can use the Replace command, which combines the Find command with a substitution feature. The Replace command searches through a document and substitutes the text you're searching for with the replacement text you specify. As Word performs the search, it stops and highlights each occurrence of the search text and lets you determine whether to substitute the replacement text by clicking the Replace button.

If you want to substitute every occurrence of the search text with the replacement text, you can click the Replace All button. When using the Replace All button with single words, keep in mind that the search text might be found within other words. To prevent Word from making incorrect substitutions in such cases, it's a good idea to select the "Find whole words only" check box along with the Replace All button. For example, suppose you want to replace the word "figure" with illustration. Unless you select the "Find whole words only" check box, Word would replace "configure" with "conillustration."

As you search through a document, you can search from the current location of the insertion point down to the end of the document, from the insertion point up to the beginning of the document, or throughout the document.

> **REFERENCE WINDOW**
>
> **Finding and Replacing Text**
> - Click the Select Browse Object button on the vertical scroll bar, and then click the Find button on the Select Browse Object menu. (You also can click Edit on the menu bar, and then click either Find or Replace.)
> - To find text, click the Find tab; or, to find and replace text, click the Replace tab.
> - Click the More button to expand the dialog box to display additional options (including the "Find whole words only" option). If you see the Less button, the additional options are already displayed.
> - In the Search list box, select Down if you want to search from the insertion point to the end of the document, select Up if you want to search from the insertion point to the beginning of the document, or select All to search the entire document.
> - Type the characters you want to find in the Find what text box.
> - If you are replacing text, type the replacement text in the Replace with text box.
> - Click the Find Next button.
> - Click the Replace button to substitute the found text with the replacement text and find the next occurrence.
> - Click the Find whole words only check box, and then click the Replace All button to substitute all occurrences of the found text with the replacement text.

Brandi wants the shortened version of the company name, "R-H Solutions," to be spelled out as "Right-Hand Solutions" every time it appears in the text.

To replace "R-H Solutions" with "Right-Hand Solutions:"

1. Click the **Select Browse Object** button near the bottom of the vertical scroll bar.

2. Click the **Find** button on the Select Browse Object menu. The Find and Replace dialog box appears.

3. Click the **Replace** tab.

4. If necessary, click the **More** button to display the additional search options.

5. If necessary, click the **Search** list arrow, and then click **All**.

6. Click the **Find what** text box, type **R-H Solutions**, press the **Tab** key, and then type **Right-Hand Solutions** in the Replace with text box. Note that because the search text is made up of more than one word, the "Find whole words only" option is unnecessary and is therefore unavailable. See Figure 2-14.

Figure 2-14 FIND AND REPLACE DIALOG BOX

- type search text here → Find what: R-H Solutions
- type replacement text here → Replace with: Right-Hand Solutions
- click to instantly replace all occurrences of search text with replacement text → Replace All
- not necessary when searching for multiple words → Find whole words only

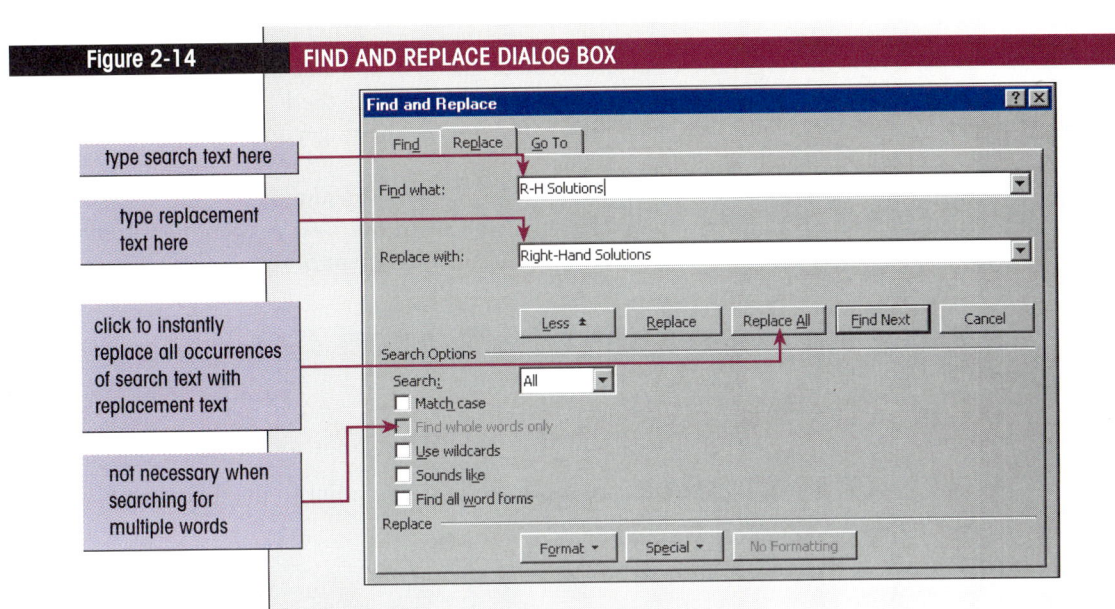

TROUBLE? If you already see the text "R-H Solutions" and "Right-Hand Solutions" in your Find and Replace dialog box, someone already performed these steps on your computer. Simply continue with Step 7.

7. Click the **Replace All** button to replace all occurrences of the search text with the replacement text. When Word finishes making the replacements, you see a dialog box telling you that six replacements were made.

8. Click **OK** to close the dialog box, and then click the **Close** button in the Find and Replace dialog box to return to the document. The full company name has been inserted into the document, as shown in Figure 2-15.

Figure 2-15 THE NAME "RIGHT-HAND SOLUTIONS" INSERTED INTO THE DOCUMENT

replacement text

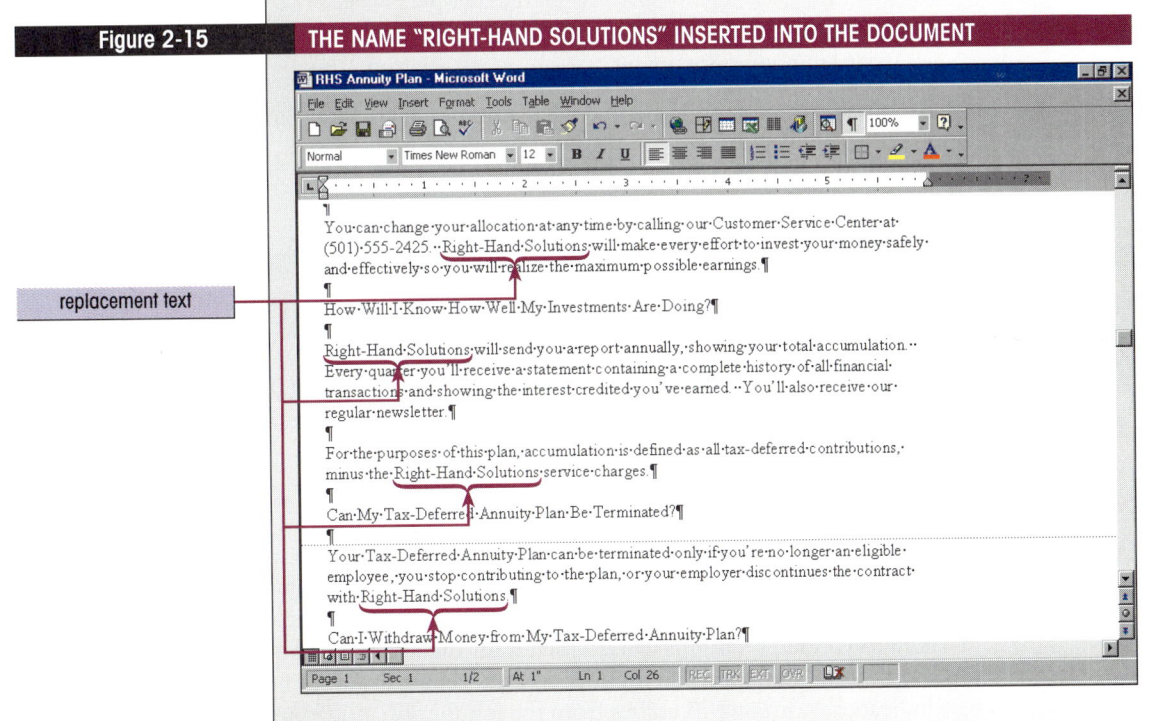

9. Click the **Save** button on the Standard toolbar to save your changes to the document.

You can also search for and replace formatting, such as bold, and special characters, such as paragraph marks, in the Find and Replace dialog box. Click in the Find what text box or the Replace with text box, enter any text if necessary, click the Format button, click Font to open the Font dialog box, and then select the formatting you want to find or replace. Complete the search or replace as usual.

You have completed the content changes Brandi suggested, but she has some other changes that will improve the plan's appearance. In the next session, you'll enhance the annuity plan by changing the width, spacing, and alignment of text.

Session 2.1 QUICK CHECK

1. Explain how to open a document and save a copy of it with a new name.
2. Which key(s) do you press to move the insertion point to the following places:
   a. down one line
   b. end of the document
   c. to the next screen
3. Describe the "select, then do" feature.
4. Define the following terms in your own words:
   a. selection bar
   b. Redo button
   c. drag and drop
5. Explain how to select a single word. Explain how to select a complete paragraph.
6. Describe a situation in which you would use the Undo button and then the Redo button.
7. True or False: You can use the Redo command to restore deleted text at a new location in your document.
8. What is the difference between cut and paste, and copy and paste?
9. List the steps involved in finding and replacing text in a document.

SESSION 2.2

In this session you will make the formatting changes Brandi suggested. You'll use a variety of formatting commands to change the margins, line spacing, text alignment, and paragraph indents. Also, you'll learn how to use the Format Painter, how to create bulleted and numbered lists, and how to change fonts, font sizes, and emphasis.

Changing the Margins

In general, it's best to begin formatting by making the changes that affect the document's overall appearance. Then you can make changes that affect only selected text. In this case, you need to adjust the margin settings of the annuity plan summary.

Word uses default margins of 1.25 inches for the left and right margins and 1 inch for the top and bottom margins. The numbers on the ruler (displayed below the Formatting toolbar) indicate the distance in inches from the left margin, not from the left edge of the paper. Unless you specify otherwise, changes you make to the margins will affect the entire document, not just the current paragraph or page.

TUTORIAL 2 EDITING AND FORMATTING A DOCUMENT   WD 2.19   WORD

> **REFERENCE WINDOW**
>
> **Changing Margins for the Entire Document**
> - With the insertion point anywhere in your document and no text selected, click File on the menu bar, and then click Page Setup.
> - If necessary, click the Margins tab to display the margin settings.
> - Use the arrows to change the settings in the Top, Bottom, Left, or Right text boxes, or type a new margin value in each text box.
> - Make sure the Apply to list box displays Whole document.
> - Click the OK button.

You need to change the top margin to 1.5 inches and the left margin to 1.75 inches, as Brandi requested. The left margin needs to be wider than usual to allow space for making holes so that the document can be inserted in a three-ring binder. In the next set of steps, you'll change the margins with the Page Setup command. You also can change margins in print layout view; you'll practice that method in the Review Assignments.

To change the margins in the annuity plan document:

1. If you took a break after the last lesson, make sure Word is running, the RHS Annuity Plan document is open, and nonprinting characters are displayed.

2. Click once anywhere in the document to make sure no text is selected.

3. Click **File** on the menu bar, and then click **Page Setup** to open the Page Setup dialog box.

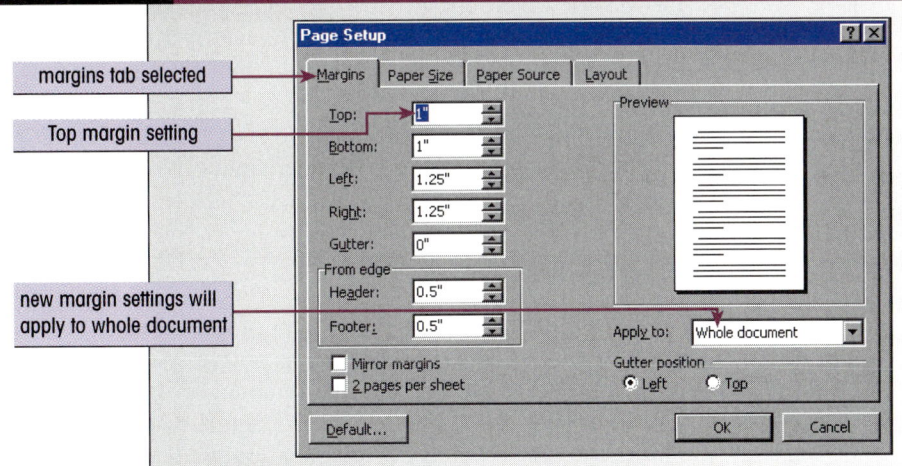

4. If necessary, click the **Margins** tab to display the margin settings. The Top margin setting is selected. See Figure 2-16.

Figure 2-16   PAGE SETUP DIALOG BOX

- margins tab selected
- Top margin setting
- new margin settings will apply to whole document

5. Type **1.5** to change the Top margin setting. (You do not have to type the inches symbol.)

6. Press the **Tab** key twice to move to the Left text box and select the current margin setting. Notice how the text area in the Preview box moves down to reflect the larger top margin.

7. Type **1.75** and then press the **Tab** key. Watch the Preview box to see how the margin increases.

8. Make sure the **Whole document** option is selected in the Apply to list box, and then click the **OK** button to return to your document. Notice that the right margin on the ruler has changed to reflect the larger margins and the reduced page area that results. See Figure 2-17.

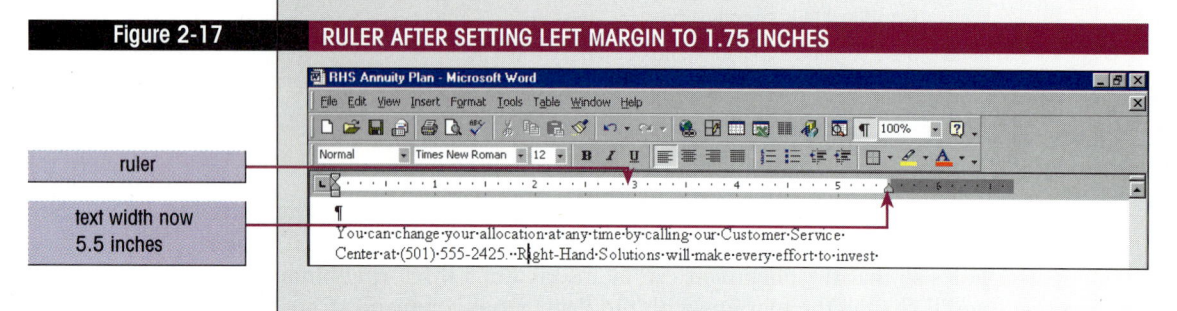

Figure 2-17   **RULER AFTER SETTING LEFT MARGIN TO 1.75 INCHES**

ruler

text width now 5.5 inches

TROUBLE? If a double dotted line and the words "Section Break" appear in your document, text was selected in the document and Whole document wasn't specified in the Apply to list box. If this occurs, click the Undo button on the Standard toolbar and then repeat Steps 1 through 8, making sure you select the Whole document option in the Apply to list box.

Now that you've made numerous changes to your document, it's a good idea to save it with a new name. That way, if the file you are working on somehow becomes corrupted, you can at least return to the earlier draft, rather than having to start all over again.

To save the document with a new name:

1. Click **File** on the menu bar, then click **Save As**.

2. Verify that the Tutorial subfolder within the Tutorial.02 folder appears in the Save in list box, change the filename to **RHS Annuity Plan Copy 2**, and then click the **Save** button. The document is saved with the new margin settings and a new name.

Next you will change the amount of space between lines of text.

Changing Line Spacing

The line spacing in a document determines the amount of vertical space between lines of text. You have a choice of three basic types of line spacing: **single spacing** (which allows for the largest character in a particular line as well as a small amount of extra space); **1.5 line spacing** (which allows for one and one-half times the space of single spacing); and **double spacing** (which allows for twice the space of single spacing). The annuity plan document is currently single-spaced because Word uses single spacing by default. Before changing the line-spacing setting, you should select the text you want to change. You can change line spacing by using the Paragraph command on the Format menu, or by using your keyboard.

TUTORIAL 2 EDITING AND FORMATTING A DOCUMENT   WD 2.21   WORD

REFERENCE WINDOW	RW

Changing Line Spacing in a Document
- Select the text you want to change.
- Click Format on the menu bar, then click Paragraph.
- Click the Line Spacing list arrow, and then click Single, 1.5 lines, or Double.

or

- Select the text you want to change.
- Press Ctrl+1 for single spacing, Ctrl+5 for 1.5 line spacing, or Ctrl+2 for double spacing.

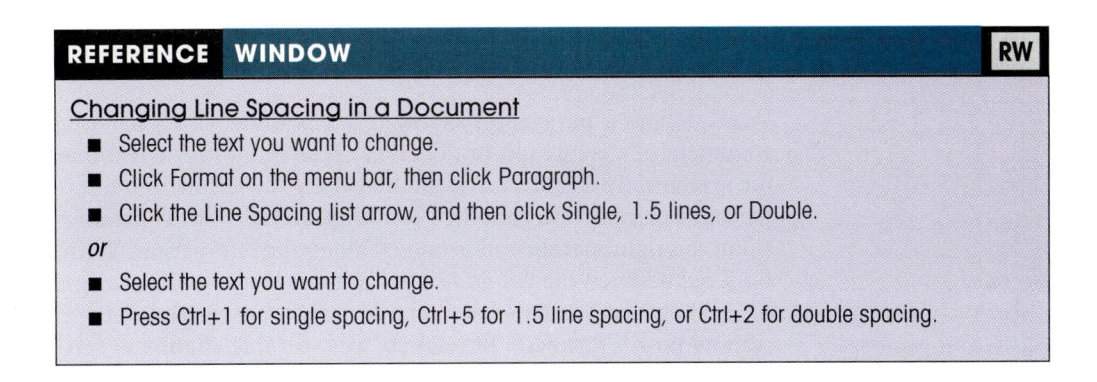

Brandi has asked you to change the line spacing for the entire annuity plan document to 1.5 line spacing. You will begin by selecting the entire document.

To change the document's line spacing:

1. Triple-click in the selection bar to select the entire document.

2. Click **Format** on the menu bar, and then click **Paragraph** to open the Paragraph dialog box.

3. If necessary, click the **Indents and Spacing** tab.

4. Click the **Line spacing** list arrow, and then click **1.5 lines**. The Preview box shows the results of the new line spacing. See Figure 2-18.

Figure 2-18   CHANGING THE DOCUMENT'S LINE SPACING

- Indents and Spacing tab
- Line spacing list arrow
- preview new line spacing here

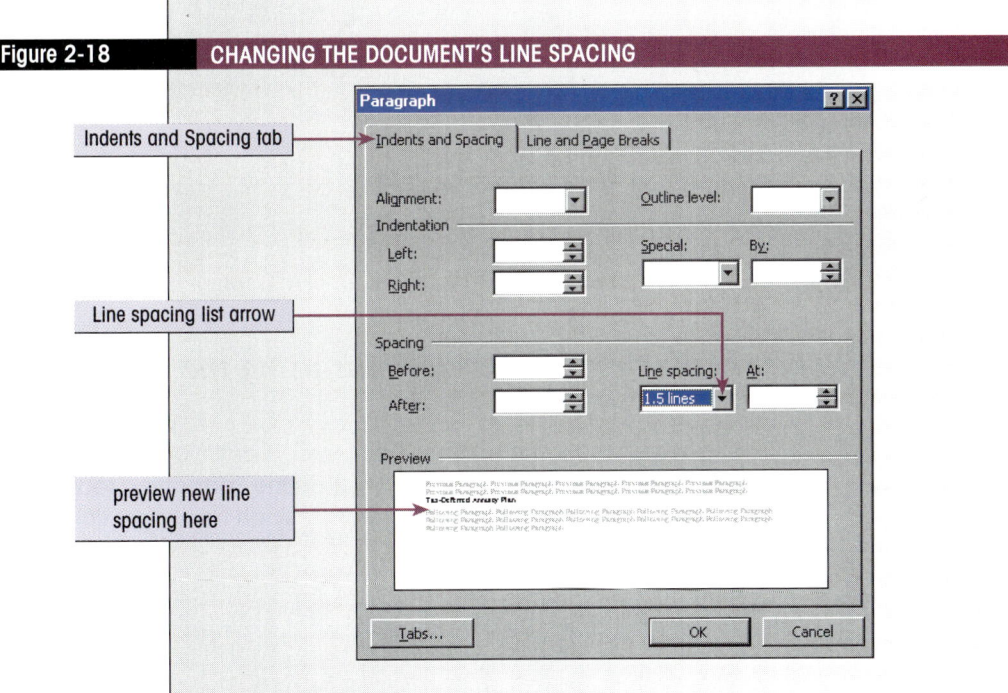

5. Click the **OK** button, and then click anywhere in the document to deselect it. Notice the additional space between every line of text in the document.

Now, you are ready to make formatting changes that affect individual paragraphs.

Aligning Text

Word defines a **paragraph** as any text that ends with a paragraph mark symbol (¶). The alignment of a paragraph or document refers to how the text lines up horizontally between the margins. By default, text is aligned along the left margin but is **ragged**, or uneven, along the right margin. This is called **left alignment**. With **right alignment**, the text is aligned along the right margin and is ragged along the left margin. With **center alignment**, text is centered between the left and right margins. With **justified alignment**, full lines of text are spaced between or aligned along both the left and the right margins. The paragraph you are reading now is justified. The easiest way to apply alignment settings is by clicking buttons on the Formatting toolbar.

Brandi indicated that the title of the annuity plan description should be centered and that the main paragraphs should be justified. First, you'll center the title.

To center-align the title:

1. Click anywhere in the title "Tax-Deferred Annuity Plan" at the beginning of the document.

2. Click the **Center** button on the Formatting toolbar. The text centers between the left and right margins. See Figure 2-19.

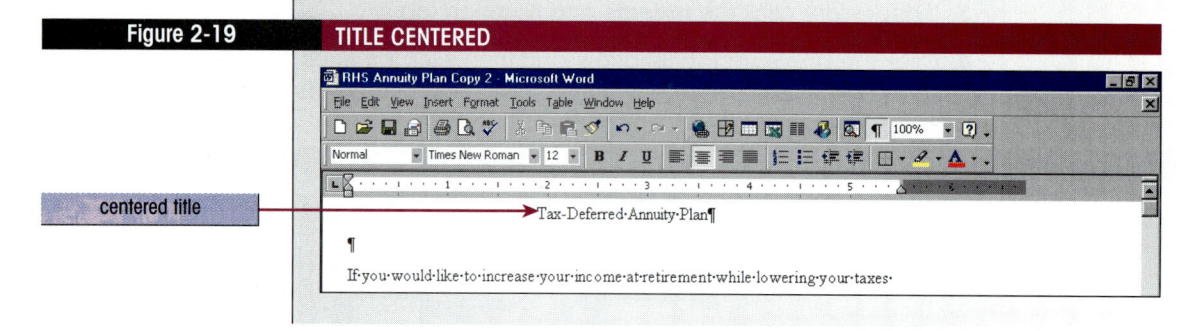

Figure 2-19   TITLE CENTERED

centered title → Tax-Deferred Annuity Plan¶

¶

If you would like to increase your income at retirement while lowering your taxes

Now, you'll justify the text in the first two main paragraphs.

To justify the first two paragraphs using the Formatting toolbar:

1. Click anywhere in the first paragraph, which begins "If you would like to increase...," and click the **Justify** button on the Formatting toolbar. The justification would be easier to see if the paragraph had more lines of text. You'll see the effects more clearly after you justify the second paragraph in the document.

2. Move the insertion point to the second main paragraph, which begins "A tax-deferred annuity allows... ."

3. Click again. The text is evenly spaced between the left and right margins. See Figure 2-20.

Figure 2-20   **TEXT JUSTIFIED USING THE FORMATTING TOOLBAR**

[Screenshot of Microsoft Word document titled "RHS Annuity Plan Copy 2" showing the Tax-Deferred Annuity Plan document with justified text. Callouts point to "click to justify text" (pointing to the justify button on the Formatting toolbar) and "justified text" (pointing to the body paragraphs).]

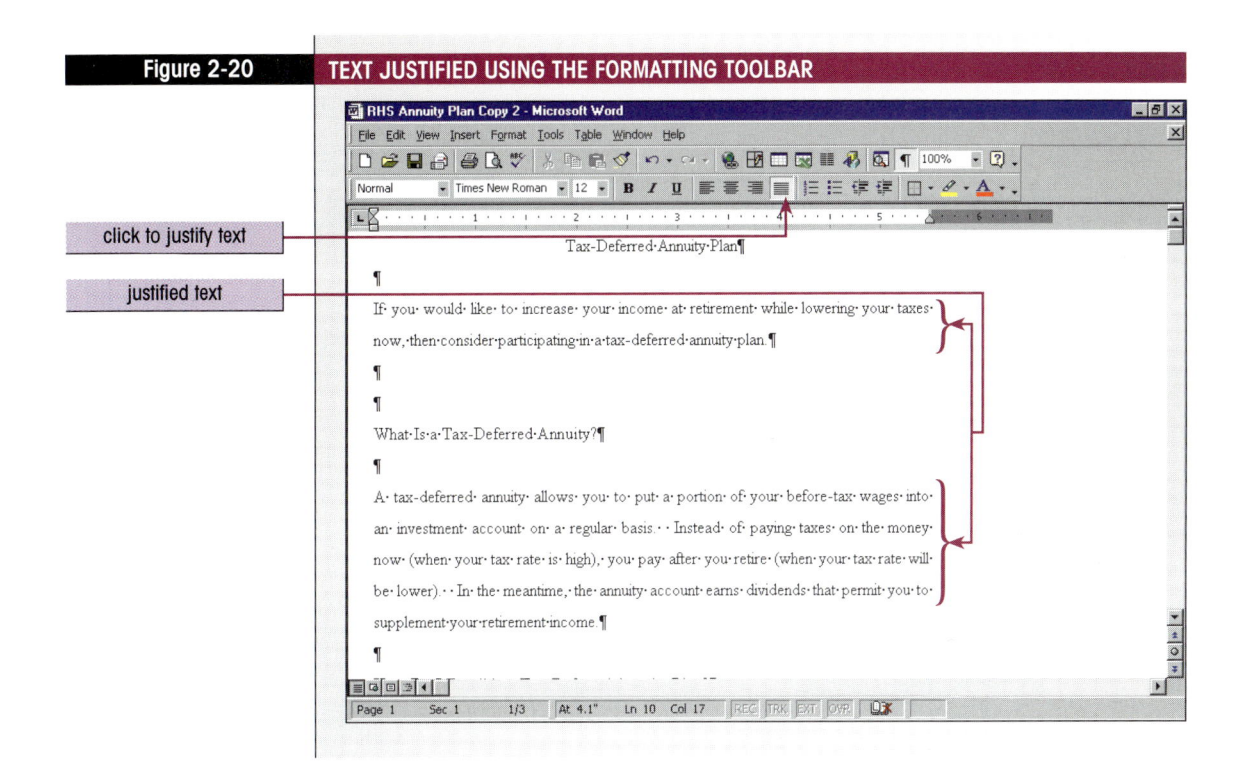

You'll justify the other paragraphs later. Now that you've learned how to change the paragraph alignment, you can turn your attention to indenting a paragraph.

Indenting a Paragraph

When you become a more experienced Word user, you might want to use some special forms of paragraph formatting, such as a **hanging indent** (where all lines except the first line of the paragraph are indented from the left margin) or a **right indent** (where all lines of the paragraph are indented from the right margin). You can select these types of indents on the Indents and Spacing tab of the Paragraph dialog box.

In this document, though, you'll need to indent only the main paragraphs 0.5 inches from the left margin. This left indent is a simple kind of paragraph indent, which requires only a quick click on the Formatting toolbar's Increase Indent button. According to Brandi's notes, you need to indent all of the main paragraphs, starting with the second paragraph.

To indent a paragraph using the Increase Indent button:

1. Make sure the insertion point is still located anywhere within the second paragraph, which begins "A tax-deferred annuity allows... ."

2. Click the **Increase Indent** button 🔲 on the Formatting toolbar twice. (Don't click the Decrease Indent button by mistake.) The entire paragraph moves right 0.5 inches each time you click the Increase Indent button. The paragraph is indented 1 inch, 0.5 inches more than Brandi wants.

3. Click the **Decrease Indent** button 🔲 on the Formatting toolbar to move the paragraph left 0.5 inches. The paragraph is now indented 0.5 inches from the left margin, as shown in Figure 2-21.

Figure 2-21: INDENTED PARAGRAPH

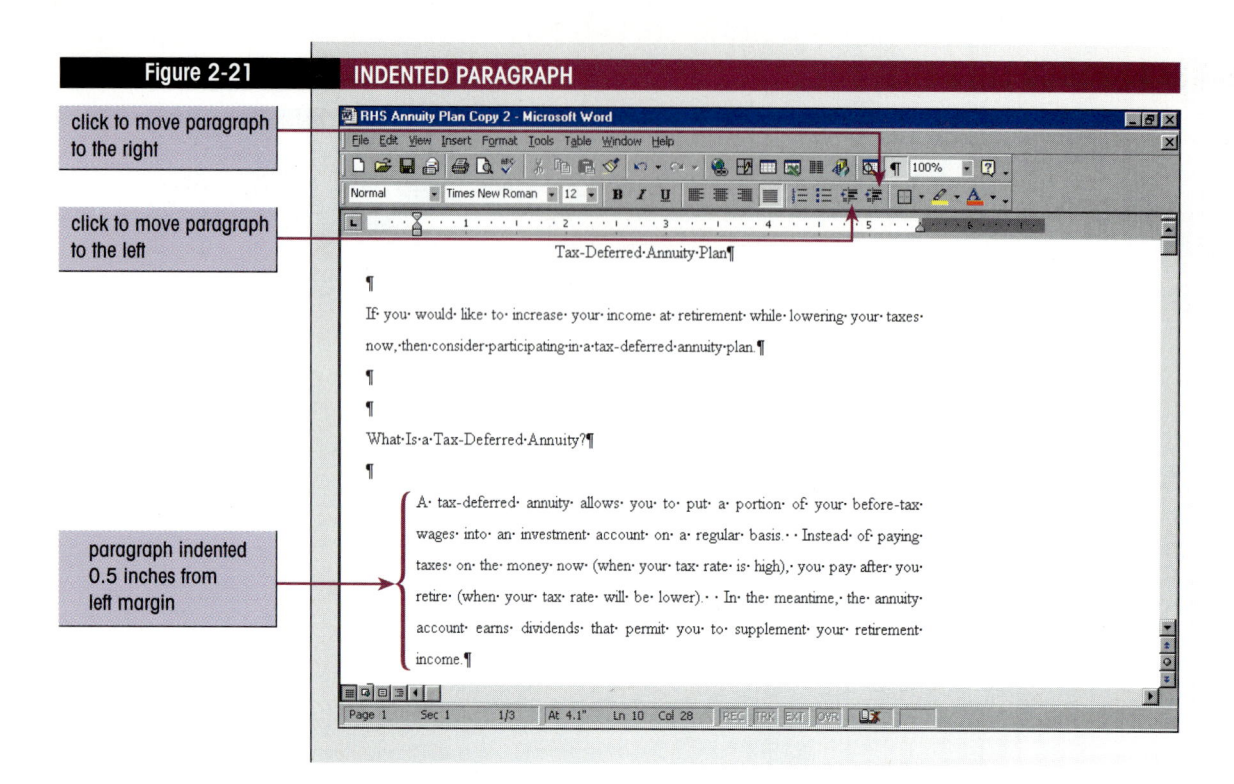

- click to move paragraph to the right
- click to move paragraph to the left
- paragraph indented 0.5 inches from left margin

You could continue to indent, and then justify, each paragraph individually, but there's an easier way—the Format Painter command. The Format Painter allows you to copy both the indentation and alignment changes to all the other main paragraphs in the document.

Using Format Painter

The **Format Painter** makes it easy to copy all the formatting features of one paragraph to one or more other paragraphs. You'll use the Format Painter now to copy the formatting of the second paragraph to other main paragraphs. Begin by highlighting the paragraph whose format you want to copy. (Note that you can't simply move the insertion point to that paragraph.)

To copy paragraph formatting with the Format Painter:

1. Double-click in the selection bar to select the second paragraph, which is indented and justified and begins "A tax-deferred annuity... ."

2. Double-click the **Format Painter** button on the Standard toolbar. The Format Painter button will stay pressed until you click the button again. When you move the pointer over text, the pointer changes to indicate that the format of the selected paragraph can be painted (or copied) onto another paragraph.

3. Scroll down, and then click anywhere in the third paragraph, which begins "As a full-time employee... ." The format of the third paragraph shifts to match the format of the selected paragraph. See Figure 2-22. As you can see, both paragraphs are now indented and justified. The pointer remains as the Format Painter pointer.

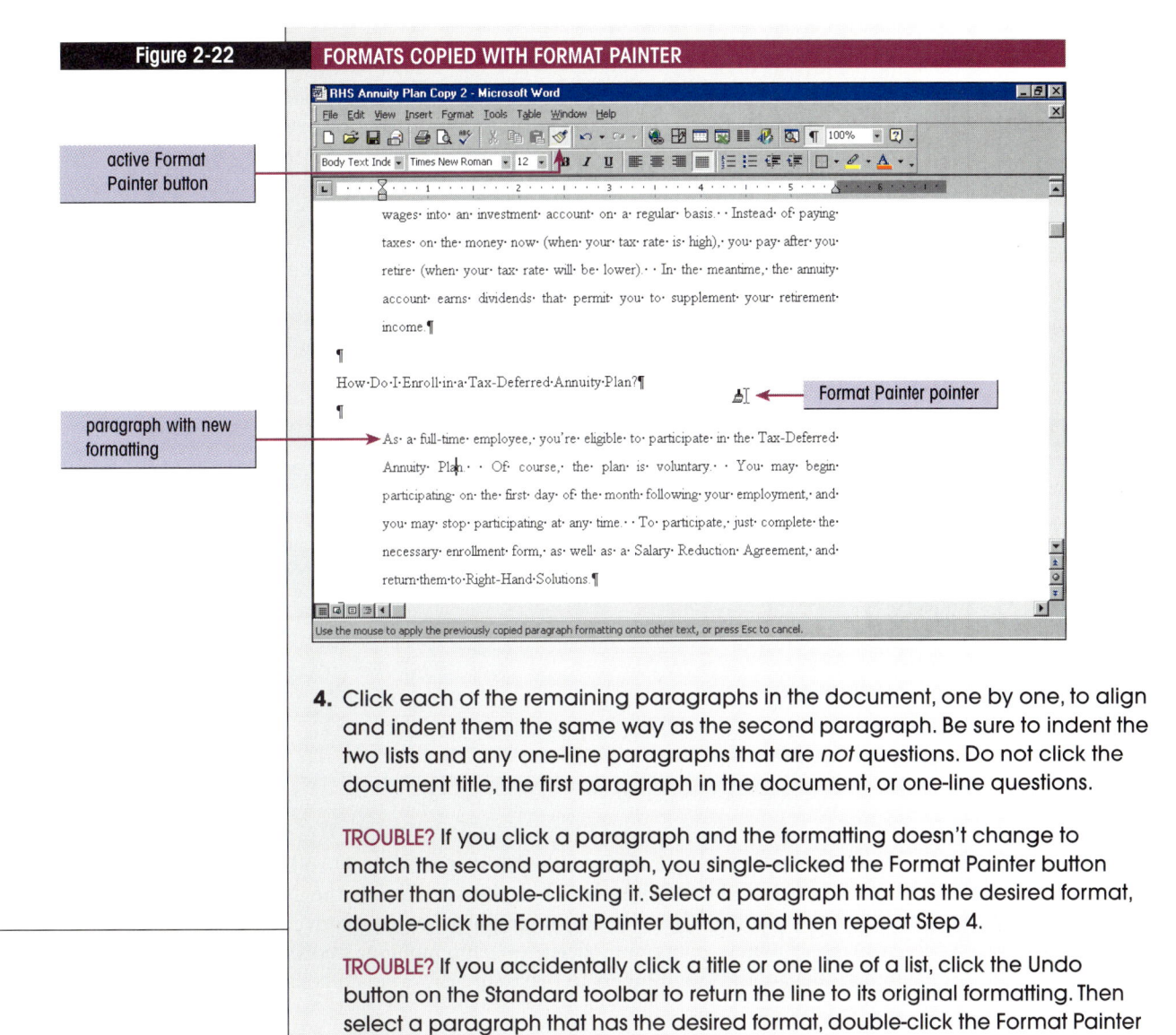

TUTORIAL 2 EDITING AND FORMATTING A DOCUMENT   WD 2.25   WORD

Figure 2-22 **FORMATS COPIED WITH FORMAT PAINTER**

- active Format Painter button
- Format Painter pointer
- paragraph with new formatting

4. Click each of the remaining paragraphs in the document, one by one, to align and indent them the same way as the second paragraph. Be sure to indent the two lists and any one-line paragraphs that are *not* questions. Do not click the document title, the first paragraph in the document, or one-line questions.

   TROUBLE? If you click a paragraph and the formatting doesn't change to match the second paragraph, you single-clicked the Format Painter button rather than double-clicking it. Select a paragraph that has the desired format, double-click the Format Painter button, and then repeat Step 4.

   TROUBLE? If you accidentally click a title or one line of a list, click the Undo button on the Standard toolbar to return the line to its original formatting. Then select a paragraph that has the desired format, double-click the Format Painter button, and finish copying the format to the main paragraphs in the document.

5. After you've formatted all the main paragraphs with the Format Painter, click ✍ to turn off the feature.

6. Click the **Save** button 🖫 on the Standard toolbar.

All the main paragraphs in the document are formatted with the correct indentation and alignment. Your next job is to make the lists easier to read by adding bullets and numbers.

Adding Bullets and Numbers

You can emphasize a list of items by adding a heavy dot, known as a **bullet**, before each item in the list. For consecutive items, you can use numbers instead of bullets. Brandi requested that you add bullets to the list of financial needs on page 3 to make them stand out.

To apply bullets to a list of items:

1. Scroll the document until you see the list of financial needs below the sentence "The following are considered to be immediate and severe financial needs."
2. Select the four items that appear in the middle of page 3 (from "medical expenses" to "Internal Revenue Service").
3. Click the **Bullets** button on the Formatting toolbar to activate the Bullets feature. A rounded bullet, a special character, appears in front of each item, and each line indents to make room for the bullet.
4. Click anywhere within the document window to deselect the text. Figure 2-23 shows the indented bulleted list.

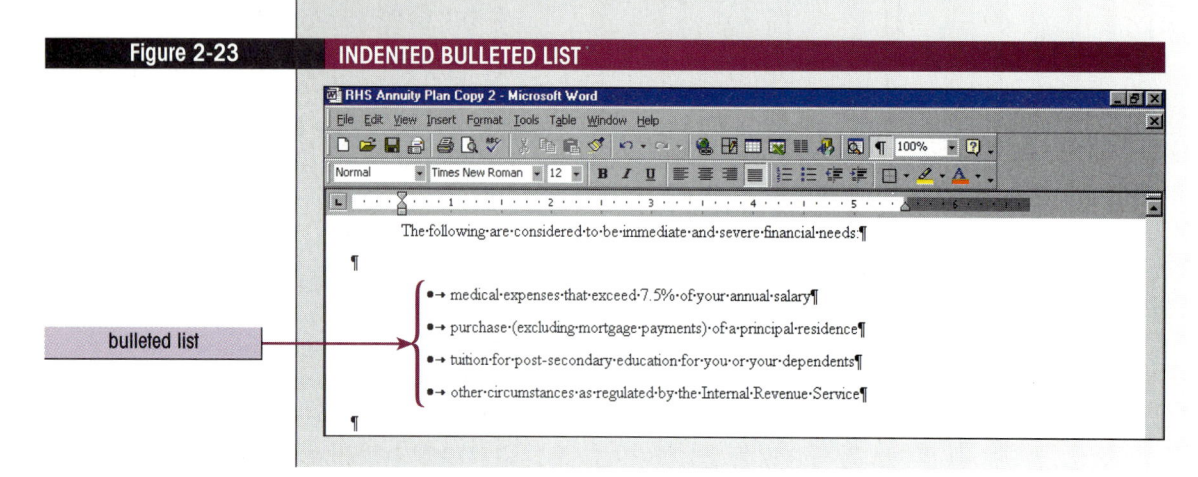

Figure 2-23   INDENTED BULLETED LIST

bulleted list

The following are considered to be immediate and severe financial needs.

- medical expenses that exceed 7.5% of your annual salary
- purchase (excluding mortgage payments) of a principal residence
- tuition for post-secondary education for you or your dependents
- other circumstances as regulated by the Internal Revenue Service

Next you need to add numbers to the list that explains when benefits can be received, in the section below the bulleted list. For this, you'll use the Numbering button, which automatically numbers the selected paragraphs with consecutive numbers and aligns them. If you insert a new paragraph, delete a paragraph, or reorder the paragraphs, Word automatically adjusts the numbers to make sure they remain consecutive.

To apply numbers to the list of items:

1. Scroll down to the next section, and then select the list that begins "reach the age..." and ends with "...become disabled."
2. Click the **Numbering** button on the Formatting toolbar. Consecutive numbers appear in front of each item in the indented list. The list is indented, similar to the bulleted list above.
3. Click anywhere in the document to deselect the text. Figure 2-24 shows the indented and numbered list.

Figure 2-24 | **INDENTED NUMBERED LIST**

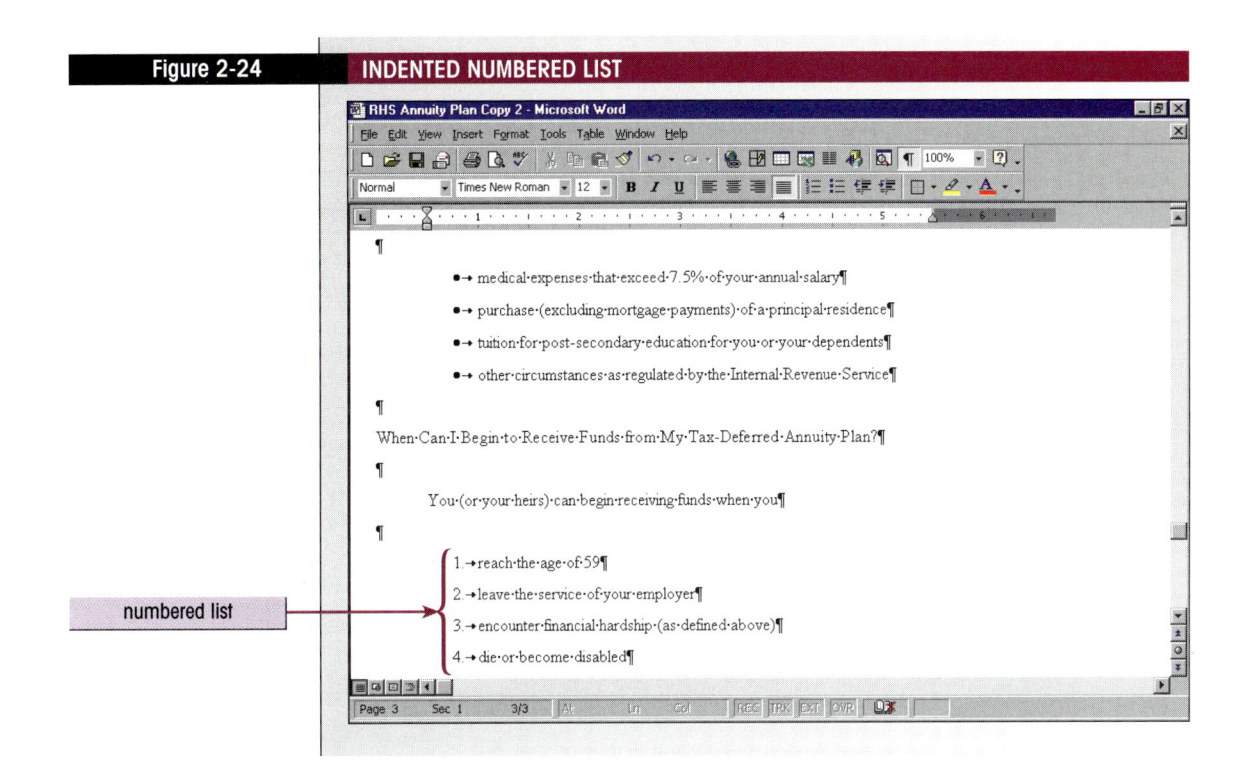

[Screenshot of Microsoft Word document showing:]

- medical expenses that exceed 7.5% of your annual salary
- purchase (excluding mortgage payments) of a principal residence
- tuition for post-secondary education for you or your dependents
- other circumstances as regulated by the Internal Revenue Service

When Can I Begin to Receive Funds from My Tax-Deferred Annuity Plan?

You (or your heirs) can begin receiving funds when you

1. reach the age of 59
2. leave the service of your employer
3. encounter financial hardship (as defined above)
4. die or become disabled

[label: numbered list]

The text of the document is now properly aligned and indented. The bullets and numbers make the lists easy to read and give readers visual clues about the type of information they contain. Next, you need to adjust the formatting of individual words.

Changing the Font and Font Size

All of Brandi's remaining changes concern changing fonts, adjusting font sizes, and emphasizing text with font styles. The first step is to change the font of the title from 12-point Times New Roman to 14-point Arial. This will make the title stand out from the rest of the text.

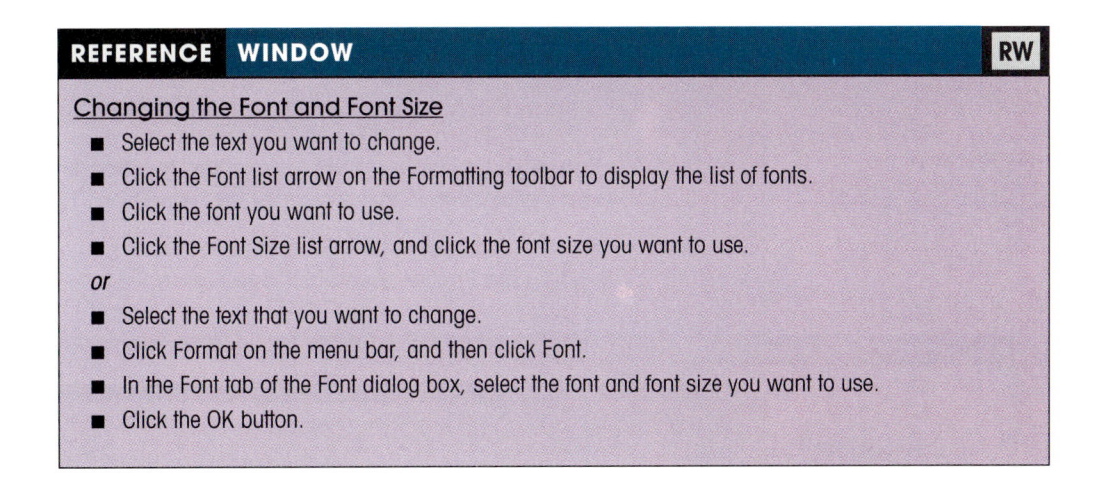

REFERENCE WINDOW | **RW**

Changing the Font and Font Size
- Select the text you want to change.
- Click the Font list arrow on the Formatting toolbar to display the list of fonts.
- Click the font you want to use.
- Click the Font Size list arrow, and click the font size you want to use.

or

- Select the text that you want to change.
- Click Format on the menu bar, and then click Font.
- In the Font tab of the Font dialog box, select the font and font size you want to use.
- Click the OK button.

Brandi wants you to change the font of the title as well as its size and style. To do this, you'll use the Formatting toolbar. Brandi wants you to use a **sans serif** font, which is a font that does not have the small horizontal lines (called serifs) at the tops and bottoms of the letters. Sans serif fonts are often used in titles so they contrast with the body text. Times New Roman is a serif font, and Arial is a sans serif font. The text you are reading now is a serif font, and the text in the steps below is a sans serif font.

To change the attributes of the title using the Font command:

1. Press **Ctrl+Home** to move to the beginning of the document, and then select the title.

2. Click the **Font** list arrow on the Formatting toolbar. A list of available fonts appears in alphabetical order, with the name of the current font highlighted in the font list and in the Font text box. See Figure 2-25. (Your list of fonts might be different from those shown.) Fonts that have been used recently might appear above a double line. Note that each name in the list is formatted with that font. For example, "Arial" appears in the Arial font, and "Times New Roman" appears in the Times New Roman font.

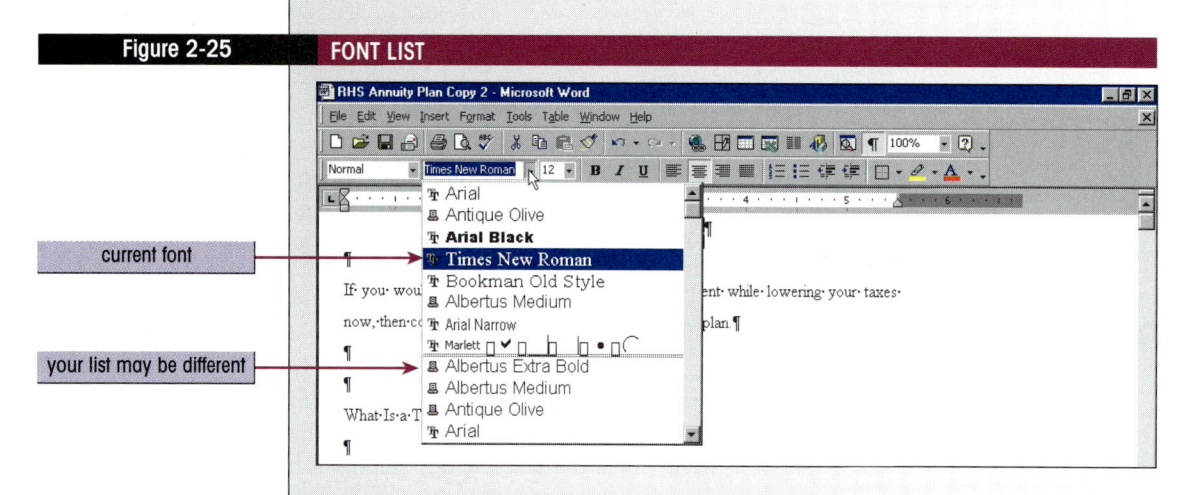

Figure 2-25   FONT LIST

- current font
- your list may be different

3. If necessary, scroll the list box until Arial appears, and then click **Arial** to select it as the new font. As you click, watch the font in the title change to reflect the new font.

   TROUBLE? If Arial doesn't appear in the font list, use another sans serif font.

4. Click the **Font Size** list arrow on the Formatting toolbar, and then click **14** in the size list. As you click, watch the title's font increase from 12 to 14 point.

5. Click the **Save** button on the Standard toolbar to save your changes, and then click within the title to deselect it. See Figure 2-26.

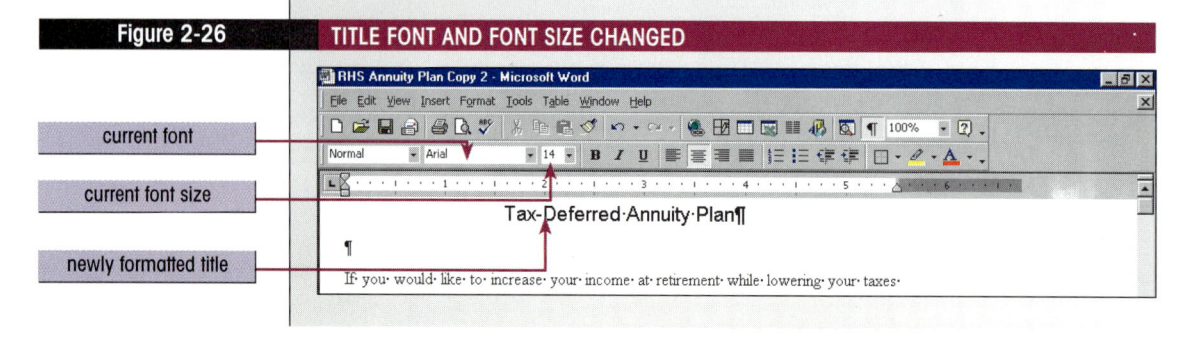

Figure 2-26   TITLE FONT AND FONT SIZE CHANGED

- current font
- current font size
- newly formatted title

TUTORIAL 2 EDITING AND FORMATTING A DOCUMENT WD 2.29 WORD

> **TROUBLE?** If your font and font size settings don't match those in Figure 2-26, you may not have selected the title. Select the title, view the font and font size settings displayed on the Formatting toolbar, and then make the necessary changes. Because of differences in fonts and monitors, the characters in your document might look different from the figure.

Emphasizing Text with Boldface, Underlining, and Italics

You can emphasize words in your document with boldface, underlining, or italics. These styles help you make specific thoughts, ideas, words, or phrases stand out. Brandi marked a few words on the document draft (shown in Figure 2-1) that need this kind of special emphasis. You add boldface, underlining, or italics by using the relevant buttons on the Formatting toolbar. Note that these buttons are toggle buttons, which means you can click them once to format the selected text, and then click again to remove the formatting from the selected text.

Bolding Text

Brandi wants to make sure that clients' employees see that the tax-deferred annuity plan can be terminated only under certain conditions. You will do this by bolding the word "only."

To change the font style to boldface:

1. Scroll down so you can view the first line of the paragraph beneath the question "Can My Tax-Deferred Annuity Plan Be Terminated?" on page 2.

2. Select the word "only" (immediately after the word "terminated").

3. Click the **Bold** button [B] on the Formatting toolbar, and then click anywhere in the document to deselect the text. The word appears in bold, as shown in Figure 2-27. After reviewing this change, you wonder if the word would look better without boldface. As you will see in the next step, you can easily remove the boldface by selecting the text and clicking the Bold button again to turn off boldfacing.

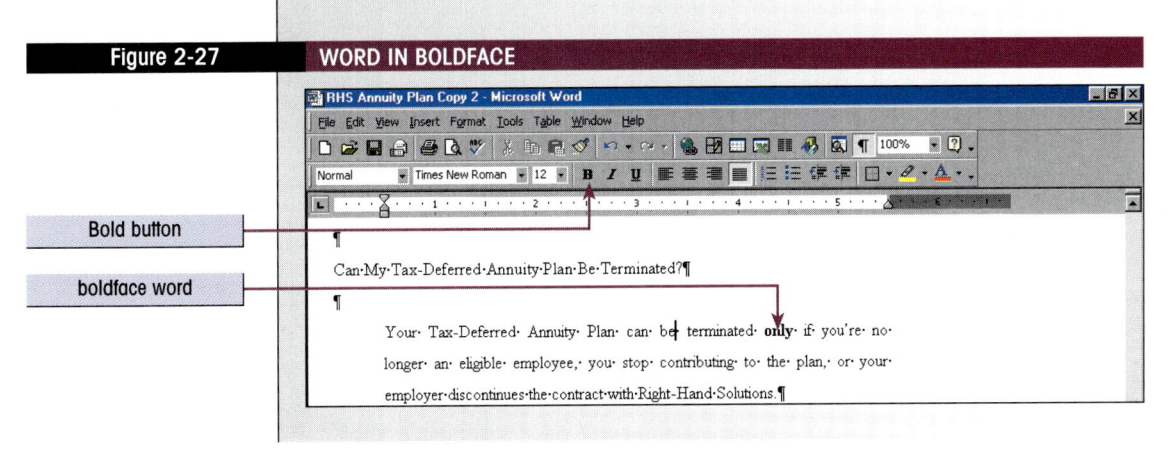

Figure 2-27 **WORD IN BOLDFACE**

Bold button

boldface word

4. Double-click the word **only** to select it, then click [B]. The word now appears without boldface. You decide you prefer to emphasize the word with boldface after all.

5. Verify that the word "only" is still selected, and then click [B]. The word appears in boldface again.

Underlining Text

The Underline command works in the same way as the Bold command. Brandi's edits indicate that the word "Note" should be inserted and underlined at the beginning of the final paragraph. You'll make both of these changes at once using the Underline command.

To underline text:

1. Press **Ctrl+End** to move the insertion point to the end of the document. Then move the insertion point to the left of the word "Get" in the first line of the final paragraph.

2. Click the **Underline** button [U] on the Formatting toolbar to turn on underlining. Notice that the Underline button remains pressed. Now, whatever text you type will be underlined on your screen and in your printed document.

3. Type **Note:** and then click [U] to turn off underlining. Notice that the Underline button is no longer pressed, and "Note:" is underlined.

4. Press the **spacebar** twice. See Figure 2-28.

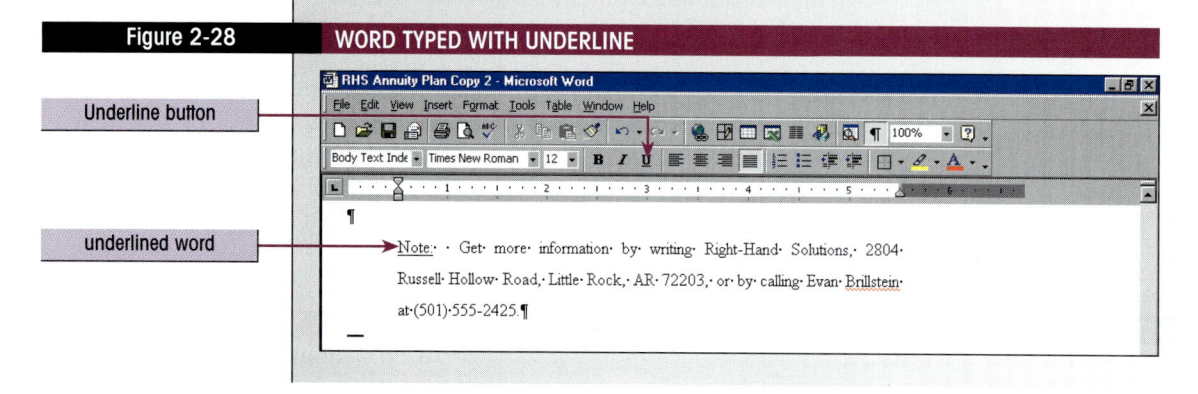

Figure 2-28   WORD TYPED WITH UNDERLINE

- Underline button
- underlined word

Italicizing Text

Next, you'll make the annuity plan conform with the other documents that Right-Hand Solutions produces by changing each question (heading) in the document to italics. This makes the document easier to read by clearly separating the sections. You'll begin with the first heading.

To italicize the question headings:

1. Press **Ctrl+Home** to return to the beginning of the document, and then select the text of the first heading, "What Is a Tax-Deferred Annuity?," by triple-clicking the text.

2. Click the **Italic** button *I* on the Formatting toolbar. The heading changes from regular to italic text.

3. Repeat Steps 1 and 2 to italicize the next heading. Now try a shorter way to italicize the text by repeating the formatting you just applied.

4. Select the next heading, and then press the **F4** key. Repeat for each of the remaining four questions (headings) in the document. The italicized headings stand out from the rest of the text and help give the document a visual structure.

Saving and Printing

You have made all the editing and formatting changes that Brandi requested for the annuity plan description. When a document is complete, it's a good idea to save it with a name that indicates that it is final. After saving the document, you can preview and print it. It's especially useful to preview a document before printing when you made a number of formatting changes because the Print Preview window makes it easy to spot text that is not aligned correctly.

To save, preview, and print the document:

1. Click **File** on the menu bar, and then click **Save As**. Save the file as **RHS Annuity Plan Final Copy** in the Tutorial subfolder, within the Tutorial.02 folder.

2. Move the insertion point to the beginning of the document.

3. Click the **Print Preview** button on the Standard toolbar, and examine the first page of the document. Use the vertical scroll bar to display the second and third pages. (If you notice any headings as the last line of a page or other formatting errors, click the Close button on the Print Preview toolbar, correct the errors in normal view, and then return to the Print Preview window. To move a heading to the next page with its paragraph, click at the beginning of the heading and press **Ctrl+Enter** to insert a manual page break.)

4. Click the **Print** button on the Print Preview toolbar. After a pause, the document prints.

5. Click the **Close** button on the Print Preview toolbar, and then click the **Close** button on the program window to close your document and exit Word.

You now have a hardcopy of the final annuity plan description, as shown in Figure 2-29.

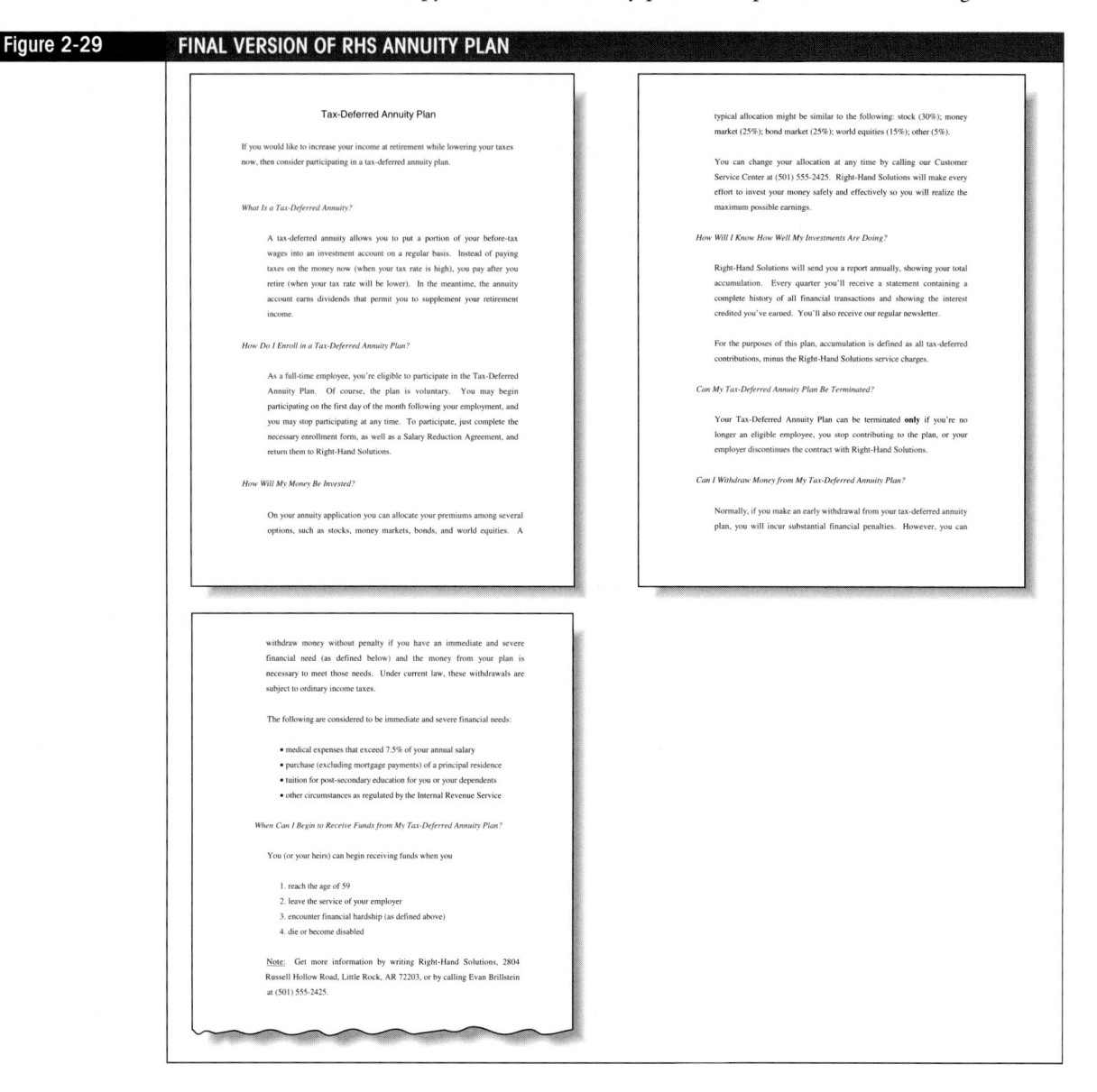

Figure 2-29　FINAL VERSION OF RHS ANNUITY PLAN

In this tutorial, you have helped Reginald plan, edit, and format the annuity plan that will appear in the employee handbooks of Right-Hand Solutions' clients. Now that you have fine-tuned the content, adjusted the text appearance and alignment, and added a bulleted list and a numbered list, the plan is visually appealing and easy to read.

You give the hardcopy to Reginald, who makes two photocopies—one for Brandi and one for the copy center, which copies and distributes the document to all clients of Right-Hand Solutions.

Session 2.2 Quick Check

1. What are Word's default margins for the left and right margins? For the top and bottom margins?
2. Describe the four types of text alignment.
3. Explain how to indent a paragraph 1 inch or more from the left margin.
4. Describe a situation in which you would use the Format Painter.
5. Explain how to add underlining to a word as you type it.
6. Explain how to transform a series of short paragraphs into a numbered list.

7. Explain how to format a title in 14-point Arial.
8. Describe the steps involved in changing the line spacing in a document.

REVIEW ASSIGNMENTS

Now that you have completed the description of the annuity plan, Brandi explains that she also wants to include a sample quarterly statement and a sample contract change notice in the client's employee handbooks to show employees how easy the statements are to read. You'll open and format this document now.

1. If necessary, start Word, make sure your Data Disk is in the appropriate disk drive, and check your screen to make sure your settings match those in the tutorial.
2. Open the file **RHSQuart** from the Review folder for Tutorial 2 on your Data Disk, and save the document as **RHS Quarterly Report**.
3. Use the Spelling and Grammar checker to correct any spelling or grammatical errors. If the Suggestions list box does not include the correct replacement, click outside the Spelling and Grammar dialog box, type the correction yourself, click Resume in the Spelling and Grammar dialog box, and continue checking the document. After you finish using the Spelling and Grammar checker, proofread the document carefully to check for any additional errors, especially words that are spelled correctly but used improperly. Pay special attention to the second main paragraph of the letter.
4. Make all edits and formatting changes marked on Figure 2-30. To substitute "Right-Hand Solutions" for "We" in the first paragraph, copy the company name from the top of the letter (without the paragraph mark) and paste it into the first paragraph as marked. (Copy and paste this text *before* you format it in Arial 14 point.)

Figure 2-30

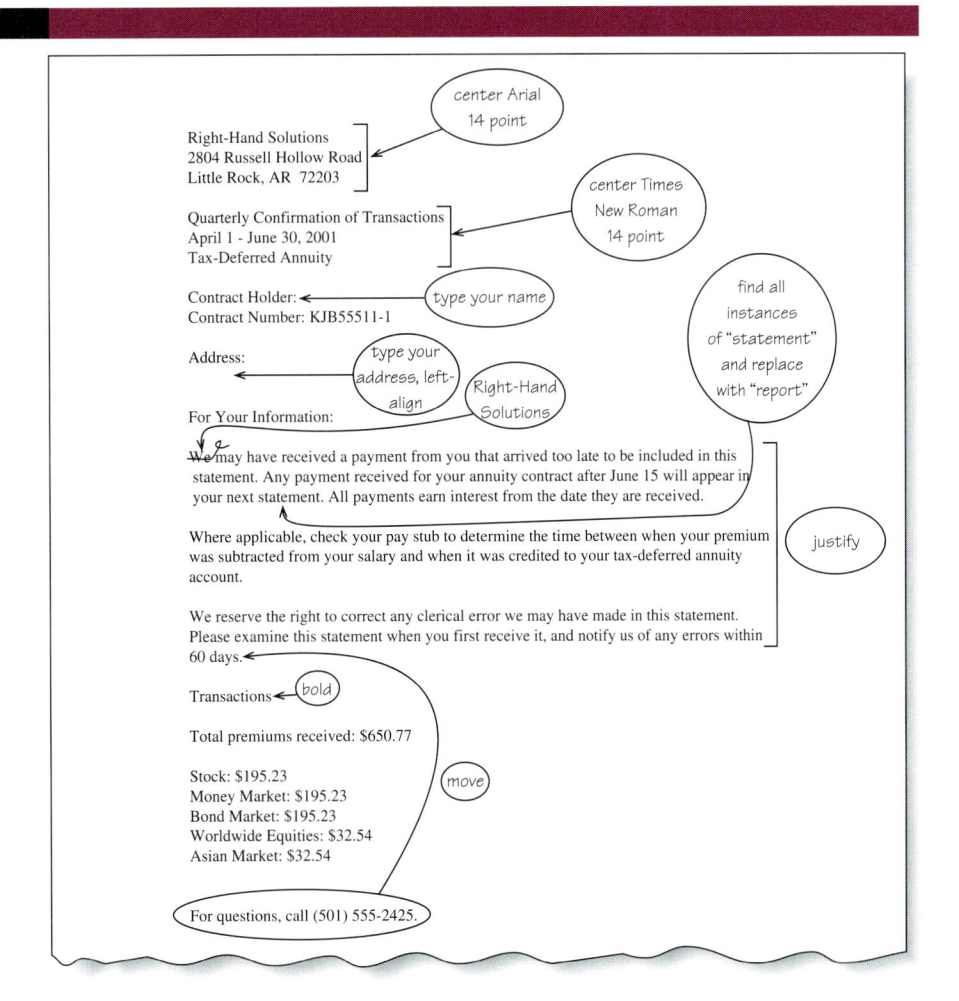

Right-Hand Solutions
2804 Russell Hollow Road
Little Rock, AR 72203

(center Arial 14 point)

Quarterly Confirmation of Transactions
April 1 - June 30, 2001
Tax-Deferred Annuity

(center Times New Roman 14 point)

Contract Holder: *(type your name)*
Contract Number: KJB55511-1

Address: *(type your address, left-align)*

(Right-Hand Solutions)

For Your Information:

(find all instances of "statement" and replace with "report")

~~We~~ may have received a payment from you that arrived too late to be included in this statement. Any payment received for your annuity contract after June 15 will appear in your next statement. All payments earn interest from the date they are received.

Where applicable, check your pay stub to determine the time between when your premium was subtracted from your salary and when it was credited to your tax-deferred annuity account.

(justify)

We reserve the right to correct any clerical error we may have made in this statement. Please examine this statement when you first receive it, and notify us of any errors within 60 days.

Transactions *(bold)*

Total premiums received: $650.77

Stock: $195.23
Money Market: $195.23
Bond Market: $195.23
Worldwide Equities: $32.54
Asian Market: $32.54

(move)

For questions, call (501) 555-2425.

5. Save the document, preview it, and then print it.
6. Close th document.
7. Open the file **RHSPort** from the Review folder for Tutorial 2 on your Data Disk, and save the file as **RHS Portfolio Changes**.

Explore

8. Make all the edits and formatting changes marked on Figure 2-31. However, instead of using the Formatting toolbar to change Current Allocation Accounts to underline 14 point, click Format on the menu bar, and then click Font to open the Font dialog box. Click the appropriate selections in the Underline style and Size list boxes. Notice that you should only replace "Right-Hand Solutions" with "RHS" in the list of Allocation Accounts. To skip an instance of "Right-Hand Solutions" without changing it, click the Find Next button in the Find and Replace dialog box.

Figure 2-31

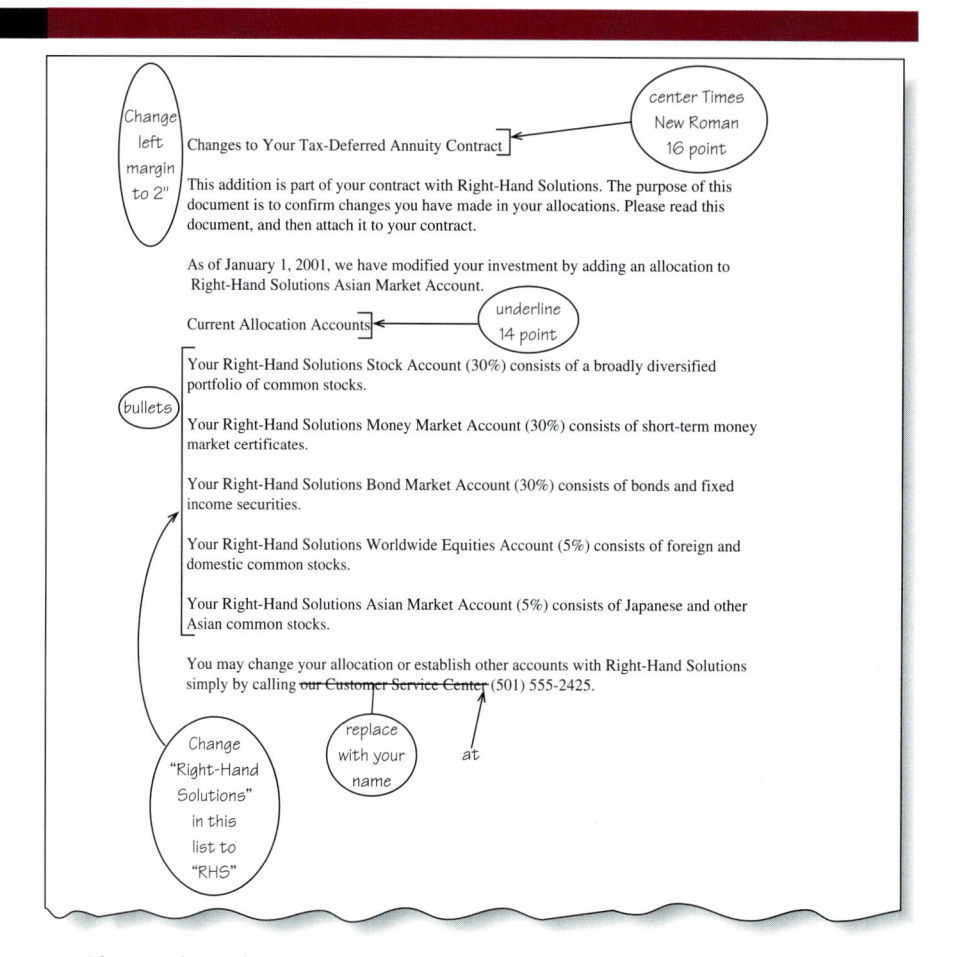

Change left margin to 2"

Changes to Your Tax-Deferred Annuity Contract — *center Times New Roman 16 point*

This addition is part of your contract with Right-Hand Solutions. The purpose of this document is to confirm changes you have made in your allocations. Please read this document, and then attach it to your contract.

As of January 1, 2001, we have modified your investment by adding an allocation to Right-Hand Solutions Asian Market Account.

Current Allocation Accounts — *underline 14 point*

bullets

Your Right-Hand Solutions Stock Account (30%) consists of a broadly diversified portfolio of common stocks.

Your Right-Hand Solutions Money Market Account (30%) consists of short-term money market certificates.

Your Right-Hand Solutions Bond Market Account (30%) consists of bonds and fixed income securities.

Your Right-Hand Solutions Worldwide Equities Account (5%) consists of foreign and domestic common stocks.

Your Right-Hand Solutions Asian Market Account (5%) consists of Japanese and other Asian common stocks.

You may change your allocation or establish other accounts with Right-Hand Solutions simply by calling ~~our Customer Service Center~~ (501) 555-2425.

Change "Right-Hand Solutions" in this list to "RHS" *replace with your name* *at*

Explore

9. Change the right margin using the ruler in print layout view:
    a. Click the Print Layout View button, and then select the entire document.
    b. Position the pointer on the ruler at the right margin, above the Right Indent marker (a small, gray triangle).
    c. Press and hold down the mouse button. A dotted line appears in the document window, indicating the current right margin. Drag the margin left to the 5-inch mark on the ruler, and then release the mouse button.
    d. Click the Normal View button to return to normal view.
    e. Save the document.

Explore

10. Change the line spacing of individual paragraphs within the document.
    a. Select the first two paragraphs in the document, immediately under the heading "Changes to Your Tax-Deferred Annuity Contract."
    b. Press Ctrl+5 to change the line spacing of the selected paragraphs to 1.5 line spacing.
    c. Save the document.

11. Cut and paste text using the Clipboard:
    a. Select the second sentence in the document ("The purpose of this document is to confirm…"), and then click the Cut button on the Standard toolbar to remove the sentence from the document. If the Clipboard toolbar appears, leave it open while you continue with the next step.
    b. Select the last sentence in the document ("You may change your allocation…"), and then click the Cut button on the Standard toolbar to remove the sentence from the document. If the Clipboard toolbar did not open at the end of the previous step, it should be open now.
    c. Move the insertion point to the beginning of the first sentence, to the left of the "T" in "This addition is part of your contract… ." Move the pointer over the icons on the Clipboard toolbar, until you find one labeled "The purpose of this document is to confirm… ." Click that icon to insert the sentence (which was originally the second sentence in the document) at the insertion point. Insert an extra space, if necessary.
    d. Repeat the previous step to insert the sentence beginning, "You may change your allocation or establish other…" at the end of the second paragraph.
    e. Click the Clear Clipboard button on the Clipboard toolbar to erase the contents of the Clipboard, and then click the Close button to close the Clipboard toolbar.
12. Click the Print Preview button on the Standard toolbar to check your work.

Explore 13. Use the Print command on the File menu to open the Print dialog box. Print two copies of the document by changing the Number of copies setting in the Print dialog box.

Explore 14. You can find out the number of words in your documents by using the Word Count command on the Tools menu. Use this command to determine the number of words in the document, and then write that number in the upper-right corner of one of the printouts.

15. Save and close the document.

CASE PROBLEMS

Case 1. Store-It-All Katie Strainchamps manages Store-It-All, a storage facility in Huntsville, Alabama. She has written the draft of a tenant-information sheet outlining Store-It-All's policies for new customers. She asks you to edit and format the document for her.

1. If necessary, start Word, make sure your Data Disk is in the appropriate disk drive, and check your screen to make sure your settings match those in the tutorials.
2. Open the file **Store** from the Tutorial 2 Cases folder on your Data Disk, and save it as **Store-It-All Policies**.
3. Use the Spelling and Grammar checker to correct any errors in the document. Then proofread the document to check for errors the Spelling and Grammar checker missed. Pay particular attention to the paragraph under "Rental Payments" and the company name throughout the document.
4. Delete the word "basic" from the first sentence of the first full paragraph. (Remember to use the Undo and Redo buttons as you work to correct any editing mistakes.)
5. Delete the second sentence in the second paragraph, which begins "You renew your contract… ."
6. Insert the bolded sentence "A bill will not be sent to you." before the first sentence under the heading "Rental Payments."
7. Under the heading "Insurance," delete the sentence in parentheses and the extra paragraph mark.
8. Change all of the margins (top, bottom, left, and right) to 1.75 inches.
9. For each paragraph following a heading, set the alignment to justify. (*Hint:* Format the first paragraph and then use the Format Painter to format each successive paragraph.)
10. Find the phrase "not negotiable" using the Find command and italicize it.
11. Indent the four-item list under the heading "Delinquent Accounts" 0.5-inch and add bullets.
12. Change both lines of the title to 14-point Arial (or another sans serif font of your choice).
13. Center and bold both lines of the title.
14. Underline all of the headings.

15. Insert two blank lines at the end of the document, and then type the following, making sure to replace "*your name*" with your first and last name: Direct all questions to *your name* in the main office.
16. Save, preview, and print the rental information sheet, and close the document.

Case 2. UpTime Matt Patterson is UpTime's marketing director for the Northeast region. The company provides productivity training for large companies across the country. Matt wants to provide interested clients with a one-page summary of UpTime's productivity training.

1. If necessary, start Word, make sure your Data Disk is in the appropriate disk drive, and check your screen to make sure your settings match those in the tutorials.
2. Open the file **UpTime** from the Tutorial 2 Cases folder on your Data Disk, and save it as **UpTime Training Summary**.
3. Change the title at the beginning of the document to a 16-point serif font other than Times New Roman. Be sure to pick a font that looks professional and is easy to read. (Remember to use the Undo and Redo buttons as you work to correct any editing mistakes.)
4. Center and bold the title.
5. Delete the word "general" from the second sentence of the first paragraph after the document title.
6. Convert the list of training components following the first paragraph to an indented, numbered list.
7. Under the heading "Personal Productivity Training Seminar," delete the third sentence from the first paragraph.
8. Under the heading "Personal Productivity Training Seminar," delete the phrase "at the seminar" from the first sentence in the second paragraph.
9. In the first paragraph under the heading "Management Productivity Training," move the first sentence (beginning with "UpTime provides management training...") to the end of the paragraph.
10. Switch the order of the first and second paragraphs under the "Field Services Technology and Training" heading.
11. Search for the text "your name," and replace it with your first and last name.
12. Change the top margin to 1.5 inches.
13. Change the left margin to 1.75 inches.
14. Bold each of the headings.
15. Italicize both occurrences of the word "free" in the second paragraph under the "Field Services Technology and Training" heading.
16. Save and preview the document.
17. Print the document, and then close the file.

Case 3. Ridge Top Thomas McGee is vice president of sales and marketing at Ridge Top, an outdoor and sporting-gear store in Conshohocken, Pennsylvania. Each year, Thomas and his staff mail a description of new products to Ridge Top's regular customers. Ralph has asked you to edit and format the first few pages of this year's new products' description.

1. If necessary, start Word, make sure your Data Disk is in the appropriate disk drive, and check your screen to make sure your settings match those in the tutorials.
2. Open the file **Ridge** from the Tutorial 2 Cases folder on your Data Disk, and save it as **Ridge Top Guide**.
3. Use the Spelling and Grammar checker to correct any errors in the document. Because of the nature of this document, it contains some words that the Word dictionary on your computer may not recognize. It also contains headings that the Spelling and Grammar checker may consider sentence fragments. As you use the Spelling and Grammar checker, use the Ignore All button, if necessary, to skip over brand names. Use the Ignore Rule button to skip over sentence fragments.

4. Delete the phrase "a great deal" from the first sentence of the paragraph below the heading "Snuggle Up to These Prices." (Remember to use the Undo and Redo buttons to correct any editing mistakes as you work.)
5. Reverse the order of the first two paragraphs under the heading, "You'll Eat Up the Prices of This Camp Cooking Gear!"
6. Cut the last sentence of the first full paragraph ("Prices are good through...") from the document. Then move the insertion point to the end of the document, press the Enter key twice, and insert the cut sentence as a new paragraph. Format it in 12-point Arial, and italicize it.
7. Format the Ridge Top tip items as a numbered list.

Explore
8. Reorder the items under the "Ridge Top Tips!" heading by moving the fourth product idea and the following paragraph to the top of the list.
9. Search for the text "your name," and replace with your first and last name.

Explore
10. Experiment with two special paragraph alignment options: first line and hanging. First, select everything from the heading "Ridge Top Guarantees Warmth at Cool Prices" through the paragraph just before the heading "Ridge Top Tips." Next, click Format on the menu bar, click Paragraph, click Indents and Spacing tab, click the Help button in the upper-right corner of the dialog box, click the Special list arrow, and review the information on the special alignment options. Experiment with both the First line and the Hanging options. When you are finished, return the document to its original format by choosing the none option.
11. Justify all the paragraphs in the document. (*Hint:* To select all paragraphs in the document at one time, click Edit on the menu bar, and then click Select All.)
12. Replace all occurrences of "RidgeTop" with "Ridge Top."
13. Apply a 12-point, bold, sans serif font to each of the headings. Be sure to pick a font that looks professional and is easy to read. (*Hint:* Use the Format Painter.)
14. Change the title's font to the same font you used for the headings, except set the size to 16 point.
15. Bold both lines of the title.
16. Underline the names and prices for all of the brandname products in the Trekker's Guide. Make sure you don't underline spaces or periods. (*Hint:* Use the Words only underline style option in the Font dialog box.)
17. Save and preview the document. Print the document, and then close the file.

Case 4. Restaurant Review Your student newspaper has asked you to review four restaurants in your area.
1. If necessary, start Word, make sure your Data Disk is in the appropriate disk drive, and check your screen to make sure your settings match those in the tutorials.
2. Write a brief summary (one to two paragraphs) for each restaurant and provide a rating for each one. Correct any spelling or grammatical errors.
3. Add a title and subtitle to your review. The subtitle should include your name.
4. Save the document as **Restaurant Review** in the Tutorial 2 Cases folder on your Data Disk, and print it.
5. Rearrange the order in which you discuss the restaurants to alphabetical order. (Remember to use the Undo and Redo buttons as you work to correct any editing mistakes.)
6. Change the top margin to 2 inches.
7. Change the left margin to 1.75 inches.
8. Center and bold the title and subtitle.
9. Change the paragraph alignment to justify.
10. Italicize the title of each restaurant.
11. Save the edited document as **Edited Restaurant Review**.
12. Print the document.
13. Save and close your document.

INTERNET ASSIGNMENTS

The purpose of the Internet Assignments is to challenge you to find information on the Internet that you can use to create effective documents. The actual assignments are updated and maintained on the Course Technology Web site. Log on to the Internet and use your Web browser to go to the Student Online Companion to accompany this text at **www.course.com/NewPerspectives/office2000**. Click the Word link, and then click the link for Tutorial 2.

QUICK CHECK ANSWERS

Session 2.1

1. Click the Open button on the Standard toolbar, or click File, click Open, and double-click the file. Click File, click Save As, select the location, type the new filename, and then click OK.
2. (a) ↓; (b) Ctrl+End; (c) Page Down
3. The process of first selecting the text to be modified, and then performing the operations such as moving, formatting, or deleting.
4. (a) The blank space in the left margin area of the document window, which allows you to easily select entire lines or large blocks of text. (b) The button on the Standard toolbar that redoes an action you previously reversed using the Undo button. (c) The process of moving text by first selecting the text, then pressing and holding the mouse button while moving the text to its new location in the document, and finally releasing the mouse button.
5. To select a single word, double-click the word, or click at the beginning of the word, and drag the pointer to the end of the word. To select a complete paragraph, triple-click in the selection bar next to the paragraph, or click at the beginning of the paragraph and drag the pointer to the end of the paragraph.
6. You might use the Undo button to remove the bold formatting you had just applied to a word. You could then use the Redo button to restore the bold formatting to the word.
7. False
8. Cut and paste removes the selected material from its original location and inserts it in a new location. Copy and paste makes a copy of the selected material and inserts the copy in a new location; the original material remains in its original location.
9. Click the Select Browse Object button, click the Find button, click the Replace tab, type the search text in the Find what text box, type the replacement text in the Replace with text box, click Find Next or click Replace all.

Session 2.2

1. The default top and bottom margins are 1 inch. The default left and right margins are 1.25 inches.
2. Align-left: each line flush left, ragged right.
   Align-right: each line flush right, ragged left.
   Center: each line centered, ragged right and left.
   Justify: each line flush left and flush right.
3. Click in the paragraph you want to indent, and then click the Increase Indent button on the Formatting toolbar once for each half-inch you want to indent.
4. You might use the Format Painter to copy the formatting of a heading with bold italic to the other headings in the document.
5. Click the Underline button on the Formatting toolbar, type the word, and then click the Underline button again to turn off underlining.
6. Select the paragraphs, and then click the Numbering button on the Formatting toolbar.
7. Select the title, click the Font list arrow, and click Arial in the list of fonts. Then click the Font Size list arrow, and click 14.
8. Select the text you want to change, click Format on the menu bar, click Paragraph, click the Line Spacing list arrow, and then click Single, 1.5, or Double. Or, select the text, and then press Ctrl+1 for single spacing, Ctrl+5 for 1.5 line spacing, or Ctrl+2 for double spacing.

New Perspectives on

MICROSOFT® EXCEL 2000

LEVEL I

TUTORIAL 1   EX 1.03
Using Worksheets to Make Business Decisions
Evaluating Sites for an Inwood Design Group Golf Course

TUTORIAL 2   EX 2.01
Creating a Worksheet
Producing a Sales Comparison Report for MSI

TUTORIAL 3   EX 3.01
Developing a Professional-Looking Worksheet
Producing a Projected Sales Report for the Pronto Salsa Company

Read This Before You Begin

To the Student

Data Disks
To complete the Level I tutorials, Review Assignments, and Case Problems, you need 1 Data Disk. Your instructor will either provide you with a Data Disk or ask you to make your own.

If you are making your own Data Disk, you will need 1 blank, formatted high-density disk. You will need to copy a set of folders from a file server or standalone computer or the Web onto your disk. Your instructor will tell you which computer, drive letter, and folders contain the files you need. You could also download the files by going to www.course.com, clicking Data Disk Files, and following the instructions on the screen.

The following table shows you which folders go on each of your disks, so that you will have enough disk space to complete all the tutorials, Review Assignments, and Case Problems:

Data Disk 1
Write this on the disk label:

Data Disk 1: Tutorials 1-3

Put these folders and all subfolders on the disk:

Tutorial.01, Tutorial.02, Tutorial.03

When you begin each tutorial, be sure you are using the correct Data Disk. Refer to the "File Finder" Chart at the back of this text for more detailed information on which files are used in which tutorials. See the inside front or inside back cover of this book for more information on Data Disk files, or ask your instructor or technical support person for assistance.

Course Labs
The Excel Level I tutorials feature an interactive Course Lab to help you understand spreadsheet concepts. There are Lab Assignments at the end of Tutorial 1 that relate to this Lab.

To start a Lab, click the **Start** button on the Windows taskbar, point to **Programs**, point to **Course Labs**, point to **New Perspectives Course Labs**, and click the name of the Lab you want to use.

Using Your Own Computer
If you are going to work through this book using your own computer, you need:

- **Computer System** Microsoft Windows 95, 98, NT, or higher must be installed on your computer. This book assumes a typical installation of Microsoft Excel.

- **Data Disk** You will not be able to complete the tutorials or exercises in this book using your own computer until you have your Data Disks.

- **Course Labs** See your instructor or technical support person to obtain the Course Lab software for use on your own computer.

Visit Our World Wide Web Site
Additional materials designed especially for you are available on the World Wide Web. Go to http://www.course.com.

To the Instructor

The Data files and Course Labs are available on the Instructor's Resource Kit for this title. Follow the instructions in the Help file on the CD-ROM to install the programs to your network or standalone computer. For information on creating Data Disks or the Course Labs, see the "To the Student" section above.

You are granted a license to copy the Data Files and Course Labs to any computer or computer network used by students who have purchased this book.

TUTORIAL 1

OBJECTIVES

In this tutorial you will:

- Start and exit Excel
- Discover how Excel is used in business
- Identify the major components of the Excel window
- Navigate an Excel workbook and worksheet
- Open, save, print, and close a worksheet
- Enter text, numbers, formulas, and functions
- Correct mistakes
- Perform what-if analyses
- Clear contents of cells
- Use the Excel Help system

LABS

Spreadsheets

USING WORKSHEETS TO MAKE BUSINESS DECISIONS

Evaluating Sites for an Inwood Design Group Golf Course

CASE

Inwood Design Group

Golf is big business in Japan. Spurred by the Japanese passion for the sport, golf enjoys unprecedented popularity in Japan. But because the country is small and mountainous, the 12 million golfers have fewer than 2,000 courses from which to choose. Fees for 18 holes on a public course average between $200 and $300; golf club memberships are bought and sold like stock shares. The market potential is phenomenal, but building a golf course in Japan is expensive because of inflated property values, difficult terrain, and strict environmental regulations.

Inwood Design Group plans to build a world-class golf course, and one of the four sites under consideration is Chiba Prefecture, Japan. Other possible sites are Kauai, Hawaii; Edmonton, Canada; and Scottsdale, Arizona. You and Mike Nagochi are members of the site selection team for Inwood. The team is responsible for collecting information on the sites, evaluating that information, and recommending the best site for the new golf course.

Your team identified five factors likely to determine the success of a golf course: Climate, Competition, Market Size, Topography, and Transportation. The team has already collected information on these factors for three of the four potential golf course sites. Mike has just returned from visiting the last site in Scottsdale, Arizona.

Using Microsoft Excel 2000 for Windows, Mike has created a worksheet that the team can use to evaluate the four sites. He needs to complete the worksheet by entering the data for the Scottsdale site. He then plans to bring the worksheet to the group's next meeting so that the team can analyze the information and recommend a site to management.

In this tutorial you will learn how to use Excel as you work with Mike to complete the Inwood site selection worksheet and with the Inwood team to select the best site for the golf course.

EX 1.03

EXCEL   EX 1.04   TUTORIAL 1 USING WORKSHEETS TO MAKE BUSINESS DECISIONS

SESSION 1.1

In this session you will learn what a spreadsheet is and how it is used in business. You will learn what Excel is and about the Excel window and its elements, how to move around a worksheet using the keyboard and the mouse, and how to open a workbook.

What Is Excel?

Excel is a computerized spreadsheet. A **spreadsheet** is an important business tool that helps you analyze and evaluate information. Spreadsheets are often used for cash flow analysis, budgeting, decision making, cost estimating, inventory management, and financial reporting. For example, an accountant might use a spreadsheet like the one in Figure 1-1 for a budget.

Figure 1-1   BUDGET SPREADSHEET

Cash Budget Forecast

	January Estimated	January Actual
Cash in Bank (Start of Month)	$1,400.00	$1,400.00
Cash in Register (Start of Month)	100.00	100.00
Total Cash	$1,500.00	$1,500.00
Expected Cash Sales	$1,200.00	$1,420.00
Expected Collections	400.00	380.00
Other Money Expected	100.00	52.00
Total Income	$1,700.00	$1,852.00
Total Cash and Income	$3,200.00	$3,352.00
All Expenses (for Month)	$1,200.00	$1,192.00
Cash Balance at End of Month	$2,000.00	$2,160.00

To produce the spreadsheet in Figure 1-1, you could manually calculate the totals and then type your results, or you could use a computer and spreadsheet program to perform the calculations and print the results. Spreadsheet programs are also referred to as electronic spreadsheets, computerized spreadsheets, or just spreadsheets.

In Excel 2000, the document you create is called a **workbook**. Each workbook is made up of individual **worksheets**, or **sheets**, just as a spiral-bound notebook is made up of sheets of paper. You will learn more about using multiple sheets later in this tutorial. For now, just keep in mind that the terms *worksheet* and *sheet* are often used interchangeably.

Starting Excel

Mike arrives at his office early because he needs to work with you to finish the worksheet and get ready for your meeting with the design team.

Start Excel and complete the worksheet that Mike will use to help the design team decide about the golf course site.

TUTORIAL 1 USING WORKSHEETS TO MAKE BUSINESS DECISIONS EX 1.05 EXCEL

To start Microsoft Excel:

1. Make sure Windows is running on your computer and the Windows desktop appears on your screen.

2. Click the **Start** button on the taskbar to display the Start menu, and then point to **Programs** to display the Programs menu.

3. Point to **Microsoft Excel** on the Programs menu. See Figure 1-2.

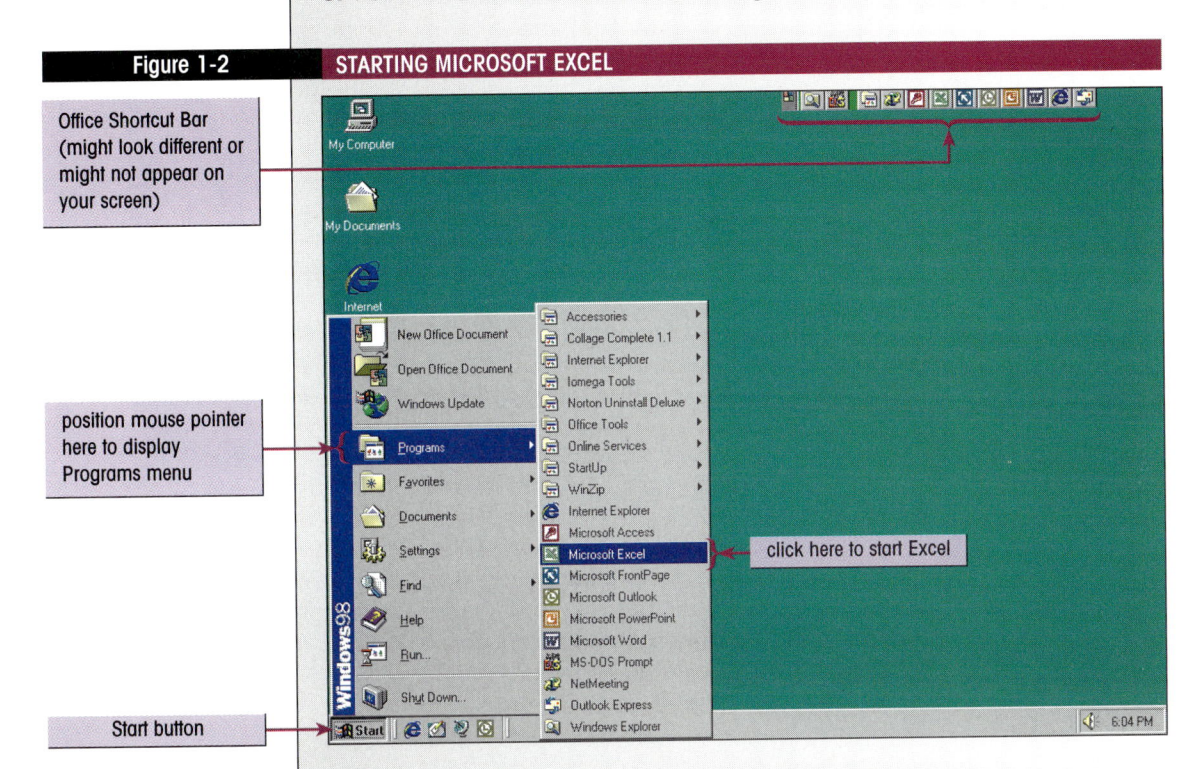

Figure 1-2   STARTING MICROSOFT EXCEL

- Office Shortcut Bar (might look different or might not appear on your screen)
- position mouse pointer here to display Programs menu
- click here to start Excel
- Start button

TROUBLE? Don't worry if your screen differs slightly. Although figures in this book were created while running Windows 98 in its default setting, these operating systems share the same basic user interface and Microsoft Excel runs equally well using Windows 95, Windows 98 in Web style, Windows NT, and Windows 2000.

TROUBLE? If the Office Shortcut Bar, which appears along the top border of the desktop in Figure 1-2, looks different on your screen or does not appear at all, your system may be set up differently. The steps in these tutorials do not require that you use the Office Shortcut Bar; therefore, the remaining figures do not display it.

4. Click **Microsoft Excel**. After a short pause, the Microsoft Excel copyright information appears in a message box and remains on the screen until the Excel program window and a blank worksheet appear. See Figure 1-3.

TROUBLE? If the Office Assistant (see Figure 1-3) window opens when you start Excel, click Help on the menu bar then click Hide the Office Assistant. You'll learn more about the Office Assistant later in this tutorial.

Figure 1-3

EXCEL PROGRAM WINDOW WITH BLANK WORKSHEET

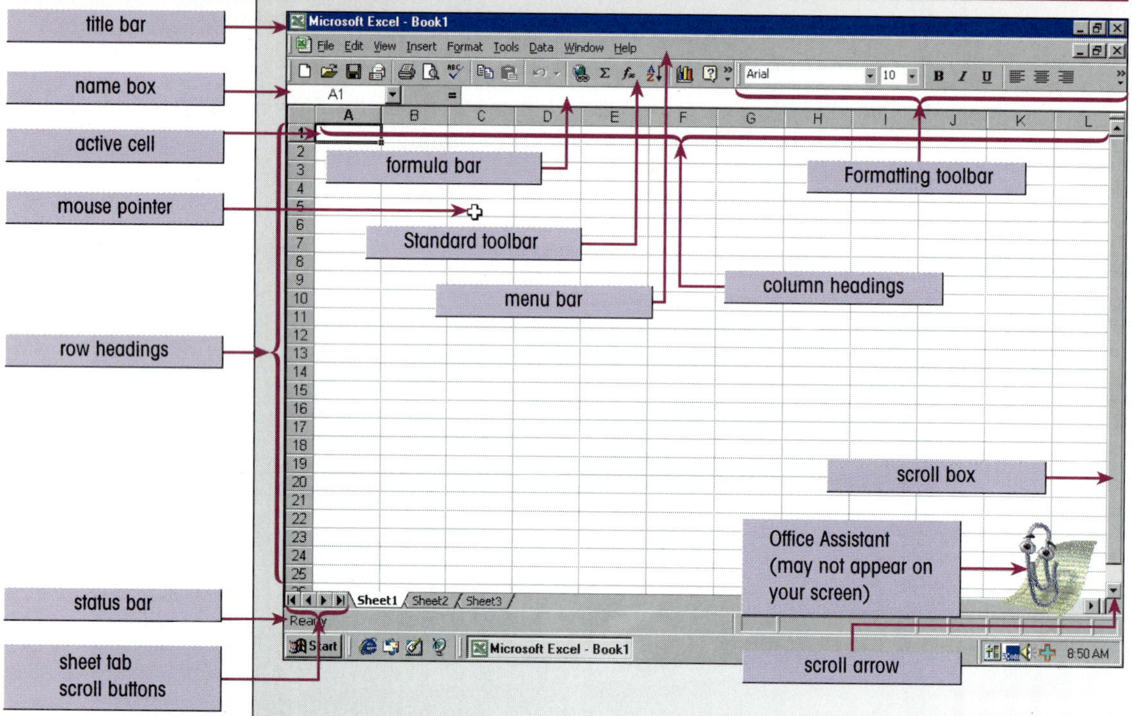

Labels: title bar, name box, active cell, mouse pointer, row headings, status bar, sheet tab scroll buttons, formula bar, Standard toolbar, menu bar, Formatting toolbar, column headings, scroll box, Office Assistant (may not appear on your screen), scroll arrow

5. If the Microsoft Excel program window does not fill the entire screen as in Figure 1-3, click the **Maximize** button ☐ in the upper-right corner of the program window. If the Book1 window is not maximized, click ☐ in the upper-right corner of the Book1 window. Your screen should now resemble Figure 1-3.

The Excel Window

The Excel window layout is consistent with the layout of other Windows programs. It contains many common features, such as the title bar, menu bar, scroll bars, and taskbar. Figure 1-3 shows these elements as well as the main components of the Excel window. Take a look at each of these Excel components so you are familiar with their location and purpose.

Toolbars

Toolbars allow you to organize the commands in Excel. The menu bar is a special toolbar at the top of the window that contains menus such as File, Edit, and View. The Standard toolbar and the Formatting toolbar are located below the menu bar. The **Standard** toolbar contains buttons corresponding to the most frequently used commands in Excel. The **Formatting** toolbar contains buttons corresponding to the commands most frequently used to improve the appearance of a worksheet.

Formula Bar

The **formula bar**, located immediately below the toolbars, displays the contents of the active cell. A **cell's contents** is the text, numbers, and formulas you enter into it. As you type or edit data, the changes appear in the formula bar. The **name box** appears at the left end of the formula bar. This area displays the cell reference for the active cell.

Workbook Window

The document window, usually called the **workbook window** or **worksheet window**, contains the sheet you are creating, editing, or using. Each worksheet consists of a series of columns identified by lettered column headings and a series of rows identified by numbered row headings. Columns are assigned alphabetic labels from A to IV (256 columns). Rows are assigned numeric labels from 1 to 65,536 (65,536 rows).

A **cell** is the rectangular area where a column and a row intersect. Each cell is identified by a **cell reference**, which is its column and row location. For example, the cell reference B6 indicates the cell where column B and row 6 intersect. The column letter is always first in the cell reference. B6 is a correct cell reference; 6B is not. The **active cell** is the cell in which you are currently working. Excel identifies the active cell with a dark border that outlines one cell. In Figure 1-3, cell A1 is the active cell. Notice that the cell reference for the active cell appears in the name box of the formula bar. You can change the active cell when you want to work elsewhere in the worksheet.

Pointer

The **pointer** is the indicator that moves on your screen as you move your mouse. The pointer changes shape to reflect the type of task you can perform at a particular location. When you click a mouse button, something happens at the pointer's location. In Figure 1-3, the pointer looks like a white plus sign ✛.

Sheet Tabs

Each worksheet has a **sheet tab** that identifies the name of the worksheet. The name on the tab of the active sheet is bold. The sheet tabs let you move quickly between the sheets in a workbook; you can simply check the sheet tab of the sheet you want to move to. By default, a new workbook consists of three worksheets. If your workbook contains many worksheets, you can use the **sheet tab scroll buttons** to scroll through the sheet tabs that are not currently visible to find the sheet you want.

Moving Around a Worksheet

Before entering or editing the contents of a cell, you need to select that cell to make it the active cell. You can select a cell using either the keyboard or the mouse.

Using the Mouse

Using the mouse, you can quickly select a cell by placing the mouse pointer on the cell and clicking the mouse button. If you need to move to a cell that's not currently on the screen, use the vertical and horizontal scroll bars to display the area of the worksheet containing the cell you are interested in, and then select the cell.

Using the Keyboard

In addition to the mouse, Excel provides you with many keyboard options for moving to different cell locations within your worksheet. Figure 1-4 shows some of the keys you can use to select a cell within your worksheet.

EXCEL EX 1.08 TUTORIAL 1 USING WORKSHEETS TO MAKE BUSINESS DECISIONS

Figure 1-4   KEYS TO MOVE AROUND THE WORKSHEET

KEYSTROKE	ACTION
↑, ↓, ←, →	Moves up, down, left, or right one cell
PgUp	Moves the active cell up one full screen
PgDn	Moves the active cell down one full screen
Home	Moves the active cell to column A of the current row
Ctrl + Home	Moves the active cell to cell A1
F5 (function key)	Opens Go To dialog box, in which you enter cell address of cell you want to make active cell

Now, try moving around the worksheet using your keyboard and mouse.

To move around the worksheet:

1. Position the mouse pointer ✛ over cell E8, then click the **left mouse** button to make it the active cell. Notice that the cell is surrounded by a black border to indicate that it is the active cell and that the name box on the formula bar displays E8.

2. Click cell **B4** to make it the active cell.

3. Press the ← key to make cell C4 the active cell.

4. Press the ↑ key to make cell C5 the active cell. See Figure 1-5.

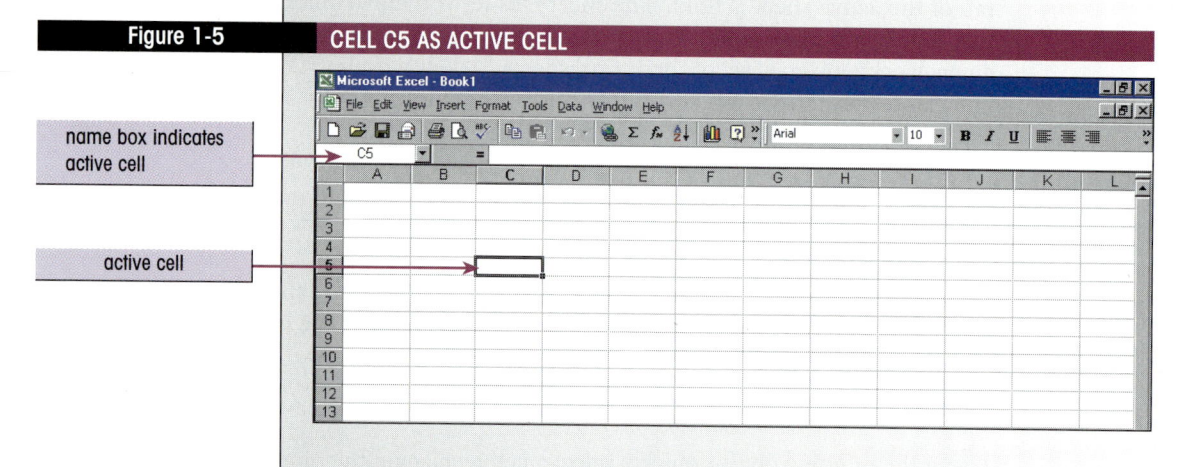

Figure 1-5   CELL C5 AS ACTIVE CELL

name box indicates active cell

active cell

5. Press the **Home** key to move to cell A5, the first cell in the current row.

6. Press **Ctrl + Home** to make cell A1 the active cell. The shortcut key Ctrl + Home can be used at any time to move to the beginning of the worksheet. Normally this is cell A1.

So far you've moved around the portion of the worksheet you can see. Many worksheets can't be viewed entirely on one screen. Next, you'll use the keyboard and mouse to bring other parts of the worksheet into view.

TUTORIAL 1 USING WORKSHEETS TO MAKE BUSINESS DECISIONS   EX 1.09   EXCEL

To bring other parts of the worksheet into view:

1. Press the **Page Down** key to move the display down one screen. The active cell is now cell A26 (the active cell on your screen may be different). Notice that the row numbers on the left side of the worksheet indicate you have moved to a different area of the worksheet. See Figure 1-6.

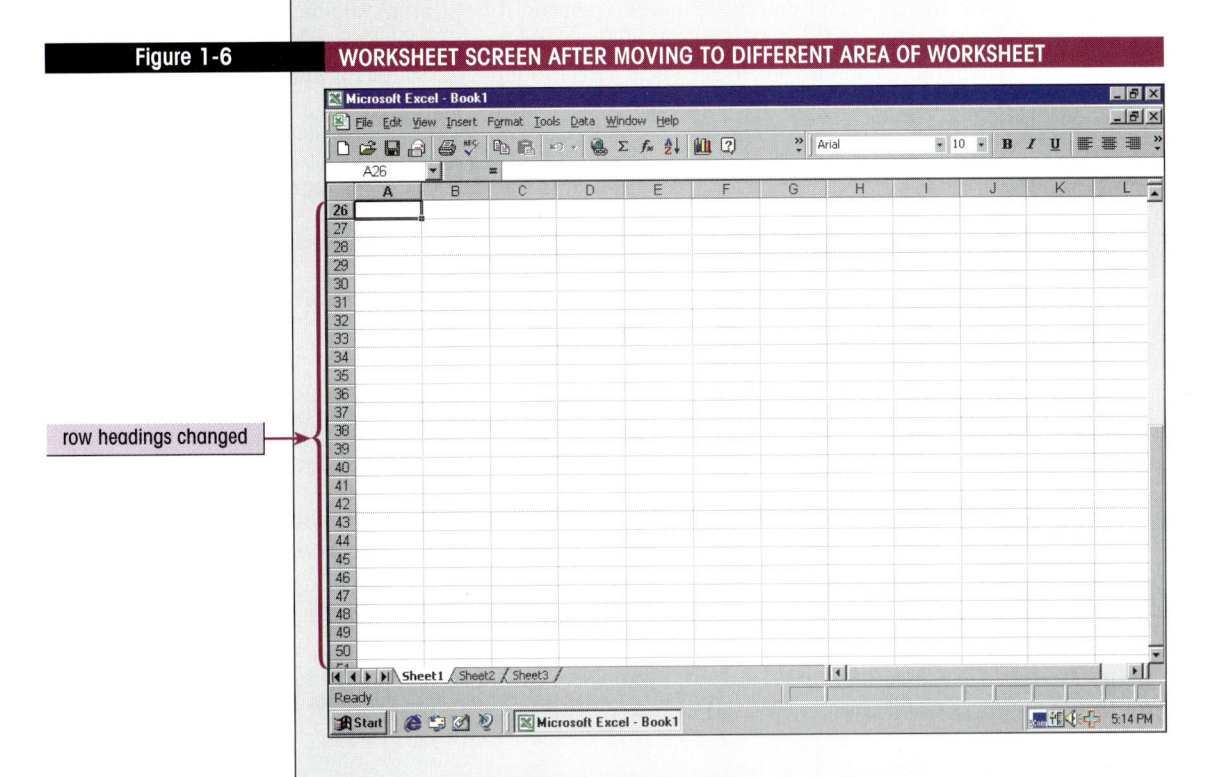

| Figure 1-6 | WORKSHEET SCREEN AFTER MOVING TO DIFFERENT AREA OF WORKSHEET |

row headings changed

2. Press the **Page Down** key again to move the display down one screen. Notice that the row numbers indicate that you have moved to a different area of the worksheet.

3. Press the **Page Up** key to move the display up one screen. The active cell is now cell A26 (the active cell on your screen may be different).

4. Click the **vertical scroll bar up arrow** button until row 12 is visible. Notice that the active cell is still A26 (the active cell on your screen may be different). Using the scroll bar changes the portion of the screen you can view without changing the active cell.

5. Click cell **C12** to make it the active cell.

6. Click the blank area above the vertical scroll box to move up a full screen.

7. Click the blank area below the vertical scroll box to move down a full screen.

8. Click the **scroll box** and drag it to the top of the scroll area to again change the area of the screen you're viewing. Notice that the ScrollTip appears telling you the current row location.

9. Press **F5** to open the Go To dialog box.

10. Type **K55** in the Reference box and then click **OK**. Cell K55 is now the active cell.

11. Press **Ctrl + Home** to make cell A1 the active cell. Now click cell **E6**.

As you know, a workbook can consist of one or more worksheets. Excel makes it easy to switch between them. Next, try moving from worksheet to worksheet.

Navigating in a Workbook

The sheet tabs let you move quickly among the different sheets in a workbook. If you can see the tab of the sheet you want, click the tab to activate the worksheet. You can also use the sheet tab scroll buttons to see sheet tabs hidden from view. Figure 1-7 describes the four tab scrolling buttons and their effects.

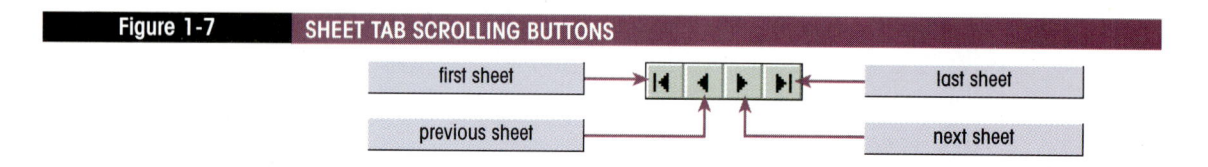

Figure 1-7   **SHEET TAB SCROLLING BUTTONS**

first sheet		last sheet
previous sheet		next sheet

Next, try moving to a new sheet.

To move to Sheet2:

1. Click the **Sheet2** tab. Sheet2, which is blank, appears in the worksheet window. Notice that the Sheet2 sheet tab is white and the name is bold, which means that Sheet2 is now the active sheet. Cell A1 is the active cell in Sheet2.

2. Click the **Sheet3** tab to make it the active sheet.

3. Click the **Sheet1** tab to make it the active sheet. Notice that cell E6 is still the active cell.

Now that you have some basic skills navigating a worksheet and workbook, you can begin working with Mike to complete the golf site selection worksheet.

Opening a Workbook

When you want to use a workbook that you previously created, you must first open it. Opening a workbook transfers a copy of the workbook file from the hard drive or 3½-inch disk to the random access memory (RAM) of your computer and displays it on your screen. When the workbook is open, the file is both in RAM and on the disk.

After you open a workbook, you can view, edit, print, or save it again on your disk.

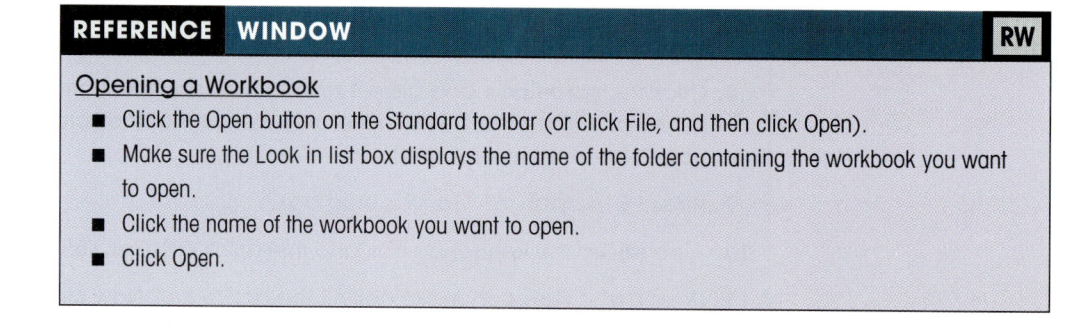

REFERENCE WINDOW   **RW**

Opening a Workbook
- Click the Open button on the Standard toolbar (or click File, and then click Open).
- Make sure the Look in list box displays the name of the folder containing the workbook you want to open.
- Click the name of the workbook you want to open.
- Click Open.

TUTORIAL 1 USING WORKSHEETS TO MAKE BUSINESS DECISIONS EX 1.11 EXCEL

Mike created a workbook to help the site selection team evaluate the four potential locations for the golf course. The workbook, Inwood, is on your Data Disk.

To open an existing workbook:

1. Place your Excel Data Disk in the appropriate drive.

   TROUBLE? If you don't have a Data Disk, you need to get one before you can proceed. Your instructor or technical support person will either give you one or ask you to make your own by following the instructions on the "Read This Before You Begin" page before this tutorial. See your instructor or technical support person for information.

2. Click the **Open** button on the Standard toolbar. The Open dialog box opens. See Figure 1-8.

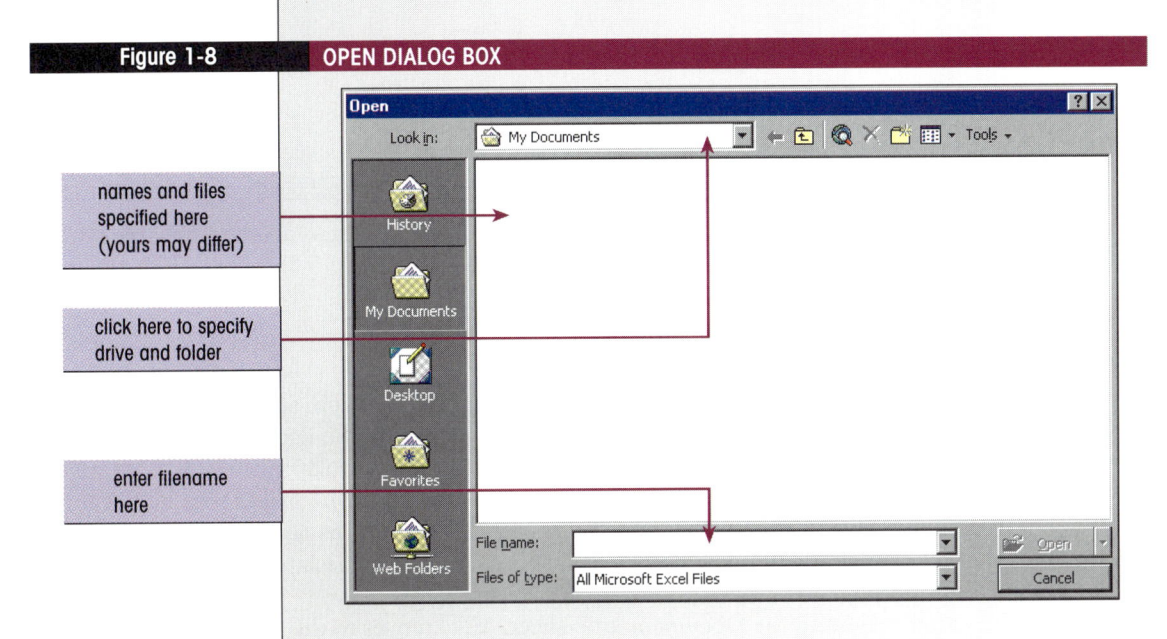

Figure 1-8 OPEN DIALOG BOX

- names and files specified here (yours may differ)
- click here to specify drive and folder
- enter filename here

3. Click the **Look in** list arrow to display the list of available drives. Locate the drive containing your Data Disk. In this text, we assume your Data Disk is a 3½-inch disk in drive A.

4. Click the drive that contains your Data Disk. A list of documents and folders on your Data Disk appears in the list box.

5. In the list of document and folder names, double-click **Tutorial.01**, double-click **Tutorial** to display that folder in the Look in list box, then click **Inwood**.

6. Click the **Open** button . (You could also double-click the filename to open the file.) The Inwood workbook opens and the first sheet in the workbook, Documentation, appears. See Figure 1-9. Notice the filename, Inwood, appears on the title bar at the top of your screen.

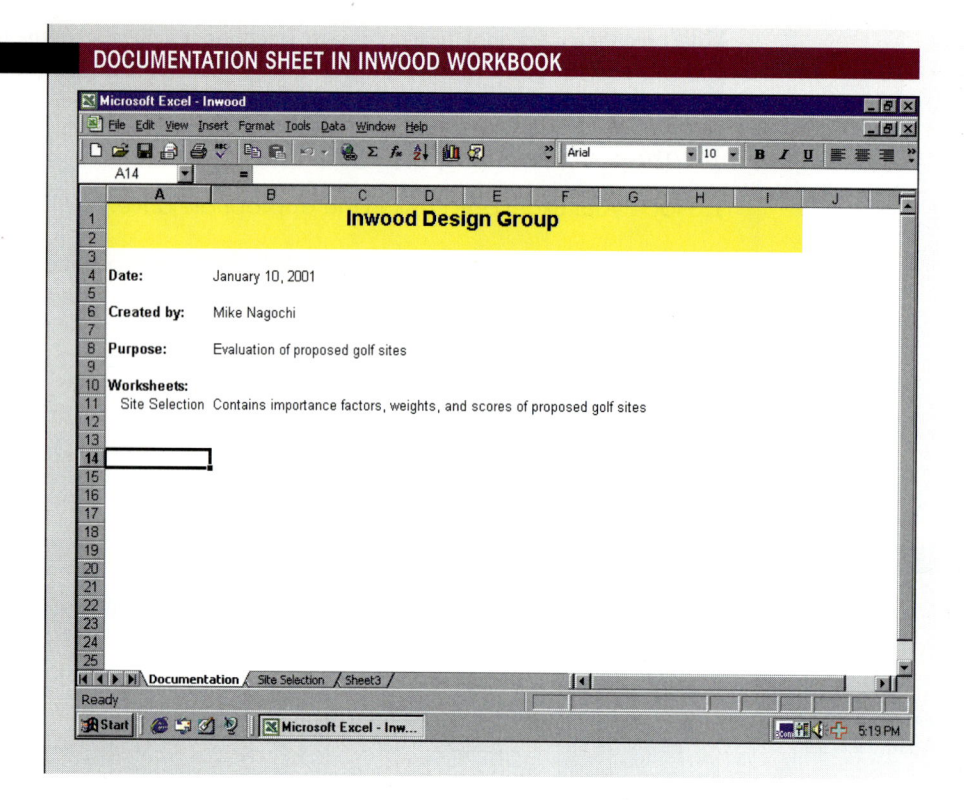

Figure 1-9   **DOCUMENTATION SHEET IN INWOOD WORKBOOK**

(Screenshot of Microsoft Excel - Inwood workbook showing the Documentation sheet with the following content:)

- **Inwood Design Group** (header in yellow)
- Date: January 10, 2001
- Created by: Mike Nagochi
- Purpose: Evaluation of proposed golf sites
- Worksheets:
  - Site Selection   Contains importance factors, weights, and scores of proposed golf sites

Layout of the Inwood Workbook

The first worksheet, Documentation, contains information about the workbook. The Documentation sheet shows who created the workbook, the date when it was created, its purpose, and a brief description of each sheet in the workbook.

Mike explains that whenever he creates a new workbook he makes sure he documents it carefully. This information is especially useful if he returns to a workbook after a long period of time (or if a new user opens it) because it provides a quick review of the workbook's purpose.

After reviewing the Documentation sheet, Mike moves to the Site Selection worksheet.

To move to the Site Selection worksheet:

1. Click the **Site Selection** sheet tab to display the worksheet Mike is preparing for the site selection team. See Figure 1-10.

Figure 1-10   **SITE SELECTION WORKSHEET**

	A	B	C	D	E
1	Factor	Importance		Raw Scores	
2		Weight	Kauai	Edmonton	Chiba
3	Climate	8	5	1	4
4	Competition	7	3	5	4
5	Market Size	10	3	4	5
6	Topography	7	4	4	1
7	Transportation	5	2	3	4
8					
9		Criteria		Weighted Scores	
10			Kauai	Edmonton	Chiba
11		Climate	40	8	32
12		Competition	21	35	28
13		Market Size	30	40	50
14		Topography	28	28	7
15		Transportation	10	15	20
16			Kauai	Edmonton	Chiba
17		Total	129	126	137

    Mike explains the general layout of the Site Selection worksheet to you. He reminds you that to this point he has only entered data for three of the four sites. He will provide the missing Scottsdale information to you. Cells C2 through E2 list three of the four sites for which he has data. Cells A3 through A7 contain the five factors on which the team's decision will be based: Climate, Competition, Market Size, Topography, and Transportation. They assign scores for Climate, Competition, Market Size, Topography, and Transportation to each location. The team uses a scale of 1 to 5 to assign a raw score for each factor. Higher raw scores indicate strength; lower raw scores indicate weakness. Cells C3 through E7 contain the raw scores for the first three locations. For example, the raw score for Kauai's Climate is 5; the two other locations have scores of 1 and 4, so Kauai, with its warm, sunny days all year, has the best climate for the golf course of the three sites visited so far. Edmonton, on the other hand, has cold weather and only received a Climate raw score of 1.

    The raw scores, however, do not provide enough information for the team to make a decision. Some factors are more important to the success of the golf course than others. The team members assigned an *importance weight* to each factor according to their knowledge of what factors contribute most to the success of a golf course. The importance weights are on a scale from 1 to 10, with 10 being most important. Mike entered the weights in cells B3 through B7. Market size, weighted 10, is the most important factor. The team believes the least important factor is Transportation, so Transportation is assigned a lower weight. Climate is important but the team considers Market Size most important. They do not use the raw scores to make a final decision; instead, they multiply each raw score by its importance weight to produce a weighted score. Which of the three sites already visited has the highest weighted score for any factor? If you look at the scores in cells C11 through E15, you see that Chiba's score of 50 for Market Size is the highest weighted score for any factor.

    Cells C17 through E17 contain the total weighted scores for the three locations. With the current weighted and raw scores, Chiba is the most promising site, with a total score of 137.

Session 1.1 Quick Check

1. A(n) _____ is the rectangular area where a column and a row intersect.
2. When you _____ a workbook, the computer copies it from your disk into RAM.
3. The cell reference _____ refers to the intersection of the fourth column and the second row.
4. To move the worksheet to the right one column:
   a. press the Enter key
   b. click the right arrow on the horizontal scroll bar
   c. press the Esc key
   d. press Ctrl + Home
5. To make Sheet2 the active worksheet, you would _____.
6. What key or keys do you press to make cell A1 the active cell?

You have now reviewed the layout of the worksheet. Now, Mike wants you to enter the data on Scottsdale. Based on his meeting with local investors and a visit to the Scottsdale site, he has assigned the following raw scores: Climate 5, Competition 2, Market Size 4, Topography 3, and Transportation 3. To complete the worksheet, you must enter the raw scores he has assigned to the Scottsdale site. You will do this in the next session.

SESSION 1.2

In this session you will learn how to enter text, values, formulas, and functions into a worksheet. You will use this data to perform what-if analyses using a worksheet. You'll also correct mistakes and use the online Help system to determine how to clear the contents of cells. Finally, you'll learn how to print a worksheet and how to close a worksheet and exit Excel.

Text, Values, Formulas, and Functions

As you have now observed, an Excel workbook can hold one or more worksheets, each containing a grid of 256 columns and 65,536 rows. The rectangular areas at the intersections of each column and row are called cells. A cell can contain a value, text, or a formula. To understand how the spreadsheet program works, you need to understand how Excel manipulates text, values, formulas, and functions.

Text

Text entries include any combination of letters, symbols, numbers, and spaces. Although text is sometimes used as data, it is more often used to describe the data contained in a worksheet. Text is often used to label columns and rows in a worksheet. For example, a projected monthly income statement contains the months of the year as column headings and income and expense categories as row labels. To enter text in a worksheet, you select the cell in which you want to enter the text by clicking the cell to select it, then typing the text. Excel automatically aligns the text on the left in a cell.

Mike's Site Selection worksheet contains a number of column heading labels. You need to enter the label for Scottsdale in the Raw Scores and Weighted Scores sections of the worksheet.

To enter a text label:

1. If you took a break after the last session, make sure Excel is running and make sure the Site Selection worksheet of the Inwood workbook is showing.

2. Click cell **F2** to make it the active cell.

3. Type **Scottsdale**, then press the **Enter** key.

   TROUBLE? If you make a mistake while typing, you can correct the error with the Backspace key. If you realize you made an error after you press the Enter key, retype the entry by repeating Steps 2 and 3.

4. Click cell **F10** and type **S**. Excel completes the entry for you based on the entries already in the column. If your data involves repetitious text, this feature, known as **AutoComplete**, can make your data entry go more quickly.

5. Press the **Enter** key to complete the entry.

6. Click cell **F16**, type **S**, and press the **Enter** key to accept Scottsdale as the entry in the cell. See Figure 1-11. Next, you need to enter the raw scores Mike assigned to Scottsdale.

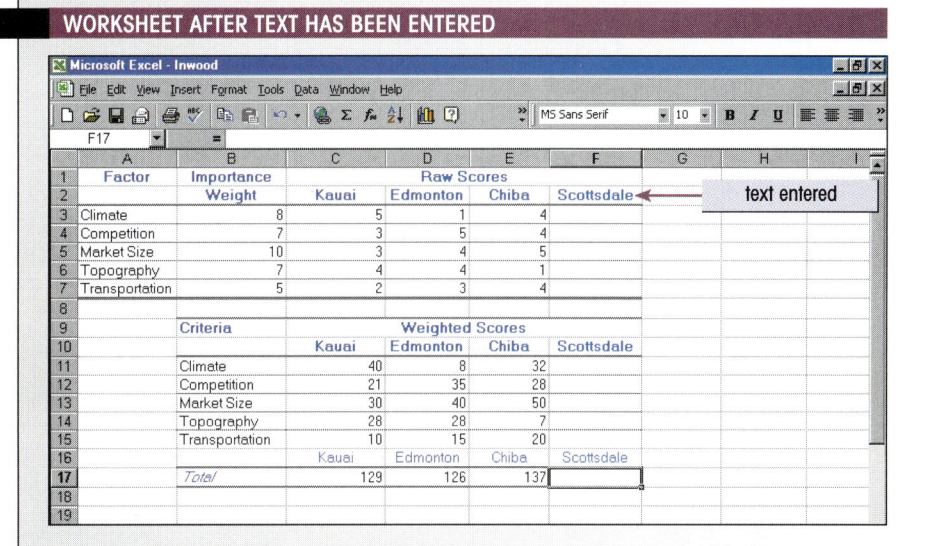

Figure 1-11   **WORKSHEET AFTER TEXT HAS BEEN ENTERED**

Values

Values are numbers that represent a quantity of some type: the number of units in inventory, stock price, an exam score, and so on. Examples of values are 378, 25.275, and -55. Values can also be dates (11/29/99) and times (4:40:31). As you type information in a cell, Excel determines whether the characters you're typing can be used as values. For example, if you type 456, Excel recognizes it as a value and it is right-justified in the cell. On the other hand, Excel treats some data commonly referred to as "numbers" as text. For example, Excel treats a telephone number (1-800-227-1240) or a Social Security number (372-70-9654) as text that cannot be used for calculations.

You need to enter the raw scores for Scottsdale.

To enter a value:

1. If necessary, click the scroll arrow so row 2 is visible. Click cell **F3**, type **5** and then press the **Enter** key. The active cell is now cell F4.

2. With cell F4 as the active cell, type **2** and press the **Enter** key.

3. Enter the value **4** for Market Size in cell F5, the value **3** for Topography in cell F6, and the value **3** for Transportation in cell F7. See Figure 1-12.

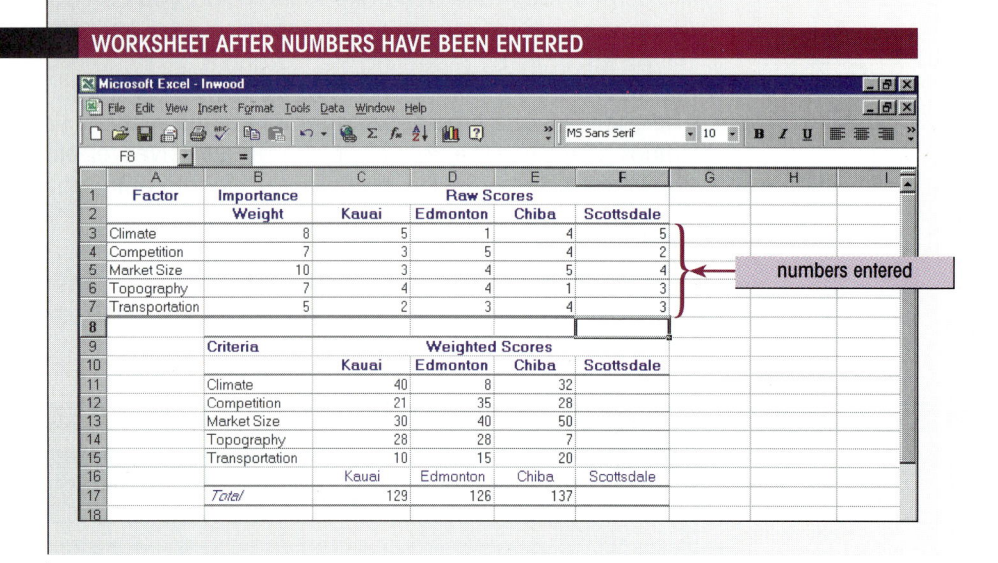

Figure 1-12 WORKSHEET AFTER NUMBERS HAVE BEEN ENTERED

Next, you enter the formulas to calculate Scottsdale's weighted score in each category.

Formulas

When you need to perform a calculation in Excel you use a formula. A **formula** is the arithmetic used to calculate values appearing in a worksheet. You can take advantage of the power of Excel by using formulas in worksheets. If you change one number in a worksheet, Excel recalculates any formula affected by the change.

An Excel formula always begins with an equal sign (=). Formulas are created by combining numbers, cell references, arithmetic operators, and/or functions. An **arithmetic operator** indicates the desired arithmetic operations. Figure 1-13 shows the arithmetic operators used in Excel.

Figure 1-13 ARITHMETIC OPERATORS USED IN FORMULAS

ARITHMETIC OPERATIONS	ARITHMETIC OPERATOR	EXAMPLE	DESCRIPTION
Addition	+	=10+A5	Adds 10 to value in cell A5
		=B1+B2+B3	Adds the values of cells B1, B2, and B3
Subtraction	–	=C9–B2	Subtracts the value in cell B2 from the value in cell C9
		=1–D2	Subtracts the value in cell D2 from 1
Multiplication	*	=C9*B9	Multiplies the value in cell C9 by the value in cell B9
		=E5*.06	Multiplies the value in E5 by the constant .06
Division	/	=C9/B9	Divides the value in cell C9 by the value in cell B9
		=D15/12	Divides the value in cell D15 by 12
Exponentiation	^	=B5^3	Raises the value stored in cell B5 to 3
		=3^B5	Raises 3 to the value stored in cell B5

The result of the formula appears in the cell where you entered the formula. To view the formula that has been entered in a cell, you must first select the cell, then look at the formula bar.

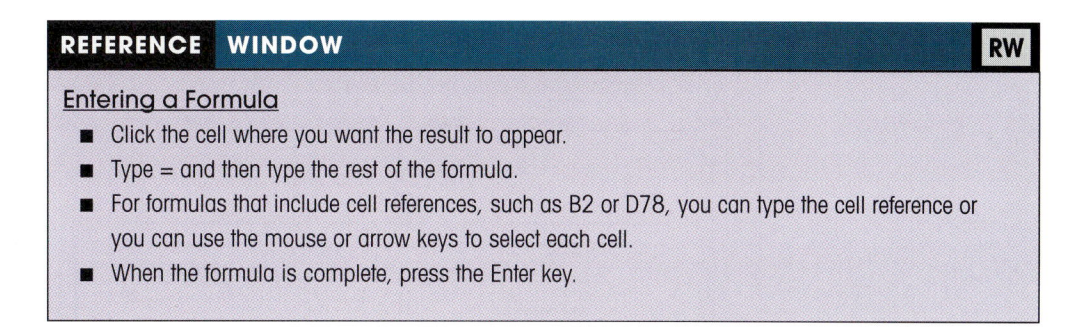

> **REFERENCE WINDOW** RW
>
> **Entering a Formula**
> - Click the cell where you want the result to appear.
> - Type = and then type the rest of the formula.
> - For formulas that include cell references, such as B2 or D78, you can type the cell reference or you can use the mouse or arrow keys to select each cell.
> - When the formula is complete, press the Enter key.

You need to enter the formulas to compute the weighted scores for the Scottsdale site. The formula multiples the raw score for a factor by the importance weight assigned to the factor. Figure 1-14 displays the formulas you need to enter into the worksheet.

Figure 1-14   FORMULAS TO CALCULATE SCOTTSDALE'S WEIGHTED SCORES

CELL	FORMULA	EXPLANATION
F11	=B3*F3	Multiplies importance weight by raw score for Climate
F12	=B4*F4	Multiplies importance weight by raw score for Competition
F13	=B5*F5	Multiplies importance weight by raw score for Market Size
F14	=B6*F6	Multiplies importance weight by raw score for Topography
F15	=B7*F7	Multiplies importance weight by raw score for Transportation

To enter the formulas to calculate each weighted score for the Scottsdale site:

1. Click cell **F11** to make it the active cell. Type **=B3*F3** to multiply the weight assigned to the Climate category by the raw score assigned to Scottsdale for the Climate category. Press the **Enter** key. The value 40 appears in cell F11.

   TROUBLE? If you make a mistake while typing, you can correct the error with the Backspace key. If you realize you made an error after you press the Enter key, repeat Step 1 to retype the entry.

2. Click cell **F11** to make it the active cell again. See Figure 1-15. Notice, the results of the formula appear in the cell, but the formula you entered appears on the formula bar.

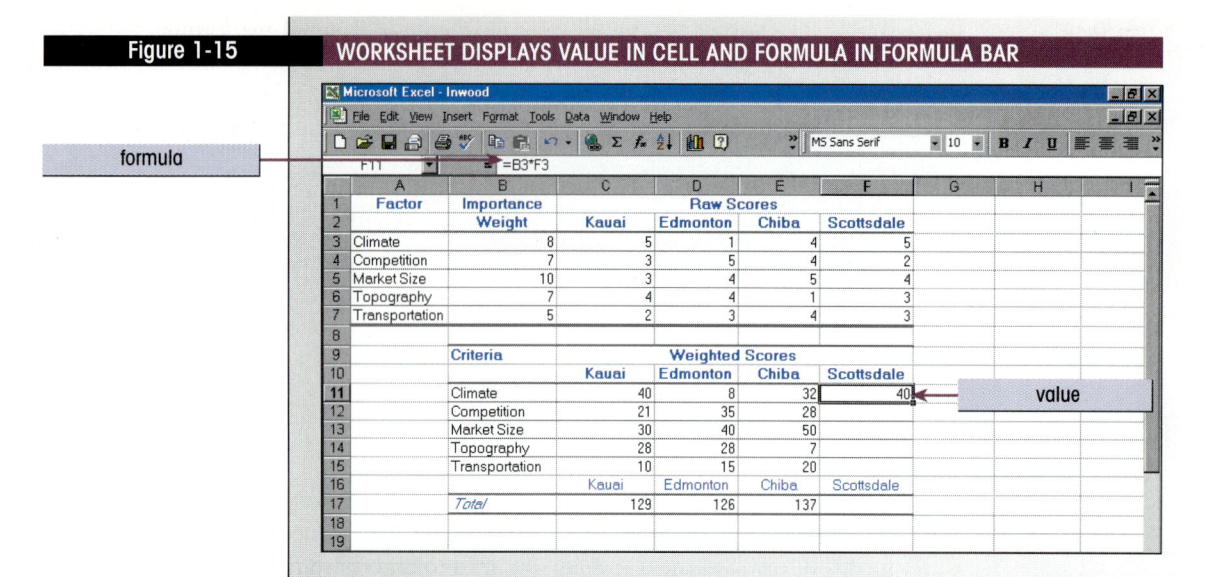

Figure 1-15 | **WORKSHEET DISPLAYS VALUE IN CELL AND FORMULA IN FORMULA BAR**

3. Click cell **F12**, type **=B4*F4**, and then press the **Enter** key. This formula multiplies the weight assigned to Competition (the contents of cell B4) by Scottsdale's raw score for Competition (cell F4). The value 14 appears in cell F12.

4. Enter the remaining formulas from Figure 1-14 into cells F13, F14, and F15. When completed, your worksheet will contain the values 40, 14, 40, 21, and 15 in cells F11 to F15.

    TROUBLE? If any value in cells F11 through F15 differs, retype the formula for that cell.

You now have to enter the formula to calculate the total weighted score for Scottsdale into the worksheet. You can use the formula =F11+F12+F13+F14+F15 to calculate the total score for the Scottsdale site. As an alternative, you can use a function to streamline this long formula.

Functions

A **function** is a predefined or built-in formula that's a shortcut for commonly used calculations. For example, the SUM function is a shortcut for entering formulas that total values in rows or columns. You can use the SUM function to create the formula =SUM(F11:F15) instead of typing the longer =F11+F12+F13+F14+F15. The SUM function in this example adds the range F11 through F15. A **range** is a group of cells, either a single cell or a rectangular block of cells. The range reference F11:F15 in the function SUM(F11:F15) refers to the rectangular block of cells beginning in the upper-left corner (F11) and ending in the lower-right corner (F15) of the range. The colon separates the upper-left corner and lower-right corner of the range. Figure 1-16 shows several examples of ranges.

TUTORIAL 1   USING WORKSHEETS TO MAKE BUSINESS DECISIONS   EX 1.19   EXCEL

Figure 1-16   EXAMPLES OF RANGES

- range D4:G4
- range B3:B9
- range D8:D8
- range I2:K12

REFERENCE WINDOW

Entering the SUM Function

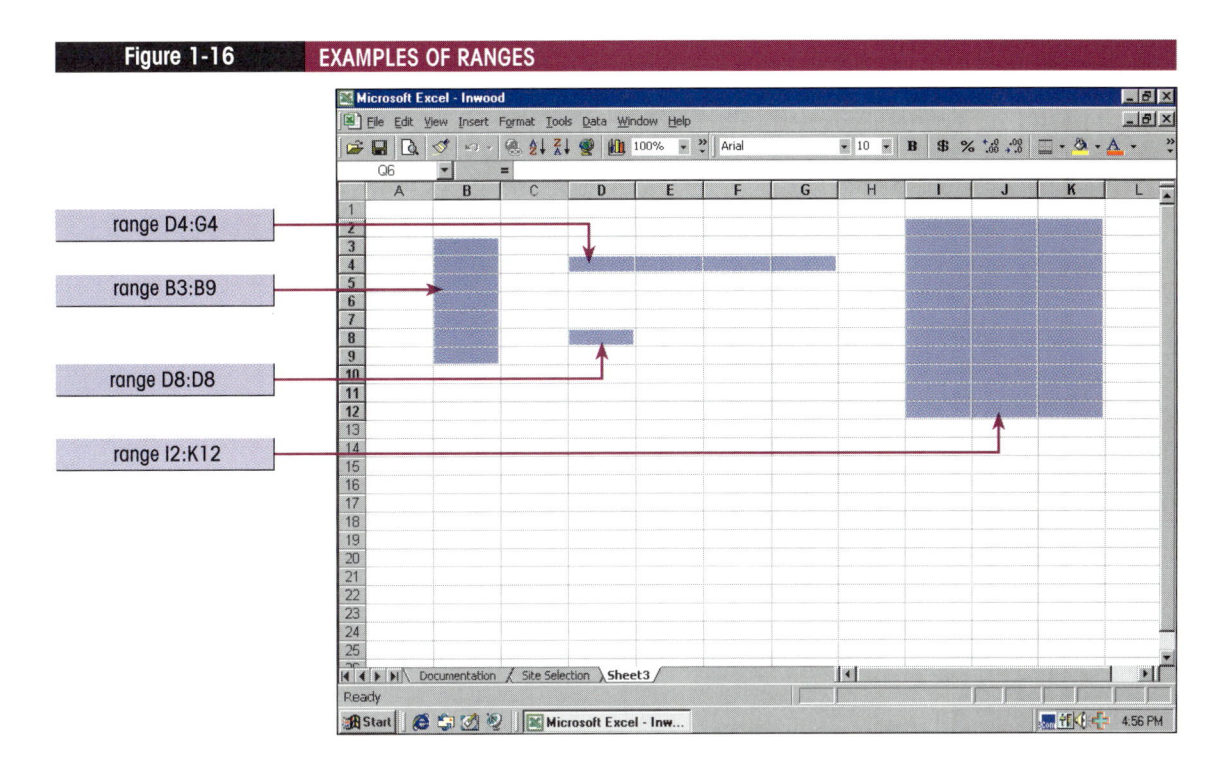

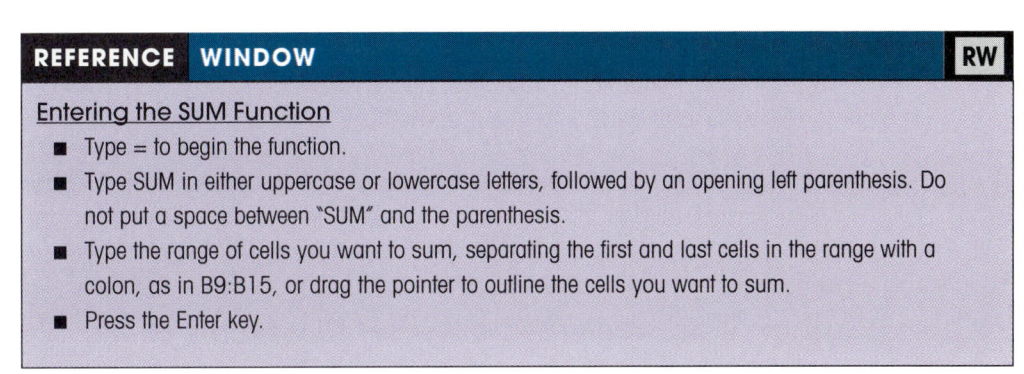

- Type = to begin the function.
- Type SUM in either uppercase or lowercase letters, followed by an opening left parenthesis. Do not put a space between "SUM" and the parenthesis.
- Type the range of cells you want to sum, separating the first and last cells in the range with a colon, as in B9:B15, or drag the pointer to outline the cells you want to sum.
- Press the Enter key.

You use the SUM function to compute the total score for the Scottsdale site.

To enter the formula using a function:

1. Click cell **F17** to make it the active cell.
2. Type **=SUM(F11:F15)**. Notice that the formula appears in the cell and the formula bar as you enter it. See Figure 1-17.

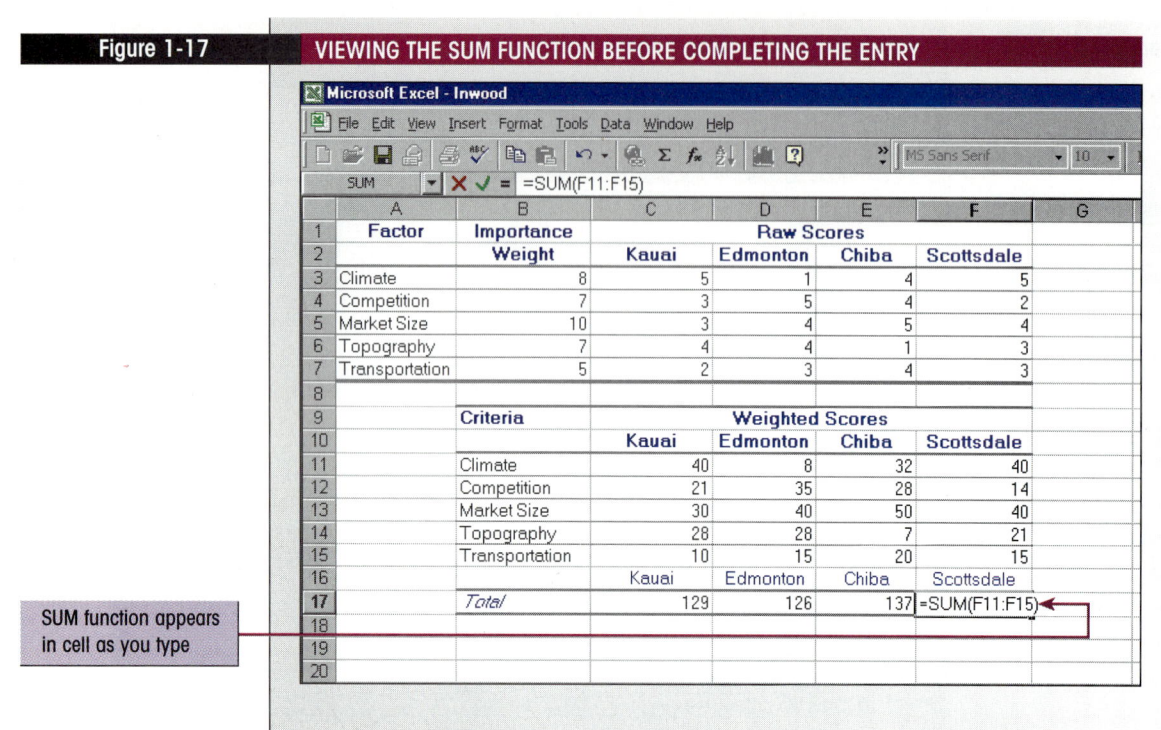

EXCEL   EX 1.20   TUTORIAL 1   USING WORKSHEETS TO MAKE BUSINESS DECISIONS

Figure 1-17   **VIEWING THE SUM FUNCTION BEFORE COMPLETING THE ENTRY**

	A	B	C	D	E	F	G
1	Factor	Importance		Raw Scores			
2		Weight	Kauai	Edmonton	Chiba	Scottsdale	
3	Climate	8	5	1	4	5	
4	Competition	7	3	5	4	2	
5	Market Size	10	3	4	5	4	
6	Topography	7	4	4	1	3	
7	Transportation	5	2	3	4	3	
8							
9		Criteria		Weighted Scores			
10			Kauai	Edmonton	Chiba	Scottsdale	
11		Climate	40	8	32	40	
12		Competition	21	35	28	14	
13		Market Size	30	40	50	40	
14		Topography	28	28	7	21	
15		Transportation	10	15	20	15	
16			Kauai	Edmonton	Chiba	Scottsdale	
17		Total	129	126	137	=SUM(F11:F15)	

SUM function appears in cell as you type

3. Press the **Enter** key to complete the formula entry and display 130, Scottsdale's total weighted score. The SUM function adds the contents of cells F11 through F15.

   TROUBLE? If 130 is not displayed in cell F17, return to Step 1 and retype formula.

The Site Selection worksheet is now complete. Mike's worksheet contains columns of information about the site selection and a chart displaying the weighted scores for each potential site. To see the chart, you must scroll the worksheet.

To scroll the worksheet to view the chart:

1. Click the **scroll arrow** button on the vertical scroll bar until the section of the worksheet containing the chart appears. See Figure 1-18.

Figure 1-18   SCROLLING THE WORKSHEET TO VIEW THE CHART

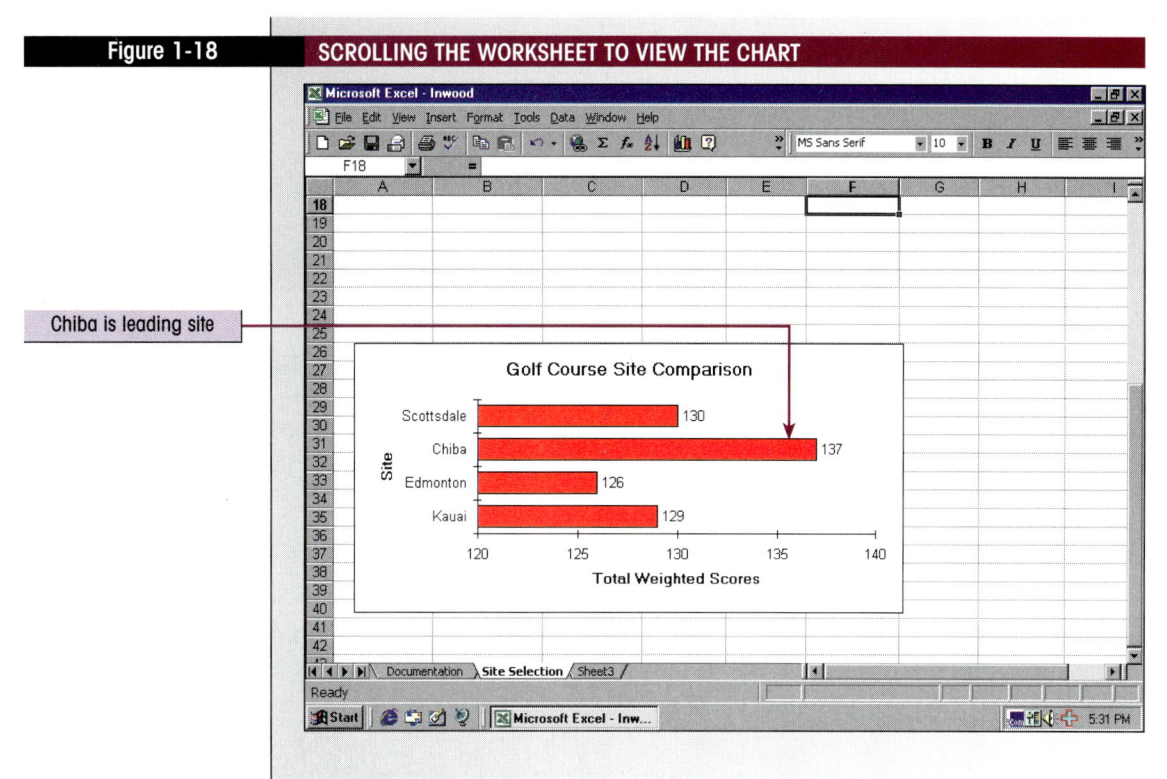

Chiba is leading site

2. After you look at the chart, click and drag the **scroll box** to the top of the vertical scroll bar.

You have completed the worksheet; Mike decides to save it before showing it to the site selection team.

Saving the Workbook

To store a workbook permanently so you can use it again without having to reenter the data and formulas, you must save it as a file on a disk. When you save a workbook, you copy it from RAM onto your disk. You'll use either the Save or the Save As command. The Save command copies the workbook onto a disk using its current filename. If a version of the file already exists, the new version replaces the old one. The Save As command asks for a filename before copying the workbook onto a disk. When you enter a new filename, you save the current file under that new name. The previous version of the file remains on the disk under its original name.

As a general rule, use the Save As command the first time you save a file or whenever you modify a file and want to save both the old and new versions. Use the Save command when you modify a file and want to save only the current version.

It is a good idea to save your file often. That way, if the power goes out or the computer stops working, you're less likely to lose your work. Because you use the Save command frequently, the Standard toolbar has a Save button ⊟, a single mouse-click shortcut for saving your workbook.

> **REFERENCE WINDOW**
>
> **Saving a Workbook with a New Filename**
> - Click File and then click Save As.
> - Change the workbook name as necessary.
> - Make sure the Save in box displays the folder in which you want to save your workbook.
> - Click the Save button.

Mike's workbook is named Inwood. The version of Inwood that you modified during this work session is on your screen. Save the modified workbook under the new name Inwood 2. This way if you want to start the tutorial from the beginning, you can open the Inwood file and start over.

To save the modified workbook under a new name:

1. Click **File** on the menu bar, and then click **Save As**. The Save As dialog box opens with the current workbook name in the File name text box.

2. Click at the end of the current workbook name, press the **spacebar**, and then type **2**. (Do not press the Enter key.)

   Before you proceed, check the other dialog box specifications to ensure that you save the workbook on your Data Disk.

3. If necessary, click the **Save in** list arrow to display the list of available drives and folders. Click the Tutorial folder in **Tutorial.01**.

4. Confirm that the Save as type text box specifies "Microsoft Excel Workbook."

5. As the number of saved worksheets begins to accumulate, you can create new folders or subfolders to store related files. You can create a new folder by clicking the New Folder button. See Figure 1-19.

6. If you need to save an Excel file in an earlier Excel format, or another format such as Lotus 1-2-3, click the drop-down area next to the Save as type box and then select the file type from the list shown.

7. When your Save As dialog box looks like the one in Figure 1-19, click the **Save** button to close the dialog box and save the workbook. Notice that the new workbook name, Inwood 2, now appears in the title bar.

TUTORIAL 1 USING WORKSHEETS TO MAKE BUSINESS DECISIONS   EX 1.23   EXCEL

| Figure 1-19 | SAVING THE WORKSHEET WITH A NEW FILENAME |

click here to create a new folder

click here to see alternative file types

new filename

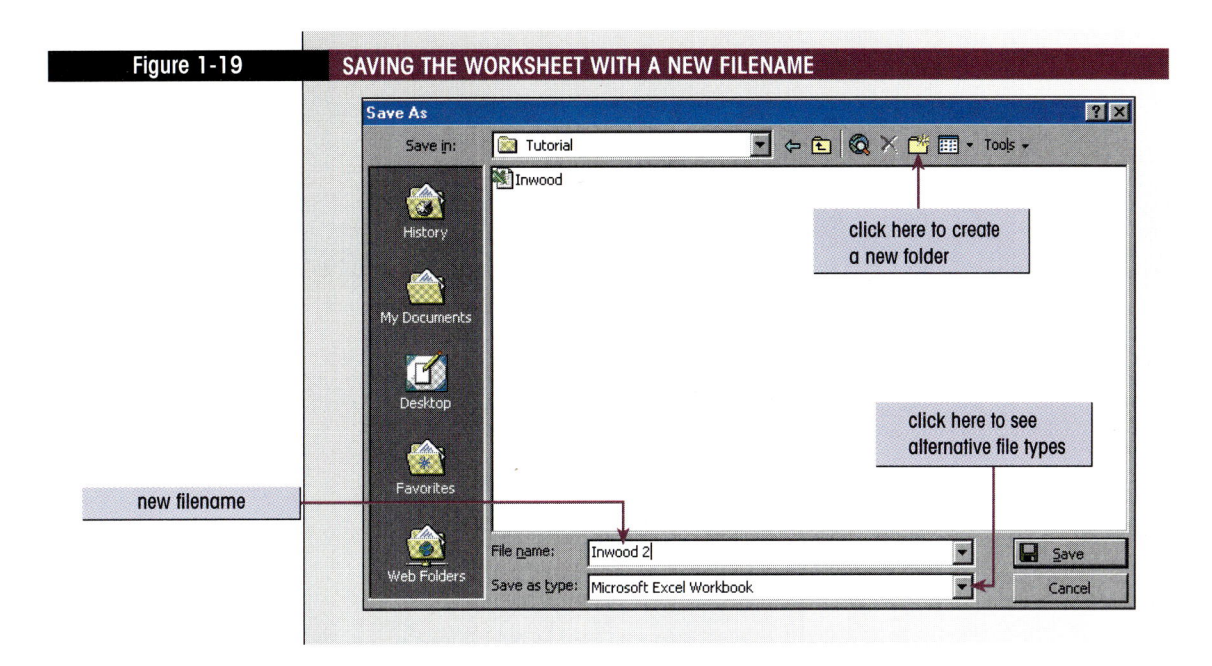

You now have two versions of the workbook: the original file—Inwood—and the modified workbook—Inwood 2.

What-if Analysis

The worksheet for site selection is now complete. Mike is ready to show it to the group. As the team examines the worksheet, you ask if the raw scores take into account recent news that a competing design group has announced plans to build a $325-million golf resort just 10 miles away from Inwood's proposed site in Chiba. Mike admits that he assigned the values before the announcement, so the raw scores do not reflect the increased competition in the Chiba market. You suggest revising the raw score for the Competition factor to reflect this market change in Chiba.

When you change a value in a worksheet, Excel automatically recalculates the worksheet and displays updated results. The recalculation feature makes Excel an extremely useful decision-making tool because it lets you quickly and easily factor in changing conditions. When you revise the contents of one or more cells in a worksheet and observe the effect this change has on all the other cells, you are performing a **what-if analysis**. In effect, you are saying, what if I change the value assigned to this factor? What effect will it have on the outcomes in the worksheet?

Because another development group has announced plans to construct a new golf course in the Chiba area, the team decides to lower Chiba's Competition raw score from 4 to 2.

To change Chiba's Competition raw score from 4 to 2:

1. Click cell **E4**. The black border around cell E4 indicates that it is the active cell. The current value of cell E4 is 4.

2. Type **2**. Notice that 2 appears in the cell and in the formula bar, along with a formula palette of three new buttons. The buttons shown in Figure 1-20—the Cancel button ✗, the Enter button ✓, and the Edit Formula button = offer alternatives for canceling, entering, and editing data and formulas.

Figure 1-20: CHANGING A CELL'S CONTENTS

Callouts: Cancel typing • same as pressing Enter key • Edit formula • new competition raw score

3. Click the **Enter** button. Excel recalculates Chiba's weighted score for the Competition factor (cell E12) and the total score for Chiba (cell E17). If necessary, click the **vertical scroll** arrow until row 17 is visible on your screen. The recalculated values are 14 and 123. See Figure 1-21.

Figure 1-21: WORKSHEET AFTER FORMULAS ARE RECALCULATED

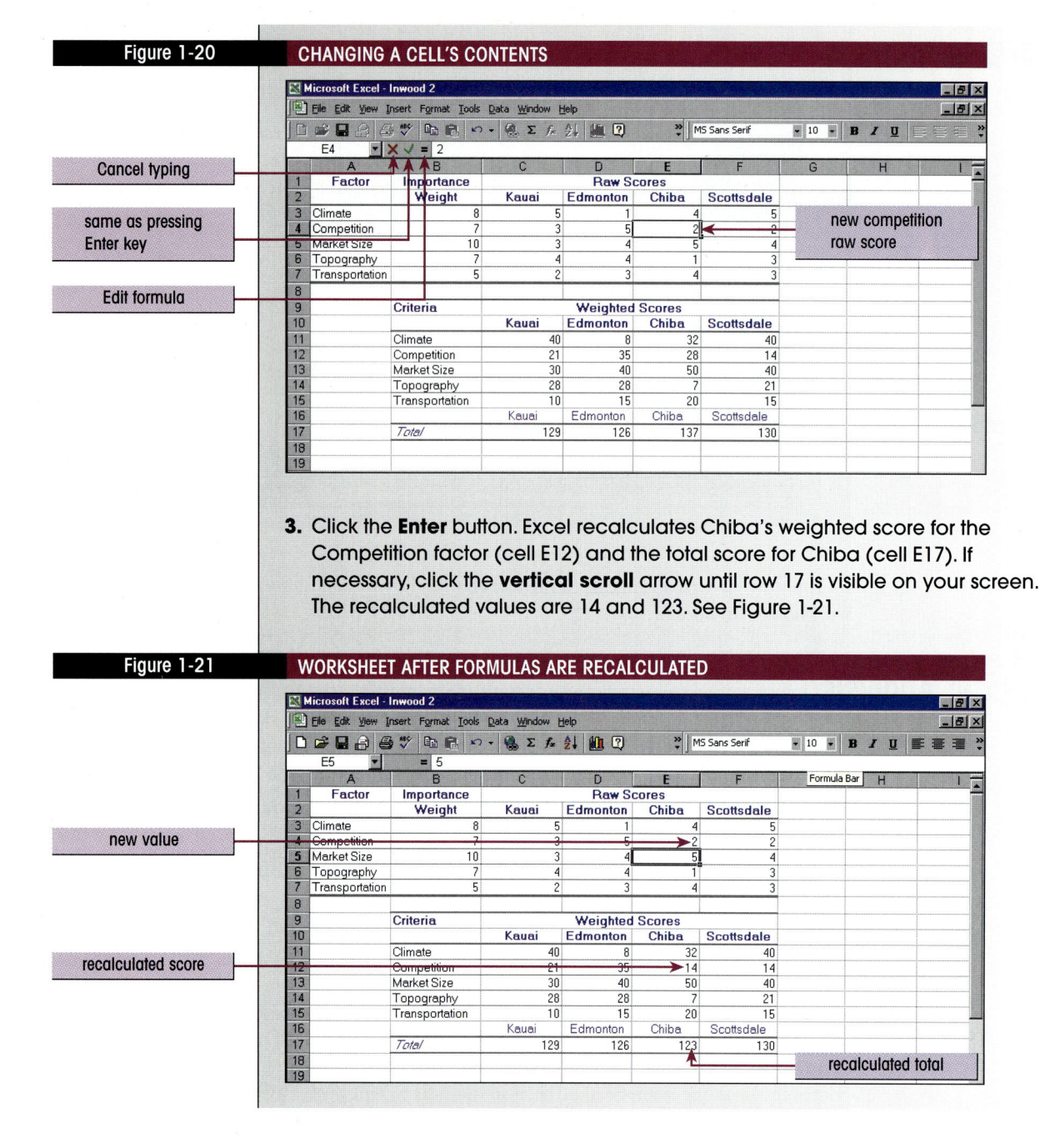

Callouts: new value • recalculated score • recalculated total

The team takes another look at the total weighted scores in row 17. Scottsdale is now the top-ranking site, with a total weighted score of 130, compared to Chiba's total weighted score of 123.

As the team continues to discuss the worksheet, several members express concern over the importance weight used for Transportation. In the current worksheet, Transportation is weighted 5 (cell B7). You remember that the group agreed to use an importance weight of 2 at a previous meeting. You ask Mike to change the importance weight for Transportation.

To change the importance weight for Transportation:

1. Click cell **B7** to make it the active cell.

2. Type **2** and press the **Enter** key. Cell B7 now contains the value 2 instead of 5. Cell B8 becomes the active cell. See Figure 1-22. Notice that the weighted scores for Transportation (row 15) and the total weighted scores for each site (row 17) have all changed.

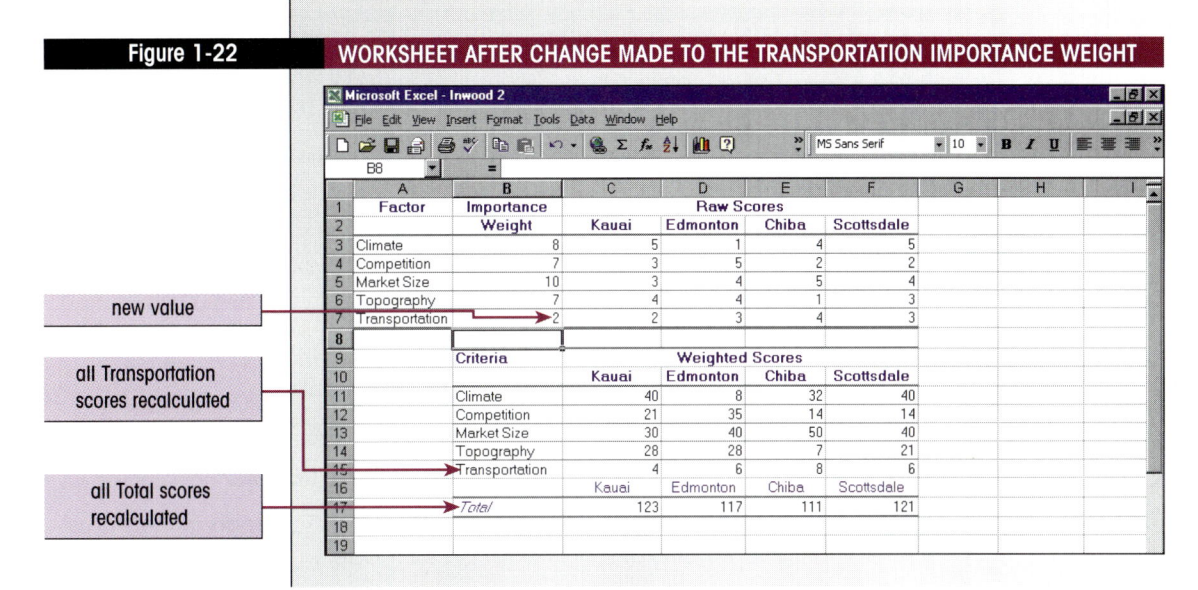

Figure 1-22 — WORKSHEET AFTER CHANGE MADE TO THE TRANSPORTATION IMPORTANCE WEIGHT

	A	B	C	D	E	F
1	Factor	Importance		Raw Scores		
2		Weight	Kauai	Edmonton	Chiba	Scottsdale
3	Climate	8	5	1	4	5
4	Competition	7	3	5	2	2
5	Market Size	10	3	4	5	4
6	Topography	7	4	4	1	3
7	Transportation	2	2	3	4	3
8						
9		Criteria		Weighted Scores		
10			Kauai	Edmonton	Chiba	Scottsdale
11		Climate	40	8	32	40
12		Competition	21	35	14	14
13		Market Size	30	40	50	40
14		Topography	28	28	7	21
15		Transportation	4	6	8	6
16			Kauai	Edmonton	Chiba	Scottsdale
17		Total	123	117	111	121

- new value
- all Transportation scores recalculated
- all Total scores recalculated

The change in the Transportation importance weight puts Kauai ahead as the most favorable site, with a total weighted score of 123.

As you enter and edit a worksheet, there are many data entry errors that can occur. The most commonly made mistake on a worksheet is a typing error. Typing mistakes are easy to correct.

Correcting Mistakes

It is easy to correct a mistake as you are typing information in a cell, before you press the Enter key. If you need to correct a mistake as you are typing information in a cell, press the Backspace key to back up and delete one or more characters. If you want to start over, press the Esc key to cancel all changes. When you are typing information in a cell, *don't* use the cursor arrow keys to edit because they move the cell pointer to another cell. One of the team members suggests changing the label "Criteria" in cell B9 to "Factors." The team members agree and you make the change to the cell.

To correct a mistake as you type:

1. Click cell **B9** to make it the active cell.

2. Type **Fak**, intentionally making an error, but don't press the Enter key.

3. Press the **Backspace** key to delete "k".

4. Type **ctors** and press the **Enter** key.

Now the word "Factors" is in cell B9. Mike suggests changing "Factors" to "Factor." The team agrees. To change a cell's contents after you press the Enter key, you use a different method. You can either retype the contents of a cell, or enter Edit mode to change the contents of a cell on the formula bar. Double-clicking a cell or pressing the F2 key puts Excel into **Edit** mode, which lets you use the Home, End, Delete, Backspace keys and the ← and → keys, and the mouse to change the text in the formula bar.

REFERENCE WINDOW | RW

Correcting Mistakes Using Edit Mode
- Double-click the cell you want to edit to begin Edit mode. The contents of the cell appear directly in the cell as well as the formula bar (or click the cell you want to edit, then press F2).
- Use Home, End, Delete, Backspace, ←, → or the mouse to edit the cell's contents either in the cell or in the formula bar.
- Press the Enter key when you finish editing.

You use Edit mode to change "Factors" to "Factor" in cell B9.

To change the word "Factors" to "Factor" in cell B9:

1. Double-click cell **B9** to begin Edit mode. Note that "Edit" appears in the status bar, reminding you that Excel is currently in Edit mode.

2. Press the **End** key if necessary to move the cursor to the right of the word "Factors," then press the **Backspace** key to delete the "s".

3. Press the **Enter** key to complete the edit.

You ask if the team is ready to recommend a site. Mike believes that, based on the best information they have, Kauai should be the recommended site and Scottsdale the alternative site. You ask for a vote, and the team unanimously agrees with Mike's recommendation.

Mike wants to have complete documentation to accompany the team's written recommendation to management, so he wants to print the worksheet.

As he reviews the worksheet one last time, he thinks that the labels in cells C16 through F16 (Kauai, Edmonton, Chiba, Scottsdale) are unnecessary and decides he wants you to delete them before printing the worksheet. You ask how to delete the contents of a cell or a group of cells. Mike is not sure, so he suggests using the Excel Help system to find the answer.

Getting Help

If you don't know how to perform a task or forget how to carry out a particular task, Excel provides an extensive on-screen help. The Excel Help system provides the same options as the Help system in other Office programs—asking help from the Office Assistant, getting help from the Help menu, and obtaining help information from Microsoft's web site. If you are not connected to the Web, you only have access to the Help files stored on your computer.

One way to get help is to use the Office Assistant, which you may have seen on your screen when you first started Excel, and which you closed earlier in this tutorial. The Office Assistant, an animated object, pops up on the screen when you click the Microsoft Excel

Help button on the Standard toolbar. The Office Assistant answers questions, offers tips, and provides help for a variety of Excel features. In addition to the Office Assistant, Figure 1-23 identifies several other ways you can get Help.

Figure 1-23   **ALTERNATIVE WAYS TO USE MICROSOFT EXCEL HELP**

ACTION*	RESULTS IN
A. Right-click Office Assistant, click Options from short-cut menu and then click Use the Office Assistant checkbox to remove check	Office Assistant no longer in use
B. On Help menu, click Microsoft Excel Help, then click Contents tab	Displays an outline of topics and subtopics on which you can get information
C. On Help menu, click Microsoft Excel Help, then click Index tab	Displays alphabetical listing of topics; enter words or phrases to scroll to an entry
D. On Help menu, click Microsoft Excel Help, then click Answer Wizard tab	Displays a Help window where a question can be entered. After clicking Search button, Excel displays a selected list of Help topics
E. Press F1	Displays Microsoft Excel Help window
F. Press Shift + F1	Pointer changes to What's This which you click when positioned over any object or menu option on the screen to see a description of the object or option

*(Alternatives B–F assume that alternative A has been implemented.)

REFERENCE WINDOW   RW

Using the Office Assistant
- Click the Microsoft Excel Help button on the Standard toolbar (or choose Microsoft Excel Help from the Help menu) to display the Office Assistant.
- Click Options to change the Office Assistant features you want to use.

  or
- Type an English-language question on a topic where you need help, and then click Search.
- Click the suggested Help topic.
- To hide the Office Assistant, right-click the Office Assistant, then click Hide.

Use the Office Assistant to get information on how to clear the contents of cells.

To get Help using the Office Assistant:

1. Click **Help** from the menu bar, then click **Show the Office Assistant** to display an animated object. If necessary, click the **Office Assistant** to display the Information Box next to the Office Assistant. See Figure 1-24.

EXCEL   EX 1.28   TUTORIAL 1   USING WORKSHEETS TO MAKE BUSINESS DECISIONS

Figure 1-24 OFFICE ASSISTANT WITH INFORMATION BOX

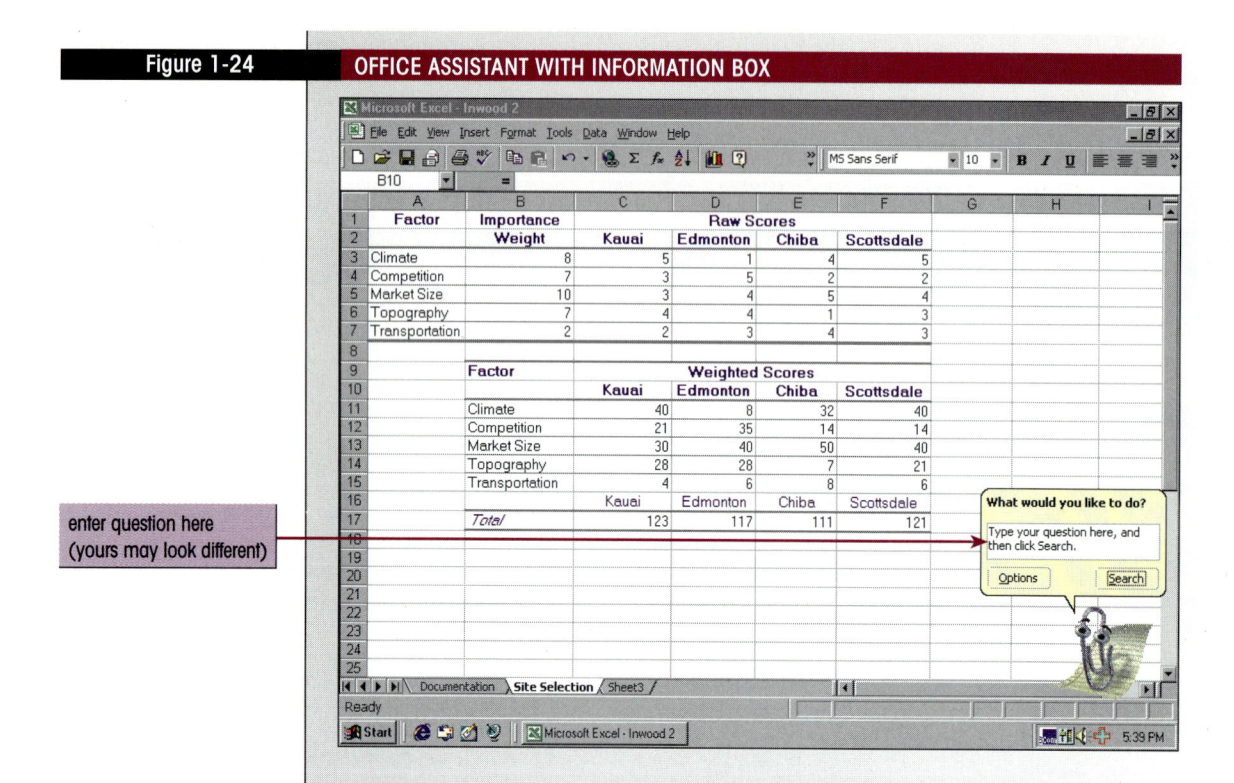

enter question here (yours may look different)

The Office Assistant can respond to an English-language question.

2. Type **how do I clear cells** in the box for your question, then click **Search** to display several possible Help topics. See Figure 1-25.

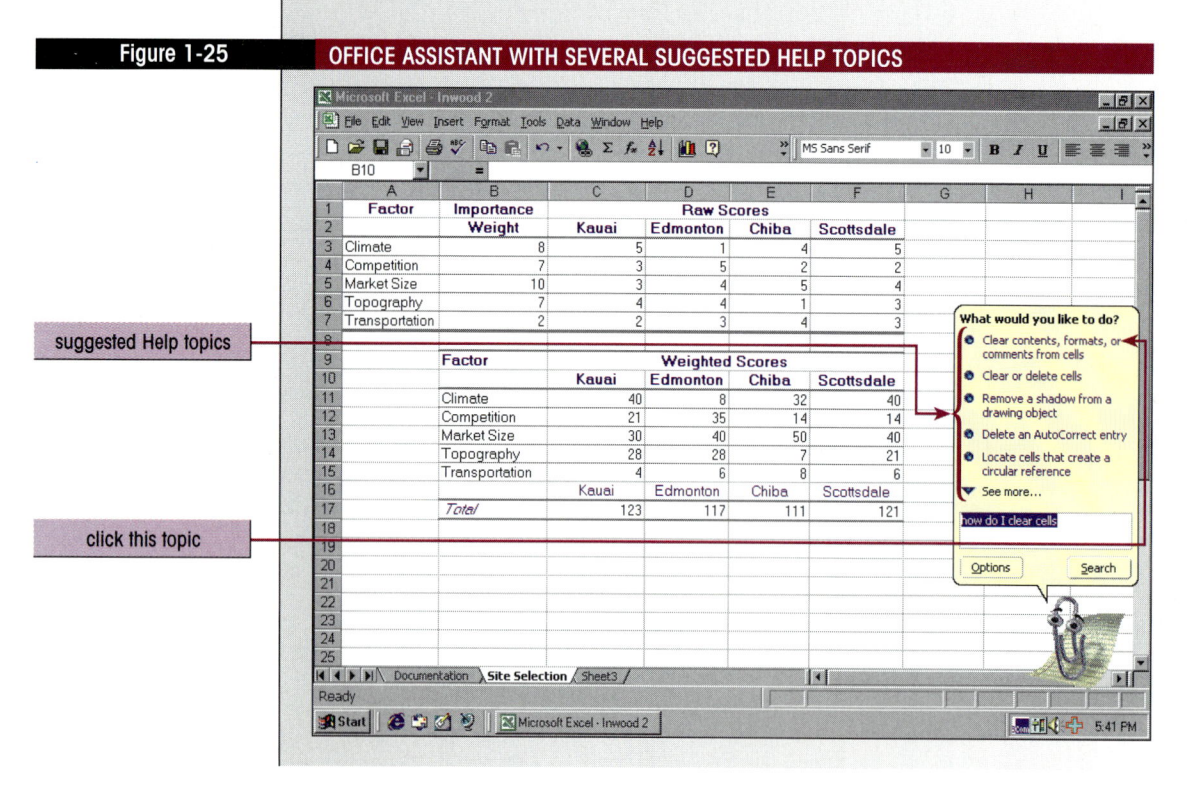

Figure 1-25 OFFICE ASSISTANT WITH SEVERAL SUGGESTED HELP TOPICS

suggested Help topics

click this topic

3. Click **Clear contents, formats, or comments from cells**, to display information on this topic. See Figure 1-26.

Figure 1-26   **EXCEL HELP DISPLAYS INFORMATION ON CLEARING CELL CONTENTS**

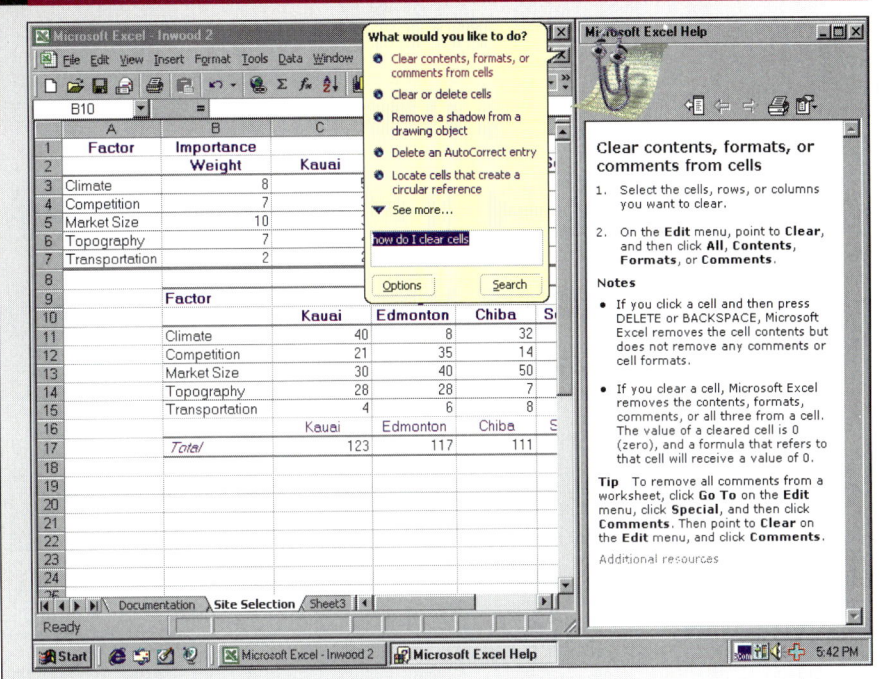

You can print the information on the topic, or you can keep the window on the screen where you can refer to it as you go through each step.

4. After reviewing the information, click the **Close** button ☒ on the Microsoft Excel Help window.

   Hide the Office Assistant.

5. Move the mouse pointer over the Office Assistant, right-click the **mouse pointer**, then click **Hide**.

After reviewing the information from the Office Assistant, you are ready to remove the labels from the worksheet.

Clearing Cell Contents

As you are building or modifying your worksheet, you may occasionally find that you have entered a label, number, or formula in a cell that you want to be empty. To erase the contents of a cell, you use either the Delete key or the Clear command on the Edit menu. Removing the contents of a cell is known as clearing a cell. Do not press the spacebar to enter a blank character in an attempt to clear a cell's contents. Excel treats a blank character as text, so even though the cell appears to be empty, it is not.

> **REFERENCE WINDOW**
>
> **Clearing Cell Contents**
> - Click the cell you want to clear, or select a range of cells you want to clear.
> - Press the Delete key.
>
> or
>
> - Click Edit, point to Clear, and then click Contents to erase only the contents of a cell, or click All to completely clear the cell contents, formatting, and notes.

You are ready to clear the labels from cells C16 through F16.

To clear the labels from cells C16 through F16:

1. Click cell **C16**. This will be the upper-left corner of the range to clear.

2. Position the cell pointer over cell C16. With the cell pointer the shape of ✚, click and drag the cell pointer to F16 to select the range C16:F16. If your pointer changes to a crosshair ✛, or an arrow, do not drag the cell pointer to F16 until the pointer changes to ✚. Note that when you select a range, the first cell in that range, cell C16 in this example, remains white and the other cells in the range are highlighted. See Figure 1-27.

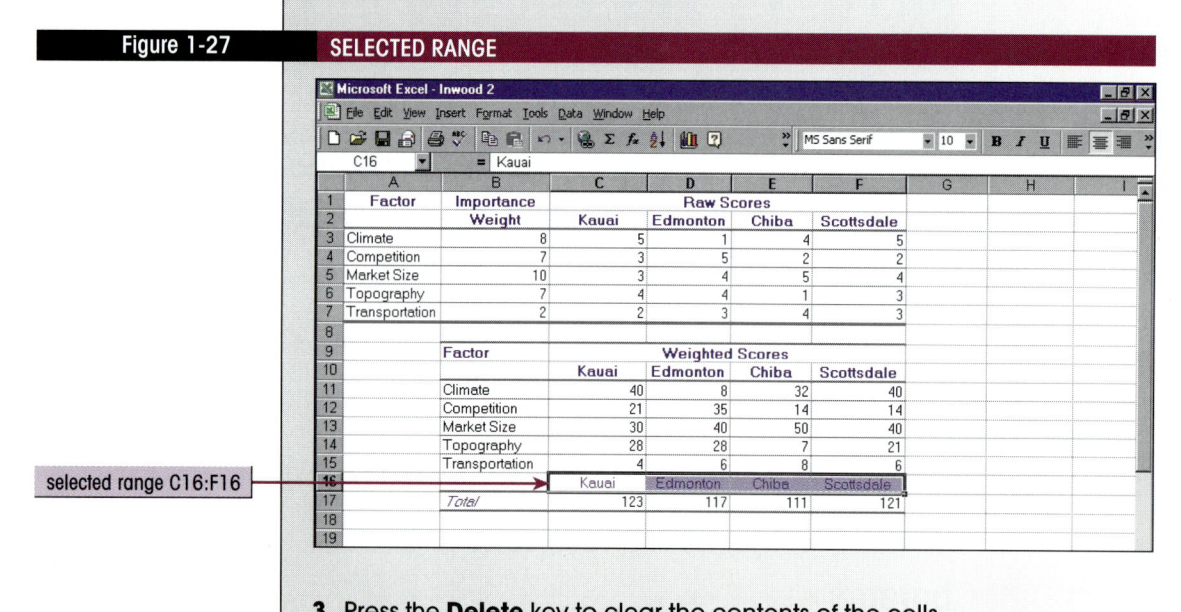

Figure 1-27 SELECTED RANGE

selected range C16:F16

3. Press the **Delete** key to clear the contents of the cells.

4. Click any cell to deselect the range.

Now that you have cleared the unwanted labels from the cells, Mike wants you to print the Site Selection worksheet.

Printing the Worksheet

You can print an Excel worksheet using either the Print command on the File menu, the Print button on the Standard toolbar, or the Print Preview command on the File menu. If you use the Print command, Excel displays a dialog box where you can specify which worksheet pages you want to print, the number of copies you want to print, and the print quality (resolution). If you use the Print button, you do not have these options; Excel prints one copy of the entire worksheet using the current print settings. If you use the Print Preview command, you can see a preview of your printout before printing the worksheet.

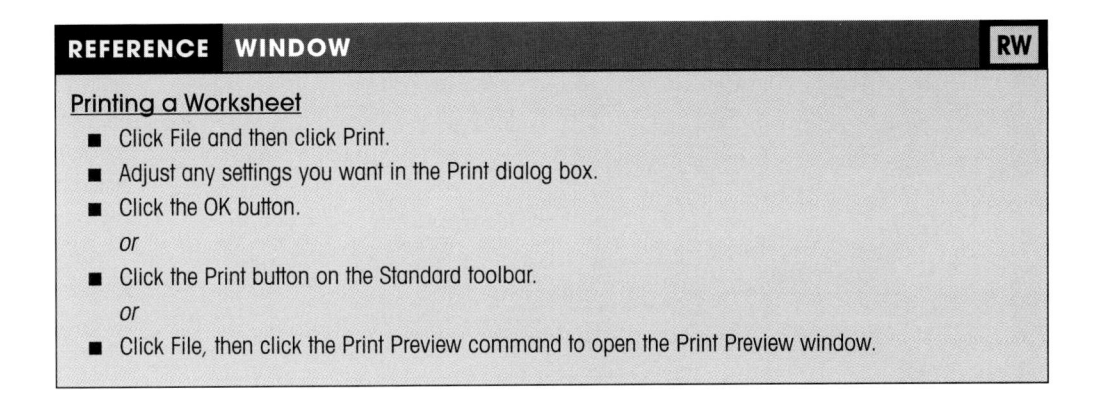

> **REFERENCE WINDOW** RW
>
> **Printing a Worksheet**
> - Click File and then click Print.
> - Adjust any settings you want in the Print dialog box.
> - Click the OK button.
>   or
> - Click the Print button on the Standard toolbar.
>   or
> - Click File, then click the Print Preview command to open the Print Preview window.

If you are printing to a shared printer, many other people may be printing documents there as well. To avoid confusion finding your printed output in an office or computer lab environment, you should first set up a method to know which document is yours. You will enter your name as the person who prepared the work in a cell on the worksheet.

> *To enter your name as the person who prepared the Site Selection worksheet:*
>
> 1. Click **Edit**, then click **Go To** to open the Go To dialog box. If necessary, click to display Go To on the menu.
> 2. Type **A40** in the Reference box and click **OK**. The active cell is now A40.
> 3. Type **Prepared by** *(enter your name here)*.
> 4. Press **Ctrl + Home** to return to cell A1.

Mike wants a printout of the entire Site Selection worksheet. You decide to select the Print command from the File menu instead of using the Print button so you can check the Print dialog box settings.

To check the print settings and then print the worksheet:

1. Make sure your printer is turned on and contains paper.

2. Click **File** on the menu bar, and then click **Print** to open the Print dialog box. See Figure 1-28.

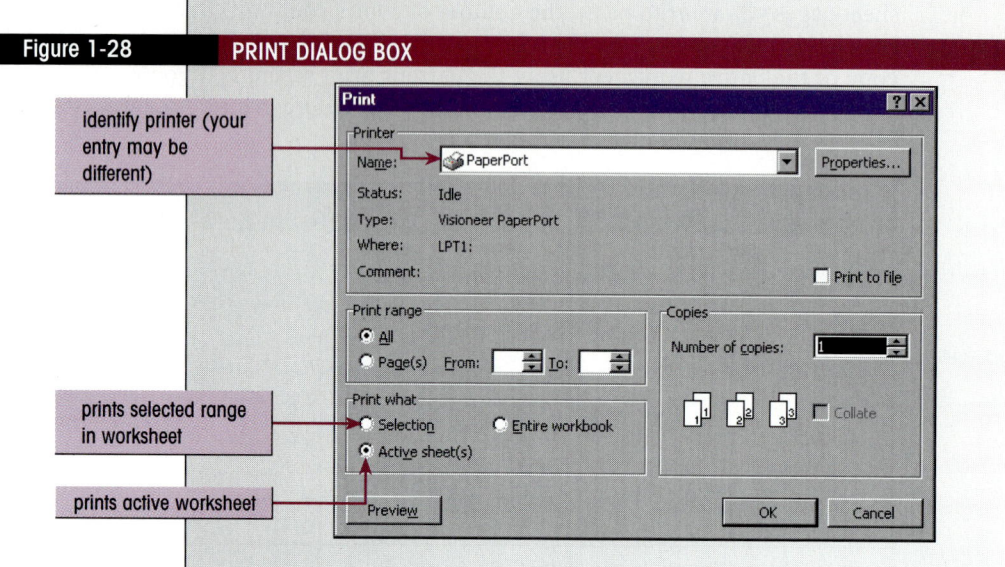

Figure 1-28   **PRINT DIALOG BOX**

- identify printer (your entry may be different)
- prints selected range in worksheet
- prints active worksheet

Now you need to select what to print. You could print the complete workbook, which would be the Documentation sheet and the Site Selection sheet. To do this, you would click the Entire workbook option button. You could also choose to print just a portion of a worksheet. For example, to print only the weighted scores data of the Site Selection worksheet, first select this range with your mouse pointer, and then select the Selection option button in the Print dialog box. In this case, Mike needs just the Site Selection worksheet.

3. If necessary, click the **Active sheet(s)** option button in the Print what section of the dialog box to print just the Site Selection worksheet, and not the Documentation sheet.

4. Make sure "1" appears in the Number of copies text box, as Mike only needs to print one copy of the worksheet.

5. Click the **OK** button to print the worksheet. See Figure 1-29.

TROUBLE? If the worksheet does not print, see your instructor or technical support person for help.

Figure 1-29   PRINTED WORKSHEET

Factor	Importance Weight	Raw Scores			
		Kauai	Edmonton	Chiba	Scottsdale
Climate	8	5	1	4	5
Competition	7	3	5	2	2
Market Size	10	3	4	5	4
Topography	7	4	4	1	3
Transportation	2	2	3	4	3

Factor	Weighted Scores			
	Kauai	Edmonton	Chiba	Scottsdale
Climate	40	8	32	40
Competition	21	35	14	14
Market Size	30	40	50	40
Topography	28	28	7	21
Transportation	4	6	8	6
Total	123	117	111	121

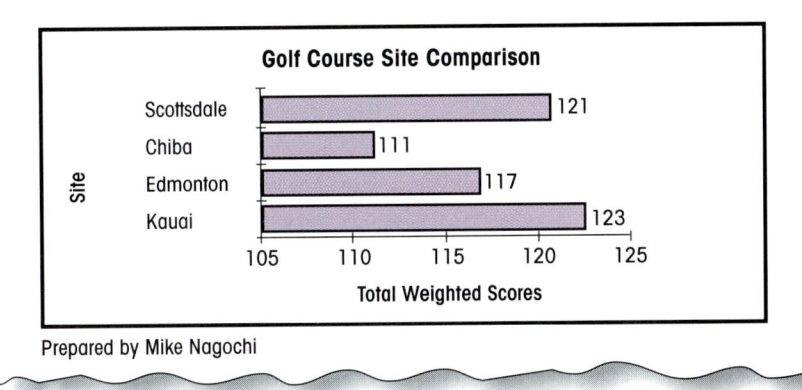

Golf Course Site Comparison

- Scottsdale: 121
- Chiba: 111
- Edmonton: 117
- Kauai: 123

Site / Total Weighted Scores

Prepared by Mike Nagochi

Mike volunteers to put together the report with the team's final recommendation, and the meeting adjourns. You and Mike are finished working with the worksheet and are ready to close the workbook.

Closing the Workbook

Closing a workbook removes it from the screen. If a workbook contains changes that have not been saved, Excel asks if you want to save your modified worksheet before closing the workbook. You can now close the workbook.

> **To close the Inwood 2 workbook:**
>
> 1. Click **File** on the menu bar, and then click **Close**. A dialog box displays the message "Do you want to save the changes you made to 'Inwood 2.xls'?" Click Yes, if you want to save the changes you made since last saving the workbook. Click No, if you do not want to keep the changes you've made to the workbook.
>
> 2. Click **Yes** to save the Inwood 2 workbook before closing it.

The Excel window stays open so you can open or create another workbook. You do not want to, so your next step is to exit Excel.

Exiting Excel

To exit Excel, you can click the Close button on the title bar, or you can use the Exit command on the File menu.

> **To exit Excel:**
>
> 1. Click the **Close** button ⊠ on the title bar. Excel closes and you return to the Windows desktop.

The Inwood site selection team has completed its work. Mike's worksheet helped the team analyze the data and recommend Kauai as the best site for Inwood's next golf course. Although the Japanese market was a strong factor in favor of locating the course in Japan's Chiba Prefecture, the mountainous terrain and competition from nearby courses reduced the site's desirability.

Session 1.2 QUICK CHECK

1. Indicate whether Excel treats the following cell entries as a value, text, or a formula:

   a. 11/09/2001
   b. Net Income
   c. 321
   d. =C11*225
   e. 200-19-1121
   f. D1-D9
   g. 44 Evans Avenue

2. You type a character and Excel finishes the entry based on entries already in the column. This feature is known as _____.

3. The formula =SUM(C3:I3) adds how many cells? Write an equivalent formula without using the SUM function.

4. What cells are included in the range D5:G7?

5. Why do you need to save a worksheet? What command do you use to save the worksheet?

6. Explain the term *what-if analysis*.

7. You can get Excel Help in any of the following ways except:

   a. clicking Help on the menu bar
   b. clicking the Help button on the Standard toolbar
   c. closing the program window
   d. pressing the F1 key

8. What key do you press to clear the contents of an active cell?

9. To print a copy of your worksheet, you use the _____ command on the _____ menu.

REVIEW ASSIGNMENTS

The other company that had planned a golf course in Chiba, Japan, has run into financial difficulties. Rumors are that the project may be canceled. A copy of the final Inwood Design Group workbook is on your Data Disk. Do the Tutorial Assignments to change this worksheet to show how the cancellation of the other project will affect your site selection.

1. If necessary, start Excel and make sure your Data Disk is in the appropriate disk drive. Open the **Inwood 3** file in the Review folder for Tutorial.01 on your Data Disk.

2. Use the Save As command to save the workbook as **Inwood 4** in the Review folder for Tutorial 1. That way you won't change the original workbook.

3. In the Site Selection worksheet, change the competition raw score for Chiba from 2 to 4. What site is ranked first?

4. The label "Topography" in cell A8 was entered incorrectly as "Topongraphy." Use Edit mode to change the "i" to "a".

5. Enter the text "Scores if the competing project in Chiba, Japan, is canceled" in cell A1.

6. Remove the raw scores for Chiba, cells E5 through E9.

7. Type your name in cell A42, then save the worksheet.

8. Print the worksheet.

9. Print the worksheet data without the chart. (*Hint*: Select the worksheet data before checking out the options in the Print dialog box.)

10. Use the What's This button . Learn more about the following Excel window components:
    a. Name box
    b. Sheet tabs
    c. Tab scrolling button (*Hint*: Click , then click each item with the Help pointer.)

11. Use the Office Assistant to learn how to delete a sheet from a workbook. Write the steps to delete a sheet. Delete Sheet3.

12. In addition to the Office Assistant, Excel offers a Help window with three sections of Help: Contents, Index, and Answer Wizard. Use the Contents tab from Microsoft Excel Help window to learn how to insert an additional worksheet into your workbook. (*Hint*: Choose Working in workbooks.) Write the steps to insert a worksheet.

13. Close the workbook and exit Excel without saving the changes.

CASE PROBLEMS

Case 1. Enrollments in the University You work 10 hours a week in the provost's office at your college. The assistant to the provost has a number of meetings today and has asked you to complete a worksheet she needs for a meeting with college deans this afternoon.

1. Open the workbook **Enroll** in the Cases folder for Tutorial.01 on your Data Disk.
2. Use the Save As command to save the workbook as **Enrollment**.
3. Complete the workbook by performing the following tasks:
   a. Enter the title "Enrollment Data for University" in cell A1.
   b. Enter the label "Total" in cell A9.
   c. Calculate the total enrollment in the University for 2001 in cell B9.
   d. Calculate the total enrollment in the University for 2000 in cell C9.
   e. Calculate the change in enrollments from 2000 to 2001. Place the results in column D. Label the column heading "Change" and use the following formula:

   Change = 2001 enrollment – 2000 enrollment

4. Type "Prepared by [your name]" in cell A12.
5. Save the workbook.
6. Print the worksheet.

Case 2. Cash Budgeting at Halpern's Appliances Fran Valence, the business manager for Halpern's Appliances, a retail appliance store, is preparing a cash budget for January. The store has a loan that must be paid the first week in February. Fran wants to determine whether the business will have enough cash to make the loan payment to the bank.

Fran sketches the projected budget so that it will have the format shown in Figure 1-30.

Figure 1-30

```
        Halpern's Appliances Cash Budget
        Projected Cash Receipts and Disbursements
        January 1, 2001
        Cash balance, January 1, 2001                       xxxx
        Projected receipts during January:
            Cash sales during month           xxxx
            Collections from credit sales     xxxx
                Total cash receipts                         xxxx
        Projected disbursements during January:
            Payments for goods purchased      xxxx
            Salaries                          xxxx
            Rent                              xxxx
            Utilities                         xxxx
                Total cash disbursements                    xxxx
        Cash balance, January 31, 2001                      xxxx
```

1. Open the workbook **Budget** in the Cases folder for Tutorial.01. Save as **BudgetSol**.
2. Enter the following formulas in cells C8, C14, and C15 of your worksheet:
   a. Total cash receipts = Cash receipts during month + Collections from credit sales
   b. Total cash disbursements = Payments for goods purchased + Salaries + Rent + Utilities
   c. Cash Balance, January 31, 2001 = Cash Balance, January 1, 2001 + Total cash receipts – Total cash disbursements
3. Enter the data in Figure 1-31 into the worksheet.
4. Type "Prepared by [your name]" in a cell two rows below the last line of the budget.

Figure 1-31

BUDGET ITEM	AMOUNT	BUDGET ITEM	AMOUNT
Cash balance at beginning of month	32000	Salaries	4800
Cash receipts during month	9000	Rent	1500
Collection from credit sales	17500	Utilities	800
Payments for goods purchased	15000		

5. Save the worksheet.

6. Print the projected cash budget.

7. After printing the budget, Fran remembers that in January the monthly rent increases by $150. Modify the projected cash budget. Print the revised cash budget.

Case 3. Selecting a Hospital Laboratory Computer System for Bridgeport Medical Center David Choi is on the Laboratory Computer Selection Committee for the Bridgeport Medical Center. After an extensive search, the committee has identified three vendors whose products appear to meet its needs. The Selection Committee has prepared an Excel worksheet to help evaluate the strengths and weaknesses of the three potential vendors. The formulas and raw scores for two of the vendors, LabStar and Health Systems, have already been entered. Now the formulas and raw scores must be entered for the third vendor, MedTech. Which vendor's system is best for the Bridgeport Medical Center? Complete these steps to find out which system is best.

1. Open the workbook **Medical** in the Cases folder for Tutorial.01.

2. Use the Save As command to save the workbook as **Medical 2** in the Cases folder for Tutorial 1. That way you won't change the original workbook for this case.

3. Examine the LAB worksheet, and type the following raw scores for MedTech: Cost = 6, Compatibility = 5, Vendor Reliability = 5, Size of Installed Base = 4, User Satisfaction = 5, Critical Functionality = 9, Additional Functionality = 8.

4. Enter the formulas to compute the weighted scores for MedTech in cells E17 to E23. See Figure 1-32.

Figure 1-32

CELL	FORMULA	CELL	FORMULA	CELL	FORMULA
E17	=B6*E6	E20	=B9*E9	E22	=B11*E11
E18	=B7*E7	E21	=B10*E10	E23	=B12*E12
E19	=B8*E8				

5. Enter the formula to compute MedTech's total weighted score.

6. In cell A2 type "Prepared by [your name]".

7. Activate the Documentation worksheet and enter information such as the name of the case, your name, date created, and purposes on this sheet.

8. Use the Save command to save the modified worksheet.

9. Print the worksheet and Documentation sheet.

10. Based on the data in the worksheet, which vendor would you recommend? Why?

11. Assume you can adjust the value for only one importance weight (cells B6 through B12). Which factor would you change and what would its new weight be in order for LabStar to have the highest weighted score? (*Hint*: Remember that the value assigned to any importance weight cannot be higher than 10.)

12. Print the modified worksheet. Close the workbook without saving it.

Case 4. Cash Counting Calculator Rob Stuben works at a local town beach in Narragansett where a fee is collected for parking. At the end of each day, the parking attendants turn in the cash they have collected, with a statement of the daily total. Rob is responsible for receiving the daily cash from each attendant, checking the accuracy of the total, and making the cash deposit to the bank.

Rob wants to set up a simple cash counter using Excel, so that he can insert the number of bills of each denomination into a worksheet and have the total cash automatically computed. By using this method he only has to count and enter the number of one-dollar bills, the number of fives, and so on.

1. Set up this worksheet for Rob. First, list all currency denominations (1, 2, 5, 10, 20, 50, 100) in the first column of your worksheet. The next column will be used to enter the count of the number of bills of each denomination (initially blank). In the third column, enter formulas to calculate totals for each denomination. That is, the number of bills multiplied by the denomination of the bill. Below this total column, enter a formula to calculate the grand total received.

   Next, you want to compare the grand total with the amount reported by an attendant. In the row below the grand total, enter the cash reported by the attendant.

   Finally, below the cash reported amount, enter the formula to calculate the difference between the grand total (calculated amount) and the cash reported by the attendant. The difference should equal zero.

2. On a separate worksheet, create a Documentation sheet. Include the title of the case, your name, date created, and the purpose of the worksheet.

3. On Rob's first day using the worksheet, the cash reported by an attendant was $1,560. Rob counted the bills and entered the following: five 50s, twenty-three 20s, forty-one 10s, sixty-five 5s, and one hundred and twenty 1s. Enter these amounts in your worksheet.

4. Type "Prepared by [your name]" in a cell two rows below the cash calculator worksheet.

5. Save the workbook in the Cases folder of Tutorial.01 using the name **CashCounter**.

6. Print the worksheet.

7. On the second day, the cash reported by an attendant was $1,395. Rob counted the bills and entered the following: two 100s, four 50s, seventeen 20s, thirty-four 10s, forty-five 5s, and ninety 1s. Delete the previous day's count and replace it with the new data.

8. Print the worksheet using the data for the second day.

9. Print the Documentation sheet.

10. Close the workbook without saving changes.

LAB ASSIGNMENTS

The New Perspectives Labs are designed to help you master some of the key computer concepts and skills presented in each chapter of the text. If you are using your school's lab computers, your instructor or technical support person should have installed the Labs software for you. If you want to use the Labs on your home computer, ask your instructor for the appropriate software. See the Read This Before You Begin page for more information on installing and starting the Lab.

Each Lab has two parts: Steps and Explore. Use Steps first to learn and review concepts. Read the information on each page and do the numbered steps. As you work through the Lab, you will be asked to answer Quick Check questions about what you have learned. At the end of the Lab, you will see a Summary Report of your answers to the Quick Checks. If your instructor wants you to turn in this Summary Report, click the Print button on the Summary Report screen.

When you have completed Steps, you can click the Explore button to complete the Lab Assignments. You can also use Explore to practice the skills you learned and to explore concepts on your own.

SPREADSHEETS Spreadsheet software is used extensively in business, education, science, and humanities to simplify tasks that involve calculations. In this Lab you will learn how spreadsheet software works. You will use spreadsheet software to examine and modify worksheets, as well as to create your own worksheets.

1. Click the Steps button to learn how spreadsheet software works. As you proceed through the Steps, answer all of the Quick Check questions that appear. After you complete the Steps, you will see a Quick Check Summary Report. Follow the instructions on the screen to print this report.

2. Click the Explore button to begin this assignment. Click OK to display a new worksheet. Click File, then click Open to display the Open dialog box. Click the file **Income.xls**, then press the Enter key to open the **Income and Expense Summary** worksheet. Notice that the worksheet contains labels and values for income from consulting and training. It also contains labels and values for expenses such as rent and salaries. The worksheet does not, however, contain formulas to calculate Total Income, Total Expenses, or Profit. Do the following:
   a. Calculate the Total Income by entering the formula =sum(C4:C5) in cell C6.
   b. Calculate the Total Expenses by entering the formula =sum(C9:C12) in C13.
   c. Calculate Profit by entering the formula =C6-C13 in cell C15.
   d. Manually check the results to make sure you entered the formulas correctly.
   e. Print your completed worksheet showing your results.

3. You can use a spreadsheet to keep track of your grade in a class. In Explore, click File, then click Open to display the Open dialog box. Click the file **Grades.xls** to open the Grades worksheet. This worksheet contains the labels and formulas necessary to calculate your grade based on four test scores. You receive a score of 88 out of 100 on the first test. On the second test, you score 42 out of 48. On the third test, you score 92 out of 100. You have not taken the fourth test yet. Enter the appropriate data in the **Grades.xls** worksheet to determine your grade after taking three tests. Print out your worksheet.

4. Worksheets are handy for answering "what if" questions. Suppose you decide to open a lemonade stand. You're interested in how much profit you can make each day. What if you sell 20 cups of lemonade? What if you sell 100? What if the cost of lemons increases?

    In Explore, open the file **Lemons.xls** and use the worksheet to answer questions a through d, then print the worksheet for question e:
    a. What is your profit if you sell 20 cups a day?
    b. What is your profit if you sell 100 cups a day?
    c. What is your profit if the price of lemons increases to $.07 and you sell 100 cups?
    d. What is your profit if you raise the price of a cup of lemonade to $.30? (Lemons still cost $.07 and assume you sell 100 cups.)
    e. Suppose your competitor boasts that she sold 50 cups of lemonade in one day and made exactly $12.00. On your worksheet adjust the cost of cups, water, lemons, and sugar, and the price per cup to show a profit of exactly $12.00 for 50 cups sold. Print this worksheet.

5. It is important to make sure the formulas in your worksheet are accurate. An easy way to test this is to enter 1's for all the values on your worksheet, then check the calculations manually. In Explore, open the worksheet **Receipt.xls**, which calculates sales receipts. Enter 1 as the value for Item 1, Item 2, Item 3, and Sales Tax %. Now, manually calculate what you would pay for three items that cost $1.00 each in a state where sales tax is 1% (.01). Do your manual calculations match those of the worksheet? If not, correct the formulas in the worksheet and print out a *formula report* of your revised worksheet.

6. In Explore, create your own worksheet showing your household budget for one month. You may make up numbers. Put a title on the worksheet. Use formulas to calculate your total income and expenses for the month. Add another formula to calculate how much money you were able to save. Print a formula report of your worksheet. Also, print your worksheet showing realistic values for one month.

INTERNET ASSIGNMENTS

The purpose of the Internet Assignments is to challenge you to find information on the Internet that you can use to create effective documents. The actual assignments are updated and maintained on the Course Technology Web site. Log on to the Internet and use your Web browser to go to the Student Online Companion to accompany this text at **www.course.com/NewPerspectives/office2000**. Click the Excel link, and then click the link for Tutorial 1.

QUICK CHECK ANSWERS

Session 1.1
1. cell
2. open
3. D2
4. b
5. click the "Sheet2" sheet tab
6. press Ctrl + Home

Session 1.2
1. a. value
   b. text
   c. value
   d. formula
   e. text
   f. text
   g. text
2. AutoComplete
3. 7; C3+D3+E3+F3+G3+H3+I3
4. D5,D6,D7,E5,E6,E7,G5,G6,G7
5. When you exit Excel, the workbook is erased from RAM. So if you want to use the workbook again, you need to save it to disk. Click File, then click Save As.
6. revising the contents of one or more cells in a worksheet and observing the effect this change has on all other cells in the worksheet
7. c
8. press the Delete key; click Edit, point to Clear, and then click Contents; click Edit, point to Clear, and then click All.
9. Print, File

TUTORIAL 2

OBJECTIVES

In this tutorial you will:

- Plan, build, test, document, preview, and print a worksheet
- Enter labels, values, and formulas
- Calculate a total using the AutoSum button
- Copy formulas using the fill handle and Clipboard
- Learn about relative, absolute, and mixed references
- Use the AVERAGE, MAX, and MIN functions to calculate values in the worksheet
- Spell check the worksheet
- Insert a row
- Reverse an action using the Undo button
- Move a range of cells
- Format the worksheet using AutoFormat
- Center printouts on a page
- Customize worksheet headers

CREATING A WORKSHEET

Producing a Sales Comparison Report for MSI

CASE

Motorcycle Specialties Incorporated

Motorcycle Specialties Incorporated (MSI), a motorcycle helmet and accessories company, provides a wide range of specialty items to motorcycle enthusiasts throughout the world. MSI has its headquarters in Atlanta, Georgia, but it markets products in North America, South America, Australia, and Europe.

The company's marketing and sales director, Sally Caneval, meets regularly with the regional sales managers who oversee global sales in each of the four regions in which MSI does business. This month, Sally intends to review overall sales in each region for the last two fiscal years and present her findings at her next meeting with the regional sales managers. She has asked you to help her put together a report that summarizes this sales information.

Specifically, Sally wants the report to show total sales for each region of the world for the two most recent fiscal years. Additionally, she wants to see the percentage change between the two years. She also wants the report to include the percentage each region contributed to the total sales of the company in 2001. Finally, she wants to include summary statistics on the average, maximum, and minimum sales for 2001.

SESSION 2.1

In this session you will learn how to plan and build a worksheet; enter labels, numbers, and formulas; and copy formulas to other cells.

Developing Worksheets

Effective worksheets are well planned and carefully designed. A well-designed worksheet should clearly identify its overall goal. It should present information in a clear, well-organized format and include all the data necessary to produce results that address the goal of the application. The process of developing a good worksheet includes the following planning and execution steps:

- determine the worksheet's purpose, what it will include, and how it will be organized
- enter the data and formulas into the worksheet
- test the worksheet
- edit the worksheet to correct any errors or make modifications
- document the worksheet
- improve the appearance of the worksheet
- save and print the completed worksheet

Planning the Worksheet

Sally begins to develop a worksheet that compares global sales by region over two years by creating a planning analysis sheet. Her planning analysis sheet helps her answer the following questions:

1. What is the goal of the worksheet? This helps to define the problem to solve.

2. What are the desired results? This information describes the output—the information required to help solve the problem.

3. What data is needed to calculate the results you want to see? This information is the input—data that must be entered.

4. What calculations are needed to produce the desired output? These calculations specify the formulas used in the worksheet.

Sally's completed planning analysis sheet is shown in Figure 2-1.

Figure 2-1 PLANNING ANALYSIS SHEET

Planning Analysis Sheet

My Goal:
To develop a worksheet to compare annual sales in each region for the last two fiscal years

What results do you want to see?
Sales by region for 2001, 2000
Total Sales for 2001, 2000
Average sales for 2001, 2000
Maximum sales for 2001, 2000
Minimum sales for 2001, 2000
Percentage change for each region
Percentage of 2001 sales for each region

What information do I need?
Sales for each region in 2001
Sales for each region in 2000

What calculations do I perform?
Percentage change = (Sales in 2001 – Sales in 2000)/ Sales in 2000
Percentage of 2001 sales = Sales in a region for 2001/Total sales 2001
Total sales for year = Sum of sales for each region
Average sales in 2001
Maximum sales in 2001
Minimum sales in 2001

Next Sally makes a rough sketch of her design, including titles, column headings, row labels, and where data values and totals should be placed. Figure 2-2 shows Sally's sketch. With these two planning tools, Sally is now ready to enter the data into Excel and build the worksheet.

Figure 2-2   **SKETCH OF WORKSHEET**

Motorcycle Specialties Incorporated
Sales Comparison 2001 with 2000

Region	Year 2001	Year 2000	% Change	% of 2001 Sales
North America	365000	314330	0.16	0.28
South America	354250	292120	0.21	0.28
Australia	251140	262000	-0.04	0.19
Europe	310440	279996	0.11	0.24
Total	1280830	1148446	0.12	

Average   320207.5
Maximum   365000
Minimum   251140

Building the Worksheet

You use Sally's planning analysis sheet, Figure 2-1, and the rough sketch shown in Figure 2-2 to guide you in preparing the sales comparison worksheet. You begin by establishing the layout of the worksheet by entering titles and column headings. Next you work on inputting the data and formulas that will calculate the results Sally needs.

To start Excel and organize your desktop:

1. Start Excel as usual.
2. Make sure your Data Disk is in the appropriate disk drive.
3. Make sure the Microsoft Excel and Book1 windows are maximized.

Entering Labels

When you build a worksheet, it's a good practice to enter the labels before entering any other data. These labels help you identify the cells where you will enter data and formulas in your worksheet. As you type a label in a cell, Excel aligns the label at the left side of the cell. Labels that are too long to fit in a cell spill over into the cell or cells to the right, if those cells are empty. If the cells to the right are not empty, Excel displays only as much of the label as fits in the cell. Begin creating the sales comparison worksheet for Sally by entering the two-line title.

To enter the worksheet title:

1. If necessary, click cell **A1** to make it the active cell.
2. Type **Motorcycle Specialties Incorporated**, and then press the **Enter** key. Since cell A1 is empty, the title appears in cell A1 and spills over into cells B1, C1, and D1. Cell A2 is now the active cell.

> **TROUBLE?** If you make a mistake while typing, remember that you can correct errors with the Backspace key. If you notice the error only after you have pressed the Enter key, then double-click the cell to activate Edit mode, and use the edit keys on your keyboard to correct the error.
>
> 3. In cell A2 type **Sales Comparison 2001 with 2000**, and then press the **Enter** key.

Next you enter the column headings defined on the worksheet sketch in Figure 2-2.

> ### To enter labels for the column headings:
>
> 1. If necessary, click cell **A3** to make it the active cell.
> 2. Type **Region** and then press the **Tab** key to complete the entry. Cell B3 is the active cell.
> 3. Type **Year 2001** in cell B3, and then press the **Tab** key.
>
>   Sally's sketch shows that three more column heads are needed for the worksheet. Enter those next.
>
> 4. Enter the remaining column heads as follows:
>
>   Cell C3: **Year 2000**
>   Cell D3: **% Change**
>   Cell E3: **% of 2001 Sales**
>
>   See Figure 2-3.
>
>   **TROUBLE?** If any cell does not contain the correct label, either edit the cell or retype the entry.

Figure 2-3   **WORKSHEET AFTER TITLES AND COLUMN HEADINGS HAVE BEEN ENTERED**

	A	B	C	D	E
1	Motorcycle Specialties Incorporated				
2	Sales Comparison 2001 with 2000				
3	Region	Year 2001	Year 2000	% Change	% of 2001 Sales
4					
5					

Recall that MSI conducts business in four different regions of the world, and the spreadsheet needs to track the sales information for each region. So Sally wants labels reflecting the regions entered into the worksheet. Enter these labels next.

> ### To enter the regions:
>
> 1. Click cell **A4**, type **North America**, and then press the **Enter** key.
> 2. In cell **A5** type **South America**, and then press the **Enter** key.
> 3. Type **Australia** in cell A6, and then **Europe** in cell A7.

The last set of labels entered identifies the summary information that will be included in the report.

TUTORIAL 2 CREATING A WORKSHEET   EX 2.05   EXCEL

To enter the summary labels:

1. In cell A8 type **Total**, and then press the **Enter** key.

2. Type the following labels into the specified cells:

   Cell A9: **Average**
   Cell A10: **Maximum**
   Cell A11: **Minimum**

   See Figure 2-4.

Figure 2-4   WORKSHEET AFTER ALL LABELS HAVE BEEN ENTERED

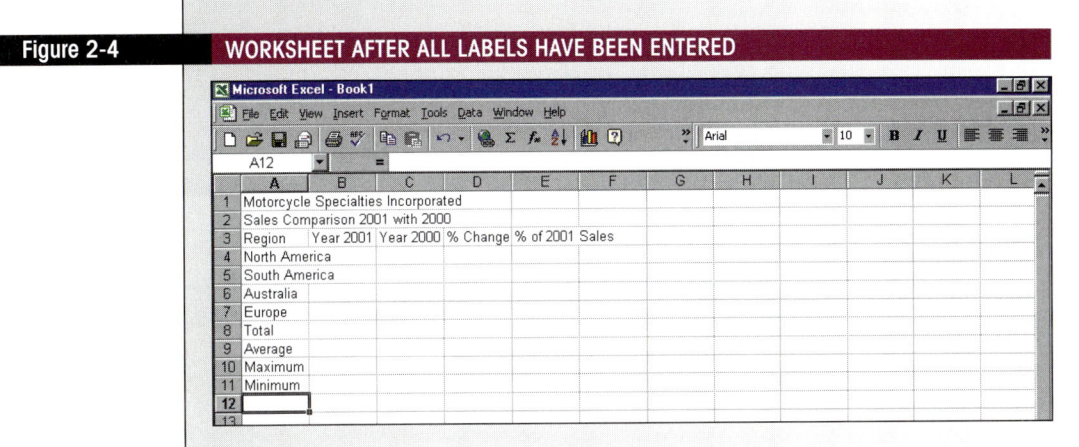

	A	B	C	D	E
1	Motorcycle Specialties Incorporated				
2	Sales Comparison 2001 with 2000				
3	Region	Year 2001	Year 2000	% Change	% of 2001 Sales
4	North America				
5	South America				
6	Australia				
7	Europe				
8	Total				
9	Average				
10	Maximum				
11	Minimum				

The labels that you just entered into the worksheet will help to identify where the data and formulas need to be placed.

Entering Data

Recall that values can be numbers, formulas, or functions. The next step in building the worksheet is to enter the data, which in this case are the numbers representing sales in each region during 2000 and 2001.

To enter the sales values for 2000 and 2001:

1. Click cell **B4** to make it the active cell. Type **365000** and then press the **Enter** key. See Figure 2-5. Notice that the region name, North America, is no longer completely visible in cell A4 because cell B4 is no longer empty. Later in the tutorial you will learn how to increase the width of a column in order to display the entire contents of cells.

Figure 2-5   WORKSHEET WITH LABEL TRUNCATED IN CELL

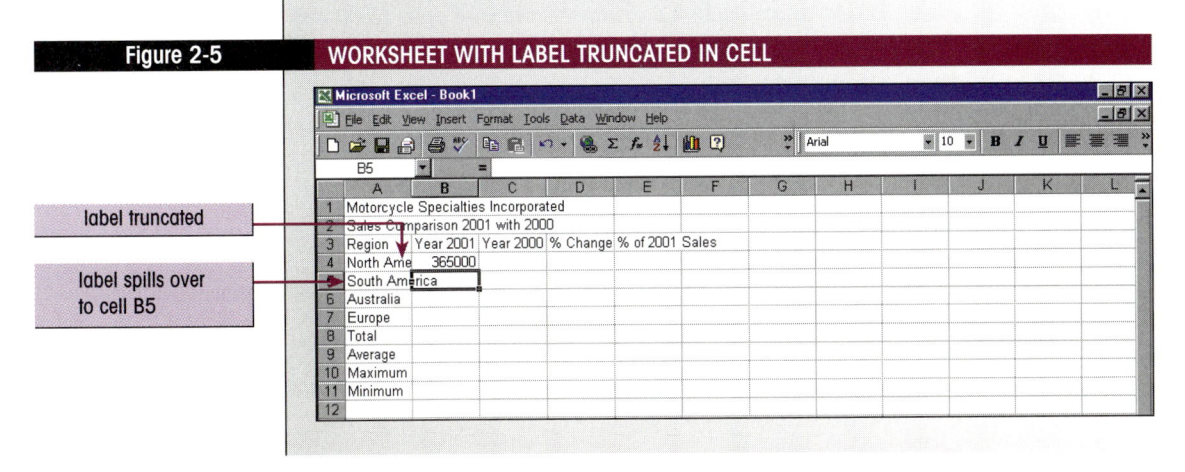

	A	B	C	D	E
1	Motorcycle Specialties Incorporated				
2	Sales Comparison 2001 with 2000				
3	Region	Year 2001	Year 2000	% Change	% of 2001 Sales
4	North Ame	365000			
5	South America				
6	Australia				
7	Europe				
8	Total				
9	Average				
10	Maximum				
11	Minimum				

label truncated → (points to cell A4)
label spills over to cell B5 → (points to cell A5)

2. In cell B5 type **354250**, and then press the **Enter** key.

3. Enter the values for cells B6, **251140**, and B7, **310440**.

   Next, type the values for sales during 2000.

4. Click cell **C4**, type **314330**, and then press the **Enter** key.

5. Enter the remaining values in the specified cells as follows:

   Cell C5: **292120**
   Cell C6: **262000**
   Cell C7: **279996**

   Your screen should now look like Figure 2-6.

Figure 2-6   WORKSHEET AFTER SALES FOR 2001 AND 2000 HAVE BEEN ENTERED

	A	B	C	D	E
1	Motorcycle Specialties Incorporated				
2	Sales Comparison 2001 with 2000				
3	Region	Year 2001	Year 2000	% Change	% of 2001 Sales
4	North America	365000	314330		
5	South America	354250	292120		
6	Australia	251140	262000		
7	Europe	310440	279996		
8	Total				
9	Average				
10	Maximum				
11	Minimum				

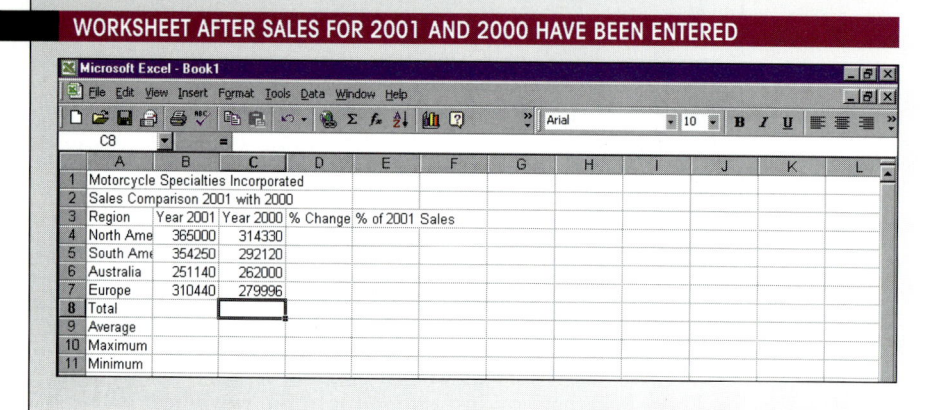

Now that you have entered the labels and data, you need to enter the formulas that will calculate the data to produce the output, or the results. The first calculation Sally wants to see is the total sales for each year. To determine total sales for 2001, you would simply sum the sales from each region for that year. In the previous tutorial you used the SUM function to calculate the weighted total score for the Scottsdale golf site by typing that function into the cell. Similarly, you can use the SUM function to calculate total sales for each year for MSI's comparison report.

Using the AutoSum Button

Since the SUM function is used more often than any other function, Excel includes the AutoSum button on the Standard toolbar. This button automatically creates a formula that contains the SUM function. To do this, Excel looks at the cells adjacent to the active cell, makes an assumption as to which cells you want to sum, and displays a formula based on its best determination about the range you want to sum. You can press the Enter key to accept the formula, or you can select a different range of cells to change the range in the formula. You want to use the AutoSum button to calculate the total sales for each year.

To calculate total sales in 2001 using the AutoSum button:

1. Click cell **B8** because this is where you want to display the total sales for 2001.

2. Click the **AutoSum** button Σ on the Standard toolbar. Excel enters a SUM function in the selected cell and determines that the range of cells to sum is B4:B7, the range directly above the selected cell. See Figure 2-7. In this case, that's exactly what you want to do.

Figure 2-7   USING THE AUTOSUM TOOL

outline of cells to be summed

range of cells to be summed

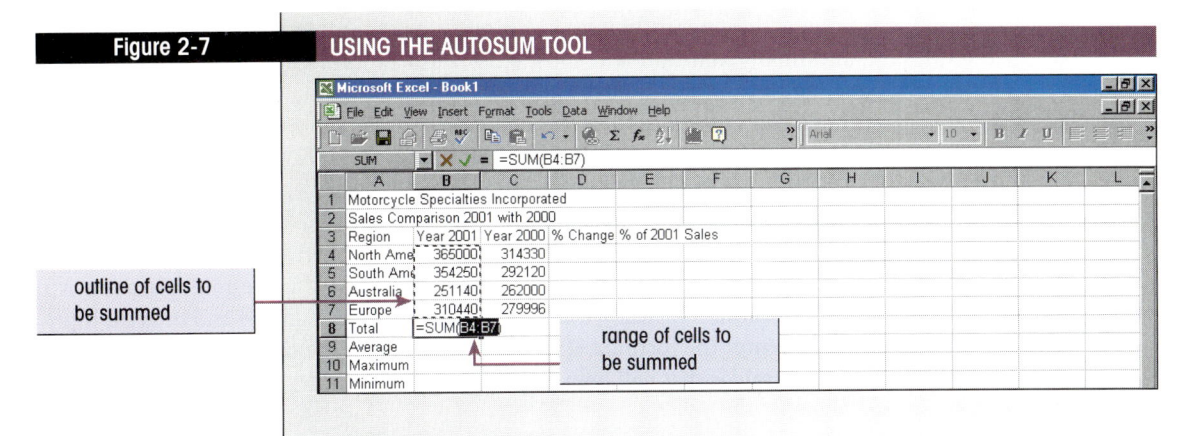

3. Press the **Enter** key to complete the formula. The result, 1280830, appears in cell B8.

Now use the same approach to calculate the total sales for 2000.

To calculate total sales in 2000 using the AutoSum button:

1. Click cell **C8** to make it the active cell.
2. Click the **AutoSum** Σ button on the Standard toolbar.
3. Press the **Enter** key to complete the formula. The result, 1148446, appears in cell C8.

Next you need to enter the formula to calculate the percentage change in sales for North America between 2001 and 2000.

Entering Formulas

Recall that a formula is an equation that performs calculations in a cell. By entering an equal sign (=) as the first entry in the cell, you are telling Excel that the numbers or symbols that follow constitute a formula, not just data. Reviewing Sally's worksheet plan, you note that you need to calculate the percentage change in sales in North America. The formula is:
Percentage change in sales for North America = (2001 sales in North America - 2000 sales in North America)/2000 sales in North America
So in looking at the worksheet, the formula in Excel would be:
=(B4-C4)/C4

If a formula contains more than one arithmetic operator, Excel performs the calculations in the standard order of precedence of operators, shown in Figure 2-8. The **order of precedence** is a set of predefined rules that Excel uses to unambiguously calculate a formula by determining which part of the formula to calculate first, which part second, and so on.

Figure 2-8   ORDER OF PRECEDENCE FOR ARITHMETIC OPERATIONS

ORDER	OPERATOR	DESCRIPTION
First	^	Exponentiation
Second	* or /	Multiplication or division
Third	+ or -	Addition or subtraction

Exponentiation is the operation with the highest precedence, followed by multiplication and division, and finally addition and subtraction. For example, because multiplication has precedence over addition, the result of the formula =3+4*5 is 23.

When a formula contains more than one operator with the same order of precedence, Excel performs the operation from left to right. Thus, in the formula =4*10/8, Excel multiplies 4 by 10 before dividing the product by 8. The result of the calculation is 5. You can add parentheses to a formula to make it easier to understand or to change the order of operations. Enclosing an expression in parentheses overrides the normal order of precedence. Excel always performs any calculations contained in parentheses first. In the formula =3+4*5, the multiplication is performed before the addition. If instead you wanted the formula to add 3+4 and then multiply the sum by 5, you would enter the formula =(3+4)*5. The result of the calculation is 35. Figure 2-9 shows examples of formulas that will help you understand the order of precedence rules.

Figure 2-9 EXAMPLES ILLUSTRATING ORDER OF PRECEDENCE RULES

FORMULA VALUE A1=10, B1=20, C1=3	ORDER OF PRECEDENCE RULE	RESULT
=A1+B1*C1	Multiplication before addition	70
=(A1+B1)*C1	Expression inside parentheses executed before expression outside	90
=A1/B1+C1	Division before addition	3.5
=A1/(B1+C1)	Expression inside parentheses executed before expression outside	.435
=A1/B1*C1	Two operators at same precedence level, leftmost operator evaluated first	1.5
=A1/(B1*C1)	Expression inside parentheses executed before expression outside	.166667

Now enter the percentage change formula as specified in Sally's planning sheet.

> **To enter the formula for the percentage change in sales for North America:**
>
> 1. Click cell **D4** to make it the active cell.
>
> 2. Type **=(B4-C4)/C4** and then press the **Enter** key. Excel performs the calculations and displays the value 0.1612 in cell D4. The formula is no longer visible in the cell. If you select the cell, the result of the formula appears in the cell, and the formula you entered appears in the formula bar.

Next you need to enter the percentage change formulas for the other regions, as well as the percentage change for the total company sales. You could type the formula =(B5-C5)/C5 in cell D5, the formula =(B6-C6)/C6 in cell D6, the formula =(B7-C7)/C7 in cell D7, and the formula =(B8-C8)/C8 in cell D8. However, this approach is time consuming and error prone. Instead, you can copy the formula you entered in cell C4 (percentage change in North American sales) into cells D5, D6, D7, and D8. Copying duplicates the cell's underlying formula into other cells, automatically adjusting cell references to reflect the new cell address. Copying formulas from one cell to another saves time and reduces the chances of entering incorrect formulas when building worksheets.

Copying a Formula Using the Fill Handle

You can copy formulas using menu commands, toolbar buttons, or the fill handle. The **fill handle** is a small black square located in the lower-right corner of the selected cell, as shown in Figure 2-10. In this section you will use the fill handle to copy the formulas. In other situations you can also use the fill handle for copying values and labels from one cell or a group of cells.

TUTORIAL 2 CREATING A WORKSHEET   EX 2.09   EXCEL

Figure 2-10	FILL HANDLE

fill handle

REFERENCE WINDOW

Copying Cell Contents with the Fill Handle
- Click the cell that contains the label, value, or formula you want to copy. If you want to copy the contents of more than one cell, select the range of cells you want to copy.
- To copy to adjacent cells, click and drag the fill handle to outline the cells where you want the copy or copies to appear, and then release the mouse button.

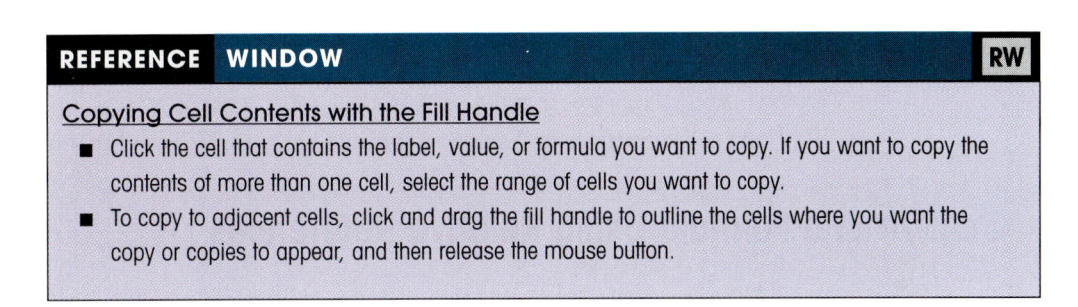

You want to copy the formula from cell D4 to cells D5, D6, D7, and D8.

To copy the formula from cell D4 to cells D5, D6, D7, and D8:

1. Click cell **D4** to make it the active cell.

2. Position the pointer over the fill handle (in the lower-right corner of cell D4) until the pointer changes to +.

3. Click and drag the pointer down the worksheet to outline cells **D5** through **D8**. See Figure 2-11.

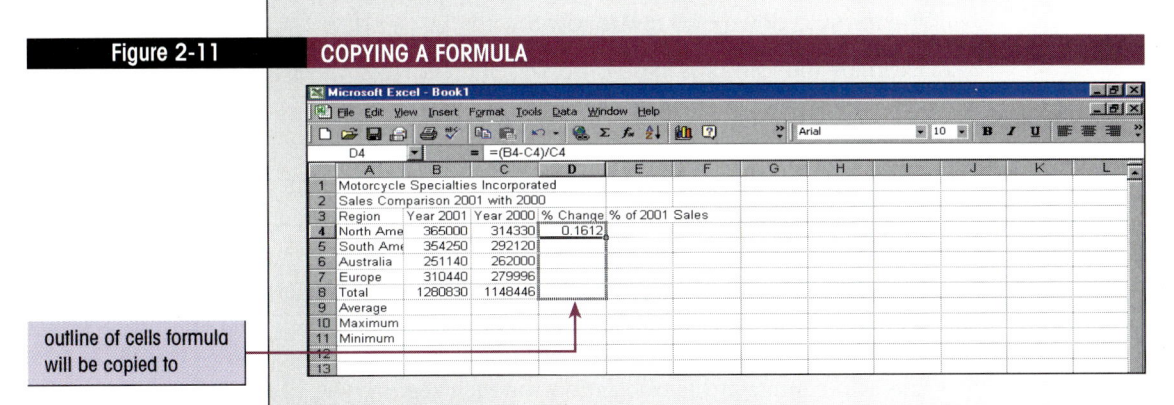

Figure 2-11	COPYING A FORMULA

outline of cells formula will be copied to

4. Release the mouse button. Excel copies the formula from D4 to cells D5 to D8. Values now appear in cells D5 through D8.

5. Click any cell to deselect the range. See Figure 2-12.

Figure 2-12 **WORKSHEET AFTER FORMULA HAS BEEN COPIED**

	A	B	C	D	E
1	Motorcycle Specialties Incorporated				
2	Sales Comparison 2001 with 2000				
3	Region	Year 2001	Year 2000	% Change	% of 2001 Sales
4	North Ame	365000	314330	0.1612	
5	South Ame	354250	292120	0.212687	
6	Australia	251140	262000	-0.04145	
7	Europe	310440	279996	0.10873	
8	Total	1280830	1148446	0.115272	
9	Average				
10	Maximum				
11	Minimum				

Notice that Excel didn't copy the formula =(B4-C4)/C4 exactly. It automatically adjusted the cell references for each new formula location. Why did that happen?

Copying a Formula Using Relative References

When you copy a formula that contains cell references, Excel automatically adjusts the cell references for the new locations. For example, when Excel copied the formula from cell D4, =(B4-C4)/C4, it automatically changed the cell references in the formula to reflect the formula's new position in the worksheet. So in cell D5 the cell references adjust to =(B5-C5)/C5. Cell references that change when copied are called **relative cell references**.

Take a moment to look at the formulas in cells D5, D6, D7, and D8.

To examine the formulas in cells D5, D6, D7, and D8:

1. Click cell **D5**. The formula =(B5-C5)/C5 appears in the formula bar.

When Excel copied the formula from cell D4 to cell D5, the cell references changed. The formula =(B4-C4)/C4 became =(B5-C5)/C5 when Excel copied the formula down one row to row 5.

2. Examine the formulas in cells D6, D7, and D8. Notice that the cell references were adjusted for the new locations.

Copying a Formula Using an Absolute Reference

According to Sally's plan, the worksheet should display the percentage that each region contributed to the total sales in 2001. For example, if the company's total sales were $100,000 and sales in North America were $25,000, then sales in North America would be 25% of total sales. To complete this calculation for each region, you need to divide each region's sales by the total company sales, as shown in the following formulas:

Contribution by North America	=B4/B8
Contribution by South America	=B5/B8
Contribution by Australia	=B6/B8
Contribution by Europe	=B7/B8

First enter the formula to calculate the percentage North America contributed to total sales.

To calculate North America's percentage of total 2001 sales:

1. Click cell **E4** to make it the active cell.

2. Type **=B4/B8** and then press the **Enter** key to display the value .284971 in cell E4.

Cell E4 displays the correct result. Sales in North America for 2001 were 365,000, which is approximately .28 of the 1,280,830 in total sales in 2001. Next, you decide to copy the formula in cell E4 to cells E5, E6, and E7.

To copy the percentage formula in cell E4 to cells E5 through E7:

1. Click cell **E4**, and then move the pointer over the fill handle in cell E4 until it changes to +.

2. Click and drag the pointer to cell **E7** and release the mouse button.

3. Click any blank cell to deselect the range. The error value "#DIV/0!" appears in cells E5 through E7. See Figure 2-13.

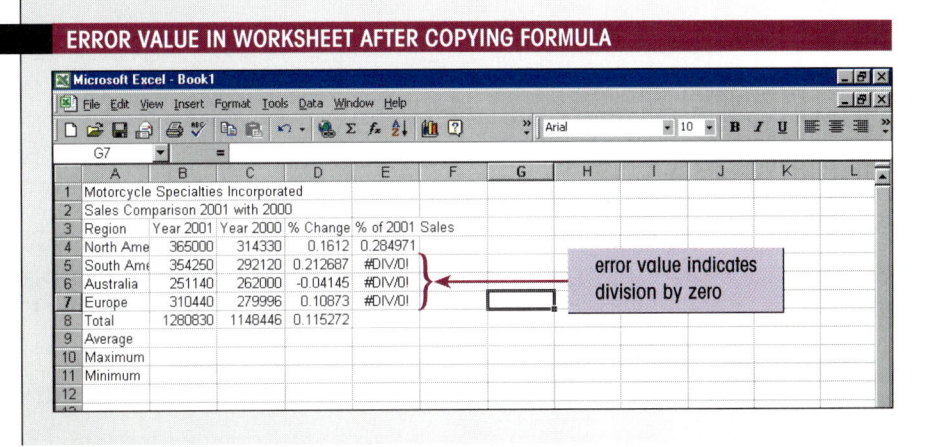

Figure 2-13   ERROR VALUE IN WORKSHEET AFTER COPYING FORMULA

	A	B	C	D	E
1	Motorcycle Specialties Incorporated				
2	Sales Comparison 2001 with 2000				
3	Region	Year 2001	Year 2000	% Change	% of 2001 Sales
4	North Ame	365000	314330	0.1612	0.284971
5	South Ame	354250	292120	0.212687	#DIV/0!
6	Australia	251140	262000	-0.04145	#DIV/0!
7	Europe	310440	279996	0.10873	#DIV/0!
8	Total	1280830	1148446	0.115272	
9	Average				
10	Maximum				
11	Minimum				

error value indicates division by zero

Something is wrong. Cells E5 through E7 display "#DIV/0!" a special constant, called an **error value.** Excel displays an error value constant when it cannot resolve the formula #DIV/0!, one of seven error value constants means that Excel was instructed to divide by zero. Take a moment to look at the formulas you copied into cells E5, E6, and E7.

To examine the formulas in cells E5 through E7:

1. Click cell **E5** and then look at the formula appearing in the formula bar, =B5/B9. The first cell reference changed from B4 in the original formula to B5 in the copied formula. That's correct because the sales data for South America is entered in cell B5. The second cell reference changed from B8 in the original formula to B9, which is not correct. The correct formula should be =B5/B8 because the total sales are in cell B8, not cell B9.

2. Look at the formulas in cells E6 and E7 and see how the cell references changed in each formula.

As you observed, the cell reference to total company sales (B8) in the original formula was changed to B9, B10, and B11 in the copied formulas. The problem with the copied formulas is that Excel adjusted *all* the cell references relative to their new location.

Absolute Versus Relative References

Sometimes when you copy a formula, you don't want Excel to change all cell references automatically to reflect their new positions in the worksheet. If you want a cell reference to point to the same location in the worksheet when you copy it, you must use an **absolute reference**. An absolute reference is a cell reference in a formula that does not change when copied to another cell.

To create an absolute reference, you insert a dollar sign ($) before the column and row of the cell reference. For example, the cell reference $B$8 is an absolute reference, whereas the cell reference B8 is a relative reference. If you copy a formula that contains the absolute reference $B$8 to another cell, the cell reference to $B$8 does not change. On the other hand, if you copy a formula containing the relative reference B8 to another cell, the reference to B8 changes. In some situations, a cell might have a **mixed reference**, such as $B8; in this case, when the formula is copied, the row number changes but the column letter does not.

To include an absolute reference in a formula, you can type a dollar sign when you type the cell reference, or you can use the F4 key to change the cell reference type while in Edit mode.

REFERENCE WINDOW RW

Changing Absolute, Mixed, and Relative References
- Double-click the cell that contains the formula you want to edit.
- Use the arrow keys to move the insertion point to the part of the cell reference you want to change.
- Press the F4 key until the reference is correct. Press the Enter key to complete the edit.

To correct the problem in your worksheet, you need to use an absolute reference, instead of a relative reference, to indicate the location of total sales in 2001. That is, you need to change the formula from =B4/B8 to =B4/$B$8. The easiest way to make this change is in Edit mode.

To change a cell reference to an absolute reference:

1. Click cell **E4** to move to the cell that contains the formula you want to edit.

2. Double-click the mouse button to edit the formula in the cell. Notice that each cell reference in the formula in cell E4 appears in a different color and the corresponding cells referred to in the formula are outlined in the same color. This feature is called **Range Finder** and is designed to make it easier for you to check the accuracy of your formula.

3. Make sure the insertion point is to the right of the division (/) operator, anywhere in the cell reference B8.

4. Press the **F4** key to change the reference to $B$8.

   TROUBLE? If your reference shows the **mixed reference** B$8 or $B8, continue to press the F4 key until you see $B$8.

5. Press the **Enter** key to update the formula in cell E4.

Cell E4 still displays .284971, which is the formula's correct result. But remember, the problem in your original formula did not surface until you copied it to cells E5 through E7. To correct the error, you need to copy the revised formula and then check the results. Although you can again use the fill handle to copy the formula, you can also copy the formula using the Clipboard and the Copy and Paste buttons on the Standard toolbar.

TUTORIAL 2 CREATING A WORKSHEET   EX 2.13   EXCEL

Copying Cell Contents Using the Copy-and-Paste Method

You can duplicate the contents of a cell or range by making a copy of the cell or range and then pasting the copy into one or more locations in the same worksheet, another worksheet, or another workbook.

When you copy a cell or range of cells, the copied material is placed on the Clipboard. You can copy labels, numbers, dates, or formulas.

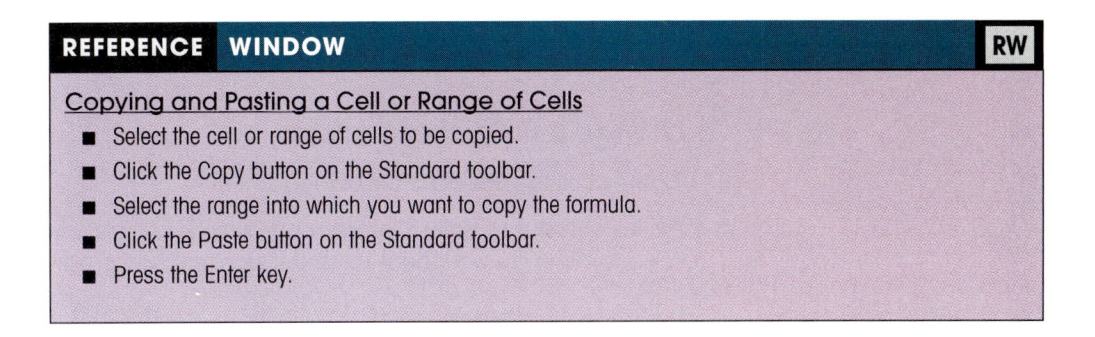

REFERENCE WINDOW	RW

Copying and Pasting a Cell or Range of Cells
- Select the cell or range of cells to be copied.
- Click the Copy button on the Standard toolbar.
- Select the range into which you want to copy the formula.
- Click the Paste button on the Standard toolbar.
- Press the Enter key.

You need to copy the formula in cell E4 to the Clipboard and then paste that formula into cells E5 through E7.

To copy the revised formula from cell E4 to cells E5 through E7:

1. Click cell **E4** because it contains the revised formula that you want to copy.

2. Click the **Copy** button on the Standard toolbar. A moving dashed line surrounds cell E4, indicating that the formula has been copied and is available to be pasted into other cells.

3. Click and drag to select cells **E5** through **E7**.

4. Click the **Paste** button on the Standard toolbar. Excel adjusts the formula and pastes it into cells E5 through E7.

5. Click any cell to deselect the range and view the formulas' results. Press the **Escape** key to clear the Clipboard and remove the dashed line surrounding cell E4. See Figure 2-14.

Figure 2-14   RESULTS OF COPYING THE FORMULA WITH AN ABSOLUTE REFERENCE

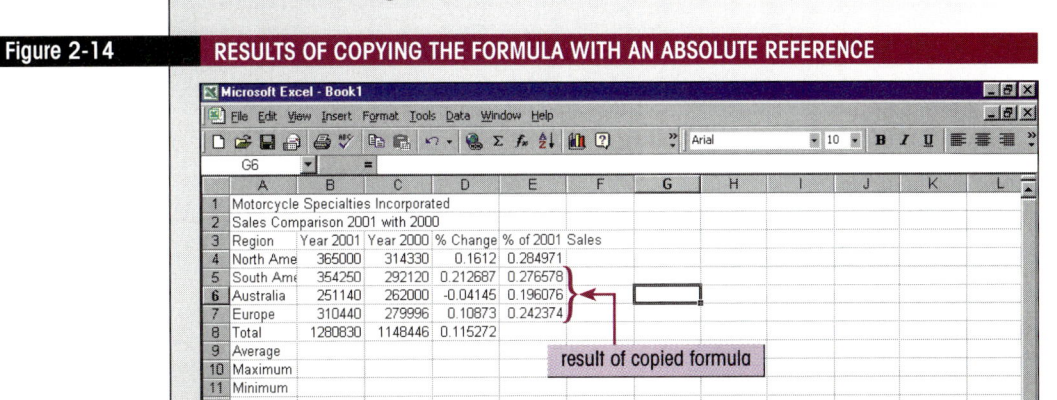

	A	B	C	D	E
1	Motorcycle Specialties Incorporated				
2	Sales Comparison 2001 with 2000				
3	Region	Year 2001	Year 2000	% Change	% of 2001 Sales
4	North Ame	365000	314330	0.1612	0.284971
5	South Ame	354250	292120	0.212687	0.276578
6	Australia	251140	262000	-0.04145	0.196076
7	Europe	310440	279996	0.10873	0.242374
8	Total	1280830	1148446	0.115272	
9	Average				
10	Maximum				
11	Minimum				

result of copied formula

Copying this formula worked. When you pasted the formula from cell E4 into the range E5:E7, Excel automatically adjusted the relative reference (B4), while using the cell reference ($B$8) for all absolute references. You have now implemented most of the design as

EXCEL   EX 2.14   TUTORIAL 2   CREATING A WORKSHEET

specified in the planning analysis sheet. Now rename the worksheet to accurately describe its contents, then save the workbook on your Data Disk before entering the formulas to compute the summary statistics.

Renaming the Worksheet

Before saving the workbook, look at the sheet tab in the lower-left corner of the worksheet window: the sheet is currently named Sheet1—the name Excel automatically uses when it opens a new workbook. Now that your worksheet is taking shape, you want to give it a more descriptive name that better indicates its contents. Change the worksheet name to Sales Comparison.

To change a worksheet name:

1. Double-click the **Sheet1** sheet tab to select it.
2. Type the new name, **Sales Comparison**, over the current name, Sheet1, and then click any cell in the worksheet. The sheet tab displays the name "Sales Comparison."

Saving the New Workbook

Now you want to save the workbook. Because this is the first time you have saved this workbook, you use the Save As command and name the file MSI Sales Report.

To save the workbook as MSI Sales Report:

1. Click **File** on the menu bar, and then click **Save As** to open the Save As dialog box.
2. In the File name text box, type **MSI Sales Report** but don't press the Enter key yet. You still need to check some other settings.
3. Click the **Save in** list arrow, and then click the drive containing your Data Disk.
4. In the folder list, select the **Tutorial** folder for **Tutorial.02**, into which you want to save the workbook. Your Save As dialog box should look like the dialog box in Figure 2-15.

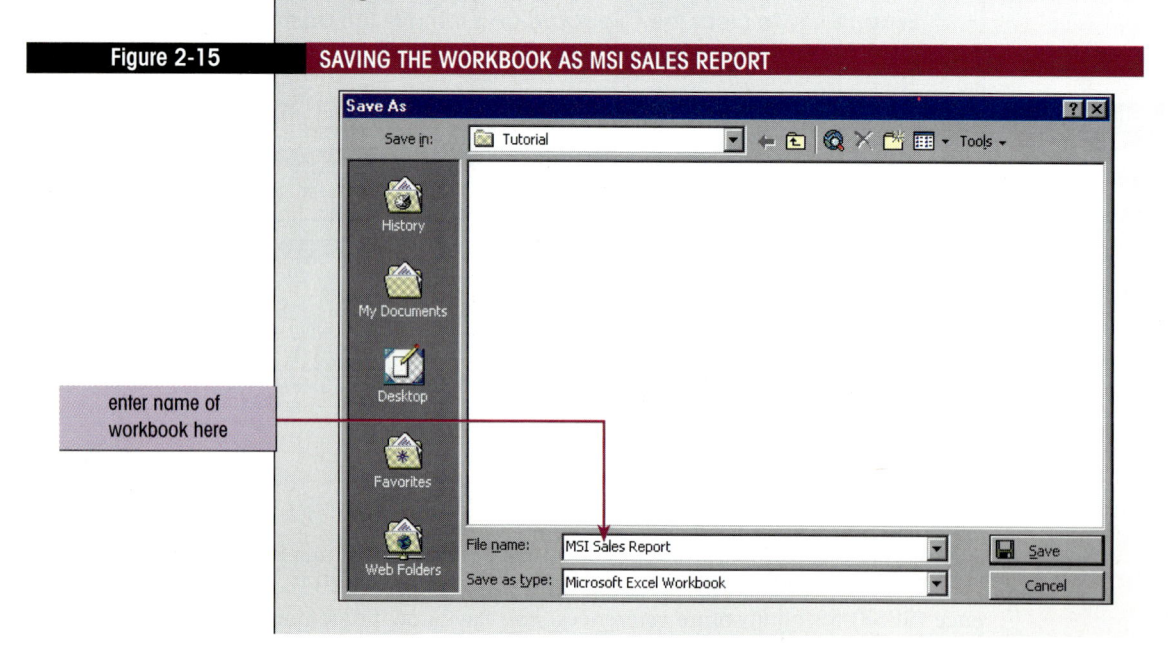

Figure 2-15   **SAVING THE WORKBOOK AS MSI SALES REPORT**

enter name of workbook here

TUTORIAL 2 CREATING A WORKSHEET   EX 2.15   EXCEL

5. Click the **Save** button to save the workbook.

   TROUBLE? If you see the message "Replace Existing MSI Sales Report," Excel found a file with the same name on the current folder. Click the Yes button to replace the file on the folder with the current version.

Session 2.1 QUICK CHECK

1. List the steps to follow to create a worksheet.
2. Describe how AutoSum works.
3. In cell D3 you have the formula =B3-C3. After you copy this formula to cell D4, the formula in cell D4 would appear in the formula bar as _____.
4. The _____ is a small black square located in the lower-right corner of a selected cell.
5. In the formula =D10*C10, D10 and C10 are examples of _____ references.
6. In the formula =A8+(1+$C$1), $C$1 is an example of a(n) _____.
7. When you copy a formula using the Copy and Paste buttons on the Standard toolbar, Excel uses the _____ to temporarily store the formula.
8. Describe the steps you take to change the name of the sheet tab.
9. What is meant by order of precedence?

Now that you have planned and built the Sales Comparison worksheet by entering labels, values, and formulas, you need to complete the worksheet by entering some functions and formatting the worksheet. You will do this in Session 2.2.

SESSION 2.2

In this session you will finish the worksheet. As you do this you will learn how to enter several statistical functions, increase the column width, insert a row between the titles and column headings, move the contents of a range to another location, and apply one of the Excel predefined formats to the report. You will also spell check the worksheet, preview, and print it.

Excel Functions

According to Sally's planning analysis sheet, you still need to enter the formulas for the summary statistics. To enter these statistics you'll use three Excel functions, AVERAGE, MAX, and MIN. The many Excel functions help you enter formulas for calculations and other specialized tasks, even if you don't know the mathematical details of the calculations. As you recall, a function is a calculation tool that performs a predefined operation. You are already familiar with the SUM function, which adds the values in a range of cells. Excel provides hundreds of functions, including a function to calculate the average of a list of numbers, a function to find a number's square root, a function to calculate loan payments, and a function to calculate the number of days between two dates.

Each function has a **syntax**, which specifies the order in which you must type the parts of the function and where to put commas, parentheses, and other punctuation. The general syntax of an Excel function is:

FUNCTION NAME(*argument1,argument2,...*)

The syntax of most functions requires you to type the function name followed by one or more arguments in parentheses. The name of the function, such as SUM or AVERAGE, describes the operation the function performs. Function **arguments** specify the values the function must use in the calculation, or the cell references that Excel must include in the calculation. For example, in the function SUM(A1:A20) the function name is SUM and the argument is A1:A20, which is the range of cells you want to total.

You can use a function in a simple formula such as =SUM(A1:A20), or a more complex formula such as =SUM(A1:A20)*52. As with all formulas, you enter the formula that contains a function in the cell where you want to display the results. The easiest way to enter a function in a cell is to use the Paste Function button on the Standard toolbar, which leads you step-by-step through the process of entering a formula containing a function.

If you prefer, you can type the function directly into the cell. Although the function name is always shown in uppercase, you can type it in either uppercase or lowercase. Also, even though parentheses enclose the arguments, you need not type the closing parenthesis if the function ends the formula. Excel automatically adds the closing parenthesis when you press the Enter key to complete the formula.

Figure 2-16 shows a few of the functions available in Excel organized by category. To learn more about functions, use the Paste Function button on the Standard toolbar or use the Help system. According to Sally's planning analysis sheet, the next step is to calculate the average regional sales for 2001.

Figure 2-16	SELECTED EXCEL FUNCTIONS		
CATEGORY	**FUNCTION NAME**	**SYNTAX**	**DEFINITION**
Finance	PMT	PMT(rate,nper,pv,fv,type)	Calculates the payment for a loan based on constant payments and a constant interest rate
	FV	FV(rate,nper,pmt,pv,type)	Returns the future value of an investment based on periodic, constant payments and a constant interest rate
Math	ROUND	ROUND(number,num_digits)	Rounds a number to a specified number of digits
	RAND	RAND( )	Returns an evenly distributed random number greater than or equal to 0 and less than 1
Logical	IF	IF(logical_test,value_if_true, value_if_false)	Returns one value if a condition you specify evaluates to TRUE and another value if it evaluates to FALSE
	AND	AND(logical1,logical2, ...)	Returns TRUE if all its arguments are TRUE; returns FALSE if one or more arguments is FALSE
Lookup and Reference	VLOOKUP	VLOOKUP(lookup_value, table_array,col_index_num, range_lookup)	Searches for a value in the leftmost column of a table, and then returns a value in the same row from a column you specify in the table
	INDIRECT	INDIRECT(ref_text,a1)	Returns the reference specified by a text string–references are immediately evaluated to display their contents
Text	CONCATENATE	CONCATENATE (text1,text2,...)	Joins several text strings into one text string
	LEFT	LEFT(text,num_chars)	Returns the first (or leftmost) character or characters in a text string
Date and Time	TODAY	TODAY( )	Returns the serial number of the current date
	YEAR	YEAR(serial_number)	Returns the year corresponding to serial number–the year is given as an integer in the range 1900-9999
Statistical	COUNT	COUNT(value1,value2, ...)	Counts the number of cells that contain numbers and numbers within the list of arguments
	STDEV	STDEV(number1,number2,...)	Estimates standard deviation based on a sample

AVERAGE Function

AVERAGE is a statistical function that calculates the average, or the arithmetic mean. The syntax for the AVERAGE function is:

AVERAGE(*number1,number2,...*)

TUTORIAL 2 CREATING A WORKSHEET   EX 2.17   **EXCEL**

Generally, when you use the AVERAGE function, *number* is a range of cells. To calculate the average of a range of cells, Excel sums the values in the range, then divides by the number of non-blank cells in the range.

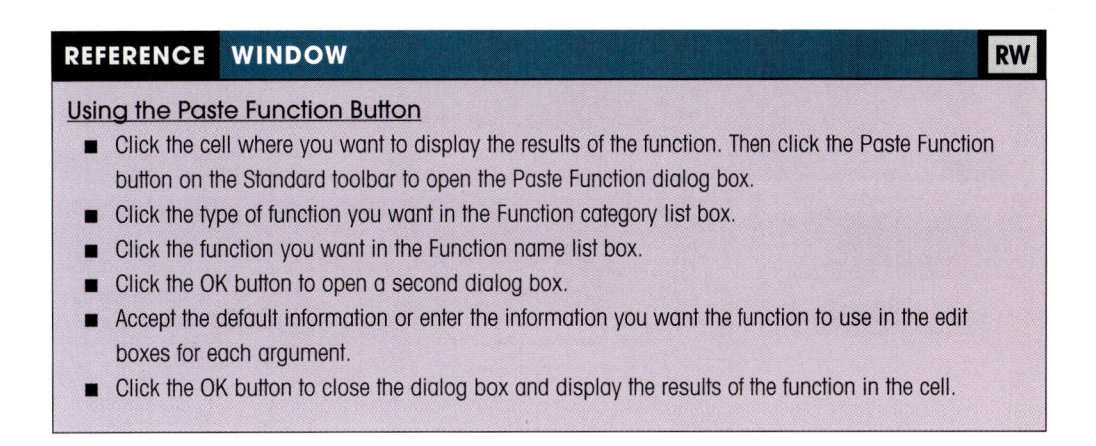

REFERENCE WINDOW

Using the Paste Function Button
- Click the cell where you want to display the results of the function. Then click the Paste Function button on the Standard toolbar to open the Paste Function dialog box.
- Click the type of function you want in the Function category list box.
- Click the function you want in the Function name list box.
- Click the OK button to open a second dialog box.
- Accept the default information or enter the information you want the function to use in the edit boxes for each argument.
- Click the OK button to close the dialog box and display the results of the function in the cell.

Sally wants you to calculate the average sales in 2001. You'll use the Paste Function button to enter the AVERAGE function, which is one of the statistical functions.

To enter the AVERAGE function using the Paste Function button:

1. If you took a break after the last session, make sure Excel is running and the MSI Sales worksheet is open. Click cell **B9** to select the cell where you want to enter the AVERAGE function.

2. Click the **Paste Function** button on the Standard toolbar to open the Paste Function dialog box.

   TROUBLE? If the Office Assistant opens and offers help on this feature, click the No option button.

3. Click **Statistical** in the Function category list box.

4. Click **AVERAGE** in the Function name list box. See Figure 2-17. The syntax for the AVERAGE function, AVERAGE(number1,number2,...), appears beneath the Function category box.

Figure 2-17   PASTE FUNCTION DIALOG BOX

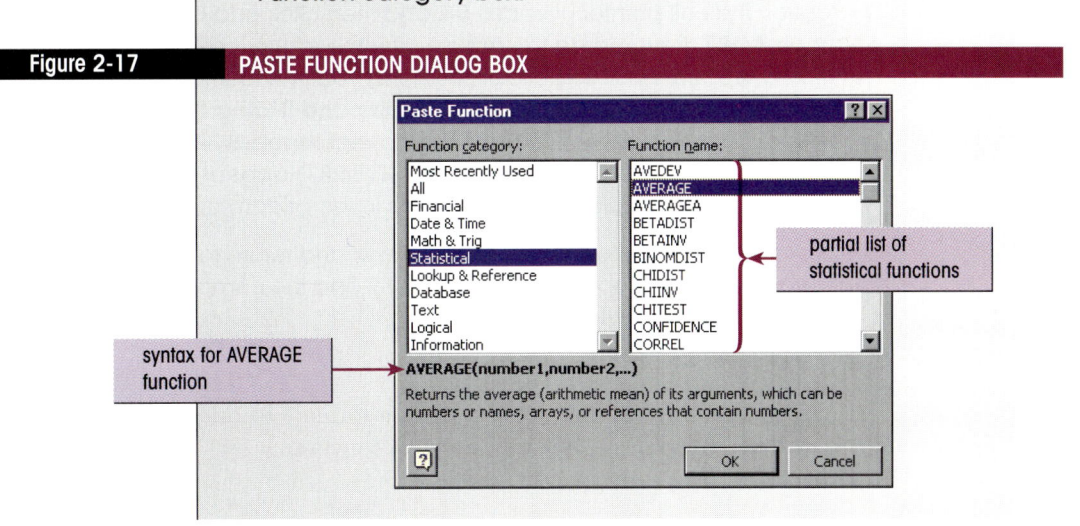

5. Click the **OK** button to open the formula palette for the Average function. The **formula palette** displays the name of the function, a text box for each argument of the function you selected, a description of the function and each argument, the current values of the arguments, the current results of the function, and the current results of the entire formula. Notice that the range B4:B8 appears in the Number1 edit box, and =AVERAGE(B4:B8) appears in the formula bar. See Figure 2-18.

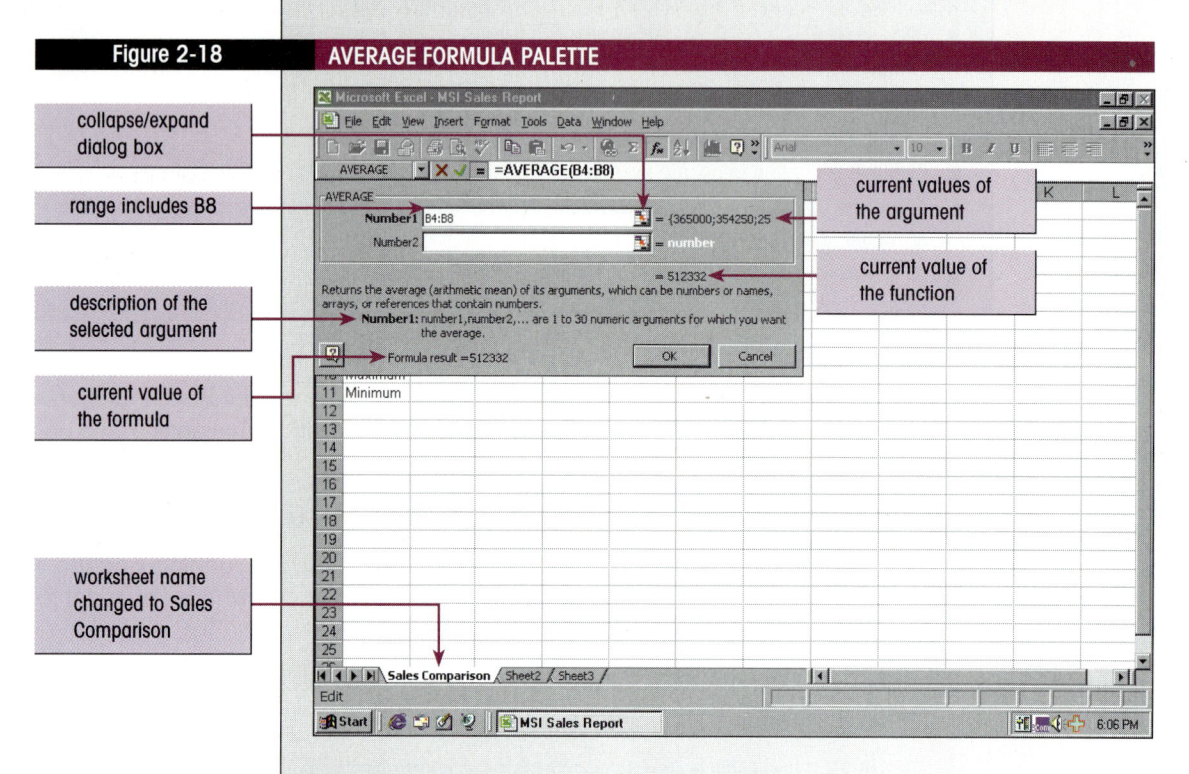

Figure 2-18 — AVERAGE FORMULA PALETTE

Callouts:
- collapse/expand dialog box
- range includes B8
- description of the selected argument
- current value of the formula
- worksheet name changed to Sales Comparison
- current values of the argument
- current value of the function

Excel has incorrectly included the total sales for 2001 (cell B8) in the range to calculate the average. The correct range is B4:B7.

6. Click the **Collapse** dialog box button to the right of the Number1 text box to collapse the dialog box to the size of one row. This makes it easier for you to identify and select the correct range.

7. Position the cell pointer over cell **B4**, and then click and drag to select the range **B4:B7**. As you drag the mouse over the range, notice that the message "4Rx1C" appears in a ScreenTip, informing you that four rows and one column have been selected, and then click the **Expand Dialog Box** button. The collapsed dialog box is restored and the correct range, B4:B7, appears in the Number1 text box. The formula =AVERAGE(B4:B7) appears in the formula bar and the formula result 320207.5 appears in the bottom of the formula palette.

8. Click the **OK** button to close the dialog box and return to the worksheet. The average, 320207.5, now appears in cell B9 and the completed function appears in the formula bar.

According to your plan, you need to enter a formula to find the largest regional sales amount in 2001. To do this, you'll use the MAX function.

MAX Function

MAX is a statistical function that finds the largest number. The syntax of the MAX function is: MAX(*number1,number2,...*)

In the MAX function, *number* can be a constant number such as 345, a cell reference such as B6, or a range of cells such as B5:B16. You can use the MAX function to simply display the largest number or to use the largest number in a calculation. Although you can use the Paste Function to enter the MAX function, this time you'll type the MAX function directly into cell B10.

To enter the MAX function by typing directly into a cell:

1. If necessary, click cell **B10** to select it as the cell into which you want to type the formula that uses the MAX function.

2. Type **=MAX(B4:B7)** and then press the **Enter** key. Cell B10 displays 365000, the largest regional sales amount in 2001.

Next you need to find the smallest regional sales amount in 2001. For that, you'll use the MIN function.

MIN Function

MIN is a statistical function that finds the smallest number. The syntax of the MIN function is: MIN(*number1,number2,...*)

You can use the MIN function to display the smallest number or to use the smallest number in a calculation.

You'll enter the MIN function directly into cell B11 using the pointing method.

Building Formulas by Pointing

Excel provides several ways to enter cell references into a formula. One is to type the cell references directly, as you have done so far in all the formulas you've entered. Another way to put a cell reference in a formula is to point to the cell reference you want to include while creating the formula. To use the **pointing method** to enter the formula, you click the cell or range of cells whose cell references you want to include in the formula. You may prefer to use this method to enter formulas because it minimizes typing errors.

Now use the pointing method to enter the formula to calculate the minimum sales.

To enter the MIN function using the pointing method:

1. If necessary, click cell **B11** to move to the cell where you want to enter the formula that uses the MIN function.

2. Type **=MIN(** to begin the formula.

3. Position the cell pointer in cell **B4**, and then click and drag to select cells **B4** through **B7**. As you drag the mouse over the range, notice that the message "4Rx1C" appears in a ScreenTip, informing you that four rows and one column have been selected. See Figure 2-19.

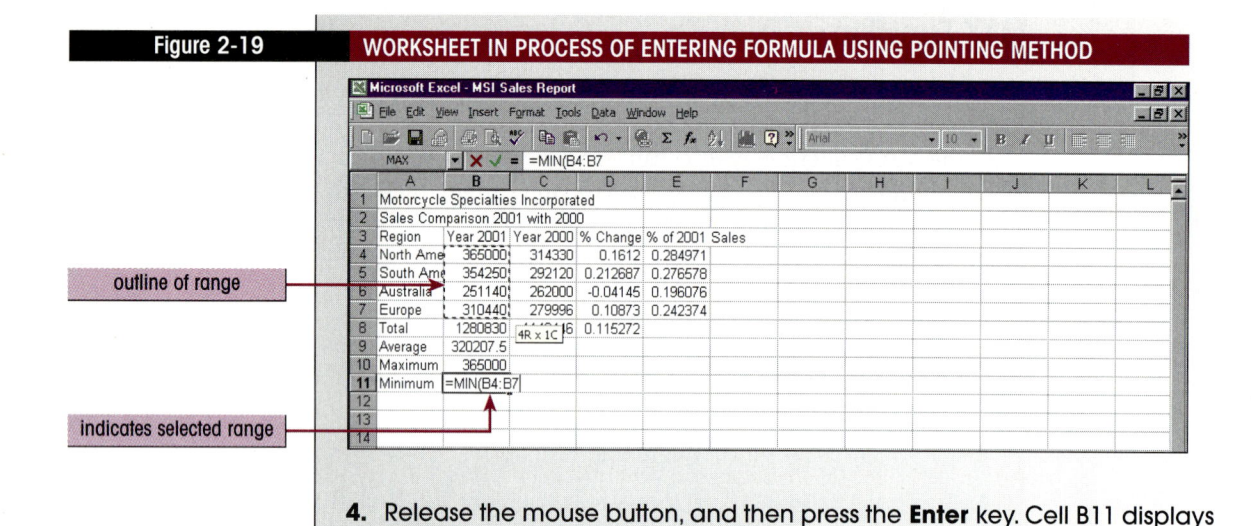

Figure 2-19 WORKSHEET IN PROCESS OF ENTERING FORMULA USING POINTING METHOD

outline of range

indicates selected range

4. Release the mouse button, and then press the **Enter** key. Cell B11 displays 251140, the smallest regional sales amount for 2001.

Now that the worksheet labels, values, formulas, and functions have been entered, Sally reviews the worksheet.

Testing the Worksheet

Before trusting a worksheet and its results, you should test it to make sure you entered the correct formulas. You want the worksheet to produce accurate results.

Beginners often expect their Excel worksheets to work correctly the first time. Sometimes they do work correctly the first time, but even well-planned and well-designed worksheets can contain errors. It's best to assume that a worksheet has errors and test it to make sure it is correct. While there are no rules for testing a worksheet, here are some approaches:

- Entering **test values**, numbers that generate a known result, to determine whether your worksheet formulas are accurate. For example, try entering a 1 into each cell. After you enter the test values, you compare the results in your worksheet with the known results. If the results on your worksheet don't match the known results, you probably made an error.
- Entering **extreme values**, such as very large or very small numbers, and observing their effect on cells with formulas.
- Working out the numbers ahead of time with pencil, paper, and calculator, and comparing these results with the output from the computer.

Sally used the third approach to test her worksheet. She had calculated her results using a calculator (Figure 2-2) and then compared them with the results on the screen (Figure 2-19). The numbers agree, so she feels confident that the worksheet she created contains accurate results.

Spell Checking the Worksheet

You can use the Excel spell check feature to help identify and correct spelling and typing errors. Excel compares the words in your worksheet to the words in its dictionary. If Excel finds a word in your worksheet not in its dictionary, it shows you the word and some suggested corrections, and you decide whether to correct it or leave it as is.

> **REFERENCE WINDOW**
>
> **Checking the Spelling in a Worksheet**
> - Click cell A1 to begin the spell check from the top of the worksheet.
> - Click the Spelling button on the Standard toolbar.
> - Change the spelling or ignore the spell check's suggestion for each identified word.
> - Click the OK button when the spell check is complete.

You have tested your numbers and formulas for accuracy. Now you can check the spelling of all text entries in the worksheet.

To check the spelling in a worksheet:

1. Click cell **A1** to begin spell checking in the first cell of the worksheet.

2. Click the **Spelling** button on the Standard toolbar to check the spelling of the text in the worksheet. A message box indicates that Excel has finished spell checking the entire worksheet. No errors were found.

   TROUBLE? If the spell check does find a spelling error in your worksheet, use the Spelling dialog box options to correct the spelling mistake and continue checking the worksheet.

Improving the Worksheet Layout

Although the numbers are correct, Sally wants to present a more polished-looking worksheet. She feels that there are a number of simple changes you can make to the worksheet that will improve its layout and make the data more readable. Specifically, she asks you to increase the width of column A so that the entire region names are visible, insert a blank row between the titles and column headings, move the summary statistics down three rows from their current location, and apply one of the predefined Excel formats to the worksheet.

Changing Column Width

Changing the column width is one way to improve the appearance of the worksheet, making it easier to read and interpret data. In Sally's worksheet, you need to increase the width of column A so that all of the labels for North America and South America appear in their cells.

Excel provides several methods for changing column width. For example, you can click a column heading or click and drag the pointer to select a series of column headings and then use the Format menu. You can also use the dividing line between column headings in the column header row. When you move the pointer over the dividing line between two column headings, the pointer changes to ↔. You can then use the pointer to drag the dividing line to a new location. You can also double-click the dividing line to make the column as wide as the longest text label or number in the column.

> **REFERENCE WINDOW**
>
> **Changing Column Width**
> - Click the column heading(s) whose width you want to change.
> - Click Format, point to Column, and then click Width.
> - In the Column Width dialog box, enter the new column width (or click AutoFit Selection to make the column(s) as wide as the longest text label or number in the column(s)).
>
> or
>
> - Drag the column heading dividing line to the right to increase column width or to the left to decrease column width.
>
> or
>
> - Double-click the column heading dividing line to make the column as wide as the longest text label or number in the column.

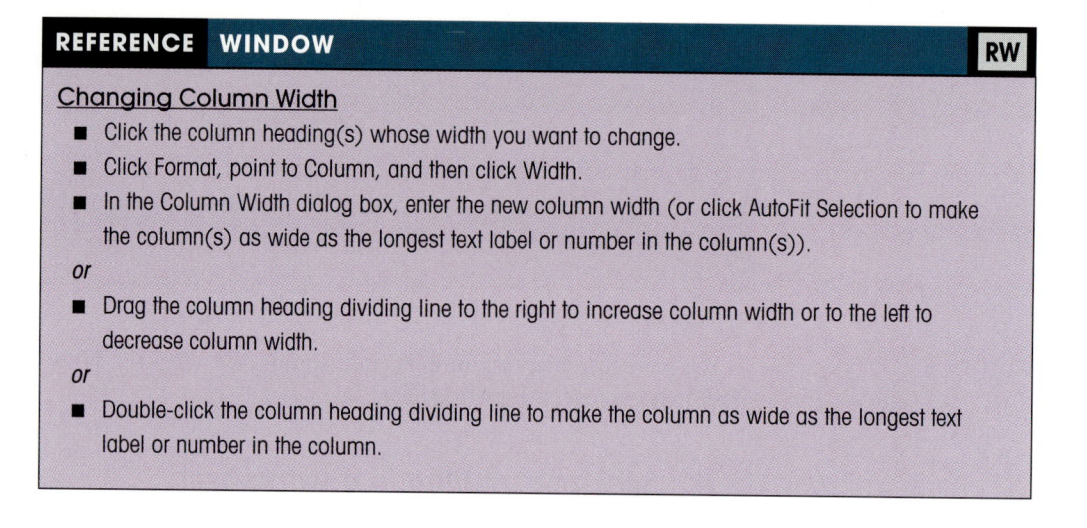

Sally has asked you to change the width of column A so that the complete region name is visible.

To change the width of column A:

1. Position the pointer ✥ on the A in the column heading area.

2. Move the pointer to the right edge of the column heading dividing columns A and B. Notice that the pointer changes to the resize arrow ↔.

3. Click and drag the resize arrow to the right, increasing the column width 12 characters or more, as indicated in the ScreenTip that pops up on the screen.

4. Release the mouse button. See Figure 2-20.

Figure 2-20   **WORKSHEET AFTER WIDTH OF COLUMN A INCREASED**

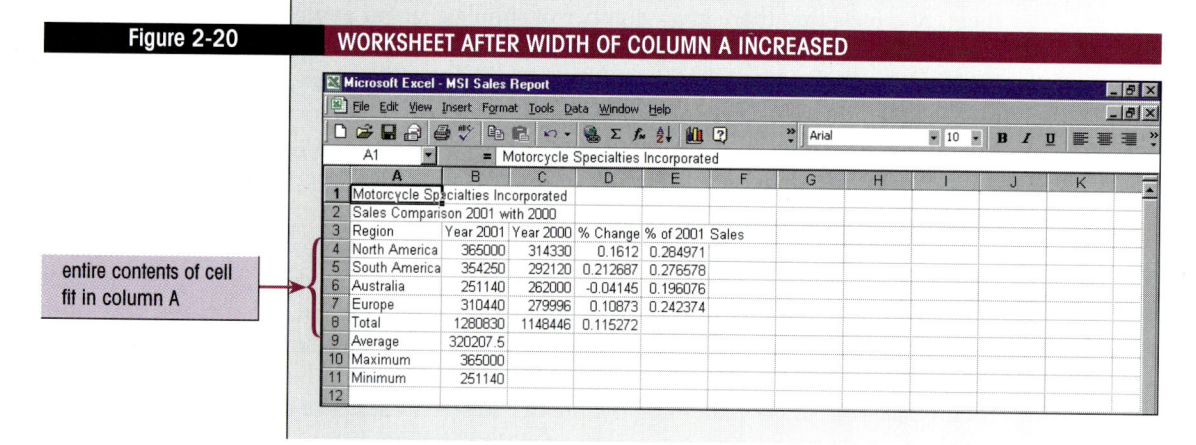

entire contents of cell fit in column A

	A	B	C	D	E
1	Motorcycle Specialties Incorporated				
2	Sales Comparison 2001 with 2000				
3	Region	Year 2001	Year 2000	% Change	% of 2001 Sales
4	North America	365000	314330	0.1612	0.284971
5	South America	354250	292120	0.212687	0.276578
6	Australia	251140	262000	-0.04145	0.196076
7	Europe	310440	279996	0.10873	0.242374
8	Total	1280830	1148446	0.115272	
9	Average	320207.5			
10	Maximum	365000			
11	Minimum	251140			

Next you need to insert a row between the title and the column heading.

Inserting a Row into a Worksheet

At times you may need to add one or more rows or columns to a worksheet to make room for new data or to make the worksheet easier to read. The process of inserting columns and rows is similar; you select the number of columns or rows you want to insert and then use

TUTORIAL 2 CREATING A WORKSHEET   EX 2.23   EXCEL

the Insert command to insert them. When you insert rows or columns, Excel repositions other rows and columns in the worksheet and automatically adjusts cell references in formulas to reflect the new location of values used in calculations.

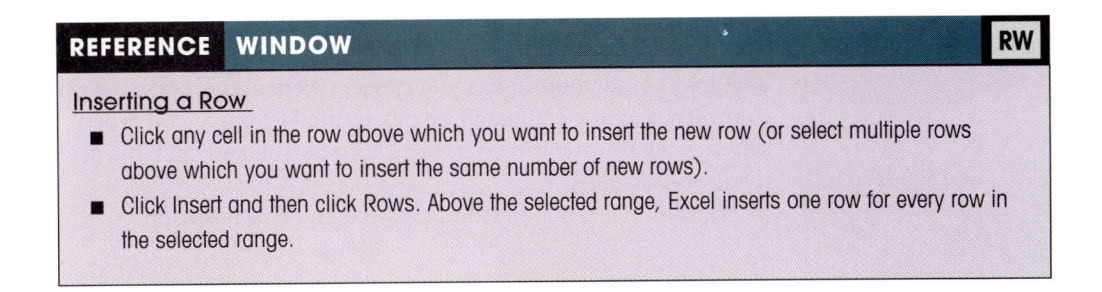

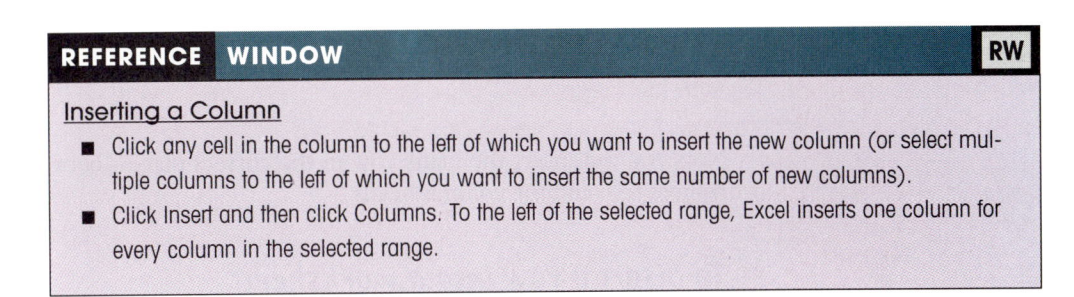

> **REFERENCE WINDOW**
>
> **Inserting a Row**
> - Click any cell in the row above which you want to insert the new row (or select multiple rows above which you want to insert the same number of new rows).
> - Click Insert and then click Rows. Above the selected range, Excel inserts one row for every row in the selected range.

> **REFERENCE WINDOW**
>
> **Inserting a Column**
> - Click any cell in the column to the left of which you want to insert the new column (or select multiple columns to the left of which you want to insert the same number of new columns).
> - Click Insert and then click Columns. To the left of the selected range, Excel inserts one column for every column in the selected range.

Sally wants one blank row between the titles and column headings in her worksheet.

To insert a row into a worksheet:

1. Click cell **A2**.

2. Click **Insert** on the menu bar, and then click **Rows**. Excel inserts a blank row above the original row 2. All other rows shift down one row. Click any cell. See Figure 2-21.

Figure 2-21   WORKSHEET AFTER ONE ROW INSERTED ABOVE ORIGINAL ROW 2

use this button to reverse action

row inserted in wrong position

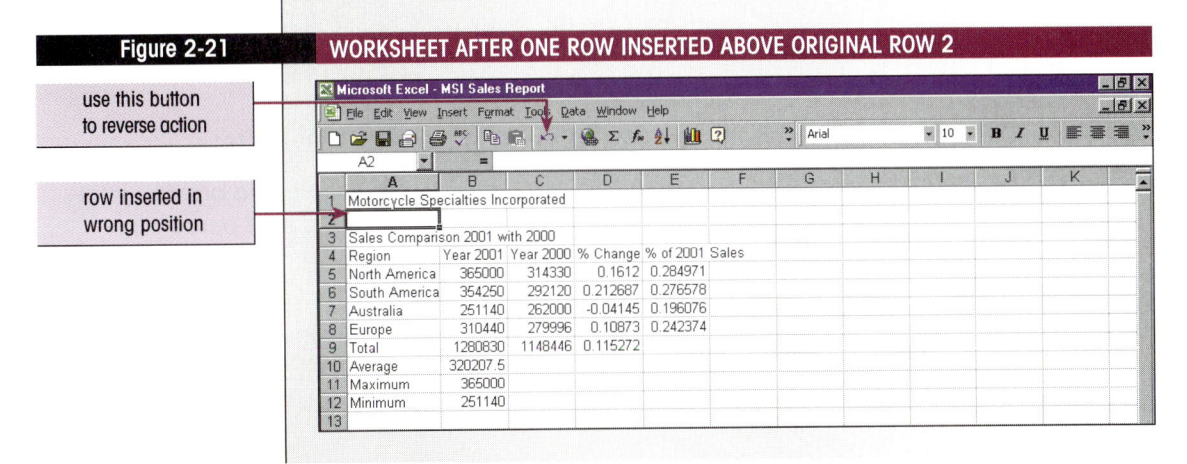

	A	B	C	D	E	F
1	Motorcycle Specialties Incorporated					
2						
3	Sales Comparison 2001 with 2000					
4	Region	Year 2001	Year 2000	% Change	% of 2001 Sales	
5	North America	365000	314330	0.1612	0.284971	
6	South America	354250	292120	0.212687	0.276578	
7	Australia	251140	262000	-0.04145	0.196076	
8	Europe	310440	279996	0.10873	0.242374	
9	Total	1280830	1148446	0.115272		
10	Average	320207.5				
11	Maximum	365000				
12	Minimum	251140				

The blank row isn't really where you wanted it. You inserted a row between the two lines of the title instead of between the title and the column heading. To correct this error you can either delete the row or use the Undo button. If you need to delete a row or column, select the row(s) or column(s) you want to delete, then click Delete on the Edit menu, or press the Delete key on your keyboard. You use the Undo button because it is a feature you find valuable in many situations.

Using the Undo Button

The Excel Undo button lets you cancel recent actions one at a time. Click the Undo button to reverse the last command or delete the last entry you typed. To reverse more than one action, click the arrow next to the Undo button and click the action you want to undo from the drop-down list.

Now use the Undo button to reverse the row insertion.

To reverse the row insertion:

1. Click the **Undo** button on the Standard toolbar to restore the worksheet to its status before the row was inserted.

Now you can insert the blank row in the correct place—between the second line of the worksheet title and the column heads.

To insert a row into a worksheet:

1. Click cell **A3** because you want to insert one row above row 3. If you wanted to insert several rows, you would select as many rows as you wanted to insert immediately below where you want the new rows inserted before using the Insert command.

2. Click **Insert** on the menu bar, and then click **Rows**. Excel inserts a blank row above the original row 3. All other rows shift down one row.

Adding a row changed the location of the data in the worksheet. For example, the percentage change in North American sales, originally in cell D4, is now in cell D5. Did Excel adjust the formulas to compensate for the new row? Check cell D5 and any other cells you want to view to verify that the cell references were adjusted.

To examine the formula in cell D5 and other cells:

1. Click cell **D5**. The formula =(B5-C5)/C5 appears in the formula bar. You originally entered the formula =(B4-C4)/C4 in cell D4 to calculate percentage change in North America. Excel automatically adjusted the cell reference to reflect the new location of the data.

2. Inspect other cells below row 3 to verify that their cell references were automatically adjusted when the new row was inserted.

Sally has also suggested moving the summary statistics down three rows from their present location to make the report easier to read. So you will need to move the range of cells containing the average, minimum, and maximum sales to a different location in the worksheet.

Moving a Range Using the Mouse

To place the summary statistics three rows below the other data in the report, you could use the Insert command to insert three blank rows between the total and average sales. Alternatively, you could use the mouse to move the summary statistics to a new location. Because you already know how to insert a row, try using the mouse to move the summary statistics to a new location. This technique is called drag and drop. You simply select the cell range you want to move and use the pointer to drag the cells' contents to the desired location.

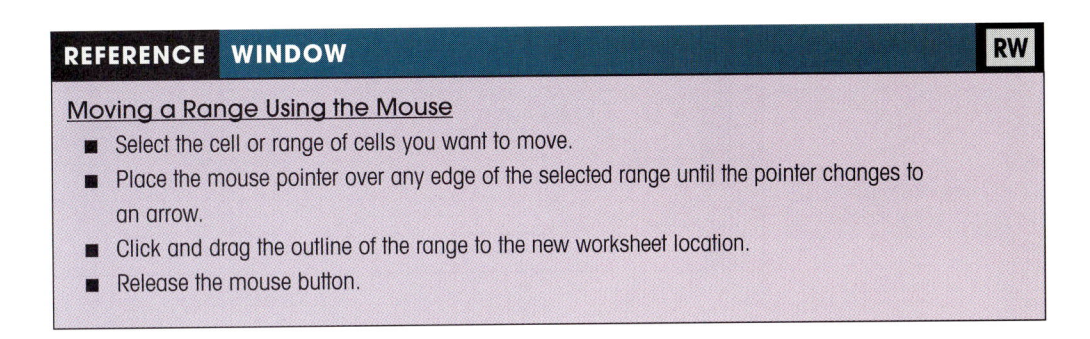

REFERENCE WINDOW

Moving a Range Using the Mouse
- Select the cell or range of cells you want to move.
- Place the mouse pointer over any edge of the selected range until the pointer changes to an arrow.
- Click and drag the outline of the range to the new worksheet location.
- Release the mouse button.

Sally has asked you to move the range A10 through B12 to the new destination area A13 through B15.

To move a range of cells using the drag-and-drop technique:

1. Select the range of cells **A10:B12**, which contains the sales summary statistics you want to move.

2. Place the mouse pointer over any edge of the selected range until the pointer changes to an arrow. See Figure 2-22.

Figure 2-22 RANGE TO BE MOVED

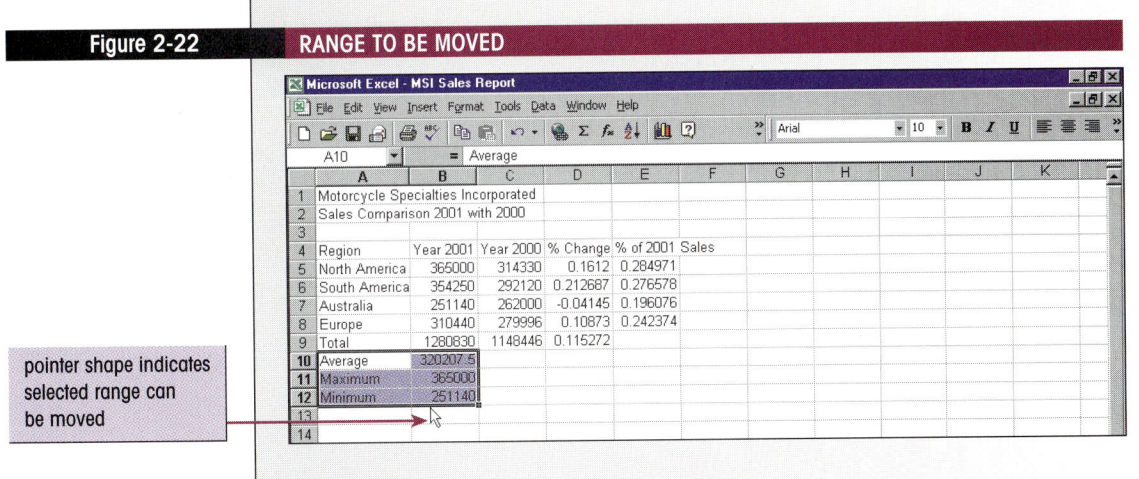

pointer shape indicates selected range can be moved

3. Click the mouse button and then hold the button down as you move (drag) the outline of the three rows down to range A13:B15. Notice how Excel displays a gray outline and a box with a range address that shows the destination of the cells.

4. Release the mouse button. Excel moves the selected cells to the designated location, A13:B15.

5. Click any cell to deselect the range. See Figure 2-23.

Figure 2-23 **WORKSHEET AFTER RANGE MOVED**

	A	B	C	D	E
1	Motorcycle Specialties Incorporated				
2	Sales Comparison 2001 with 2000				
3					
4	Region	Year 2001	Year 2000	% Change	% of 2001 Sales
5	North America	365000	314330	0.1612	0.284971
6	South America	354250	292120	0.212687	0.276578
7	Australia	251140	262000	-0.04145	0.196076
8	Europe	310440	279996	0.10873	0.242374
9	Total	1280830	1148446	0.115272	
10					
11					
12					
13	Average	320207.5			
14	Maximum	365000			
15	Minimum	251140			

new location for summary statistics

Next Sally wants you to use the Excel AutoFormat feature to improve the worksheet's appearance by emphasizing the titles and aligning numbers in cells.

Using AutoFormat

The AutoFormat feature lets you change the appearance of your worksheet by selecting from a collection of predefined worksheet formats. Each worksheet format in the AutoFormat collection gives your worksheet a more professional appearance by applying attractive fonts, borders, colors, and shading to a range of data. AutoFormat also adjusts column widths, row heights, and the alignment of text in cells to improve the appearance of the worksheet.

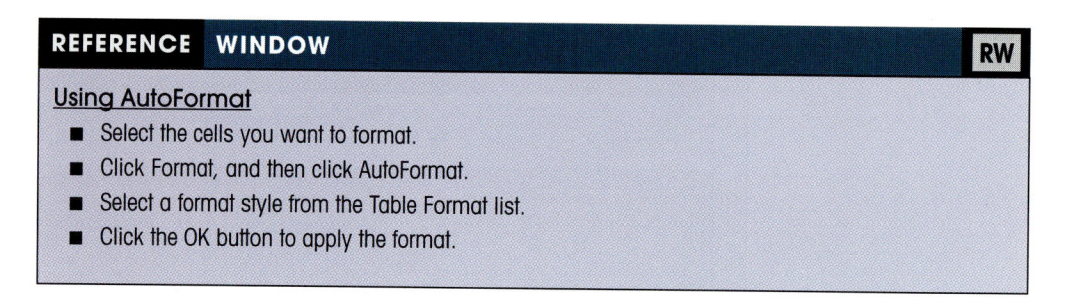

REFERENCE WINDOW   RW

Using AutoFormat
- Select the cells you want to format.
- Click Format, and then click AutoFormat.
- Select a format style from the Table Format list.
- Click the OK button to apply the format.

Now you'll use AutoFormat's Simple format to improve the worksheet's appearance.

To apply AutoFormat's Simple format:

1. Select cells **A1:E9** as the range you want to format using AutoFormat.

2. Click **Format** on the menu bar, and then click **AutoFormat**. The AutoFormat dialog box opens. See Figure 2-24.

Figure 2-24 **AUTOFORMAT DIALOG BOX**

click here to preview other Autoformats

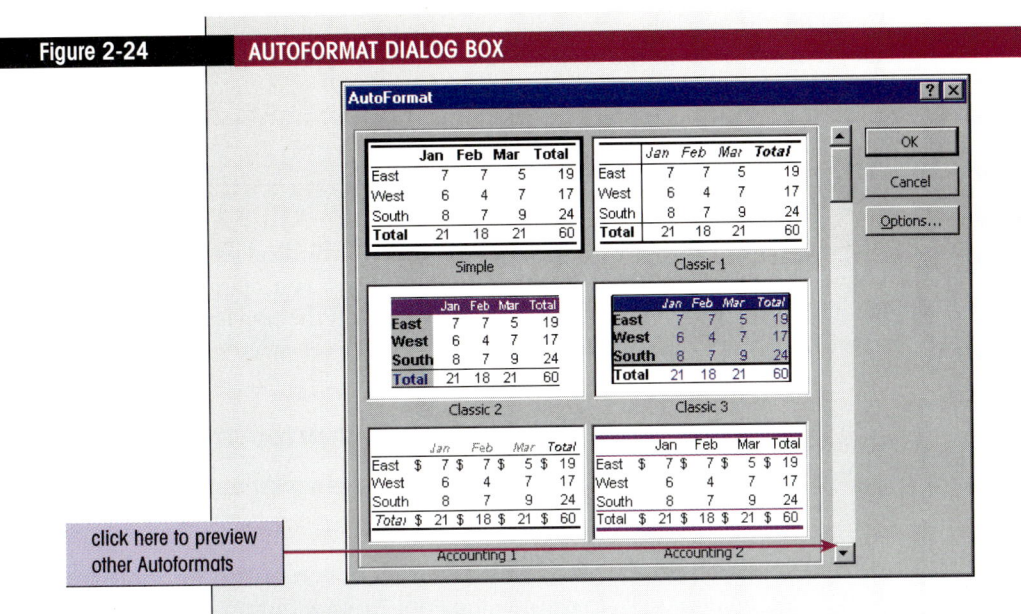

3. The dialog box displays a preview of how each format will appear when applied to a worksheet. Notice the dark border around the Simple format indicating it is the selected format.

4. Click the **OK** button to apply the Simple format.

5. Click any cell to deselect the range. Figure 2-25 shows the newly formatted worksheet.

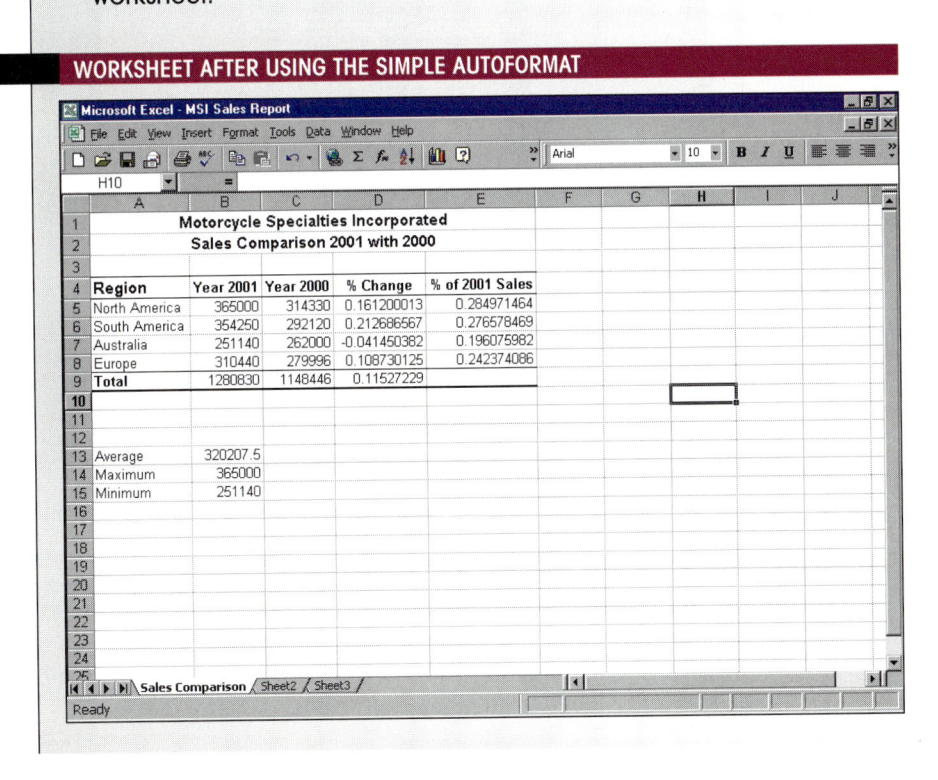

Figure 2-25 **WORKSHEET AFTER USING THE SIMPLE AUTOFORMAT**

	A	B	C	D	E
1		Motorcycle Specialties Incorporated			
2		Sales Comparison 2001 with 2000			
3					
4	Region	Year 2001	Year 2000	% Change	% of 2001 Sales
5	North America	365000	314330	0.161200013	0.284971464
6	South America	354250	292120	0.212686567	0.276578469
7	Australia	251140	262000	-0.041450382	0.196075982
8	Europe	310440	279996	0.108730125	0.242374086
9	Total	1280830	1148446	0.11527229	
10					
11					
12					
13	Average	320207.5			
14	Maximum	365000			
15	Minimum	251140			

You show the worksheet to Sally. She's impressed with the improved appearance and decides to hand it out to the regional sales managers at their next meeting. She asks you to print it so she can make copies.

Previewing the Worksheet Using Print Preview

Before you print a worksheet, you can use the Excel Print Preview window to see how it will look when printed. The Print Preview window shows you margins, page breaks, headers, and footers that are not always visible on the screen. If the preview isn't what you want, you can close the Print Preview window and change the worksheet before printing it.

To preview the worksheet before you print it:

1. Click the Print Preview button to display the worksheet in the Print Preview window. See Figure 2-26.

   TROUBLE? If you do not see the Print Preview button on the Standard toolbar, click More Buttons to display the Print Preview button.

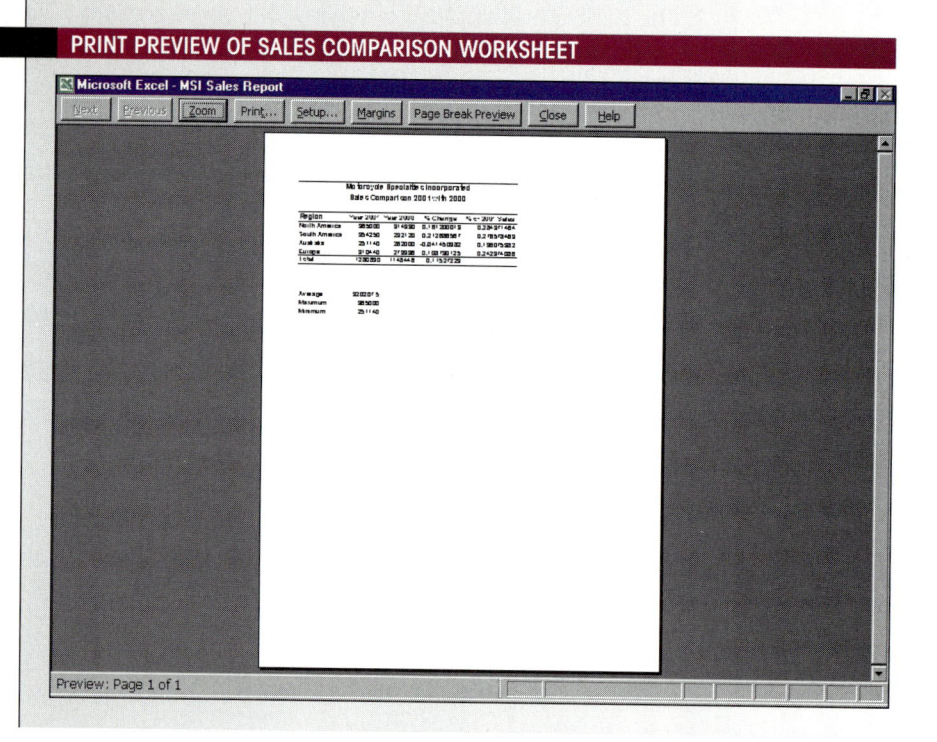

Figure 2-26 PRINT PREVIEW OF SALES COMPARISON WORKSHEET

When Excel displays a full page in the Print Preview window, you might have difficulty seeing the text of the worksheet because it is so small. Don't worry if the preview isn't completely readable. One purpose of the Print Preview window is to see the overall layout of the worksheet and how it will fit on the printed page. If you want a better view of the text, you can use the Zoom button.

> ### To display an enlarged section of the Print Preview window:
>
> 1. Click the **Zoom** button to display an enlarged section of the Print Preview.
> 2. Click the **Zoom** button again to return to the full-page view.

Notice that the Print Preview window contains several other buttons. Figure 2-27 describes each of these buttons.

Figure 2-27	DESCRIPTION OF PRINT PREVIEW BUTTONS
CLICKING THIS BUTTON	RESULTS IN
Next	Moving forward one page
Previous	Moving backward one page
Zoom	Magnifying the Print Preview screen to zoom in on any portion of the page; click again to return to full-page preview
Print	Printing the document
Setup	Displaying the Page Setup dialog box
Margins	Changing the width of margins, columns in the worksheet and the position of headers and footers
Page Break Preview	Showing where page breaks occur in the worksheet and which area of the worksheet will be printed; you can adjust where data will print by inserting or moving page breaks
Close	Closing the Print Preview window
Help	Activating Help

Looking at the worksheet in Print Preview, you observe that it is not centered on the page. By default, Excel prints a worksheet at the upper left of the page's print area. You can specify that the worksheet be centered vertically, horizontally, or both.

Centering the Printout

Worksheet printouts generally look more professional centered on the printed page. You decide that Sally would want you to center the sales comparison worksheet both horizontally and vertically on the printed page.

> ### To center the printout:
>
> 1. In Print Preview, click the **Setup** button to open the Page Setup dialog box.
> 2. Click the **Margins** tab. See Figure 2-28. Notice that the preview box displays a worksheet positioned at the upper-left edge of the page.

Figure 2-28 — MARGINS TAB OF PAGE SETUP DIALOG BOX

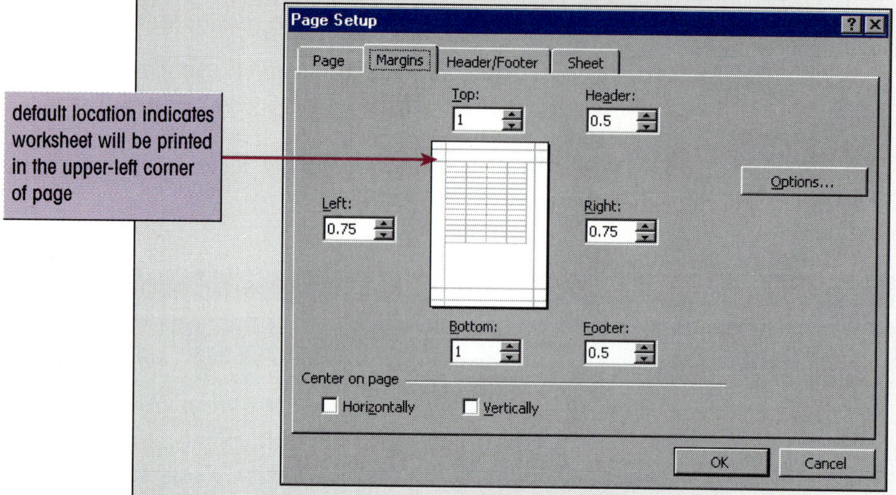

default location indicates worksheet will be printed in the upper-left corner of page

3. Click the **Horizontally** check box in the Center on page section to place a check in it.

4. Click the **Vertically** check box to place a check in it.

   Notice that the sample window shows that the worksheet is now centered vertically and horizontally on the page.

5. Click the **OK** button to return to the Print Preview window. Notice that the output in the Print Preview window is centered vertically and horizontally.

   TROUBLE? If you see only the worksheet name, click the Zoom button to view the entire page.

Adding Headers and Footers

Headers and footers can provide useful documentation on your printed worksheet, such as the name of the person who created the worksheet, the date it was printed, and its filename. The **header** is text printed in the top margin of every worksheet page. A **footer** is text printed in the bottom margin of every page. Headers and footers are not displayed in the worksheet window. To see them, you must preview or print the worksheet.

Excel uses formatting codes in headers and footers to represent the items you want to print. Formatting codes produce dates, times, and filenames that you might want a header or footer to include. Using formatting codes instead of typing the date, time, filename and so on provides flexibility. For example, if you use a formatting code for date, the current date appears on the printout whenever the worksheet is printed. You can type these codes, or you can click a formatting code button to insert the code. Figure 2-29 shows the formatting codes and the buttons for inserting them.

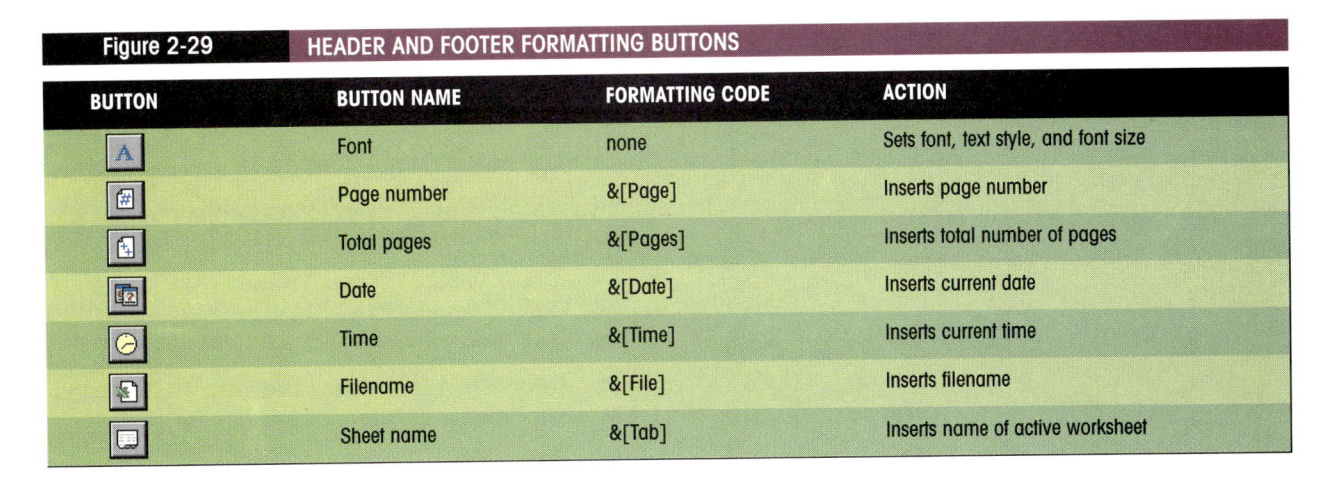

Figure 2-29 HEADER AND FOOTER FORMATTING BUTTONS

BUTTON	BUTTON NAME	FORMATTING CODE	ACTION
A	Font	none	Sets font, text style, and font size
#	Page number	&[Page]	Inserts page number
	Total pages	&[Pages]	Inserts total number of pages
	Date	&[Date]	Inserts current date
	Time	&[Time]	Inserts current time
	Filename	&[File]	Inserts filename
	Sheet name	&[Tab]	Inserts name of active worksheet

Sally asks you to add a custom header that includes the filename and today's date. She also wants you to add a custom footer that displays the preparer's name.

To add a header and a footer to your worksheet:

1. In the Print Preview window, click the **Setup** button to open the Page Setup dialog box, and then click the **Header/Footer** tab.

2. Click the **Custom Header** button to open the Header dialog box.

3. With the insertion point in the Left section box, click the **Filename** button. The code &(File) appears in the Left section box.

   TROUBLE? If you clicked the wrong code, double-click the code, press the Delete key, then repeat Steps 2 and 3.

4. Click the **Right section** box to move the insertion point to the Right section box.

5. Click the **Date** button. The code &(Date) appears in the Right section box. See Figure 2-30.

Figure 2-30 INSERTING FORMATTING CODES INTO THE HEADER DIALOG BOX

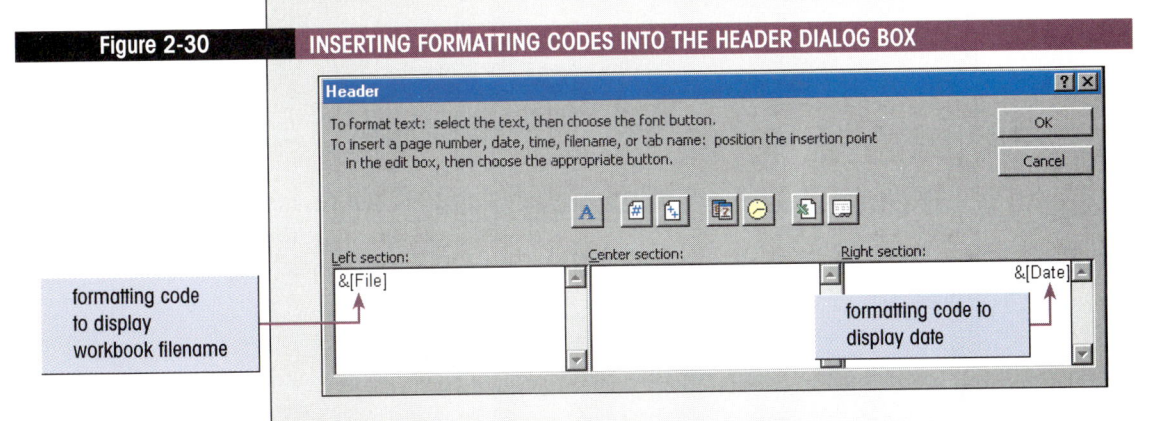

Header dialog box showing:
- Left section: &[File] — formatting code to display workbook filename
- Center section: (empty)
- Right section: &[Date] — formatting code to display date

TROUBLE? If you clicked the wrong code, double-click the code, press the Delete key, and then repeat Step 5.

6. Click the **OK** button to complete the header and return to the Page Setup dialog box. Notice that the header shows the filename on the left and the date on the right.

7. Click the **Custom Footer** button to open the Footer dialog box.

8. Click the **Center section** box to move the insertion point to the Center section box.

9. Type **Prepared by** (*enter your name here*).

10. Click the **OK** button to complete the footer and return to the Page Setup dialog box. Notice that the footer shows your name in the bottom, center of the page.

11. Click the **OK** button to return to the Print Preview window. The new header and footer appear in the Print Preview window.

12. Click the **Close** button to exit the Print Preview window and return to the worksheet.

You'll use the Print button on the Standard toolbar to print one copy of the worksheet with the current settings. First, save the worksheet before printing it.

To save your page setup settings with the worksheet and print the worksheet:

1. Click the **Save** button on the Standard toolbar.

2. Click the **Print** button on the Standard toolbar. See Figure 2-31.

   TROUBLE? If you see a message that indicates that you have a printer problem, click the Cancel button to cancel printing. Check your printer to make sure it is turned on and is online; also make sure it has paper. Then go back and try Step 2 again. If you have no printer available, click the Cancel button.

Figure 2-31   PRINTED WORKSHEET

Region	Year 2001	Year 2000	% Change	% of 2001 Sales
North America	365000	314330	0.161200013	0.284971464
South America	354250	292120	0.212686567	0.276578469
Australia	251140	262000	-0.041450382	0.196075982
Europe	310440	279996	0.108730125	0.242374086
Total	1280830	1148446	0.11527229	

Motorcycle Specialties Incorporated
Sales Comparison 2001 with 2000

Average	320207.5
Maximum	365000
Minimum	251140

Sally reviews the printed worksheet and is satisfied with its appearance. Now she asks for a second printout without the average, minimum, and maximum statistics.

Setting the Print Area

By default, Excel prints the entire worksheet. There are situations in which you are interested in printing a portion of the worksheet. To do this, you first select the area you want to print, and then use the Set Print Area command to define the print area.

To print a portion of the worksheet:

1. Select the range **A1:E9**.
2. Click **File**, point to Print Area, and then click **Set Print Area**.
3. Click the **Print Preview** button. Notice the average, minimum and maximum values are not included in the print preview window.
4. Click **Close** to return to the worksheet.
5. Click any cell outside the highlighted range. Notice the range A1: E9 is surrounded with a dashed line indicating the current print area for the worksheet.

If you want to print the entire worksheet once a print area has been set, you need to remove the current print area. Select File, point to Print Area, and click the Clear Print Area to remove the print area. Now the entire worksheet will print.

Documenting the Workbook

Documenting the workbook provides valuable information to those using the workbook. Documentation includes external documentation as well as notes and instructions within the workbook. This information could be as basic as who created the worksheet and the date it was created, or it could be more detailed, including formulas, summaries, and layout information.

Depending on the use of the workbook, the required amount of documentation varies. Sally's planning analysis sheet and sketch for the sales comparison worksheet are one form of external documentation. This information can be useful to someone who would need to modify the worksheet in any way because it states the goals, required input, output, and the calculations used.

One source of internal documentation would be a worksheet placed as the first worksheet in the workbook, such as the Documentation worksheet in Tutorial 1 to determine the best location for the new Inwood golf course. In more complex workbooks, this sheet may also include an index of all worksheets in the workbook, instructions on how to use the worksheets, where to enter data, how to save the workbook, and how to print reports. This documentation method is useful because the information is contained directly in the workbook and can easily be viewed upon opening the workbook, or printed if necessary. Another source of internal documentation is the **Property** dialog box. This dialog box enables you to electronically capture information such as the name of the workbook's creator, the creation date, the number of revisions, and other information related to the workbook.

If you prefer, you can include documentation on each sheet of the workbook. One way is to attach notes to cells by using the Comments command to explain complex formulas, list assumptions, and enter reminders.

The worksheet itself can be used as documentation. Once a worksheet is completed, it is a good practice to print and file a hardcopy of your work as documentation. This hardcopy file should include a printout of each worksheet displaying the values and another printout of the worksheet displaying the cell formulas.

Sally asks you to include a note in the worksheet that will remind her that the sales in Europe do not include an acquisition that was approved in December. You suggest inserting a cell comment.

Adding Cell Comments

Cell comments can help users remember assumptions, explain complex formulas, or place reminders related to the contents of a specific cell.

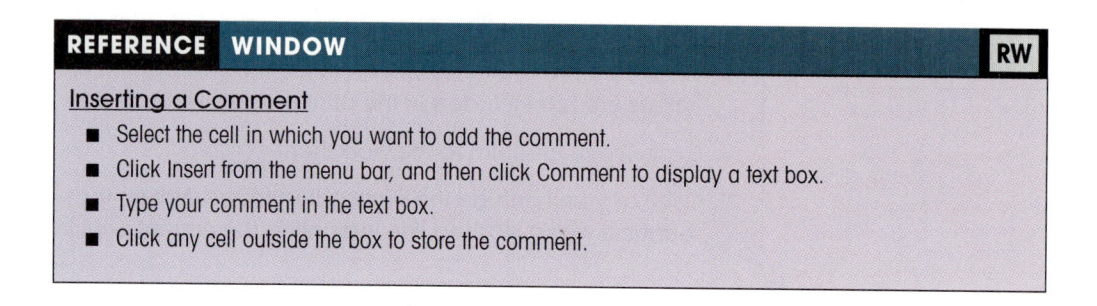

REFERENCE WINDOW

Inserting a Comment
- Select the cell in which you want to add the comment.
- Click Insert from the menu bar, and then click Comment to display a text box.
- Type your comment in the text box.
- Click any cell outside the box to store the comment.

Use the cell comment to insert the note for Sally.

To add a comment to a cell:

1. Click cell **B8**.

2. Click **Insert** and then click **Comment** to display a text box.

   TROUBLE? If the Comment item does not appear on the Insert menu, click ⌄ to view additional items on the Insert menu.

   Now enter your comment in the text box.

3. Type **Does not include sales from company acquired in December**. See Figure 2-32.

Figure 2-32 INSERTING A CELL COMMENT

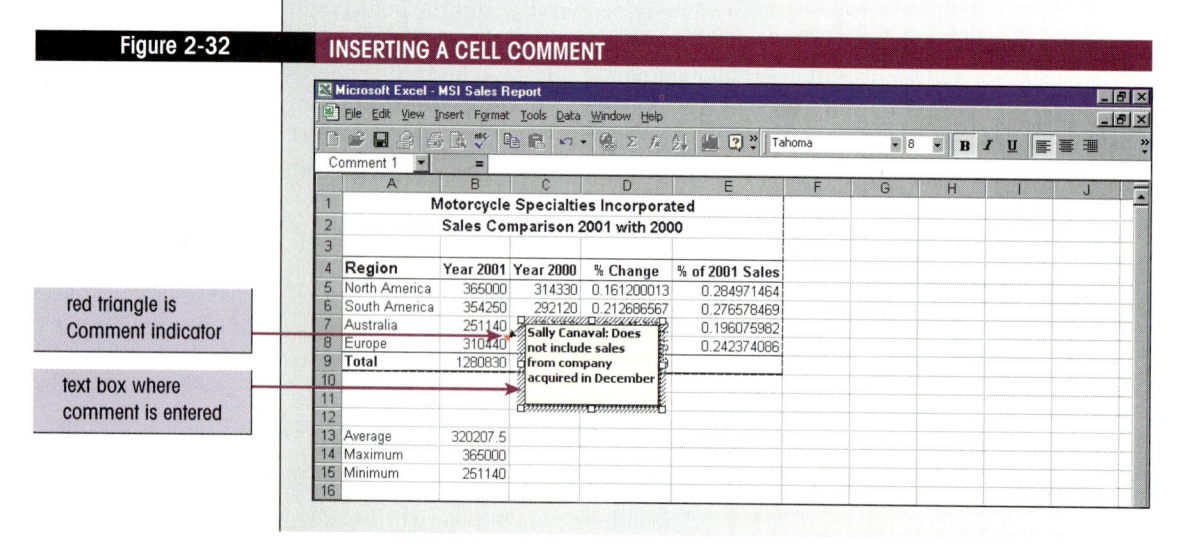

4. Click any cell outside the text box. The comment disappears. Notice, the **Comment indicator**, a tiny red triangle, appears in the upper-right corner of the cell indicating the cell contains a comment.

   Now view the comment.

   TROUBLE? If the comment remains on the screen, click View, then click Comments.

5. Move the mouse pointer over cell **B8**. The Comment appears, preceded by the name of the user who made the comment.

6. Move the mouse pointer to another cell. The comment disappears.

7. Save the workbook.

Once a comment is inserted, you can edit or delete the comment by right-clicking the cell and selecting Edit Comment or Delete Comment from the shortcut menu.

Now Sally asks for a printout of the worksheet formulas for her file.

Displaying and Printing Worksheet Formulas

You can document the formulas you entered in a worksheet by displaying and printing them. When you display formulas, Excel shows the formulas you entered in each cell instead of showing the results of the calculations. You want a printout of the formulas in your worksheet for documentation.

To display worksheet formulas:

1. Click **Tools** on the menu bar, and then click **Options** to open the Options dialog box.

2. Click the **View** tab, and then click the **Formulas** check box in the Window options section to select it.

3. Click the **OK** button to return to the worksheet. The width of each column nearly doubles to accommodate the underlying formulas. See Figure 2-33.

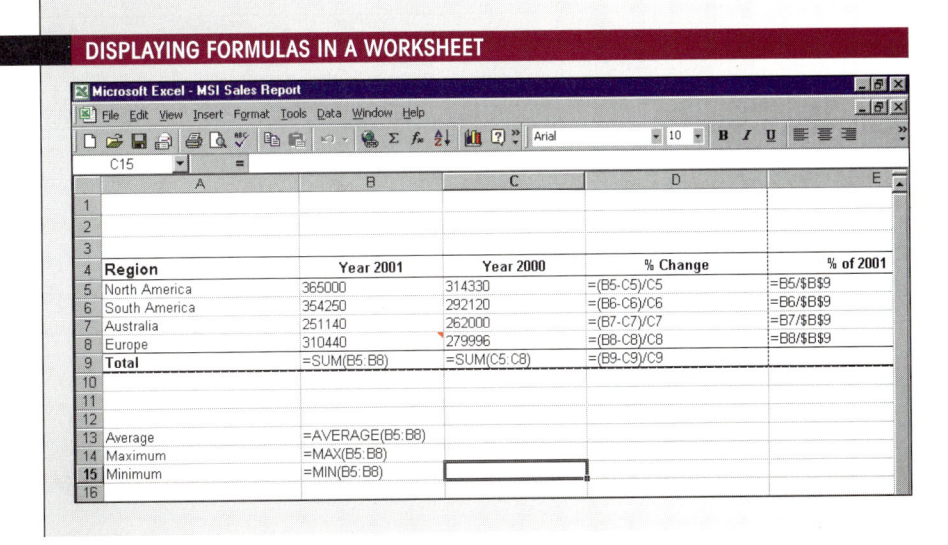

Figure 2-33 | **DISPLAYING FORMULAS IN A WORKSHEET**

	A	B	C	D	E
4	Region	Year 2001	Year 2000	% Change	% of 2001
5	North America	365000	314330	=(B5-C5)/C5	=B5/$B$9
6	South America	354250	292120	=(B6-C6)/C6	=B6/$B$9
7	Australia	251140	262000	=(B7-C7)/C7	=B7/$B$9
8	Europe	310440	279996	=(B8-C8)/C8	=B8/$B$9
9	Total	=SUM(B5:B8)	=SUM(C5:C8)	=(B9-C9)/C9	
10					
11					
12					
13	Average	=AVERAGE(B5:B8)			
14	Maximum	=MAX(B5:B8)			
15	Minimum	=MIN(B5:B8)			
16					

> You may find the keyboard shortcut, Ctrl + ` (` is found next to the 1 in the upper-left area of the keyboard) easier to use when displaying formulas. Press the shortcut key once to display formulas and again to display results.

Now print the worksheet displaying the formulas. Before printing the formulas, you need to change the appropriate settings in the Page Setup dialog box to show the gridlines and the row/column headings, center the worksheet on the page, and fit the printout on a single page.

To adjust the print setups to display formulas:

1. Click **File** on the menu bar, and then click **Page Setup** to open the Page Setup dialog box.

2. Click the **Sheet** tab to view the sheet options, and then click the **Row and Column Headings** check box in the Print section to print the row numbers and column letters along with the worksheet results.

3. Click the **Gridlines** check box to select that option.

4. Click the **Page** tab and then click the **Landscape** option button. This option prints the worksheet with the paper positioned so it is wider than it is tall.

5. Click the **Fit to** option button in the Scaling section of the Page tab. This option reduces the worksheet when you print it, so it fits on the specific number of pages in the Fit to check box. The default is 1.

6. Click the **Print Preview** button to open the Print Preview window.

7. Click the **Print** button. See Figure 2-34. Notice that your printout does not include the formulas for average, minimum and maximum because the print area is still set for the range A1:E9.

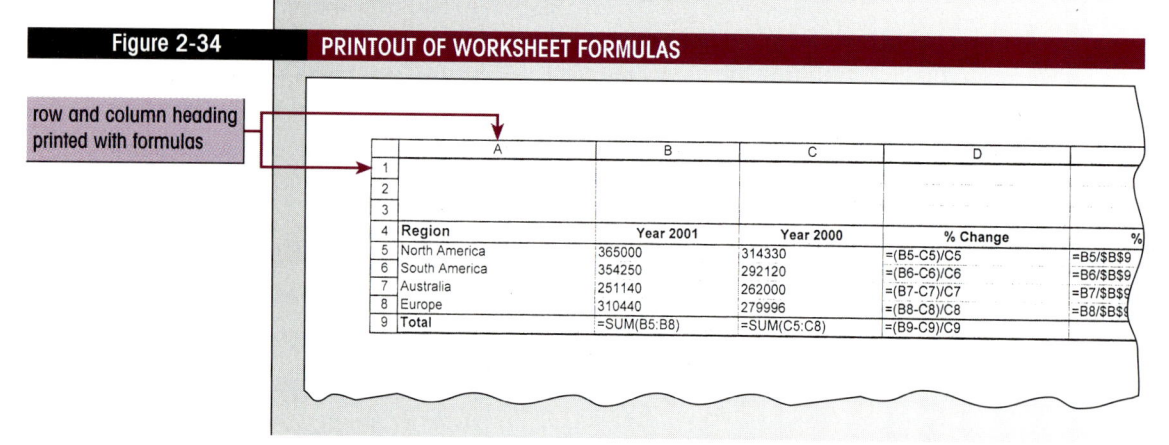

Figure 2-34   PRINTOUT OF WORKSHEET FORMULAS

row and column heading printed with formulas

	A	B	C	D	
1					
2					
3					
4	Region	Year 2001	Year 2000	% Change	%
5	North America	365000	314330	=(B5-C5)/C5	=B5/$B$9
6	South America	354250	292120	=(B6-C6)/C6	=B6/$B$9
7	Australia	251140	262000	=(B7-C7)/C7	=B7/$B$9
8	Europe	310440	279996	=(B8-C8)/C8	=B8/$B$9
9	Total	=SUM(B5:B8)	=SUM(C5:C8)	=(B9-C9)/C9	

After printing the formulas, return the worksheet so it displays the worksheet values.

To display the worksheet values:

1. Press **Ctrl + `** to display the worksheet values.

2. Close the workbook without saving it, and then exit Excel.

Session 2.2 QUICK CHECK

1. What is meant by syntax?
2. In the function MAX(A1:A8), identify the function name. Identify the argument(s).
3. Describe how you use the pointing method to create a formula that includes the SUM function.
4. Describe how to insert a row or a column.
5. To reverse your most recent action, which button should you click?
   a. 💾
   b. 📂
   c. ↩
6. To move a range of cells, you must _____ the range first.
7. _____ is a command that lets you change your worksheet's appearance by selecting a collection of predefined worksheet formats.
8. A _____ is text that is printed in the top margin of every worksheet page.
9. A _____ is a tiny red triangle in the upper-right corner of a cell that indicates the cell contains a _____.
10. To display formulas instead of values in your worksheet, what command should you choose?
11. If your worksheet has too many columns to fit on one printed page, you should try _____ orientation.

You have planned, built, formatted, and documented Sally's sales comparison worksheet. It is ready for her to present to the regional sales managers at their next meeting.

REVIEW ASSIGNMENTS

After Sally meets with the regional sales managers for MSI, she decides it would be a good idea to provide the managers with their own copy of the sales comparison worksheet, so they can update the report with next year's sales data and also modify it to use for their own sales tracking purposes. Before passing it on to them, she wants to provide more documentation and add some additional information that the managers thought would be useful to them. Complete the following for Sally:

1. Start Windows and Excel, if necessary. Insert your Data Disk into the appropriate disk drive. Make sure the Excel and Book1 windows are maximized.
2. Open the workbook **MSI 1** in the Review folder for Tutorial 2 on your Data Disk.
3. Save your workbook as **MSI Sales Report 2** in the Review folder for Tutorial 2 on your Data Disk.
4. Make Sheet2 the active sheet. Use Sheet2 to include information about the workbook. Insert the information in Figure 2-35 into Sheet2. Increase the width of column A as necessary.

Figure 2-35

CELL	TEXT ENTRY
A1	Motorcycle Specialties Incorporated
A3	Created by:
A4	Date Created:
A6	Purpose:
B3	enter your name
B4	enter today's date
B6	Sales report comparing sales by region 2001 with 2000

5. Change the name of the worksheet from **Sheet2** to **Documentation** and print the Documentation sheet.

Explore

6. Move the Documentation sheet so it is the first sheet in the workbook.

7. Make Sales Comparison the active sheet.

8. Insert a row between Australia and Europe. Add the following data (Africa, 125000, 100000) in columns A, B, and C. Copy the formulas for % Change and % of 2001 Sales into the row containing the data for Africa.

9. Open the Office Assistant and then enter the search phrase "Insert a column" to obtain instructions on inserting a new column into a worksheet. Insert a new column between columns C and D.

10. In cell D4, enter the heading "Change".

11. In cell D5, enter the formula to calculate the change in sales for North America from 2000 to 2001. (*Hint*: Check that the figure in cell D5 is 50670.)

12. Copy the formula in D5 to the other regions and total (D6 through D10) using the fill handle.

13. Calculate summary statistics for the year 2000. In cell C14 display the average sales, in cell C15 display the maximum, and in cell C16 display the minimum.

14. Save the workbook.

15. Print the sales comparison worksheet.

16. a. Insert the following comment into cell F4: "Divide 2001 sales in each region by total sales in 2001".
    b. Use the Office Assistant to learn how to print comments to a cell. List the steps.

17. a. Insert a new sheet into the workbook using the Worksheet command from the Insert menu. Activate the **Sales Comparison** sheet and select the range A1:E10. Copy the selected range to the Clipboard. Activate Sheet1 and paste the selected range to the corresponding cells in Sheet1. Apply a different AutoFormat to this range. Print Sheet1. *Note:* If the Office Clipboard toolbar appears, you can use the Office Assistant to learn "About collecting and pasting multiple items" in the Office Clipboard.
    b. Use the Delete Sheet command from the Edit menu to delete Sheet1.
    c. Save the workbook.

CASE PROBLEMS

Case 1. Annual Stockholders' Meeting at MJ Inc. Jeanne Phelp, chief financial officer (CFO) of MJ Incorporated is responsible for preparing the annual financial reports and mailing them to stockholders before the annual stockholder's meeting. She has completed some of the work for the annual meeting and is now in the process of finishing a report comparing the changes in net income between the current year and last year. Now you can help her complete this report.

1. Use columns A through D to enter the title, labels, and constants from Figure 2-36 into a worksheet.

Figure 2-36

MJ INCORPORATED INCOME STATEMENT

	2001	2000	PERCENTAGE CHANGE
Net Sales	1818500	1750500	
Cost of Goods Sold	1005500	996000	
Gross Profit			
Selling and Administrative expenses	506000	479000	
Income from Operations			
Interest expense	18000	19000	
Income before taxes			
Income tax expense	86700	77000	
Net Income			
Outstanding shares	20000	20000	
Earnings Per Share			

2. Complete the income statement for 2001 and 2000 by entering the following formulas for each year:
   - Gross profit = Net sales – Cost of goods sold
   - Income from operations = Gross profit – Selling and administrative expenses
   - Income before taxes = Income from operations – Interest expense
   - Net income = Income before taxes – Income tax expense

3. Compute the percentage change between the two years for each item in the income statement.

4. Compute earnings per share (net income / outstanding shares).

5. In cell B4 add the cell comment "Unaudited results".

6. Select an AutoFormat to improve the appearance of your worksheet.

7. Prepare a Documentation sheet, and then place it as the first sheet in the workbook.

8. Save the workbook as **MJ Income** in the Cases folder for Tutorial 2 on your Data Disk. *Note:* The workbook should open so the user can see the contents of the Documentation sheet. (*Hint:* Make the Documentation sheet the active sheet before you save the workbook.)

9. Add your name and date in the custom footer, then print the worksheet, centered horizontally and vertically.

10. Print the Documentation sheet.

11. Save the worksheet, and then print the formulas for the worksheet. Include row and column headings in the output. Do not save the workbook after printing the formulas.

Case 2. Compiling Data on the U.S. Airline Industry The editor of *Aviation Week and Space Technology* has asked you to research the current status of the U.S. airline industry. You collect information on the revenue-miles and passenger-miles for each major U.S. airline (Figure 2-37).

Figure 2-37 REVENUE-MILES AND PASSENGER MILES FOR MAJOR U.S. AIRLINES

AIRLINE	REVENUE-MILES (IN 1000S OF MILES)	PASSENGER-MILES (IN 1000S OF MILES)
American	26000	2210000
Continental	9300	620500
Delta	21500	1860000
Northwest	20800	1900500
US Airways	9850	1540000
United	35175	3675000

You want to calculate the following summary information to use in the article:

- total revenue-miles for the U.S. airline industry
- total passenger-miles for the U.S. airline industry
- each airline's share of the total revenue-miles
- each airline's share of the total passenger-miles
- average revenue-miles for U.S. airlines
- average passenger-miles for U.S. airlines

In order to provide the editor with your researched information, complete these steps:

1. Open a new workbook and then enter the title, column and row labels, and data from Figure 2-37.

2. Enter the formulas to compute the total and average revenue-miles and passenger-miles. Use the SUM and AVERAGE functions where appropriate. Remember to include row labels to describe each statistic.

3. Add a column to display each airline's share of the total revenue-miles. Remember to include a column heading. You decide the appropriate location for this data.

4. Add a column to display each airline's share of the total passenger-miles. Remember to include a column heading. You decide the appropriate location for this data.

5. In a cell two rows after the row of data you entered, insert a line reading : "Compiled by: XXXX", where XXXX is your name.

6. Rename the worksheet tab Mileage Data.

7. Save the worksheet as **Airline** in the Cases folder for Tutorial 2.

8. Print the worksheet. Make sure you center the report, do not include gridlines, and place the date in the upper-right corner of the header.

9. Select an AutoFormat to improve the appearance of your output.

10. Save your workbook.

11. Print the worksheet, centered on the page.

12. Save the worksheet and then print the formulas for the worksheet. Include row and column headings in the printout.

Case 3. Fresh Air Sales Incentive Program Carl Stambaugh is assistant sales manager at Fresh Air Inc., a manufacturer of outdoors and expedition clothing. Fresh Air sales representatives contact retail chains and individual retail outlets to sell the Fresh Air line.

This year, to stimulate sales, Carl has decided to run a sales incentive program for sales representatives. Each sales representative has been assigned a sales goal 12% higher than his or her total sales last year. All sales representatives who reach this new goal will be awarded an all-expenses-paid trip for two to Cozumel, Mexico.

Carl wants to track the results of the sales incentive program with an Excel worksheet. He has asked you to complete the worksheet by adding the formulas to compute:

- actual sales in 2001 for each sales representative
- sales goal in 2001 for each sales representative
- percentage of goal reached for each sales representative

He also wants a printout before he presents the worksheet at the next sales meeting. Complete these steps:

1. Open the workbook **Fresh** in the Cases folder for Tutorial 2 on your Data Disk. Maximize the worksheet window and then save the workbook as **Fresh Air Sales Incentives** in the Cases folder for Tutorial 2.

2. Complete the worksheet by adding the following formulas:
   a. 2001 actual for each employee = Sum of actual sales for each quarter
   b. Goal 2001 for each employee = 2000 Sales X (1 + Goal % increase)
   c. % goal reached for each employee = 2001 actual / 2001 goal

   (*Hint:* Use the Copy command. Review relative versus absolute references.)

3. At the bottom of the worksheet (three rows after the last sales rep), add the average, maximum, and minimum statistics for columns C through I.

4. Make formatting changes using an Autoformat to improve the appearance of the worksheet. Begin the formatting in row 6.

5. In cell C4, insert the cell comment "entered sales goal values between 10 and 15 percent".

6. Save the workbook.

7. Print the worksheet. Make sure you center the worksheet horizontally, add an appropriate header, and place your name, course, and date in the footer. Print the worksheet so it fits on one page.

8. Add a Documentation sheet. Save the workbook and then print the Documentation worksheet.

9. Change the sales goal to 14 percent. Print the worksheet.

Explore

10. As you scroll down the worksheet, the column headings no longer appear on the screen, making it difficult to know what each column represents. Use the Office Assistant to look up "Keep column labels visible." Implement this feature in your worksheet. Save the workbook. Explain the steps you take to keep the columns visible.

11. Print the formulas in columns H, I, and J. The printout should include row and column headings. Use the Set Print Area command so you only print the formulas in these three columns. Do not save the workbook after you complete this step.

Case 4. Stock Portfolio for Juan Cortez Your close friend, Juan Cortez, works as an accountant at a local manufacturing company. While in college, with a double major in accounting and finance, Juan dabbled in the stock market and expressed an interest in becoming a financial planner and running his own firm. To that end, he has continued his professional studies in the evenings with the aim of becoming a certified financial planner. He has already begun to provide financial planning services to a few clients. Because of his hectic schedule as a full-time accountant, part-time student, and part-time financial planner, Juan finds it difficult to keep up with the data-processing needs for his clients. You have offered to assist him.

Juan asks you to set up a worksheet to keep track of a stock portfolio for one of his clients.

Open a new workbook and do the following:

1. Figure 2-38 shows the data you will enter into the workbook. For each stock, you will enter the name, number of shares purchased, and purchase price. Periodically, you will also enter the current price of each stock so Juan can review the changes with his clients.

Figure 2-38

STOCK	NO. OF SHARES	PURCHASE PRICE	COST	CURRENT PRICE	CURRENT VALUE	GAINS/LOSSES
Excite	100	67.30		55.50		
Yahoo	250	121		90.625		
Netscape	50	24.50		26.375		
Microsoft	100	89.875		105.375		
Intel	50	69		83		

2. In addition to entering the data, you need to make the following calculations:
   a. Cost = No. of shares * Purchase price
   b. Current value = No. of shares * Current price
   c. Gains/Losses = Current value minus cost
   d. Totals for cost, Current value, and Gains/Losses

   Enter the formulas to calculate the cost, current value, gains/losses, and totals.

3. In the cell where you enter the label for Current Price, insert the cell comment "As of 9/1/2001".

4. Apply an AutoFormat that improves the appearance of the worksheet.

5. Add a Documentation sheet to the workbook.

6. Save the workbook as **Portfolio** in the Cases folder for Tutorial 2.

7. Print the worksheet. Make sure you center the worksheet horizontally and add an appropriate header and footer.

8. Print the Documentation sheet.

9. Clear the prices in the Current Price column of the worksheet.

10. Enter the following prices:

Excite	57.250
Yahoo	86.625
Netscape	30.75
Microsoft	102.375
Intel	84.375

    Print the worksheet.

11. Print the formulas for the worksheet. Make sure you include row and column headings in the printed output.

12. From the financial section of your newspaper, look up the current price of each stock (all these stocks are listed on the NASDAQ Stock Exchange). Enter these prices in the worksheet. Print the worksheet.

INTERNET ASSIGNMENTS

The purpose of the Internet Assignments is to challenge you to find information on the Internet that you can use to create effective documents. The actual assignments are updated and maintained on the Course Technology Web site. Log on to the Internet and use your Web browser and go to the Student Online Companion to accompany this text at **www.course.com/NewPerspectives/office2000**. Click the Excel link, and then click the link for Tutorial 2.

QUICK CHECK ANSWERS

Session 2.1

1. Determine the purpose of the worksheet, enter the data and formulas, test the worksheet; correct errors, improve the appearance, document the worksheet, save and print.

2. Select the cell where you want the sum to appear. Click the AutoSum button. Excel suggests a formula that includes the SUM function. To accept the formula press the Enter key.

3. =B4-C4

4. fill handle

5. Cell references; if you were to copy the formula to other cells, these cells are relative references.

6. absolute reference

7. Windows clipboard

8. Double-click the sheet tab, then type the new name, and then press the Enter key or click any cell in the worksheet to accept the entry.

9. Order of precedence is a set of predefined rules that Excel uses to unambiguously calculate a formula by determining which part of the formula to calculate first, which part second, and so on.

Session 2.2

1. Syntax specifies the set of rules that determine the order and punctuation of formulas and functions in Excel.

2. MAX is the function name; A1:A8 is the argument.

3. Assuming you are entering a formula with a function, first select the cell where you want to place a formula, type =, the function name and a left parenthesis, and then click and drag over the range of cells to be used in the formula. Press the Enter key.

4. Click any cell in the row above which you want to insert a row. Click Insert, then click Rows.

5. c

6. select

7. AutoFormat

8. header

9. comment indicator, comment

10. Click Tools, click Options, and then in the View tab, click the Formula check box.

11. landscape

TUTORIAL 3

OBJECTIVES

In this tutorial you will:

- Format data using the Number, Currency, Accounting, and Percentage formats
- Align cell contents
- Center text across columns
- Change fonts, font style, and font size
- Clear formatting from cells
- Delete cells from a worksheet
- Use borders and color for emphasis
- Add text box and graphics to a worksheet using the Drawing toolbar
- Remove gridlines from the worksheet
- Print in landscape orientation
- Hide and unhide rows and columns

DEVELOPING A PROFESSIONAL-LOOKING WORKSHEET

Producing a Projected Sales Report for the Pronto Salsa Company

CASE

Pronto Salsa Company

Anne Castelar owns the Pronto Salsa Company, a successful business located in the heart of Tex-Mex country. She is working on a plan to add a new product, de Chili Guero Four-Alarm Red Hot, to Pronto's gourmet salsa line.

Anne wants to take out a bank loan to purchase additional food-processing equipment to handle the requirements of the increased salsa production. She has an appointment with her loan officer at 2:00 p.m. today. To prepare for the meeting, Anne creates a worksheet to show the projected sales of the new salsa and the expected effect on profits. Although the numbers and formulas are in place on the worksheet, Anne has no time to format the worksheet to create the greatest impact. She planned to do that now, but an unexpected problem with today's produce shipment requires her to leave the office for a few hours. Anne asks you to complete the worksheet. She shows you a printout of the unformatted worksheet and explains that she wants the finished worksheet to look very professional—like those you see in business magazines. She also asks you to make sure that the worksheet emphasizes the profits expected from sales of the new salsa.

EX 3.01

EXCEL   EX 3.02   TUTORIAL 3 DEVELOPING A PROFESSIONAL-LOOKING WORKSHEET

SESSION 3.1

In this session you will learn how to make your worksheets easier to understand through various formatting techniques. You will format values using Currency, Number, and Percentage formats. You will also change font styles and font sizes, and change the alignment of data within cells and across columns. As you perform all these tasks, you'll find the Format Painter button an extremely useful tool.

Opening the Workbook

After Anne leaves, you develop the worksheet plan in Figure 3-1 and the worksheet format plan in Figure 3-2.

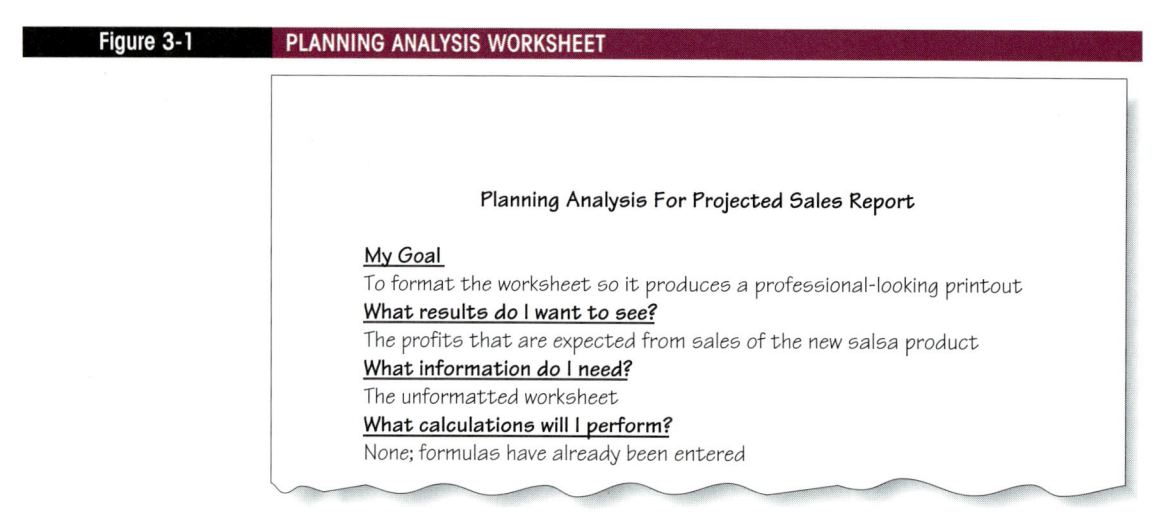

Figure 3-1   PLANNING ANALYSIS WORKSHEET

Planning Analysis For Projected Sales Report

My Goal
To format the worksheet so it produces a professional-looking printout
What results do I want to see?
The profits that are expected from sales of the new salsa product
What information do I need?
The unformatted worksheet
What calculations will I perform?
None; formulas have already been entered

Figure 3-2   FORMAT PLAN

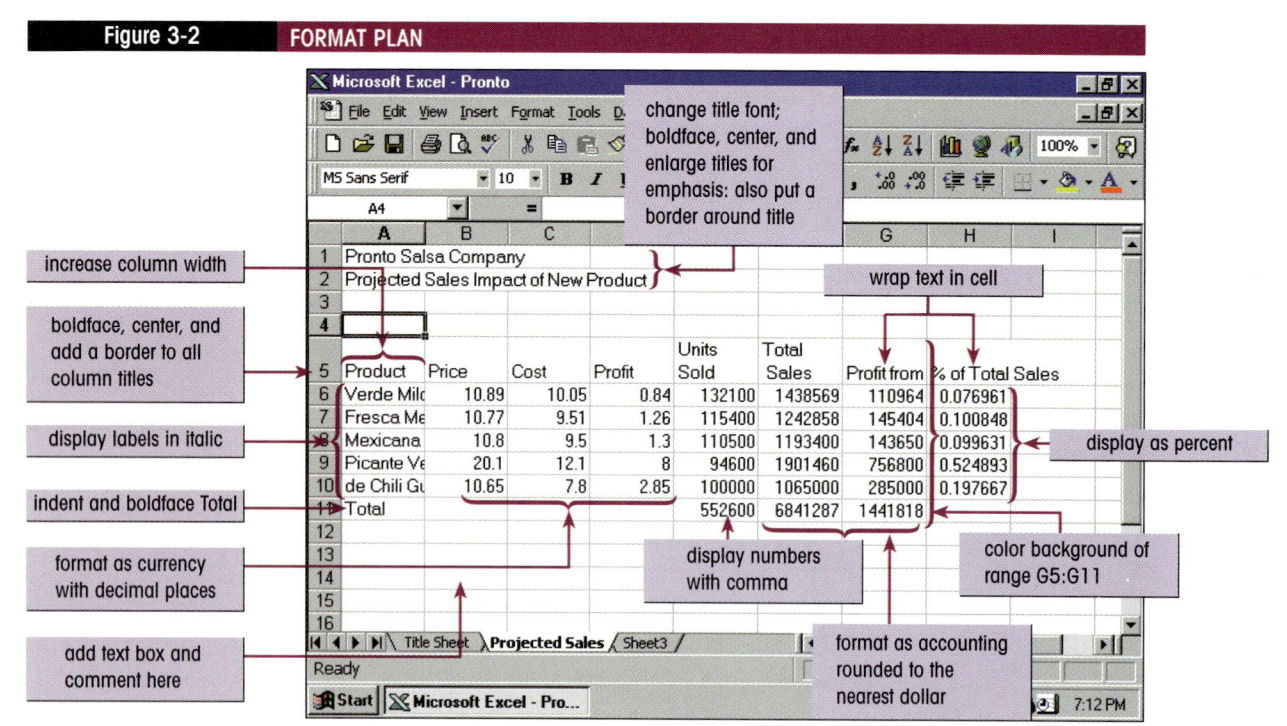

Callouts pointing to the worksheet screenshot:
- increase column width
- boldface, center, and add a border to all column titles
- display labels in italic
- indent and boldface Total
- format as currency with decimal places
- add text box and comment here
- change title font; boldface, center, and enlarge titles for emphasis: also put a border around title
- wrap text in cell
- display numbers with comma
- display as percent
- color background of range G5:G11
- format as accounting rounded to the nearest dollar

Worksheet data (Projected Sales sheet):

	A	B	C	D	E	F	G
1	Pronto Salsa Company						
2	Projected Sales Impact of New Product						
5	Product	Price	Cost	Profit	Units Sold	Total Sales	Profit from |% of Total Sales
6	Verde Mild	10.89	10.05	0.84	132100	1438569	110964	0.076961
7	Fresca Me	10.77	9.51	1.26	115400	1242858	145404	0.100848
8	Mexicana	10.8	9.5	1.3	110500	1193400	143650	0.099631
9	Picante Ve	20.1	12.1	8	94600	1901460	756800	0.524893
10	de Chili Gu	10.65	7.8	2.85	100000	1065000	285000	0.197667
11	Total				552600	6841287	1441818	

Anne has already entered all the formulas, numbers, and labels. Your main task is to format this information so it is easy to read and understand, and appears professional. This can be accomplished on two levels—by formatting the detailed data in the worksheet and by enhancing the appearance of the worksheet as a whole.

On the data level, you decide that the numbers should be formatted according to their use. For example, the product prices need to appear as dollar values, the column and row labels need to fit within their cells, and the labels need to stand out more. To enhance the worksheet as a whole, you need to structure it so that related information is visually grouped together using lines and borders. Anne also wants certain areas of the worksheet containing key information to stand out, color may be a useful tool for this.

With all that needs to be done before Anne's 2:00 p.m. meeting, you decide that the best place to begin is with formatting the data within the worksheet. Once that is done, you will work to improve the worksheet's overall organization and appearance.

Now that the planning is done, you are ready to start Excel and open the workbook of unformatted data that Anne created.

To start Excel and organize your desktop:

1. Start Excel as usual.
2. Make sure your Data Disk is in the appropriate disk drive.
3. Make sure the Microsoft Excel and Book1 windows are maximized.

Now you need to open Anne's file and begin formatting the worksheet. Anne stored the workbook as Pronto, but before you begin to change the workbook, save it using the filename Pronto Salsa Company. This way, the original workbook, Pronto, remains unchanged in case you want to work through this tutorial again.

To open the Pronto workbook and save the workbook as Pronto Salsa Company:

1. Click the **Open** button on the Standard toolbar to open the Open dialog box.
2. Open the Pronto workbook in the Tutorial folder for Tutorial 3 on your Data Disk.
3. Click **File** on the menu bar, and then click **Save As** to open the Save As dialog box.
4. In the File name text box, change the filename to **Pronto Salsa Company**.
5. Click the **Save** button to save the workbook under the new filename. The new filename, Pronto Salsa Company, appears in the title bar.

   TROUBLE? If you see the message "Replace existing file?", click the Yes button to replace the old version of Pronto Salsa Company with your new version.

6. Click the **Projected Sales** sheet tab. See Figure 3-3.

Figure 3-3 **PRONTO SALSA COMPANY WORKSHEET**

	A	B	C	D	E	F	G	H
1	Pronto Salsa Company							
2	Projected Sales Impact of New Product							
3								
4					Units	Total		
5	Product	Price	Cost	Profit	Sold	Sales	Profit from	% of Total Sales
6	Verde Mild	10.89	10.05	0.84	132100	1438569	110964	0.076961
7	Fresca Me	10.77	9.51	1.26	115400	1242858	145404	0.100848
8	Mexicana	10.8	9.5	1.3	110500	1193400	143650	0.099631
9	Picante Ve	20.1	12.1	8	94600	1901460	756800	0.524893
10	de Chili Gu	10.65	7.8	2.85	100000	1065000	285000	0.197667
11	Total				552600	6841287	1441818	

EXCEL   EX 3.04   TUTORIAL 3 DEVELOPING A PROFESSIONAL-LOOKING WORKSHEET

Studying the worksheet, you notice that the numbers are difficult to read. You decide to improve the appearance of the numbers in worksheet cells first.

Formatting Worksheet Data

Formatting is the process of changing the appearance of the data in worksheet cells. Formatting can make your worksheets easier to understand, and draw attention to important points.

In the previous tutorial you used AutoFormat to improve the appearance of your worksheet. AutoFormat applies a predefined format to a selected range in a worksheet. AutoFormat is easy to use, but its predefined format might not suit every application. If you decide to customize a worksheet's format, you can use the extensive Excel formatting options. When you select your own formats, you can format an individual cell or a range of cells.

Formatting changes only the appearance of the worksheet; it does not change the text or numbers stored in the cells. For example, if you format the number .123653 using a Percentage format that displays only one decimal place, the number appears in the worksheet as 12.4%; however, the original number, .123653, remains stored in the cell. When you enter data into cells, Excel applies an automatic format, referred to as the General format. The **General format** aligns numbers at the right side of the cell, uses a minus sign for negative values, and displays numbers without trailing zeros to the right of the decimal point. You can change the General format by using AutoFormat, the Format menu, the Shortcut menu, or toolbar buttons.

There are many ways to access the Excel formatting options. The Format menu provides access to all formatting commands.

The Shortcut menu provides quick access to the Format dialog box. To display the Shortcut menu, make sure the pointer is positioned within the range you have selected to format, and then click the right mouse button.

The Formatting toolbar contains formatting buttons, including the style and alignment buttons, and the Font Style and Font Size boxes, as shown in Figure 3-4.

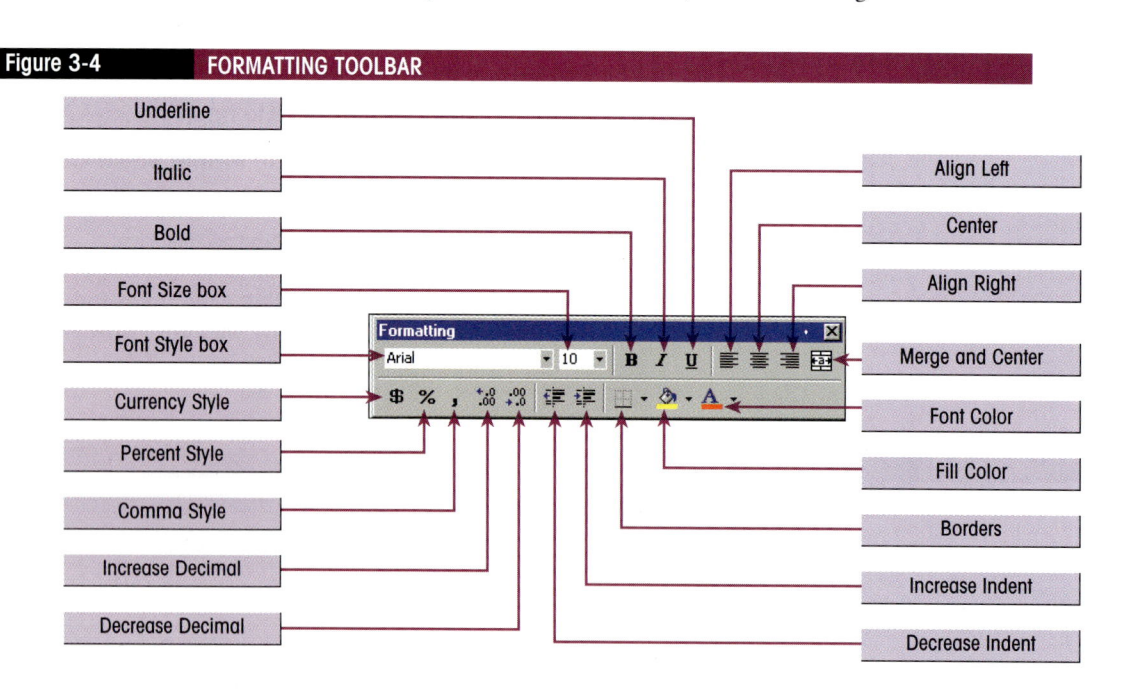

Figure 3-4 FORMATTING TOOLBAR

Labels: Underline, Italic, Bold, Font Size box, Font Style box, Currency Style, Percent Style, Comma Style, Increase Decimal, Decrease Decimal, Align Left, Center, Align Right, Merge and Center, Font Color, Fill Color, Borders, Increase Indent, Decrease Indent

Most experienced Excel users develop a preference for which menu or buttons they use to access the Excel formatting options; however, most beginners find it easy to remember that all formatting options are available from the Format menu.

Looking at Anne's worksheet, you decide to change the appearance of the numbers first.

Changing the Appearance of Numbers

When the data in the worksheet appears as numbers, you want each number to appear in a style appropriate for what it is representing. The Excel default General format is often not the most appropriate style. For example, dollar values may require the dollar symbol ($) and thousand separators, and these can be applied to numerical data simply by changing the data's format. You can also use formatting to standardize the number of decimal places appearing in a cell. Excel has a variety of predefined number formats. Figure 3-5 describes some of the most commonly used formats.

Figure 3-5	COMMONLY USED NUMBER FORMATS
CATEGORY	**DISPLAY OPTION**
General	Excel default Number format; displays numbers without dollar signs, commas, or trailing decimal places
Number	Sets decimal places, negative number display, and comma separator
Currency	Sets decimal places and negative number display, and inserts dollar signs and comma separators
Accounting	Specialized monetary value format used to align dollar signs, decimal places, and comma separators
Date	Sets date or date and time display
Percentage	Inserts percent sign to the right of a number with a set number of decimal places

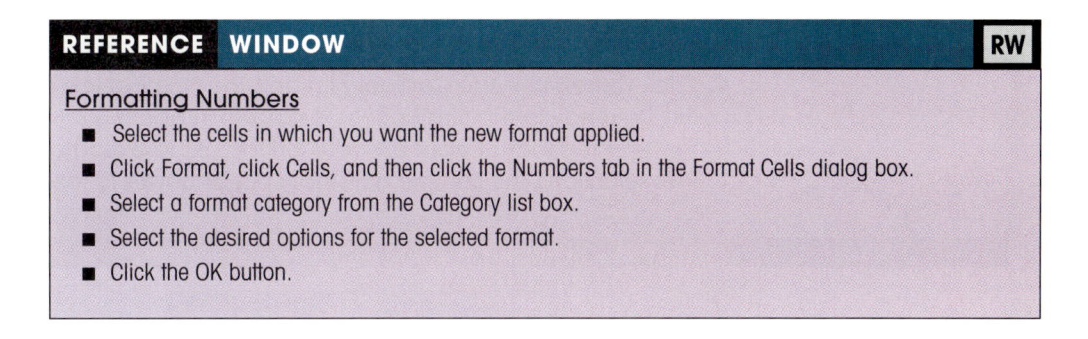

> **REFERENCE WINDOW** RW
>
> **Formatting Numbers**
> - Select the cells in which you want the new format applied.
> - Click Format, click Cells, and then click the Numbers tab in the Format Cells dialog box.
> - Select a format category from the Category list box.
> - Select the desired options for the selected format.
> - Click the OK button.

To change the number formatting, you select the cell or range of cells to be reformatted, and then use the Format Cells command or the Formatting toolbar buttons to apply a different format.

Currency and Accounting Formats

In reviewing Anne's unformatted worksheet, you recognize that there are several columns of data that represent currency. You decide to apply the Currency format to the Price, Cost, and Profit columns.

You have several options when formatting values as currency. You need to decide the number of decimal places you want visible; whether or not you want to see the dollar sign; and how you want negative numbers to look. Keep in mind that if you want the currency symbols and decimal places to line up within a column, you should choose the Accounting format rather than the Currency format.

In the Pronto Salsa Company worksheet, you want to apply the Currency format to the values in columns B, C, and D. The numbers will be formatted to include a dollar sign with two decimal places. You also decide to put parentheses around negative numbers in the worksheet.

To format columns B, C, and D using the Currency format:

1. Select the range **B6:D10**.

2. Click **Format** on the menu bar, and then click **Cells** to open the Format Cells dialog box.

3. If necessary, click the **Number** tab. See Figure 3-6.

Figure 3-6   **NUMBER TAB OF FORMAT CELLS DIALOG BOX**

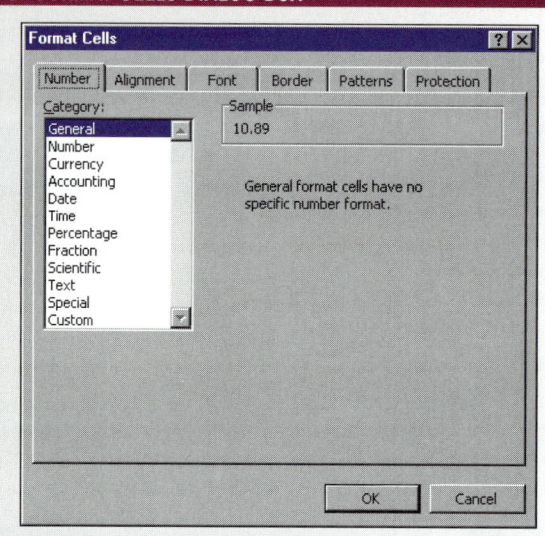

4. Click **Currency** in the Category list box. The Number tab changes to display the Currency formatting options, as shown in Figure 3-7. Notice that a sample of the selected format appears near the top of the dialog box. As you make further selections, the sample automatically changes to reflect your choices.

Figure 3-7   **SELECTING A CURRENCY FORMAT**

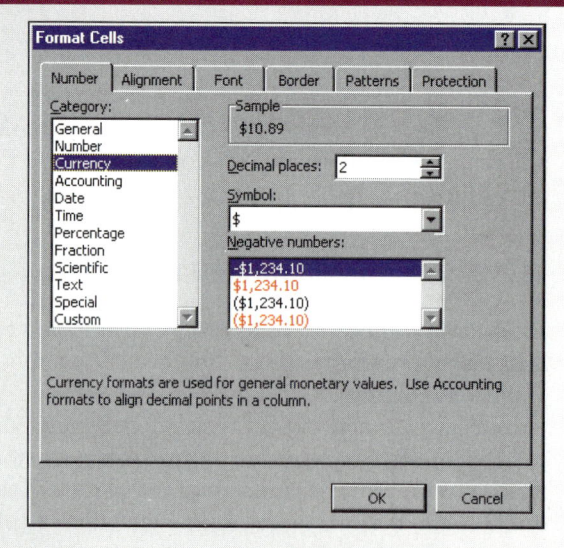

Notice that 2 decimal places is the default setting. A dollar sign ($) appears in the Symbol list box, indicating that the dollar sign will appear. If you are using a different currency, click the down arrow in the Symbol list box to select the currency symbol you want to use. Given the current options selected, you only need to select a format for negative numbers.

5. Click the third option **($1,234.10)** in the Negative numbers list box.

6. Click the **OK** button to format the selected range.

7. Click any cell to deselect the range and view the new formatting. See Figure 3-8.

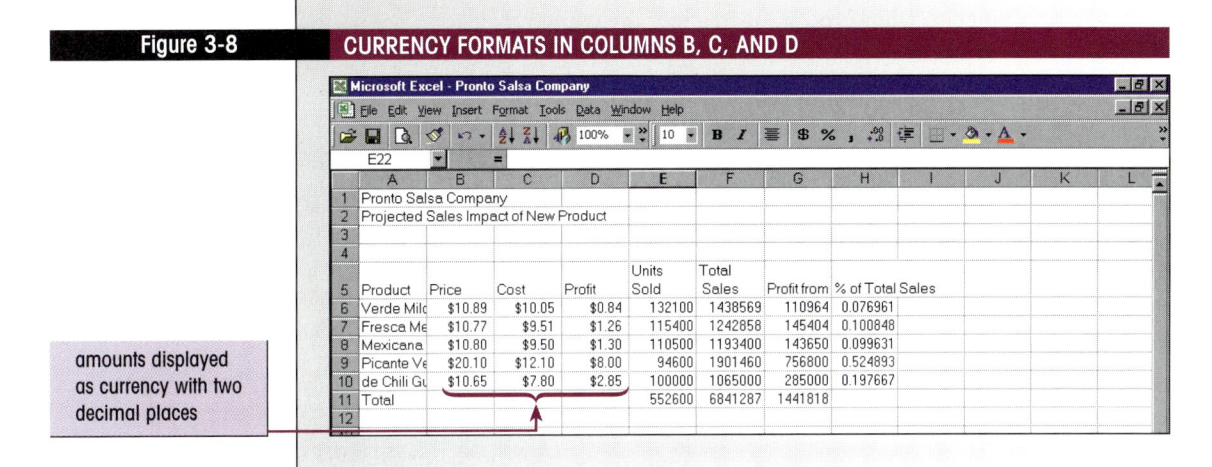

Figure 3-8 — CURRENCY FORMATS IN COLUMNS B, C, AND D

Product	Price	Cost	Profit	Units Sold	Total Sales	Profit from	% of Total Sales
Verde Mild	$10.89	$10.05	$0.84	132100	1438569	110964	0.076961
Fresca Me	$10.77	$9.51	$1.26	115400	1242858	145404	0.100848
Mexicana	$10.80	$9.50	$1.30	110500	1193400	143650	0.099631
Picante Ve	$20.10	$12.10	$8.00	94600	1901460	756800	0.524893
de Chili Gu	$10.65	$7.80	$2.85	100000	1065000	285000	0.197667
Total				552600	6841287	1441818	

amounts displayed as currency with two decimal places

When your worksheet has large dollar amounts, you might want to use a Currency or Accounting format that does not display any decimal places. To do this you use the Decrease Decimal button on the Formatting toolbar, or change the decimal places setting in the Format Cells dialog box. Currency values appearing with no decimal places are rounded to the nearest dollar: $15,612.56 becomes $15,613; $16,507.49 becomes $16,507; and so on.

You decide to format the Total Sales column as using the Accounting style format rounded to the nearest dollar. The Accounting style format lines up the currency symbol and decimal points in a column.

To format cells F6 through F11 using the Accounting style format rounded to the nearest dollar:

1. Select the range **F6:F11**.

2. Click **Format** on the menu bar, and then click **Cells** to open the Format Cells dialog box.

3. If necessary, click the **Number** tab.

4. Click **Accounting** in the Category list box.

5. Click the **Decimal places** spin box down arrow twice to change the setting to 0 decimal places. Notice that the sample format changes to reflect the new settings.

6. Click the **OK** button to apply the format. Notice that Excel automatically increased the column width to accommodate the formatted numbers.

7. Click any cell to deselect the range.

After formatting the Total Sales figures in column F, you realize you should have used the same format for the numbers in column G. To save time, you simply copy the formatting from column F to column G.

The Format Painter Button

The Format Painter button on the Standard toolbar lets you copy formats quickly from one cell or range to another. You simply click a cell containing the formats you want to copy, click the Format Painter button, and then use the click-and-drag technique to select the range to which you want to apply the copied formats.

To copy the format from cell F6:

1. Click cell **F6** because it contains the format you want to copy.

2. Click the **Format Painter** button on the Standard toolbar. As you move the pointer over the worksheet cells, notice that the pointer turns to .

   TROUBLE? If you do not see the Format Painter button on the Standard toolbar, click More Buttons to display the Format Painter button.

3. Position over cell G6, and then click and drag to select cells **G6:G11**. When you release the mouse button, you notice that cells G6:G11 contain number symbols (######) instead of values. This is because the formatting change has caused the data to exceed the width of the cell.

4. Click any cell to deselect the range and view the formatted Profit from Sales column. See Figure 3-9.

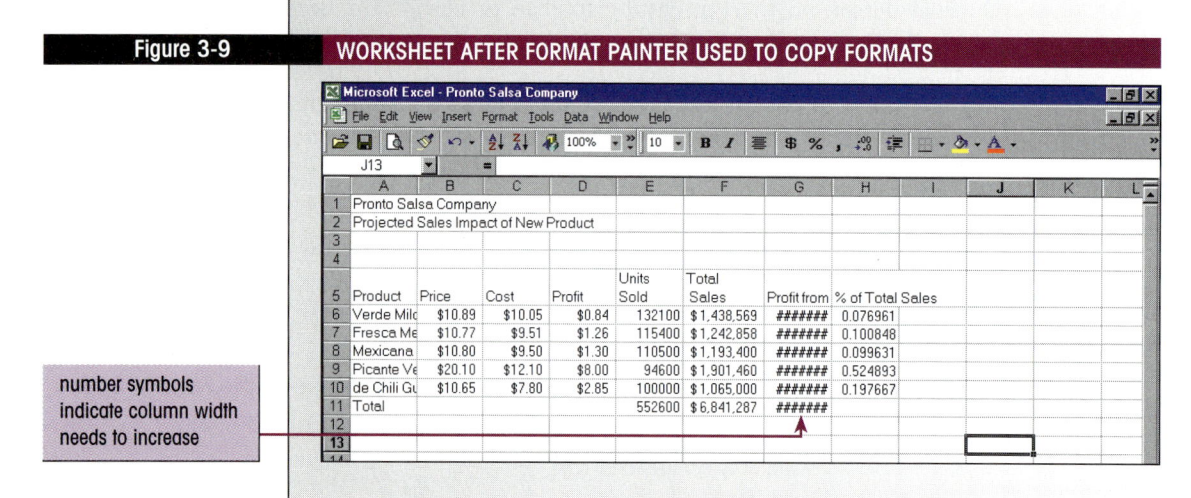

Figure 3-9 **WORKSHEET AFTER FORMAT PAINTER USED TO COPY FORMATS**

number symbols indicate column width needs to increase

As you review the changes on the screen, you notice that cells G6:G11 contain number symbols (######) instead of values. This is because the formatting change has caused the data to exceed the width of the cell.

Number Symbol (###) Replacement

If a number is too long to fit within a cell's boundaries, Excel displays a series of number symbols (###) in the cell. The number symbols indicate that the number of digits in the value exceeds the cell's width. The number or formula is still stored in the cell, but the current cell width is not large enough to display the value. To display the value, you just need to increase the column width. One way you can do this is to use the Shortcut menu.

To replace the number symbols by increasing the column width:

1. Position the mouse pointer over the column heading for column G, and then right-click to display the Shortcut menu.

2. Click **Column Width** to open the Column Width dialog box.

3. Type **11** in the Column Width box.

4. Click the **OK** button to view the total sales.

5. Click any cell to view the formatted data. See Figure 3-10.

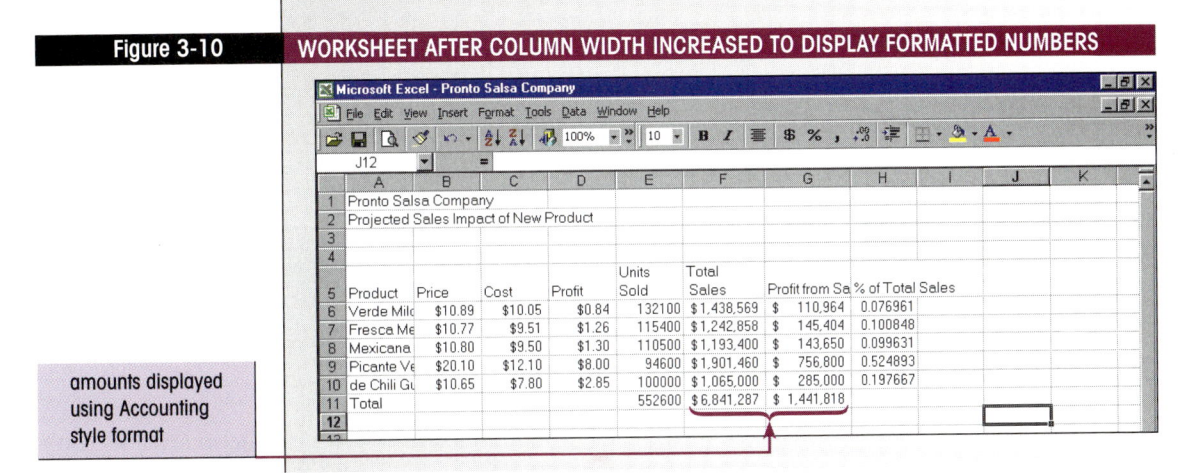

Figure 3-10   WORKSHEET AFTER COLUMN WIDTH INCREASED TO DISPLAY FORMATTED NUMBERS

amounts displayed using Accounting style format

Now the cells containing price, cost, profit, total sales, and profit from sales are formatted using the currency and accounting styles. Next you want to apply formats to the numbers in columns E and H so they are easier to read.

Number Formats

Like Currency formats, the Excel Number formats offer many options. You can select Number formats to specify

- the number of decimal places that are visible
- whether to display a comma to delimit thousands, millions, and billions
- whether to display negative numbers with a minus sign, parentheses, or red numerals

To access all Excel Number formats, you can use the Number tab in the Format Cells dialog box. You can also use the Comma Style button, the Increase Decimal button, and the Decrease Decimal button on the Formatting toolbar to select some Number formats.

Looking at your planning sheet and sketch, you can see that the numbers in column E need to be made easier to read by changing the format to include commas.

To format the contents in column E with a comma and no decimal places:

1. Select the range **E6:E11**.

2. Click the **Comma Style** button on the Formatting toolbar to apply the Comma Style. The default for the Comma Style is to display numbers with two places to the right of the decimal. Click the **Decrease Decimal** button on the Formatting toolbar to decrease the number of decimal places to zero.

   TROUBLE? If you do not see the Comma Style button on the Standard toolbar, click More Buttons to display the Comma Style button.

3. Click any cell to deselect the range and view the formatted Units Sold column. See Figure 3-11.

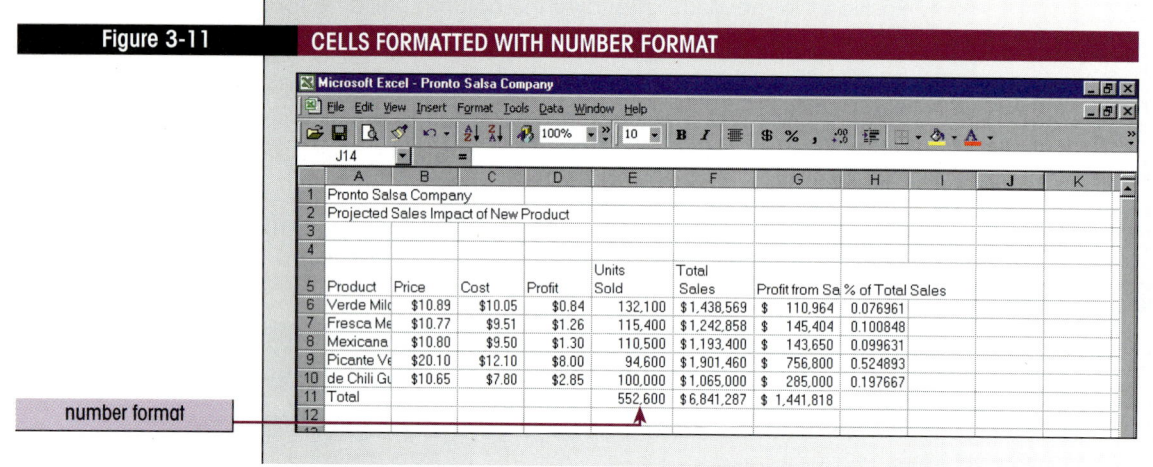

Figure 3-11
CELLS FORMATTED WITH NUMBER FORMAT

number format

Looking at the numbers in column H, you realize that they are difficult to interpret and decide that you do not need to display so many decimal places. These numbers would be much more readable as percentages; what are your options for displaying percentages?

Percentage Format

When formatting values as percentages, you need to select how many decimal places you want visible. The Percentage format with no decimal places displays the number 0.18037 as 18%. The Percentage format with two decimal places displays the same number as 18.04%. If you want to use the Percentage format with two decimal places, you select this option using the Number tab in the Format Cells dialog box. You can also use the Percent Style button on the Formatting toolbar, and then click the Increase Decimal button twice to add two decimal places.

Your format plan (see Figure 3-2) specifies a Percentage format with no decimal places for the values in column H. You could use the Number tab to choose this format, but it's faster to use the Percent Style button on the Formatting toolbar.

To format the values in column H as percentages with no decimal places:

1. Select the range **H6:H10**.
2. Click the **Percent Style** button on the Formatting toolbar.
3. Click any cell to deselect the range and view the Percent Style. See Figure 3-12.

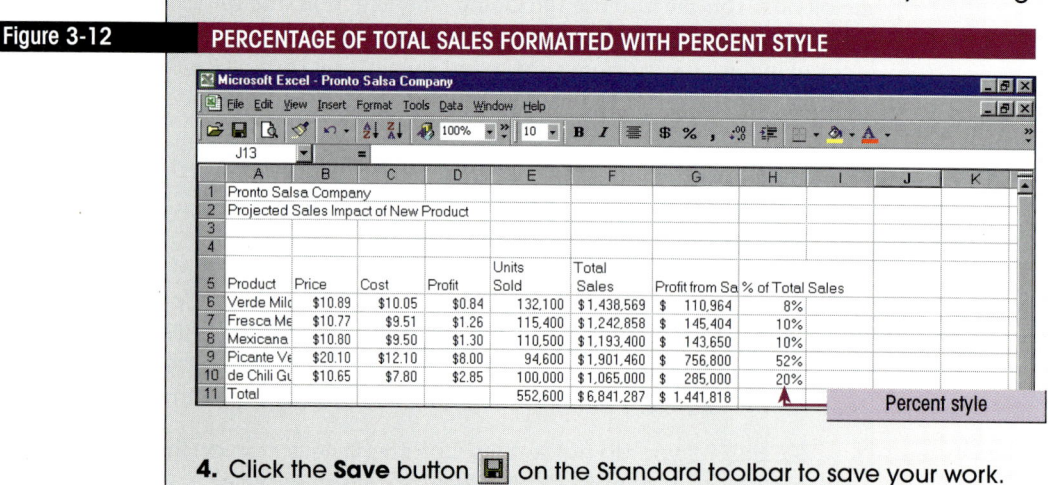

Figure 3-12
PERCENTAGE OF TOTAL SALES FORMATTED WITH PERCENT STYLE

Percent style

4. Click the **Save** button on the Standard toolbar to save your work.

You review the worksheet. You have now formatted all the numbers in the worksheet appropriately. The next step in formatting Anne's worksheet is to improve the alignment of the data in the cells.

Aligning Cell Contents

The **alignment** of data in a cell is the position of the data relative to the right and left edges of the cell. Cell contents can be aligned on the left or right side of the cell, or centered in the cell. When you enter numbers and formulas, Excel automatically aligns them on the cell's right side. Excel automatically aligns text entries on the cell's left side. The default Excel alignment does not always create the most readable worksheet. As a general rule, you should center column titles, format columns of numbers so that the decimal places are in line, and leave columns of text aligned on the left. You can change the alignment of cell data using the four alignment tools on the Formatting toolbar, or you can access additional alignment options by selecting the Alignment tab in the Format Cells dialog box.

To center the column titles within a cell:

1. Select the range **A5:H5**.

2. Click the **Center** button on the Formatting toolbar to center the cell contents.

3. Click any cell to deselect the range and view the centered titles. See Figure 3-13.

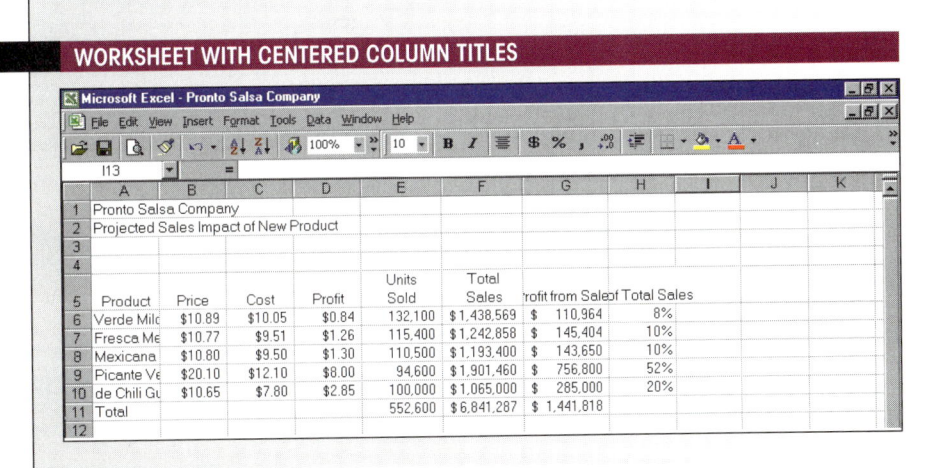

Figure 3-13   WORKSHEET WITH CENTERED COLUMN TITLES

Notice that the column titles in columns G and H are not fully visible. Although you could widen the column widths of these two columns to display the entire text, the Excel Wrap Text option enables you to display a label within a cell's existing width.

Wrapping Text in a Cell

As you know, if you enter a label that's too wide for the active cell, Excel extends the label past the cell border and into the adjacent cells—provided those cells are empty. If you select the Wrap Text option, Excel will display your label entirely within the active cell. To accommodate the label, the height of the row in which the cell is located is increased, and the text is "wrapped" onto the additional lines.

Now wrap the column titles in columns G and H.

To wrap text within a cell:

1. Select the range **G5:H5**.

2. Click **Format** on the menu bar, and then click **Cells** to open the Format Cells dialog box.

3. Click the **Alignment** tab. See Figure 3-14.

Figure 3-14	ALIGNMENT TAB OF FORMAT CELLS DIALOG BOX

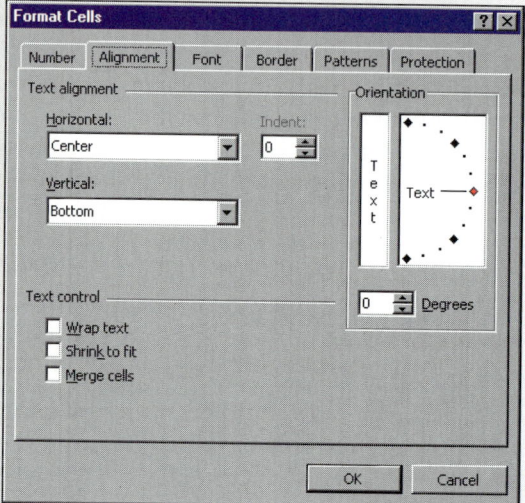

4. Click the **Wrap text** check box in the Text control area to select that option.

5. Click the **OK** button to apply the text wrapping.

6. Click any cell to deselect the range and view the entire text displayed in the cell. See Figure 3-15.

Figure 3-15	WRAPPING TEXT IN A CELL

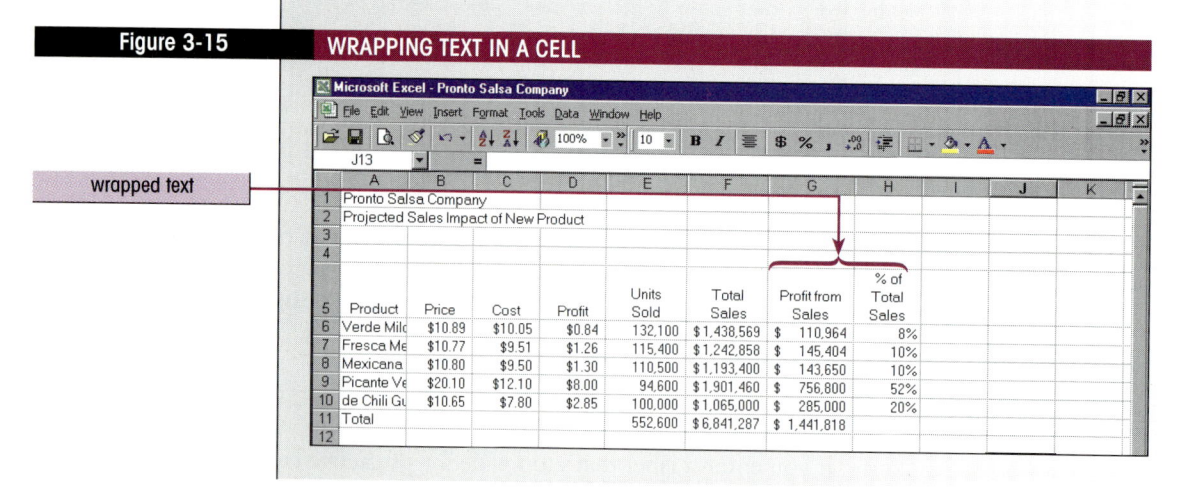

Now you are ready to center the main worksheet titles.

Centering Text Across Cells

Sometimes you might want to center the contents from one cell across more than one column. This is particularly useful for centering a title at the top of a worksheet. Now you use the Center Across Selection option in the Alignment tab from the Format Cells dialog box to center the worksheet titles in cells A1 and A2 across columns A through H.

To center the worksheet titles across columns A through H:

1. Select the range **A1:H2**.

2. Click **Format**, click **Cells**, and then, if necessary, click the **Alignment** tab in the Format Cells dialog box.

3. Click the arrow next to the **Horizontal** text alignment list box to display the horizontal text alignment options.

4. Click the **Center Across Selection** option to center the title lines across columns A through H.

5. Click the **OK** button.

6. Click any cell to deselect the range. See Figure 3-16.

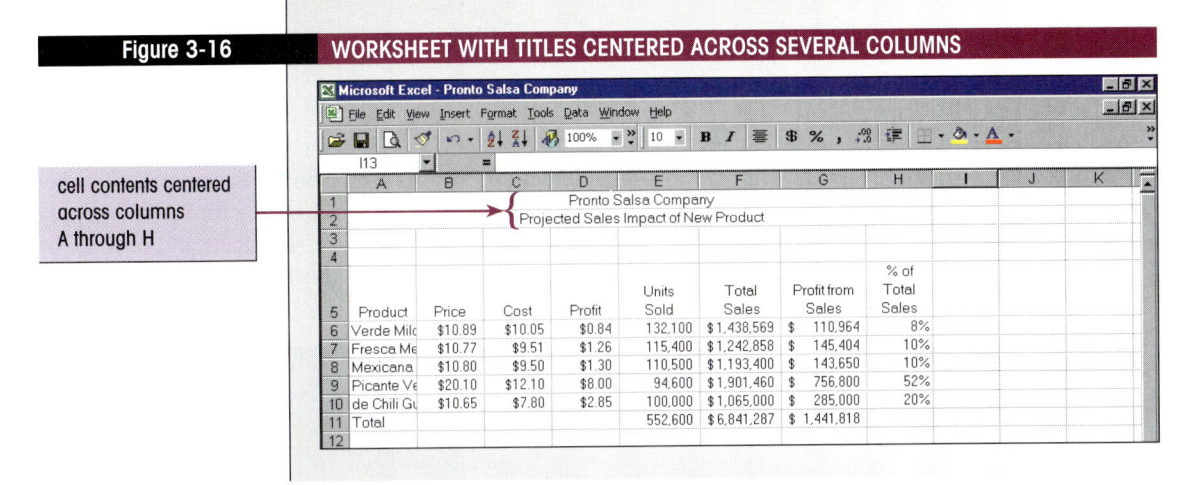

Figure 3-16 | **WORKSHEET WITH TITLES CENTERED ACROSS SEVERAL COLUMNS**

cell contents centered across columns A through H

Indenting Text Within a Cell

When you type text in a cell it is left-aligned. You can indent text from the left edge by using the Increase Indent button on the Formatting toolbar or the Index spinner button in the Alignment tab of the Format Cells dialog box. You decide to indent the word "Total" to provide a visual cue of the change from detail to summary information.

To indent text within a cell:

1. Click cell **A11** to make it the active cell.

2. Click the **Increase Indent** button on the Formatting toolbar to indent the word "Total" within the cell.

3. Click the **Save** button on the Standard toolbar to save the worksheet.

You check your plan and confirm that you selected formats for all worksheet cells containing data and that the data within the cells is aligned properly. The formatting of the worksheet contents is almost complete. Your next task is to improve the appearance of the labels by changing the font style of the title and the column headings.

You decide to use the Bold button on the Formatting toolbar to change some titles in the worksheet to boldface.

Changing the Font, Font Style, and Font Size

A font is a set of letters, numbers, punctuation marks, and symbols with a specific size and design. Figure 3-17 shows some examples. A font can have one or more of the following font styles: regular, italic, bold, and bold italic.

Figure 3-17   SELECTED FONTS

FONT	REGULAR STYLE	ITALIC STYLE	BOLD STYLE	BOLD ITALIC STYLE
Times	AaBbCc	*AaBbCc*	**AaBbCc**	***AaBbCc***
Courier	AaBbCc	*AaBbCc*	**AaBbCc**	***AaBbCc***
Garamond	AaBbCc	*AaBbCc*	**AaBbCc**	***AaBbCc***
Helvetica Condensed	AaBbCc	*AaBbCc*	**AaBbCc**	***AaBbCc***

Most fonts are available in many sizes, and you can also select font effects, such as strikeout, underline, and color. The Formatting toolbar provides tools for changing font style by applying boldface, italics, underline, and increasing or decreasing font size. To access and preview other font effects, you can open the Format Cells dialog box from the Format menu.

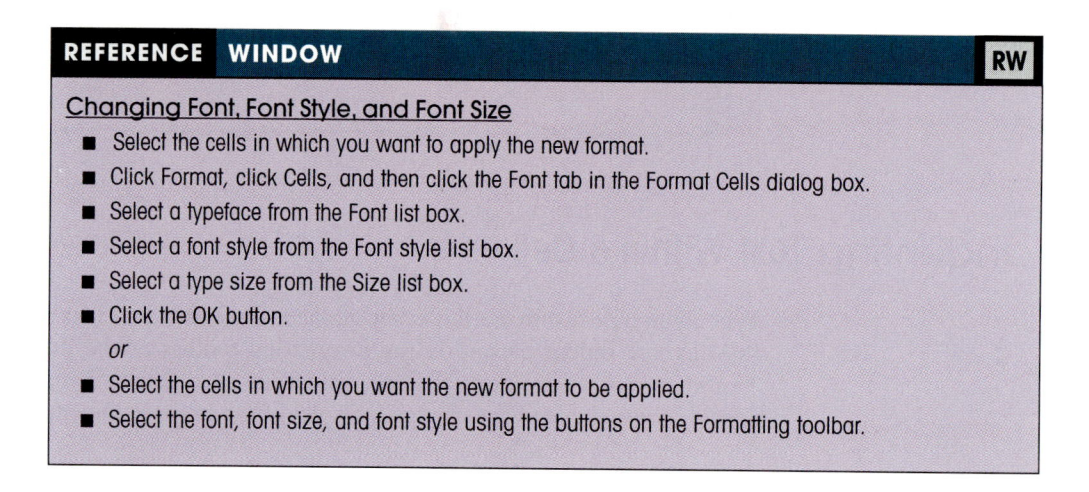

REFERENCE WINDOW   RW

Changing Font, Font Style, and Font Size
- Select the cells in which you want to apply the new format.
- Click Format, click Cells, and then click the Font tab in the Format Cells dialog box.
- Select a typeface from the Font list box.
- Select a font style from the Font style list box.
- Select a type size from the Size list box.
- Click the OK button.

or

- Select the cells in which you want the new format to be applied.
- Select the font, font size, and font style using the buttons on the Formatting toolbar.

You begin by formatting the word "Total" in cell A11 in boldface letters.

To apply the boldface font style:

1. If necessary, click cell **A11**.

2. Click the **Bold** button [B] on the Formatting toolbar to set the font style to boldface. Notice that when a style like bold is applied to a cell's content, the toolbar button appears depressed to indicate that the style is applied to the active cell.

You also want to display the column titles in boldface. To do this, first select the range you want to format, and then click the Bold button to apply the format.

To display the column titles in boldface:

1. Select the range **A5:H5**.

2. Click the **Bold** button **B** on the Formatting toolbar to apply the boldface font style.

3. Click any cell to deselect the range.

Next you want to change the font and size of the worksheet titles for emphasis. You use the Font dialog box (instead of the toolbar) so you can preview your changes. Remember, although the worksheet titles appear to be in columns A through F, they are just spilling over from column A. To format the titles, you need to select only cells A1 and A2—the cells where the titles were originally entered.

To change the font and font size of the worksheet titles:

1. Select the range **A1:A2**. Although the title is centered within the range A1:H2, the values are stored in cells A1 and A2.

2. Click **Format** on the menu bar, and then click **Cells** to open the Format Cells dialog box.

3. Click the **Font** tab. See Figure 3-18.

Figure 3-18   **FONT TAB IN FORMAT CELLS DIALOG BOX**

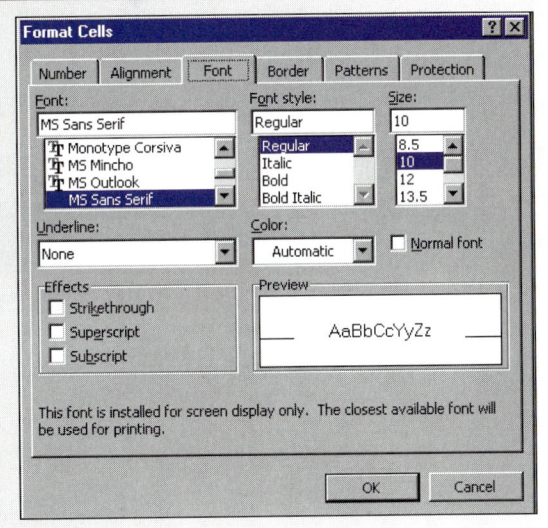

4. Use the Font box scroll bar to find the Times New Roman font. Click the **Times New Roman** font to select it.

5. Click **Bold** in the Font style list box.

6. Click **14** in the Size list box. A sample of the font appears in the Preview box.

7. Click the **OK** button to apply the new font, font style, and font size to the worksheet titles.

8. Click any cell to deselect the titles. See Figure 3-19.

EXCEL EX 3.16 TUTORIAL 3 DEVELOPING A PROFESSIONAL-LOOKING WORKSHEET

Figure 3-19 TITLES AFTER NEW FONT, FONT STYLE, AND FONT SIZE APPLIED

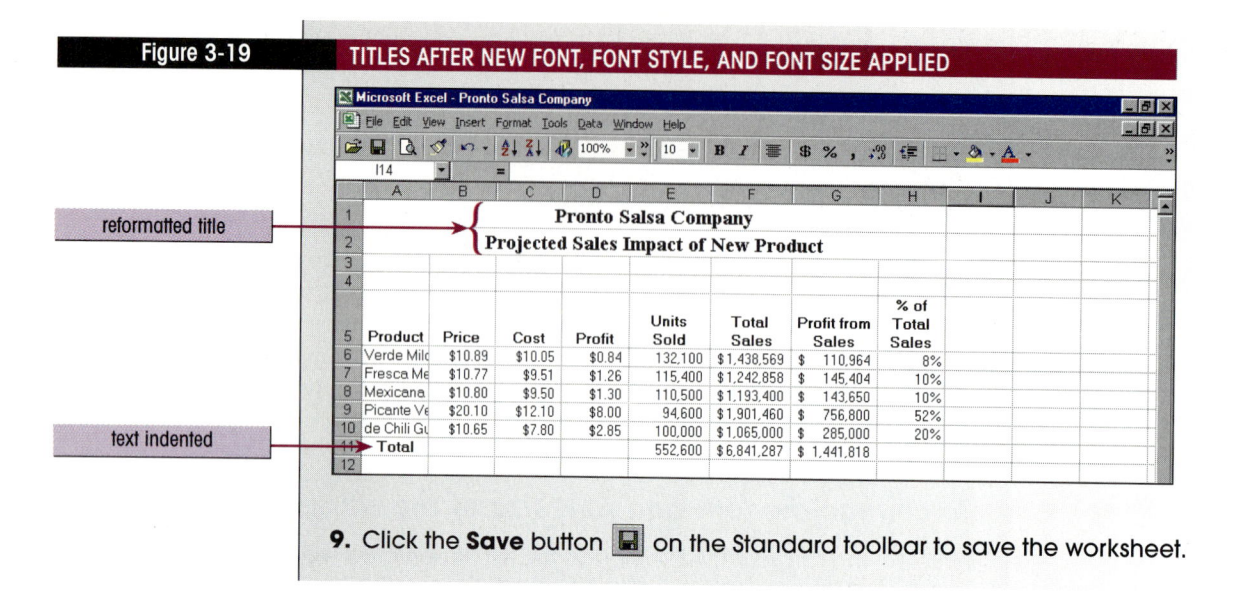

reformatted title

text indented

9. Click the **Save** button on the Standard toolbar to save the worksheet.

Next you decide to display the products names in italics.

To italicize the row labels:

1. Select the range **A6:A10**.

2. Click the **Italic** button on the Formatting toolbar to apply the italic font style.

3. Click any cell to deselect the range and view the formatting you have done so far. See Figure 3-20.

Figure 3-20 BOLD AND ITALIC FORMATS APPLIED

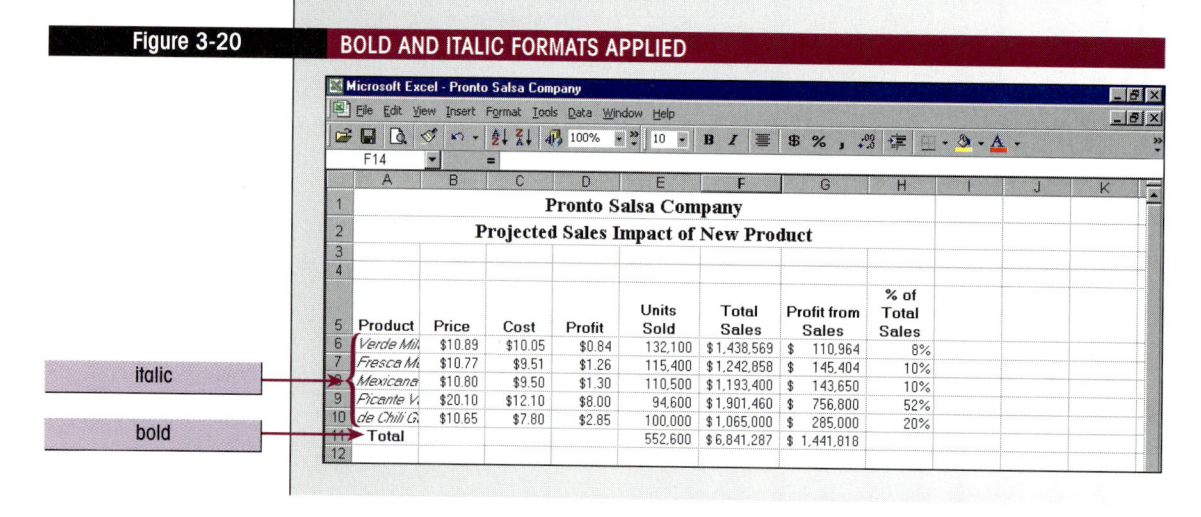

italic

bold

You hope Anne will approve of the Times New Roman font—it looks like the font on the Pronto salsa jar labels and would like to use it to create a style that can be applied to other worksheets.

Using Styles

A **style** is a saved collection of formatting, such as font, font size, pattern, and alignment that you combine, name and save as a group. A style can include from one to six attributes—Number, font, Alignment, Border, Pattern, and Protection. Once you have saved a style, you can apply it to a cell or range to achieve consistency in formatting. Excel has six predefined styles—Comma, Comma[0], Currency, currency[0], Normal, and Percent. By default, every cell in a worksheet is automatically formatted with the Normal style, which you use whenever you start typing in a new worksheet.

You can create a style in two ways: by using an example of the cell that has the formats you want associated with the style; or manually, by choosing formats from the Style dialog box and selecting the format you want associated with the style.

Although you won't create a style in this tutorial, you can follow the steps in the reference window if you want to create a style.

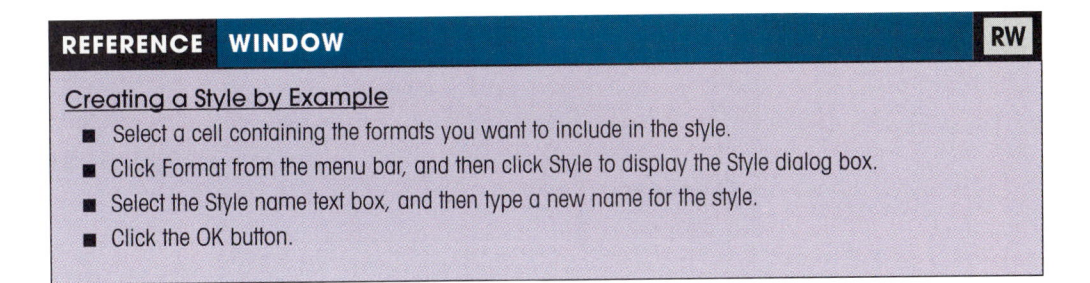

REFERENCE WINDOW — RW

Creating a Style by Example
- Select a cell containing the formats you want to include in the style.
- Click Format from the menu bar, and then click Style to display the Style dialog box.
- Select the Style name text box, and then type a new name for the style.
- Click the OK button.

Clearing Formats from Cells

Anne reviews the worksheet and decides the italics format applied to the product names is not necessary. She asks you to remove the formatting from cells A6:A10. Although you could use Undo to remove the last step, you'll use the Edit, Clear command which erases formatting while leaving the cell's content intact. This command can be issued at any time to clear formatting from a cell.

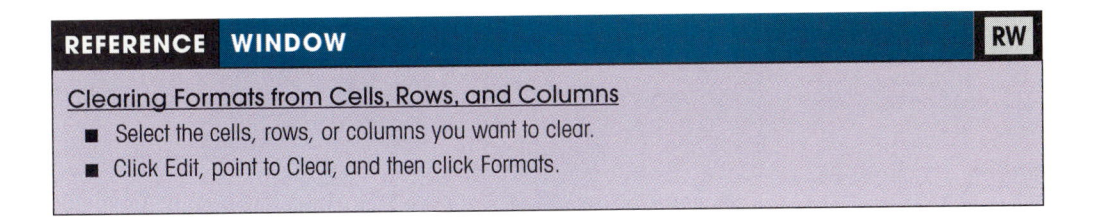

REFERENCE WINDOW — RW

Clearing Formats from Cells, Rows, and Columns
- Select the cells, rows, or columns you want to clear.
- Click Edit, point to Clear, and then click Formats.

To clear the formatting of a cell:

1. Select cells A6:A10, the cells whose format you want to clear.

2. Click **Edit**, point to **Clear** and then click **Formats** to return the cell to its default (General) format. Notice the contents of the cells have not been erased.

3. Click any cell to deselect and view the product names in Regular style.

Deleting Cells from a Worksheet

Anne again reviews the worksheet and decides to remove the Cost data, range C5:C11, from the worksheet. You will use the Delete command from the Edit menu to remove these cells from the worksheet. When you delete one or more cells from a worksheet, you remove the space occupied by these cells and must specify if you want the cells beneath the deleted cells to shift up or the cells to the right of the deleted cells to shift to the left.

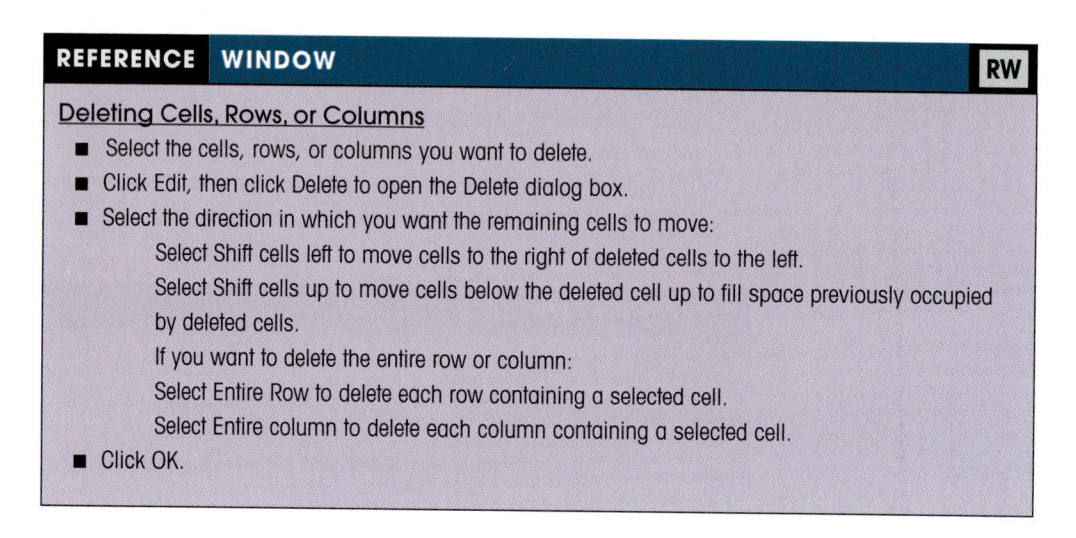

> **REFERENCE WINDOW**   RW
>
> **Deleting Cells, Rows, or Columns**
> - Select the cells, rows, or columns you want to delete.
> - Click Edit, then click Delete to open the Delete dialog box.
> - Select the direction in which you want the remaining cells to move:
>   Select Shift cells left to move cells to the right of deleted cells to the left.
>   Select Shift cells up to move cells below the deleted cell up to fill space previously occupied by deleted cells.
>   If you want to delete the entire row or column:
>   Select Entire Row to delete each row containing a selected cell.
>   Select Entire column to delete each column containing a selected cell.
> - Click OK.

To delete cells from the worksheet

1. Select the range **C5:C11**, the cells to be deleted from the worksheet.
2. Click **Edit**, click **Delete** to open the Delete dialog box. See Figure 3-21.

Figure 3-21   DELETE DIALOG BOX

3. If necessary, click the **Shift cells left** option button.
4. Click OK. Notice all the cells from D5:H6 shift left one column.
5. Click any cell to observe that the Cost data no longer appears in the worksheet. See Figure 3-22. Save the worksheet.

TUTORIAL 3 DEVELOPING A PROFESSIONAL-LOOKING WORKSHEET   EX 3.19   EXCEL

Figure 3-22 WORKSHEET AFTER COST CELLS DELETED

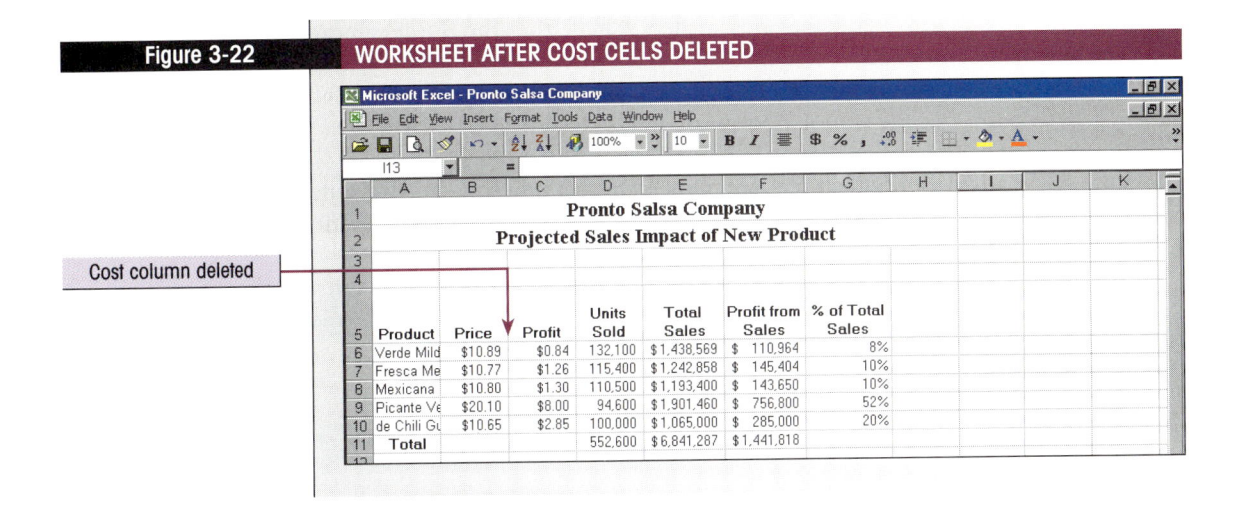

Cost column deleted

Session 3.1 QUICK CHECK

1. List three ways you can access formatting commands, options, and tools.
2. If the number .05765 is in a cell, what will Excel display if you:
   a. format the number using the Percentage format with one decimal place?
   b. format the number using the Currency format with 2 decimal places and the dollar sign?
3. The _____ copies formats quickly from one cell or range to another.
4. A series of ####### in a cell indicates _____.
5. Explain two ways to completely display a label that currently is not entirely displayed.
6. Explain why Excel might display 3,045.39 in a cell, but 3045.38672 in the formula bar.
7. What are the general rules you should follow for aligning column headings, numbers, and text labels?
8. List the options available on the Formatting toolbar for aligning data.

Now that you have finished formatting the data in the worksheet, you need to enhance the worksheet's appearance and readability as a whole. You will do this in Session 3.2 by applying borders, colors, and a text box.

SESSION 3.2

In this session you will learn how to enhance a worksheet's overall appearance by adding borders and color. You will use the Drawing toolbar to add a text box and graphic to the worksheet and use landscape orientation to print the worksheet.

Adding and Removing Borders

A worksheet is often divided into zones that visually group related information. Lines, called **borders**, can help to distinguish different zones of the worksheet and add visual interest.

You can create lines and borders using either the Borders button on the Formatting toolbar or the Border tab in the Format Cells dialog box. You can place a border around a single cell or a group of cells using the Outline option. To create a horizontal line, you place a border at the top or bottom of a cell. To create a vertical line, you place a border on the right or left side of a cell.

The Border tab lets you choose from numerous border styles, including different line thicknesses, double lines, dashed lines, and colored lines. With the Borders button, your choice of border styles is more limited.

To remove a border from a cell or group of cells, you can use the Border tab in the Format Cells dialog box. To remove all borders from a selected range of cells, select the None button in the Presets area.

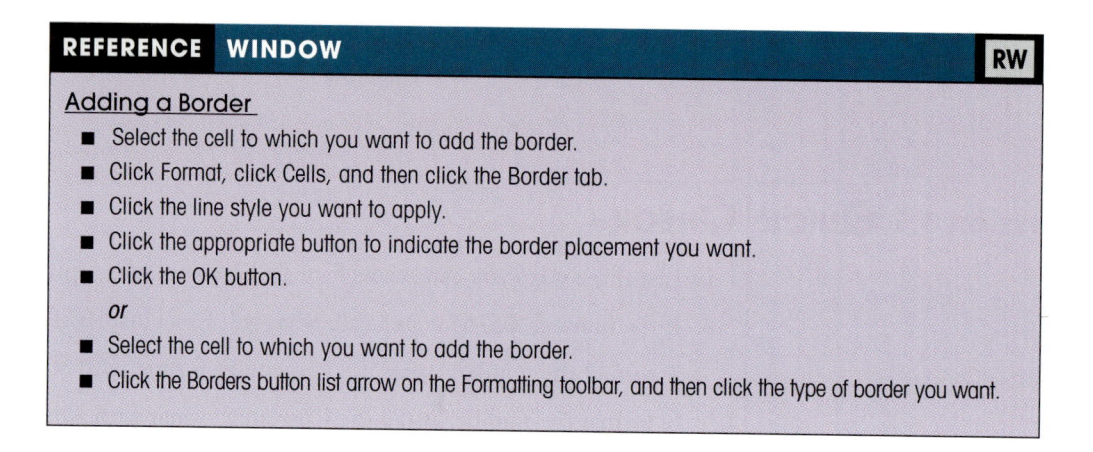

REFERENCE WINDOW

Adding a Border
- Select the cell to which you want to add the border.
- Click Format, click Cells, and then click the Border tab.
- Click the line style you want to apply.
- Click the appropriate button to indicate the border placement you want.
- Click the OK button.

or

- Select the cell to which you want to add the border.
- Click the Borders button list arrow on the Formatting toolbar, and then click the type of border you want.

You decide that a thick line under all column titles will separate them from the data in the columns. To do this, you use the Borders button on the Formatting toolbar.

To underline column titles:

1. If you took a break after the last session, make sure Excel is running and the Projected Sales worksheet of the Pronto Salsa Company workbook is open.
2. Select the range **A5:G5**.
3. Click the **Borders** button list arrow on the Formatting toolbar. The Borders palette appears. See Figure 3-23.

Figure 3-23   **BORDERS PALETTE**

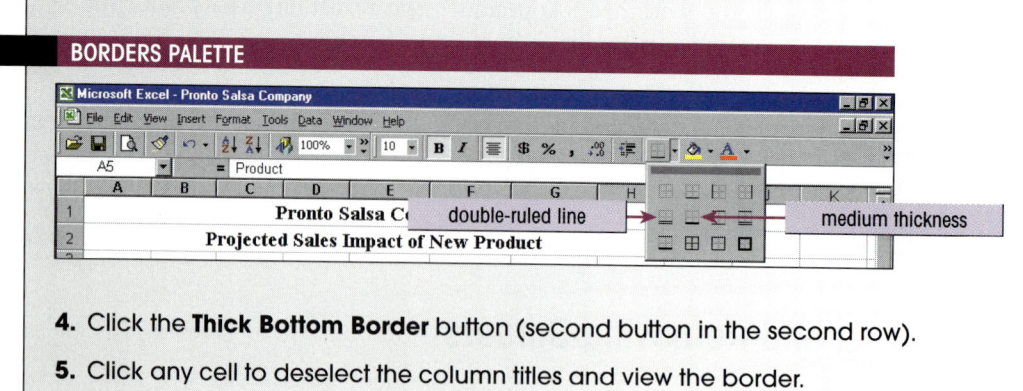

double-ruled line   *medium thickness*

4. Click the **Thick Bottom Border** button (second button in the second row).
5. Click any cell to deselect the column titles and view the border.

TUTORIAL 3 DEVELOPING A PROFESSIONAL-LOOKING WORKSHEET   EX 3.21   EXCEL

You also want a line to separate the data from the totals in row 11, and a double-ruled line below the totals for added emphasis. This time you use the Border tab in the Format Cells dialog box to apply borders to cells.

To add a line separating the data and the totals and a double-ruled line below the totals:

1. Select the range **A11:G11**.
2. Click **Format** on the menu bar, click **Cells**, and then click the **Border** tab in the Format Cells dialog box. See Figure 3-24

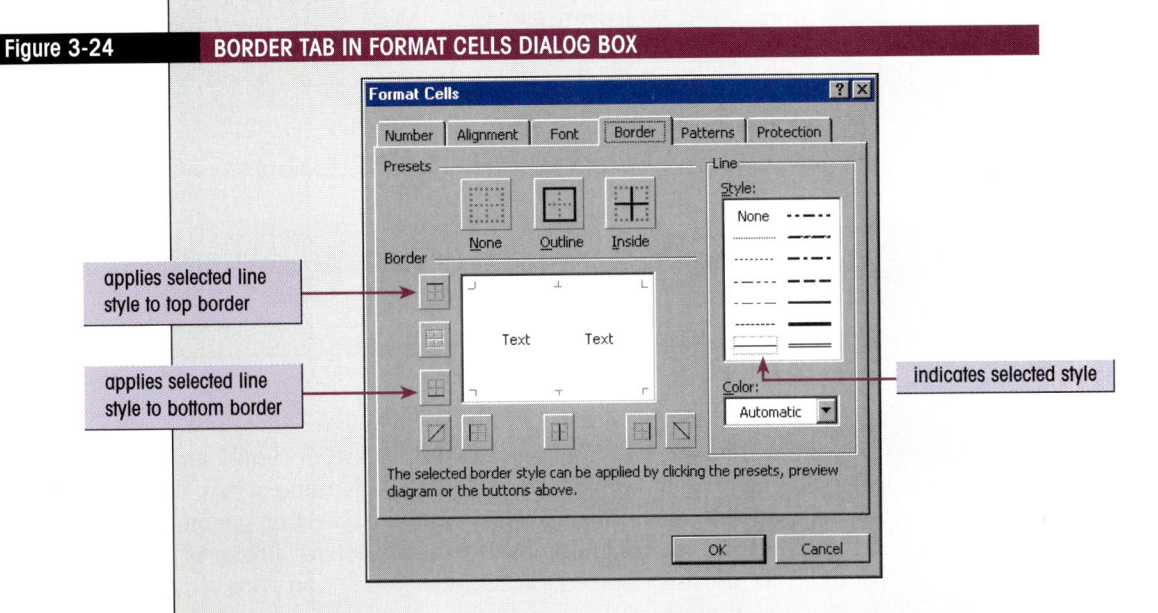

Figure 3-24   BORDER TAB IN FORMAT CELLS DIALOG BOX

- applies selected line style to top border
- applies selected line style to bottom border
- indicates selected style

3. Click the **medium thick line** in the Line Style box (third from the bottom in the second column).
4. Click the **top border** button. A thick line appears at the top of the Border preview window.
5. Click the **double-ruled line** in the Line Style box.
6. Click the **bottom border** button. A double-ruled line appears at the bottom of the Border preview window.
7. Click the **OK** button to apply the borders.
8. Click any cell to deselect the range and view the borders. See Figure 3-25.

Figure 3-25: BORDERS APPLIED TO WORKSHEET

(Screenshot showing Pronto Salsa Company worksheet with "double-ruled line" annotation pointing to row above Total, and "medium thickness" annotation pointing to right border of data area.)

Product	Price	Profit	Units Sold	Total Sales	Profit from Sales	% of Total Sales
Verde Mild	$10.89	$0.84	132,100	$1,438,569	$ 110,964	8%
Fresca Me	$10.77	$1.26	115,400	$1,242,858	$ 145,404	10%
Mexicana	$10.80	$1.30	110,500	$1,193,400	$ 143,650	10%
Picante Ve	$20.10	$8.00	94,600	$1,901,460	$ 756,800	52%
de Chili Gu	$10.65	$2.85	100,000	$1,065,000	$ 285,000	20%
Total			552,600	$6,841,287	$1,441,818	

9. Click the **Save** button on the Standard toolbar to save the worksheet.

In addition to borders, you want to add color to emphasize the Profit from Sales column.

Using Color for Emphasis

Patterns and colors provide visual interest, emphasize worksheet zones, or indicate data-entry areas. The way you intend to use the worksheet should guide your use of patterns or colors. If you print the worksheet in color and distribute a hard copy of it, or if you plan to use a color projection device to display your worksheet on screen, you can take advantage of the Excel color formatting options. If you do not have a color printer, you can use patterns because it is difficult to predict how colors you see on your screen will translate into gray shades on your printout.

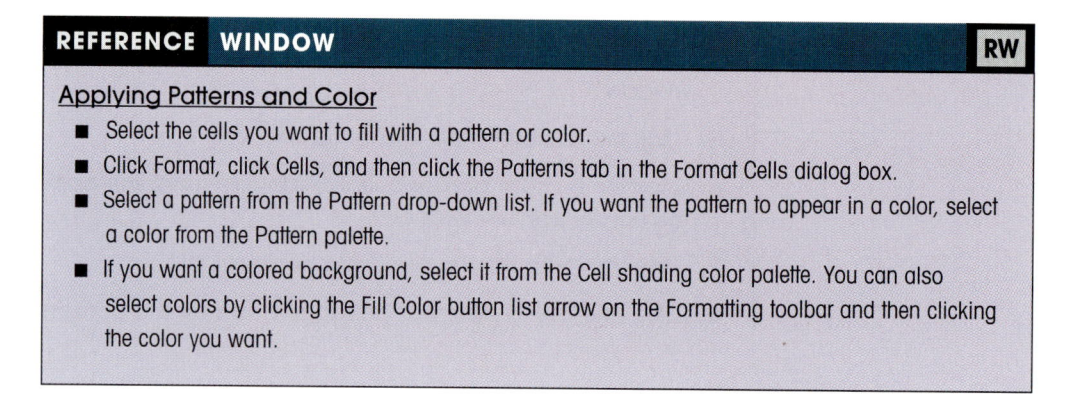

REFERENCE WINDOW

Applying Patterns and Color
- Select the cells you want to fill with a pattern or color.
- Click Format, click Cells, and then click the Patterns tab in the Format Cells dialog box.
- Select a pattern from the Pattern drop-down list. If you want the pattern to appear in a color, select a color from the Pattern palette.
- If you want a colored background, select it from the Cell shading color palette. You can also select colors by clicking the Fill Color button list arrow on the Formatting toolbar and then clicking the color you want.

You want your worksheet to look good when you print it in black and white on the office laser printer, but you also want it to look good on the screen when you show it to Anne. You decide that a yellow background will enable the Profit from Sales column to stand out and looks fairly good both on the screen and the printout. You apply this format using the Patterns tab in the Format Cells dialog box.

TUTORIAL 3 DEVELOPING A PROFESSIONAL-LOOKING WORKSHEET   EX 3.23   EXCEL

To apply a color to the Profit from Sales column:

1. Select the range **F5:F11**.

2. Click **Format** on the menu bar, click **Cells**, and then click the **Patterns** tab in the Format Cells dialog box. See Figure 3-26. A color palette appears.

Figure 3-26   COLOR PALETTE IN PATTERNS TAB OF FORMAT CELLS DIALOG BOX

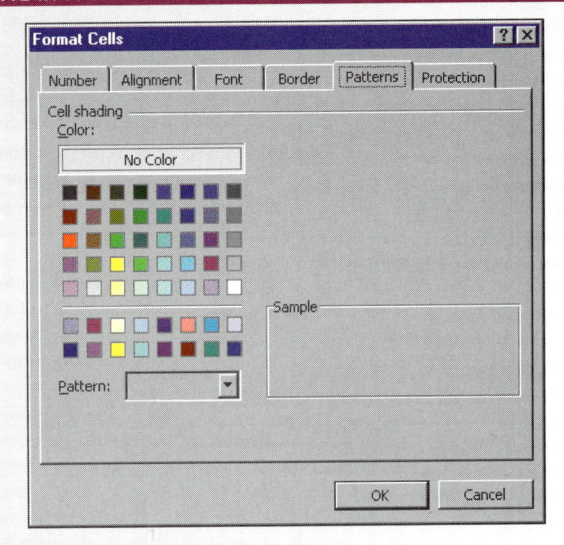

3. Click the **yellow square** in the fourth row (third square from the left) of the Cell shading Color palette.

4. Click the **OK** button to apply the color.

5. Click any cell to deselect the range and view the color in the Profit from Sales column. See Figure 3-27.

Figure 3-27   WORKSHEET AFTER APPLYING COLOR TO A COLUMN

	A	B	C	D	E	F	G
1				Pronto Salsa Company			
2				Projected Sales Impact of New Product			
3							
4							
5	Product	Price	Profit	Units Sold	Total Sales	Profit from Sales	% of Total Sales
6	Verde Mild	$10.89	$0.84	132,100	$1,438,569	$ 110,964	8%
7	Fresca Me	$10.77	$1.26	115,400	$1,242,858	$ 145,404	10%
8	Mexicana	$10.80	$1.30	110,500	$1,193,400	$ 143,650	10%
9	Picante Ve	$20.10	$8.00	94,600	$1,901,460	$ 756,800	52%
10	de Chili Gu	$10.65	$2.85	100,000	$1,065,000	$ 285,000	20%
11	Total			552,600	$6,841,287	$1,441,818	

yellow background

You can also use buttons on the Formatting toolbar to change the color for the cell background (Fill Color button) and text in a cell (Text Color button).

Now that you have finished formatting labels and values, you can change the width of column A to best display the information in that column. To do this, you use Excel's Automatic Adjustment feature to change the width of a column to fit the widest entry in a cell.

To change the column width to fit the contents of a column:

1. Position the pointer over the column boundary between column A and column B. The pointer changes to ↔.

2. Double-click the boundary. The column width automatically adjusts to accommodate the widest entry in column A. See Figure 3-28.

Figure 3-28   **RESULTS OF CHANGING COLUMN WIDTH**

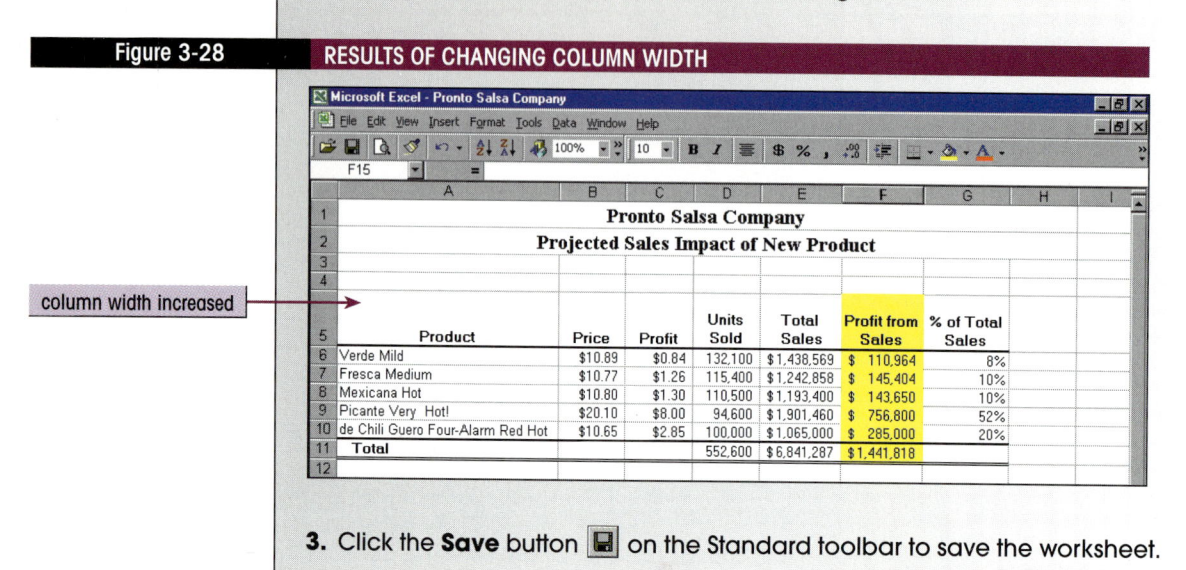

column width increased

3. Click the **Save** button on the Standard toolbar to save the worksheet.

Using the Drawing Toolbar for Emphasis

The Excel Text Box feature lets you display notes, comments, and headings in a worksheet. A **text box** is like an electronic Post-it note that appears on top of the worksheet cells.

To add a text box you use the Text Box button, which is located on the Drawing toolbar, and type the note in the text box.

Activating the Drawing Toolbar

Excel provides many toolbars. You have been using two: the Standard toolbar and the Formatting toolbar. Some of the other toolbars include the Chart toolbar, the Drawing toolbar, and the Visual Basic toolbar. To activate a toolbar, it's usually easiest to use the toolbar Shortcut menu, but to activate the Drawing toolbar, you can simply click the Drawing button on the Standard toolbar. When you finish using a toolbar, you can easily remove it from the worksheet.

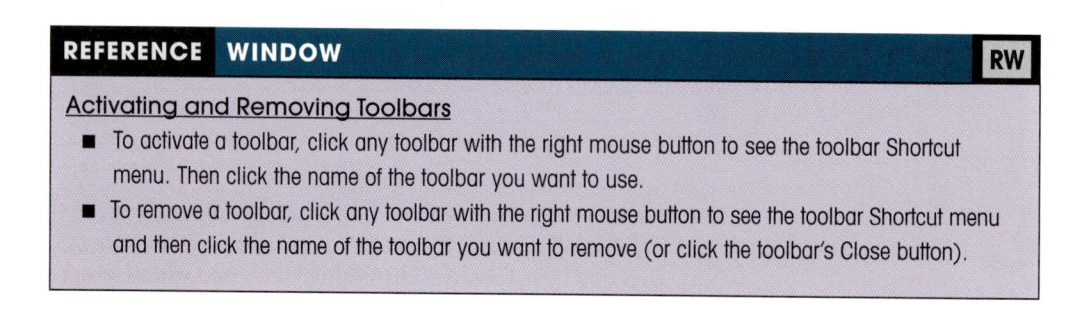

REFERENCE WINDOW   RW

Activating and Removing Toolbars

- To activate a toolbar, click any toolbar with the right mouse button to see the toolbar Shortcut menu. Then click the name of the toolbar you want to use.
- To remove a toolbar, click any toolbar with the right mouse button to see the toolbar Shortcut menu and then click the name of the toolbar you want to remove (or click the toolbar's Close button).

You need the Drawing toolbar to accomplish your next formatting task. (If your Drawing toolbar is already active, skip the following step.)

To display the Drawing toolbar:

1. Click the **Drawing** button on the Standard toolbar.

The toolbar might appear in any location in the worksheet window; this is called a **floating** toolbar. You don't want the toolbar obstructing your view of the worksheet, so drag it to the bottom of the worksheet window to **anchor** it there. (If your toolbar is already anchored at the bottom of the worksheet window, or at the top, skip the next set of steps.)

To anchor the Drawing toolbar to the bottom of the worksheet window:

1. Position the pointer on the title bar of the Drawing toolbar.
2. Click and drag the toolbar to the bottom of the screen.
3. Release the mouse button to attach the Drawing toolbar to the bottom of the worksheet window. See Figure 3-29.

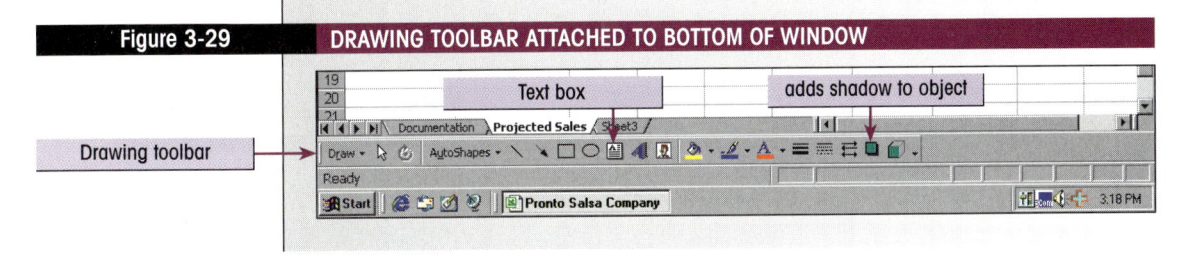

Figure 3-29　DRAWING TOOLBAR ATTACHED TO BOTTOM OF WINDOW

Now that the Drawing toolbar is where you want it, you proceed with your plan to add a comment to the worksheet.

Adding a Text Box

A **text box** is a drawing tool that contains text. It sits on top of the cells in a worksheet and is useful for drawing attention to important points in a worksheet or chart. With Excel you can use a variety of drawing tools, such as boxes, lines, circles, arrows, and text boxes to add graphic objects to your worksheet. To move, modify, or delete a graphic object, you first select it by moving the pointer over the object, then click it. Small square handles indicate that the object is selected. Use these handles to adjust the object's size, change its location, or delete it.

EXCEL   EX 3.26   TUTORIAL 3   DEVELOPING A PROFESSIONAL-LOOKING WORKSHEET

> **REFERENCE WINDOW**
>
> **Adding a Text Box**
> - Click the Text Box button on the Drawing toolbar.
> - Position the pointer where you want the text box to appear in the worksheet.
> - Click and drag to outline the size and shape of the text box.
> - Type the text for the text box.
> - Click outside the text box.

You want to draw attention to the low price and high profit margin of the new salsa product. To do this, you plan to add a text box to the bottom of the worksheet that contains a note about expected profits.

To add a text box:

1. Click the **Text Box** button on the Drawing toolbar. As you move the pointer inside the worksheet area, the pointer changes to ↓. Position the crosshair of the pointer at the top of cell **A13** to mark the upper-left corner of the text box.

2. Click and drag ✛ to cell **C18**, and then release the mouse button to mark the lower-right corner of the text box. See Figure 3-30.

   You are ready to type the text into the text box.

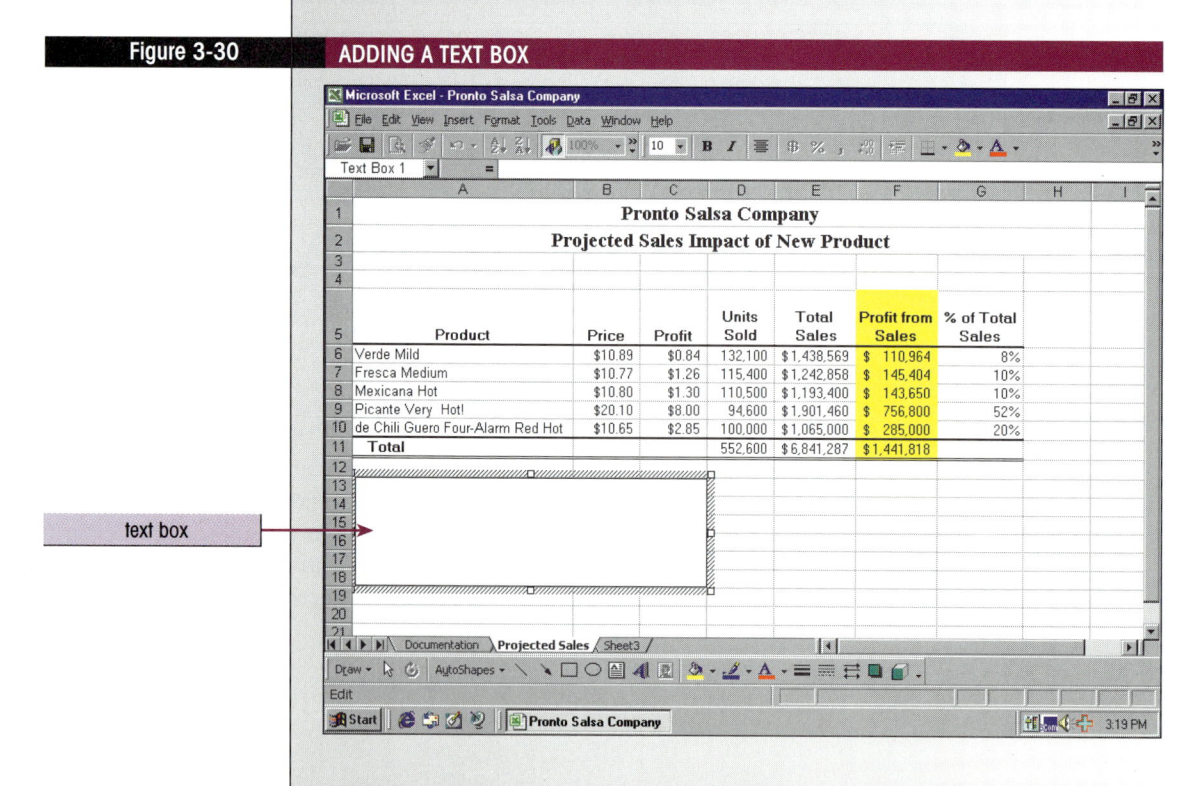

Figure 3-30   ADDING A TEXT BOX

3. Make sure the insertion point is in the text box and then type **Notice the high profit margin of the de Chili Guero Four-Alarm Red Hot. It has the second highest profit per unit.**

You want to use a different font style to emphasize the name of the new salsa product in the text box.

To italicize the name of the new salsa product:

1. Position I in the text box just before the word "de Chili."
2. Click and drag I to the end of the word "Hot," and then release the mouse button.

    TROUBLE? If the size of your text box differs slightly from the one in the figure, the lines of text might break differently. So don't worry if the text in your text box is not arranged exactly like the text in the figure.

3. Click the **Italic** button *I* on the Formatting toolbar.
4. Click any cell to deselect the product name, which now appears italicized.

You decide to change the text box size so that there is no empty space at the bottom.

To change the text box size:

1. Click the **text box** to select it and display the patterned border with handles.
2. Position the pointer on the center handle at the bottom of the text box. The pointer changes to ↕.
3. Click and drag ↕ up to shorten the box, and then release the mouse button.

You want to change the text box a bit more by adding a drop shadow to it.

To add a shadow to the text box:

1. Make sure the text box is still selected. (Look for the patterned border and handles.)
2. Click the **Shadow** button on the Drawing toolbar to display the gallery of Shadow options. See Figure 3-31.

EXCEL   EX 3.28   TUTORIAL 3 DEVELOPING A PROFESSIONAL-LOOKING WORKSHEET

Figure 3-31   SHADOW STYLE OPTIONS

reduced height of text box

click Shadow Style 6

3. Click **Shadow Style 6** (second style from the left in the second row).

4. Click any cell. See Figure 3-32.

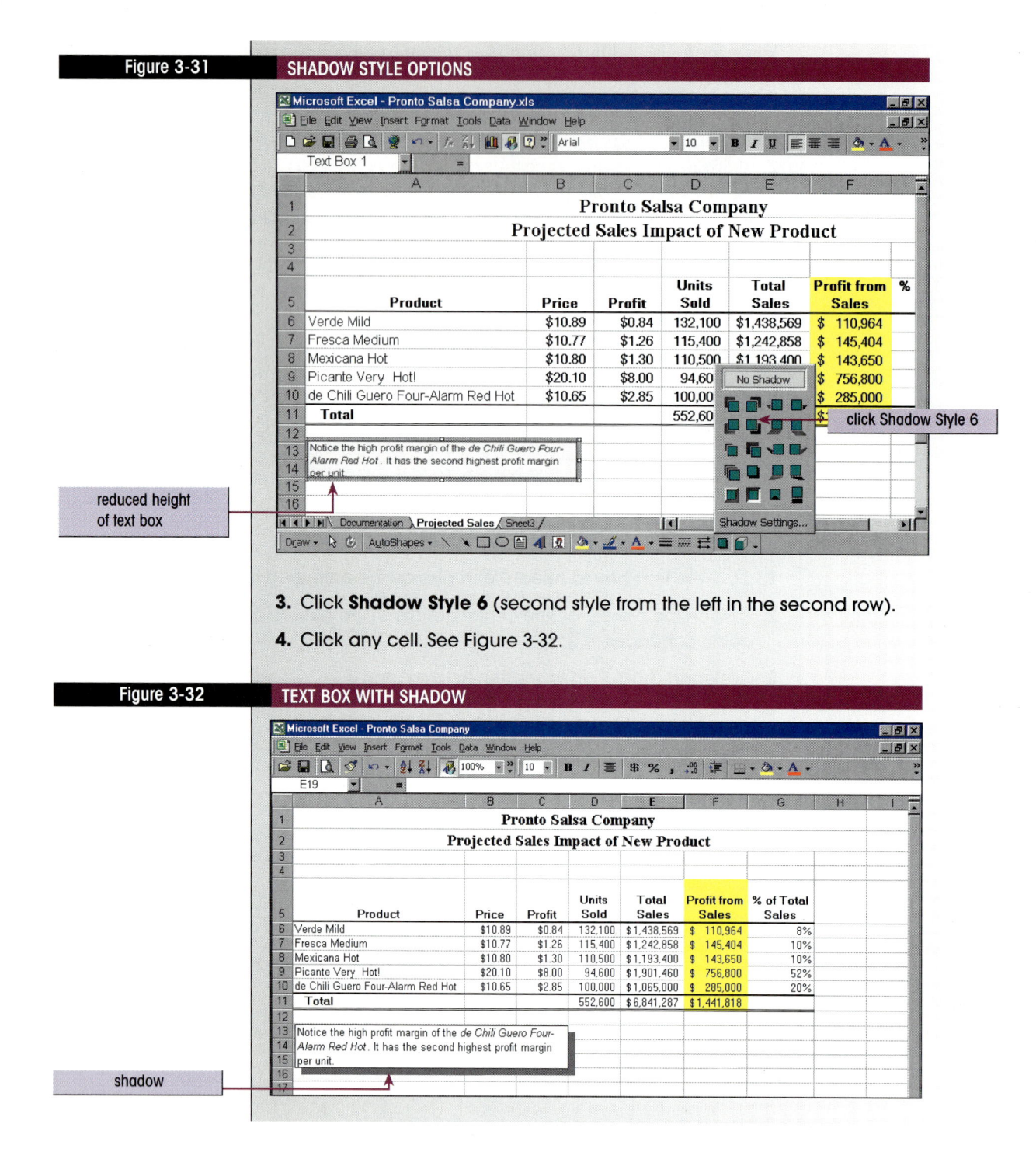

Figure 3-32   TEXT BOX WITH SHADOW

shadow

Adding an Arrow

You decide to add an arrow pointing from the text box to the row with information on the new salsa.

To add an arrow:

1. Click the **Arrow** button on the Drawing toolbar. As you move the mouse pointer inside the worksheet, the pointer changes to +.

2. Position + on the top edge of the text box in cell **B12**. To ensure a straight line, press and hold the **Shift** key as you drag to cell **B10**, and then release the mouse button.

3. Click any cell to deselect the arrow. See Figure 3-33.

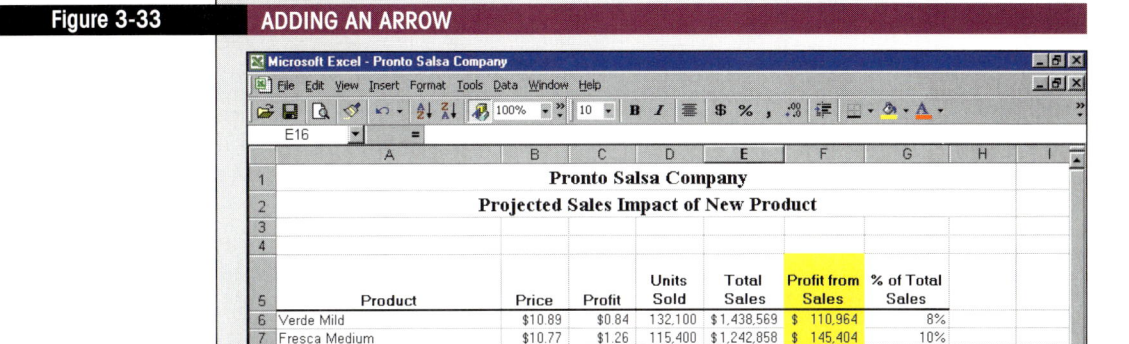

Figure 3-33   ADDING AN ARROW

	A	B	C	D	E	F	G
1			Pronto Salsa Company				
2			Projected Sales Impact of New Product				
3							
4							
5	Product	Price	Profit	Units Sold	Total Sales	Profit from Sales	% of Total Sales
6	Verde Mild	$10.89	$0.84	132,100	$1,438,569	$ 110,964	8%
7	Fresca Medium	$10.77	$1.26	115,400	$1,242,858	$ 145,404	10%
8	Mexicana Hot	$10.80	$1.30	110,500	$1,193,400	$ 143,650	10%
9	Picante Very Hot!	$20.10	$8.00	94,600	$1,901,460	$ 756,800	52%
10	de Chili Guero Four-Alarm Red Hot	$10.65	$2.85	100,000	$1,065,000	$ 285,000	20%
11	Total			552,600	$6,841,287	$1,441,818	
12							
13	Notice the high profit margin of the *de Chili Guero Four-*						
14	*Alarm Red Hot*. It has the second highest profit margin						
15	per unit.						

You want the arrow to point to cell C10 instead of B10, so you need to reposition it.

Like a text box, an arrow is an Excel object. To modify the arrow object, you must select it. When you do so, two small square handles appear on it. You can reposition either end of the arrow by dragging one of the handles.

To reposition the arrow:

1. Move the pointer over the arrow object until the pointer changes to ↖.

2. Click the **arrow**. Handles appear at each end of the arrow.

3. Move the pointer to the top handle on the arrowhead until the pointer changes to ↗.

4. Click and drag + to cell **C10**, and then release the mouse button.

5. Click any cell to deselect the arrow object. See Figure 3-34.

EXCEL   EX 3.30   TUTORIAL 3   DEVELOPING A PROFESSIONAL-LOOKING WORKSHEET

| Figure 3-34 | MOVING AN ARROW |

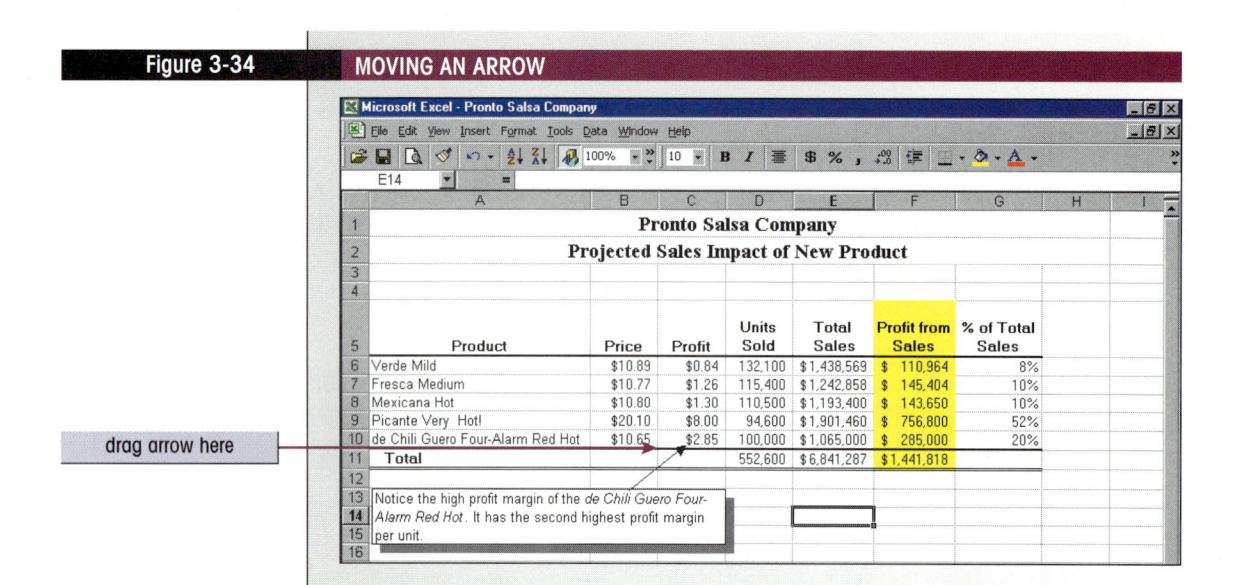

(Screenshot of Microsoft Excel - Pronto Salsa Company worksheet showing the Projected Sales Impact of New Product with a callout "drag arrow here" pointing to the arrow between the text box and cell F10.)

Now that the text box is finished, you can remove the Drawing toolbar from the worksheet.

To remove the Drawing toolbar:

1. Click the **Drawing** button on the Standard toolbar. The Drawing toolbar is removed from the window, and the Drawing button no longer appears depressed (selected).

2. Press **Ctrl + Home** to make cell A1 the active cell.

3. Click the **Save** button on the Standard toolbar to save your work.

You have now made all the formatting changes and enhancements to Anne's worksheet. She has just returned to the office, and you show her the completed worksheet. She is very pleased with how professional the worksheet looks, but she thinks of one more way to improve the appearance of the worksheet. She asks you to remove the gridlines from the worksheet display.

Controlling the Display of Gridlines

Although normally the boundaries of each cell are outlined in black, Anne has decided the worksheet will have more of a professional appearance if you remove the gridlines. To remove the gridline display, you deselect the Gridlines option in the View tab of the Options dialog box.

To remove the display of gridlines in the worksheet:

1. Click **Tools** on the menu bar, click **Options**, and if necessary, then click the **View** tab in the Options dialog box.

2. Click the **Gridlines** check box in the Window option to remove the check and deselect the option.

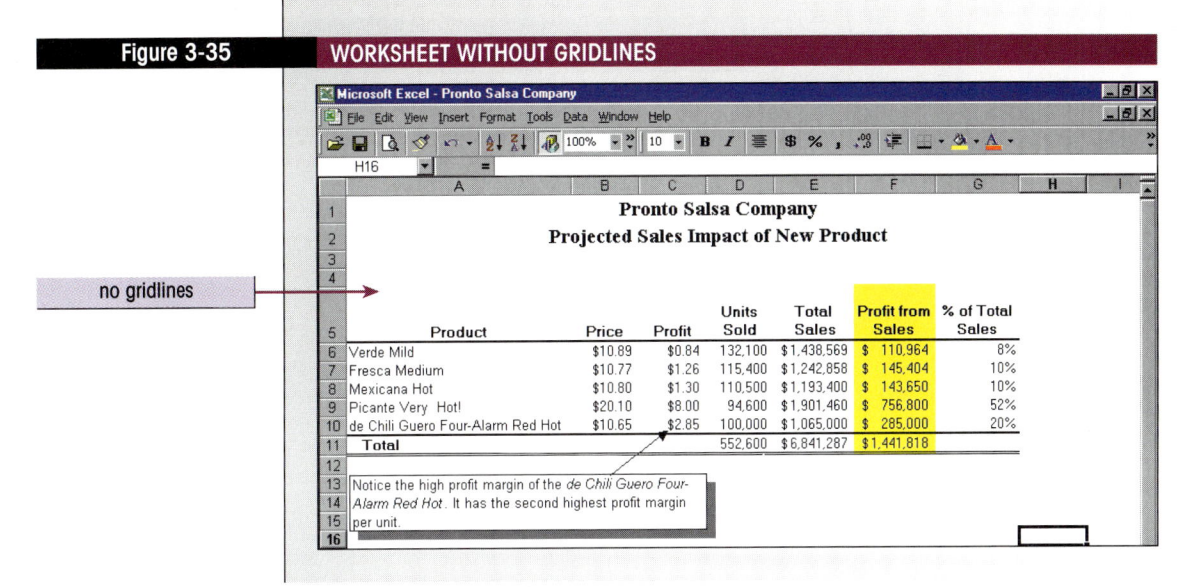

TUTORIAL 3 DEVELOPING A PROFESSIONAL-LOOKING WORKSHEET   EX 3.31

3. Click the **OK** button to display the worksheet without gridlines. See Figure 3-35.

Figure 3-35   **WORKSHEET WITHOUT GRIDLINES**

no gridlines

Now you are ready to print the worksheet.

Printing the Worksheet

Before you print a worksheet, you can use the Excel Print Preview window to see how it will look when printed. Recall that the Print Preview window shows you margins, page breaks, headers, and footers that are not always visible on the screen.

To preview the worksheet before you print it:

1. Click the **Print Preview** button on the Standard toolbar to display the first worksheet page in the Print Preview window. See Figure 3-36.

EXCEL   EX 3.32   TUTORIAL 3   DEVELOPING A PROFESSIONAL-LOOKING WORKSHEET

Figure 3-36   PRINT PREVIEW

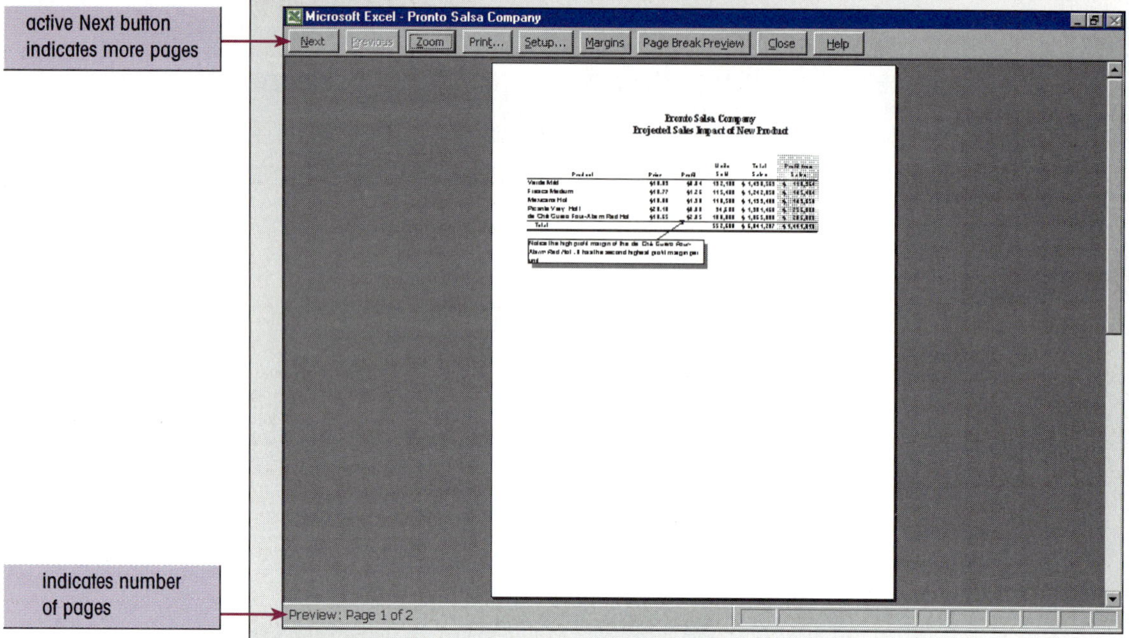

active Next button indicates more pages

indicates number of pages

2. Click the **Next** button to preview the second worksheet page. Only one column appears on this page.

3. Click the **Previous** button to preview the first page again.

Looking at the Print Preview, you see that the worksheet is too wide to fit on a single page. You realize that if you print the worksheet horizontally (lengthwise), it will fit on a single sheet of paper.

Portrait and Landscape Orientations

Excel provides two print orientations, **portrait** and **landscape**. Portrait orientation prints the worksheet with the paper positioned so it is taller than it is wide. Landscape orientation prints the worksheet with the paper positioned so it is wider than it is tall. Because some worksheets are wider than they are tall, landscape orientation is very useful.

You can specify print orientation using the Page Setup command on the File menu or using the Setup button in the Print Preview window. Use the landscape orientation for the Projected Sales worksheet.

To change the print orientation to landscape:

1. In the Print Preview window, click the **Setup** button to open the Page Setup dialog box. If necessary, click the **Page** tab.

2. Click the **Landscape** option button in the Orientation section to select this option.

3. Click the **OK** button to return to the Print Preview window. See Figure 3-37. Notice the landscape orientation; that is, the page is wider than it is tall. The worksheet will now print on one page.

Figure 3-37 **LANDSCAPE ORIENTATION**

Next button is not active

indicates 1 page

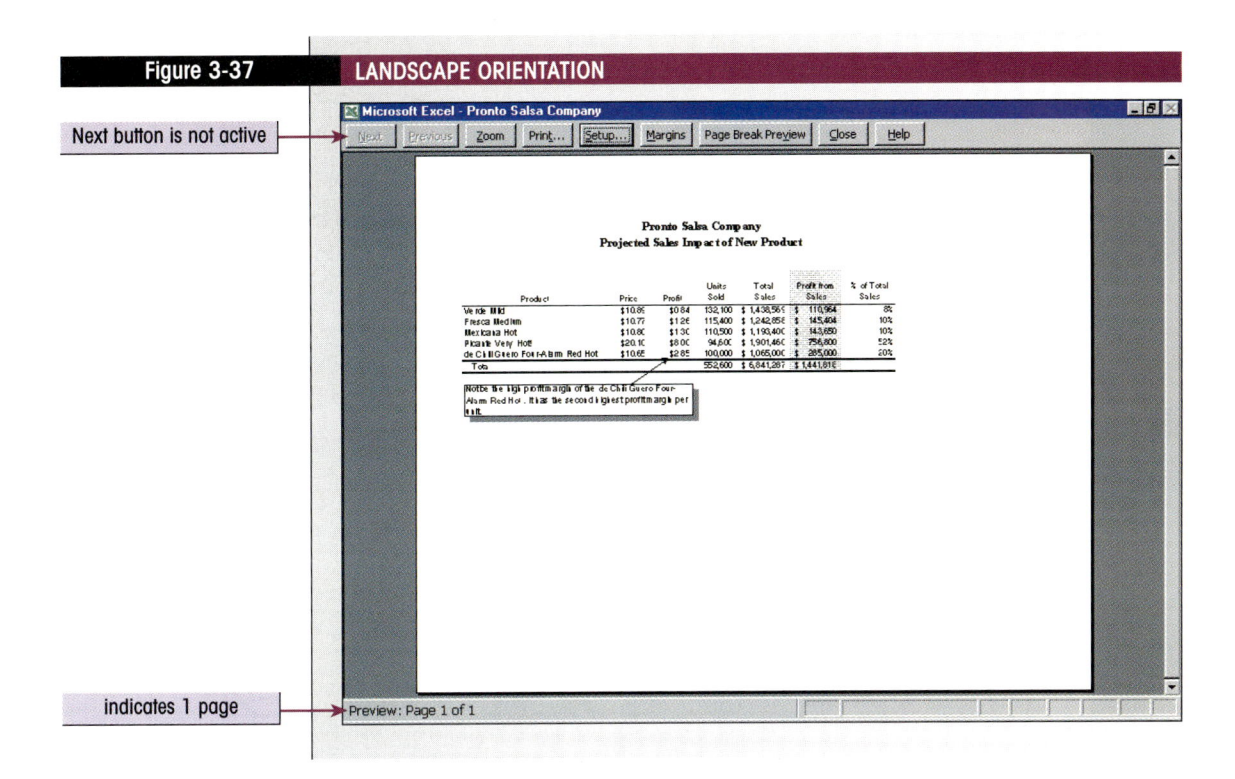

Before printing the worksheet, center the output on the page, and use the header/footer tab to document the printed worksheet.

To center the printed output:

1. Click the **Setup** button to open the Page Setup dialog box. Click the **Margins** tab.
2. Click the **Center on page Horizontally** check box to place a check in it and select that option.

Next modify the printed footer by adding your name in the center section.

To insert a custom footer for the worksheet:

1. Click the **Header/Footer** tab, and then click the **Custom footer** to open the Footer dialog box.
2. In the **Center section** box, type **Prepared by (enter your name here)**.
3. Click the **OK** button to complete the footer and return to the Page Setup dialog box.
4. Click the **OK** button to return to the Print Preview window.
5. Click the **Close** button to return to the worksheet.

The worksheet is ready to print, but you should always save your work before printing.

To save your Page Setup settings and print the worksheet:

1. Click the **Save** button on the Standard toolbar.

2. Click the **Print** button on the Standard toolbar to print the worksheet. See Figure 3-38.

   TROUBLE? If you see a message that indicates that you have a printer problem, click the Cancel button to cancel the printout. Check your printer to make sure it is turned on and is online; also make sure it has paper. Then go back and try Step 2 again. If you have no printer available, click the Cancel button.

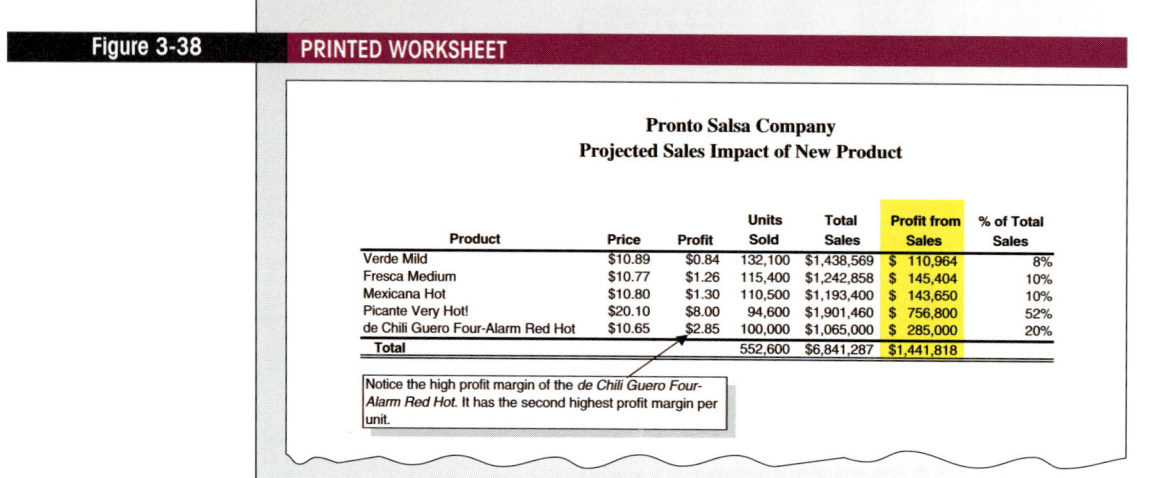

Figure 3-38   PRINTED WORKSHEET

Pronto Salsa Company
Projected Sales Impact of New Product

Product	Price	Profit	Units Sold	Total Sales	Profit from Sales	% of Total Sales
Verde Mild	$10.89	$0.84	132,100	$1,438,569	$ 110,964	8%
Fresca Medium	$10.77	$1.26	115,400	$1,242,858	$ 145,404	10%
Mexicana Hot	$10.80	$1.30	110,500	$1,193,400	$ 143,650	10%
Picante Very Hot!	$20.10	$8.00	94,600	$1,901,460	$ 756,800	52%
de Chili Guero Four-Alarm Red Hot	$10.65	$2.85	100,000	$1,065,000	$ 285,000	20%
Total			552,600	$6,841,287	$1,441,818	

Notice the high profit margin of the *de Chili Guero Four-Alarm Red Hot*. It has the second highest profit margin per unit.

TROUBLE? If the title for the last two columns didn't print completely, you need to increase the row height for row 5. Select row 5, drag the border below row 5 until the row height is 42.75 or greater (check the reference area of the formula bar), and then click the Print button.

Hiding and Unhiding Rows and Columns

Anne asks for one more printout, this one omitting the Units Sold column. The printout will include the product name, price, profit, total sales, profit from sales and % of total sales.

Hiding rows and columns is useful if you don't want to display certain information when the worksheet is open, or don't want to print certain information in the worksheet.

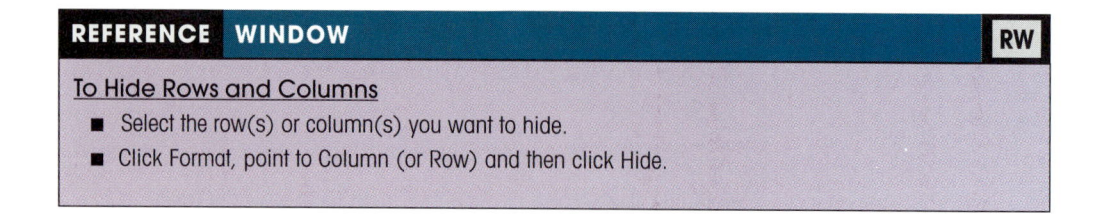

REFERENCE WINDOW

To Hide Rows and Columns

- Select the row(s) or column(s) you want to hide.
- Click Format, point to Column (or Row) and then click Hide.

To hide the Units Sold column:

1. Click the column header in column D. Notice the entire column is selected.
2. Click **Format**, point to **Column** and then click **Hide.**
3. Click any cell to observe that column D is hidden. See Figure 3-39.

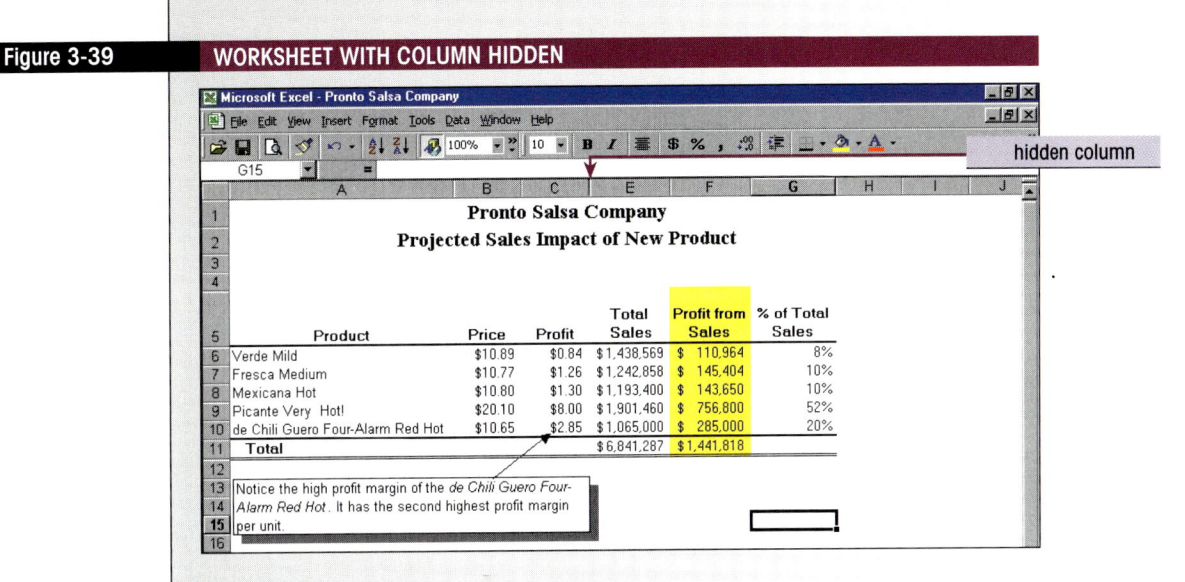

Figure 3-39 | **WORKSHEET WITH COLUMN HIDDEN**

4. Print the report.

Before saving the workbook, unhide the hidden column.

To unhide the hidden column:

1. Position the pointer over the column header in column C.
2. Click and drag the pointer to the column header in column E. Notice that columns C and E are highlighted.
3. Click **Format**, point to **Column**, and then click **Unhide**. Column D is no longer hidden.
4. Click any cell to view column D.

   Now that you are done formatting the worksheet, close the workbook and exit Excel.

5. Save, then Close the workbook and exit Excel.

You have completed formatting the Projected Sales worksheet and are ready to give it to Anne to check over before she presents it at her meeting with the bank loan officer.

Session 3.2 Quick Check

1. List two ways you can place a double-ruled line at the bottom of a range of cells.

2. Describe how to activate the Drawing toolbar.

3. To move, modify, or delete an object, you must _____ it first.

4. A _____ is a block of text that is placed in the worksheet.

5. _____ orientation prints the worksheet with the paper positioned so it is taller than it is wide, and _____ orientation prints so the paper is positioned wider than it is tall.

6. An arrow is an example of a _____.

7. What steps are needed to remove the gridlines from the worksheet display?

Review Assignments

After you show Anne the Projected Sales worksheet, the two of you discuss alternative ways to improve the worksheet's appearance. You decide to make some of these changes and give Anne the choice between two formatted worksheets. Do the following:

1. Start Windows and Excel, if necessary. Insert your Data Disk into the appropriate disk drive. Make sure the Excel and Book1 windows are maximized. Open the workbook **Pronto2** in the Review folder for Tutorial 3, and then save it as **Pronto3**.

2. Right-align the column heading in the Projected Sales worksheet.

3. Make the contents of cells A10:G10 bold to emphasize the new product. Make any necessary column-width adjustments.

4. Apply a yellow color to the range A1:G2.

5. Right-align the label in cell A11.

Explore 6. Draw borders around the data in A1:G10 so it appears in a grid.

7. Replace the name currently in the footer with your name so that it appears on the printout of the worksheet. Make sure the footer also prints the date and filename. Place the sheet name in the center section of the custom header.

8. Make sure the Page Setup menu settings are set for centered horizontally and vertically.

9. Preview the printout to make sure it fits on one page. Save and print the worksheet.

Explore 10. Fill the text box with the color yellow so that it appears as a "yellow sticky note." (*Hint:* select the text box by clicking on one of the selection handles. Use the Fill Color button on the Drawing toolbar.)

11. Change the color of the two-line title to blue (the text, not the background color).

12. In Step 4 you applied the color yellow to the cells A1 through G2. Remove the yellow color so that the background is the same as the rest of your worksheet.

13. If you've completed Steps 10, 11, or 12, save the worksheet as **Pronto4**.

Explore 14. a. Study the worksheet shown in Figure 3-40. Then open the Office Assistant and inquire about rotating data and merging cells.

Figure 3-40

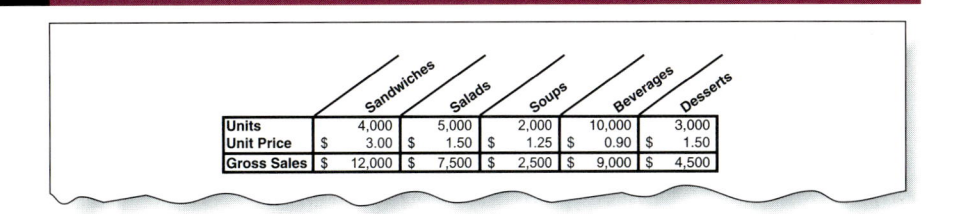

	Sandwiches	Salads	Soups	Beverages	Desserts
Units	4,000	5,000	2,000	10,000	3,000
Unit Price	$ 3.00	$ 1.50	$ 1.25	$ 0.90	$ 1.50
Gross Sales	$ 12,000	$ 7,500	$ 2,500	$ 9,000	$ 4,500

  b. Open the workbook **Explore3** in the Tutorial 3 Review folder and then save it as **Explore3 Solution** in the same folder.
  c. Use the Rotate Text formatting feature to change the worksheet so it is similar to Figure 3-40. Make any other changes to make the worksheet as similar as possible to the one shown in Figure 3-40.
  d. Save and then print the worksheet.

CASE PROBLEMS

Case 1. Jenson Sports Wear Quarterly Sales Carol Roberts is the national sales manager for Jenson Sports Wear, a company that sells sportswear to major department stores. She has been using an Excel worksheet to track the results of her staff's sales incentive program. She has asked you to format the worksheet so it looks professional. She also wants a printout before she presents the worksheet at the next sales meeting. Complete these steps to format and print the worksheet:

1. Start Windows and Excel, if necessary. Insert your Data Disk into the appropriate disk drive. Make sure the Excel and Book1 windows are maximized. Open the workbook **Running** in the Cases folder for Tutorial 3 on your Data Disk. Maximize the worksheet window and then save the workbook as **Running2**.

2. Complete the worksheet by doing the following:
   a. Calculating totals for each product
   b. Calculating quarterly subtotals for the Shoes and Shirts departments
   c. Calculating totals for each quarter and an overall total

3. Modify the worksheet so it is formatted as shown in Figure 3-41.

4. Use the Page Setup dialog box to center the output both horizontally and vertically.

5. Add the filename, your name, and the date in the custom footer and delete both the formatting code &[File] from the Center section of the header.

6. Save the workbook.

7. Preview the worksheet and adjust the page setup as necessary for the printed results you want.

8. Print the worksheet. Your printout should fit on one page.

Explore 9. Place the note "Leading product" in a text box. Remove the border from the text box. (*Hint*: Use the Format Textbox dialog box—Colors and Lines Tab.) Draw an oval object around the text box. (*Hint*: Use the Oval tool on the Drawing toolbar and right-click to determine which command sends the oval object to the back.) Draw an arrow from the edge of the oval to the number in the worksheet representing the leading product. Save and print the worksheet. Your printout should fit on one page.

Figure 3-41

	Sports Wear Inc. Quarterly Sales by Product				
Shoes	Qtr 1	Qtr 2	Qtr 3	Qtr 4	Total
Running	2,250	2,550	2,650	2,800	10,250
Tennis	2,800	1,500	2,300	2,450	9,050
Basketball	1,250	1,400	1,550	1,550	5,750
Subtotal	$ 6,300	$ 5,450	$ 6,500	$ 6,800	$ 25,050
Shirts	Qtr 1	Qtr 2	Qtr 3	Qtr 4	Total
Tee	1,000	1,150	1,250	1,150	4,550
Polo	2,100	2,200	2,300	2,400	9,000
Sweat	250	250	275	300	1,075
Subtotal	$ 3,350	$ 3,600	$ 3,825	$ 3,850	$ 14,625
Grand Total	$ 9,650	$ 9,050	$ 10,325	$ 10,650	$ 39,675

Case 2. State Recycling Campaign Fred Birnbaum is working as an intern in the state's Waste Disposal Department. They have a pilot project on recycling for three counties (Seacoast, Metro, and Pioneer Valley). You have been asked to complete the worksheet, summarizing the results of the pilot program and formatting it for presentation to their board of directors.

1. Start Windows and Excel, if necessary. Insert your Data Disk into the appropriate disk drive. Make sure the Excel and Book1 windows are maximized. Open the workbook **Recycle** in the Cases folder for Tutorial 3 on your Data Disk, and then save it as **Recycle2**.

2. Add two columns to calculate yearly totals for tons and a dollar value for each material in each county.

3. Insert three rows at the top of the worksheet to include:
   State Recycling Project
   Material Reclamation 1999
   <blank row>

4. Format the worksheet until you feel confident that the board of directors will be impressed with the appearance of the report.

5. Rename the worksheet **Recycle Data**.

6. Save the worksheet.

7. Print the worksheet centered horizontally and vertically on the page using landscape orientation. Include your name in the custom footer.

8. Remove the gridlines from the display. Use the Border tab of the Format Cells dialog box to place the recycle data in a grid. Save the workbook as **Recycle3**.

Explore

9. Change the magnification of the sheet so you can view the recycle data on the screen without having to scroll. (*Hint*: Use the Zoom control on the Standard toolbar.)

Case 3. State Government Expenditures Ken Dry, an assistant to the governor, has started an Excel worksheet summarizing current and proposed expenditures for all the state agencies. Ken has been called away on an emergency and asked you to complete the worksheet. He left the following note:

The column headings and agency and division names have been entered in the worksheet. Column A includes Divisions, which appear as the rows with no expenditure data in columns B and C. Agencies are those rows that include expenditure data in columns B and C. For example, the first division is General Government and the first agency within this division is Administration; the next division is Human Services and its first agency is Children and Families, and so on. See Figure 3-42.

You need to modify the worksheet by:

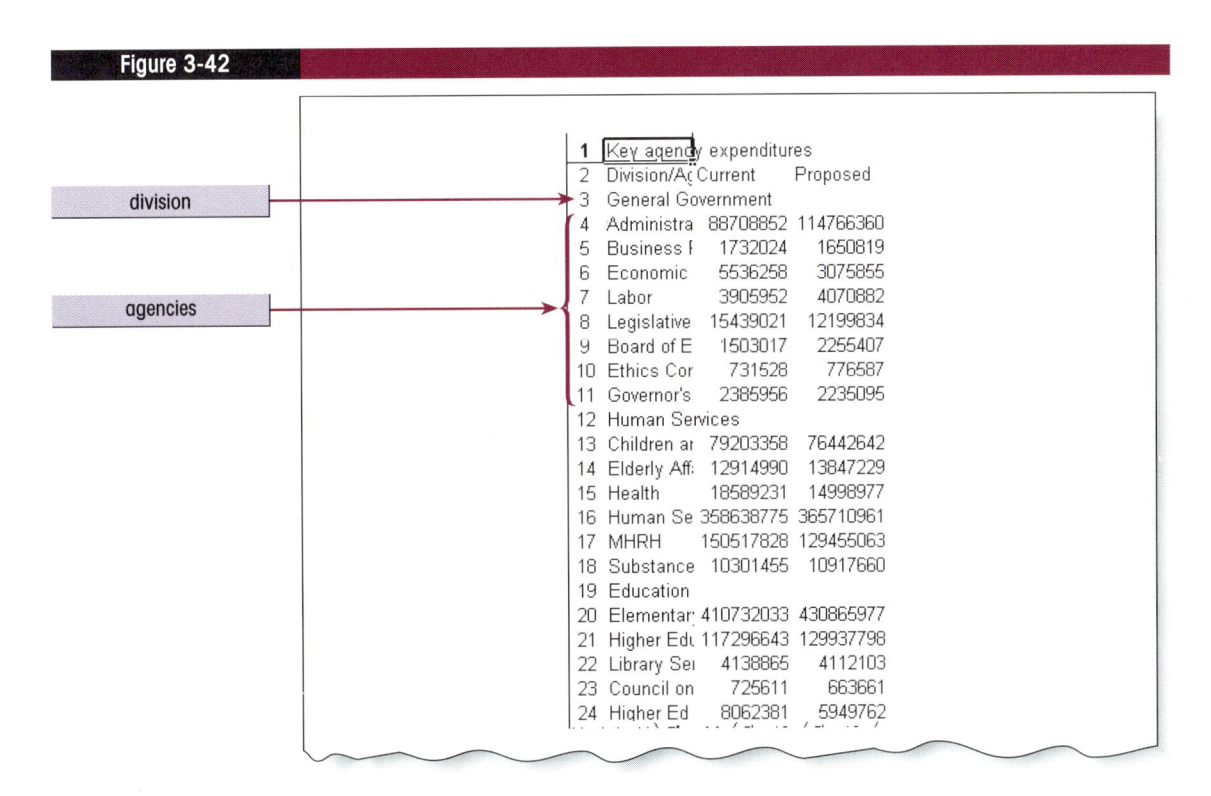

Figure 3-42

	A	B	C
1	Key agency expenditures		
2	Division/A	Current	Proposed
3	General Government		
4	Administra	88708852	114766360
5	Business F	1732024	1650819
6	Economic	5536258	3075855
7	Labor	3905952	4070882
8	Legislative	15439021	12199834
9	Board of E	1503017	2255407
10	Ethics Cor	731528	776587
11	Governor's	2385956	2235095
12	Human Services		
13	Children ar	79203358	76442642
14	Elderly Aff	12914990	13847229
15	Health	18589231	14998977
16	Human Se	358638775	365710961
17	MHRH	150517828	129455063
18	Substance	10301455	10917660
19	Education		
20	Elementar	410732033	430865977
21	Higher Edu	117296643	129937798
22	Library Ser	4138865	4112103
23	Council on	725611	663661
24	Higher Ed	8062381	5949762

(row 3 labeled "division"; rows 4–11 labeled "agencies")

- Calculating overall government totals (for all agencies) for both current and proposed expenditures

- Calculating totals for each division. Remember that the agencies in a division follow in the rows below the division name (if necessary, you can insert rows to provide room for totals).

- Add the following calculations in columns D, E, and F:
  a. percentage change between current and proposed (next year's) expenditures (column D)
  b. for proposed expenditures-percentage of agency's expenditures in a division to total expenditures in that division; for example, Administration is 81.4% of the General Government division expenditures and Children and Families is 12.4% of Health and Services (column E)
  c. for proposed expenditures-percentage of agency's expenditures to total government expenditures; for example, Administration is 7.5% of overall government expenditures, while Business Regulation is .1% of overall government expenditures (column F)

Do the following:

1. Open the workbook **StateGov.xls** in the Cases folder for Tutorial 3, and then save it as **State Government**.

2. Use the note left by Ken to complete the worksheet.

3. Your output will be handed out at a press conference, so you need to improve the appearance of the worksheet so it will look more professional.

4. Assign a descriptive sheet name to Sheet1.

5. Print your report on one page. Include your name, class, and date in the print footer and the sheet name as part of the print header.

6. Include a Documentation sheet in your workbook. In this sheet, include the title of the project, your name, date completed, and brief purpose. Print this sheet.

7. Save the workbook.

8. Print the formulas that underlie the worksheet. Save the worksheet before you display the formulas in the worksheet. Print the formulas on one page and include row and column headings as part of the printout.

Case 4. Ortiz Marine Services Vince DiOrio is an information systems major at a local college. He works three days a week at a nearby marina, Ortiz Marine Services, to help pay for his tuition. Vince works in the business office, and his responsibilities range from making coffee to keeping the company's books.

Recently, Jim Ortiz, the owner of the marina, asked Vince if he could help computerize the payroll for their employees. He explained that the employees work a different number of hours each week for different rates of pay. Jim does the payroll manually now and finds it time-consuming. Moreover, whenever he makes an error, he is embarrassed and annoyed at having to take the additional time to correct it. Jim was hoping Vince could help him.

Vince immediately agrees to help. He tells Jim that he knows how to use Excel and that he can build a worksheet that will save him time and reduce errors. Jim and Vince meet. They review the present payroll process and discuss the desired outcomes of the payroll spreadsheet. Figure 3-43 is a sketch of the output Jim wants to get.

Figure 3-43

```
Ortiz Marine Service Payroll
Week Ending
```

Employee	Hours	Pay Rate	Gross Pay	Federal Withholding	State Withholding	Total Deductions	Net Pay
Bramble	16	6					
Juarez	25	6.25					
Smith	30	8					
DiOrio	25	7.75					
Smiken	10	5.90					
Cortez	30	7					
Fulton	20	6					
Total							

Do the following:

1. Create the worksheet sketched in Figure 3-43.

2. Use the following formulas in your workbook to calculate total hours, gross pay, federal withholding, state withholding, total deductions and net pay for the company:

   a. Gross pay is hours times pay rate.
   b. Federal withholding is 15% of gross pay.
   c. State withholding is 4% of gross pay.
   d. Total deductions is the sum of federal and state withholding.
   e. Net pay is the difference between gross pay and total deductions.

3. Apply the formatting techniques learned in this tutorial to create a professional-looking workbook.

4. Assign a descriptive sheet name.

5. Create a Documentation sheet.

6. Save the workbook as **Payroll** in the Cases folder for Tutorial 3.

7. Print the worksheet, including appropriate headers and footers.

8. Remove the hours for the seven employees.

9. Enter the following hours: 18 for Bramble, 25 for Juarez, 35 for Smith, and 20 for DiOrio, 15 for Smiken, 35 for Cortez, and 22 for Fulton.

10. Print the new worksheet.

11. Print the formulas on one page. Include row and column headers in the printed output.

INTERNET ASSIGNMENTS

The purpose of the Internet Assignments is to challenge you to find information on the Internet that you can use to create effective spreadsheets. The actual assignments are updated and maintained on the Course Technology Web site. Log on to the Internet and use your Web browser to go to the Student Online Companion to accompany this text at **www.course.com/NewPerspectives/Office2000**. Click the Excel link, and then click the link for Tutorial 3.

Quick Check Answers

Session 3.1

1. click Format, click Cells; right-click mouse in cell you want to format; use buttons on the Formatting toolbar
2. a. 5.8%   b. $0.06
3. Format Painter button
4. The column width of a cell is not wide enough to display the numbers, and you need to increase the column width.
5. Position the mouse pointer over the column header, right-click the mouse and click Column Width. Enter the new column width in the Column Width dialog box. Position the mouse pointer over the right edge of the column you want to modify, and then click and drag to increase the column width.
6. The data in the cell is formatted with the Comma style using two decimal places.
7. center column headings, right-align numbers, and left-align text
8. Left align button, Center button, Right align button, and Merge and Center button

Session 3.2

1. use the Borders tab on the Format Cells dialog box, or the Borders button on the Formatting toolbar
2. click the Drawing button on the Standard toolbar
3. select
4. text box
5. Portrait; landscape
6. drawing object
7. click Tools, click Options, click View tab, and then remove the check from the Gridlines check box

LEVEL I

New Perspectives on

MICROSOFT®
ACCESS 2000

TUTORIAL 1 AC 1.03
Introduction to Microsoft Access 2000
Viewing and Working with a Table Containing Customer Data

TUTORIAL 2 AC 2.01
Maintaining a Database
Creating, Modifying, and Updating an Order Table

TUTORIAL 3 AC 3.01
Querying a Database
Retrieving Information About Restaurant Customers and Their Orders

Read This Before You Begin

To the Student

Data Disks

To complete the Level I tutorials, Review Assignments, and Case Problems, you need 4 Data Disks. Your instructor will either provide you with these Data Disks or ask you to make your own.

If you are making your own Data Disks, you will need 4 blank, formatted high-density disks. You will need to copy a set of folders from a file server or standalone computer or the Web onto your disks. Your instructor will tell you which computer, drive letter, and folders contain the files you need. You could also download the files by going to www.course.com, clicking Data Disk Files, and following the instructions on the screen.

The following table shows you which folders go on each of your disks, so that you will have enough disk space to complete all the tutorials, Review Assignments, and Case Problems:

Data Disk 1
Write this on the disk label:
Data Disk 1: Tutorial files
Put this folder from the Disk 1 folder on the disk:
Tutorial

Data Disk 2
Write this on the disk label:
Data Disk 2: Review files
Put this folder from the Disk 2 folder on the disk:
Review

Data Disk 3
Write this on the disk label:
Data Disk 3: Case Problem 1 files
Put this folder from the Disk 3 folder on the disk:
Cases

Data Disk 4
Write this on the disk label:
Data Disk 4: Case Problem 2
Put this folder from the Disk 4 folder on the disk:
Cases

Data Disk 5
Write this on the disk label:
Data Disk 5: Case Problem 3
Put this folder from the Disk 5 folder on the disk:
Cases

Data Disk 6
Write this on the disk label:
Data Disk 6: Case Problem 4
Put this folder from the Disk 6 folder on the disk:
Cases

When you begin each tutorial, be sure you are using the correct Data Disk. Refer to the "File Finder" Chart at the back of this text for more detailed information on which files are used in which tutorials. These Access Level I tutorials use the same files for Tutorials 1-3. If you are completing the Level II tutorials, you will need to create new Data Disks for those tutorials. See the inside front or inside back cover of this book for more information on Data Disk files, or ask your instructor or technical support person for assistance.

Course Labs

The Access Level I tutorials features an interactive Course Lab to help you understand database concepts. There are Lab Assignments at the end of Tutorial 1 that relate to this Lab.

To start a Lab, click the **Start** button on the Windows taskbar, point to **Programs**, point to **Course Labs**, point to **New Perspectives Course Labs**, and click the name of the Lab you want to use.

Using Your Own Computer

If you are going to work through this book using your own computer, you need:

- **Computer System** Microsoft Windows 95, 98, NT, or higher must be installed on your computer. This book assumes a typical installation of Microsoft Access.

- **Data Disks** You will not be able to complete the tutorials or exercises in this book using your own computer until you have your Data Disks.

- **Course Labs** See your instructor or technical support person to obtain the Course Lab software for use on your own computer.

Visit Our World Wide Web Site

Additional materials designed especially for you are available on the World Wide Web.
Go to http://www.course.com.

To the Instructor

The Data Files and Course Labs are available on the Instructor's Resource Kit for this title. Follow the instructions in the Help file on the CD-ROM to install the programs to your network or standalone computer. For information on creating Data Disks or the Course Labs, see the "To the Student" section above.

You are granted a license to copy the Data Files and Course Labs to any computer or computer network used by students who have purchased this book.

TUTORIAL 1

OBJECTIVES

In this tutorial you will:

- Define the terms field, record, table, relational database, primary key, and foreign key
- Start and exit Access
- Open an existing database
- Identify the components of the Access and Database windows
- Open, navigate, and print a table
- Create, run, and print a query
- Create and print a form
- Use the Access Help system
- Create, preview, and print a report
- Compact a database

LAB

Databases

INTRODUCTION TO MICROSOFT ACCESS 2000

Viewing and Working with a Table Containing Customer Data

CASE

Valle Coffee

Ten years ago, Leonard Valle became the president of Algoman Imports, a small distributor of inexpensive coffee beans to supermarkets in western Michigan. At that time the company's growth had leveled off, so during his first three years Leonard took several dramatic, risky steps in an attempt to increase sales and profits. First, he changed the inexpensive coffee bean varieties that Algoman Imports had been distributing to a selection of gourmet varieties from Central and South America, Africa, and several island nations. Second, he purchased facilities and equipment so that the company could roast, grind, flavor, and package the coffee beans instead of buying them already roasted and packaged whole. Because the company could now control the quality of the finest gourmet coffees, Leonard stopped distributing to supermarkets and shifted sales to restaurants and offices throughout the area.

Within two years, company sales and profits soared; consequently, Leonard took over ownership of the company. He changed the company name to Valle Coffee, continued expanding into other markets and geographic areas (specifically, Ohio and Indiana), and expanded the company's line of coffee flavors and blends.

Part of Valle Coffee's success can be credited to its use of computers in all aspects of its business, including financial management, inventory control, shipping, receiving, production, and sales. Several months ago the company upgraded to Microsoft Windows and **Microsoft Access 2000** (or simply **Access**), a computer program used to enter, maintain, and retrieve related data in a format known as a database. Barbara Hennessey, office manager at Valle Coffee, and her staff use Access to maintain company data such as customer orders and billing, coffee supplier orders and payments, and advertising placements and payments. Barbara recently created a database named Restaurant to track the company's restaurant customers, their orders, and related data such as the products they order. She asks for your help in completing and maintaining this database.

SESSION 1.1

In this session, you will learn key database terms and concepts, start Access and open an existing database, identify components of the Access and Database windows, open and navigate a table, print a table, and exit Access.

Introduction to Database Concepts

Before you begin working on Barbara's database and using Access, you need to understand a few key terms and concepts associated with databases.

Organizing Data

Data is a valuable resource to any business. At Valle Coffee, for example, important data includes customers' names and addresses, and order dates and amounts. Organizing, storing, maintaining, retrieving, and sorting this type of data are critical activities that enable a business to find and use information effectively. Before storing data on a computer, however, you first must organize the data.

Your first step in organizing data is to identify the individual fields. A **field** is a single characteristic or attribute of a person, place, object, event, or idea. For example, some of the many fields that Valle Coffee tracks are customer number, customer name, customer address, customer phone number, order number, billing date, and invoice amount.

Next, you group related fields together into tables. A **table** is a collection of fields that describe a person, place, object, event, or idea. Figure 1-1 shows an example of a Customer table consisting of four fields: Customer #, Customer Name, Customer Address, and Phone Number.

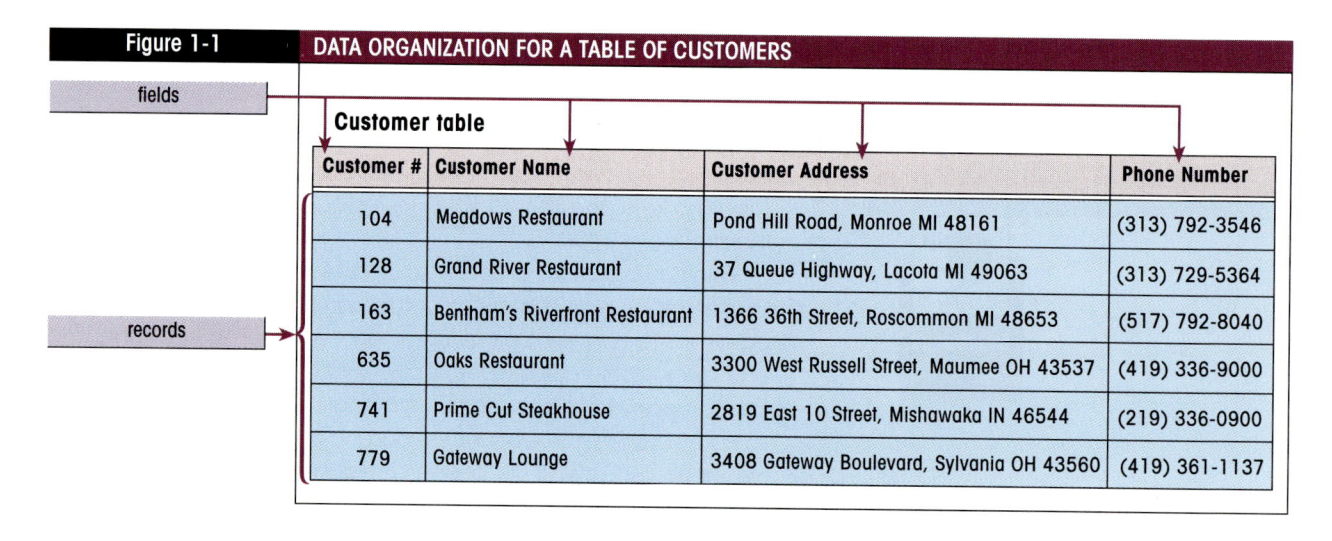

Figure 1-1 DATA ORGANIZATION FOR A TABLE OF CUSTOMERS

Customer table

Customer #	Customer Name	Customer Address	Phone Number
104	Meadows Restaurant	Pond Hill Road, Monroe MI 48161	(313) 792-3546
128	Grand River Restaurant	37 Queue Highway, Lacota MI 49063	(313) 729-5364
163	Bentham's Riverfront Restaurant	1366 36th Street, Roscommon MI 48653	(517) 792-8040
635	Oaks Restaurant	3300 West Russell Street, Maumee OH 43537	(419) 336-9000
741	Prime Cut Steakhouse	2819 East 10 Street, Mishawaka IN 46544	(219) 336-0900
779	Gateway Lounge	3408 Gateway Boulevard, Sylvania OH 43560	(419) 361-1137

The specific value, or content, of a field is called the **field value**. In Figure 1-1, the first set of field values for Customer #, Customer Name, Customer Address, and Phone Number are, respectively, 104; Meadows Restaurant; Pond Hill Road, Monroe MI 48161; and (313) 792-3546. This set of field values is called a **record**. In the Customer table, the data for each customer is stored as a separate record. Six records are shown in Figure 1-1; each row of field values is a record.

Databases and Relationships

A collection of related tables is called a **database**, or a **relational database**. Valle Coffee's Restaurant database will contain two related tables: the Customer table, which Barbara has already created, and the Order table, which you will create in Tutorial 2. Sometimes you might want information about customers and the orders they placed. To obtain this information you must have a way to connect records in the Customer table to records in the Order table. You connect the records in the separate tables through a **common field** that appears in both tables. In the sample database shown in Figure 1-2, each record in the Customer table has a field named Customer #, which is also a field in the Order table. For example, Oaks Restaurant is the fourth customer in the Customer table and has a Customer # of 635. This same Customer # field value, 635, appears in three records in the Order table. Therefore, Oaks Restaurant is the customer that placed these three orders.

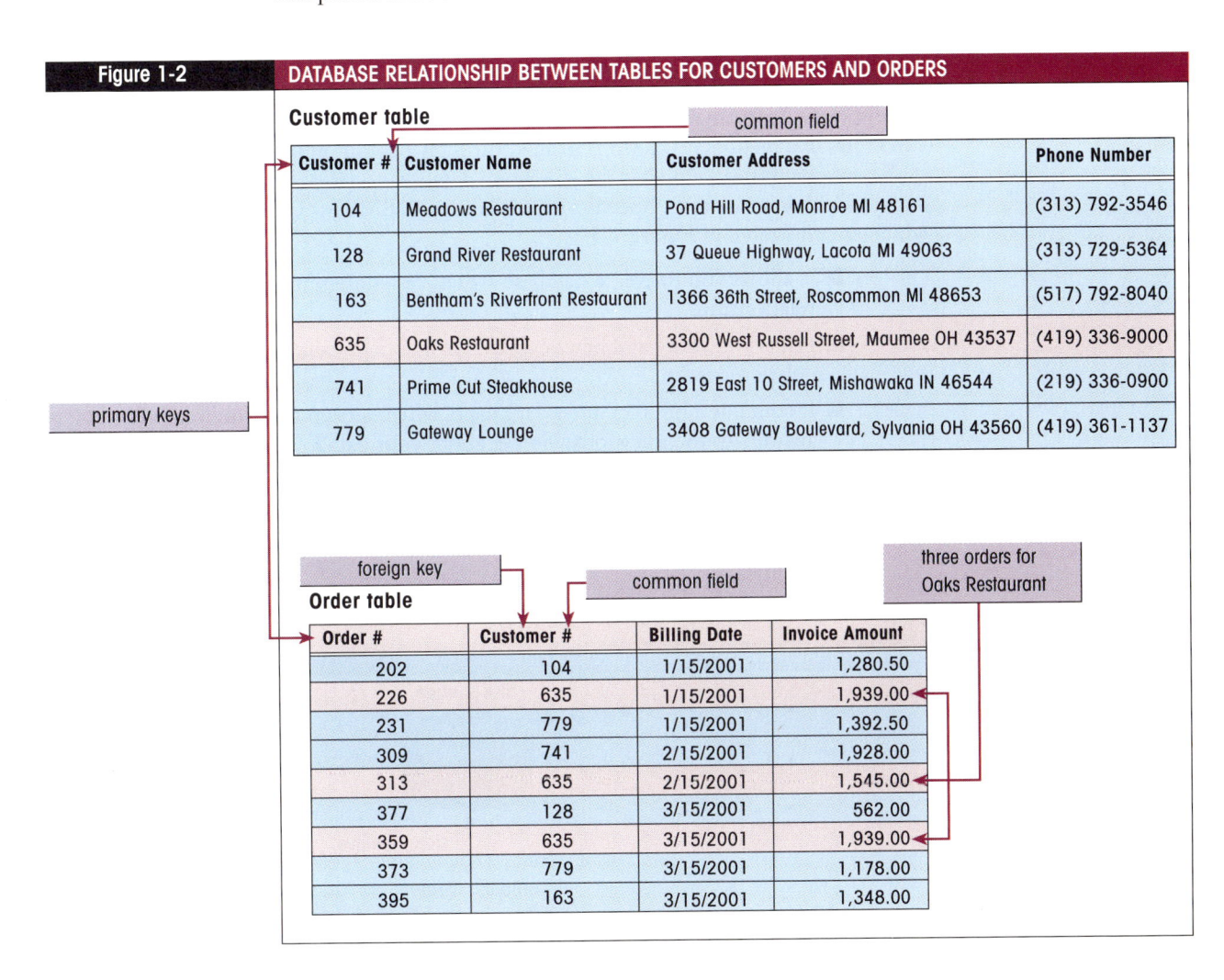

Figure 1-2 DATABASE RELATIONSHIP BETWEEN TABLES FOR CUSTOMERS AND ORDERS

Customer table (primary keys; common field)

Customer #	Customer Name	Customer Address	Phone Number
104	Meadows Restaurant	Pond Hill Road, Monroe MI 48161	(313) 792-3546
128	Grand River Restaurant	37 Queue Highway, Lacota MI 49063	(313) 729-5364
163	Bentham's Riverfront Restaurant	1366 36th Street, Roscommon MI 48653	(517) 792-8040
635	Oaks Restaurant	3300 West Russell Street, Maumee OH 43537	(419) 336-9000
741	Prime Cut Steakhouse	2819 East 10 Street, Mishawaka IN 46544	(219) 336-0900
779	Gateway Lounge	3408 Gateway Boulevard, Sylvania OH 43560	(419) 361-1137

Order table (foreign key; common field; three orders for Oaks Restaurant)

Order #	Customer #	Billing Date	Invoice Amount
202	104	1/15/2001	1,280.50
226	635	1/15/2001	1,939.00
231	779	1/15/2001	1,392.50
309	741	2/15/2001	1,928.00
313	635	2/15/2001	1,545.00
377	128	3/15/2001	562.00
359	635	3/15/2001	1,939.00
373	779	3/15/2001	1,178.00
395	163	3/15/2001	1,348.00

Each Customer # in the Customer table must be unique, so that you can distinguish one customer from another and identify the customer's specific orders in the Order table. The Customer # field is referred to as the primary key of the Customer table. A **primary key** is a field, or a collection of fields, whose values uniquely identify each record in a table. In the Order table, Order # is the primary key.

When you include the primary key from one table as a field in a second table to form a relationship between the two tables, it is called a **foreign key** in the second table, as shown in

Figure 1-2. For example, Customer # is the primary key in the Customer table and a foreign key in the Order table. Although the primary key Customer # has unique values in the Customer table, the same field as a foreign key in the Order table does not have unique values. The Customer # value 635, for example, appears three times in the Order table because the Oaks Restaurant placed three orders. Each foreign key value, however, must match one of the field values for the primary key in the other table. In the example shown in Figure 1-2, each Customer # value in the Order table must match a Customer # value in the Customer table. The two tables are related, enabling users to tie together the facts about customers with the facts about orders.

Relational Database Management Systems

To manage its databases, a company purchases a database management system. A **database management system** (**DBMS**) is a software program that lets you create databases and then manipulate data in them. Most of today's database management systems, including Access, are called relational database management systems. In a **relational database management system**, data is organized as a collection of tables. As stated earlier, a relationship between two tables in a relational DBMS is formed through a common field.

A relational DBMS controls the storage of databases on disk by carrying out data creation and manipulation requests. Specifically, a relational DBMS provides the following functions, which are illustrated in Figure 1-3:

- It allows you to create database structures containing fields, tables, and table relationships.
- It lets you easily add new records, change field values in existing records, and delete records.
- It contains a built-in query language, which lets you obtain immediate answers to the questions you ask about your data.
- It contains a built-in report generator, which lets you produce professional-looking, formatted reports from your data.
- It provides protection of databases through security, control, and recovery facilities.

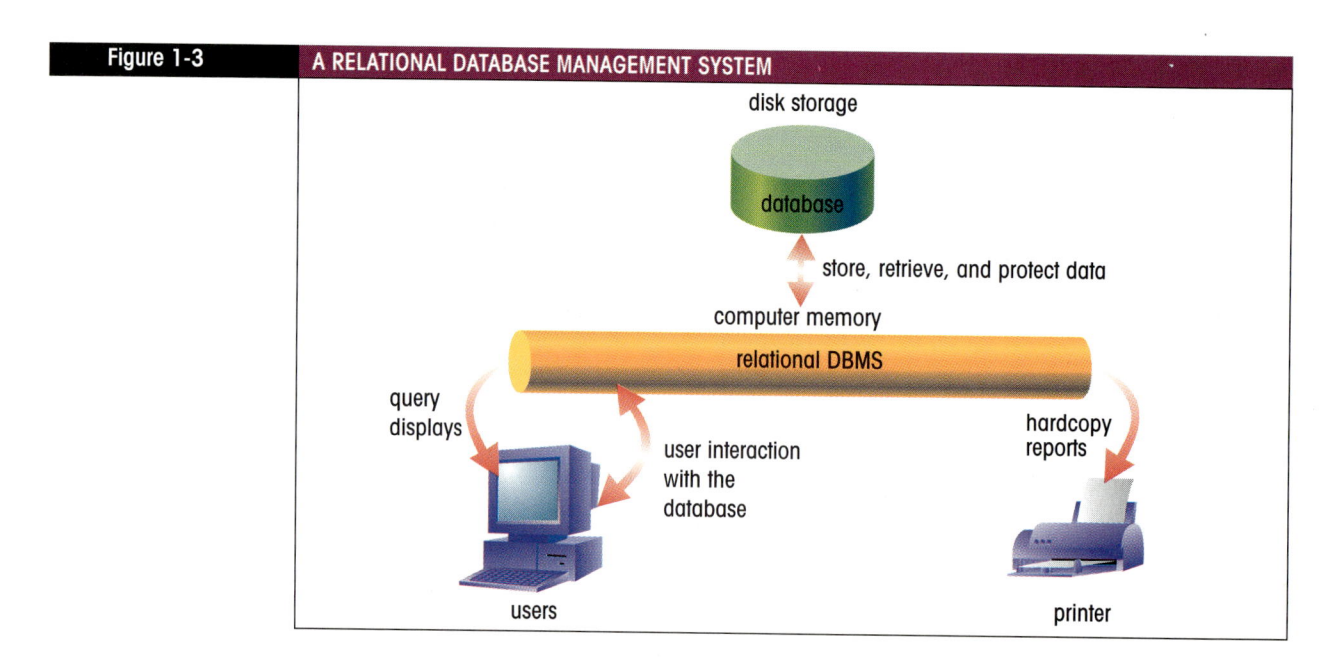

Figure 1-3   A RELATIONAL DATABASE MANAGEMENT SYSTEM

A company like Valle Coffee benefits from a relational DBMS because it allows several users working in different departments to share the same data. More than one user can enter data into a database, and more than one user can retrieve and analyze data that was entered by others. For example, Valle Coffee will keep only one copy of the Customer table, and all employees will be able to use it to meet their specific needs for customer information.

Finally, unlike other software programs, such as spreadsheets, a DBMS can handle massive amounts of data and can easily form relationships among multiple tables. Each Access database, for example, can be up to two gigabytes in size and can contain up to 32,768 objects (tables, queries, and so on).

Now that you've learned some database terms and concepts, you're ready to start Access and open the Restaurant database.

Starting Access

You start Access in the same way that you start other Windows programs—using the Start button on the taskbar.

To start Access:

1. Make sure Windows is running on your computer and the Windows desktop appears on your screen.

2. Click the **Start** button on the taskbar to display the Start menu, and then point to **Programs** to display the Programs menu.

3. Point to **Microsoft Access** on the Programs menu. See Figure 1-4.

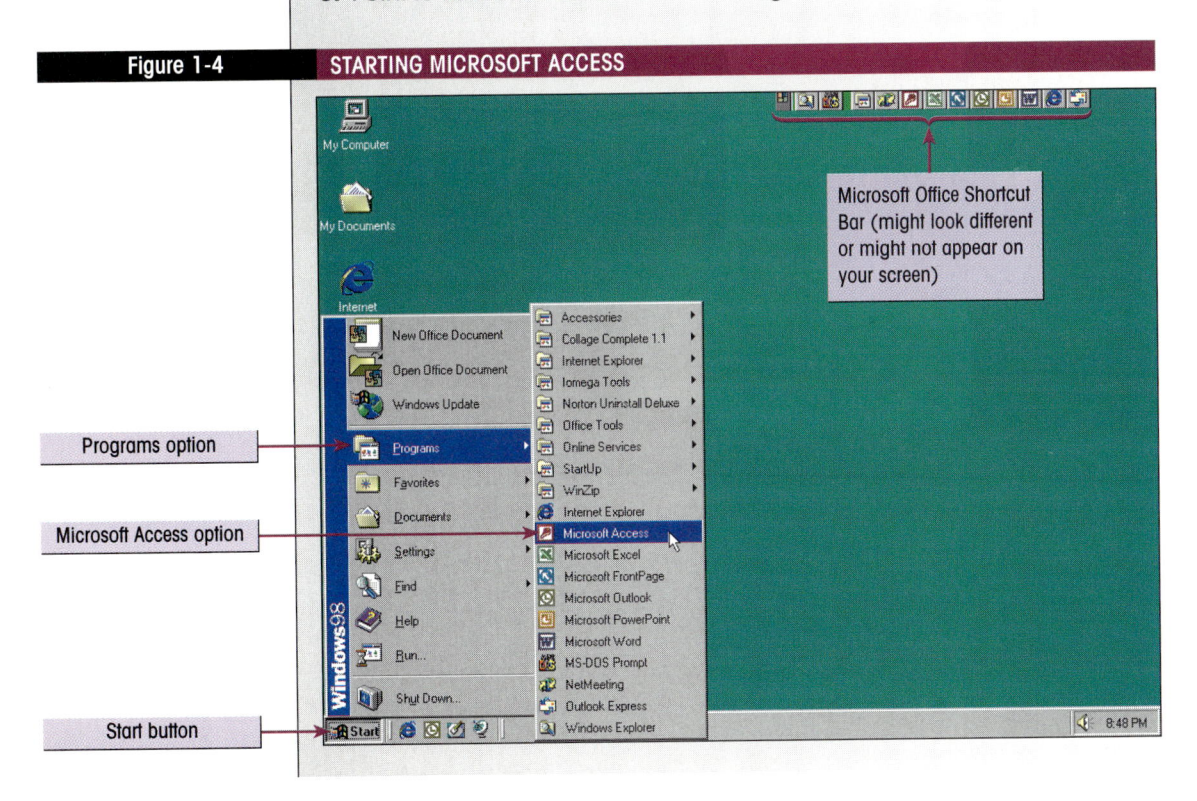

Figure 1-4   STARTING MICROSOFT ACCESS

TROUBLE? Don't worry if your screen differs slightly from the figure. Although the figures in this book were created on a computer running Windows 98 in its default settings, the different Windows operating systems share the same basic user interface, and Microsoft Access runs equally well using Windows 95, Windows 98 in Web Style, Windows NT, or Windows 2000.

TROUBLE? If you don't see the Microsoft Access option on the Programs menu, ask your instructor or technical support person for help.

TROUBLE? The Office Shortcut Bar, which appears along the top border of the desktop in Figure 1-4, might look different on your screen, or it might not appear at all, depending on how your system is set up. Because these tutorials do not require you to use the Office Shortcut Bar, it has been omitted from the remaining figures in this text.

4. Click **Microsoft Access** to start Access. After a short pause, the Access copyright information appears in a message box and remains on the screen until the Access window is displayed. See Figure 1-5.

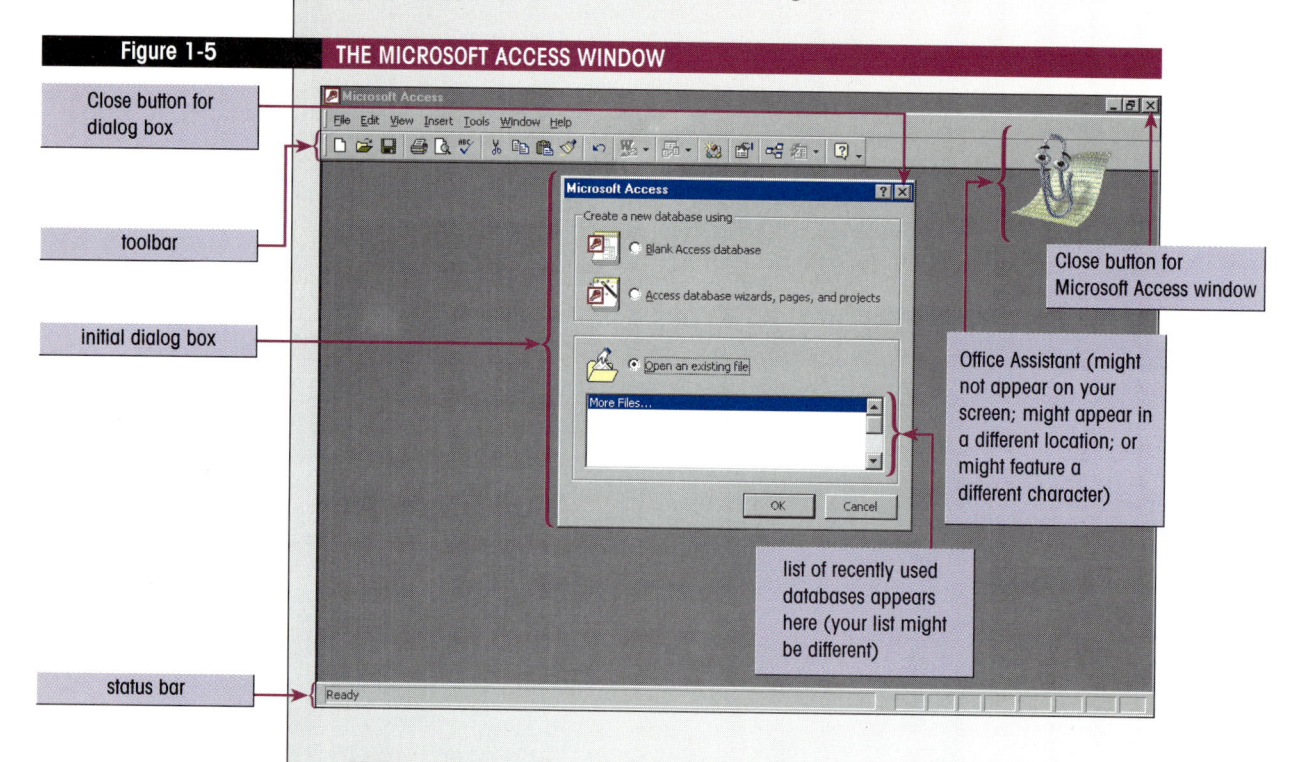

Figure 1-5   THE MICROSOFT ACCESS WINDOW

- Close button for dialog box
- toolbar
- initial dialog box
- status bar
- Close button for Microsoft Access window
- Office Assistant (might not appear on your screen; might appear in a different location; or might feature a different character)
- list of recently used databases appears here (your list might be different)

TROUBLE? Depending on how your system is set up, the Office Assistant (see Figure 1-5) might open when you start Access. If it opens, right-click the Office Assistant to display the shortcut menu, and then click Hide. You'll learn more about the Office Assistant later in this tutorial. If you've started Access immediately after installing it, you'll need to click the Start Using Microsoft Access option, which the Office Assistant displays, before hiding the Office Assistant.

When you start Access, the Access window contains a dialog box that allows you to create a new database or open an existing database. You can click the "Blank Access database" option button to create a new database on your own, or you can click the "Access database wizards, pages, and projects" option button and let a Wizard guide you through the steps for creating a database. In this case, you need to open an existing database.

TUTORIAL 1 INTRODUCTION TO MICROSOFT ACCESS 2000 AC 1.09 ACCESS

Opening an Existing Database

To open an existing database, you can select the name of a database in the list of recently opened databases (if the list appears), or you can click the More Files option to open a database not listed. You need to open an existing database—the Restaurant database on your Data Disk.

To open the Restaurant database:

1. Make sure you have created your copy of the Access Data Disk, and then place your Data Disk in the appropriate disk drive.

    TROUBLE? If you don't have a Data Disk, you need to get one before you can proceed. Your instructor will either give you one or ask you to make your own. (See your instructor for information.) In either case, be sure that you have made a backup copy of your Data Disk before you begin working, so that the original Data Files will be available on the copied disk in case you need to start over because of an error or problem.

2. In the Microsoft Access dialog box, make sure the **Open an existing file** option button is selected. Also, if your dialog box contains a list of files, make sure the **More Files** option is selected.

3. Click the **OK** button to display the Open dialog box. See Figure 1-6.

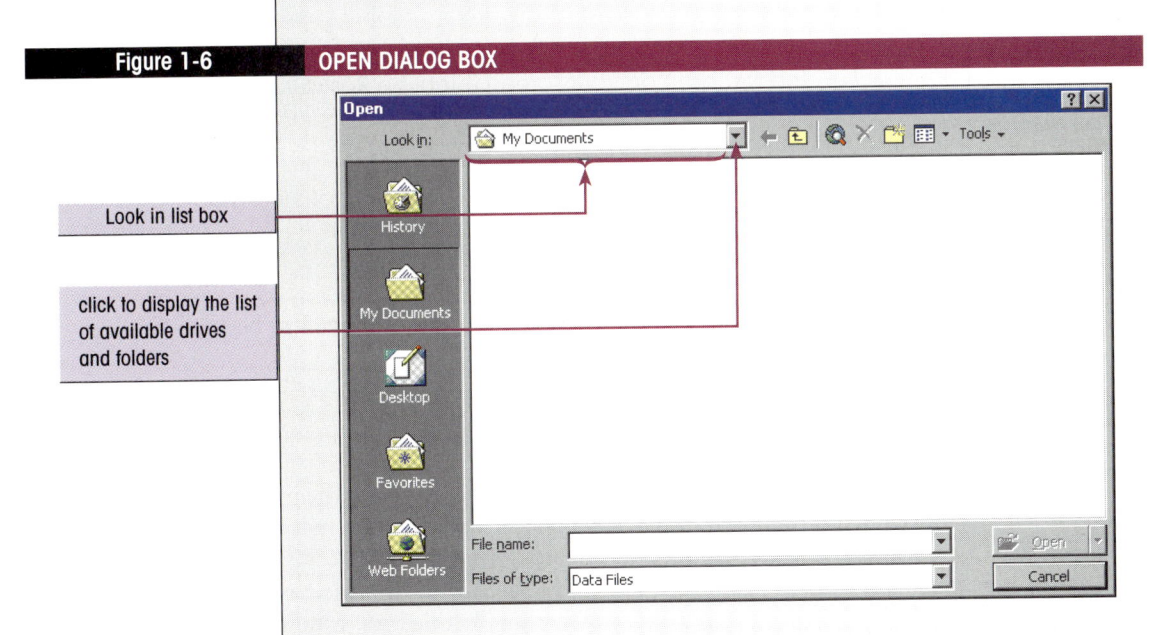

| Figure 1-6 | OPEN DIALOG BOX |

- Look in list box
- click to display the list of available drives and folders

TROUBLE? The list of folders and files on your screen might be different from the list in Figure 1-6, which does not contain any items.

4. Click the **Look in** list arrow, and then click the drive that contains your Data Disk.

5. Click **Tutorial** in the list box (if necessary), and then click the **Open** button to display a list of the files in the Tutorial folder.

6. Click **Restaurant** in the list box, and then click the **Open** button. The Restaurant database opens in the Access window. See Figure 1-7.

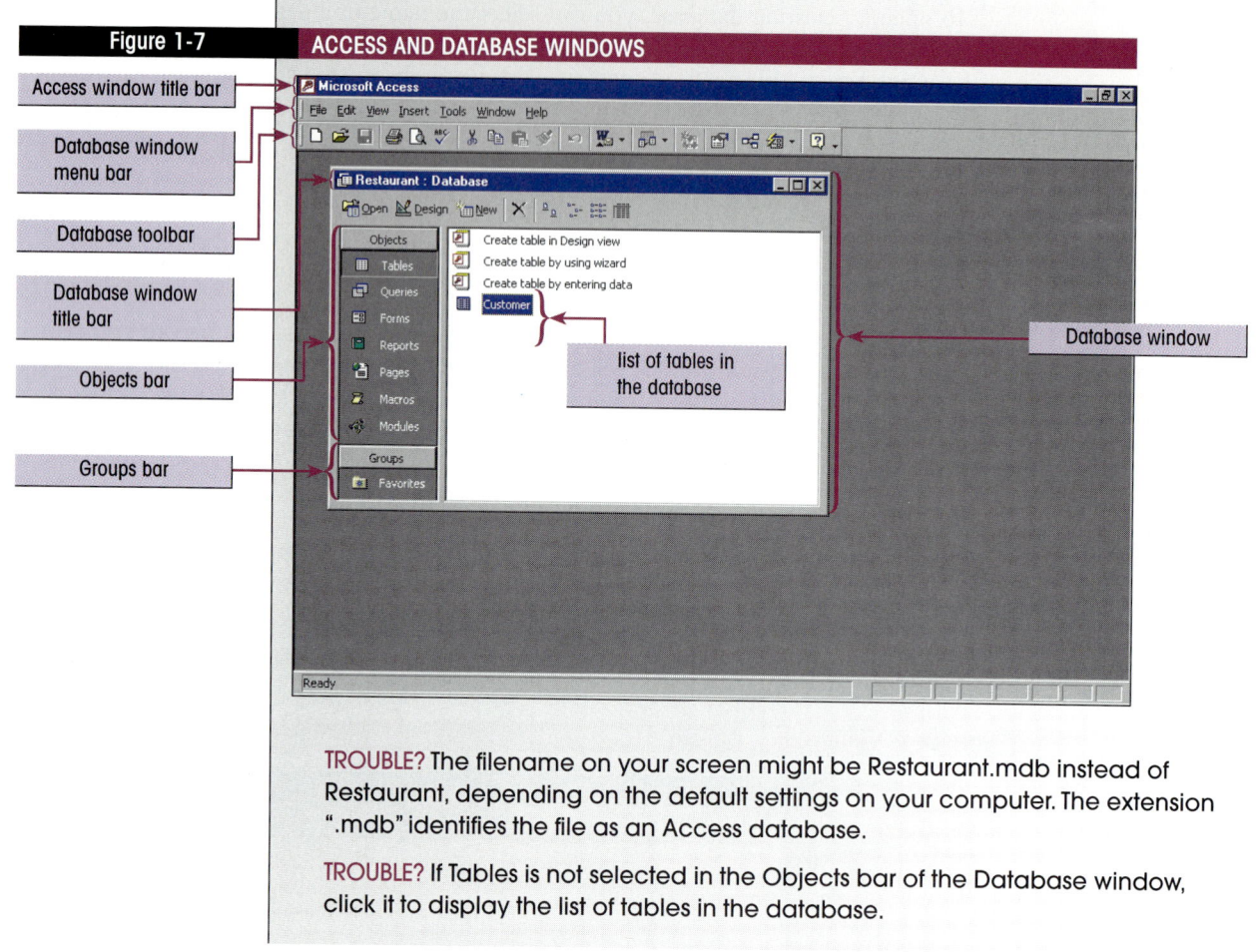

Figure 1-7   ACCESS AND DATABASE WINDOWS

Labels: Access window title bar; Database window menu bar; Database toolbar; Database window title bar; Objects bar; Groups bar; list of tables in the database; Database window

TROUBLE? The filename on your screen might be Restaurant.mdb instead of Restaurant, depending on the default settings on your computer. The extension ".mdb" identifies the file as an Access database.

TROUBLE? If Tables is not selected in the Objects bar of the Database window, click it to display the list of tables in the database.

Before you can begin working with the database, you need to become familiar with the components of the Access and Database windows.

The Access and Database Windows

The **Access window** is the program window that appears when you start the program. The **Database window** appears when you open a database; this window is the main control center for working with an open Access database. Except for the Access window title bar, all screen components now on your screen are associated with the Database window (see Figure 1-7). Most of these screen components—including the title bars, window sizing buttons, menu bar, toolbar, and status bar—are the same as the components in other Windows programs.

The Database window provides a variety of options for viewing and manipulating database objects. Each item in the **Objects bar** controls one of the major object groups—such as tables, queries, forms, and reports—in an Access database. The **Groups bar** allows you to organize different types of database objects into groups, with shortcuts to those objects, so that you can work with them more easily.

The Database window also provides a toolbar with buttons for quickly creating, opening, and managing objects, as well as shortcut options for some of these tasks.

Barbara has already created the Customer table in the Restaurant database. She asks you to open the Customer table and view its contents.

Opening an Access Table

As noted earlier, tables contain all the data in a database. Tables are the fundamental objects for your work in Access. To view, add, change, or delete data in a table, you first must open the table. You can open any Access object by using the Open button in the Database window.

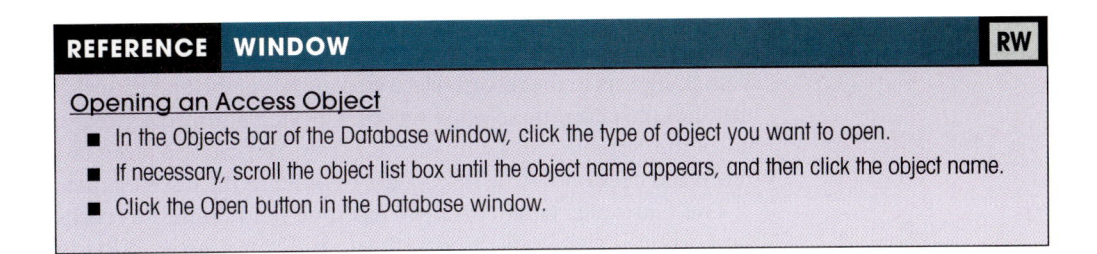

> **REFERENCE WINDOW**
>
> **Opening an Access Object**
> - In the Objects bar of the Database window, click the type of object you want to open.
> - If necessary, scroll the object list box until the object name appears, and then click the object name.
> - Click the Open button in the Database window.

You need to open the Customer table, which is the only table currently in the Restaurant database.

To open the Customer table:

1. If the Customer table is not highlighted, click **Customer** to select it.
2. Click the **Open** button in the Database window. The Customer table opens in Datasheet view on top of the Database and Access windows. See Figure 1-8.

Figure 1-8 TABLE DISPLAYED IN DATASHEET VIEW

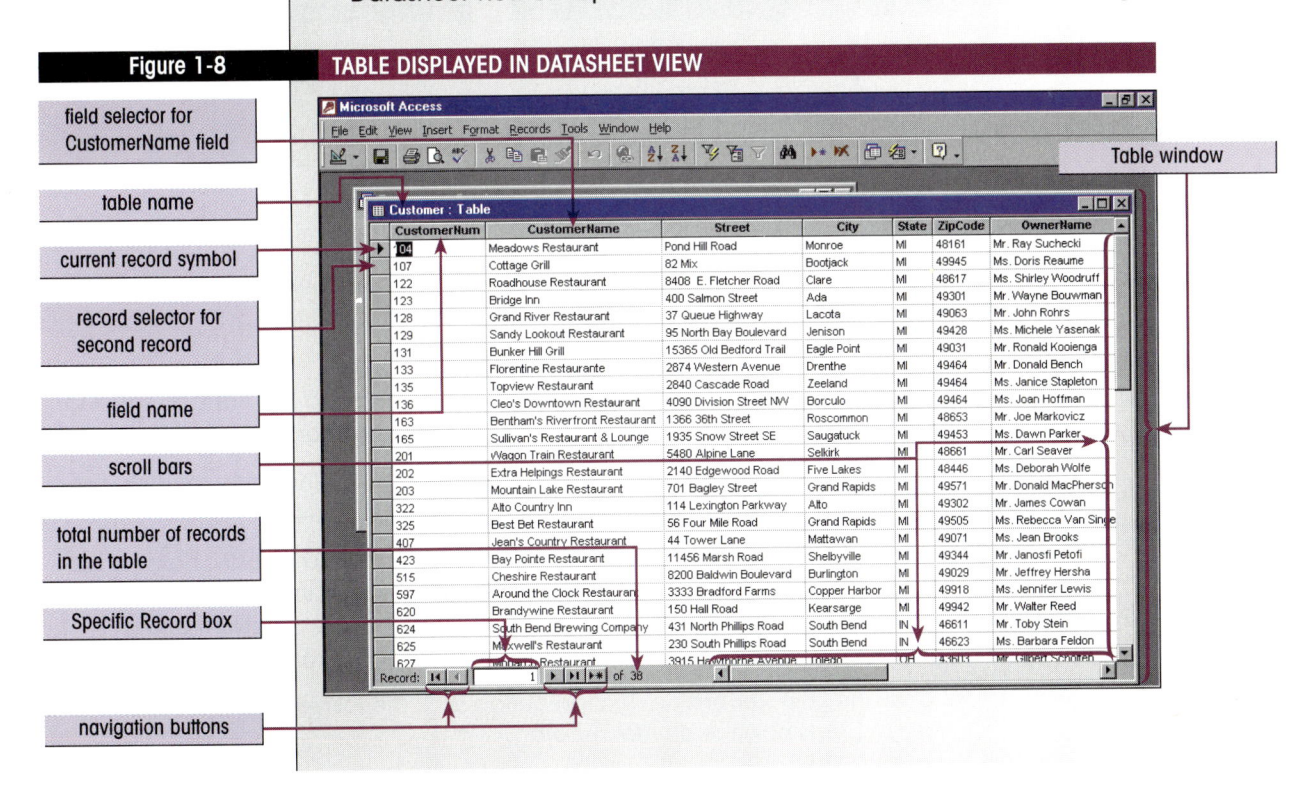

Callouts:
- field selector for CustomerName field
- table name
- current record symbol
- record selector for second record
- field name
- scroll bars
- total number of records in the table
- Specific Record box
- navigation buttons
- Table window

Datasheet view shows a table's contents as a **datasheet** in rows and columns, similar to a table or spreadsheet. Each row is a separate record in the table, and each column contains the field values for one field in the table. Each column is headed by a field name inside a field selector, and each row has a record selector to its left. Clicking a **field selector** or a **record selector** selects that entire column or row (respectively), which you can then manipulate. A field selector is also called a **column selector**, and a record selector is also called a **row selector**.

Navigating an Access Datasheet

When you first open a datasheet, Access selects the first field value in the first record. Notice that this field value is highlighted and that a darkened triangle symbol, called the current record symbol, appears in the record selector to the left of the first record. The **current record symbol** identifies the currently selected record. Clicking a record selector or field value in another row moves the current record symbol to that row. You can also move the pointer over the data on the screen and click one of the field values to position the insertion point.

The Customer table currently has nine fields and 38 records. To view fields or records not currently visible in the datasheet, you can use the horizontal and vertical scroll bars shown in Figure 1-8 to navigate through the data. The **navigation buttons**, also shown in Figure 1-8, provide another way to move vertically through the records. Figure 1-9 shows which record becomes the current record when you click each navigation button. The **Specific Record box**, which appears between the two sets of navigation buttons, displays the current record number. The total number of records in the table appears to the right of the navigation buttons.

Figure 1-9   NAVIGATION BUTTONS

NAVIGATION BUTTON	RECORD SELECTED	NAVIGATION BUTTON	RECORD SELECTED
⏮	First Record	⏭	Last Record
◀	Previous Record	▶*	New Record
▶	Next Record		

Barbara suggests that you use the various navigation techniques to move through the Customer table and become familiar with its contents.

To navigate the Customer datasheet:

1. Click the right scroll arrow in the horizontal scroll bar a few times to scroll to the right and view the remaining fields in the Customer table.

2. Drag the scroll box in the horizontal scroll bar back to the left to return to the previous display of the datasheet.

3. Click the **Next Record** navigation button ▶. The second record is now the current record, as indicated by the current record symbol in the second record selector. Also, notice that the second record's value for the CustomerNum field is highlighted, and "2" (for record number 2) appears in the Specific Record box.

4. Click the **Last Record** navigation button ⏭. The last record in the table, record 38, is now the current record.

> 5. Click the **Previous Record** navigation button. Record 37 is now the current record.
>
> 6. Click the **First Record** navigation button. The first record is now the current record.

Next, Barbara asks you to print the Customer table so that you can refer to it as you continue working with the Restaurant database.

Printing a Table

In Access you can print a table using either the Print command on the File menu or the Print button on the toolbar. The Print command opens a dialog box in which you can specify print settings. The Print button prints the table using the current settings. You'll use the Print button to print the Customer table.

> ### To print the Customer table:
>
> 1. Click the **Print** button on the Table Datasheet toolbar. Because all of the fields can't fit across one page, the table prints on two pages. You'll learn how to specify different print settings in later tutorials.

Now that you've viewed and printed the Customer table, you can exit Access.

Exiting Access

To exit Access, you simply click the Close button on the Access window title bar. When exiting, Access closes any open tables and the open database before closing the program.

> ### To exit Access:
>
> 1. Click the **Close** button on the Access window title bar. The Customer table and the Restaurant database close, Access closes, and you return to the Windows desktop.

Now that you've become familiar with Access and the Restaurant database, you're ready to work with the data stored in the database.

Session 1.1 QUICK CHECK

1. A(n) _____ is a single characteristic of a person, place, object, event, or idea.
2. You connect the records in two separate tables through a(n) _____ that appears in both tables.

3. The _____, whose values uniquely identify each record in a table, is called a _____ when it is placed in a second table to form a relationship between the two tables.

4. In a table, the rows are called _____, and the columns are called _____.

5. The _____ identifies the selected record in an Access table.

6. Describe the two methods for navigating through a table.

SESSION 1.2

In this session, you will create and print a query; create and print a form; use the Help system; and create, preview, and print a report.

Kim Carpenter, the director of marketing at Valle Coffee, wants a list of all restaurant customers so that her staff can call customers to check on their satisfaction with Valle Coffee's services and products. She doesn't want the list to include all the fields in the Customer table (such as Street and ZipCode). To produce this list for Kim, you need to create a query using the Customer table.

Creating and Printing a Query

A **query** is a question you ask about the data stored in a database. In response to a query, Access displays the specific records and fields that answer your question. When you create a query, you tell Access which fields you need and what criteria Access should use to select the records. Then Access displays only the information you want, so you don't have to navigate through the entire database for the information.

You can design your own queries or use an Access **Query Wizard**, which guides you through the steps to create a query. The Simple Query Wizard allows you to select records and fields quickly, and is an appropriate choice for producing the customer list Kim wants.

To start the Simple Query Wizard:

1. Insert your Data Disk in the appropriate disk drive.

2. Start Access, make sure the **Open an existing file** option button is selected and the **More Files** option is selected, and then click the **OK** button to display the Open dialog box.

3. Click the **Look in** list arrow, click the drive that contains your Data Disk, click **Tutorial** in the list box, and then click the **Open** button to display the list of files in the Tutorial folder.

4. Click **Restaurant** in the list box, and then click the **Open** button.

5. Click **Queries** in the Objects bar of the Database window to display the Queries list. The Queries list box does not contain any queries yet.

TUTORIAL 1 INTRODUCTION TO MICROSOFT ACCESS 2000   AC 1.15

You need to use the Simple Query Wizard to create the query for Kim. You can choose this Wizard either by clicking the New button, which opens a dialog box from which you can choose among several different Wizards to create your query, or by double-clicking the "Create query by using wizard" option, which automatically starts the Simple Query Wizard.

6. Double-click **Create query by using wizard**. The first Simple Query Wizard dialog box opens. See Figure 1-10.

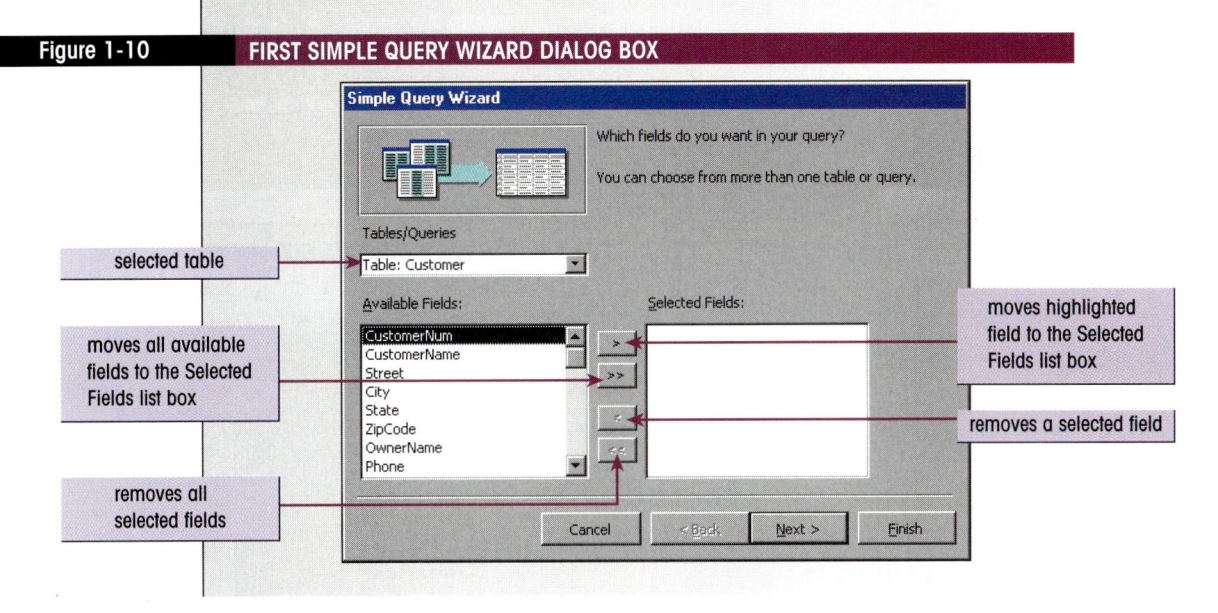

Figure 1-10   **FIRST SIMPLE QUERY WIZARD DIALOG BOX**

- selected table
- moves all available fields to the Selected Fields list box
- removes all selected fields
- moves highlighted field to the Selected Fields list box
- removes a selected field

Because Customer is the only object currently in the Restaurant database, it is listed in the Tables/Queries box. You could click the Tables/Queries list arrow to choose another table or a query on which to base the query you're creating. The Available Fields list box lists the fields in the selected table (in this case, Customer). You need to select fields from this list to include them in the query. To select fields one at a time, click a field and then click the > button. The selected field moves from the Available Fields list box on the left to the Selected Fields list box on the right. To select all the fields, click the >> button. If you change your mind or make a mistake, you can remove a field by clicking it in the Selected Fields list box and then clicking the < button. To remove all selected fields, click the << button.

Each Wizard dialog box contains buttons on the bottom that allow you to move to the previous dialog box (Back button), move to the next dialog box (Next button), or cancel the creation process (Cancel button) and return to the Database window. You can also finish creating the object (Finish button) and accept the Wizard's defaults for the remaining options.

Kim wants her list to include data from only the following fields: CustomerNum, CustomerName, City, State, OwnerName, and Phone. You need to select these fields to be included in the query.

To create the query using the Simple Query Wizard:

1. Click **CustomerNum** in the Available Fields list box (if necessary), and then click the > button. The CustomerNum field moves to the Selected Fields list box.

2. Repeat Step 1 for the fields **CustomerName**, **City**, **State**, **OwnerName**, and **Phone**, and then click the **Next** button. The second, and final, Simple Query Wizard dialog box opens and asks you to choose a name for your query. This name will appear in the Queries list in the Database window. You'll change the suggested name (Customer Query) to "Customer List."

3. Click at the end of the highlighted name, use the Backspace key to delete the word "Query," and then type **List**. Now you can view the query results.

4. Click the **Finish** button to complete the query. Access displays the query results in Datasheet view.

5. Click the **Maximize** button on the Query window to maximize the window. See Figure 1-11.

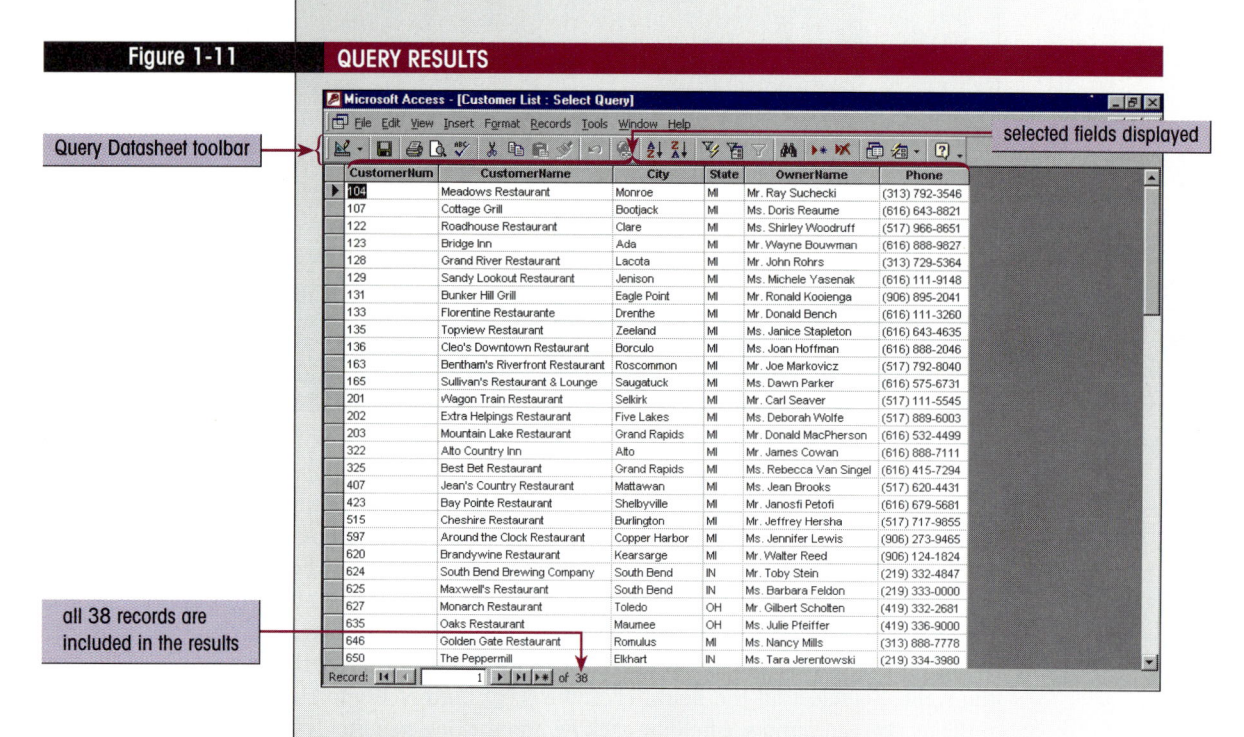

Figure 1-11   QUERY RESULTS

Query Datasheet toolbar

selected fields displayed

CustomerNum	CustomerName	City	State	OwnerName	Phone
104	Meadows Restaurant	Monroe	MI	Mr. Ray Suchecki	(313) 792-3546
107	Cottage Grill	Bootjack	MI	Ms. Doris Reaume	(616) 643-8821
122	Roadhouse Restaurant	Clare	MI	Ms. Shirley Woodruff	(517) 966-8651
123	Bridge Inn	Ada	MI	Mr. Wayne Bouwman	(616) 888-9827
128	Grand River Restaurant	Lacota	MI	Mr. John Rohrs	(313) 729-5364
129	Sandy Lookout Restaurant	Jenison	MI	Ms. Michele Yasenak	(616) 111-9148
131	Bunker Hill Grill	Eagle Point	MI	Mr. Ronald Kooienga	(906) 895-2041
133	Florentine Restaurante	Drenthe	MI	Mr. Donald Bench	(616) 111-3260
135	Topview Restaurant	Zeeland	MI	Ms. Janice Stapleton	(616) 643-4635
136	Cleo's Downtown Restaurant	Borculo	MI	Ms. Joan Hoffman	(616) 888-2046
163	Bentham's Riverfront Restaurant	Roscommon	MI	Mr. Joe Markovicz	(517) 792-8040
165	Sullivan's Restaurant & Lounge	Saugatuck	MI	Ms. Dawn Parker	(616) 575-6731
201	Wagon Train Restaurant	Selkirk	MI	Mr. Carl Seaver	(517) 111-5545
202	Extra Helpings Restaurant	Five Lakes	MI	Ms. Deborah Wolfe	(517) 889-6003
203	Mountain Lake Restaurant	Grand Rapids	MI	Mr. Donald MacPherson	(616) 532-4499
322	Alto Country Inn	Alto	MI	Mr. James Cowan	(616) 888-7111
325	Best Bet Restaurant	Grand Rapids	MI	Ms. Rebecca Van Singel	(616) 415-7294
407	Jean's Country Restaurant	Mattawan	MI	Ms. Jean Brooks	(517) 620-4431
423	Bay Pointe Restaurant	Shelbyville	MI	Mr. Janosfi Petofi	(616) 679-5681
515	Cheshire Restaurant	Burlington	MI	Mr. Jeffrey Hersha	(517) 717-9855
597	Around the Clock Restaurant	Copper Harbor	MI	Ms. Jennifer Lewis	(906) 273-9465
620	Brandywine Restaurant	Kearsarge	MI	Mr. Walter Reed	(906) 124-1824
624	South Bend Brewing Company	South Bend	IN	Mr. Toby Stein	(219) 332-4847
625	Maxwell's Restaurant	South Bend	IN	Ms. Barbara Feldon	(219) 333-0000
627	Monarch Restaurant	Toledo	OH	Mr. Gilbert Scholten	(419) 332-2681
635	Oaks Restaurant	Maumee	OH	Ms. Julie Pfeiffer	(419) 336-9000
646	Golden Gate Restaurant	Romulus	MI	Ms. Nancy Mills	(313) 888-7778
650	The Peppermill	Elkhart	IN	Ms. Tara Jerentowski	(219) 334-3980

Record: 1 of 38

all 38 records are included in the results

The datasheet displays the six selected fields for each record in the Customer table. The fields are shown in the order you selected them, from left to right.

The records are currently listed in order by the primary key field (CustomerNum). Kim prefers the records to be listed in order by state so that her staff members can focus on all records for the customers in a particular state. To display the records in the order Kim wants, you need to sort the query results by the State field.

To sort the query results:

1. Click to position the insertion point anywhere in the State column. This establishes the State column as the current field.

2. Click the **Sort Ascending** button on the Query Datasheet toolbar. Now the records are sorted in ascending alphabetical order by the values in the State field. All the records for Indiana are listed first, followed by the records for Michigan and then Ohio.

Kim asks for a printed copy of the query results so that she can bring the customer list to a meeting with her staff members. To print the query results, you can use the Print button on the Query Datasheet toolbar.

To print the query results:

1. Click the **Print** button on the Query Datasheet toolbar to print one copy of the query results with the current settings.

2. Click the **Close** button on the menu bar to close the query.

   A dialog box opens and asks if you want to save changes to the design of the query. This box opens because you changed the sort order of the query results.

3. Click the **Yes** button to save the query design changes and return to the Database window. Notice that the Customer List query now appears in the Queries list box. In addition, because you maximized the Query window, now the Database window is also maximized. You need to restore the window.

4. Click the **Restore** button on the menu bar to restore the Database window.

The query results are not stored in the database; however, the query design is stored as part of the database with the name you specified. You can re-create the query results at any time by running the query again. You'll learn more about creating and running queries in Tutorial 3.

After Kim leaves for her staff meeting, Barbara asks you to create a form for the Customer table so that her staff members can use the form to enter and work with data easily in the table.

Creating and Printing a Form

A **form** is an object you use to maintain, view, and print records in a database. Although you can perform these same functions with tables and queries, forms can present data in customized and useful ways.

In Access, you can design your own forms or use a Form Wizard to create forms for you automatically. A **Form Wizard** is an Access tool that asks you a series of questions, and then creates a form based on your answers. The quickest way to create a form is to use an **AutoForm Wizard**, which places all the fields from a selected table (or query) on a form automatically, without asking you any questions, and then displays the form on the screen.

Barbara wants a form for the Customer table that will show all the fields for one record at a time, with fields listed one below another. This type of form will make it easier for her staff to focus on all the data for a particular customer. You'll use the AutoForm: Columnar Wizard to create the form.

To create the form using an AutoForm Wizard:

1. Click **Forms** in the Objects bar of the Database window to display the Forms list. The Forms list box does not contain any forms yet.

2. Click the **New** button in the Database window to open the New Form dialog box. See Figure 1-12.

Figure 1-12   NEW FORM DIALOG BOX

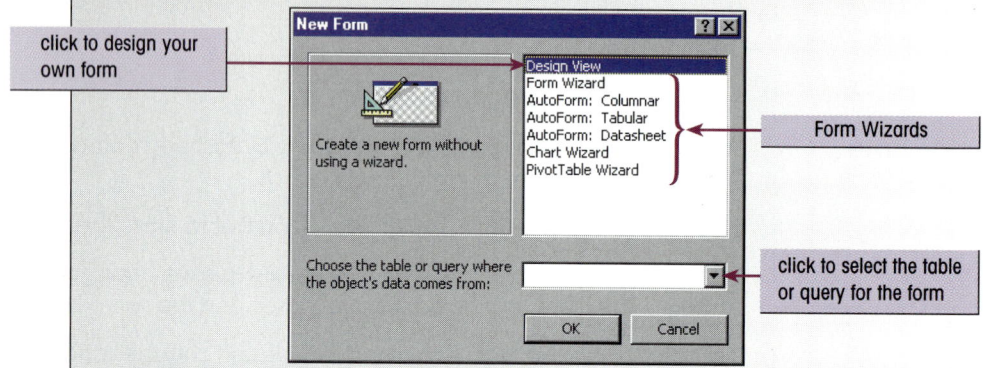

click to design your own form

Form Wizards

click to select the table or query for the form

The top list box provides options for designing your own form or creating a form using one of the Form Wizards. In the bottom list box, you choose the table or query that will supply the data for the form.

3. Click **AutoForm: Columnar** to select this AutoForm Wizard.

4. Click the list arrow for choosing the table or query on which to base the form, and then click **Customer**.

5. Click the **OK** button. The AutoForm Wizard creates the form and displays it in Form view. See Figure 1-13.

Figure 1-13   FORM CREATED BY THE AUTOFORM: COLUMNAR WIZARD

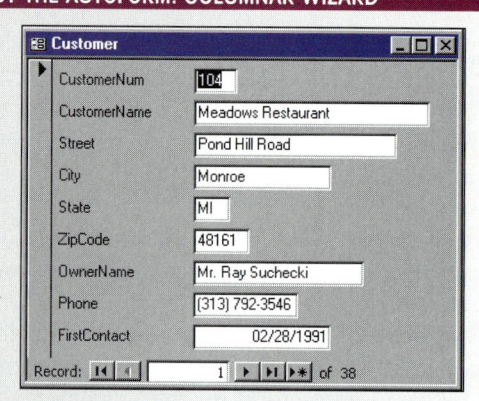

CustomerNum	104
CustomerName	Meadows Restaurant
Street	Pond Hill Road
City	Monroe
State	MI
ZipCode	48161
OwnerName	Mr. Ray Suchecki
Phone	(313) 792-3546
FirstContact	02/28/1991

Record: 1 of 38

TROUBLE? The background of your form might look different from the one shown in Figure 1-13, depending on your computer's settings. If so, don't worry. You will learn how to change the form's style later in this text. For now, continue with the tutorial.

The form displays one record at a time in the Customer table. Access displays the field values for the first record in the table and selects the first field value (CustomerNum).

Each field name appears on a separate line and on the same line as its field value, which appears in a box. The widths of the boxes are different to accommodate the different sizes of the displayed field values; for example, compare the small box for the State field value with the larger box for the CustomerName field value. The AutoForm: Columnar Wizard automatically placed the field names and values on the form and supplied the background style.

Also, notice that the Form window contains navigation buttons, similar to those available in Datasheet view, which you can use to display different records in the form.

Barbara asks you to print the data for the Embers Restaurant, which is the last record in the table. After printing this record in the form, you'll save the form with the name "Customer Data" in the Restaurant database. Then the form will be available for later use. You'll learn more about creating and customizing forms in Tutorial 4.

To print the form with data for the last record, and then save and close the form:

1. Click the **Last Record** navigation button . The last record in the table, record 38 for Embers Restaurant, is now the current record.

2. Click **File** on the menu bar, and then click **Print**. The Print dialog box opens.

3. Click the **Selected Record(s)** option button, and then click the **OK** button to print only the current record in the form.

4. Click the **Save** button on the Form View toolbar. The Save As dialog box opens.

5. In the Form Name text box, click at the end of the highlighted word "Customer," press the **spacebar**, type **Data**, and then press the **Enter** key. Access saves the form as Customer Data in your Restaurant database and closes the dialog box.

6. Click the **Close** button on the Form window title bar to close the form and return to the Database window. Note that the Customer Data form is now listed in the Forms list box.

Kim returns from her staff meeting with another request. She wants the same customer list you produced earlier when you created the Customer List query, but she'd like the information presented in a more readable format. She suggests you use the Access Help system to learn about formatting data in reports.

Getting Help

The Access Help system provides the same options as the Help system in other Windows programs—the Help Contents, the Answer Wizard, and the Help Index—which are available from the Microsoft Access Help window. The Access Help system also provides additional ways to get help as you work—the Office Assistant and the What's This? command. You'll learn how to use the Office Assistant next in this section. The What's This? command provides context-sensitive Help information. When you choose this command from the Help menu, the pointer changes to the Help pointer , which you can then use to click any object or option on the screen to see a description of the object.

Finding Information with the Office Assistant

The Office Assistant is an interactive guide to finding information in the Help system. You can ask the Office Assistant a question, and then it will search the Help system to find an answer.

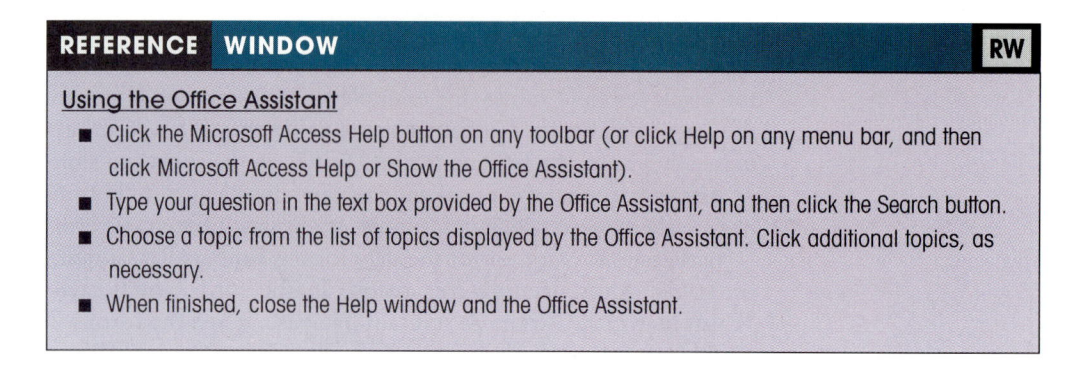

> **REFERENCE WINDOW**
>
> **Using the Office Assistant**
> - Click the Microsoft Access Help button on any toolbar (or click Help on any menu bar, and then click Microsoft Access Help or Show the Office Assistant).
> - Type your question in the text box provided by the Office Assistant, and then click the Search button.
> - Choose a topic from the list of topics displayed by the Office Assistant. Click additional topics, as necessary.
> - When finished, close the Help window and the Office Assistant.

You'll use the Office Assistant to get Help about creating reports in Access. Because you chose to hide the Office Assistant earlier in this tutorial, you need to redisplay it first.

To get Help about reports:

1. Click the **Microsoft Access Help** button on the Database toolbar. The Office Assistant appears and displays a text box in which you can type your question. See Figure 1-14.

Figure 1-14   **USING THE OFFICE ASSISTANT**

- type your question in this text box (your text might not be selected)
- Office Assistant (your Office Assistant character might be different)
- click to have the Office Assistant search for an answer

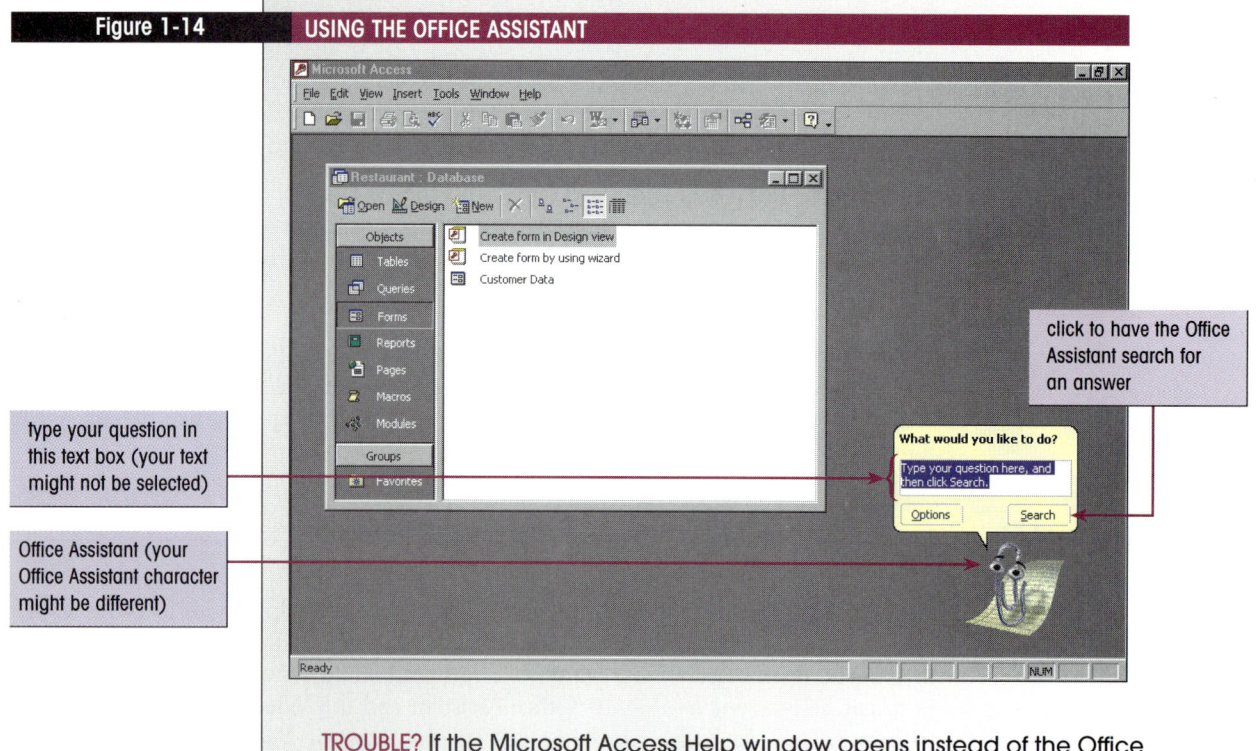

TROUBLE? If the Microsoft Access Help window opens instead of the Office Assistant, click the Close button ☒ to close the Help window, click Help on the menu bar, and then click Show the Office Assistant. If you don't see the text box and the Search button, click the Office Assistant.

TROUBLE? Your Office Assistant might appear in a different location on your screen. You can click and drag the Office Assistant to move it to another location, if you want.

TUTORIAL 1 INTRODUCTION TO MICROSOFT ACCESS 2000   AC 1.21

You need to find information about creating reports in Access. To do so, you can simply begin to type your question.

2. Type **How do I create a report?** and then click the **Search** button. The Office Assistant displays a list of relevant topics. See Figure 1-15.

Figure 1-15   LIST OF RELATED TOPICS

3. In the list of topics, click **Create a report**. The Office Assistant opens the topic in the Microsoft Access Help window, which opens on the left or right side of your screen. To see more of the Help window, you can maximize it.

4. Click the **Maximize** button on the Microsoft Access Help window.

5. After reading the displayed text, click the topic **Create a report by using AutoReport**. The Help window for using AutoReport opens. Because the Office Assistant might block the text in the Help window, you'll hide it again.

6. Right-click the **Office Assistant** to display the shortcut menu, click **Hide**, and then click anywhere in the Help window to redisplay the entire window, if necessary. The full text of the Help topic is now visible. See Figure 1-16.

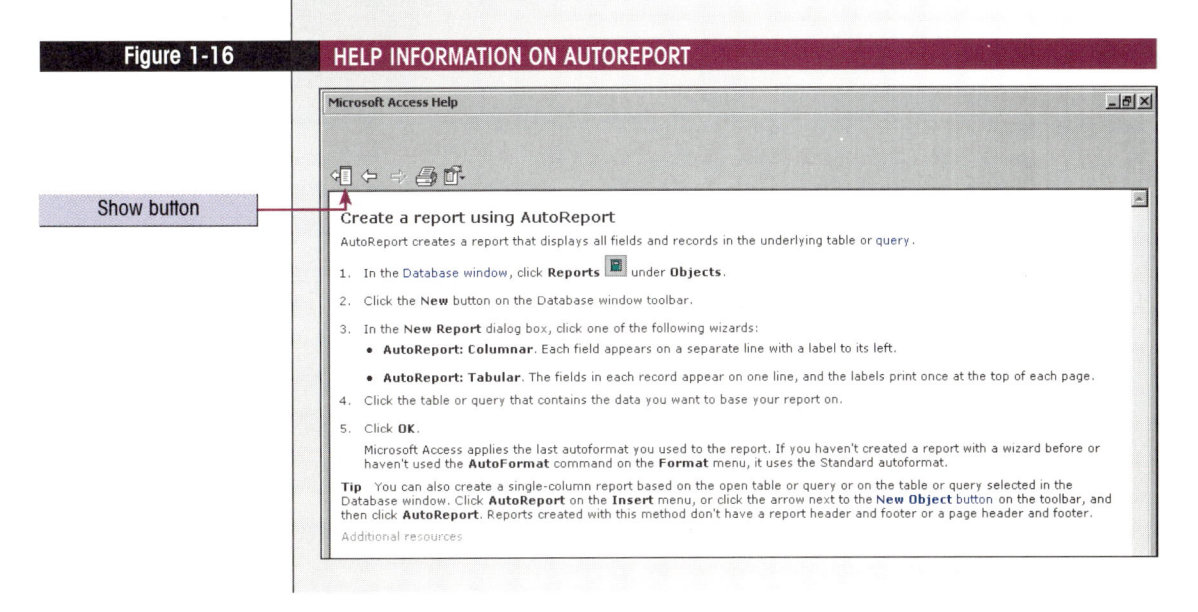

Figure 1-16   HELP INFORMATION ON AUTOREPORT

Show button

TROUBLE? If the Microsoft Access Help window minimizes when you hide the Office Assistant, click the Microsoft Access Help program button on the taskbar to restore the window.

7. Read the information displayed in the Help window. Note that the AutoReport feature is similar to the AutoForm feature you used earlier. You'll use the AutoReport: Columnar Wizard to create the report for Kim.

As mentioned earlier, the Help system in Access provides different ways to find information, including the Contents, Answer Wizard, and Index features. To gain access to these features, you need to use the Show button in the Microsoft Access Help window (see Figure 1-16).

To display the additional Help features:

1. Click the **Show** button on the toolbar in the Microsoft Access Help window. The Contents, Answer Wizard, and Index tabs appear in the left frame of the window. See Figure 1-17.

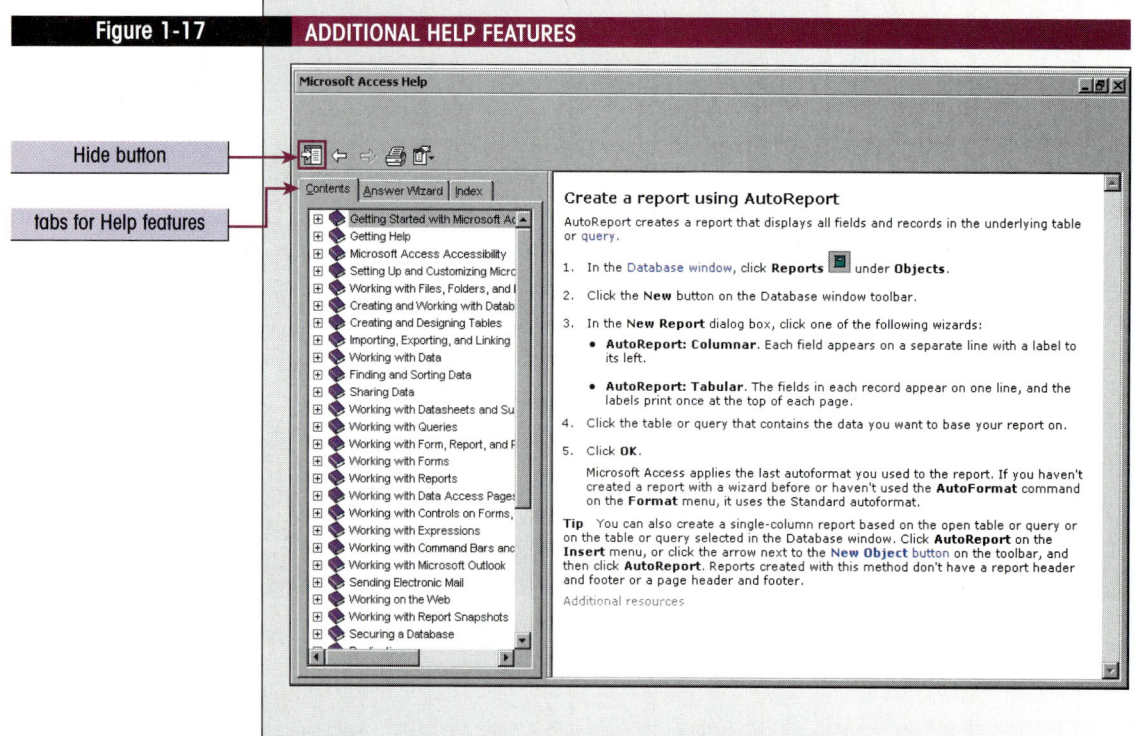

Figure 1-17 ADDITIONAL HELP FEATURES

Hide button

tabs for Help features

Note that the Show button is now labeled the Hide button, which you could click to remove the display of the tabs. You'll have a chance to use some of these additional Help tools in the exercises at the end of this tutorial. For now, you can close the Microsoft Access Help window and create the report for Kim.

2. Click the **Close** button on the Microsoft Access Help window title bar to exit Help and return to the Database window.

Creating, Previewing, and Printing a Report

A **report** is a formatted printout (or screen display) of the contents of one or more tables in a database. Although you can print data from tables, queries, and forms, reports provide you with the greatest flexibility for formatting printed output.

Kim wants a report showing the same information contained in the Customer List query that you created earlier. However, she wants the data for each customer to be grouped together, with one customer record below another, as shown in the report sketch in Figure 1-18. You'll use the AutoReport: Columnar Wizard to produce the report for Kim.

Figure 1-18	SKETCH OF KIM'S REPORT

Customer List

CustomerNum _____
CustomerName _____
City _____
State ___
OwnerName _____
Phone _____

CustomerNum _____
CustomerName _____
City _____
State ___
OwnerName _____
Phone _____

•   •
•   •
•   •

To create the report using the AutoReport: Columnar Wizard:

1. Click **Reports** in the Objects bar of the Database window, and then click the **New** button in the Database window to open the New Report dialog box, which is similar to the New Form dialog box you saw earlier.

2. Click **AutoReport: Columnar** to select this Wizard for creating the report.

   Because Kim wants the same data as in the Customer List query, you need to choose that query as the basis for the report.

3. Click the list arrow for choosing the table or query on which to base the report, and then click **Customer List**.

4. Click the **OK** button. The AutoReport Wizard creates the report and displays it in Print Preview, which shows exactly how the report will look when printed.

   To view the report better, you'll maximize the window and change the Zoom setting so that you can see the entire page.

5. Click the **Maximize** button on the Report window, click the **Zoom** list arrow (next to the value 100%) on the Print Preview toolbar, and then click **Fit**. The entire first page of the report is displayed in the window. See Figure 1-19.

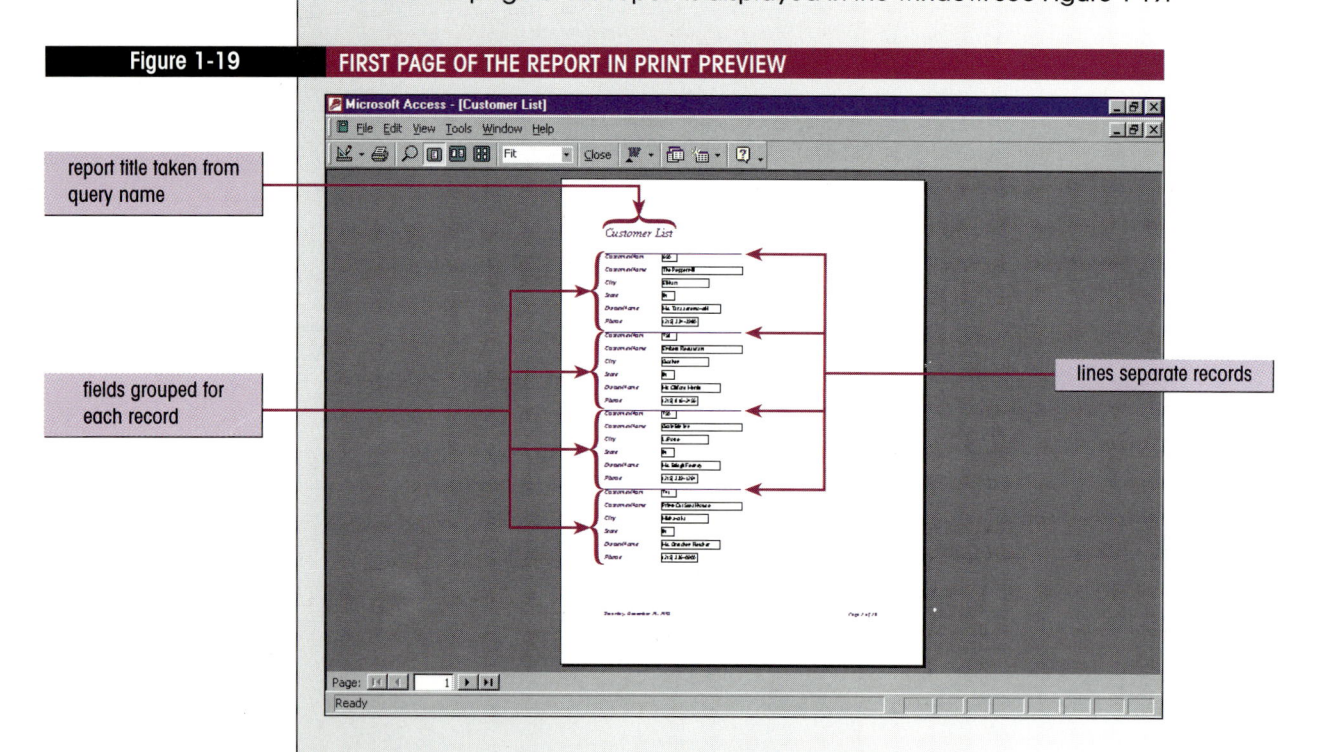

Figure 1-19 FIRST PAGE OF THE REPORT IN PRINT PREVIEW

- report title taken from query name
- fields grouped for each record
- lines separate records

Each field from the Customer List query appears on its own line, with the corresponding field value to the right, in a box. Lines separate one record from the next, visually grouping all the fields for each record. The name of the query—Customer List—appears as the report title.

TROUBLE? The background of your report might look different from the one shown in Figure 1-19, depending on your computer's settings. If so, don't worry. You will learn how to change the report's style later in this text.

The report spans multiple pages. Kim asks you to print just the first page of the report so that she can review its format. After printing the report page, you'll close the report without saving it because you can easily re-create it at any time. In general, it's best to save an object—report, form, or query—only if you anticipate using the object frequently or if it is time-consuming to create, because these objects use considerable storage space on your disk. You'll learn more about creating and customizing reports in Tutorial 4.

To print the first report page, and then close the report:

1. Click **File** on the menu bar, and then click **Print**. The Print dialog box opens. You need to change the print settings to print only the first page of the report.

2. In the Print Range section, click the **Pages** option button, type **1** in the From text box, press the **Tab** key, and then type **1** in the To text box.

3. Click the **OK** button to print the first page of the report. Now you can close the report.

4. Click the **Close** button ⊠ on the menu bar. *Do not* click the Close button on the Print Preview toolbar.

   TROUBLE? If you clicked the Close button on the Print Preview toolbar, you switched to Design view. Simply click the Close button ⊠ on the menu bar, and then continue with the tutorial.

   A dialog box opens and asks if you want to save the changes to the report design.

5. Click the **No** button to close the report without saving it.

When you work in an Access database and create and manipulate objects, such as queries, forms, and reports, the size of your database increases. To free up disk space and make a database a more manageable size, Access provides a way for you to compact a database.

Compacting a Database

Whenever you open an Access database and work in it, the size of the database increases. Likewise, when you delete records or database objects—such as queries, forms, and reports—the space occupied by the deleted records or objects on disk does not become available for other records or objects. To make the space available, you must compact the database. **Compacting** a database rearranges the data and objects in a database to make its size smaller. Unlike making a copy of a database file, which you do to protect your database against loss or damage, you compact a database to make it smaller, thereby making more space available on your disk.

Compacting and Repairing a Database

When you compact a database, Access repairs the database at the same time. In many cases, Access detects that a database is damaged when you try to open it and gives you the option to compact and repair it at that time. If you think your database might be damaged because it is behaving unpredictably, you can use the "Compact and Repair Database" option to fix it. With your database file open, choose the Database Utilities option from the Tools menu, and then choose the Compact and Repair Database option.

Compacting a Database Automatically

Access also allows you to set an option for your database file so that every time you close the database, it will be compacted automatically.

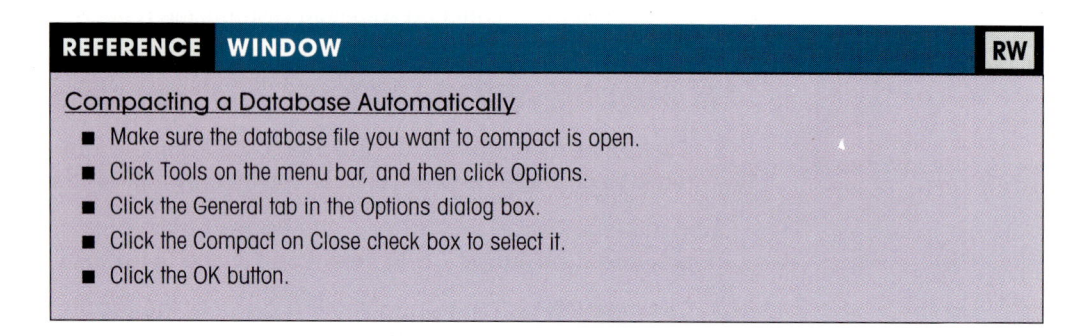

REFERENCE WINDOW

Compacting a Database Automatically
- Make sure the database file you want to compact is open.
- Click Tools on the menu bar, and then click Options.
- Click the General tab in the Options dialog box.
- Click the Compact on Close check box to select it.
- Click the OK button.

You'll set the compact option now for the Restaurant database. Then, every time you subsequently open and close the Restaurant database, Access will compact the database file for you. After setting this option, you'll exit Access.

To set the option for compacting the Restaurant database:

1. Make sure the Restaurant Database window is open on your screen.

2. Click **Tools** on the menu bar, and then click **Options**. The Options dialog box opens.

3. Click the **General** tab in the dialog box, and then click the **Compact on Close** check box to select it. See Figure 1-20.

Figure 1-20 GENERAL TAB OF THE OPTIONS DIALOG BOX

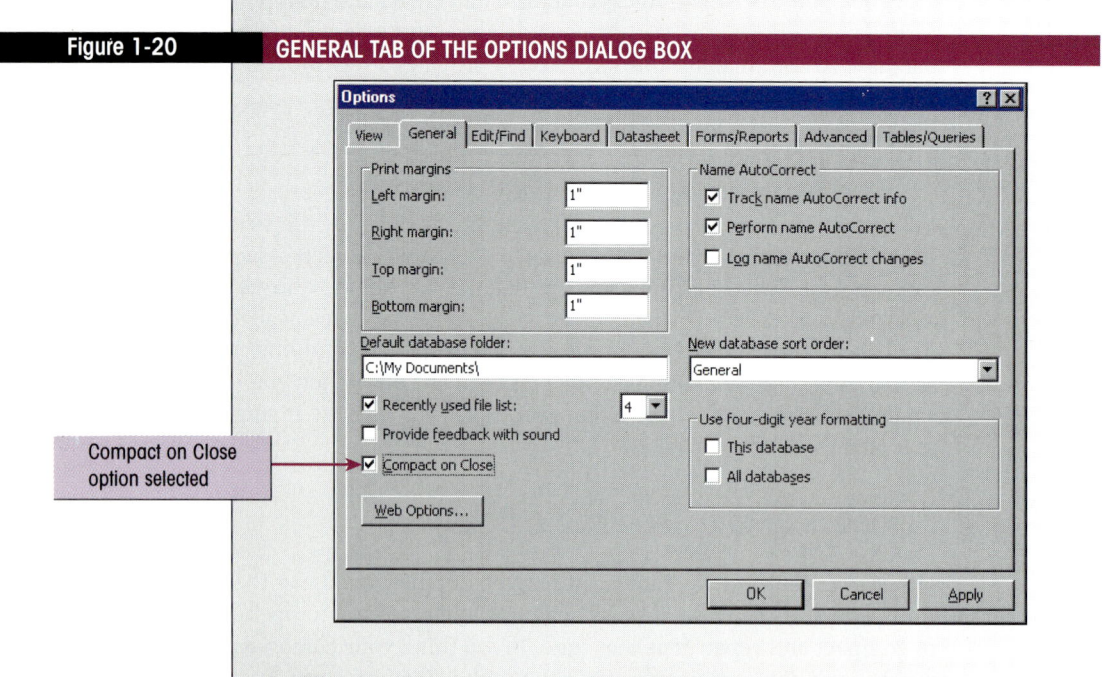

Compact on Close option selected

4. Click the **OK** button to set the option. Now you can exit Access.

5. Click the **Close** button ⊠ on the Access window title bar to exit Access. When you exit, Access closes the Restaurant database file and compacts it automatically.

Backing Up and Restoring a Database

As noted earlier, you make a backup copy of a database file to protect your database against loss or damage. You can make the backup copy using one of several methods: Windows Explorer, My Computer, Microsoft Backup, or other backup software. If you back up your database file to a floppy disk, and the file size exceeds the size of the disk, you cannot use Windows Explorer or My Computer; you must use Microsoft Backup or some other backup software so that you can copy the file over more than one disk.

To restore a database file that you have backed up, choose the same method you used to make the backup copy. For example, if you used the Microsoft Backup tool (which is one of the System Tool Accessories available from the Programs menu), you must choose the Restore option for this tool to copy the database file to your database folder. If the existing database file and the backup copy have the same name, restoring the backup copy might replace the existing file. If you want to save the existing file, rename it before you restore it.

With the Customer table in place, Barbara can continue to build the Restaurant database and use it to store, manipulate, and retrieve important data for Valle Coffee. In the following tutorials, you'll help Barbara complete and maintain the database, and you'll use it to meet the specific information needs of other Valle Coffee employees.

Session 1.2 QUICK CHECK

1. A(n) _____ is a question you ask about the data stored in a database.
2. Unless you specify otherwise, the records resulting from a query are listed in order by the _____.
3. The quickest way to create a form is to use a(n) _____.
4. Describe the form created by the AutoForm: Columnar Wizard.
5. Describe how you use the Office Assistant to get Help.
6. After creating a report, the AutoReport Wizard displays the report in _____.

REVIEW ASSIGNMENTS

In the Review Assignments, you'll work with the **Customer** database, which is similar to the database you worked with in the tutorial. Complete the following:

1. Make sure your Data Disk is in the disk drive.

2. Start Access and open the **Customer** database, which is located in the Review folder on your Data Disk.

Explore

3. In the Microsoft Access Help window, display and then select the Contents tab. (*Hint*: Click any topic displayed in the Office Assistant list box to open the Microsoft Access Help window.) Double-click the topic "Creating and working with Databases." Click the topic "Databases: What they are and how they work," and then click the related graphic for the topic. Read the displayed information. When finished, close the window to return to the Contents tab. Repeat this procedure for the similarly worded topics for tables, queries, forms, and reports. When finished reading all the topics, close the Microsoft Access Help window.

Explore 4. Use the Office Assistant to ask the following question: "How do I rename a table?" Choose the topic "Rename a database object" and read the displayed information. Close the Microsoft Access Help window and hide the Office Assistant. Then, in the **Customer** database, rename the **Table1** table as **Customers**.

5. Open the **Customers** table.

Explore 6. In the Microsoft Access Help window, display and then select the Index tab. (*Hint*: Click any topic displayed in the Office Assistant list box to open the Help window.) Type the keyword "print" in the Type keywords text box, and then click the Search button. Click the topic "Print a report." Read the displayed information, click the button for more information at the end of the first paragraph (>>), and then read the information. Close the Microsoft Access Help window. Print the **Customers** table datasheet in landscape orientation. Close the **Customers** table.

7. Use the Simple Query Wizard to create a query that includes the City, CustomerName, OwnerName, and Phone fields (in that order) from the **Customers** table. Name the query **Customer Phone List**. Sort the query results in ascending order by City. Print the query results, and then close and save the query.

8. Use the AutoForm: Columnar Wizard to create a form for the **Customers** table.

Explore 9. Use context-sensitive Help to find out how to move to a particular record and display it in the form. Choose the What's This? command from the Help menu, and then use the Help pointer to click the number 1 in the Specific Record box at the bottom of the form. Read the displayed information. Click to close the Help box, and then use the Specific Record box to move to record 28 (for The Peppermill) in the **Customers** table.

10. Print the form for the current record (28), save the form as **Customer Info**, and then close the form.

Explore 11. Use the AutoReport: Tabular Wizard to create a report based on the **Customers** table. Print the first page of the report, and then close and save the report as **Customers**.

12. Set the option for compacting the **Customer** database on close.

13. Exit Access.

CASE PROBLEMS

Case 1. Ashbrook Mall Information Desk Ashbrook Mall is a large, modern mall located in Phoenix, Arizona. The Mall Operations Office is responsible for everything that happens within the mall and anything that affects the mall's operation. Among the independent operations groups that report to the Mall Operations Office are the Maintenance Group, the Mall Security Office, and the Information Desk. You will be helping the Information Desk personnel.

One important service provided by the Information Desk is to maintain a catalog of current job openings at stores within the mall. Sam Bullard, the director of the Mall Operations Office, recently created an Access database named **MallJobs** to store this information. You'll help Sam complete and maintain this database. Complete the following:

1. Make sure your Data Disk is in the disk drive.

2. Start Access and open the **MallJobs** database, which is located in the Cases folder on your Data Disk.

3. Open the **Store** table, print the table datasheet, and then close the table.

4. Use the Simple Query Wizard to create a query that includes the StoreName, Contact, and Extension fields (in that order) from the **Store** table. Name the query **Contact List**. Print the query results, and then close the query.

Explore 5. Use the AutoForm: Tabular Wizard to create a form for the **Store** table. Print the form, save it as **Store Info**, and then close it.

Explore 6. Use the AutoReport: Columnar Wizard to create a report based on the **Store** table. Maximize the Report window and change the Zoom setting to Fit. Use the Two Pages button on the Print Preview toolbar to view both pages of the report in Print Preview. Print the first page of the report, and then close and save it as **Stores**.

7. Set the option for compacting the **MallJobs** database on close.

8. Exit Access.

Case 2. Professional Litigation User Services Professional Litigation User Services (PLUS) is a company that creates all types of visual aids for judicial proceedings. Clients are usually private law firms, although the District Attorney's office has occasionally contracted for its services. PLUS creates graphs, maps, timetables, and charts, both for computerized presentations and in large-size form for presentation to juries. PLUS also creates videos, animations, presentation packages, and slide shows—in short, anything of a visual nature that can be used in a judicial proceeding to make, clarify, or support a point.

Raj Jawahir, a new employee at PLUS, is responsible for tracking the daily payments received from the firm's clients. He created an Access database named **Payments**, and needs your help in working with this database. Complete the following:

1. Make sure your Data Disk is in the disk drive.

2. Start Access and open the **Payments** database, which is located in the Cases folder on your Data Disk.

3. Open the **Firm** table, print the table datasheet, and then close the table.

4. Use the Simple Query Wizard to create a query that includes the FirmName, PLUSAcctRep, and Extension fields (in that order) from the **Firm** table. Name the query **AcctRep List**.

Explore 5. Sort the query results in descending order by the PLUSAcctRep field. (*Hint*: Use a toolbar button.)

Explore 6. Use the Office Assistant to ask the following question: "How do I select multiple records?" Choose the topic "Selecting fields and records in Datasheet view." Hide the Office Assistant, read the displayed information, and then close the Help window. Select the first 10 records in the datasheet (all the records with the value "Tyler, Olivia" in the PLUSAcctRep field), and then print just the selected records. Close the query, and save your changes to the design.

7. Use the AutoForm: Columnar Wizard to create a form for the **Firm** table. Move to record 25, and then print the form for the current record only. Save the form as **Firm Info** and then close the form.

8. Use the AutoReport: Columnar Wizard to create a report based on the **Firm** table. Maximize the Report window and change the Zoom setting to Fit.

Explore 9. Use the View menu to view all eight pages of the report at the same time in Print Preview.

10. Print just the first page of the report, and then close and save the report as **Firms**.

11. Set the option for compacting the **Payments** database on close.

12. Exit Access.

Case 3. Best Friends Best Friends is a not-for-profit organization that trains hearing and service dogs for people with disabilities. Established in 1989 in Boise, Idaho, by Noah and Sheila Warnick, Best Friends is modeled after Paws With A Cause®, the original and largest provider of hearing and service dogs in the United States. Like Paws With A Cause® and other such organizations, Best Friends strives to provide "Dignity Through Independence."

To raise funds for Best Friends, Noah and Sheila periodically conduct walk-a-thons. The events have become so popular that Noah and Sheila created an Access database named **Walks** to track walker and pledge data. You'll help them complete and maintain the **Walks** database. Complete the following:

1. Make sure your Data Disk is in the disk drive.

2. Start Access and open the **Walks** database, which is located in the Cases folder on your Data Disk.

3. Open the **Walker** table, print the table datasheet, and then close the table.

Explore 4. Use the Simple Query Wizard to create a query that includes all the fields in the **Walker** table *except* the Phone field. (*Hint*: Use the `>>` and `<` buttons to select the necessary fields.) In the second Simple Query Wizard dialog box, make sure the Detail option button is selected. (This second dialog box opens because the table contains numeric values.) Name the query **Walker Distance**.

Explore 5. Sort the results in descending order by the Distance field. (*Hint*: Use a toolbar button.) Print the query results, and then close and save the query.

6. Use the AutoForm: Columnar Wizard to create a form for the **Walker** table. Move to record 16, and then print the form for the current record only. Save the form as **Walker Info**, and then close it.

7. Use the AutoReport: Columnar Wizard to create a report based on the **Walker** table. Maximize the Report window and change the Zoom setting to Fit.

Explore 8. Use the View menu to view all six pages of the report at the same time in Print Preview.

9. Print just the first page of the report, and then close and save the report as **Walkers**.

10. Set the option for compacting the **Walks** database on close.

11. Exit Access.

Case 4. Lopez Lexus Dealerships Maria and Hector Lopez own a chain of Lexus dealerships throughout Texas. They have used a computer in their business for several years to handle payroll and typical accounting functions. Because of the dealership's phenomenal expansion, both in the number of car locations and the number of cars handled, they created an Access database named **Lexus** to track their car inventory. You'll help them work with and maintain this database. Complete the following:

1. Make sure your Data Disk is in the disk drive.

2. Start Access and open the **Lexus** database, which is located in the Cases folder on your Data Disk.

3. Open the **Cars** table.

Explore 4. Print the **Cars** table datasheet in landscape orientation, and then close the table.

Explore 5. Use the Simple Query Wizard to create a query that includes the Model, Class, Year, LocationCode, Cost, and SellingPrice fields (in that order) from the **Cars** table. In the second Simple Query Wizard dialog box, make sure the Detail option button is selected. (This second dialog box opens because the table contains numeric values.) Name the query **Cost vs Selling**.

Explore 6. Sort the query results in descending order by SellingPrice. (*Hint*: Use a toolbar button.)

7. Print the query results, and then close and save the query.

8. Use the AutoForm: Columnar Wizard to create a form for the **Cars** table. Move to record 3, and then print the form for the current record only. Save the form as **Car Info**, and then close it.

Explore 9. Use the AutoReport: Tabular Wizard to create a report based on the **Cars** table. Maximize the Report window and change the Zoom setting to Fit. Use the Two Pages button on the Print Preview toolbar to view both pages of the report in Print Preview. Print the first page of the report in landscape orientation, and then close and save the report as **Cars**.

10. Set the option for compacting the **Lexus** database on close.

11. Exit Access.

INTERNET ASSIGNMENTS

The purpose of the Internet Assignments is to challenge you to find information on the Internet that you can use to create effective documents. The actual assignments are updated and maintained on the Course Technology Web site. Log on to the Internet and use your Web browser to go to the Student Online Companion to accompany this text at **www.course.com/NewPerspectives/office2000**. Click the Access link, and then click the link for Tutorial 1.

LAB ASSIGNMENTS

These Lab Assignments are designed to accompany the interactive Course Lab called Databases. To start the Databases Lab, click the Start button on the Windows taskbar, point to Programs, point to Course Labs, point to New Perspectives Applications, and then click Databases. If you do not see Course Labs on your Programs menu, see your instructor or technical support person.

Databases This Databases Lab demonstrates the essential concepts of file and database management systems. You will use the Lab to search, sort, and report the data contained in a file of classic books.

1. Click the Steps button to review basic database terminology and to learn how to manipulate the classic books database. As you proceed through the Steps, answer all of the Quick Check questions that appear. After you complete the Steps, you will see a Quick Check summary report. Follow the instructions on the screen to print this report.

2. Click the Explore button. Make sure you can apply basic database terminology to describe the classic books database by answering the following questions:
   a. How many records does the file contain?
   b. How many fields does each record contain?
   c. What are the contents of the Catalog # field for the book written by Margaret Mitchell?
   d. What are the contents of the Title field for the record with Thoreau in the Author field?
   e. Which field has been used to sort the records?

3. In Explore, manipulate the database as necessary to answer the following questions:
   a. When the books are sorted by title, what is the first record in the file?
   b. Use the Search button to search for all the books in the West location. How many do you find?
   c. Use the Search button to search for all the books in the Main location that are checked in. What do you find?

4. Use the Report button to print out a report that groups the books by Status and sorts them by Title. On your report, circle the four field names. Draw a box around the summary statistics showing which books are currently checked in and which books are currently checked out.

QUICK CHECK ANSWERS

Session 1.1
1. field
2. common field
3. primary key; foreign key
4. records; fields
5. current record symbol
6. Use the horizontal and vertical scroll bars to view fields or records not currently visible in the datasheet; use the navigation buttons to move vertically through the records.

Session 1.2
1. query
2. primary key
3. AutoForm Wizard
4. The form displays each field name on a separate line to the left of its field value, which appears in a box; the widths of the boxes represent the size of the fields.
5. Click the Microsoft Access Help button on any toolbar (or choose Microsoft Access Help or Show the Office Assistant from the Help menu), type a question in the text box, click the Search button, and then choose a topic from the list displayed.
6. Print Preview

TUTORIAL 2

OBJECTIVES

In this tutorial you will:

- Learn the guidelines for designing databases and Access tables
- Create and save a table
- Define fields and specify the primary key
- Add records to a table
- Modify the structure of a table
- Delete, move, and add fields
- Change field properties
- Copy records from another Access database
- Delete and change records

MAINTAINING A DATABASE

Creating, Modifying, and Updating an Order Table

CASE

Valle Coffee

The Restaurant database currently contains only one table—the Customer table—which stores data about Valle Coffee's restaurant customers. Barbara also wants to track information about each order placed by each restaurant customer. This information includes the order's billing date and invoice amount. Barbara asks you to create a second table in the Restaurant database, named Order, in which to store the order data.

Some of the order data Barbara needs is already stored in another Valle Coffee database. After creating the Order table and adding some records to it, you'll copy the records from the other database into the Order table. Then you'll maintain the Order table by modifying it and updating it to meet Barbara's specific data requirements.

SESSION 2.1

In this session, you will learn the guidelines for designing databases and Access tables. You'll also learn how to create a table, define the fields for a table, select the primary key for a table, save the table structure, and add records to a table datasheet.

Guidelines for Designing Databases

A database management system can be a useful tool, but only if you first carefully design the database so that it meets the needs of its users. In database design, you determine the fields, tables, and relationships needed to satisfy the data and processing requirements. When you design a database, you should follow these guidelines:

- **Identify all the fields needed to produce the required information.** For example, Barbara needs information about customers and orders. Figure 2-1 shows the fields that satisfy those information requirements.

Figure 2-1 · BARBARA'S DATA REQUIREMENTS

CustomerName	BillingDate
OrderNum	OwnerName
Street	InvoiceAmt
City	PlacedBy
State	Phone
ZipCode	FirstContact
CustomerNum	

- **Group related fields into tables.** For example, Barbara grouped the fields relating to customers into the Customer table. The other fields are grouped logically into the Order table, which you will create, as shown in Figure 2-2.

Figure 2-2 · BARBARA'S FIELDS GROUPED INTO CUSTOMER AND ORDER TABLES

Customer table	Order table
CustomerNum	OrderNum
CustomerName	BillingDate
Street	PlacedBy
City	InvoiceAmt
State	
ZipCode	
OwnerName	
Phone	
FirstContact	

- **Determine each table's primary key.** Recall that a primary key uniquely identifies each record in a table. Although a primary key is not mandatory in Access, it's usually a good idea to include one in each table. Without a primary key, selecting the exact record you want can be a problem. For some tables, one of the fields, such as a Social Security number or credit card number, naturally serves the function of a primary key. For other tables, two or more fields might be needed to function as the primary key.

In these cases, the primary key is referred to as a **composite key**. For example, a school grade table would use a combination of student number and course code to serve as the primary key. For a third category of tables, no single field or combination of fields can uniquely identify a record in a table. In these cases, you need to add a field whose sole purpose is to serve as the primary key.

For Barbara's tables, CustomerNum is the primary key for the Customer table, and OrderNum will be the primary key for the Order table.

- **Include a common field in related tables.** You use the common field to connect one table logically with another table. For example, Barbara's Customer and Order tables will include the CustomerNum field as a common field. Recall that when you include the primary key from one table as a field in a second table to form a relationship, the field is called a foreign key in the second table; therefore, the CustomerNum field will be a foreign key in the Order table. With this common field, Barbara can find all orders placed by a customer; she can use the CustomerNum value for a customer and search the Order table for all orders with that CustomerNum value. Likewise, she can determine which customer placed a particular order by searching the Customer table to find the one record with the same CustomerNum value as the corresponding value in the Order table.

- **Avoid data redundancy.** Data redundancy occurs when you store the same data in more than one place. With the exception of common fields to connect tables, you should avoid redundancy because it wastes storage space and can cause inconsistencies, if, for instance, you type a field value one way in one table and a different way in the same table or in a second table. Figure 2-3 shows an example of incorrect database design that illustrates data redundancy in the Order table; the Customer Name field is redundant, and one value was entered incorrectly, in three different ways.

Figure 2-3 — INCORRECT DATABASE DESIGN WITH DATA REDUNDANCY

Customer table

Customer Number	Customer Name	Customer Address	Phone Number
104	Meadows Restaurant	Pond Hill Road, Monroe MI 48161	(313) 792-3546
128	Grand River Restaurant	37 Queue Highway, Lacota MI 49063	(313) 729-5364
163	Bentham's Riverfront Restaurant	1366 36th Street, Roscommon MI 48653	(517) 792-8040
635	Oaks Restaurant	3300 West Russell Street, Maumee OH 43537	(419) 336-9000
741	Prime Cut Steakhouse	2819 East 10 Street, Mishawaka IN 46544	(219) 336-0900
779	Gateway Lounge	3408 Gateway Boulevard, Sylvania OH 43560	(419) 361-1137

Order table

Order Number	Customer Number	Customer Name	Billing Date	Invoice Amount
202	104	Meadows Restaurant	01/15/2001	1,280.50
226	635	Oakes Restaurant	01/15/2001	1,939.00
231	779	Gateway Lounge	01/15/2001	1,392.50
309	741	Prime Cut Steakhouse	02/15/2001	1,928.00
313	635	Stokes Inn	02/15/2001	1,545.00
377	128	Grand River Restaurant	03/15/2001	562.00
359	635	Raks Restaurant	03/15/2001	1,939.00
373	779	Gateway Lounge	03/15/2001	1,178.00
395	163	Bentham's Riverfront Restaurant	03/15/2001	1,348.00

inconsistent data

data redundancy

- **Determine the properties of each field.** You need to identify the **properties**, or characteristics, of each field so that the DBMS knows how to store, display, and process the field. These properties include the field's name, maximum number of characters or digits, description, valid values, and other field characteristics. You will learn more about field properties later in this tutorial.

The Order table you need to create will contain the fields shown in Figure 2-2. Before you create the table, you first need to learn some guidelines for designing Access tables.

Guidelines for Designing Access Tables

As just noted, the last step of database design is to determine the properties, such as the name and data type, of each field. Access has rules for naming fields, choosing data types, and defining other properties for fields.

Naming Fields and Objects

You must name each field, table, and other object in an Access database. Access then stores these items in the database, using the names you supply. It's best to choose a field or object name that describes the purpose or contents of the field or object, so that later you can easily remember what the name represents. For example, the two tables in the Restaurant database will be named Customer and Order, because these names suggest their contents.

The following rules apply to naming fields and objects:

- A name can be up to 64 characters long.
- A name can contain letters, numbers, spaces, and special characters, except for a period (.), exclamation mark (!), accent grave (`), and square brackets ([ ]).
- A name cannot start with a space.
- A table or query name must be unique within a database. A field name must be unique within a table, but it can be used again in another table.

In addition, experienced users of databases follow these tips for naming fields and objects:

- Capitalize the first letter of each word in the name.
- Avoid extremely long names because they are difficult to remember and reference.
- Use standard abbreviations, such as Num for Number, Amt for Amount, and Qty for Quantity.
- Do not use spaces in field names because these names will appear in column headings on datasheets and on labels on forms and reports. By not using spaces you'll be able to show more fields on these objects at one time.

Assigning Field Data Types

You must assign a data type for each field. The **data type** determines what field values you can enter for the field and what other properties the field will have. For example, the Order table will include a BillingDate field, so you will assign the date/time data type to this field because it will store date values. Then Access will allow you to enter and manipulate only dates or times as values in the BillingDate field.

Figure 2-4 lists the 10 data types available in Access, describes the field values allowed for each data type, explains when you should use each data type, and indicates the field size of each data type.

Figure 2-4 — DATA TYPES FOR FIELDS

DATA TYPE	DESCRIPTION	FIELD SIZE
Text	Allows field values containing letters, digits, spaces, and special characters. Use for names, addresses, descriptions, and fields containing digits that are not used in calculations.	0 to 255 characters; 50 characters default
Memo	Allows field values containing letters, digits, spaces, and special characters. Use for long comments and explanations.	1 to 64,000 characters; exact size is determined by entry
Number	Allows positive and negative numbers as field values. Numbers can contain digits, a decimal point, commas, a plus sign, and a minus sign. Use for fields that you will use in calculations, except calculations involving money.	1 to 15 digits
Date/Time	Allows field values containing valid dates and times from January 1, 100 to December 31, 9999. Dates can be entered in mm/dd/yy (month, day, year) format, several other date formats, or a variety of time formats such as 10:35 PM. You can perform calculations on dates and times, and you can sort them. For example, you can determine the number of days between two dates.	8 bytes
Currency	Allows field values similar to those for the number data type. Unlike calculations with number data type decimal values, calculations performed using the currency data type are not subject to round-off error.	Accurate to 15 digits on the left side of the decimal separator and to 4 digits on the right side
AutoNumber	Consists of integers with values controlled by Access. Access automatically inserts a value in the field as each new record is created. You can specify sequential numbering or random numbering. This guarantees a unique field value, so that such a field can serve as a table's primary key.	9 digits
Yes/No	Limits field values to yes and no, on and off, or true and false. Use for fields that indicate the presence or absence of a condition, such as whether an order has been filled, or if an employee is eligible for the company dental plan.	1 character
OLE Object	Allows field values that are created in other programs as objects, such as photographs, video images, graphics, drawings, sound recordings, voice-mail messages, spreadsheets, and word-processing documents. These objects can be linked or embedded.	1 gigabyte maximum; exact size depends on object size
Hyperlink	Consists of text or combinations of text and numbers stored as text and used as a hyperlink address. A hyperlink address can have up to three parts: the text that appears in a field or control; the path to a file or page; and a location within the file or page. Hyperlinks help you to connect your application easily to the Internet or an intranet.	Up to 64,000 characters total for the three parts of a hyperlink data type
Lookup Wizard	Creates a field that lets you look up a value in another table or in a predefined list of values.	Same size as the primary key field used to perform the lookup

Assigning Field Sizes

The **field size** property defines a field value's maximum storage size for text, number, and AutoNumber fields only. The other data types have no field size property because their storage size is either a fixed, predetermined amount or is determined automatically by the field value itself, as shown in Figure 2-4. A text field has a default field size of 50 characters; you can also set its field size by entering a number in the range 1 to 255. For example, the OrderNum and CustomerNum fields in the Order table will be text fields with sizes of 3 each.

When you use the number data type to define a field, you should set the field's field size property based on the largest value that you expect to store in that field. Access processes smaller data sizes faster using less memory, so you can optimize your database's performance and its storage space by selecting the correct field size for each field. For example, it would be wasteful to use the Long Integer setting when defining a field that will only store whole numbers ranging from 0 to 255, because the Long Integer setting will use four bytes of storage space. A better choice would be the Byte setting, which uses one byte of storage space to store the same values. Other field size property settings for number fields are:

- **Byte**: Stores whole numbers (numbers with no fractions) from 0 to 255 in one byte
- **Integer**: Stores whole numbers from -32,768 to 32,767 in two bytes
- **Long Integer** (default): Stores whole numbers from -2,147,483,648 to 2,147,483,647 in four bytes
- **Single**: Stores positive and negative numbers to precisely seven decimal places and uses four bytes
- **Double**: Stores positive and negative numbers to precisely 15 decimal places and uses eight bytes
- **Replication ID**: Establishes a unique identifier for replication of tables, records, and other objects and uses 16 bytes
- **Decimal**: Stores positive and negative numbers to precisely 28 decimal places and uses 12 bytes

Barbara documented the design for the Order table by listing each field's name, data type, size (if applicable), and description, as shown in Figure 2-5. Note that Barbara assigned the text data type to the OrderNum field (the table's primary key), to the CustomerNum field (a foreign key to the Customer table), and to the PlacedBy field. BillingDate will have the date/time data type, and InvoiceAmt will have the currency data type.

Figure 2-5 — DESIGN FOR THE ORDER TABLE

Field Name	Data Type	Field Size	Description
OrderNum	Text	3	primary key
CustomerNum	Text	3	foreign key
BillingDate	Date/Time		
PlacedBy	Text	25	person who placed order
InvoiceAmt	Currency		

With Barbara's design, you are ready to create the Order table.

Creating a Table

Creating a table consists of naming the fields and defining the properties for the fields, specifying a primary key (and a foreign key, if applicable) for the table, and then saving the table structure. You will use Barbara's design (Figure 2-5) as a guide for creating the Order table. First, you need to open the Restaurant database.

TUTORIAL 2 MAINTAINING A DATABASE   AC 2.07

To open the Restaurant database:

1. Place your Data Disk in the appropriate disk drive.

2. Start Access. The Access window opens with the initial dialog box.

3. Make sure that the **Open an existing file** option button and the **More Files** option are selected, and then click the **OK** button to display the Open dialog box.

4. Click the **Look in** list arrow, and then click the drive that contains your Data Disk.

5. Click **Tutorial** in the list box, and then click the **Open** button to display a list of the files in the Tutorial folder.

6. Click **Restaurant** in the list box, and then click the **Open** button. The Restaurant database opens in the Access window.

7. Make sure that **Tables** is selected in the Objects bar of the Database window.

The Customer table is listed in the Tables list box. Now you'll create the Order table in the Restaurant database.

To begin creating the Order table:

1. Click the **New** button in the Database window. The New Table dialog box opens. See Figure 2-6.

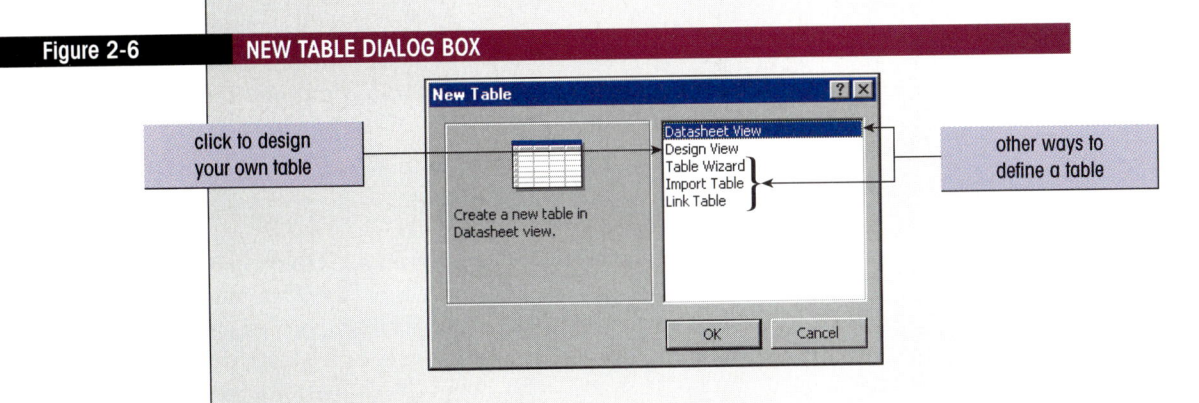

Figure 2-6   NEW TABLE DIALOG BOX

click to design your own table

other ways to define a table

In Access, you can create a table from entered data (Datasheet View), define your own table (Design View), use a Wizard to automate the table creation process (Table Wizard), or use a Wizard to import or link data from another database or other data source (Import Table or Link Table). For the Order table, you will define your own table.

2. Click **Design View** in the list box, and then click the **OK** button. The Table window opens in Design view. See Figure 2-7.

ACCESS   AC 2.08   TUTORIAL 2   MAINTAINING A DATABASE

Figure 2-7 TABLE WINDOW IN DESIGN VIEW

- Table window menu bar
- Table Design toolbar
- current row symbol
- other field properties will appear here
- default table name
- row selectors
- Table window Maximize button
- Table Design grid
- Help for using the current property

Note that you could have double-clicked the option "Create table in Design view" in the Database window to open the Table window in Design view.

You use Design view to define or modify a table structure or the properties of the fields in a table. If you create a table without using a Wizard, you enter the fields and their properties for your table directly in this window.

Defining Fields

Initially, the default table name, Table1, appears on the Table window title bar, the current row symbol is positioned in the first row selector of the Table Design grid, and the insertion point is located in the first row's Field Name box. The purpose or characteristics of the current property (Field Name, in this case) appear in the lower-right section of the Table window. You can display more complete information about the current property by pressing the F1 key.

You enter values for the Field Name, Data Type, and Description field properties in the upper half of the Table window. You select values for all other field properties, most of which are optional, in the lower half of the window. These other properties will appear when you move to the first row's Data Type text box.

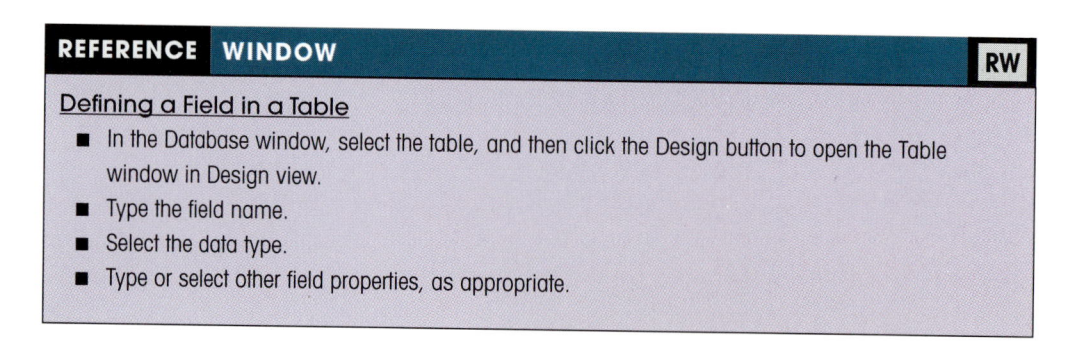

REFERENCE WINDOW   RW

Defining a Field in a Table
- In the Database window, select the table, and then click the Design button to open the Table window in Design view.
- Type the field name.
- Select the data type.
- Type or select other field properties, as appropriate.

The first field you need to define is OrderNum.

To define the OrderNum field:

1. Type **OrderNum** in the first row's Field Name text box, and then press the **Tab** key (or press the **Enter** key) to advance to the Data Type text box. The default data type, Text, appears highlighted in the Data Type text box, which now also contains a list arrow, and field properties for a text field appear in the lower half of the window. See Figure 2-8.

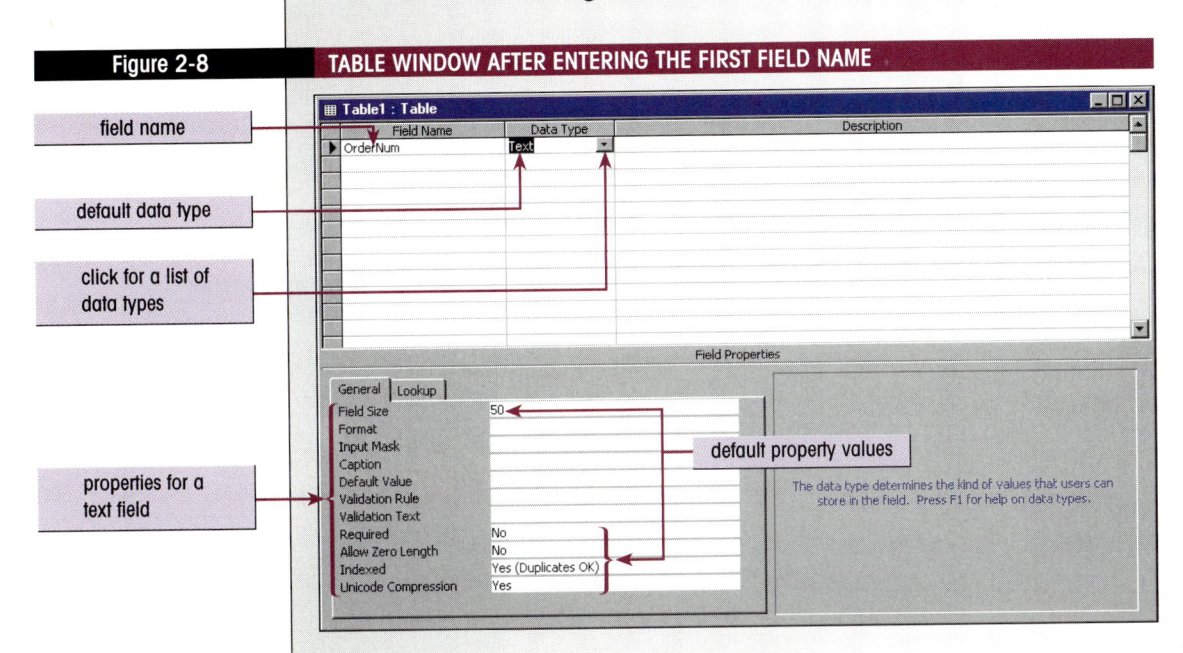

Figure 2-8   TABLE WINDOW AFTER ENTERING THE FIRST FIELD NAME

- field name
- default data type
- click for a list of data types
- properties for a text field
- default property values

Notice that the lower-right section of the window now provides an explanation for the current property, Data Type.

TROUBLE? If you make a typing error, you can correct it by clicking the mouse to position the insertion point, and then using either the Backspace key to delete characters to the left of the insertion point or the Delete key to delete characters to the right of the insertion point. Then type the correct text.

Because order numbers will not be used for calculations, you will assign the text data type to the OrderNum field instead of the number data type, and then enter the Description property value as "primary key." You can use the Description property to enter an optional description for a field to explain its purpose or usage. A field's Description property can be up to 255 characters long, and its value appears in the status bar when you view the table datasheet.

2. Press the **Tab** key to accept Text as the field's data type and move to the Description text box, and then type **primary key** in the Description text box.

The Field Size property has a default value of 50, which you will change to a value of 3, because order numbers at Valle Coffee contain three digits. When you select or enter a value for a property, you *set* the property. The Required property has a default value of No, which means that a value does not need to be entered for the field. Because Barbara doesn't want an order entered without an order number, you will change the Required property to Yes. (Refer to the Access Help system for a complete description of all the properties available for the different data types.)

3. Select **50** in the Field Size text box either by dragging the pointer or double-clicking the mouse, and then type **3**.

4. Click the **Required** text box to position the insertion point there. A list arrow appears on the right side of the Required text box.

5. Click the **Required** list arrow. Access displays the Required list box. See Figure 2-9.

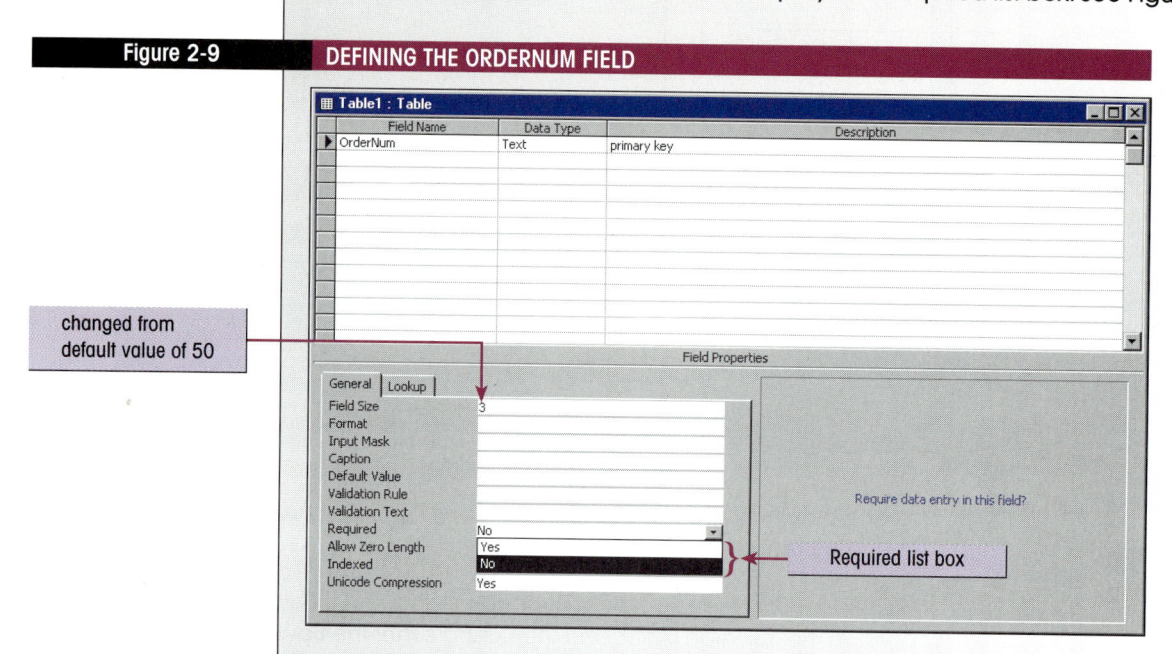

Figure 2-9   DEFINING THE ORDERNUM FIELD

changed from default value of 50

Required list box

When you position the insertion point or select text in many Access text boxes, Access displays a list arrow, which you can click to display a list box with options. You can display the list arrow and the list box simultaneously if you click the text box near its right side.

6. Click **Yes** in the list box. The list box closes, and Yes is now the value for the Required property. The definition of the first field is complete.

Barbara's Order table design shows CustomerNum as the second field. You will define CustomerNum as a text field with a Description of "foreign key" and a Field Size of 3, because customer numbers at Valle Coffee contain three digits. Because it's possible that a record for an order might need to be entered for a customer not yet added to the database, Barbara asks you to leave the Required property at its default value of No.

To define the CustomerNum field:

1. Place the insertion point in the second row's Field Name text box, type **CustomerNum** in the text box, and then press the **Tab** key to advance to the Data Type text box.

   Customer numbers are not used in calculations, so you'll assign the text data type to the field, and then enter its Description value as "foreign key."

2. Press the **Tab** key to accept Text as the field's data type and to move to the Description text box, and then type **foreign key** in the Description text box.

   Next, you'll change the Field Size property to 3. Note that when defining the fields in a table, you can move between the top and bottom panes of the table window by pressing the F6 key.

3. Press the **F6** key to move to the bottom pane (Field Properties). The current entry for the Field Size property, 50, is highlighted.

4. Type **3** to set the Field Size property. You have completed the definition of the second field. See Figure 2-10.

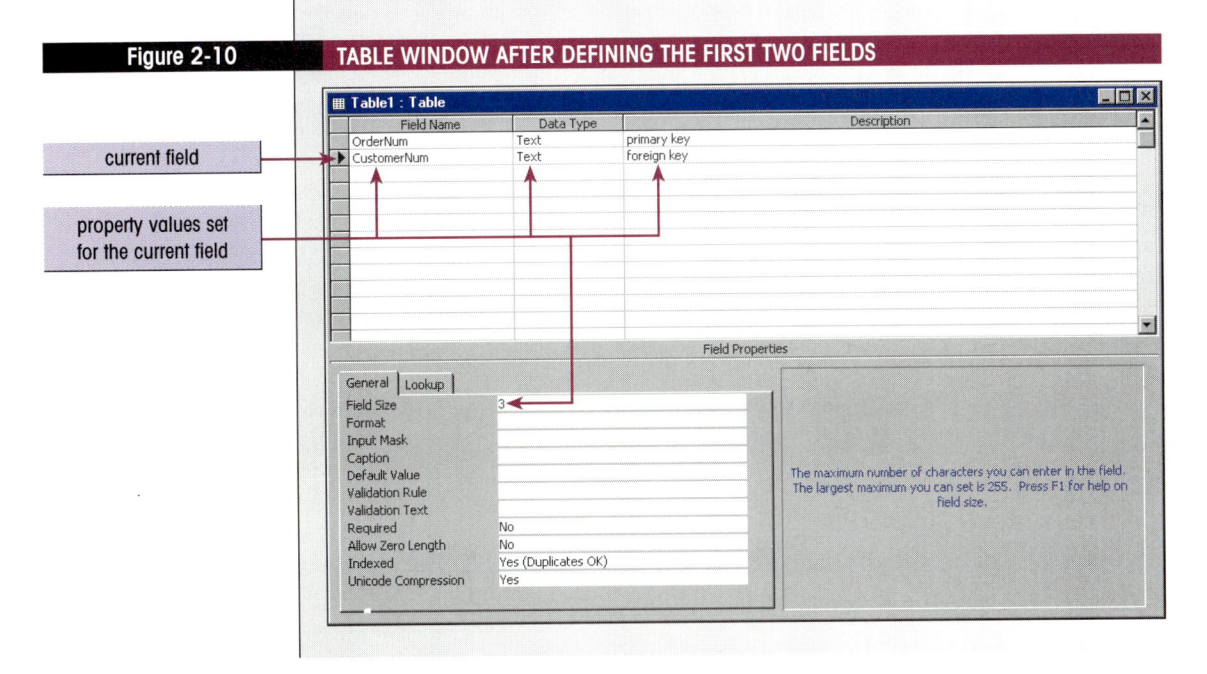

Figure 2-10   TABLE WINDOW AFTER DEFINING THE FIRST TWO FIELDS

Field Name	Data Type	Description
OrderNum	Text	primary key
CustomerNum	Text	foreign key

current field

property values set for the current field

Field Properties

General | Lookup

Field Size: 3
Format:
Input Mask:
Caption:
Default Value:
Validation Rule:
Validation Text:
Required: No
Allow Zero Length: No
Indexed: Yes (Duplicates OK)
Unicode Compression: Yes

The maximum number of characters you can enter in the field. The largest maximum you can set is 255. Press F1 for help on field size.

Using Barbara's Order table design in Figure 2-5, you can now complete the remaining field definitions: BillingDate with the date/time data type, PlacedBy with the text data type, and InvoiceAmt with the currency data type.

To define the BillingDate field:

1. Place the insertion point in the third row's Field Name text box, type **BillingDate** in the text box, and then press the **Tab** key to advance to the Data Type text box.

2. Click the **Data Type** list arrow, click **Date/Time** in the list box, and then press the **Tab** key to advance to the Description text box.

If you've assigned a descriptive field name and the field does not fulfill a special function (such as primary key), you usually do not enter a value for the optional Description property. BillingDate is a field that does not require a value for its Description property.

Barbara wants the values in the BillingDate field to be displayed in a format showing the month, day, and year as in the following example: 01/15/2001. You use the Format property to control the display of a field value.

3. In the Field Properties section, click the right side of the **Format** text box to display the list of predefined formats. As noted in the right section of the window, you can either choose a predefined format or enter a custom format.

    TROUBLE? If you see a list arrow instead of a list of predefined formats, click the list arrow to display the list.

    None of the predefined formats matches the layout Barbara wants for the BillingDate values. Therefore, you need to create a custom date format. Figure 2-11 shows some of the symbols available for custom date and time formats. (A complete description of all the custom formats is available in Help.)

Figure 2-11

SYMBOLS FOR SOME CUSTOM DATE FORMATS

SYMBOL	DESCRIPTION
/	date separator
d	day of the month in one or two numeric digits, as needed (1 to 31)
dd	day of the month in two numeric digits (01 to 31)
ddd	first three letters of the weekday (Sun to Sat)
dddd	full name of the weekday (Sunday to Saturday)
w	day of the week (1 to 7)
ww	week of the year (1 to 53)
m	month of the year in one or two numeric digits, as needed (1 to 12)
mm	month of the year in two numeric digits (01 to 12)
mmm	first three letters of the month (Jan to Dec)
mmmm	full name of the month (January to December)
yy	last two digits of the year (01 to 99)
yyyy	full year (0100 to 9999)

Barbara wants the dates to be displayed with a two-digit month (mm), a two-digit day (dd), and a four-digit year (yyyy). You'll enter this custom format now.

4. Click the **Format** list arrow to close the list of predefined formats, and then type **mm/dd/yyyy** in the Format text box. See Figure 2-12.

TUTORIAL 2 MAINTAINING A DATABASE   AC 2.13   **ACCESS**

Figure 2-12   SPECIFYING THE CUSTOM DATE FORMAT

current field

custom date format entered

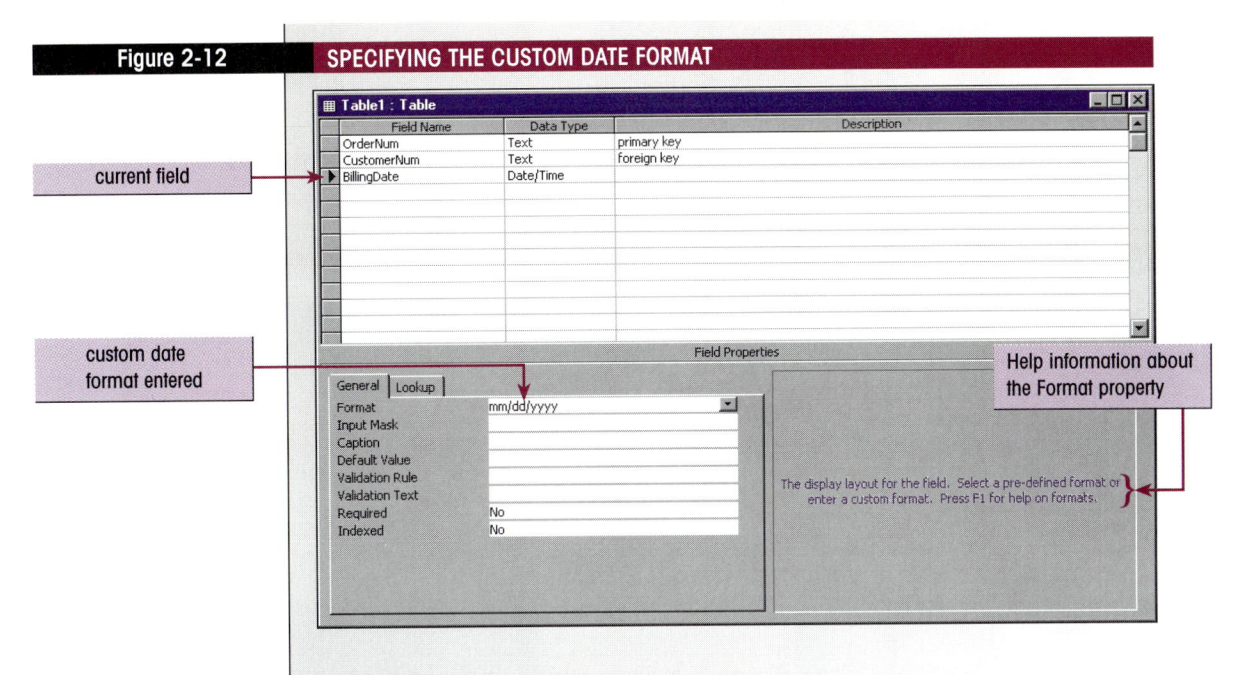

Help information about the Format property

Barbara does not want to require that a value be entered for the BillingDate field, so you have completed the definition of the field.

Now you're ready to finish the Order table design by defining the PlacedBy and InvoiceAmt fields.

To define the PlacedBy and InvoiceAmt fields:

1. Place the insertion point in the fourth row's Field Name text box.

2. Type **PlacedBy** in the Field Name text box, and then press the **Tab** key to advance to the Data Type text box.

   This field will contain names, so you'll assign the text data type to it. Also, Barbara wants to include the description "person who placed order" to clarify the contents of the field.

3. Press the **Tab** key to accept Text as the field's data type and to move to the Description text box, and then type **person who placed order** in the Description text box.

   Next, you'll change the Field Size property's default value of 50 to 25, which should be long enough to accommodate all names.

4. Press the **F6** key to move to and select 50 in the Field Size text box, and then type **25**.

   The definition of the PlacedBy field is complete. Next, you'll define the fifth and final field, InvoiceAmt. This field will contain dollar amounts, so you'll assign the currency data type to it.

5. Place the insertion point in the fifth row's Field Name text box.

6. Type **InvoiceAmt** in the Field Name text box, and then press the **Tab** key to advance to the Data Type text box.

You can select a value from the Data Type list box as you did for the BillingDate field. Alternatively, you can type the property value in the text box or type just the first character of the property value.

7. Type **c**. The value in the fifth row's Data Type text box changes to "currency," with the letters "urrency" highlighted. See Figure 2-13.

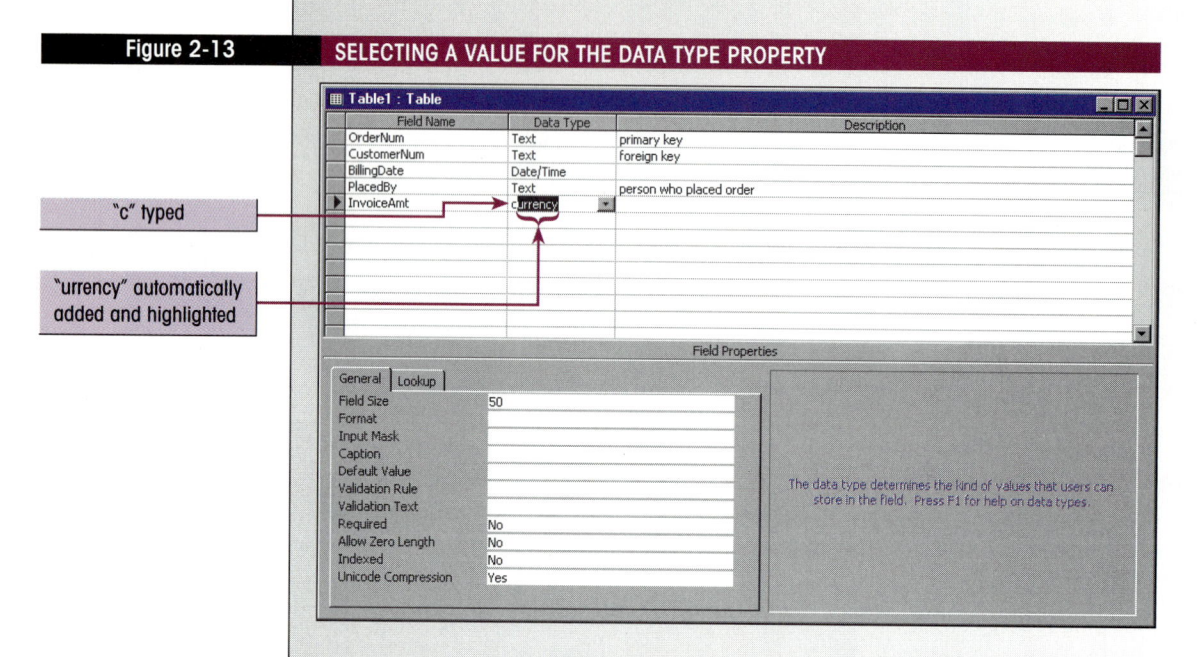

Figure 2-13   SELECTING A VALUE FOR THE DATA TYPE PROPERTY

"c" typed

"urrency" automatically added and highlighted

8. Press the **Tab** key to advance to the Description text box. Access changes the value for the Data Type property to Currency.

In the Field Properties section, notice the default values for the Format, Decimal Places, and Default Value properties. For a field with a Format property value of Currency, two decimal places are provided when the Decimal Places property value is set to Auto. These properties, combined with the Default Value property of 0, specify that values in the InvoiceAmt field will initially appear as follows: $0.00. This is the format Barbara wants for the InvoiceAmt field, so you are finished defining the fields for the Order table.

Next, you need to specify the primary key for the Order table.

Specifying the Primary Key

Although Access does not require a table to have a primary key, including a primary key offers several advantages:

- A primary key uniquely identifies each record in a table.
- Access does not allow duplicate values in the primary key field. If a record already exists with an OrderNum value of 143, for example, Access prevents you from adding another record with this same value in the OrderNum field. Preventing duplicate values ensures the uniqueness of the primary key field and helps to avoid data redundancy.

- Access forces you to enter a value for the primary key field in every record in the table. This is known as **entity integrity**. If you do not enter a value for a field, you have actually given the field what is known as a **null value**. You cannot give a null value to the primary key field because entity integrity prevents Access from accepting and processing that record.
- Access stores records on disk in the same order as you enter them but displays them in order by the field values of the primary key. If you enter records in no specific order, you are ensured that you will later be able to work with them in a more meaningful, primary key sequence.
- Access responds faster to your requests for specific records based on the primary key.

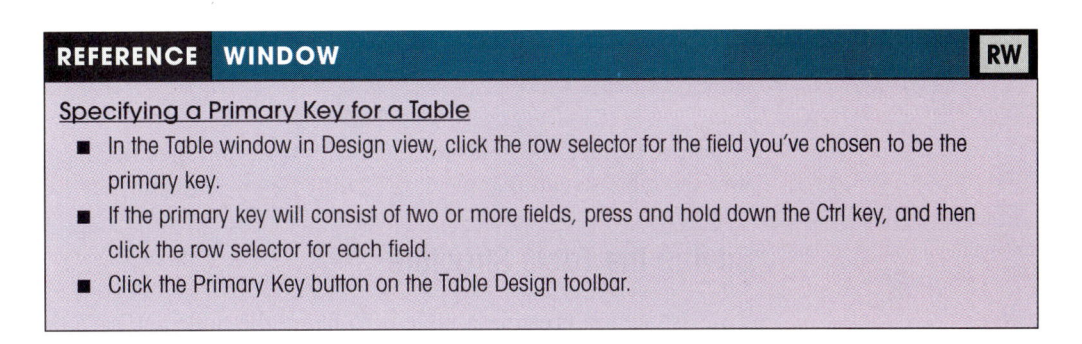

REFERENCE WINDOW

Specifying a Primary Key for a Table
- In the Table window in Design view, click the row selector for the field you've chosen to be the primary key.
- If the primary key will consist of two or more fields, press and hold down the Ctrl key, and then click the row selector for each field.
- Click the Primary Key button on the Table Design toolbar.

According to Barbara's design, you need to specify OrderNum as the primary key for the Order table.

To specify OrderNum as the primary key:

1. Position the pointer on the row selector for the OrderNum field until the pointer changes to ➡. See Figure 2-14.

Figure 2-14   SPECIFYING ORDERNUM AS THE PRIMARY KEY

Labels: Primary Key button, pointer, row selector

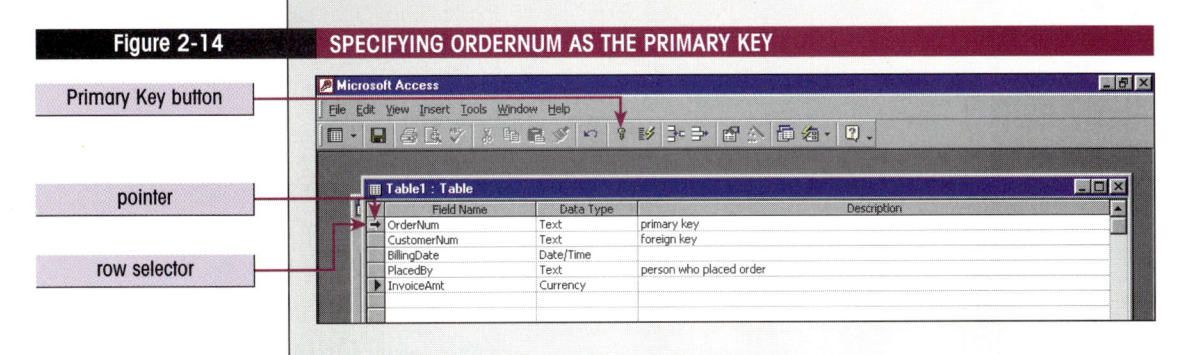

2. Click the mouse button. The entire first row of the Table Design grid is highlighted.

3. Click the **Primary Key** button on the Table Design toolbar, and then click to the right of InvoiceAmt in the fifth row's Field Name text box to deselect the first row. A key symbol appears in the row selector for the first row, indicating that the OrderNum field is the table's primary key. See Figure 2-15.

ACCESS   AC 2.16   TUTORIAL 2   MAINTAINING A DATABASE

| Figure 2-15 | ORDERNUM SELECTED AS THE PRIMARY KEY |

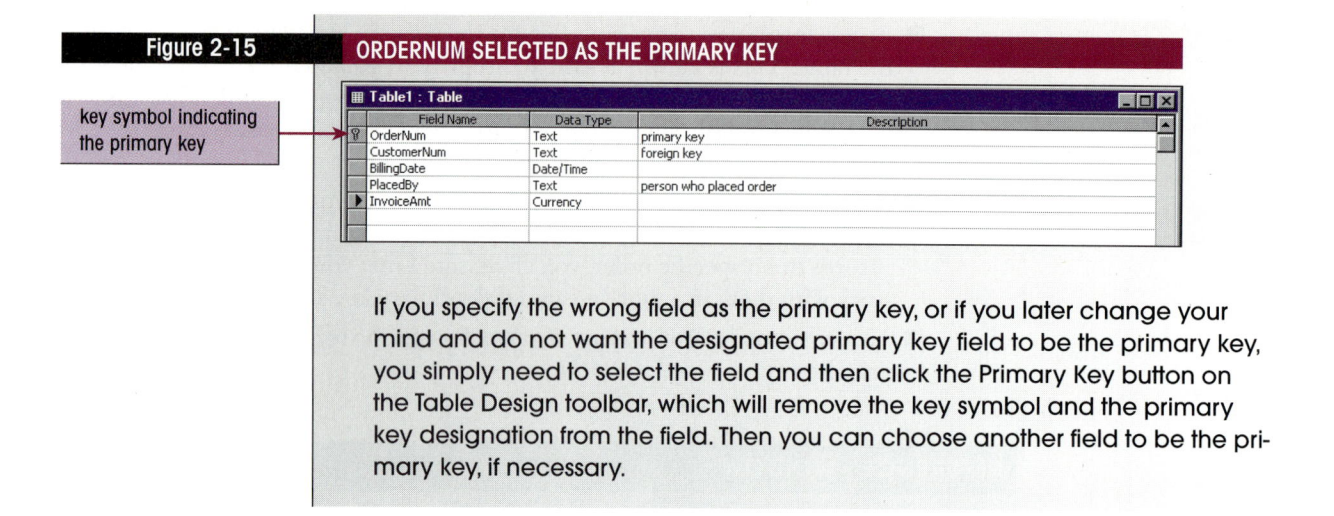

key symbol indicating the primary key

Field Name	Data Type	Description
OrderNum	Text	primary key
CustomerNum	Text	foreign key
BillingDate	Date/Time	
PlacedBy	Text	person who placed order
InvoiceAmt	Currency	

If you specify the wrong field as the primary key, or if you later change your mind and do not want the designated primary key field to be the primary key, you simply need to select the field and then click the Primary Key button on the Table Design toolbar, which will remove the key symbol and the primary key designation from the field. Then you can choose another field to be the primary key, if necessary.

You've defined the fields for the Order table and specified its primary key, so you can now save the table structure.

Saving the Table Structure

The last step in creating a table is to name the table and save the table's structure on disk. Once the table is saved, you can use it to enter data in the table.

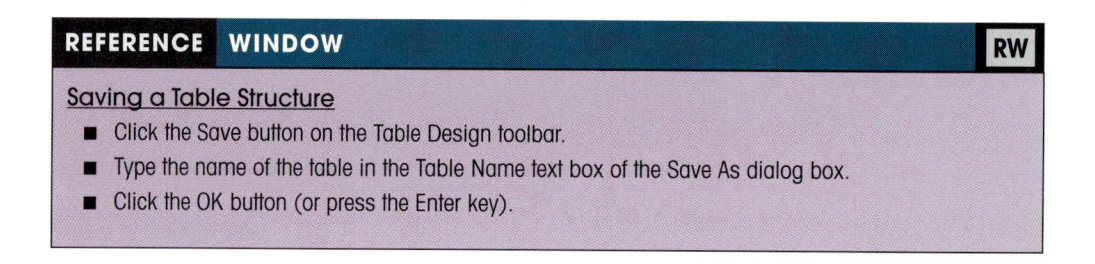

REFERENCE WINDOW   RW

Saving a Table Structure
- Click the Save button on the Table Design toolbar.
- Type the name of the table in the Table Name text box of the Save As dialog box.
- Click the OK button (or press the Enter key).

You need to save the table you've defined as "Order."

To name and save the Order table:

1. Click the **Save** button on the Table Design toolbar. The Save As dialog box opens.

2. Type **Order** in the Table Name text box, and then press the **Enter** key. Access saves the table with the name Order in the Restaurant database on your Data Disk. Notice that Order appears instead of Table1 in the Table window title bar.

Next, Barbara asks you to add the two records shown in Figure 2-16 to the Order table. These two records contain data for orders that two customers recently placed with Valle Coffee.

| Figure 2-16 | RECORDS TO BE ADDED TO THE ORDER TABLE |

OrderNum	CustomerNum	BillingDate	PlacedBy	InvoiceAmt
323	624	02/15/2001	Isabelle Rouy	$1,986.00
201	107	01/15/2001	Matt Gellman	$854.00

Adding Records to a Table

You can add records to an Access table in several ways. A table datasheet provides a simple way for you to add records. As you learned in Tutorial 1, a datasheet shows a table's contents in rows and columns. Each row is a separate record in the table, and each column contains the field values for one field in the table. To view a table datasheet, you first must change from Design view to Datasheet view.

You'll switch to Datasheet view and add the two records in the Order table datasheet.

To add the records in the Order table datasheet:

1. Click the **View** button for Datasheet view on the Table Design toolbar. The Table window opens in Datasheet view. See Figure 2-17.

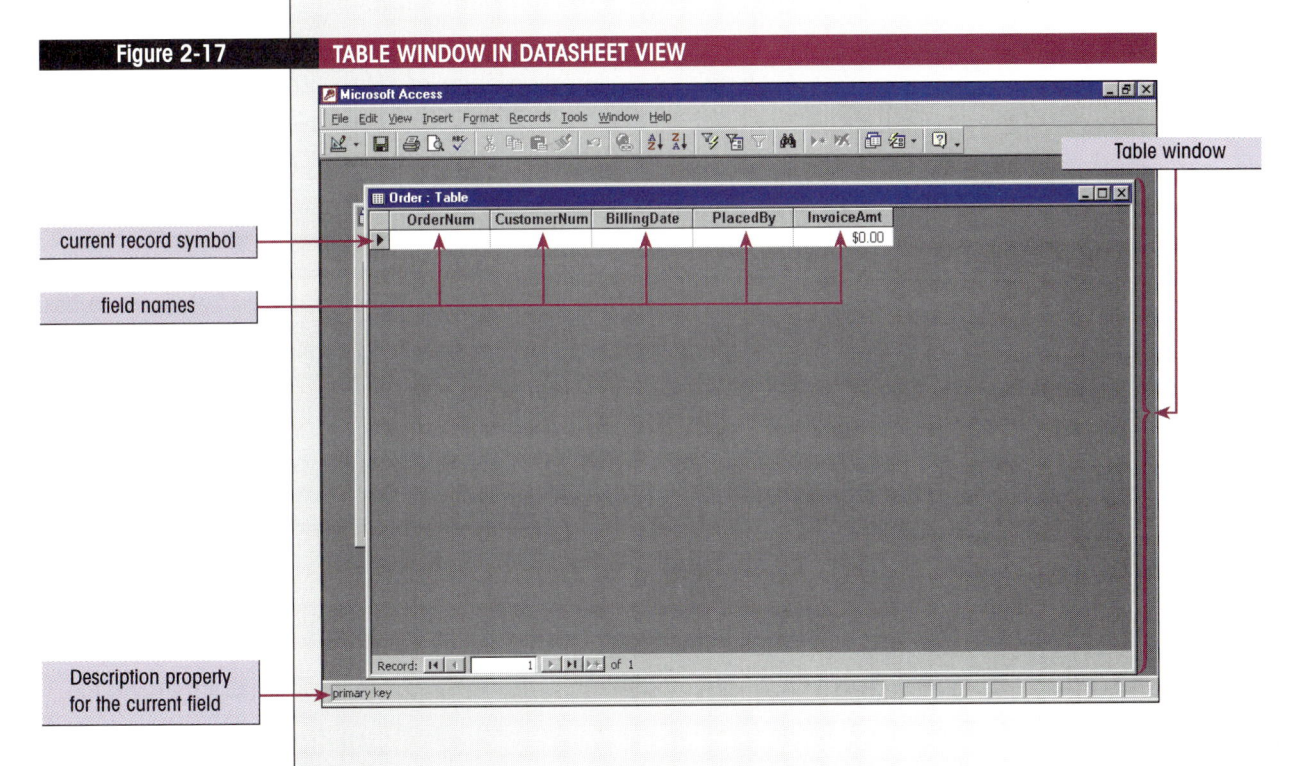

| Figure 2-17 | TABLE WINDOW IN DATASHEET VIEW |

The table's five field names appear at the top of the datasheet. The current record symbol in the first row's record selector identifies the currently selected record, which contains no data until you enter the first record. The insertion point is located in the first row's OrderNum field, whose Description property appears in the status bar.

2. Type **323**, which is the first record's OrderNum field value, and then press the **Tab** key. Each time you press the Tab key, the insertion point moves to the right to the next field in the record. See Figure 2-18.

Figure 2-18 | **DATASHEET FOR ORDER TABLE AFTER ENTERING THE FIRST FIELD VALUE**

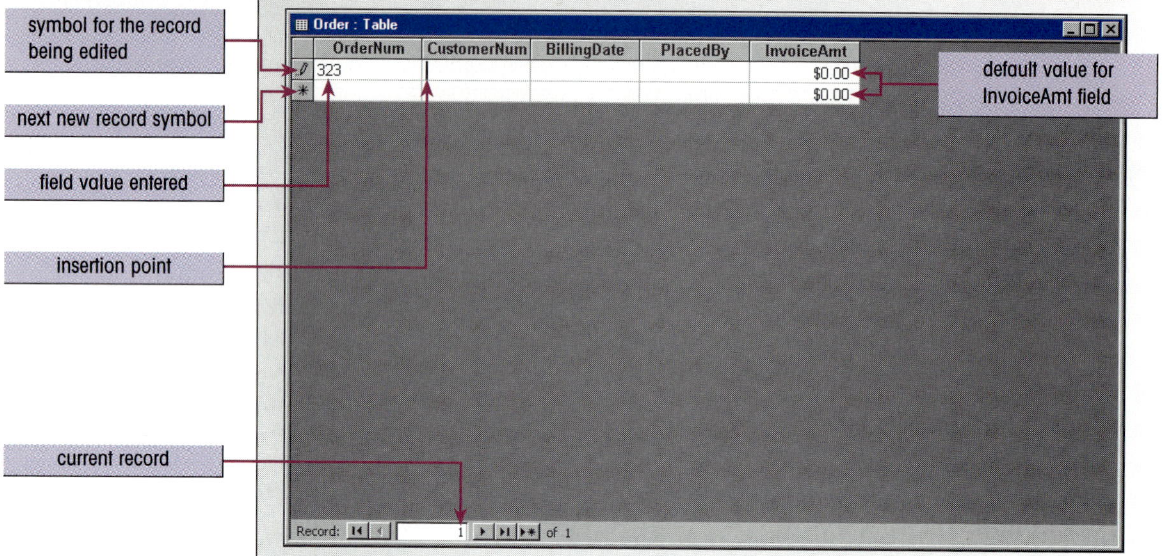

- symbol for the record being edited
- next new record symbol
- field value entered
- insertion point
- current record
- default value for InvoiceAmt field

> **TROUBLE?** If you make a mistake when typing a value, use the Backspace key to delete characters to the left of the insertion point, or the Delete key to delete characters to the right of the insertion point. Then type the correct text. If you want to correct a value by replacing it entirely, double-click the value to select it, and then type the correct value.

The pencil symbol in the first row's record selector indicates that the record is being edited. The star symbol in the second row's record selector identifies the second row as the next one available for a new record. The InvoiceAmt column displays "$0.00," the default value for the field, as specified by the field's properties.

3. Type **624** and then press the **Tab** key. The insertion point moves to the right side of the BillingDate field.

Recall that you specified a custom format for the BillingDate field, mm/dd/yyyy. However, when you enter the digits for the year, you only need to enter the final two digits; you do not have to enter all four digits. For example, for a field value containing the year 1999, you only need to enter "99" and Access will store and automatically display the full four digits, as specified by the custom format.

4. Type **02/15/01** and then press the **Tab** key. Access displays the BillingDate field value as "02/15/2001" and the insertion point moves to the PlacedBy field.

5. Type **Isabelle Rouy** and then press the **Tab** key. The insertion point moves to the InvoiceAmt field, whose field value is highlighted.

Notice that field values for text fields are left-aligned in their boxes, and field values for date/time and currency fields are right-aligned in their boxes. If the default value of $0.00 is correct for the InvoiceAmt field, you can press the Tab key to accept the value and advance to the beginning of the next record. Otherwise, type the field value for the InvoiceAmt field. You do not need to type the dollar sign, commas, or decimal point (for whole dollar amounts) because Access adds these symbols automatically for you.

6. Type **1986** and then press the **Tab** key. Access displays $1,986.00 for the InvoiceAmt field, stores the first completed record in the Order table, removes the pencil symbol from the first row's record selector, advances the insertion point to the second row's OrderNum text box, and places the current record symbol in the second row's record selector.

Now you can enter the values for the second record.

7. Type **201** in the OrderNum field, press the **Tab** key to move to the CustomerNum field, type **107** in the CustomerNum field, and then press the **Tab** key. The insertion point moves to the right side of the BillingDate field.

8. Type **01/15/01** and then press the **Tab** key. The insertion point moves to the PlacedBy field.

9. Type **Matt Gellman** and then press the **Tab** key. The value in the InvoiceAmt field is now highlighted.

10. Type **854** and then press the **Tab** key. Access changes the InvoiceAmt field value to $854.00, saves the record in the Order table, and moves the insertion point to the beginning of the third row. See Figure 2-19.

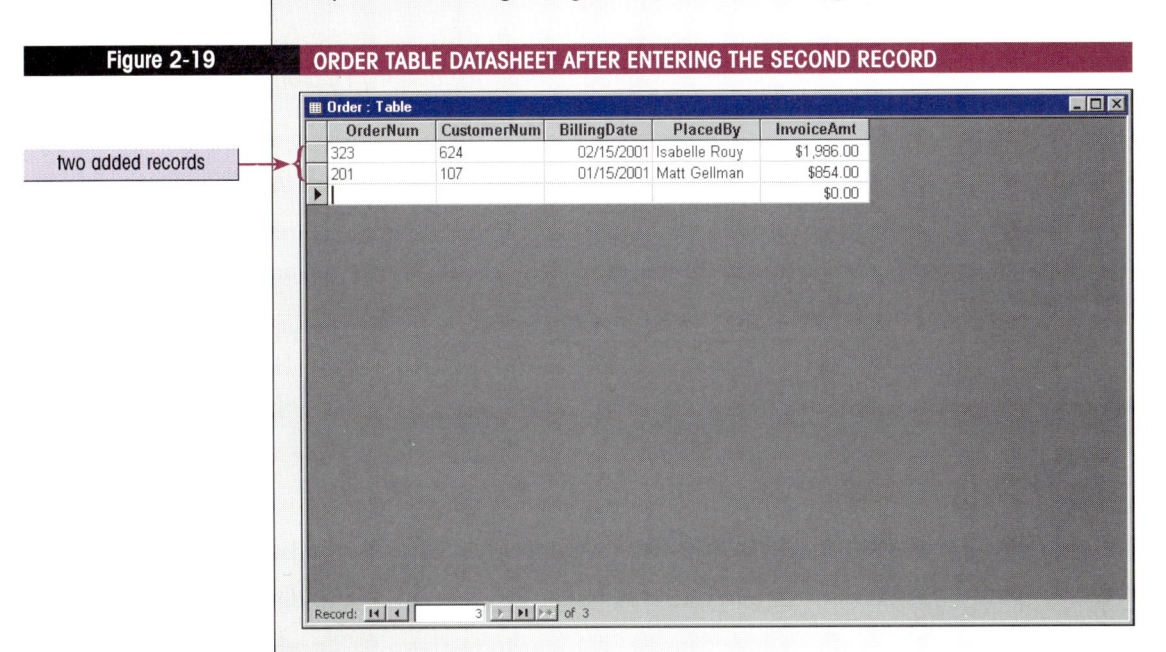

Figure 2-19   **ORDER TABLE DATASHEET AFTER ENTERING THE SECOND RECORD**

two added records

OrderNum	CustomerNum	BillingDate	PlacedBy	InvoiceAmt
323	624	02/15/2001	Isabelle Rouy	$1,986.00
201	107	01/15/2001	Matt Gellman	$854.00
				$0.00

Record: 3 of 3

Notice that "Record 3 of 3" appears around the navigation buttons, even though the table contains only two records. Access is anticipating that you will enter a new record, which would be the third of three records in the table. If you moved the insertion point to the second record, the display would change to "Record 2 of 2."

Even though the Order table contains only two records, Barbara asks you to print the table datasheet so that she can bring it with her to a staff meeting. She wants to show the table design to her staff members to make sure that it will meet their needs for tracking order data.

You'll use the Print button on the Table Datasheet toolbar to print one copy of the Order table with the current settings.

> ### To print the Order table:
>
> **1.** Click the **Print** button 🖨 on the Table Datasheet toolbar.
>
> Notice that the two records are currently listed in the order in which you entered them. However, once you close the table or change to another view, and then redisplay the table datasheet, the records will be listed in primary key order by the values in the OrderNum field.

You have created the Order table in the Restaurant database and added two records to the table, which Access saved automatically to the database on your Data Disk.

Saving a Database

Notice the Save button on the Table Datasheet toolbar. This Save button, unlike the Save buttons in other Windows programs, does not save the active document (database) to your disk. Instead, you use the Save button to save the design of a table, query, form, or report, or to save datasheet format changes. Access does not have a button or option you can use to save the active database.

Access saves the active database to your disk automatically, both on a periodic basis and whenever you close the database. This means that if your database is stored on a disk in drive A, you should never remove the disk while the database file is open. If you do remove the disk, Access will encounter problems when it tries to save the database, which might damage the database.

The Order table is now complete. In Session 2.2, you'll continue to work with the Order table by modifying its structure and entering and maintaining data in the table.

Session 2.1 QUICK CHECK

1. What guidelines should you follow when you design a database?
2. What is the purpose of the data type property for a field?
3. For which three types of fields can you assign a field size?
4. Why did you define the OrderNum field as a text field instead of a number field?
5. A(n) _____ value, which results when you do not enter a value for a field, is not permitted for a primary key.
6. What does a pencil symbol in a datasheet's row selector represent? A star symbol?

SESSION 2.2

In this session, you will modify the structure of a table by deleting, moving, and adding fields and changing field properties; copy records from another Access database; and update a database by deleting and changing records.

Modifying the Structure of an Access Table

Even a well-designed table might need to be modified. For example, the government at all levels and the competition place demands on a company to track more data and to modify the data it already tracks. Access allows you to modify a table's structure in Design view: you can add and delete fields, change the order of fields, and change the properties of the fields.

After meeting with her staff members and reviewing the structure of the Order table and the format of the field values in the datasheet, Barbara has several changes she wants you to make to the table. First, she has decided that it's not necessary to keep track of the name of the person who placed a particular order, so she wants you to delete the PlacedBy field. Also, she thinks that the InvoiceAmt field should remain a currency field, but she wants the dollar signs removed from the displayed field values in the datasheet. She also wants the BillingDate field moved to the end of the table. Finally, she wants you to add a yes/no field, named Paid, to the table to indicate whether or not the customer has paid for the order. The Paid field will be inserted between the CustomerNum and InvoiceAmt fields. Figure 2-20 shows Barbara's modified design for the Order table.

Figure 2-20   **MODIFIED DESIGN FOR THE ORDER TABLE**

Field Name	Data Type	Field Size	Description
OrderNum	Text	3	primary key
CustomerNum	Text	3	foreign key
Paid	Yes/No		
InvoiceAmt	Currency		
BillingDate	Date/Time		

You'll begin modifying the table by deleting the PlacedBy field.

Deleting a Field

After you've defined a table structure and added records to the table, you can delete a field from the table structure. When you delete a field, you also delete all the values for the field from the table. Therefore, you should make sure that you need to delete a field and that you delete the correct field.

REFERENCE WINDOW   **RW**

Deleting a Field from a Table Structure

- In the Table window in Design view, right-click the row selector for the field you want to delete, to select the field and display the shortcut menu.
- Click Delete Rows on the shortcut menu.

You need to delete the PlacedBy field from the Order table structure.

To delete the PlacedBy field:

1. If you took a break after the previous session, make sure that Access is running and that the Order table of the Restaurant database is open.

2. Click the **View** button for Design view on the Table Datasheet toolbar. The Table window for the Order table opens in Design view.

3. Position the pointer on the row selector for the PlacedBy field until the pointer changes to ➡.

4. Right-click to select the entire row for the field and display the shortcut menu, and then click **Delete Rows**.

   A dialog box opens asking you to confirm the deletion.

5. Click the **Yes** button to close the dialog box and to delete the field and its values from the table. See Figure 2-21.

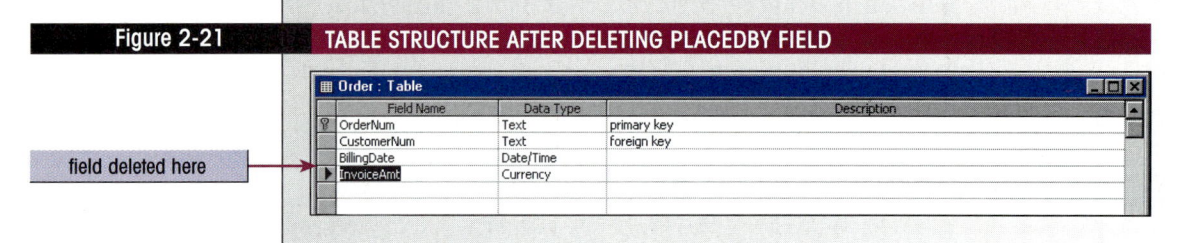

Figure 2-21   **TABLE STRUCTURE AFTER DELETING PLACEDBY FIELD**

Field Name	Data Type	Description
OrderNum	Text	primary key
CustomerNum	Text	foreign key
BillingDate	Date/Time	
InvoiceAmt	Currency	

field deleted here

You have deleted the PlacedBy field in the Table window, but the change doesn't take place in the table on disk until you save the table structure. Because you have other modifications to make to the table, you'll wait until you finish them all before saving the modified table structure to disk.

Moving a Field

To move a field, you use the mouse to drag it to a new location in the Table window in Design view. Your next modification to the Order table structure is to move the BillingDate field to the end of the table, as Barbara requested.

To move the BillingDate field:

1. Click the **row selector** for the BillingDate field to select the entire row.

2. Place the pointer in the row selector for the BillingDate field, click the pointer, and then drag the pointer to the row selector below the InvoiceAmt row selector. See Figure 2-22.

TUTORIAL 2 MAINTAINING A DATABASE   AC 2.23   ACCESS

| Figure 2-22 | MOVING A FIELD IN THE TABLE STRUCTURE |

selected field

position the move pointer in this row selector

Field Name	Data Type	Description
OrderNum	Text	primary key
CustomerNum	Text	foreign key
BillingDate	Date/Time	
InvoiceAmt	Currency	

move pointer

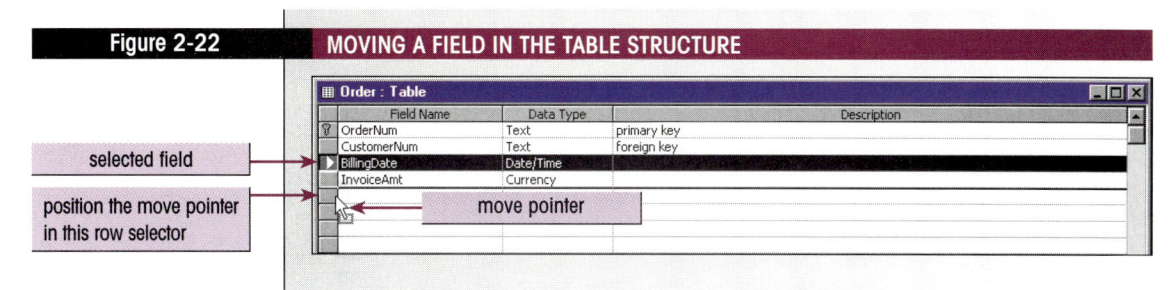

3. **Release** the mouse button. Access moves the BillingDate field below the InvoiceAmt field in the table structure.

   TROUBLE? If the BillingDate field did not move, repeat Steps 1 through 3, making sure you firmly hold down the mouse button during the drag operation.

Adding a Field

Next, you need to add the Paid field to the table structure between the CustomerNum and InvoiceAmt fields. To add a new field between existing fields, you must insert a row. You begin by selecting the field that will be below the new field you want to insert.

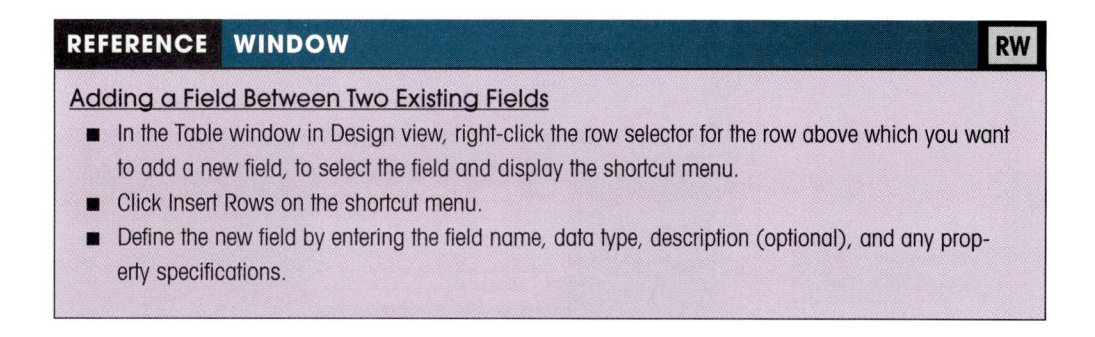

REFERENCE WINDOW   RW

Adding a Field Between Two Existing Fields
- In the Table window in Design view, right-click the row selector for the row above which you want to add a new field, to select the field and display the shortcut menu.
- Click Insert Rows on the shortcut menu.
- Define the new field by entering the field name, data type, description (optional), and any property specifications.

To add the Paid field to the Order table:

1. Right-click the **row selector** for the InvoiceAmt field to select this field and display the shortcut menu, and then click **Insert Rows**. Access adds a new, blank row between the CustomerNum and InvoiceAmt fields. See Figure 2-23.

| Figure 2-23 | AFTER INSERTING A ROW IN THE TABLE STRUCTURE |

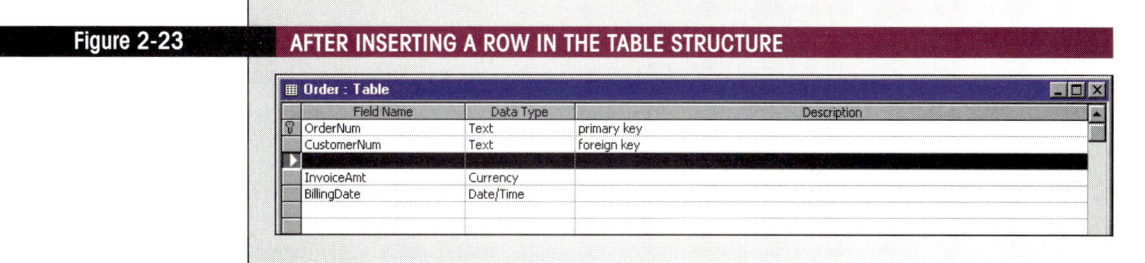

Field Name	Data Type	Description
OrderNum	Text	primary key
CustomerNum	Text	foreign key
InvoiceAmt	Currency	
BillingDate	Date/Time	

You'll define the Paid field in the new row for the Order table. Access will add this new field to the Order table structure between the CustomerNum and InvoiceAmt fields.

2. Click the **Field Name** text box for the new row, type **Paid**, and then press the **Tab** key.

   The Paid field will be a yes/no field that will specify whether or not an invoice has been paid.

3. Type **y**. Access completes the data type as "yes/No."

4. Press the **Tab** key to select the yes/no data type and to move to the Description text box.

   Notice that Access changes the value in the Data Type text box from "yes/No" to "Yes/No." Barbara wants the Paid field to have a Default Value property value of "No," so you need to set this property.

5. In the Field Properties section, click the **Default Value** text box, type **no**, and then click the **Description** text box for the Paid field. Notice that Access changes the Default Value property value from "no" to "No." See Figure 2-24.

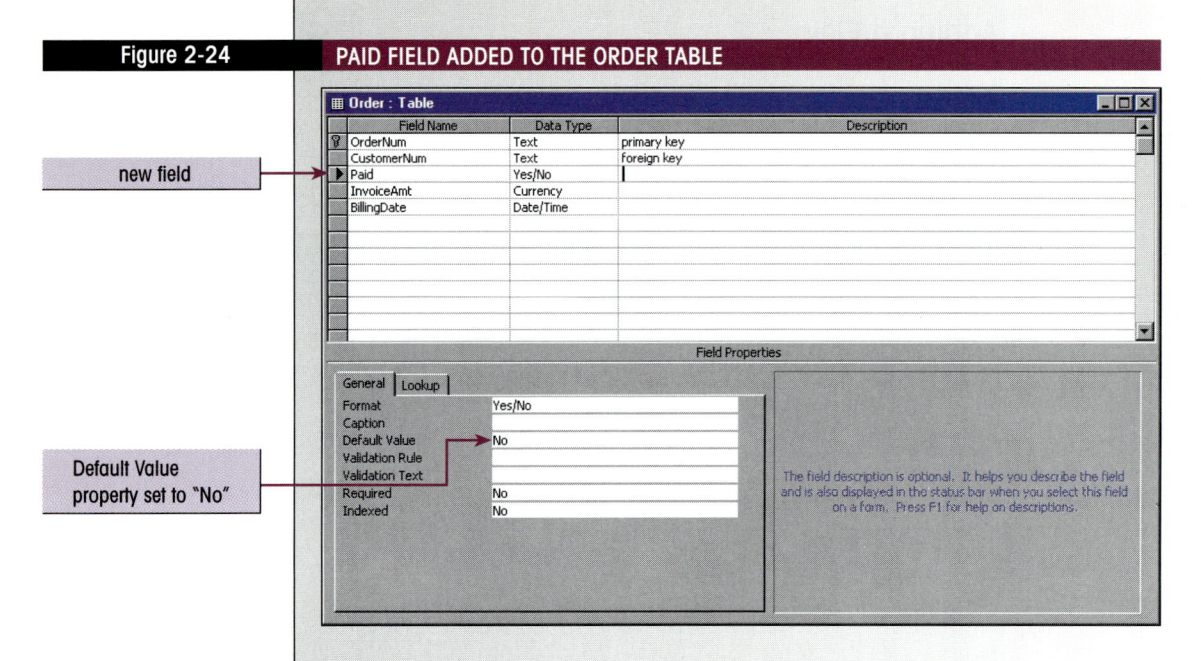

Figure 2-24   **PAID FIELD ADDED TO THE ORDER TABLE**

Field Name	Data Type	Description
OrderNum	Text	primary key
CustomerNum	Text	foreign key
Paid	Yes/No	
InvoiceAmt	Currency	
BillingDate	Date/Time	

new field → Paid

Field Properties

General | Lookup
Format: Yes/No
Caption:
Default Value: No ← *Default Value property set to "No"*
Validation Rule:
Validation Text:
Required: No
Indexed: No

The field description is optional. It helps you describe the field and is also displayed in the status bar when you select this field on a form. Press F1 for help on descriptions.

Because its field name clearly indicates its purpose, you do not need to enter a description for the Paid field.

You've completed adding the Paid field to the Order table in Design view. As with the other changes you've made, however, the Paid field is not added to the Order table in the Restaurant database until you save the changes to the table structure.

Changing Field Properties

Barbara's last modification to the table structure is to remove the dollar signs from the InvoiceAmt field values displayed in the datasheet—repeated dollar signs are unnecessary and they clutter the datasheet. As you learned earlier when defining the BillingDate field, you use the Format property to control the display of a field value.

To change the Format property of the InvoiceAmt field:

1. Click the **Description** text box for the InvoiceAmt field. The InvoiceAmt field is now the current field.

2. Click the right side of the **Format** text box to display the Format list box. See Figure 2-25.

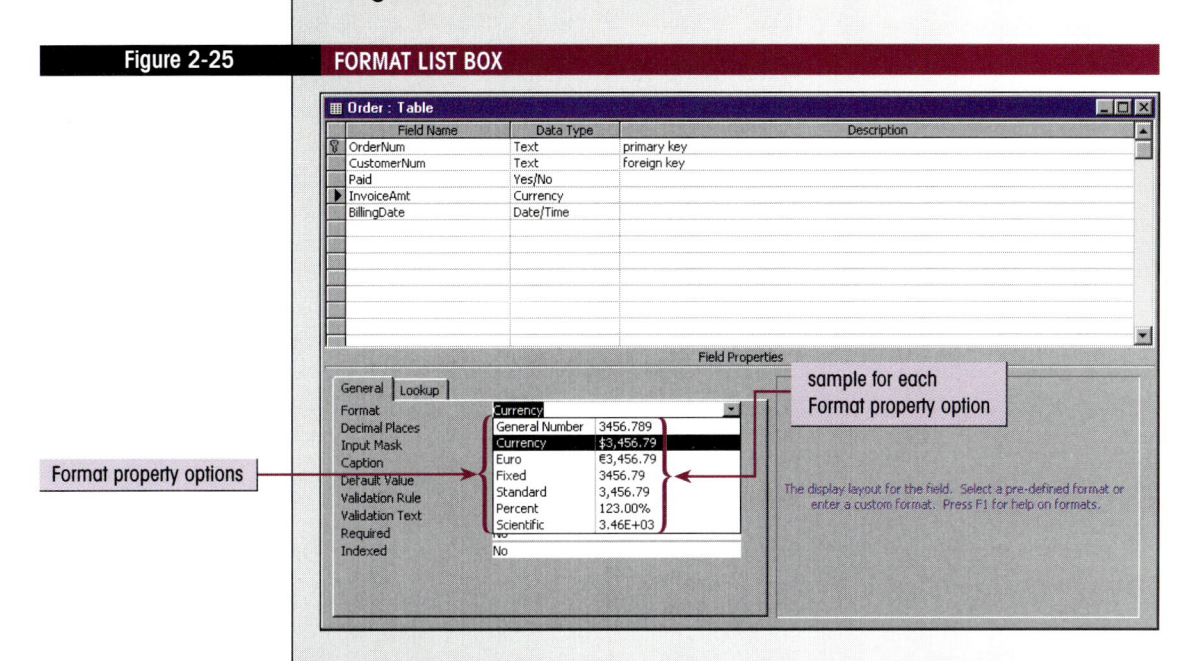

Figure 2-25   **FORMAT LIST BOX**

To the right of each Format property option is a field value whose appearance represents a sample of the option. The Standard option specifies the format Barbara wants for the InvoiceAmt field.

3. Click **Standard** in the Format list box to accept this option for the Format property.

Barbara wants you to add a third record to the Order table datasheet. Before you can add the record, you must save the modified table structure, and then switch to the Order table datasheet.

To save the modified table structure, and then switch to the datasheet:

1. Click the **Save** button on the Table Design toolbar. The modified table structure for the Order table is stored in the Restaurant database.

2. Click the **View** button for Datasheet view on the Table Design toolbar. The Order table datasheet opens. See Figure 2-26.

Figure 2-26 DATASHEET FOR THE MODIFIED ORDER TABLE

- records in primary key order
- check box for a yes/no field
- dollar signs removed
- field moved
- field added

OrderNum	CustomerNum	Paid	InvoiceAmt	BillingDate
201	107	☐	854.00	01/15/2001
323	624	☐	1,986.00	02/15/2001
*		☐	0.00	

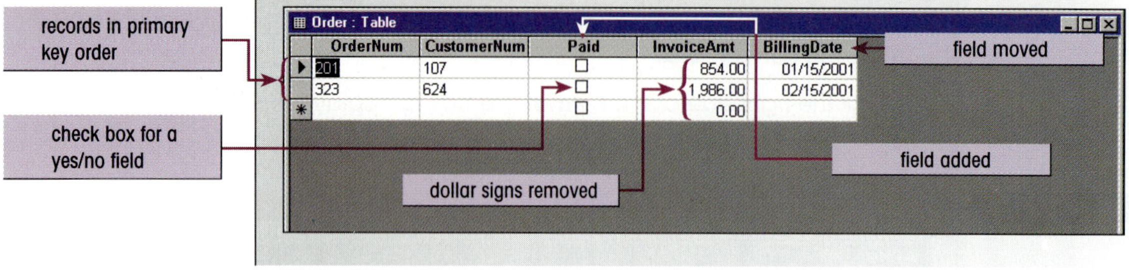

Notice that the PlacedBy field no longer appears in the datasheet, the BillingDate field is now the rightmost column, the InvoiceAmt field values do not contain dollar signs, and the Paid field appears between the CustomerNum and InvoiceAmt fields. The Paid column contains check boxes to represent the yes/no field values. Empty check boxes signify "No," which is the default value you assigned to the Paid field. A "Yes" value is indicated by a check mark in the check box. Also notice that the records appear in ascending order based on the value in the OrderNum field, the Order table's primary key, even though you did not enter the records in this order.

Barbara asks you to add a third record to the table. This record is for an order that has been paid.

To add the record to the modified Order table:

1. Click the **New Record** button on the Table Datasheet toolbar. The insertion point is located in the OrderNum field for the third row, which is the next row available for a new record.

2. Type **211**. The pencil symbol appears in the row selector for the third row, and the star appears in the row selector for the fourth row. Recall that these symbols represent a record being edited and the next available record, respectively.

3. Press the **Tab** key. The insertion point moves to the CustomerNum field.

4. Type **201** and then press the **Tab** key. The Paid field is now the current field.

    Recall that the default value for this field is "No," which means the check box is initially empty. For yes/no fields with check boxes, you press the Tab key to leave the check box unchecked; you press the spacebar or click the check box to add or remove a check mark in the check box. Because the invoice for this order has been paid, you need to insert a check mark in the check box.

5. Press the **spacebar**. A check mark appears in the check box.

6. Press the **Tab** key. The value in the InvoiceAmt field is now highlighted.

7. Type **703.5** and then press the **Tab** key. The insertion point moves to the BillingDate field.

8. Type **01/15/01** and then press the **Tab** key. Access saves the record in the Order table and moves the insertion point to the beginning of the fourth row. See Figure 2-27.

TUTORIAL 2 MAINTAINING A DATABASE   AC 2.27

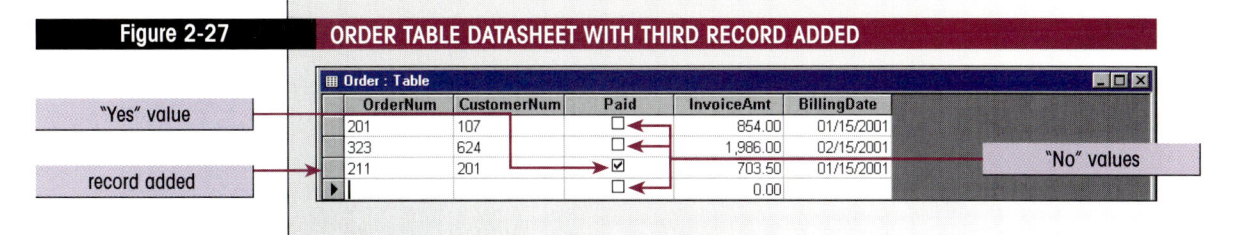

| Figure 2-27 | ORDER TABLE DATASHEET WITH THIRD RECORD ADDED |

"Yes" value →

record added →

OrderNum	CustomerNum	Paid	InvoiceAmt	BillingDate
201	107	☐	854.00	01/15/2001
323	624	☐	1,986.00	02/15/2001
211	201	☑	703.50	01/15/2001
		☐	0.00	

← "No" values

As you add records, Access places them at the end of the datasheet. If you switch to Design view, then return to the datasheet, or if you close the table and then open the datasheet, Access will display the records in primary key sequence.

You have modified the Order table structure and added one record. Instead of typing the remaining records in the Order table, Barbara suggests that you copy them from a table that already exists in another database, and then paste them into the Order table.

Copying Records from Another Access Database

You can copy and paste records from a table in the same database or in a different database only if the tables have the same structure—that is, the tables contain the same fields in the same order. Barbara's Valle database in the Tutorial folder on your Data Disk has a table named Restaurant Order that has the same table structure as the Order table. The records in the Restaurant Order table are the records Barbara wants you to copy into the Order table.

Other programs, such as Microsoft Word and Microsoft Excel, allow you to have two or more documents open at a time. However, you can have only one Access database open at a time. Therefore, you need to close the Restaurant database, open the Restaurant Order table in the Valle database, select and copy the table records, close the Valle database, reopen the Order table in the Restaurant database, and then paste the copied records.

To copy the records from the Restaurant Order table:

1. Click the **Close** button ☒ on the Table window title bar to close the Order table, and then click the **Close** button ☒ on the Database window title bar to close the Restaurant database.

2. Click the **Open** button on the Database toolbar to display the Open dialog box.

3. If necessary, display the list of files on your Data Disk, and then open the **Tutorial** folder.

4. Open the database file named **Valle**. The Database window opens, showing the tables for the Valle database.

    Notice that the Valle database contains two tables: the Restaurant Customer table and the Restaurant Order table. The Restaurant Order table contains the records you need to copy.

5. Click **Restaurant Order** in the Tables list box, and then click the **Open** button in the Database window. The datasheet for the Restaurant Order table opens. See Figure 2-28. Note that this table contains a total of 102 records.

Figure 2-28 | DATASHEET FOR THE VALLE DATABASE'S RESTAURANT ORDER TABLE

click here to select all records

OrderNum	CustomerNum	Paid	InvoiceAmt	BillingDate
200	135	✓	871.35	01/15/2001
202	104	✓	1,280.50	01/15/2001
203	122	✓	1,190.00	01/15/2001
204	123	✓	1,055.00	01/15/2001
205	128	✓	654.50	01/15/2001
206	129	✓	1,392.50	01/15/2001
207	131	✓	1,604.50	01/15/2001
208	133	✓	1,784.00	01/15/2001
209	136	☐	1,106.00	01/15/2001
210	163	✓	1,223.00	01/15/2001
212	203	✓	1,220.50	01/15/2001
213	325	✓	1,426.50	01/15/2001
214	407	☐	1,070.50	01/15/2001
215	741	✓	1,852.00	01/15/2001
216	515	✓	1,309.50	01/15/2001
217	597	✓	1,963.50	01/15/2001
218	627	✓	1,530.00	01/15/2001
219	652	✓	1,578.00	01/15/2001
220	202	✓	1,248.50	01/15/2001
221	625	☐	1,607.00	01/15/2001
222	624	✓	1,986.00	01/15/2001
223	687	✓	1,129.00	01/15/2001

Record: 1 of 102

total number of records in the table

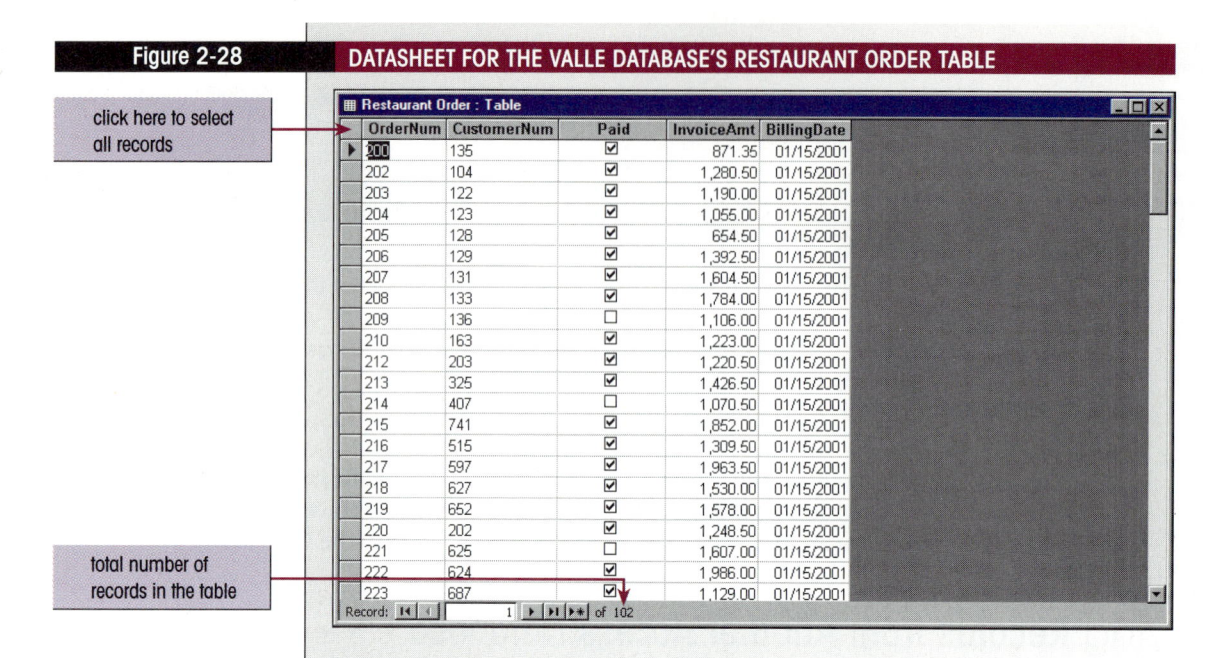

Barbara wants you to copy all the records in the Restaurant Order table. You can select all records by clicking the row selector for the field name row.

6. Click the **row selector** for the field name row (see Figure 2-28). All the records in the table are now highlighted, which means that Access has selected all of them.

7. Click the **Copy** button on the Table Datasheet toolbar. All of the records are copied to the Windows Clipboard.

   TROUBLE? If a Clipboard toolbar opens, click its Close button to close it, and then continue with Step 8.

8. Click the **Close** button on the Table window title bar. A dialog box opens asking if you want to save the data you copied on the Windows Clipboard.

9. Click the **Yes** button in the dialog box. The dialog box closes, and then the table closes.

10. Click the **Close** button on the Database window title bar to close the Valle database.

To finish copying and pasting the records, you must open the Order table and paste the copied records into the table.

To paste the copied records into the Order table:

1. Click **File** on the menu bar, and then click **Restaurant** in the list of recently opened databases. The Database window opens, showing the tables for the Restaurant database.

2. In the Tables list box, click **Order** (if necessary) and then click the **Open** button in the Database window. The datasheet for the Order table opens.

   You must paste the records at the end of the table.

3. Click the **row selector** for row four, which is the next row available for a new record.

4. Click the **Paste** button on the Table Datasheet toolbar. A dialog box opens, asking if you are sure you want to paste the records (102 in all).

5. Click the **Yes** button. All the records are pasted from the Windows Clipboard, and the pasted records remain highlighted. See Figure 2-29. Notice that the table now contains a total of 105 records—the three original records plus the 102 copied records.

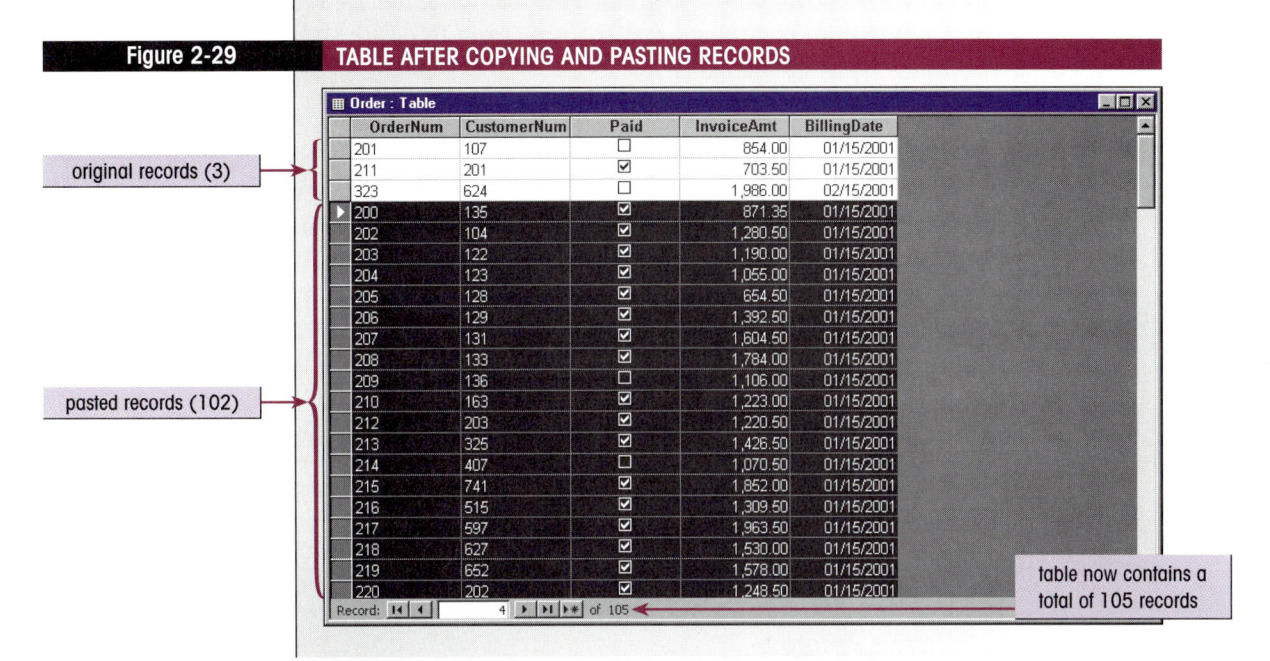

Figure 2-29 TABLE AFTER COPYING AND PASTING RECORDS

original records (3)

pasted records (102)

table now contains a total of 105 records

Using the Office Clipboard

When you copied records from the Valle database and pasted them into the Restaurant database, you used the Windows Clipboard. The **Windows Clipboard** is a temporary storage area for data that is cut or copied to it from any Windows program. The data is stored on the Clipboard until you either close Windows or cut or copy something else to the Clipboard.

When you need to copy multiple pieces of data from one program to another—or within the same program (such as Access)—you can use the Office Clipboard. The **Office Clipboard** lets you cut or copy up to 12 different items from any Office 2000 program so that you can paste these items into different locations later. For example, if you need to copy the records from Barbara's Valle database, and then open another database and copy additional records from it, you could copy each set of records to the Office Clipboard, open the Restaurant database, and then paste these two different sets of records in two actions. If you used the Windows Clipboard to copy the same records, you would only be able to paste the records from the second database, because the first set of records would be deleted as soon as you performed the second copy operation.

The Office Clipboard appears automatically as a Clipboard toolbar as soon as you cut or copy two items to it. When the Clipboard toolbar opens, you will see a Copy button, Paste All button, and a Clear Clipboard button, along with icons that represent each item that you either cut or copied to the Clipboard. To paste an item in a new location, such as pasting records copied from one table to another, you select the location in which to paste the item, and then click the icon that contains the data to paste. In Access, the Paste All button is not available all the time, but you can still paste groups of items by inserting them individually.

You've completed copying and pasting the records between the two tables. Now that you have all the records in the Order table, Barbara examines the records to make sure they are correct. She finds one record that she wants you to delete and another record that needs changes to its field values.

Updating a Database

Updating, or **maintaining**, a database is the process of adding, changing, and deleting records in database tables to keep them current and accurate. You've already added records to the Order table. Now Barbara wants you to delete and change records.

Deleting Records

To delete a record, you need to select the record in Datasheet view, and then delete it using the Delete Record button on the Table Datasheet toolbar or the Delete Record option on the shortcut menu.

REFERENCE WINDOW   RW

Deleting a Record
- In the Table window in Datasheet view, click the row selector for the record you want to delete, and then click the Delete Record button on the Table Datasheet toolbar (or right-click the row selector for the record, and then click Delete Record on the shortcut menu).
- In the dialog box asking you to confirm the deletion, click the Yes button.

Barbara asks you to delete the record whose OrderNum is 200 because this record was entered in error; it represents an order from an office customer, not a restaurant customer, and therefore does not belong in the Restaurant database. The fourth record in the table has an OrderNum value of 200. This record is the one you need to delete.

To delete the record:

1. Right-click the **row selector** for row four. Access selects the fourth record and displays the shortcut menu. See Figure 2-30.

Figure 2-30 DELETING A RECORD

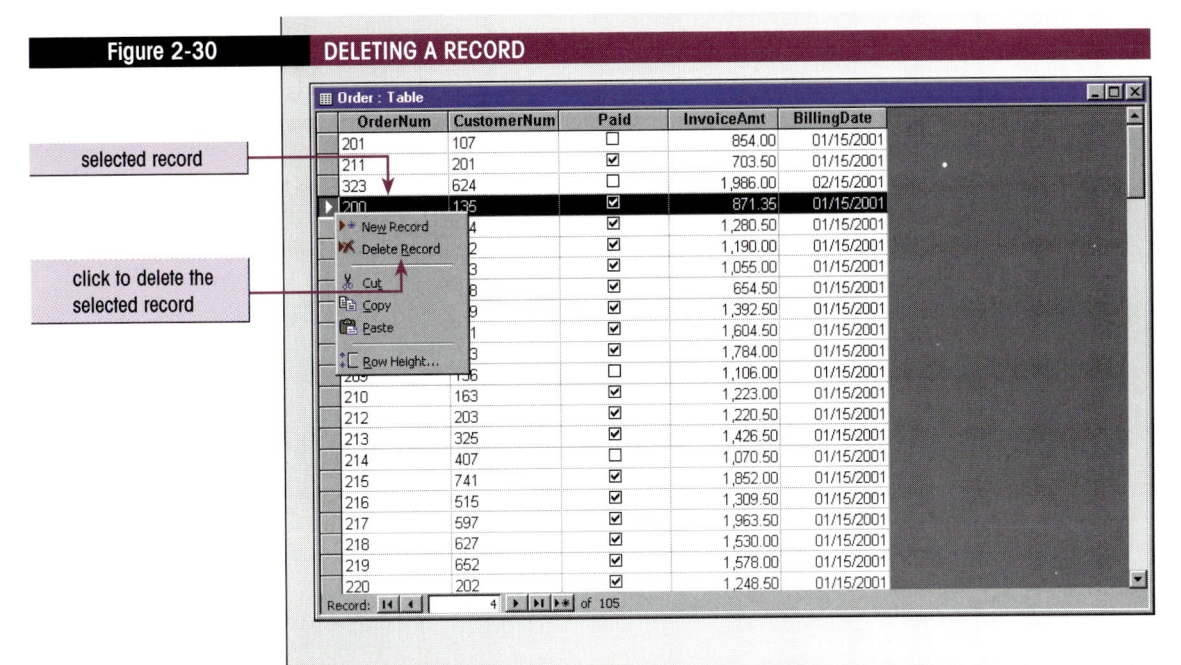

selected record

click to delete the selected record

OrderNum	CustomerNum	Paid	InvoiceAmt	BillingDate
201	107	☐	854.00	01/15/2001
211	201	☑	703.50	01/15/2001
323	624	☐	1,986.00	02/15/2001
200	135	☑	871.35	01/15/2001
		☑	1,280.50	01/15/2001
		☑	1,190.00	01/15/2001
		☑	1,055.00	01/15/2001
		☑	654.50	01/15/2001
		☑	1,392.50	01/15/2001
		☑	1,604.50	01/15/2001
		☑	1,784.00	01/15/2001
		☐	1,106.00	01/15/2001
210	163	☑	1,223.00	01/15/2001
212	203	☑	1,220.50	01/15/2001
213	325	☑	1,426.50	01/15/2001
214	407	☐	1,070.50	01/15/2001
215	741	☑	1,852.00	01/15/2001
216	515	☑	1,309.50	01/15/2001
217	597	☑	1,963.50	01/15/2001
218	627	☑	1,530.00	01/15/2001
219	652	☑	1,578.00	01/15/2001
220	202	☑	1,248.50	01/15/2001

Shortcut menu options: New Record, Delete Record, Cut, Copy, Paste, Row Height...

Record: 4 of 105

2. Click **Delete Record** on the shortcut menu. Access deletes the record and opens a dialog box asking you to confirm the deletion.

   TROUBLE? If you selected the wrong record for deletion, click the No button. Access ends the deletion process and redisplays the deleted record. Repeat Steps 1 and 2 to delete the correct record.

3. Click the **Yes** button to confirm the deletion and close the dialog box.

Barbara's final update to the Order table involves changes to field values in one of the records.

Changing Records

To change the field values in a record, you first must make the record the current record. Then you position the insertion point in the field value to make minor changes or select the field value to replace it entirely. In Tutorial 1, you used the mouse with the scroll bars and the navigation buttons to navigate through the records in a datasheet. You can also use keystroke combinations and the F2 key to navigate a datasheet and to select field values.

The **F2 key** is a toggle that you use to switch between navigation mode and editing mode:

- In **navigation mode**, Access selects an entire field value. If you type while you are in navigation mode, your typed entry replaces the highlighted field value.

- In **editing mode**, you can insert or delete characters in a field value based on the location of the insertion point.

Figure 2-31 shows some of the navigation mode and editing mode keystroke techniques.

Figure 2-31 — NAVIGATION MODE AND EDITING MODE KEYSTROKE TECHNIQUES

PRESS	TO MOVE THE SELECTION IN NAVIGATION MODE	TO MOVE THE INSERTION POINT IN EDITING MODE
←	Left one field value at a time	Left one character at a time
→	Right one field value at a time	Right one character at a time
Home	Left to the first field value in the record	To the left of the first character in the field value
End	Right to the last field value in the record	To the right of the last character in the field value
↑ or ↓	Up or down one record at a time	Up or down one record at a time and switch to navigation mode
Tab or Enter	Right one field value at a time	Right one field value at a time and switch to navigation mode
Ctrl + Home	To the first field value in the first record	To the left of the first character in the field value
Ctrl + End	To the last field value in the last record	To the right of the last character in the field value

The record Barbara wants you to change has an OrderNum field value of 397. Some of the values were entered incorrectly for this record, and you need to enter the correct values.

To modify the record:

1. Make sure the OrderNum field value for the fourth record is still highlighted, indicating that the table is in navigation mode.

2. Press **Ctrl + End**. Access displays records from the end of the table and selects the last field value in the last record. This field value is for the BillingDate field.

3. Press the **Home** key. The first field value in the last record is now selected. This field value is for the OrderNum field.

4. Press the ↑ key. The OrderNum field value for the previous record is selected. This record is the one you need to change.

   Barbara wants you to change these field values in the record: OrderNum to 398, CustomerNum to 165, Paid to "Yes" (checked), and InvoiceAmt to 1426.50. You do not need to change the BillingDate.

5. Type **398**, press the **Tab** key, type **165**, press the **Tab** key, press the **spacebar** to insert a check mark in the Paid check box, press the **Tab** key, and then type **1426.5**. The changes to the record are complete.

6. Press the ↓ key to save the changes to the record and make the next record the current record. See Figure 2-32.

Figure 2-32 TABLE AFTER CHANGING FIELD VALUES IN A RECORD

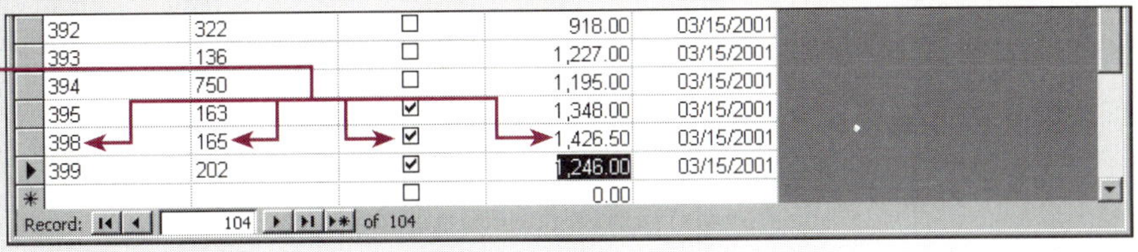

field values changed

392	322	☐	918.00	03/15/2001
393	136	☐	1,227.00	03/15/2001
394	750	☐	1,195.00	03/15/2001
395	163	☑	1,348.00	03/15/2001
398	165	☑	1,426.50	03/15/2001
▶ 399	202	☑	1,246.00	03/15/2001
*		☐	0.00	

Record: 14 ◀ | 104 | ▶ ▶| ▶* of 104

You've completed all of Barbara's updates to the Order table. Barbara asks you to print only the first page of data from the Order table datasheet so that she can show the revised table structure to her staff members. After you print the page, you can exit Access.

To print the first page of Order table data, and then exit Access:

1. Click **File** on the menu bar, and then click **Print** to open the Print dialog box.

2. In the Print Range section, click the **Pages** option button, type **1** in the From text box, press the **Tab** key, and then type **1** in the To text box.

3. Click the **OK** button to print the first page of data.

   Now you can exit Access.

4. Click the **Close** button ⊠ on the Access window title bar to close the Order table and the Restaurant database and to exit Access.

Barbara and her staff members approve of the revised table structure for the Order table. They are confident that the table will allow them to easily track order data for Valle Coffee's restaurant customers.

Session 2.2 QUICK CHECK

1. What is the effect of deleting a field from a table structure?
2. How do you insert a field between existing fields in a table structure?
3. A field with the _____ data type can appear in the table datasheet as a check box.
4. Which property do you use to control the display appearance of a field value?
5. Why must you close an open database when you want to copy records to it from a table in another database?
6. What is the difference between navigation mode and editing mode?

REVIEW ASSIGNMENTS

Barbara needs a database to track the coffee products offered by Valle Coffee. She asks you to create the database by completing the following:

1. Make sure your Data Disk is in the disk drive, and then start Access.

Explore 2. In the initial Microsoft Access dialog box, click the Blank Access database option button, and then click the OK button. In the File New Database dialog box, select the Review folder on your Data Disk, and then enter the name **Valle Products** for the database in the File name text box. Click the Create button to create the new database.

Explore 3. Display the Table window in Design view (if necessary), and then create a table using the table design shown in Figure 2-33.

Figure 2-33

Field Name	Data Type	Description	Field Size	Other Properties
ProductCode	Text	primary key	4	
CoffeeCode	Text	foreign key	4	
Price	Currency	price for this product		Format: Fixed Decimal Places: 2
Decaf	Text	D if decaf, Null if regular	1	Default Value: D
BackOrdered	Yes/No	back-ordered from supplier?		

4. Specify ProductCode as the primary key, and then save the table as **Product**.
5. Add the product records shown in Figure 2-34 to the **Product** table. (*Hint*: You must type the decimal point when entering the Price field values.)

Figure 2-34

ProductCode	CoffeeCode	Price	Decaf	BackOrdered
2316	JRUM	8.99		Yes
9754	HAZL	40.00	D	Yes
9309	COCO	9.99	D	No

6. Make the following changes to the structure of the **Product** table:
   a. Add a new field between the CoffeeCode and Price fields, using these properties:
      Field Name: WeightCode
      Data Type: Text
      Description: foreign key
      Field Size: 1
   b. Move the Decaf field so that it appears between the WeightCode and Price fields.
   c. Save the revised table structure.
7. Use the **Product** datasheet to update the database as follows:
   a. Enter these WeightCode values for the three records: A for ProductCode 2316, A for ProductCode 9309, and E for ProductCode 9754.
   b. Add a record to the **Product** datasheet with these field values:
      ProductCode: 9729
      CoffeeCode: COLS
      WeightCode: E
      Decaf: D
      Price: 39.75
      BackOrdered: Yes
8. Close the **Product** table, and then set the option for compacting the **Valle Products** database on close.

9. Barbara created a database with her name as the database name. The **Coffee Product** table in that database has the same format as the **Product** table you created. Copy all the records from the **Coffee Product** table in the **Barbara** database (located in the Review folder on your Data Disk) to the end of your **Product** table.

Explore 10. Because you added a number of records to the database, its size has increased. Compact the database manually using the Compact and Repair Database option.

11. Reopen the **Product** datasheet. The records now appear in primary key order by ProductCode. Then delete the record with the ProductCode 2372 from the **Product** table.

12. Delete the BackOrdered field from the **Product** table structure.

Explore 13. Use the Access Help system to learn how to resize datasheet columns to fit the data, and then resize all columns in the datasheet for the **Product** table so that each column fits its data. Scroll the datasheet to make sure all field values are fully displayed. For any field values that are not fully displayed, make sure the field values are visible on the screen, and then resize the appropriate columns again.

14. Print the first page of data from the **Product** table datasheet, and then save and close the table.

Explore 15. Create a table named **Weight**, based on the data shown in Figure 2-35, according to the following steps:

Figure 2-35

WeightCode	Weight/Size
A	1 lb pkg
B	6 lb case
C	24 ct 1.5 oz pkg
D	44 ct 1.25 oz pkg
E	44 ct 1.5 oz pkg
F	88 ct 1.25 oz pkg
G	88 ct 1.5 oz pkg

a. Select the Datasheet View option in the New Table dialog box.
b. Enter the seven records shown in Figure 2-35. (Do *not* enter the field names at this point.)
c. Switch to Design view, supply the table name, and then answer No if asked if you want to create a primary key.
d. Type the following field names and set the following properties:
   WeightCode
   Description: primary key
   Field Size: 1
   Weight/Size
   Description: weight in pounds or size in packages (number and weight) per case
   Field Size: 17
e. Specify the primary key, save the table structure changes, and then switch back to Datasheet view. If you receive any warning messages, answer Yes to continue.
f. Resize both datasheet columns to fit the data (use Access Help to learn how to resize datasheet columns, if necessary); then save, print, and close the datasheet.

Explore 16. Create a table named **Coffee** using the Import Table Wizard, which is available in the New Table dialog box. The table you need to import is named **Coffee.dbf** and is located in the Review folder on your Data Disk. This table has a dBASE 5 file type. (You'll need to change the entry in the Files of type list box to display the file in the list.) After importing the table, complete the following:

a. Change all field names to use the Valle Coffee convention of uppercase and lowercase letters, and then enter the following Description property values:
   CoffeeCode: primary key
   Decaf: is this coffee available in decaf?

b. Change the Format property of the Decaf field to Yes/No.
c. Specify the primary key, and then save the table structure changes.
d. Switch to Datasheet view, and then resize all columns in the datasheet to fit the data. (Use Access Help to learn how to resize datasheet columns, if necessary.) Be sure to scroll through the table to make sure that all field values are fully displayed.
e. Save, print, and then close the datasheet.
17. Close the **Valle Products** database, and then exit Access.

CASE PROBLEMS

Case 1. Ashbrook Mall Information Desk Sam Bullard, the director of the Mall Operations Office at Ashbrook Mall, uses the **MallJobs** database to maintain information about current job openings at stores in the mall. Sam asks you to help him maintain the database by completing the following:

1. Make sure your Data Disk is in the disk drive.
2. Start Access and open the **MallJobs** database located in the Cases folder on your Data Disk.
3. Create a table using the table design shown in Figure 2-36.

Figure 2-36

Field Name	Data Type	Description	Field Size
Job	Text	primary key	5
Store	Text	foreign key	3
Hours/Week	Text		20
Position	Text		35
ExperienceReq	Yes/No		

4. Specify Job as the primary key, and then save the table as **Job**.
5. Add the job records shown in Figure 2-37 to the **Job** table.

Figure 2-37

Job	Store	Hours/Week	Position	ExperienceReq
10037	TH	negotiable	Salesclerk	Yes
10053	BR	16-32	Server	No
10022	BE	35-45	Assistant Manager	Yes

6. Sam created a database named **Openings** that contains a table with job data named **Current Jobs**. The **Job** table you created has the same format as the **Current Jobs** table. Copy all the records from the **Current Jobs** table in the **Openings** database (located in the Cases folder on your Data Disk) to the end of your **Job** table.
7. Modify the structure of the **Job** table by completing the following:
   a. Delete the ExperienceReq field.
   b. Move the Hours/Week field so that it follows the Position field.

Explore 8. Use the Access Help system to learn how to resize datasheet columns to fit the data, and then switch to Datasheet view and resize all columns in the datasheet for the **Job** table.

9. Use the **Job** datasheet to update the database as follows:
   a. For Job 10048, change the Position value to Clerk, and change the Hours/Week value to 25-35.
   b. Add a record to the **Job** datasheet with the following field values:
      Job: 10034
      Store: JB
      Position: Salesclerk
      Hours/Week: negotiable
   c. Delete the record for Job 10031.
10. Switch to Design view, and then switch back to Datasheet view so that the records appear in primary key sequence by Job.
11. Print the **Job** table datasheet, and then save and close the table.
12. Close the **MallJobs** database, and then exit Access.

Case 2. Professional Litigation User Services (PLUS) Raj Jawahir is responsible for tracking the daily payments received from PLUS clients. You'll help him maintain the **Payments** database by completing the following:

1. Make sure your Data Disk is in the disk drive.
2. Start Access and open the **Payments** database located in the Cases folder on your Data Disk.
3. Create a table named **Payment** using the table design shown in Figure 2-38. (*Hint:* Make sure that you include spaces between the components of the custom format for the DatePaid field.)

Figure 2-38

Field Name	Data Type	Description	Field Size	Other Properties
Payment#	Text	primary key	5	
Firm#	Text	foreign key	4	
DatePaid	Date/Time			Format: mmm dd yyyy (custom format)
AmtPaid	Currency			Format: Standard

4. Add the payment records shown in Figure 2-39 to the **Payment** table.

Figure 2-39

Payment#	Firm#	DatePaid	AmtPaid
10031	1111	06/03/2001	2500.00
10002	1147	06/01/2001	1700.00
10015	1151	06/02/2001	2000.00

5. Modify the structure of the **Payment** table by completing the following:
   a. Add a new field between the Payment# and Firm# fields, using these properties:
      Field Name: Deposit#
      Data Type: Text
      Field Size: 3
   b. Move the DatePaid field so that it follows the AmtPaid field.
6. Use the **Payment** datasheet to update the database as follows:
   a. Enter these Deposit# values for the three records: 101 for Payment# 10002, 102 for Payment# 10015, and 103 for Payment# 10031.
   b. Add a record to the **Payment** datasheet with these field values:
      Payment#:   10105
      Deposit#:   117
      Firm#:   1103
      AmtPaid: 1,750.00
      DatePaid: 06/20/2001

7. Raj created a database named **PlusPays** that contains recent payments in the **Payment Records** table. The **Payment** table you created has the same format as the **Payment Records** table. Copy all the records from the **Payment Records** table in the **PlusPays** database (located in the Cases folder on your Data Disk) to the end of your **Payment** table.

Explore 8. Use the Access Help system to learn how to resize datasheet columns to fit the data, and then resize all columns in the datasheet for the **Payment** table.

9. For Payment# 10002, change the AmtPaid value to 1300.00.
10. Delete the record for Payment# 10096.
11. Print the first page of data from the **Payment** table datasheet, and then save and close the table.
12. Close the **Payments** database, and then exit Access.

Case 3. Best Friends Noah and Sheila Warnick continue to track information about participants in the walk-a-thons held to benefit Best Friends. Help them maintain the **Walks** database by completing the following:

1. Make sure your Data Disk is in the disk drive.
2. Start Access and open the **Walks** database located in the Cases folder on your Data Disk.

Explore 3. Create a table named **Pledge** using the Import Table Wizard. The table you need to import is named **Pledge.db** and is located in the Cases folder on your Data Disk. This table has a Paradox file type. (You'll need to change the entry in the Files of type list box to display the file in the list.) After importing the table, complete the following:
   a. Change all field names to use uppercase and lowercase letters, as appropriate, and then enter the following Description property values:
      PledgeNo: primary key
      WalkerID: foreign key
      PerMile: amount pledged per mile
   b. Specify the primary key, and then save the table structure changes.
   c. Switch to Datasheet view, and then resize all columns in the datasheet to fit the data. (Use Access Help to learn how to resize datasheet columns, if necessary.)

Explore 4. Modify the structure of the **Pledge** table by completing the following:
   a. Add a new field between the PaidAmt and PerMile fields, using these properties:
      Field Name: DatePaid
      Data Type: Date/Time
      Format: mm/dd/yyyy (custom format)
   b. Change the Data Type of both the PledgeAmt field and the PaidAmt field to Currency. For each of these fields, choose the Fixed format.
   c. Save the table structure. Answer Yes to any warning messages.

5. Use the **Pledge** datasheet to update the database as follows:
   a. Enter these DatePaid values for the five records: 09/15/2001 for PledgeNo 1, 09/01/2001 for PledgeNo 2, 08/25/2001 for PledgeNo 3, 09/20/2001 for PledgeNo 4, and 08/14/2001 for PledgeNo 5. Resize the DatePaid column to fit the data.
   b. Add a record to the **Pledge** datasheet with these field values:
      PledgeNo: 6
      Pledger: Gene Delsener
      WalkerID: 138
      PledgeAmt: 50
      PaidAmt: 50
      DatePaid: 09/18/2001
      PerMile: 0
   c. Enter the value 133 in the WalkerID field for PledgeNo 1.
   d. Change both the PledgeAmt value and the PaidAmt value for PledgeNo 3 to 25.00.
   e. Change the WalkerID value for PledgeNo 5 to 165.

6. Print the **Pledge** table datasheet, and then save and close the table.
7. Close the **Walks** database, and then exit Access.

Case 4. Lopez Lexus Dealerships Maria and Hector Lopez use the **Lexus** database to track the car inventory in the chain of Lexus dealerships they own. You'll help them maintain the **Lexus** database by completing the following:

1. Make sure your Data Disk is in the disk drive.
2. Start Access and open the **Lexus** database located in the Cases folder on your Data Disk.

Explore

3. Use the Import Spreadsheet Wizard to create a new table named **Locations**. The data you need to import is contained in the **Lopez** workbook, which is a Microsoft Excel file located in the Cases folder on your Data Disk.
   a. Select the Import Table option in the New Table dialog box.
   b. Change the entry in the Files of type list box to display the list of Excel workbook files in the Cases folder.
   c. Select the **Lopez** file and then click the Import button.
   d. In the Import Spreadsheet Wizard dialog boxes, choose the option for using column headings as field names; select the option for choosing your own primary key, and specify LocationCode as the primary key; and enter the table name (**Locations**). Otherwise, accept the Wizard's choices for all other options for the imported data.

Explore

4. Use the Access Help system to learn how to resize datasheet columns to fit the data, and then open the **Locations** table and resize all columns in the datasheet.
5. Modify the structure of the **Locations** table by completing the following:
   a. For the LocationCode field, enter a Description property of "primary key," change the Field Size to 2, and change the Required property to Yes.
   b. For the LocationName field, change the Field Size to 25.
   c. For the ManagerName field, change the Field Size to 35.
   d. Save the table. If you receive any warning messages about lost data or integrity rules, click the Yes button.
6. Use the **Locations** datasheet to update the database as follows:
   a. For LocationCode A2, change the ManagerName value to Curran, Edward.
   b. Add a record to the **Locations** datasheet with these field values:
      LocationCode: H2
      LocationName: Houston
      ManagerName: Cohen, Molly
   c. Delete the record for LocationCode L2.
7. Print the **Locations** table datasheet, and then close the table.

Explore

8. Use the Table Wizard to create a new table named **Managers** based on the sample **Employees** table, which is a sample table in the Business category, as follows:
   a. Add the following sample fields to your table (in the following order): SocialSecurityNumber, LastName, Region, DateHired, and Salary. Do *not* click the Next button yet.
   b. Click Last Name in the "Fields in my new table" list, click the Rename Field button in the first Table Wizard dialog box, and then change the LastName field name to ManagerName. Click the Next button.
   c. Change the default table name to **Managers**. Select the option to create your own primary key, and then select an appropriate field as your primary key. (*Hint:* Select a field that will contain unique numbers, and then select the correct option button that represents your data.) Click the Next button, and then click the Finish button in the final Table Wizard dialog box.
   d. Enter the following data into the **Managers** table:
      Social Security Number: 789-00-8642
      ManagerName: Evans, Hannah
      Region: Austin
      DateHired: 05/31/96
      Salary: 52,000
   e. Resize all columns in the datasheet to fit the data.
9. Print the **Managers** table datasheet, and then save and close the table.
10. Close the **Lexus** database, and then exit Access.

INTERNET ASSIGNMENTS

The purpose of the Internet Assignments is to challenge you to find information on the Internet that you can use to create effective documents. The actual assignments are updated and maintained on the Course Technology Web site. Log on to the Internet and use your Web browser to go to the Student Online Companion to accompany this text at **www.course.com/NewPerspectives/office2000**. Click the Access link, and then click the link for Tutorial 2.

QUICK CHECK ANSWERS

Session 2.1

1. Identify all the fields needed to produce the required information, group related fields into tables, determine each table's primary key, include a common field in related tables, avoid data redundancy, and determine the properties of each field.
2. The data type determines what field values you can enter for the field and what other properties the field will have.
3. text, number, and AutoNumber fields
4. Order numbers will not be used for calculations.
5. null
6. the record being edited; the next row available for a new record

Session 2.2

1. The field and all its values are removed from the table.
2. In Design view, right-click the row selector for the row above which you want to insert the field, click Insert Rows on the shortcut menu, and then define the new field.
3. yes/no
4. Format property
5. Access allows you to have only one database open at a time.
6. In navigation mode, the entire field value is selected, and anything you type replaces the field value; in editing mode, you can insert or delete characters in a field value based on the location of the insertion point.

TUTORIAL 3

OBJECTIVES

In this tutorial you will:

- Learn how to use the Query window in Design view
- Create, run, and save queries
- Define a relationship between two tables
- Sort data in a query
- Filter data in a query
- Specify an exact match condition in a query
- Change a datasheet's appearance
- Use a comparison operator to match a range of values
- Use the And and Or logical operators
- Perform calculations in a query using calculated fields, aggregate functions, and record group calculations

QUERYING A DATABASE

Retrieving Information About Restaurant Customers and Their Orders

CASE

Valle Coffee

At a recent company meeting, Leonard Valle and other Valle Coffee employees discussed the importance of regularly monitoring the business activity of the company's restaurant customers. For example, Kim Carpenter and her marketing staff track customer activity to develop new strategies for promoting Valle Coffee products. Barbara Hennessey and her office staff need to track information about all the orders for which bills were sent out on a specific date, so that they can determine whether the bills have been paid. In addition, Leonard is interested in analyzing the payment history of restaurant customers to determine which customers pay their invoices in a timely manner, which customers have higher invoice amounts, and so on. All of these informational needs can be satisfied by queries that retrieve information from the Restaurant database.

SESSION 3.1

In this session, you will use the Query window in Design view to create, run, and save queries; define a one-to-many relationship between two tables; sort data with a toolbar button and in Design view; and filter data in a query datasheet.

Introduction to Queries

As you learned in Tutorial 1, a query is a question you ask about data stored in a database. For example, Kim might create a query to find records in the Customer table for only those customers in a specific state. When you create a query, you tell Access which fields you need and what criteria Access should use to select the records.

Access provides powerful query capabilities that allow you to:

- display selected fields and records from a table
- sort records
- perform calculations
- generate data for forms, reports, and other queries
- update data in the tables in a database
- find and display data from two or more tables

Most questions about data are generalized queries in which you specify the fields and records you want Access to select. These common requests for information, such as "Which customers have unpaid bills?" or "Which type of coffee sells best in Ohio?" are called **select queries**. The answer to a select query is returned in the form of a datasheet.

More specialized, technical queries, such as finding duplicate records in a table, are best formulated using a Query Wizard. A Query Wizard prompts you for information by asking a series of questions and then creates the appropriate query based on your answers. In Tutorial 1, you used the Simple Query Wizard to display only some of the fields in the Customer table; Access provides other Query Wizards for more complex queries. For common, informational queries, it is easier for you to design your own query than to use a Query Wizard.

Kim wants you to create a query to display the customer number, customer name, city, owner name, and first contact information for each record in the Customer table. She needs this information for a market analysis her staff is completing on Valle Coffee's restaurant customers. You'll open the Query window to create the query for Kim.

Query Window

You use the Query window in Design view to create a query. In Design view you specify the data you want to view by constructing a query by example. Using **query by example (QBE)**, you give Access an example of the information you are requesting. Access then retrieves the information that precisely matches your example.

For Kim's query, you need to display data from the Customer table. You'll begin by starting Access, opening the Restaurant database, and displaying the Query window in Design view.

To start Access, open the Restaurant database, and open the Query window in Design view:

1. Place your Data Disk in the appropriate disk drive.

2. Start Access and open the **Restaurant** database located in the Tutorial folder on your Data Disk. The Restaurant database is displayed in the Database window.

3. Click **Queries** in the Objects bar of the Database window, and then click the **New** button. The New Query dialog box opens. See Figure 3-1.

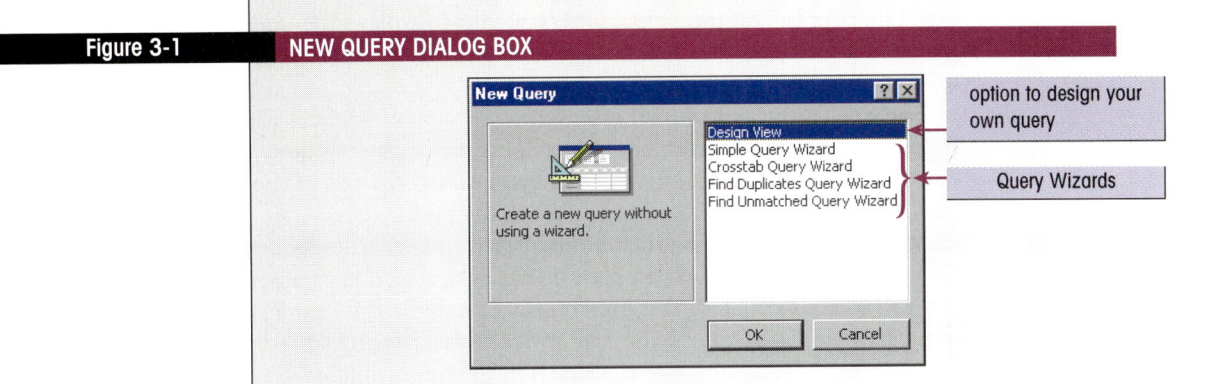

Figure 3-1   NEW QUERY DIALOG BOX

- option to design your own query
- Query Wizards

You'll design your own query instead of using a Query Wizard.

4. If necessary, click **Design View** in the list box.

5. Click the **OK** button. Access opens the Show Table dialog box on top of the Query window. (Note that you could also have double-clicked the option "Create query in Design view" from the Database window.) Notice that the title bar of the Query window shows that you are creating a select query.

The query you are creating will retrieve data from the Customer table, so you need to add this table to the Select Query window.

6. Click **Customer** in the Tables list box (if necessary), click the **Add** button, and then click the **Close** button. Access places the Customer table's field list in the Select Query window and closes the Show Table dialog box.

To display more of the fields you'll be using for creating queries, you'll maximize the Select Query window.

7. Click the **Maximize** button on the Select Query window title bar. See Figure 3-2.

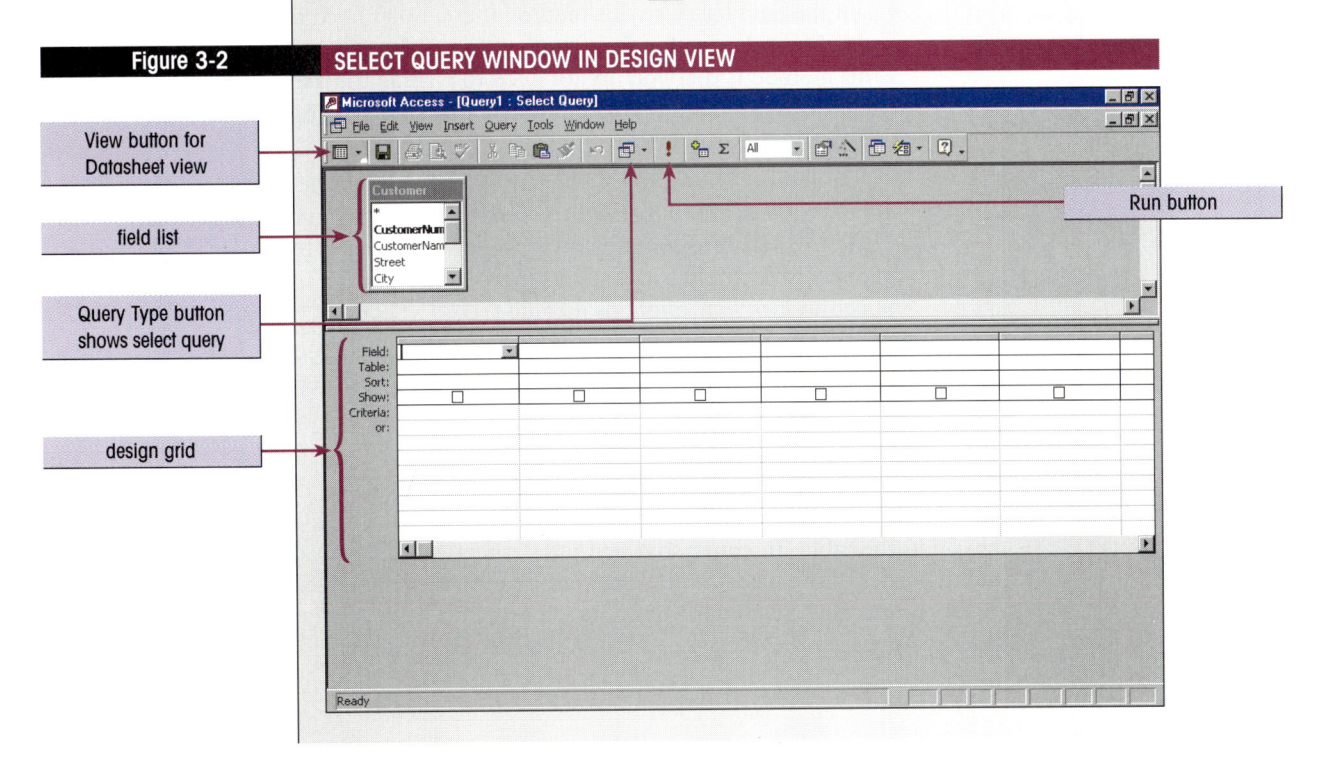

Figure 3-2   SELECT QUERY WINDOW IN DESIGN VIEW

- View button for Datasheet view
- field list
- Query Type button shows select query
- design grid
- Run button

In Design view, the Select Query window contains the standard title bar, menu bar, status bar, and the Query Design toolbar. On the toolbar, the Query Type button shows a select query; the icon on this button changes according to the type of query you are creating. The title bar on the Select Query window displays the query type, Select Query, and the default query name, Query1. You'll change the default query name to a more meaningful one later when you save the query.

The Select Query window in Design view contains a field list and the design grid. The **field list**, which appears in the upper-left area of the window, contains the fields for the table you are querying. The table name appears at the top of the list box, and the fields are listed in the order in which they appear in the table.

In the **design grid**, you include the fields and record selection criteria for the information you want to see. Each column in the design grid contains specifications about a field you will use in the query. You can choose a single field for your query by dragging its name from the field list to the design grid in the lower portion of the window. Alternatively, you can double-click a field name to place it in the next available design grid column.

When you are constructing a query, you can see the query results at any time by clicking the View button or the Run button on the Query Design toolbar. In response, Access displays the datasheet, which contains the set of fields and records that results from answering, or **running**, the query. The order of the fields in the datasheet is the same as the order of the fields in the design grid. Although the datasheet looks just like a table datasheet and appears in Datasheet view, a query datasheet is temporary, and its contents are based on the criteria you establish in the design grid. In contrast, a table datasheet shows the permanent data in a table. However, you can update data while viewing a query datasheet, just as you can when working in a table datasheet or a form.

If the query you are creating includes every field from the specified table, you can use one of the following three methods to transfer all the fields from the field list to the design grid:

- Click and drag each field individually from the field list to the design grid. Use this method if you want the fields in your query to appear in an order that is different from the order in the field list.

- Double-click the asterisk in the field list. Access places the table name followed by a period and an asterisk (as in "Customer.*") in the design grid, which signifies that the order of the fields will be the same in the query as it is in the field list. Use this method if you don't need to sort the query or specify conditions for the records you want to select. The advantage of using this method is that you do not need to change the query if you add or delete fields from the underlying table structure. Such changes are reflected automatically in the query.

- Double-click the field list title bar to highlight all the fields, and then click and drag one of the highlighted fields to the design grid. Access places each field in a separate column and arranges the fields in the order in which they appear in the field list. Use this method rather than the previous one if you need to sort your query or include record selection criteria.

Now you'll create and run Kim's query to display selected fields from the Customer table.

Creating and Running a Query

The default table datasheet displays all the fields in the table, in the same order as they appear in the table. In contrast, a query datasheet can display selected fields from a table, and the order of the fields can be different from that of the table.

Kim wants the CustomerNum, CustomerName, City, OwnerName, and FirstContact fields to appear in the query results. You'll add each of these fields to the design grid.

TUTORIAL 3 QUERYING A DATABASE   AC 3.05   ACCESS

To select the fields for the query, and then run the query:

1. Drag **CustomerNum** from the Customer field list to the design grid's first column Field text box, and then release the mouse button. See Figure 3-3.

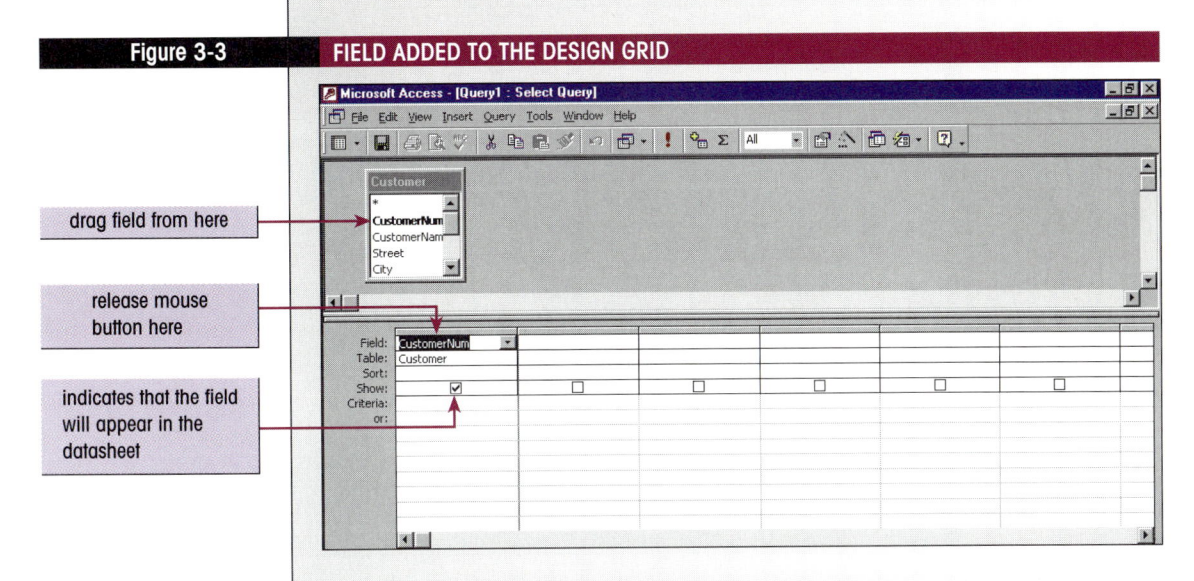

Figure 3-3   **FIELD ADDED TO THE DESIGN GRID**

- drag field from here
- release mouse button here
- indicates that the field will appear in the datasheet

In the design grid's first column, the field name CustomerNum appears in the Field text box, the table name Customer appears in the Table text box, and the check mark in the Show check box indicates that the field will be displayed in the datasheet when you run the query. Sometimes you might not want to display a field and its values in the query results. For example, if you are creating a query to show all customers located in Michigan, and you assign the name "Customers in Michigan" to the query, you do not need to include the State field value for each record in the query results—every State field value would be "MI" for Michigan. Even if you choose not to include a field in the display of the query results, you can still use the field as part of the query to select specific records or to specify a particular sequence for the records in the datasheet.

2. Double-click **CustomerName** in the Customer field list. Access adds this field to the second column of the design grid.

3. Scrolling the Customer field list as necessary, repeat Step 2 for the **City**, **OwnerName**, and **FirstContact** fields to add these fields to the design grid in that order.

Having selected the fields for Kim's query, you can now run the query.

TROUBLE? If you double-click the wrong field and accidentally add it to the design grid, you can remove the field from the grid. Select the field's column by clicking the pointer ↓ on the bar above the Field text box for the field you want to delete, click Edit on the menu bar, and then click Delete Columns.

4. Click the **Run** button on the Query Design toolbar. Access runs the query and displays the results in Datasheet view. See Figure 3-4.

Figure 3-4
DATASHEET DISPLAYED AFTER RUNNING THE QUERY

selected fields displayed

CustomerNum	CustomerName	City	OwnerName	FirstContact
104	Meadows Restaurant	Monroe	Mr. Ray Suchecki	02/28/1991
107	Cottage Grill	Bootjack	Ms. Doris Reaume	04/03/1991
122	Roadhouse Restaurant	Clare	Ms. Shirley Woodruff	04/12/1991
123	Bridge Inn	Ada	Mr. Wayne Bouwman	04/17/1992
128	Grand River Restaurant	Lacota	Mr. John Rohrs	04/20/1992
129	Sandy Lookout Restaurant	Jenison	Ms. Michele Yasenak	04/27/1992
131	Bunker Hill Grill	Eagle Point	Mr. Ronald Koolenga	05/01/1992
133	Florentine Restaurante	Drenthe	Mr. Donald Bench	05/03/1993
135	Topview Restaurant	Zeeland	Ms. Janice Stapleton	05/11/1993
136	Cleo's Downtown Restaurant	Borculo	Ms. Joan Hoffman	05/11/1993
163	Bentham's Riverfront Restaurant	Roscommon	Mr. Joe Markovicz	05/18/1994
165	Sullivan's Restaurant & Lounge	Saugatuck	Ms. Dawn Parker	05/19/1994
201	Wagon Train Restaurant	Selkirk	Mr. Carl Seaver	05/25/1994
202	Extra Helpings Restaurant	Five Lakes	Ms. Deborah Wolfe	05/25/1995
203	Mountain Lake Restaurant	Grand Rapids	Mr. Donald MacPherson	08/25/1995
322	Alto Country Inn	Alto	Mr. James Cowan	06/02/1996
325	Best Bet Restaurant	Grand Rapids	Ms. Rebecca Van Singel	06/12/1996
407	Jean's Country Restaurant	Mattawan	Ms. Jean Brooks	09/18/1996
423	Bay Pointe Restaurant	Shelbyville	Mr. Janosfi Petofi	10/24/1996
515	Cheshire Restaurant	Burlington	Mr. Jeffrey Hersha	12/11/1996
597	Around the Clock Restaurant	Copper Harbor	Ms. Jennifer Lewis	06/24/1997
620	Brandywine Restaurant	Kearsarge	Mr. Walter Reed	07/02/1997
624	South Bend Brewing Company	South Bend	Mr. Toby Stein	07/17/1997
625	Maxwell's Restaurant	South Bend	Ms. Barbara Feldon	07/19/1997
627	Monarch Restaurant	Toledo	Mr. Gilbert Scholten	07/29/1997
635	Oaks Restaurant	Maumee	Ms. Julie Pfeiffer	09/13/1998
646	Golden Gate Restaurant	Romulus	Ms. Nancy Mills	11/12/1998
650	The Peppermill	Elkhart	Ms. Tara Jerentowski	11/16/1998

38 records selected — Record: 1 of 38

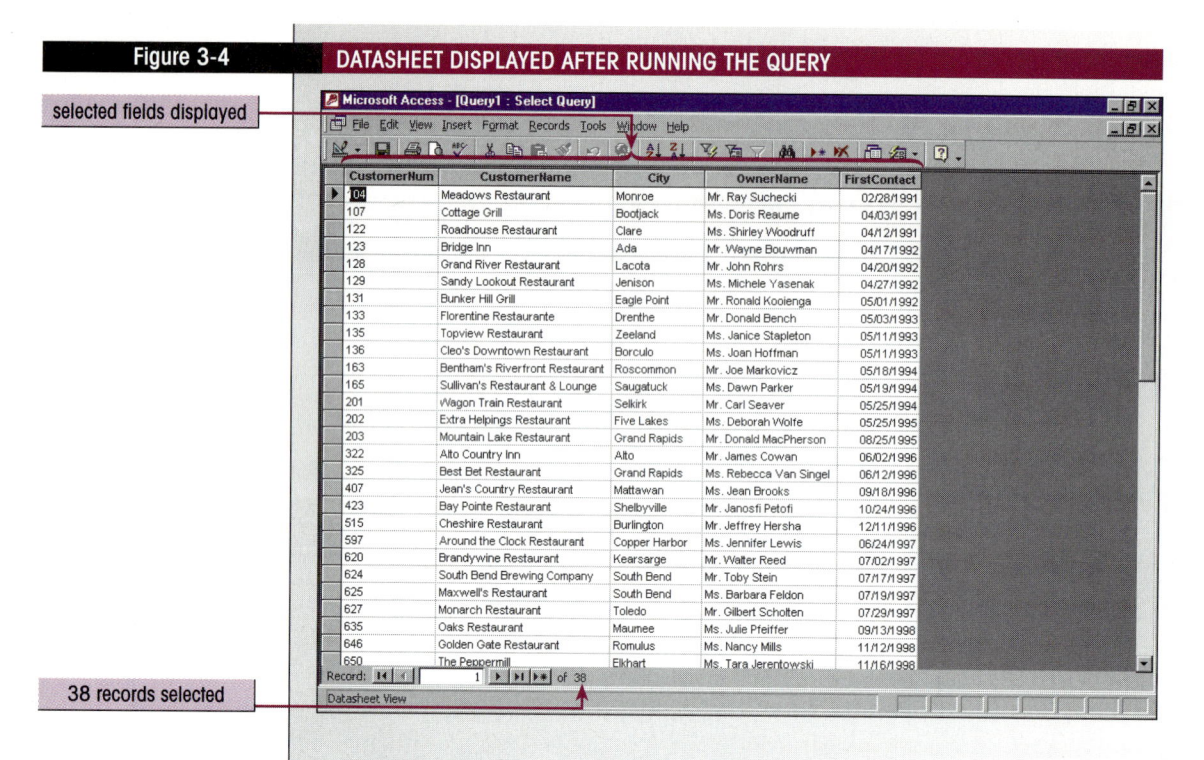

The five fields you added to the design grid appear in the datasheet, and the records are displayed in primary key sequence by customer number. Access selected a total of 38 records for display in the datasheet.

Kim asks you to save the query as "Customer Analysis" so that she can easily retrieve the same data again.

5. Click the **Save** button on the Query Datasheet toolbar. The Save As dialog box opens.

6. Type **Customer Analysis** in the Query Name text box, and then press the **Enter** key. Access saves the query with the specified name in the Restaurant database on your Data Disk and displays the name in the title bar.

7. Click the **Close** button on the menu bar to close the query and return to the Database window. Note that the Customer Analysis query appears in the list of queries.

8. Click the **Restore** button on the menu bar to return the Database window to its original size.

Barbara also wants to view specific information in the Restaurant database. However, she needs to see data from both the Customer table and the Order table at the same time. To view data from two tables at the same time, you need to define a relationship between the tables.

Defining Table Relationships

One of the most powerful features of a relational database management system is its ability to define relationships between tables. You use a common field to relate one table to another. The process of relating tables is often called performing a **join**. When you join tables that have a common field, you can extract data from them as if they were one larger table. For example, you can join the Customer and Order tables by using the CustomerNum field in both tables as the common field. Then you can use a query, form, or report to extract selected data from each table, even though the data is contained in two separate tables, as shown in Figure 3-5. In the Orders query shown in Figure 3-5, the OrderNum, Paid, and InvoiceAmt columns are fields from the Order table, and the CustomerName and State columns are fields from the Customer table. The joining of records is based on the common field of CustomerNum. The Customer and Order tables have a type of relationship called a one-to-many relationship.

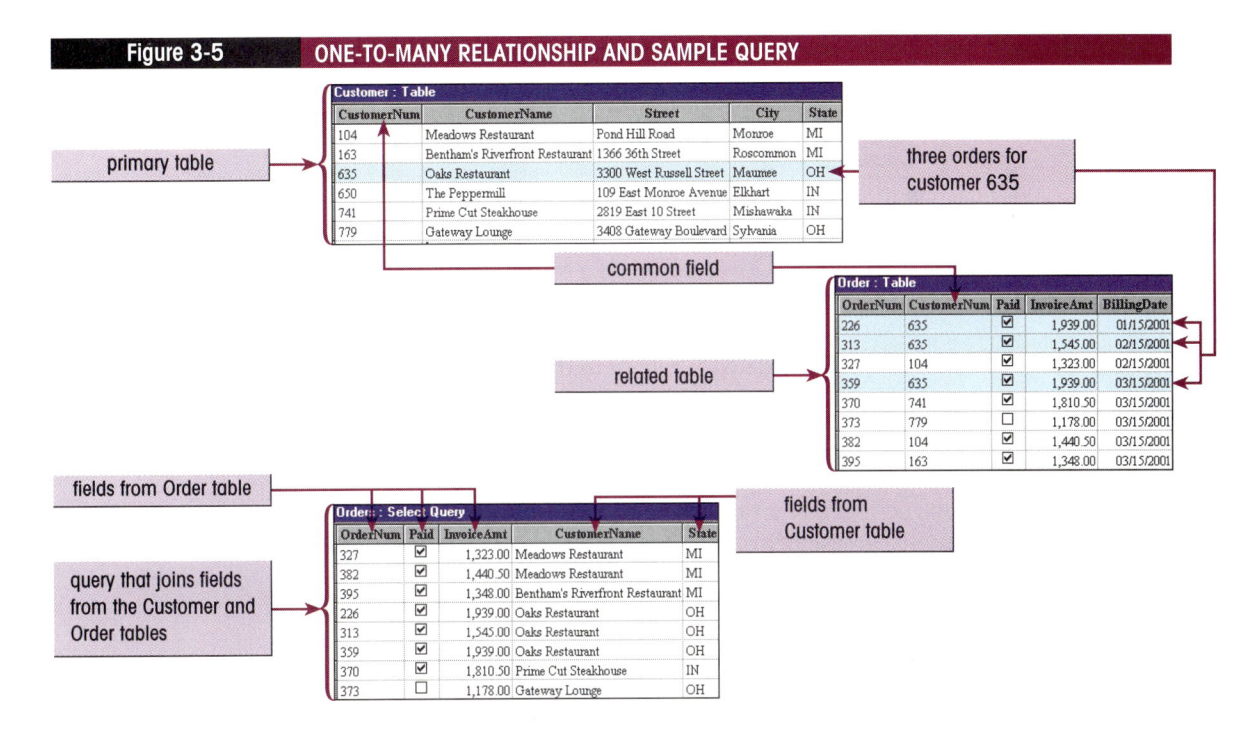

Figure 3-5 ONE-TO-MANY RELATIONSHIP AND SAMPLE QUERY

One-to-Many Relationships

A **one-to-many relationship** exists between two tables when one record in the first table matches zero, one, or many records in the second table, and when one record in the second table matches exactly one record in the first table. For example, as shown in Figure 3-5, customer 635 has three orders, customer 650 has zero orders, customers 163, 741, and 779 each have one order, and customer 104 has two orders. Every order has a single matching customer.

Access refers to the two tables that form a relationship as the primary table and the related table. The **primary table** is the "one" table in a one-to-many relationship; in Figure 3-5, the Customer table is the primary table because there is only one customer for each order. The **related table** is the "many" table; in Figure 3-5, the Order table is the related table because there can be many orders for each customer.

Because related data is stored in two tables, inconsistencies between the tables can occur. Consider the following scenarios:

- Barbara adds an order to the Order table for customer 107, Cottage Grill. This order does not have a matching record in the Customer table. The data is inconsistent, and the order record is considered to be an **orphaned** record.
- Barbara changes Oaks Restaurant from customer number 635 to 997 in the Customer table. Three orphaned records for customer 635 now exist in the Order table, and the database is inconsistent.

- Barbara deletes the record for Meadows Restaurant, customer 104, in the Customer table because this customer is no longer a Valle Coffee customer. The database is again inconsistent; two records for customer 104 in the Order table have no matching record in the Customer table.

You can avoid these problems by specifying referential integrity between tables when you define their relationships.

Referential Integrity

Referential integrity is a set of rules that Access enforces to maintain consistency between related tables when you update data in a database. Specifically, the referential integrity rules are as follows:

- When you add a record to a related table, a matching record must already exist in the primary table.
- If you attempt to change the value of the primary key in the primary table, Access prevents this change if matching records exist in a related table. However, if you choose the **cascade updates** option, Access permits the change in value to the primary key and changes the appropriate foreign key values in the related table.
- When you delete a record in the primary table, Access prevents the deletion if matching records exist in a related table. However, if you choose the **cascade deletes** option, Access deletes the record in the primary table and all records in related tables that have matching foreign key values.

Now you'll define a one-to-many relationship between the Customer and Order tables so that you can use fields from both tables to create a query that will retrieve the information Barbara wants.

Defining a Relationship Between Two Tables

When two tables have a common field, you can define a relationship between them in the Relationships window. The **Relationships window** illustrates the relationships among a database's tables. In this window you can view or change existing relationships, define new relationships between tables, and rearrange the layout of the tables.

You need to open the Relationships window and define the relationship between the Customer and Order tables. You'll define a one-to-many relationship between the two tables, with Customer as the primary table and Order as the related table, and with CustomerNum as the common field (the primary key in the Customer table and a foreign key in the Order table).

To define a one-to-many relationship between the two tables:

1. Click the **Relationships** button on the Database toolbar. The Show Table dialog box opens on top of the Relationships window. See Figure 3-6.

TUTORIAL 3 QUERYING A DATABASE   AC   3.09   ACCESS

| Figure 3-6 | SHOW TABLE DIALOG BOX |

Relationships window
add both tables

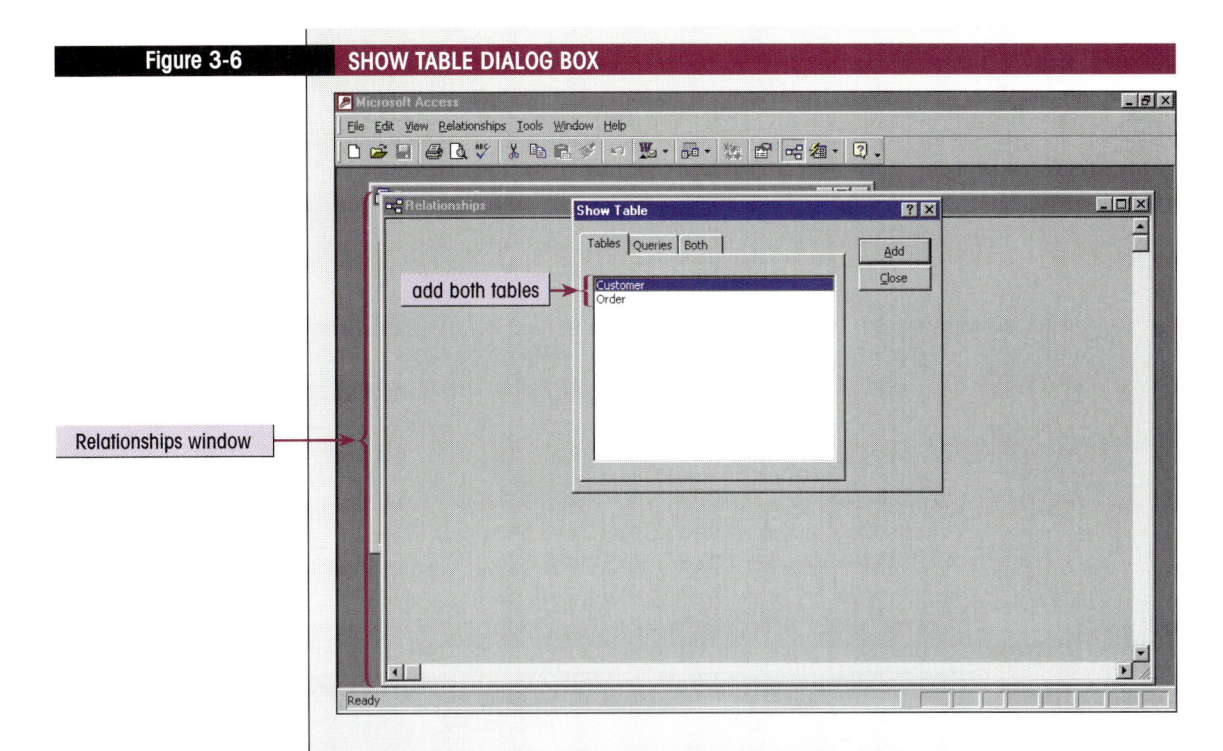

You must add each table participating in a relationship to the Relationships window.

2. Click **Customer** (if necessary) and then click the **Add** button. The Customer table is added to the Relationships window.

3. Click **Order** and then click the **Add** button. The Order table is added to the Relationships window.

4. Click the **Close** button in the Show Table dialog box to close it and reveal the entire Relationships window.

To form the relationship between the two tables, you drag the common field of CustomerNum from the primary table to the related table. Then Access opens the Edit Relationships dialog box, in which you select the relationship options for the two tables.

5. Click **CustomerNum** in the Customer table list, and drag it to **CustomerNum** in the Order table list. When you release the mouse button, the Edit Relationships dialog box opens. See Figure 3-7.

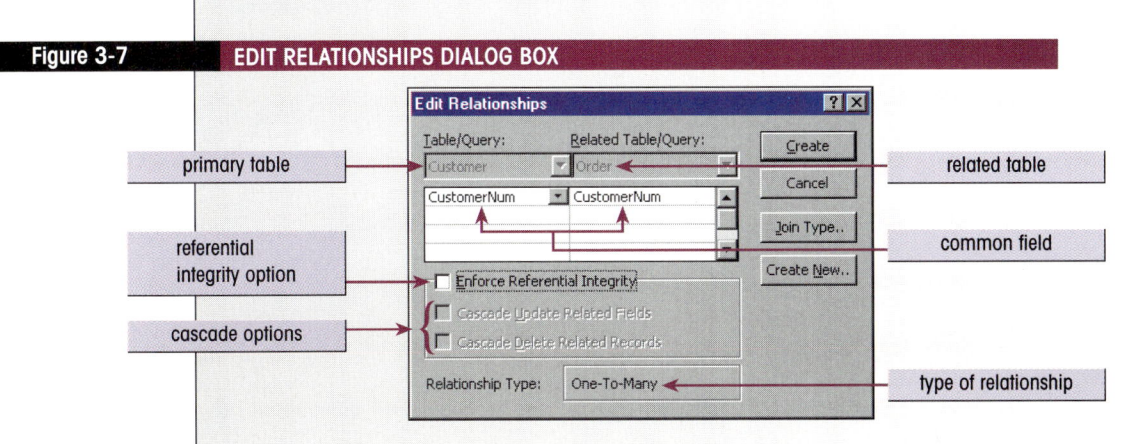

| Figure 3-7 | EDIT RELATIONSHIPS DIALOG BOX |

primary table
related table
referential integrity option
common field
cascade options
type of relationship

The primary table, related table, and common field appear at the top of the dialog box. The type of relationship, one-to-many, appears at the bottom of the dialog box. When you click the Enforce Referential Integrity check box, the two cascade options become available. If you select the Cascade Update Related Fields option, Access will change the appropriate foreign key values in the related table when you change a primary key value in the primary table. If you select the Cascade Delete Related Records option, when you delete a record in the primary table, Access will delete all records in the related table that have a matching foreign key value.

6. Click the **Enforce Referential Integrity** check box, click the **Cascade Update Related Fields** check box, and then click the **Cascade Delete Related Records** check box. You have now selected all the necessary relationship options.

7. Click the **Create** button to define the one-to-many relationship between the two tables and close the dialog box. The completed relationship appears in the Relationships window. See Figure 3-8.

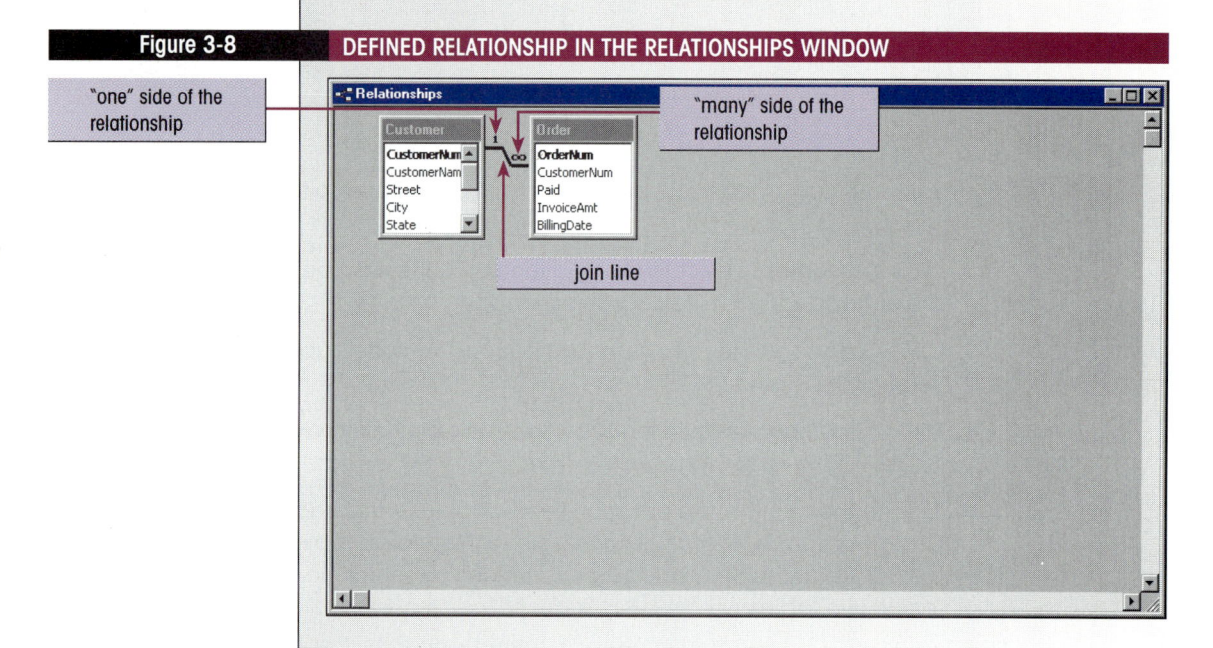

Figure 3-8 — DEFINED RELATIONSHIP IN THE RELATIONSHIPS WINDOW

"one" side of the relationship

"many" side of the relationship

join line

The **join line** connects the CustomerNum fields, which are common to the two tables. The common field joins the two tables, which have a one-to-many relationship. The "one" side of the relationship has the digit 1 at its end, and the "many" side of the relationship has the infinity symbol ∞ at its end. The two tables are still separate tables, but you can use the data in them as if they were one table.

8. Click the **Save** button on the Relationship toolbar to save the layout in the Relationships window.

9. Click the **Close** button on the Relationships window title bar. The Relationships window closes, and you return to the Database window.

TUTORIAL 3 QUERYING A DATABASE   AC 3.11

Now that you have joined the Customer and Order tables, you can create a query to produce the information Barbara wants. As part of her system for tracking payments received from restaurant customers, Barbara needs a query that displays the CustomerName, City, and State fields from the Customer table and the BillingDate, InvoiceAmt, and Paid fields from the Order table.

To create, run, and save the query using the Customer and Order tables:

1. With the Queries object selected in the Database window, double-click **Create query in Design view**. The Show Table dialog box opens on top of the Query window in Design view.

   You need to add both tables to the Query window.

2. Click **Customer** in the Tables list box (if necessary), click the **Add** button, click **Order**, click the **Add** button, and then click the **Close** button. The Customer and Order field lists appear in the Query window, and the Show Table dialog box closes. Note that the one-to-many relationship that exists between the two tables is shown in the Query window. Also, notice that the join line is thick at both ends; this signifies that you selected the option to enforce referential integrity. If you had not selected this option, the join line would be thin at both ends and neither the "1" nor the infinity symbol would appear, even though there is a one-to-many relationship between the two tables.

   You need to place the CustomerName, City, and State fields from the Customer field list into the design grid, and then place the BillingDate, InvoiceAmt, and Paid fields from the Order field list into the design grid.

3. Double-click **CustomerName** in the Customer field list to place CustomerName in the design grid's first column Field text box.

4. Repeat Step 3 to add the **City** and **State** fields from the Customer table, and then add the **BillingDate**, **InvoiceAmt**, and **Paid** fields (in that order) from the Order table, so that these fields are placed in the second through sixth columns of the design grid.

   The query specifications are complete, so you can now run the query.

5. Click the **Run** button ! on the Query Design toolbar. Access runs the query and displays the results in the datasheet.

6. Click the **Maximize** button ▢ on the Query window. See Figure 3-9.

Figure 3-9 DATASHEET FOR THE QUERY BASED ON THE CUSTOMER AND ORDER TABLES

fields from the Customer table

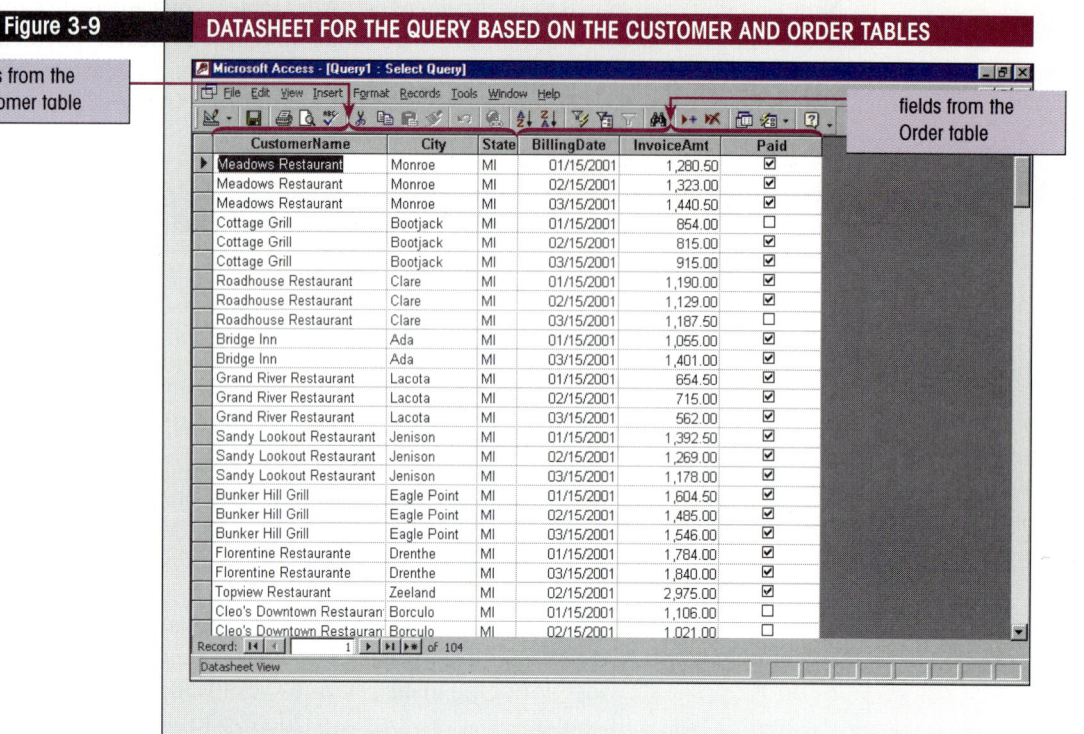

fields from the Order table

CustomerName	City	State	BillingDate	InvoiceAmt	Paid
Meadows Restaurant	Monroe	MI	01/15/2001	1,280.50	☑
Meadows Restaurant	Monroe	MI	02/15/2001	1,323.00	☑
Meadows Restaurant	Monroe	MI	03/15/2001	1,440.50	☑
Cottage Grill	Bootjack	MI	01/15/2001	854.00	☐
Cottage Grill	Bootjack	MI	02/15/2001	815.00	☑
Cottage Grill	Bootjack	MI	03/15/2001	915.00	☑
Roadhouse Restaurant	Clare	MI	01/15/2001	1,190.00	☑
Roadhouse Restaurant	Clare	MI	02/15/2001	1,129.00	☑
Roadhouse Restaurant	Clare	MI	03/15/2001	1,187.50	☐
Bridge Inn	Ada	MI	01/15/2001	1,055.00	☑
Bridge Inn	Ada	MI	03/15/2001	1,401.00	☑
Grand River Restaurant	Lacota	MI	01/15/2001	654.50	☑
Grand River Restaurant	Lacota	MI	02/15/2001	715.00	☑
Grand River Restaurant	Lacota	MI	03/15/2001	562.00	☑
Sandy Lookout Restaurant	Jenison	MI	01/15/2001	1,392.50	☑
Sandy Lookout Restaurant	Jenison	MI	02/15/2001	1,269.00	☑
Sandy Lookout Restaurant	Jenison	MI	03/15/2001	1,178.00	☑
Bunker Hill Grill	Eagle Point	MI	01/15/2001	1,604.50	☑
Bunker Hill Grill	Eagle Point	MI	02/15/2001	1,485.00	☑
Bunker Hill Grill	Eagle Point	MI	03/15/2001	1,546.00	☑
Florentine Restaurante	Drenthe	MI	01/15/2001	1,784.00	☑
Florentine Restaurante	Drenthe	MI	03/15/2001	1,840.00	☑
Topview Restaurant	Zeeland	MI	02/15/2001	2,975.00	☑
Cleo's Downtown Restauran	Borculo	MI	01/15/2001	1,106.00	☐
Cleo's Downtown Restauran	Borculo	MI	02/15/2001	1,021.00	☐

Only the six selected fields from the Customer and Order tables appear in the datasheet. The records are displayed in order according to the values in the primary key field, CustomerNum, even though this field is not included in the query datasheet.

Barbara plans on frequently tracking the data retrieved by the query, so she asks you to save the query as "Customer Orders."

7. Click the **Save** button on the Query Datasheet toolbar. The Save As dialog box opens.

8. Type **Customer Orders** in the Query Name text box, and then press the **Enter** key. Access saves the query with the specified name and displays the name in the Query window title bar.

Barbara decides she wants the records displayed in alphabetical order by customer name. Because your query displays data in order by the field value of CustomerNum, the primary key for the Customer table, you need to sort the records by CustomerName to display the data in the order Barbara wants.

Sorting Data in a Query

Sorting is the process of rearranging records in a specified order or sequence. Often you need to sort data before displaying or printing it, to meet a specific request. For example, Barbara might want to review order information arranged by the Paid field because she needs to know which orders are still unpaid. On the other hand, Leonard might want to view order information arranged by the InvoiceAmt totals for each customer, because he tracks company sales.

When you sort data in a database, you do not change the sequence of the records in the underlying tables. Only the records in the query datasheet are rearranged according to your specifications.

To sort records, you must select the **sort key**, which is the field used to determine the order of records in the datasheet. In this case, Barbara wants the data sorted by the customer name, so you need to specify the CustomerName field as the sort key. Sort keys can be text, number, date/time, currency, AutoNumber, yes/no, or Lookup Wizard fields, but not memo, OLE object, or hyperlink fields. You sort records in either ascending (increasing) or descending (decreasing) order. Figure 3-10 shows the results of each type of sort for different data types.

Figure 3-10 SORTING RESULTS FOR DIFFERENT DATA TYPES

DATA TYPE	ASCENDING SORT RESULTS	DESCENDING SORT RESULTS
Text	A to Z	Z to A
Number	lowest to highest numeric value	highest to lowest numeric value
Date/Time	oldest to most recent date	most recent to oldest date
Currency	lowest to highest numeric value	highest to lowest numeric value
AutoNumber	lowest to highest numeric value	highest to lowest numeric value
Yes/No	yes (check mark in check box) then no values	no then yes values

Access provides several methods for sorting data in a table or query datasheet and in a form. One method, clicking the toolbar sort buttons, lets you sort the displayed records quickly.

Using a Toolbar Button to Sort Data

The **Sort Ascending** and **Sort Descending** buttons on the toolbar allow you to sort records immediately, based on the selected field. First you select the column on which you want to base the sort, and then you click the appropriate sort button on the toolbar to rearrange the records in either ascending or descending order. Unless you save the datasheet or form after you've sorted the records, the rearrangement of records is temporary.

Recall that in Tutorial 1 you used the Sort Ascending button to sort query results by the State field. You'll use this same button to sort the Customer Orders query results by the CustomerName field.

To sort the records using a toolbar sort button:

1. Click any visible CustomerName field value to establish this field as the current field.

2. Click the **Sort Ascending** button on the Query Datasheet toolbar. The records are rearranged in ascending order by customer name. See Figure 3-11.

Figure 3-11   SORTING RECORDS ON A SINGLE FIELD IN A DATASHEET

(Screenshot of Microsoft Access - [Customer Orders : Select Query] showing records sorted in ascending order by CustomerName. Callouts point to the Sort Descending button, Sort Ascending button, and "records sorted in ascending order by CustomerName.")

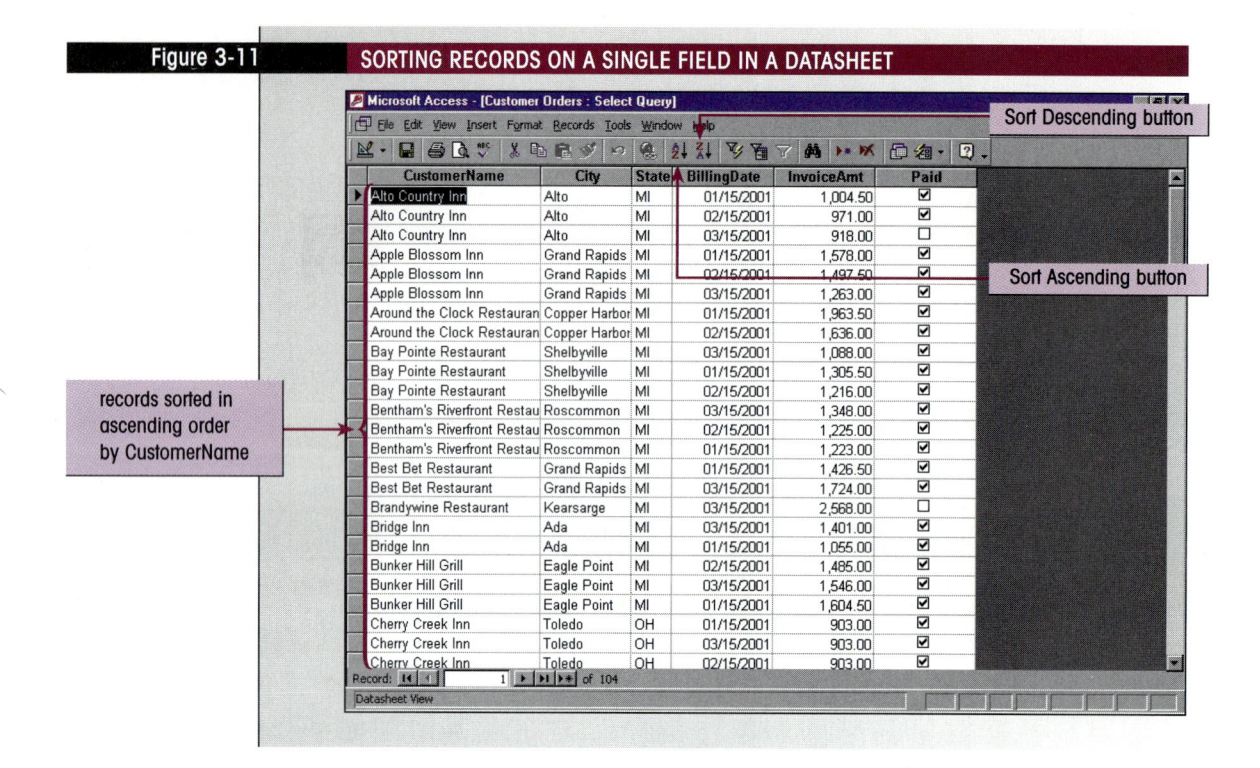

After viewing the query results, Barbara decides that she'd prefer to see the records arranged by the value in the Paid field, so that she can identify the paid invoices more easily. She wants to view all the unpaid invoices before the paid invoices (descending order for the Paid field, which is a yes/no field); plus, she wants to display the records within each group in increasing value of the InvoiceAmt field. To do this you need to sort using two fields.

Sorting Multiple Fields in Design View

Sort keys can be unique or nonunique. A sort key is **unique** if the value of the sort key field for each record is different. The CustomerNum field in the Customer table is an example of a unique sort key because each customer record has a different value in this field. A sort key is **nonunique** if more than one record can have the same value for the sort key field. For example, the Paid field in the Order table is a nonunique sort key because more than one record has the same Paid value.

When the sort key is nonunique, records with the same sort key value are grouped together, but they are not in a specific order within the group. To arrange these grouped records in a specific order, you can specify a **secondary sort key**, which is a second sort key field. The first sort key field is called the **primary sort key**. Note that the primary sort key is not the same as a table's primary key field. A table has at most one primary key, which must be unique, whereas any field in a table can serve as a primary sort key.

Access lets you select up to 10 different sort keys. When you use the toolbar sort buttons, the sort key fields must be in adjacent columns in the datasheet. You highlight the columns, and Access sorts first by the first column and then by each other highlighted column in order from left to right.

Barbara wants the records sorted first by the Paid field and then by the InvoiceAmt field. Although the two fields are adjacent, they are in the wrong order in your current query design. If you used a toolbar sort button, the InvoiceAmt field would be the primary sort key instead of the Paid field. You could move the InvoiceAmt field to the right of the Paid field in the query datasheet. However, you can specify only one type of sort—either ascending or descending—for selected columns in the query datasheet. This is not what Barbara wants; she wants the Paid field values to be sorted in descending order and the InvoiceAmt field values to be sorted in ascending order.

In this case, you need to specify the sort keys for the query in Design view. Any time you want to sort on multiple fields that are nonadjacent or in the wrong order, but you do not want to rearrange the columns in the query datasheet to accomplish the sort, you must specify the sort keys in Design view.

In the Query window in Design view, Access first uses the sort key that is leftmost in the design grid. Therefore, you must arrange the fields you want to sort from left to right in the design grid, with the primary sort key being the leftmost sort key field.

REFERENCE WINDOW

Sorting a Query Datasheet
- In the query datasheet, select the field or adjacent fields on which you want to sort.
- Click the Sort Ascending button or the Sort Descending button on the Query Datasheet toolbar.

or

- In Design view, position the fields serving as sort keys from left (primary sort key) to right, and then select the sort order for each sort key.

To achieve the results Barbara wants, you need to switch to Design view, move the InvoiceAmt field to the right of the Paid field, and then specify the sort order for the two fields.

To select the two sort keys in Design view:

1. Click the **View** button for Design view on the Query Datasheet toolbar to open the query in Design view.

   First, you'll move the InvoiceAmt field to the right of the Paid field.

2. If necessary, click the right arrow in the design grid's horizontal scroll bar a few times to scroll to the right so that both the InvoiceAmt and Paid fields, as well as the next empty column, are completely visible.

3. Position the pointer above the InvoiceAmt field name until the pointer changes to ↓, and then click to select the field. See Figure 3-12.

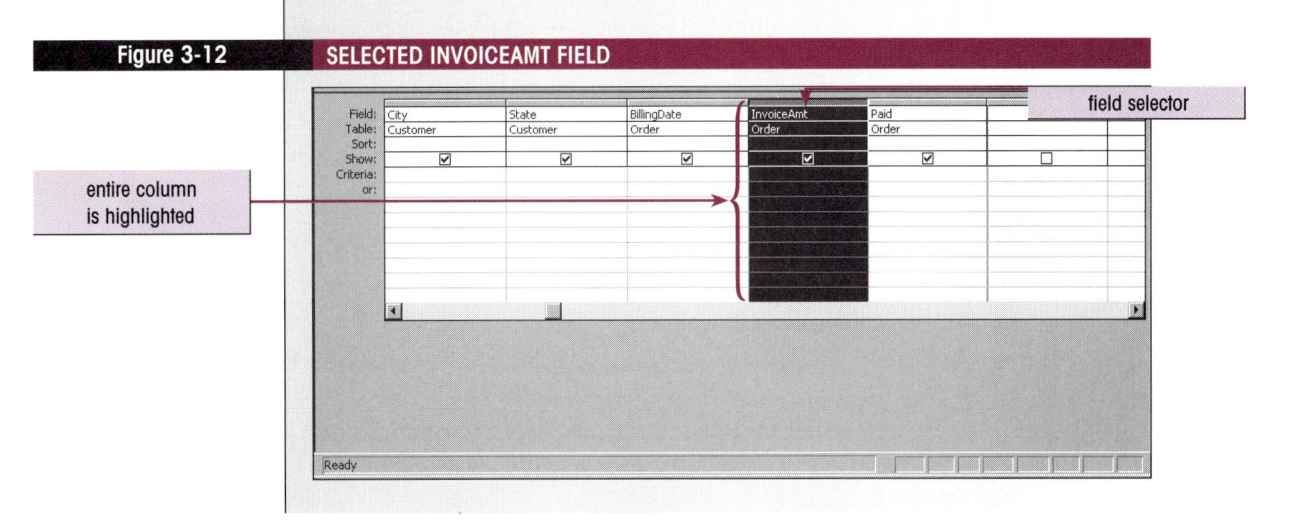

Figure 3-12   SELECTED INVOICEAMT FIELD

4. Position the pointer in the field selector at the top of the highlighted column, and then click and drag the pointer to the right until the vertical line on the right of the Paid field is highlighted. See Figure 3-13.

Figure 3-13   DRAGGING THE FIELD IN THE DESIGN GRID

drag pointer to here

line is highlighted

5. Release the mouse button. The InvoiceAmt field moves to the right of the Paid field.

The fields are now in the correct order for the sort. Next, you need to specify a descending sort order for the Paid field and an ascending sort order for the InvoiceAmt field.

6. Click the **Paid Sort** text box, click the **Sort** list arrow that appears, and then click **Descending**. You've selected a descending sort order for the Paid field, which will be the primary sort key. The Paid field is a yes/no field, and a descending sort order for this type of field displays all the no (unpaid) values before the yes (paid) values.

7. Click the **InvoiceAmt Sort** text box, click the **Sort** list arrow, click **Ascending**, and then click the **Criteria** text box for the InvoiceAmt field. You've selected an ascending sort order for the InvoiceAmt field, which will be the secondary sort key. See Figure 3-14.

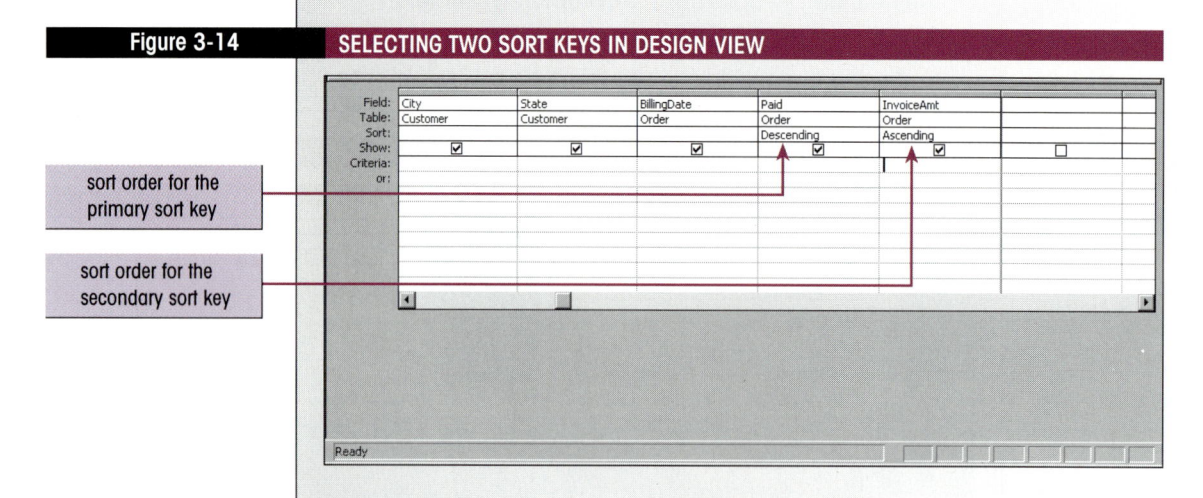

Figure 3-14   SELECTING TWO SORT KEYS IN DESIGN VIEW

sort order for the primary sort key

sort order for the secondary sort key

You have finished your query changes, so now you can run the query and then save the modified query with the same query name.

8. Click the **Run** button on the Query Design toolbar. Access runs the query and displays the query datasheet. The records appear in descending order, based on the values of the Paid field. Within groups of records with the same Paid field value, the records appear in ascending order by the values of the InvoiceAmt field. See Figure 3-15.

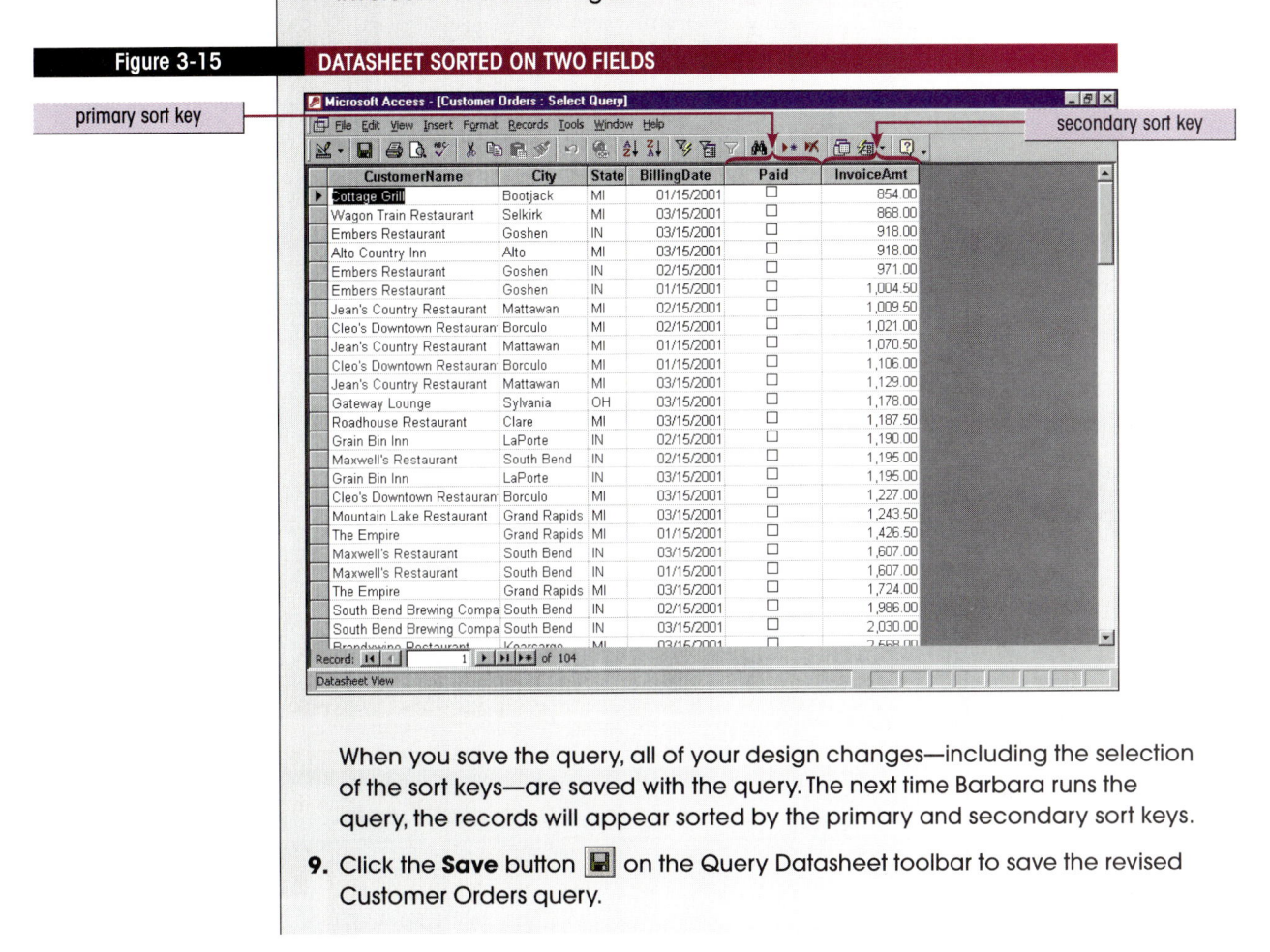

Figure 3-15 — DATASHEET SORTED ON TWO FIELDS

primary sort key ... *secondary sort key*

CustomerName	City	State	BillingDate	Paid	InvoiceAmt
Cottage Grill	Bootjack	MI	01/15/2001	☐	854.00
Wagon Train Restaurant	Selkirk	MI	03/15/2001	☐	868.00
Embers Restaurant	Goshen	IN	03/15/2001	☐	918.00
Alto Country Inn	Alto	MI	03/15/2001	☐	918.00
Embers Restaurant	Goshen	IN	02/15/2001	☐	971.00
Embers Restaurant	Goshen	IN	01/15/2001	☐	1,004.50
Jean's Country Restaurant	Mattawan	MI	02/15/2001	☐	1,009.50
Cleo's Downtown Restauran	Borculo	MI	02/15/2001	☐	1,021.00
Jean's Country Restaurant	Mattawan	MI	01/15/2001	☐	1,070.50
Cleo's Downtown Restauran	Borculo	MI	01/15/2001	☐	1,106.00
Jean's Country Restaurant	Mattawan	MI	03/15/2001	☐	1,129.00
Gateway Lounge	Sylvania	OH	03/15/2001	☐	1,178.00
Roadhouse Restaurant	Clare	MI	03/15/2001	☐	1,187.50
Grain Bin Inn	LaPorte	IN	02/15/2001	☐	1,190.00
Maxwell's Restaurant	South Bend	IN	02/15/2001	☐	1,195.00
Grain Bin Inn	LaPorte	IN	03/15/2001	☐	1,195.00
Cleo's Downtown Restauran	Borculo	MI	03/15/2001	☐	1,227.00
Mountain Lake Restaurant	Grand Rapids	MI	03/15/2001	☐	1,243.50
The Empire	Grand Rapids	MI	01/15/2001	☐	1,426.50
Maxwell's Restaurant	South Bend	IN	03/15/2001	☐	1,607.00
Maxwell's Restaurant	South Bend	IN	01/15/2001	☐	1,607.00
The Empire	Grand Rapids	MI	03/15/2001	☐	1,724.00
South Bend Brewing Compa	South Bend	IN	02/15/2001	☐	1,986.00
South Bend Brewing Compa	South Bend	IN	03/15/2001	☐	2,030.00
Brandywine Restaurant	Kearsarge	MI	03/15/2001	☐	2,568.00

Record: 1 of 104

When you save the query, all of your design changes—including the selection of the sort keys—are saved with the query. The next time Barbara runs the query, the records will appear sorted by the primary and secondary sort keys.

9. Click the **Save** button on the Query Datasheet toolbar to save the revised Customer Orders query.

Barbara wants to concentrate on the unpaid orders in the datasheet. Selecting only the unpaid orders is a temporary change that Barbara wants in the datasheet, so you do not need to switch to Design view and change the query. Instead, you can apply a filter.

Filtering Data

A **filter** is a set of restrictions you place on the records in an open datasheet or form to *temporarily* isolate a subset of the records. A filter lets you view different subsets of displayed records so that you can focus on only the data you need. Unless you save a query or form with a filter applied, an applied filter is not available the next time you run the query or open the form. The simplest technique for filtering records is Filter By Selection. **Filter By Selection** lets you select all or part of a field value in a datasheet or form, and then display only those records that contain the selected value in the field. Another technique for filtering records is to use **Filter By Form**, which changes your datasheet to display empty fields. Then you can select a value from the list arrow that appears when you click any blank field to apply a filter that selects only those records containing that value.

| REFERENCE WINDOW | RW |

Using Filter By Selection
- In the datasheet or form, select all or part of the field value that will be the basis for the filter.
- Click the Filter By Selection button on the toolbar.

For Barbara's request, you need to select an unchecked box in the Paid field, which represents an unpaid order, and then use Filter By Selection to display only those query records with this same value.

To display the records using Filter By Selection:

1. Click any check box that is unchecked in the Paid column. When you click the check box, you select the field value, but you also change the check box from unchecked to checked. Because you've changed an unpaid order to a paid order, you need to click the same check box a second time.

2. Click the same check box a second time. The field value changes back to unchecked, which is now the selected field value.

3. Click the **Filter By Selection** button on the Query Datasheet toolbar. Access displays the filtered results. Only the 25 query records that have an unchecked Paid field value appear in the datasheet; these records are the unpaid order records. Note that the status bar display (FLTR), the area next to the navigation buttons, and the selected Remove Filter button on the toolbar all indicate that the records have been filtered. See Figure 3-16.

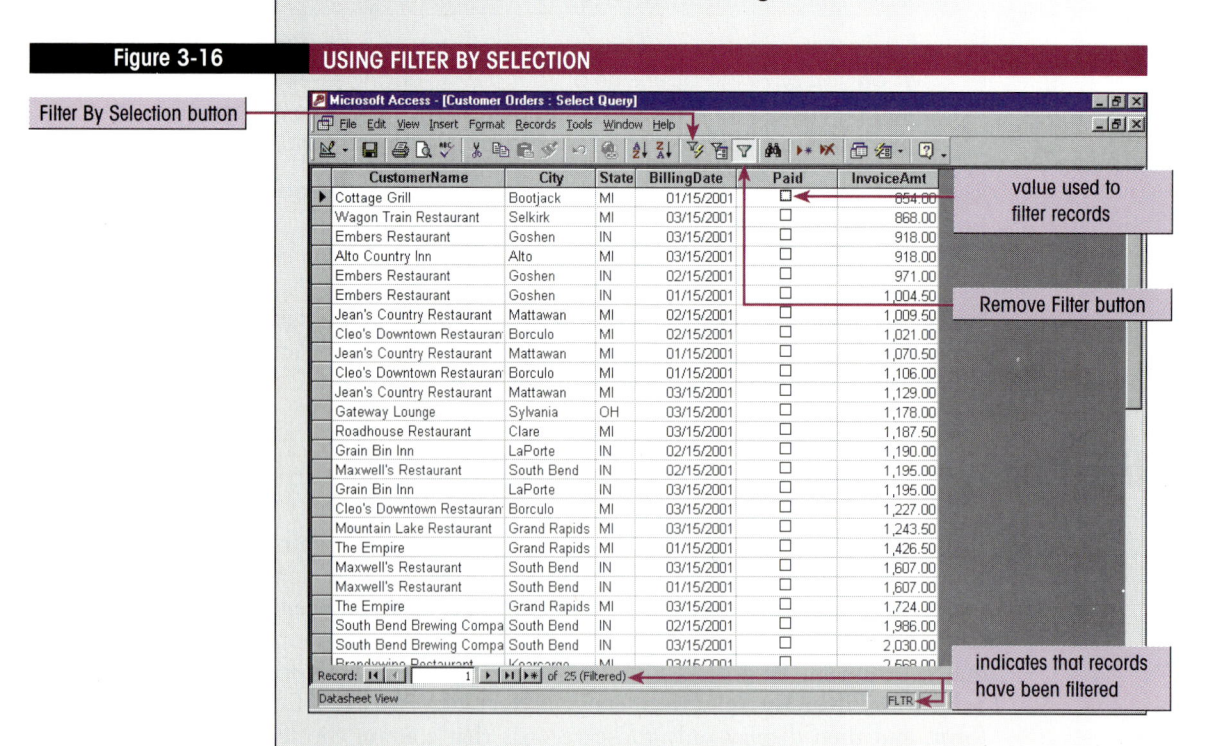

Figure 3-16 USING FILTER BY SELECTION

Barbara asks you to print the current datasheet so that she can give the printout to a staff member who is tracking unpaid orders.

4. Click the **Print** button on the Query Datasheet toolbar to print the datasheet.

   Now you can redisplay all the query records by clicking the Remove Filter button; this button works as a toggle to switch between the filtered and nonfiltered displays.

5. Click the **Remove Filter** button on the Query Datasheet toolbar. Access redisplays all the records in the query datasheet.

6. Click the **Save** button on the Query Datasheet toolbar, and then click the **Close** button on the menu bar to save and close the query and return to the Database window.

7. Click the **Restore** button on the menu bar to return the Database window to its original size.

The queries you've created will help Valle Coffee employees retrieve just the information they want to view. In the next session, you'll continue to create queries to meet their information needs.

Session 3.1 QUICK CHECK

1. What is a select query?
2. Describe the field list and the design grid in the Query window in Design view.
3. How are a table datasheet and a query datasheet similar? How are they different?
4. The _____ is the "one" table in a one-to-many relationship, and the _____ is the "many" table in the relationship.
5. _____ is a set of rules that Access enforces to maintain consistency between related tables when you update data in a database.
6. For a date/time field, what is ascending sort order?
7. When must you define multiple sort keys in Design view instead of in the query datasheet?
8. A(n) _____ is a set of restrictions you place on the records in an open datasheet or form to isolate a subset of records temporarily.

SESSION 3.2

In this session, you will specify an exact match condition in a query, change a datasheet's appearance, use a comparison operator to match a range of values, use the And and Or logical operators to define multiple selection criteria for queries, and perform calculations in queries.

Barbara wants to display customer and order information for all orders billed on 01/15/2001, so that she can see which orders have been paid. For this request, you need to create a query that displays selected fields from the Order and Customer tables and selected records that satisfy a condition.

Defining Record Selection Criteria for Queries

Just as you can display selected fields from a table in a query datasheet, you can display selected records. To tell Access which records you want to select, you must specify a condition as part of the query. A **condition** is a criterion, or rule, that determines which records are selected. To define a condition for a field, you place the condition in the field's Criteria text box in the design grid.

A condition usually consists of an operator, often a comparison operator, and a value. A **comparison operator** asks Access to compare the values of a database field to the condition value and to select all the records for which the relationship is true. For example, the condition >1000.00 for the InvoiceAmt field selects all records in the Order table having InvoiceAmt field values greater than 1000.00. Figure 3-17 shows the Access comparison operators.

Figure 3-17   ACCESS COMPARISON OPERATORS

OPERATOR	MEANING	EXAMPLE
=	equal to (optional; default operator)	="Hall"
<	less than	<#1/1/99#
<=	less than or equal to	<=100
>	greater than	>"C400"
>=	greater than or equal to	>=18.75
<>	not equal to	<>"Hall"
Between ... And...	between two values (inclusive)	Between 50 And 325
In ()	in a list of values	In ("Hall", "Seeger")
Like	matches a pattern that includes wildcards	Like "706*"

Specifying an Exact Match

For Barbara's request, you need to create a query that will display only those records in the Order table with the value 01/15/2001 in the BillingDate field. This type of condition is called an **exact match** because the value in the specified field must match the condition exactly in order for the record to be included in the query results. You'll use the Simple Query Wizard to create the query, and then you'll specify the exact match condition.

To create the query using the Simple Query Wizard:

1. If you took a break after the previous session, make sure that Access is running, the Restaurant database is open, and the Queries object is selected in the Database window.

2. Double-click **Create query by using wizard**. Access opens the first Simple Query Wizard dialog box, in which you select the tables (or queries) and fields for the query.

3. Click the **Tables/Queries** list arrow, and then click **Table: Order**. The fields in the Order table appear in the Available Fields list box. See Figure 3-18.

Figure 3-18 FIRST SIMPLE QUERY WIZARD DIALOG BOX

selected table

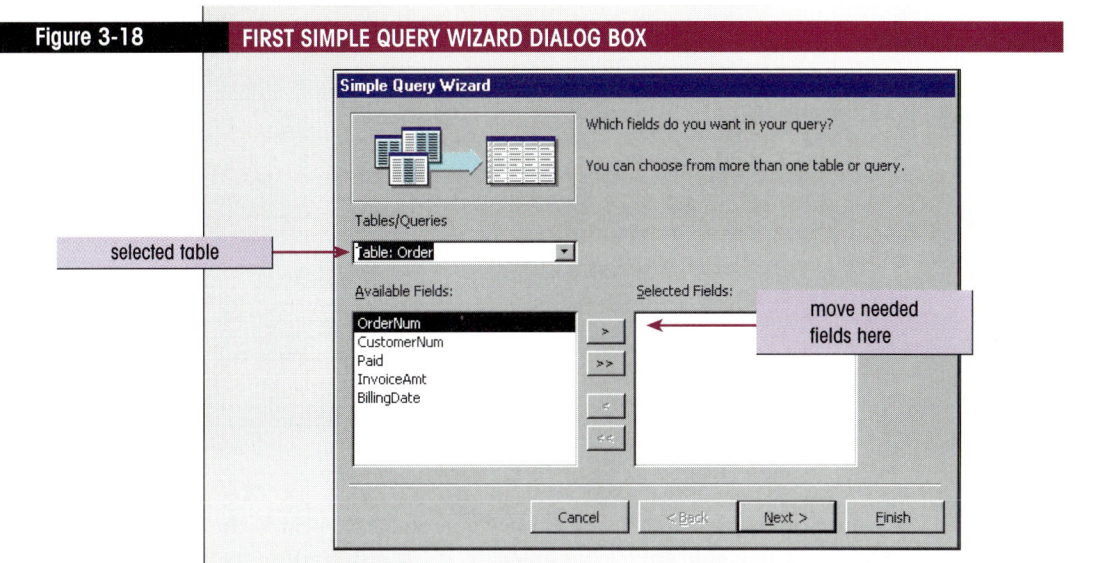

move needed fields here

Except for the CustomerNum field, you will include all fields from the Order table in the query.

4. Click the **>>** button. All the fields from the Available Fields list box move to the Selected Fields list box.

5. Click **CustomerNum** in the Selected Fields list box, click the **<** button to move the CustomerNum field back to the Available Fields list box, and then click **BillingDate** in the Selected Fields list box.

   Barbara also wants certain information from the Customer table included in the query results.

6. Click the **Tables/Queries** list arrow, and then click **Table: Customer**. The fields in the Customer table now appear in the Available Fields list box. Notice that the fields you selected from the Order table remain in the Selected Fields list box.

7. Click **CustomerName** in the Available Fields list box, and then click the **>** button to move CustomerName to the Selected Fields list box.

8. Repeat Step 7 to move the **State**, **OwnerName**, and **Phone** fields into the Selected Fields list box.

9. Click the **Next** button to open the second Simple Query Wizard dialog box, in which you choose whether the query will display records from the selected tables or a summary of those records. Summary options show calculations such as average, minimum, maximum, and so on. Barbara wants to view the details for the records, not a summary.

10. Make sure the **Detail (shows every field of every record)** option button is selected, and then click the **Next** button to open the last Simple Query Wizard dialog box, in which you choose a name for the query and complete the Wizard. You need to enter a condition for the query, so you'll want to modify the query's design.

11. Type **January Orders**, click the **Modify the query design** option button, and then click the **Finish** button. Access saves the query as January Orders and opens the query in Design view. See Figure 3-19.

Figure 3-19: QUERY IN DESIGN VIEW

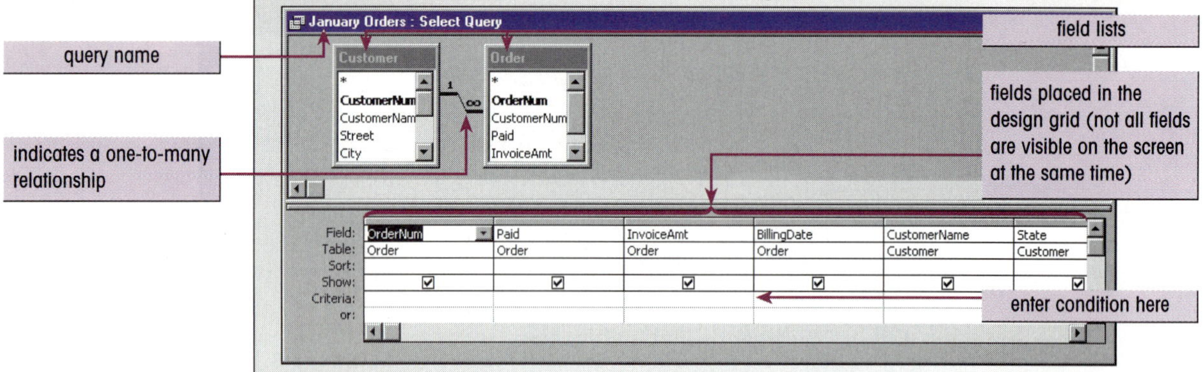

- query name
- indicates a one-to-many relationship
- field lists
- fields placed in the design grid (not all fields are visible on the screen at the same time)
- enter condition here

The field lists for the Customer and Order tables appear in the top portion of the window, and the join line indicating a one-to-many relationship connects the two tables. The selected fields appear in the design grid. Not all of the fields are visible in the grid; to see the other selected fields, you need to scroll to the right using the horizontal scroll bar.

To display the information Barbara wants, you need to enter the condition for the BillingDate field in its Criteria text box. Barbara wants to display only those records with a billing date of 01/15/2001.

To enter the exact match condition, and then run the query:

1. Click the **BillingDate Criteria** text box, type **1/15/01**, and then press the **Enter** key. The condition changes to #1/15/01#. (Note that you do not have to type the date as 01/15/2001; if you did, Access would still change the condition to #1/15/01#.)

   Access automatically placed number signs (#) before and after the condition. You must place date and time values inside number signs when using these values as selection criteria. If you omit the number signs, however, Access will include them automatically.

2. Click the **Run** button on the Query Design toolbar. Access runs the query and displays the selected field values for only those records with a BillingDate field value of 01/15/2001. A total of 36 records are selected and displayed in the datasheet. See Figure 3-20.

Figure 3-20: DATASHEET DISPLAYING SELECTED FIELDS AND RECORDS

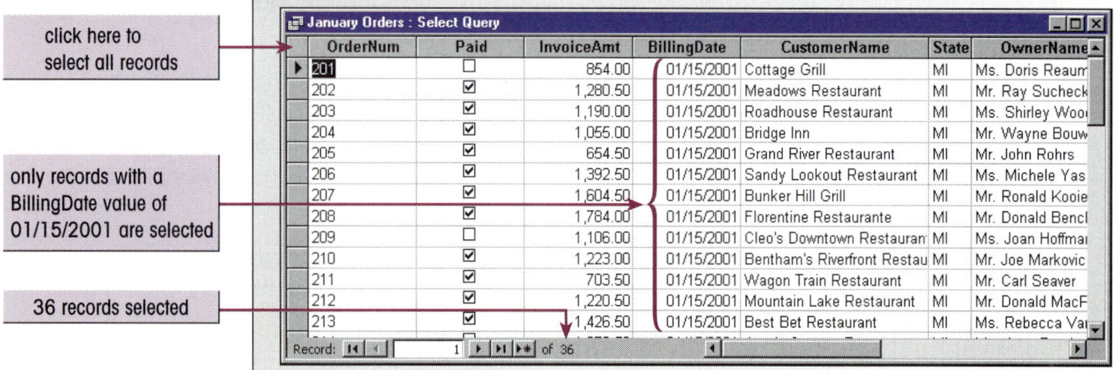

- click here to select all records
- only records with a BillingDate value of 01/15/2001 are selected
- 36 records selected

Barbara would like to see more fields and records on the screen at one time. She asks you to maximize the datasheet, change the datasheet's font size, and resize all the columns to their best fit.

Changing a Datasheet's Appearance

You can change the characteristics of a datasheet, including the font type and size of text in the datasheet, to improve its appearance or readability. You also can resize the datasheet columns to view more columns on the screen at the same time.

You'll maximize the datasheet, change the font size from the default 10 points to 8, and then resize the datasheet columns.

To change the font size and resize columns in the datasheet:

1. Click the **Maximize** button on the Query window title bar.

2. Click the **record selector** to the left of the field names at the top of the datasheet (see Figure 3-20) to select the entire datasheet.

3. Click **Format** on the menu bar, and then click **Font** to open the Font dialog box.

4. Scroll the Size list box, click **8**, and then click the **OK** button. The font size for the entire datasheet changes to 8.

   Next you need to resize the columns to their best fit—that is, so each column is just wide enough to fit the longest value in the column.

5. Position the pointer in the OrderNum field selector. When the pointer changes to ↓, click to select the entire column and deselect all other columns.

6. Click the horizontal scroll right arrow until the Phone field is fully visible, and then position the pointer in the Phone field selector until the pointer changes to ↓.

7. Press and hold the **Shift** key, and then click the mouse button. All the columns are selected. Now you can resize all of them at once.

8. Position the pointer at the right edge of the Phone field selector until the pointer changes to ↔. See Figure 3-21.

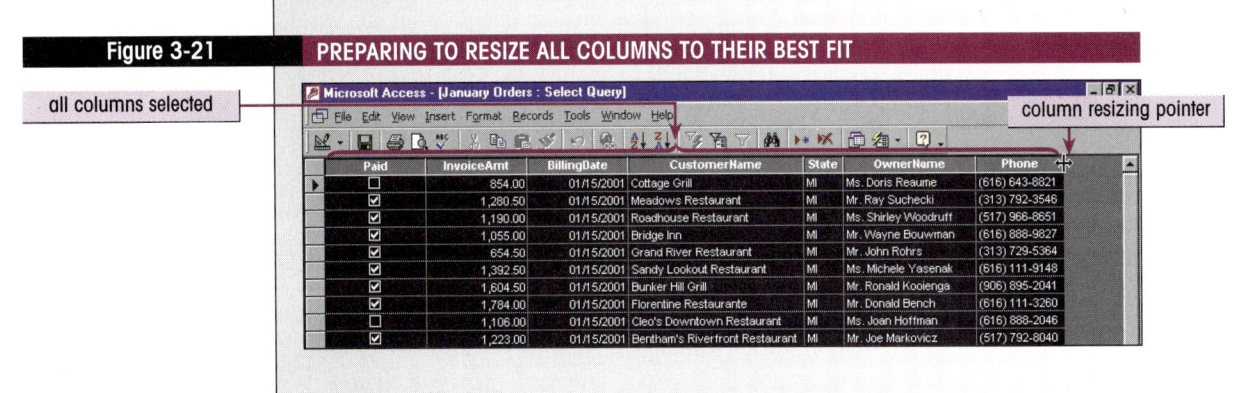

Figure 3-21   **PREPARING TO RESIZE ALL COLUMNS TO THEIR BEST FIT**

all columns selected

column resizing pointer

9. Double-click the mouse button. All columns are resized to their best fit, which makes each column just large enough to fit the longest *visible* field value in the column, including the field name at the top of the column. Scroll through the datasheet and resize individual columns as needed to display all field values completely.

10. If necessary, scroll to the left so that the OrderNum field is visible, and then click any field value box (except a Paid field value) to deselect all columns. See Figure 3-22.

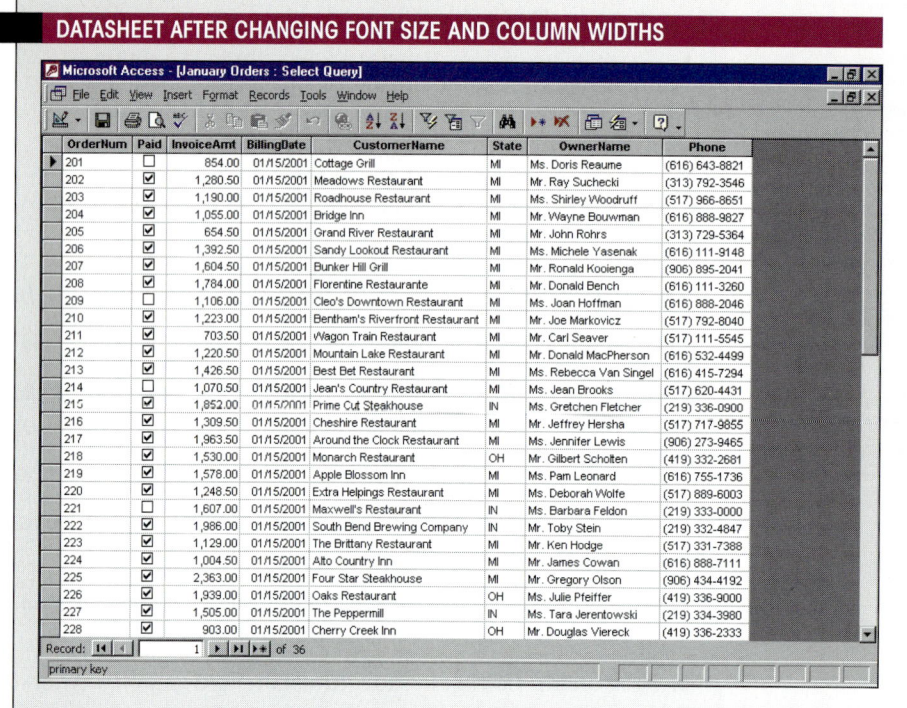

Figure 3-22   **DATASHEET AFTER CHANGING FONT SIZE AND COLUMN WIDTHS**

TROUBLE? Your screen might show more or fewer columns, depending on the monitor you are using.

11. Click the **Save** button on the Query Datasheet toolbar, and then click the **Close** button on the menu bar. Access saves and closes the query, and you return to the Database window.

After viewing the query results, Barbara decides that she would like to see the same fields, but only for those records whose InvoiceAmt exceeds $2,000. She wants to note this information and pass it along to her staff members so that they can contact those customers with higher outstanding invoices. To create the query needed to produce these results, you need to use a comparison operator to match a range of values—in this case, any InvoiceAmt value greater than $2,000.

Using a Comparison Operator to Match a Range of Values

Once you create and save a query, you can click the Open button to run it again, or you can click the Design button to change its design. Because the design of the query you need to create next is similar to the January Orders query, you will change its design, run the query to test it, and then save the query with a new name, which keeps the January Orders query intact.

To change the January Orders query design to create a new query:

1. Click the **January Orders** query in the Database window (if necessary), and then click the **Design** button to open the January Orders query in Design view.

2. Click the **InvoiceAmt Criteria** text box, type **>2000**, and then press the **Tab** key. See Figure 3-23.

Figure 3-23   CHANGING A QUERY'S DESIGN TO CREATE A NEW QUERY

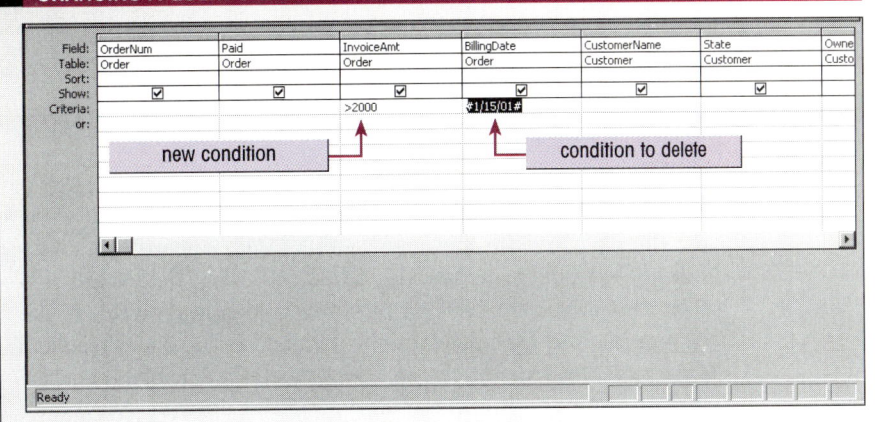

Barbara's new condition specifies that a record will be selected only if its InvoiceAmt field value exceeds 2000. Before you run the query, you need to delete the condition for the BillingDate field.

3. With the BillingDate field condition highlighted, press the **Delete** key. Now there is no condition for the BillingDate field.

4. Click the **Run** button on the Query Design toolbar. Access runs the query and displays the selected fields for only those records with an InvoiceAmt field value greater than 2000. A total of four records are selected. See Figure 3-24.

Figure 3-24   RUNNING THE MODIFIED QUERY

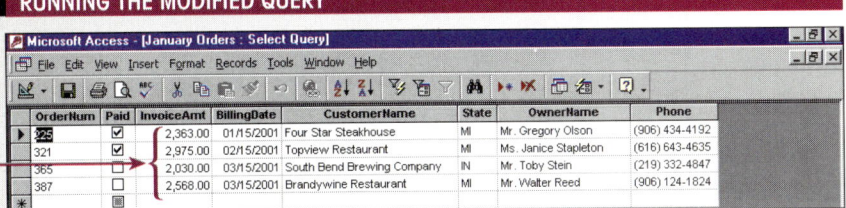

only records with an InvoiceAmt value greater than 2000 are selected

OrderNum	Paid	InvoiceAmt	BillingDate	CustomerName	State	OwnerName	Phone
225	✓	2,363.00	01/15/2001	Four Star Steakhouse	MI	Mr. Gregory Olson	(906) 434-4192
321	✓	2,975.00	02/15/2001	Topview Restaurant	MI	Ms. Janice Stapleton	(616) 643-4635
365	☐	2,030.00	03/15/2001	South Bend Brewing Company	IN	Mr. Toby Stein	(219) 332-4847
387	☐	2,568.00	03/15/2001	Brandywine Restaurant	MI	Mr. Walter Reed	(906) 124-1824

Of the records retrieved, Barbara notes that order numbers 365 and 387 have not yet been paid and the amount of each. She gives this information to her staff.

So that Barbara can display this information again, as necessary, you'll save the query as High Invoice Amounts.

5. Click **File** on the menu bar, and then click **Save As** to open the Save As dialog box.

6. In the text box for the new query name, type **High Invoice Amounts**. Notice that the As text box specifies that you are saving the data as a query.

7. Click the **OK** button to save the query using the new name. The new query name appears in the Query window title bar.

8. Click the **Close** button ☒ on the menu bar. The Database window becomes the active window.

Leonard asks Barbara for a list of the orders billed on 01/15/2001 that are still unpaid. He wants to know which customers are slow in paying their invoices. To produce this data, you need to create a query containing two conditions—one for the order's billing date and another to indicate that the order is unpaid.

Defining Multiple Selection Criteria for Queries

Multiple conditions require you to use **logical operators** to combine two or more conditions. When you want a record selected only if two or more conditions are met, you need to use the **And logical operator**. In this case, Leonard wants to see only those records with a BillingDate field value of 01/15/2001 *and* a Paid field value of No. If you place conditions in separate fields in the *same* Criteria row of the design grid, all the conditions in that row must be met in order for a record to be included in the query results. However, if you place conditions in *different* Criteria rows, a record will be selected if at least one of the conditions is met. If none of the conditions is met, then Access does not select the record. When you place conditions in different Criteria rows, you are using the **Or logical operator**. Figure 3-25 illustrates the difference between the And and Or logical operators.

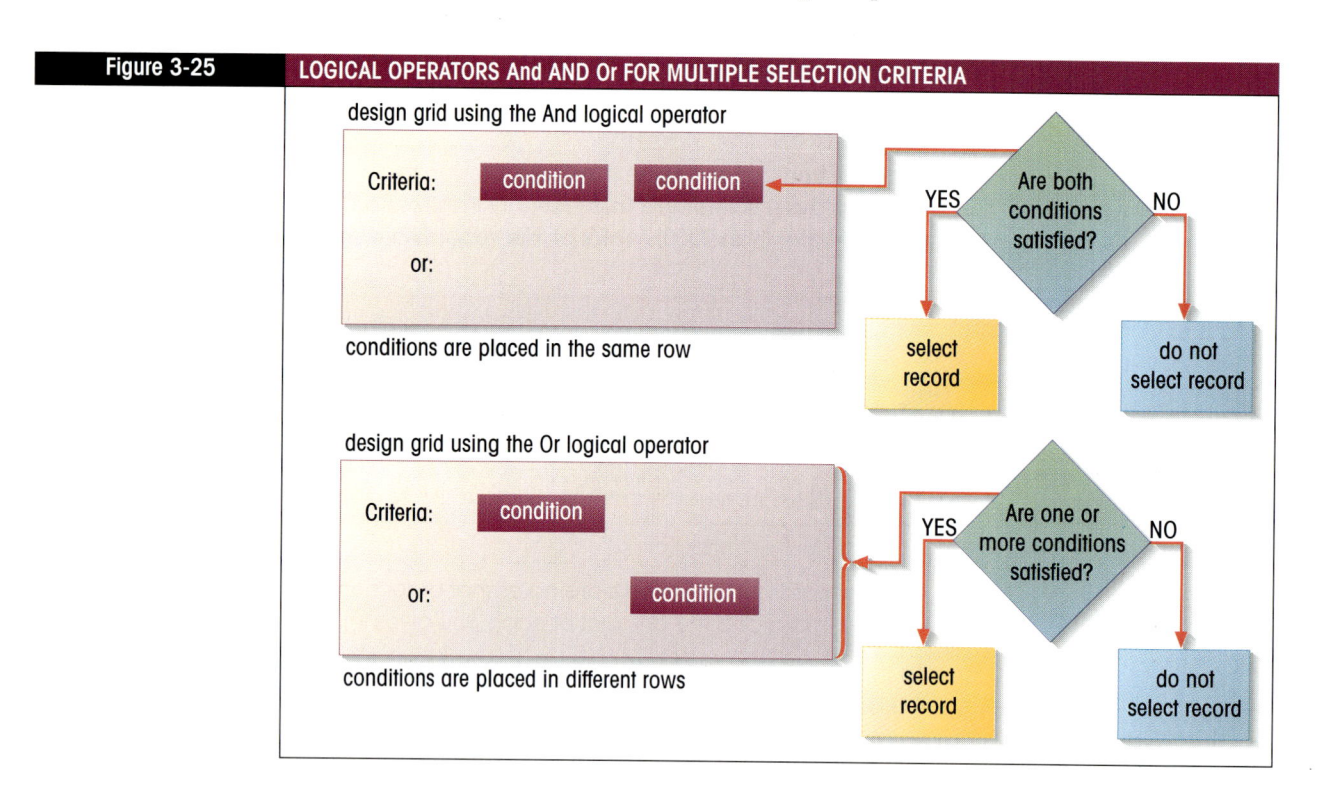

Figure 3-25 LOGICAL OPERATORS And AND Or FOR MULTIPLE SELECTION CRITERIA

design grid using the And logical operator

Criteria:	condition	condition
or:		

conditions are placed in the same row

Are both conditions satisfied? YES → select record   NO → do not select record

design grid using the Or logical operator

Criteria:	condition	
or:		condition

conditions are placed in different rows

Are one or more conditions satisfied? YES → select record   NO → do not select record

The And Logical Operator

To create Leonard's query, you need to modify the existing January Orders query to show only the unpaid orders billed on 01/15/2001. For the modified query, you must add a second condition in the same Criteria row. The condition #1/15/01# for the BillingDate field finds records billed on the specified date, and the condition "No" in the Paid field finds records whose invoices have not been paid. Because the conditions appear in the same Criteria row, the query will select records only if both conditions are met.

After modifying the query, you'll save it and then rename it as "Unpaid January Orders," overwriting the January Orders query, which Barbara no longer needs.

To modify the January Orders query and use the And logical operator:

1. With the Queries object selected in the Database window, click **January Orders** (if necessary), and then click the **Design** button to open the query in Design view.

2. Click the **Paid Criteria** text box, type **no**, and then press the **Tab** key. See Figure 3-26.

Figure 3-26 QUERY TO FIND UNPAID JANUARY ORDERS

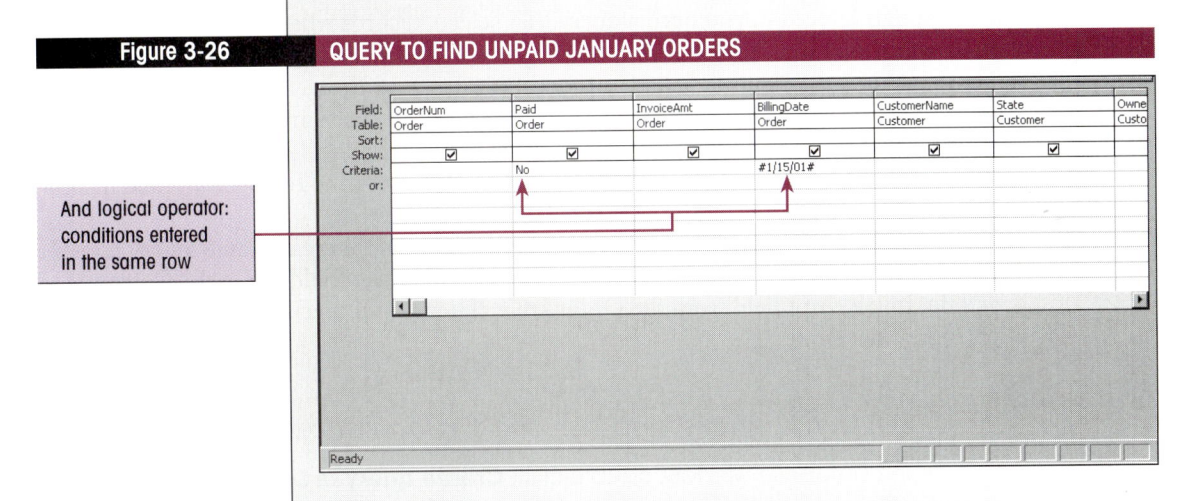

And logical operator: conditions entered in the same row

The condition for the BillingDate field is already entered, so you can run the query.

3. Click the **Run** button on the Query Design toolbar. Access runs the query and displays in the datasheet only those records that meet both conditions: a BillingDate field value of 01/15/2001 and a Paid field value of No. A total of six records are selected. See Figure 3-27.

Figure 3-27 RESULTS OF QUERY USING THE AND LOGICAL OPERATOR

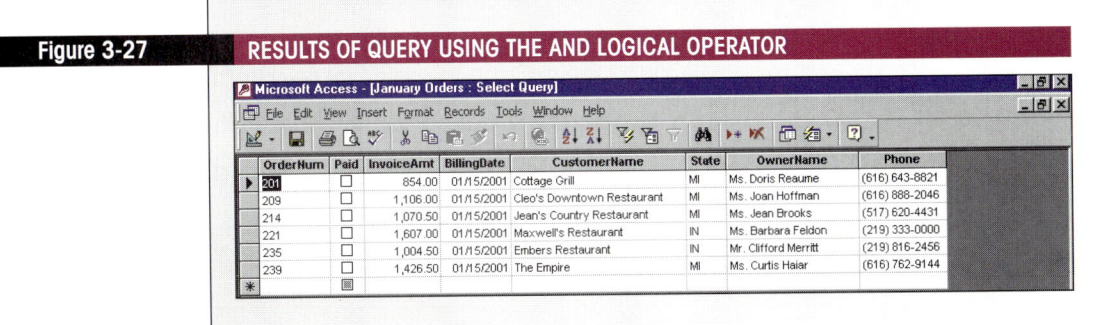

OrderNum	Paid	InvoiceAmt	BillingDate	CustomerName	State	OwnerName	Phone
201	☐	854.00	01/15/2001	Cottage Grill	MI	Ms. Doris Reaume	(616) 643-8821
209	☐	1,106.00	01/15/2001	Cleo's Downtown Restaurant	MI	Ms. Joan Hoffman	(616) 888-2046
214	☐	1,070.50	01/15/2001	Jean's Country Restaurant	MI	Ms. Jean Brooks	(517) 620-4431
221	☐	1,607.00	01/15/2001	Maxwell's Restaurant	IN	Ms. Barbara Feldon	(219) 333-0000
235	☐	1,004.50	01/15/2001	Embers Restaurant	IN	Mr. Clifford Merritt	(219) 816-2456
239	☐	1,426.50	01/15/2001	The Empire	MI	Ms. Curtis Haiar	(616) 762-9144

> Now you can save the changes to the query and rename it.
>
> 4. Click the **Save** button 🔳 on the Query Datasheet toolbar, and then click the **Close** button ✖ on the menu bar.
>
> 5. Right-click **January Orders** in the Queries list box, and then click **Rename** on the shortcut menu.
>
> 6. Click to position the insertion point to the left of the word "January," type **Unpaid**, press the **spacebar**, and then press the **Enter** key. The query name is now Unpaid January Orders.

Leonard also wants to determine which restaurant customers are most valuable to Valle Coffee. Specifically, he wants to see a list of those customers who have been placing orders for many years or who place orders for a substantial amount of money, so that he can call the customers personally and thank them for their business. To create this query, you need to use the Or logical operator.

The Or Logical Operator

For Leonard's request, you need a query that selects records when either one of two conditions is satisfied or when both conditions are satisfied. That is, a record is selected if the FirstContact field value is less than 01/1/1994 (to find those customers who have been doing business with Valle Coffee the longest) *or* if the InvoiceAmt field value is greater than 2000 (to find those customers who spend more money). You will enter the condition for the FirstContact field in one Criteria row and the condition for the InvoiceAmt field in another Criteria row, thereby using the Or logical operator.

To display the information Leonard wants to view, you'll create a new query containing the CustomerName, OwnerName, Phone, and FirstContact fields from the Customer table and the InvoiceAmt field from the Order table. Then you'll specify the conditions using the Or logical operator.

> *To create the query and use the Or logical operator:*
>
> 1. In the Database window, double-click **Create query in Design view**. The Show Table dialog box opens on top of the Query window in Design view.
>
> 2. Click **Customer** in the Tables list box (if necessary), click the **Add** button, click **Order**, click the **Add** button, and then click the **Close** button. The Customer and Order field lists appear in the Query window and the Show Table dialog box closes.
>
> 3. Double-click **CustomerName** in the Customer field list to add the CustomerName field to the design grid's first column Field text box.
>
> 4. Repeat Step 3 to add the **OwnerName**, **Phone**, and **FirstContact** fields from the Customer table, and then add the **InvoiceAmt** field from the Order table.
>
>   Now you need to specify the first condition, <1/1/94, in the FirstContact field.
>
> 5. Click the **FirstContact Criteria** text box, type **<1/1/94** and then press the **Tab** key.
>
>   Because you want records selected if either of the conditions for the FirstContact or InvoiceAmt fields is satisfied, you must enter the condition for the InvoiceAmt field in the "or" row of the design grid.
>
> 6. Press the ▼ key, and then type **>2000** in the "or" text box for InvoiceAmt. See Figure 3-28.

Figure 3-28   QUERY WINDOW WITH THE OR LOGICAL OPERATOR

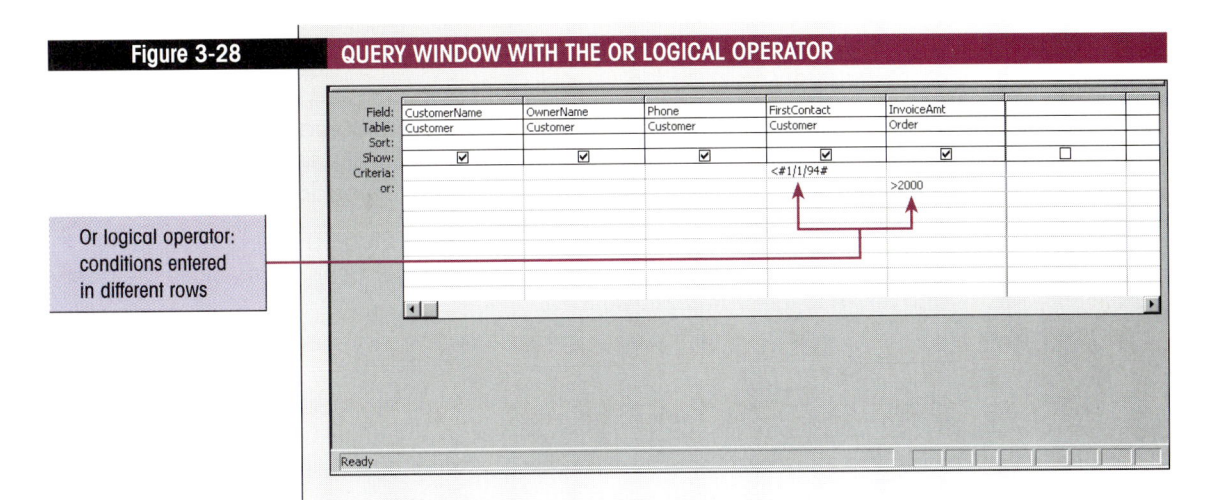

Or logical operator: conditions entered in different rows

The query specifications are complete, so now you can run the query.

7. Click the **Run** button on the Query Design toolbar. Access runs the query and displays only those records that meet either condition: a FirstContact field value less than 01/1/1994 or an InvoiceAmt field value greater than 2000. A total of 29 records are selected.

   Leonard wants the list displayed in alphabetical order by CustomerName.

8. Click any visible CustomerName field value to establish this field as the current field, and then click the **Sort Ascending** button on the Query Datasheet toolbar.

9. Resize all datasheet columns to their best fit. Be sure to scroll through the entire datasheet to make sure that all values are completely displayed. Deselect all columns when finished resizing, and then return to the top of the datasheet. See Figure 3-29.

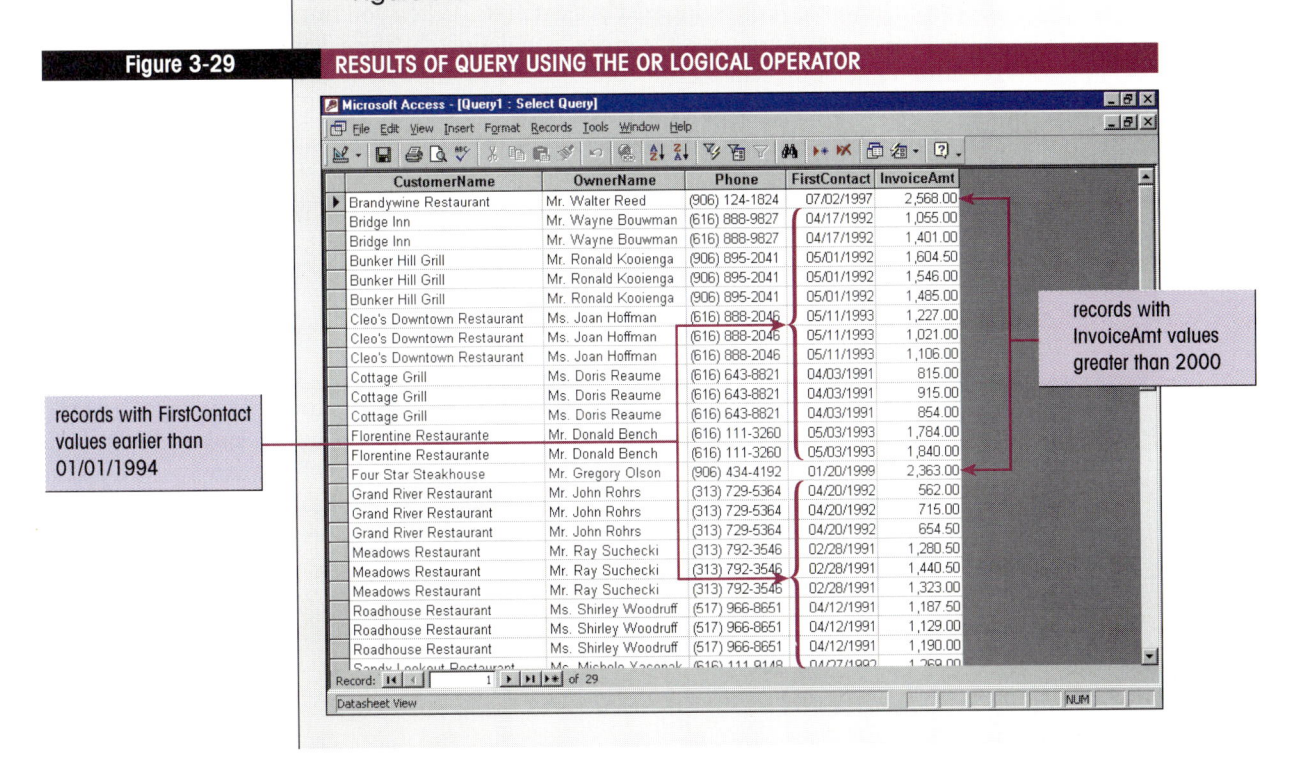

Figure 3-29   RESULTS OF QUERY USING THE OR LOGICAL OPERATOR

records with FirstContact values earlier than 01/01/1994

records with InvoiceAmt values greater than 2000

> Now you'll save the query as Top Customers, print the query results, and then close the query.
>
> 10. Click the **Save** button on the Query Datasheet toolbar, type **Top Customers** in the Query Name text box, and then press the **Enter** key. Access saves the query with the specified name in the Restaurant database.
>
> 11. Click the **Print** button on the Query Datasheet toolbar to print the query results, and then click the **Close** button on the menu bar to close the query and return to the Database window.

Next, Leonard asks Barbara if the Restaurant database can be used to perform calculations. He is considering adding a 2% late charge to the unpaid invoices billed in January, and he wants to know exactly what these charges would be.

Performing Calculations

In addition to using queries to retrieve, sort, and filter data in a database, you can use a query to perform calculations. To perform a calculation, you define an **expression** containing a combination of database fields, constants, and operators. For numeric expressions, the data types of the database fields must be number, currency, or date/time; the constants are numbers such as .02 (for the 2% late charge); and the operators can be arithmetic operators (+ – * /) or other specialized operators. In complex expressions you can enclose calculations in parentheses to indicate which one should be performed first. In expressions without parentheses, Access calculates in the following order of precedence: multiplication and division before addition and subtraction. When operators have equal precedence, Access calculates them in order from left to right.

To perform a calculation in a query, you add a calculated field to the query. A **calculated field** is a field that displays the results of an expression. A calculated field appears in a query datasheet; however, it does not exist in a database. When you run a query that contains a calculated field, Access evaluates the expression defined by the calculated field and displays the resulting value in the datasheet.

Creating a Calculated Field

To produce the information Leonard wants, you need to open the Unpaid January Orders query and create a calculated field that will multiply each InvoiceAmt field value by .02 to account for the 2% late charge Leonard is considering.

To enter an expression for a calculated field, you can type it directly in a Field text box in the design grid. Alternatively, you can open the Zoom box or Expression Builder and use either one to enter the expression. The **Zoom box** is a large text box for entering text, expressions, or other values. **Expression Builder** is an Access tool that contains an expression box for entering the expression, buttons for common operators, and one or more lists of expression elements, such as table and field names. Unlike a Field text box, which is too small to show an entire expression at one time, the Zoom box and Expression Builder are large enough to display lengthy expressions. In most cases Expression Builder provides the easiest way to enter expressions.

| REFERENCE WINDOW | RW |

Using Expression Builder
- Display the query in Design view.
- In the design grid, position the insertion point in the Field text box of the field for which you want to create an expression.
- Click the Build button on the Query Design toolbar.
- Use the expression elements and common operators to build the expression, or type the expression directly.
- Click the OK button.

You'll begin by opening the Unpaid January Orders query in Design view and modifying it to show only the information Leonard wants to view.

To modify the Unpaid January Orders query:

1. In the Database window, click **Unpaid January Orders**, and then click the **Design** button.

   Leonard wants to see only the OrderNum, CustomerName, and InvoiceAmt fields. So, you'll first delete the unnecessary fields, and then uncheck the Show boxes for the Paid and BillingDate fields. You need to keep these two fields in the query because they specify the conditions for the query; however, Leonard does not want them to appear in the query results.

2. Scroll the design grid to the right until the last three fields—State, OwnerName, and Phone—are visible.

3. Position the pointer on the State field until the pointer changes to ↓, click and hold down the mouse button, drag the mouse to the right to highlight the State, OwnerName, and Phone fields, and then release the mouse button.

4. Press the **Delete** key to delete the three selected fields.

5. Scroll the design grid back to the left, click the **Show** check box for the Paid field to remove the check mark, and then click the **Show** check box for the BillingDate field to remove the check mark.

   Next you'll move the InvoiceAmt field to the right of the CustomerName field so that the InvoiceAmt values will appear next to the calculated field values in the query results.

6. Make sure both the InvoiceAmt field and the empty field to the right of the CustomerName field are visible in the design grid.

7. Select the InvoiceAmt field, and then use the pointer to drag the field to the right of the CustomerName field.

8. If necessary, scroll the design grid so that the empty field to the right of InvoiceAmt is visible, and then click anywhere in the design grid to deselect the InvoiceAmt field. See Figure 3-30.

Figure 3-30 — MODIFIED QUERY BEFORE ADDING THE CALCULATED FIELD

InvoiceAmt field positioned to the right of CustomerName

Show boxes unchecked

calculated field will go here

Now you're ready to use Expression Builder to enter the calculated field in the Unpaid January Orders query.

To add the calculated field to the Unpaid January Orders query:

1. Position the insertion point in the Field text box to the right of the InvoiceAmt field, and then click the **Build** button on the Query Design toolbar. The Expression Builder dialog box opens. See Figure 3-31.

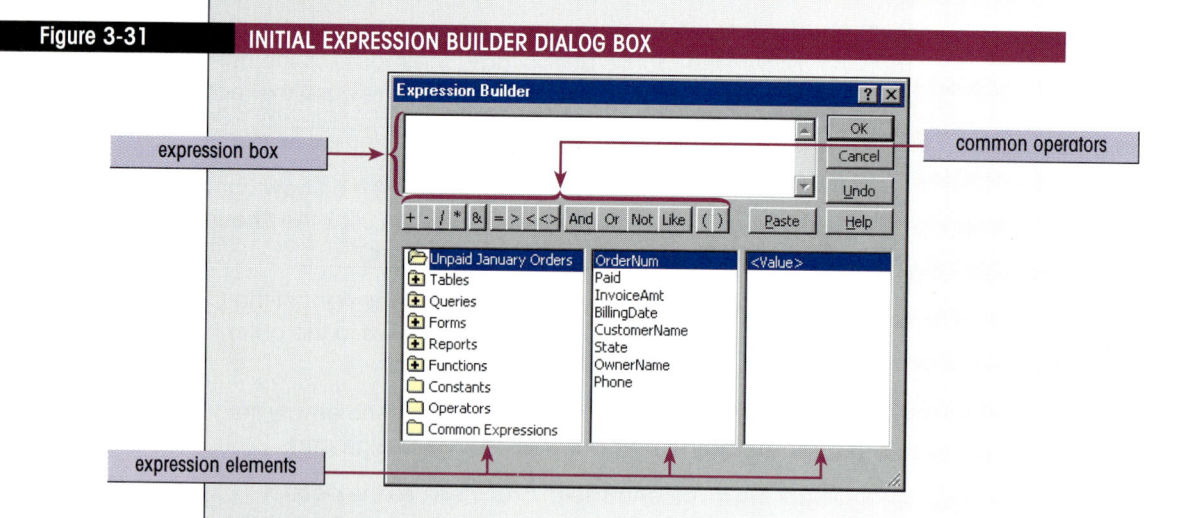

Figure 3-31 — INITIAL EXPRESSION BUILDER DIALOG BOX

expression box

common operators

expression elements

You use the common operators and expression elements to help you build an expression. Note that the Unpaid January Orders query is already selected in the list box on the lower left; the fields included in the query are listed in the center box.

The expression for the calculated field will multiply the InvoiceAmt field values by the numeric constant .02 (which represents a 2% late charge). To include a field in the expression, you select the field and then click the Paste button. To include a numeric constant, you simply type the constant in the expression.

2. Click **InvoiceAmt** and then click the **Paste** button. [InvoiceAmt] appears in the expression box.

   To include the multiplication operator in the expression, you click the asterisk (*) button.

3. Click the ***** button in the row of common operators, and then type **.02**. You have completed the entry of the expression. See Figure 3-32.

| Figure 3-32 | COMPLETED EXPRESSION FOR THE CALCULATED FIELD |

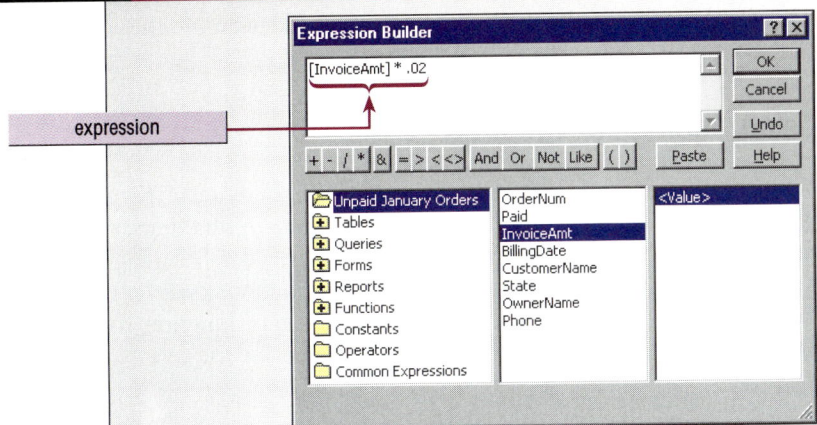

Note that you also could have typed the expression directly into the expression box, instead of clicking the field name and the operator.

4. Click the **OK** button. Access closes the Expression Builder dialog box and adds the expression to the design grid in the Field text box for the calculated field.

   Next, you need to specify a name for the calculated field as it will appear in the query results.

5. Press the **Home** key to position the insertion point to the left of the expression.

   You'll enter the name LateCharge, which is descriptive of the field's contents; then you'll run the query.

6. Type **LateCharge:**. *Make sure you include the colon following the field name. The colon is needed to separate the field name from its expression.*

   Now you can run the query.

7. Click the **Run** button on the Query Design toolbar. Access runs the query and displays the query datasheet, which contains the three specified fields and the calculated field with the name "LateCharge." See Figure 3-33.

| Figure 3-33 | DATASHEET DISPLAYING THE CALCULATED FIELD |

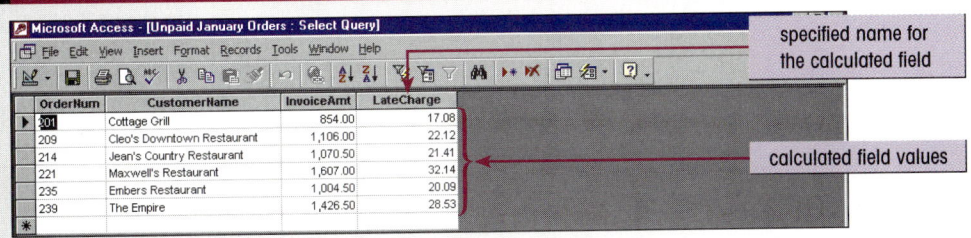

> You'll save the query as Unpaid With Late Charge, and then close it.
>
> 8. Click **File** on the menu bar, click **Save As**, type **Unpaid With Late Charge**, press the **Enter** key, and then click the **Close** button ⊠ on the menu bar. The Database window becomes the active window.

Barbara prepares a report of Valle Coffee's restaurant business for Leonard on a regular basis. The information in the report includes a summary of the restaurant orders. Barbara lists the total invoice amount for all orders, the average invoice amount, and the total number of orders. She asks you to create a query to determine these statistics from data in the Order table.

Using Aggregate Functions

You can calculate statistical information, such as totals and averages, on the records selected in a query. To do this, you use the Access aggregate functions. **Aggregate functions** perform arithmetic operations on selected records in a database. Figure 3-34 lists the most frequently used aggregate functions. Aggregate functions operate on the records that meet a query's selection criteria. You specify an aggregate function for a specific field, and the appropriate operation applies to that field's values for the selected records.

Figure 3-34	FREQUENTLY USED AGGREGATE FUNCTIONS	
AGGREGATE FUNCTION	**DETERMINES**	**DATA TYPES SUPPORTED**
Avg	Average of the field values for the selected records	AutoNumber, Currency, Date/Time, Number
Count	Number of records selected	AutoNumber, Currency, Date/Time, Memo, Number, OLE Object, Text, Yes/No
Max	Highest field value for the selected records	AutoNumber, Currency, Date/Time, Number, Text
Min	Lowest field value for the selected records	AutoNumber, Currency, Date/Time, Number, Text
Sum	Total of the field values for the selected records	AutoNumber, Currency, Date/Time, Number

To display the total, average, and count of all the invoice amounts in the Order table, you will use the Sum, Avg, and Count aggregate functions for the InvoiceAmt field.

> ### To calculate the total, average, and count of all invoice amounts:
>
> 1. Double-click **Create query in Design view**. Access opens the Show Table dialog box on top of the Query window in Design view.
>
> 2. Click **Order**, click the **Add** button, and then click the **Close** button. The Order field list is added to the top of the Query window, and the dialog box closes.
>
>   To perform the three calculations on the InvoiceAmt field, you need to add the field to the design grid three times.
>
> 3. Double-click **InvoiceAmt** in the Order field list three times to add three copies of the field to the design grid.

You need to select an aggregate function for each InvoiceAmt field. When you click the Totals button on the Query Design toolbar, a row labeled "Total" is added to the design grid. The Total row provides a list of the aggregate functions that you can select.

4. Click the **Totals** button Σ on the Query Design toolbar. A new row labeled "Total" appears between the Table and Sort rows in the design grid. See Figure 3-35.

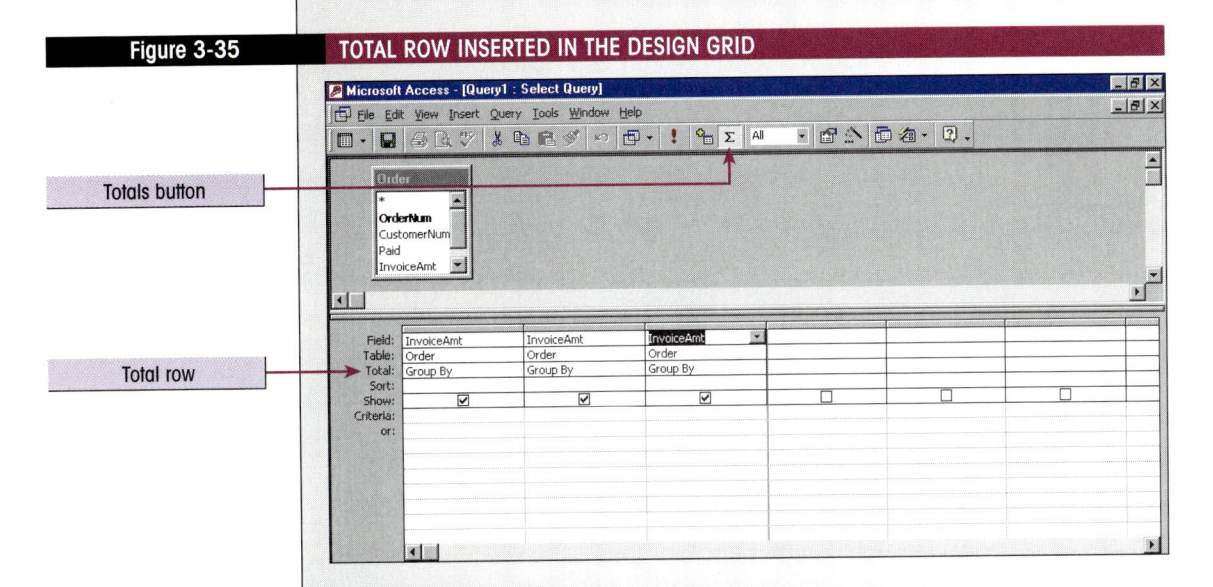

Figure 3-35 **TOTAL ROW INSERTED IN THE DESIGN GRID**

- Totals button
- Total row

In the Total row, you specify the aggregate function you want to use for a field.

5. Click the right side of the first column's **Total** text box, and then click **Sum**. This field will calculate the total of all the InvoiceAmt field values.

When you run the query, Access automatically will assign a datasheet column name of "SumOfInvoiceAmt" for this field. You can change the datasheet column name to a more descriptive or readable name by entering the name you want in the Field text box. However, you must also keep the field name InvoiceAmt in the Field text box, because it identifies the field whose values will be summed. The Field text box will contain the datasheet column name you specify followed by the field name (InvoiceAmt) with a colon separating the two names.

6. Position the insertion point to the left of InvoiceAmt in the first column's Field text box, and then type **Total of Invoices:**. Be sure you include the colon at the end.

7. Click the right side of the second column's **Total** text box, and then click **Avg**. This field will calculate the average of all the InvoiceAmt field values.

8. Position the insertion point to the left of InvoiceAmt in the second column's Field text box, and then type **Average of Invoices:**.

9. Click the right side of the third column's **Total** text box, and then click **Count**. This field will calculate the total number of invoices (orders).

10. Position the insertion point to the left of InvoiceAmt in the third column's Field text box, and then type **Number of Invoices:**.

The query design is complete, so you can run the query.

11. Click the **Run** button on the Query Design toolbar. Access runs the query and displays one record containing the three aggregate function values. The single row of summary statistics represents calculations based on the 104 records selected in the query.

    You need to resize the three columns to their best fit to see the column names.

12. Resize each column by double-clicking the pointer on the right edge of each column's field selector; then position the insertion point at the start of the field value in the first column. See Figure 3-36.

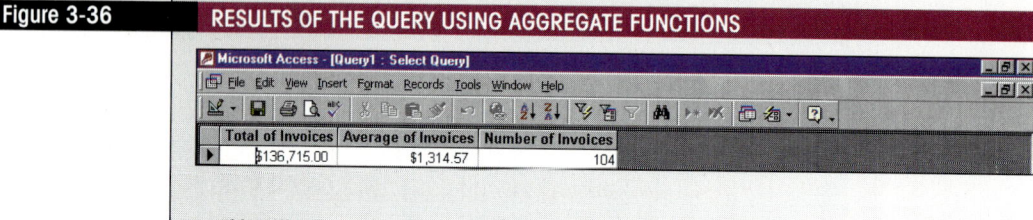

Figure 3-36   RESULTS OF THE QUERY USING AGGREGATE FUNCTIONS

Total of Invoices	Average of Invoices	Number of Invoices
$136,715.00	$1,314.57	104

You'll save the query as Invoice Statistics.

13. Click the **Save** button on the Query Datasheet toolbar, type **Invoice Statistics**, and then press the **Enter** key.

Barbara's report to Leonard also includes the same invoice statistics (total, average, and count) for each month. Because Valle Coffee sends invoices to its restaurant customers once a month, each invoice in a month has the same billing date. Barbara asks you to display the invoice statistics for each different billing date in the Order table.

Using Record Group Calculations

In addition to calculating statistical information on all or selected records in selected tables, you can calculate statistics for groups of records. For example, you can determine the number of customers in each state or the total invoice amounts by billing date.

To create a query for Barbara's latest request, you can modify the current query by adding the BillingDate field and assigning the Group By operator to it. The **Group By operator** divides the selected records into groups based on the values in the specified field. Those records with the same value for the field are grouped together, and the datasheet displays one record for each group. Aggregate functions, which appear in the other columns of the design grid, provide statistical information for each group.

You need to modify the current query to add the Group By operator for the BillingDate field. This will display the statistical information grouped by billing date for the 104 selected records in the query.

To add the BillingDate field with the Group By operator, and then run the query:

1. Click the **View** button for Design view on the Query Datasheet toolbar to switch to Design view.

2. Scroll the Order field list, if necessary, and then double-click **BillingDate** to add the field to the design grid. Group By, which is the default option in the Total row, appears for the BillingDate field.

   You've completed the query changes, so you can run the query.

3. Click the **Run** button on the Query Design toolbar. Access runs the query and displays three records—one for each BillingDate group. Each record contains the three aggregate function values and the BillingDate field value for the group. Again, the summary statistics represent calculations based on the 104 records selected in the query. See Figure 3-37.

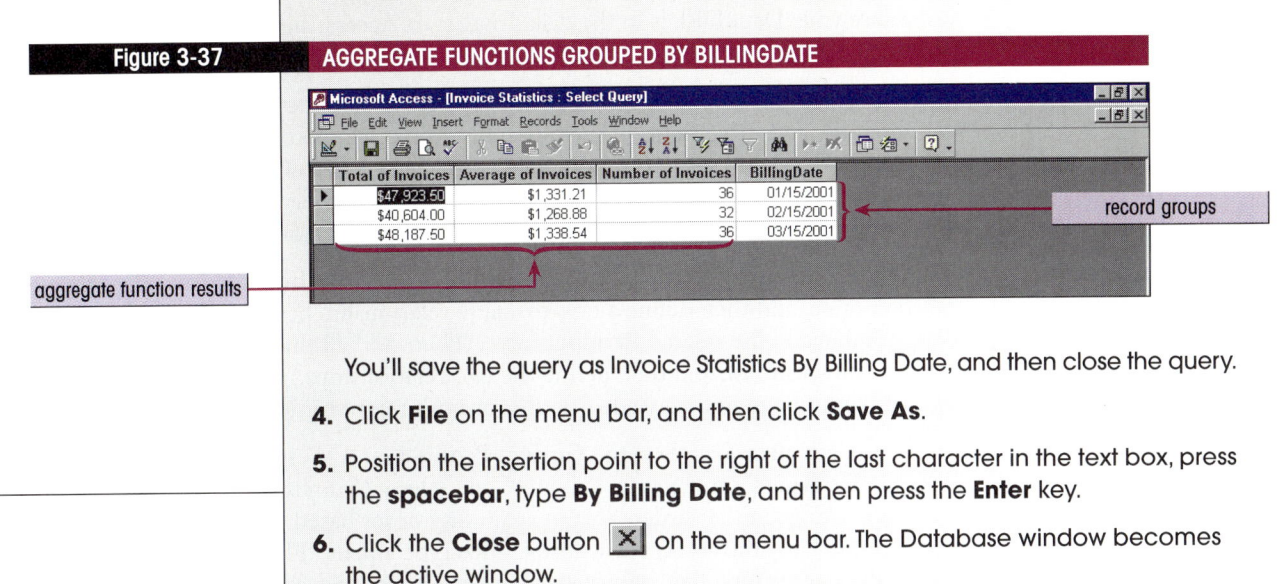

Figure 3-37   AGGREGATE FUNCTIONS GROUPED BY BILLINGDATE

Total of Invoices	Average of Invoices	Number of Invoices	BillingDate
$47,923.50	$1,331.21	36	01/15/2001
$40,604.00	$1,268.88	32	02/15/2001
$48,187.50	$1,338.54	36	03/15/2001

aggregate function results   *record groups*

You'll save the query as Invoice Statistics By Billing Date, and then close the query.

4. Click **File** on the menu bar, and then click **Save As**.

5. Position the insertion point to the right of the last character in the text box, press the **spacebar**, type **By Billing Date**, and then press the **Enter** key.

6. Click the **Close** button on the menu bar. The Database window becomes the active window.

7. Click the **Close** button on the Access window title bar to close the Restaurant database and to exit Access.

The queries you've created and saved will help Leonard, Barbara, Kim, and other employees monitor and analyze the business activity of Valle Coffee's restaurant customers. Now any employee can run the queries at any time, modify them as needed, or use them as the basis for designing new queries to meet additional information requirements.

Session 3.2 QUICK CHECK

1. A(n) _____ is a criterion, or rule, that determines which records are selected for a query datasheet.

2. In the design grid, where do you place the conditions for two different fields when you use the And logical operator? The Or logical operator?

3. To perform a calculation in a query, you define a(n) _____ containing a combination of database fields, constants, and operators.

4. How does a calculated field differ from a table field?

5. What is an aggregate function?

6. The _____ operator divides selected records into groups based on the values in a field.

REVIEW ASSIGNMENTS

Barbara needs information from the **Valle Products** database, and she asks you to query the database by completing the following:

1. Make sure your Data Disk is in the disk drive, start Access, and then open the **Valle Products** database located in the Review folder on your Data Disk.

2. Create a select query based on the **Product** table. Display the ProductCode, WeightCode, and Price fields in the query results; sort in descending order based on the Price field values; and select only those records whose CoffeeCode value equals BRUM. (*Hint*: Do not display the CoffeeCode field values in the query results.) Save the query as **BRUM Coffee**, run the query, print the query datasheet, and then close the query.

Explore

3. Define a one-to-many relationship between the primary **Coffee** table and the related **Product** table, and then define a one-to-many relationship between the primary **Weight** table and the related **Product** table. (*Hint*: Add all three tables to the Relationships window, and then define the two relationships.) Select the referential integrity option and both cascade options for both relationships.

4. Create a select query based on the **Coffee**, **Product**, and **Weight** tables. Select the fields CoffeeType, CoffeeName, ProductCode, Decaf (from the **Product** table), Price, and Weight/Size, in that order. Sort in ascending order based on the CoffeeName field values. Select only those records whose CoffeeType equals "Flavored." (*Hint*: Do not display the CoffeeType field values in the query results.) Save the query as **Flavored Coffees**, and then run the query. Resize all columns in the datasheet to fit the data. Print the datasheet, and then save the query.

5. Use the Office Assistant to learn about Filter By Form. (*Hint:* Ask the Office Assistant the question, "How do I use Filter By Form," and then click the topic "Filter records by entering values in a blank view of your form or datasheet.") Read the topic, and then close the Microsoft Access Help window.

Explore

6. Use the Filter By Form button on the Query Datasheet toolbar to filter the records that have a Weight/Size of "1 lb pkg," and then apply the filter. Print the query datasheet.

Explore

7. Remove the filter to display all records, and then save and close the query.

Explore

8. Create a query based on the **Product** table that shows all products that do not have a WeightCode field value of A, and whose Price field value is greater than 50; display all fields except Decaf from the **Product** table. Save the query as **Pricing**, and then run the query.

Explore

9. Open the **Pricing** query in Design view. Create a calculated field named NewPrice that displays the results of increasing the Price values by 3%. Display the results in descending order by NewPrice. Save the query as **New Prices**, run the query, resize all columns in the datasheet to fit the data, print the query datasheet, and then save and close the query.

10. Open the **Flavored Coffees** query in Design view. Modify the query to display only those records with a CoffeeType field value of "Flavored" or with a Price field value greater than 50. Save the query as **Flavored Plus Higher Priced**, and then run the query. Resize all columns in the datasheet to fit the data, print the query datasheet, and then save and close the query.

Explore

11. Create a new query based on the **Product** table. Use the Min and Max aggregate functions to find the lowest and highest values in the Price field. Name the two aggregate fields Lowest Price and Highest Price, respectively. Save the query as **Lowest And Highest Prices**, run the query, and then print the query datasheet.

Explore 12. Open the **Lowest And Highest Prices** query in Design view. Use the Show Table button on the Query Design toolbar to open the Show Table dialog box, and then add the **Weight** table to the query. Modify the query so that the records are grouped by the Weight/Size field. Save the query as **Lowest And Highest Prices By Weight/Size**, run the query, print the query datasheet, and then close the query.

13. Close the **Valle Products** database, and then exit Access.

CASE PROBLEMS

Case 1. Ashbrook Mall Information Desk Sam Bullard wants to view specific information about jobs available at the Ashbrook Mall. He asks you to query the **MallJobs** database by completing the following:

1. Make sure your Data Disk is in the disk drive, start Access, and then open the **MallJobs** database located in the Cases folder on your Data Disk.

2. Define a one-to-many relationship between the primary **Store** table and the related **Job** table. Select the referential integrity option and both cascade options for the relationship.

3. Create a select query based on the **Store** and **Job** tables. Display the StoreName, Location, Position, and Hours/Week fields, in that order. Sort in ascending order based on the StoreName field values. Run the query, save the query as **Store Jobs**, and then print the datasheet.

4. Use Filter By Selection to temporarily display only those records with a Location field value of A3 in the **Store Jobs** query datasheet. Print the datasheet and then remove the filter. Save and close the query.

5. Open the **Store Jobs** query in Design view. Modify the query to display only those records with a Position value of Server. Run the query, save the query as **Server Jobs**, and then print the datasheet.

6. Open the **Server Jobs** query in Design view. Modify the query to display only those records with a Position value of Server and with an Hours/Week value of 20-25. Run the query, save it with the same name, print the datasheet, and then close the query.

7. Close the **MallJobs** database, and then exit Access.

Case 2. Professional Litigation User Services (PLUS) Raj Jawahir is completing an analysis of the payment history of PLUS clients. To help him find the information he needs, you'll query the **Payments** database by completing the following:

1. Make sure your Data Disk is in the disk drive, start Access, and then open the **Payments** database located in the Cases folder on your Data Disk.

2. Define a one-to-many relationship between the primary **Firm** table and the related **Payment** table. Select the referential integrity option and both cascade options for the relationship.

3. Create a select query based on the **Firm** and **Payment** tables. Display the fields Firm# (from the **Firm** table), FirmName, AmtPaid, and DatePaid, in that order. Sort in descending order based on the AmtPaid field values. Select only those records whose AmtPaid is greater than 2500. Save the query as **Large Payments**, and then run the query. Print the datasheet and then close the query.

4. For all payments on 06/01/2001, display the Payment#, AmtPaid, DatePaid, and FirmName fields. Save the query as **June 1 Payments**, and then run the query. Switch to Design view, modify the query so that the DatePaid values do not appear in the query results, and then save the modified query. Run the query, print the query results, and then close the query.

Explore

5. For all firms that have Olivia Tyler as a PLUS account representative, display the FirmName, FirmContact, AmtPaid, and DatePaid fields. Save the query as **Tyler Accounts**, run the query, print the query results, and then close the query.

6. For all payments made on 06/10/2001 or 06/11/2001, display the fields DatePaid, AmtPaid, FirmName, and Firm# (from the **Firm** table). Display the results in ascending order by DatePaid and then in descending order by AmtPaid. Save the query as **Selected Dates**, run the query, print the query datasheet, and then close the query.

Explore

7. Use the **Payment** table to display the highest, lowest, total, average, and count of the AmtPaid field for all payments. Then do the following:
   a. Specify column names of HighestPayment, LowestPayment, TotalPayments, AveragePayment, and #Payments. Save the query as **Payment Statistics**, and then run the query. Resize all datasheet columns to their best fit, save the query, and then print the query results.
   b. Change the query to display the same statistics grouped by DatePaid. Save the query as **Payment Statistics By Date**, run the query, and then print the query results.
   c. Change the **Payment Statistics By Date** query to display the same statistics by DatePaid, then by Deposit#. Save the query as **Payment Statistics By Date By Deposit**, run the query, print the query results using landscape orientation, and then save and close the query.

8. Close the **Payments** database, and then exit Access.

Case 3. Best Friends Noah and Sheila Warnick want to find specific information about the walk-a-thons they conduct for Best Friends. You'll help them find the information in the **Walks** database by completing the following:

1. Make sure your Data Disk is in the disk drive, start Access, and then open the **Walks** database located in the Cases folder on your Data Disk.

2. Define a one-to-many relationship between the primary **Walker** table and the related **Pledge** table. Select the referential integrity option and both cascade options for the relationship.

3. For all walkers with a PledgeAmt field value of greater than 30, display the WalkerID, LastName, PledgeNo, and PledgeAmt fields. Sort the query in ascending order by PledgeAmt. Save the query as **Large Pledges**, run the query, print the query datasheet, and then close the query.

4. For all walkers who pledged less than $15 or who pledged $5 per mile, display the Pledger, PledgeAmt, PerMile, LastName, FirstName, and Distance fields. Save the query as **Pledged Or Per Mile**, run the query, and then print the query datasheet. Change the query to select all walkers who pledged less than $15 and who pledged $5 per mile. Save the query as **Pledged And Per Mile**, and then run the query. Describe the results. Close the query.

Explore

5. For all pledges, display the WalkerID, Pledger, Distance, PerMile, and PledgeAmt fields. Save the query as **Difference**. Create a calculated field named CalcPledgeAmt that displays the results of multiplying the Distance and PerMile fields; then save the query. Create a second calculated field named Difference that displays the results of subtracting the CalcPledgeAmt field from the PledgeAmt field. Format the calculated fields as fixed. (*Hint*: Choose the Properties option on the shortcut menu for the selected field.) Display the results in ascending order by PledgeAmt. Save the modified query, and then run the query. Resize all datasheet columns to their best fit, print the query results, and then save and close the query.

6. Use the **Pledge** table to display the total, average, and count of the PledgeAmt field for all pledges. Then do the following:
   a. Specify column names of TotalPledge, AveragePledge, and #Pledges.

   Explore
   b. Change properties so that the values in the TotalPledge and AveragePledge columns display two decimal places and the fixed format. (*Hint*: Choose the Properties option on the shortcut menu for the selected field.)
   c. Save the query as **Pledge Statistics**, run the query, resize all datasheet columns to their best fit, and then print the query datasheet. Save the query.

   Explore
   d. Change the query to display the sum, average, and count of the PledgeAmt field for all pledges by LastName. (*Hint*: Use the Show Table button on the Query Design toolbar to add the **Walker** table to the query.) Save the query as **Pledge Statistics By Walker**, run the query, print the query datasheet, and then close the query.

7. Close the **Walks** database, and then exit Access.

Case 4. Lopez Lexus Dealerships Maria and Hector Lopez want to analyze data about the cars and different locations for their Lexus dealerships. Help them query the **Lexus** database by completing the following:

1. Make sure your Data Disk is in the disk drive, start Access, and then open the **Lexus** database located in the Cases folder on your Data Disk.

2. Define a one-to-many relationship between the primary **Locations** table and the related **Cars** table. Select the referential integrity option and both cascade options for the relationship.

3. For all vehicles, display the Model, Class, Year, LocationCode, and SellingPrice fields. Save the query as **Car Info**, and then run the query. Resize all datasheet columns to their best fit. In Datasheet view, sort the query results in descending order by the SellingPrice field. Print the query datasheet, and then save and close the query.

4. For all vehicles manufactured in 2000, display the Model, Year, Cost, SellingPrice, and LocationName fields. Sort the query in ascending order by Cost. Save the query as **2000 Cars**, and then run the query. Modify the query to remove the display of the Year field values from the query results. Save the modified query, run the query, print the query datasheet, and then close the query.

Explore
5. For all vehicles located in Laredo or with a transmission of M5, display the Model, Year, Cost, SellingPrice, Transmission, LocationCode, and LocationName fields. Save the query as **Location Or Trans**, run the query, and then print the query datasheet using landscape orientation. Change the query to select all vehicles located in Laredo and with a transmission of M5. Save the query as **Location And Trans**, run the query, print the query datasheet in landscape orientation, and then close the query.

6. For all vehicles, display the Model, Class, Year, Cost, and SellingPrice fields. Save the query as **Profit**. Then create a calculated field named Profit that displays the difference between the vehicle's selling price and cost. Display the results in descending order by Profit. Save the query, run the query, print the query datasheet, and then close the query.

Explore
7. Use the **Cars** table to determine the total cost, average cost, total selling price, and average selling price of all vehicles. Use the Index tab in online Help to look up the word "caption"; then choose the topic "Change a field name in a query." Read the displayed information, and then choose and read the subtopic "Display new field names by changing the Caption property." Close the Help window. Set the Caption property of the four fields to Total Cost, Average Cost, Total Selling Price, and Average Selling Price, respectively. Save the query as **Car Statistics**, run the query, resize all datasheet columns to their best fit, print the query datasheet, and then save the query again. Revise the query

to show the car statistics grouped by LocationName. (*Hint*: Use the Show Table button on the Query Design toolbar to display the Show Table dialog box.) Set the Caption property of the LocationName field to Location. Save the revised query as **Car Statistics By Location**, run the query, print the query datasheet, and then close the query.

Explore

8. Use the Answer Wizard to ask the following question: "How do I create a Top Values query?" Choose the topic "Display only the highest or lowest values in the query's results." Read the displayed information, and then close the Help window. Open the **Profit** query in Design view, and then modify the query to display only the top five values for the Profit field. Save the query as **Top Profit**, run the query, print the query datasheet, and then close the query.

9. Close the **Lexus** database, and then exit Access.

INTERNET ASSIGNMENTS

The purpose of the Internet Assignments is to challenge you to find information on the Internet that you can use to create effective documents. The actual assignments are updated and maintained on the Course Technology Web site. Log on to the Internet and use your Web browser to go to the Student Online Companion to accompany this text at **www.course.com/NewPerspectives/office2000**. Click the Access link, and then click the link for Tutorial 3.

QUICK CHECK ANSWERS

Session 3.1

1. a general query in which you specify the fields and records you want Access to select
2. The field list contains the table name at the top of the list box and the table's fields listed in the order in which they appear in the table; the design grid displays columns that contain specifications about a field you will use in the query.
3. A table datasheet and a query datasheet look the same, appearing in Datasheet view, and can be used to update data in a database. A table datasheet shows the permanent data in a table, whereas a query datasheet is temporary and its contents are based on the criteria you establish in the design grid.
4. primary table; related table
5. referential integrity
6. oldest to most recent date
7. when you want to perform different types of sorts (both ascending and descending, for example) on multiple fields, and when you want to sort on multiple fields that are nonadjacent or in the wrong order, but you do not want to rearrange the columns in the query datasheet to accomplish the sort
8. filter

Session 3.2

1. condition
2. in the same Criteria row; in different Criteria rows
3. expression
4. A calculated field appears in a query datasheet but does not exist in a database, as does a table field.
5. a function that performs an arithmetic operation on selected records in a database
6. Group By

LEVEL I

New Perspectives on

MICROSOFT®
POWERPOINT®
2000

TUTORIAL 1   PPT 1.03

Using PowerPoint to Create Presentations
Presentation to Reach Potential Customers of Inca Imports International

Read This Before You Begin

To the Student

Data Disks
To complete the Level I tutorials, Review Assignments, and Case Problems in this book, you need one Data Disk. Your instructor will either provide you with a Data Disk or ask you to make your own.

If you are making your own Data Disk, you will need one blank, formatted high-density disk. You will need to copy a set of folders from a file server or standalone computer or the Web onto your disks. Your instructor will tell you which computer, drive letter, and folders contain the files you need. You could also download the files by going to www.course.com, clicking Data Disk Files, and following the instructions on the screen.

The following table shows you which folders go on your disks, so that you will have enough disk space to complete all the tutorials, Review Assignments, and Case Problems:

Data Disk 1
Write this on the disk label:
Data Disk 1: Level I Tutorial 1
Put these folders on the disk:
Tutorial.01

When you begin each tutorial, be sure you are using the correct Data Disk. See the inside front or inside back cover of this book for more information on Data Disk files, or ask your instructor or technical support person for assistance.

Using Your Own Computer
If you are going to work through this book using your own computer, you need:

- **Computer System** Microsoft PowerPoint 2000 and Windows 95 or higher must be installed on your computer. This book assumes a complete installation of PowerPoint 2000.

- **Data Disks** You will not be able to complete the tutorials or exercises in this book using your own computer until you have Data Disks.

Visit Our World Wide Web Site
Additional materials designed especially for you are available on the World Wide Web. Go to http://www.course.com.

To the Instructor

The Data files are available on the Instructor's Resource Kit for this title. Follow the instructions in the Help file on the CD-ROM to install the programs to your network or standalone computer. For information on creating Data Disks, see the "To the Student" section above.

You are granted a license to copy the Data Files to any computer or computer network used by students who have purchased this book.

TUTORIAL 1

OBJECTIVES

In this tutorial you will:

- Start and exit PowerPoint
- Identify the components of the PowerPoint window
- Open and view an existing presentation
- Create a presentation using the AutoContent Wizard
- Edit text of the presentation in the Outline Pane and the Slide Pane
- Insert and delete slides
- Check the spelling and style in a presentation
- Use the PowerPoint Help system
- Create notes
- Save, preview, and print a presentation

USING POWERPOINT TO CREATE PRESENTATIONS

Presentation to Reach Potential Customers of Inca Imports International

CASE

Inca Imports International

Three years ago Patricia Cuevas and Angelena Cristenas began an import business called Inca Imports International. Working with suppliers in South America, particularly in Ecuador and Peru, the company imports fresh fruits and vegetables to North America during the winter and spring (which are summer and fall in South America) and sells them to small grocery stores in the Los Angeles area.

Inca Imports now has 34 employees and is a healthy and growing company. It has recently made plans to construct a distribution facility in Quito, Ecuador, and to launch a marketing campaign to position itself for further expansion. Patricia (president of Inca Imports) assigned Carl Vetterli (vice president of sales and marketing) the task of identifying potential customers and developing methods to reach them. Carl has scheduled a meeting with Patricia, Angelena (vice president of operations), Enrique Hoffmann (director of marketing), and other colleagues to review the results of his market research and to find ways of helping sales representatives increase sales.

Carl decides he wants to prepare two separate presentations for this meeting. His first presentation will include a demographic profile of Inca Imports' current customers, the results of a customer satisfaction survey, a vision statement of the company's future growth, a list of options for attracting new clients, and recommendations for a marketing strategy. Carl has already prepared this presentation, using many of PowerPoint's special features. For his second presentation, he wants a brainstorming session on how to help Inca Imports' sales representatives improve their sales effectiveness. He has not prepared this presentation, and asks you to help him create it.

SESSION 1.1

In this session, you'll learn how to start and exit PowerPoint, identify the parts of the PowerPoint window, and open and view an existing presentation. You'll also learn how to create a new presentation using the AutoContent Wizard and how to insert and modify text in both the Slide Pane and the Outline Pane.

What Is PowerPoint?

PowerPoint is a powerful presentation graphics program that provides everything you need to produce an effective presentation in the form of black-and-white or color overheads, 35 mm photographic slides, or on-screen slides. You may have already seen your instructors use PowerPoint presentations to enhance their classroom lectures.

Using PowerPoint, you can prepare each component of a presentation: individual slides, speaker notes, an outline of the presentation, and audience handouts. The presentation you'll create for Carl will include slides, notes, and handouts. Before you begin creating this presentation, however, you'll first preview Carl's existing presentation. You'll learn about some of PowerPoint's capabilities that can help make your presentations more interesting and effective.

Starting PowerPoint

You start PowerPoint in the same way that you start other Windows 98 programs—using the Start button on the taskbar.

To start PowerPoint:

1. Make sure Windows 98 is running on your computer, and that the Windows 98 desktop appears on your screen.

   TROUBLE? If you're running Windows NT Workstation on your computer or network, don't worry. Although the figures in this book were created while running Windows 98, Windows NT and Windows 98 share the same interface, and PowerPoint 2000 runs equally well under either operating system.

2. Click the **Start** button on the taskbar to display the Start menu, and then point to **Programs** to display the Programs menu.

3. Point to **Microsoft PowerPoint** on the Programs menu. See Figure 1-1.

TUTORIAL 1 USING POWERPOINT TO CREATE PRESENTATIONS   PPT 1.05   **POWERPOINT**

Figure 1-1   **STARTING MICROSOFT POWERPOINT**

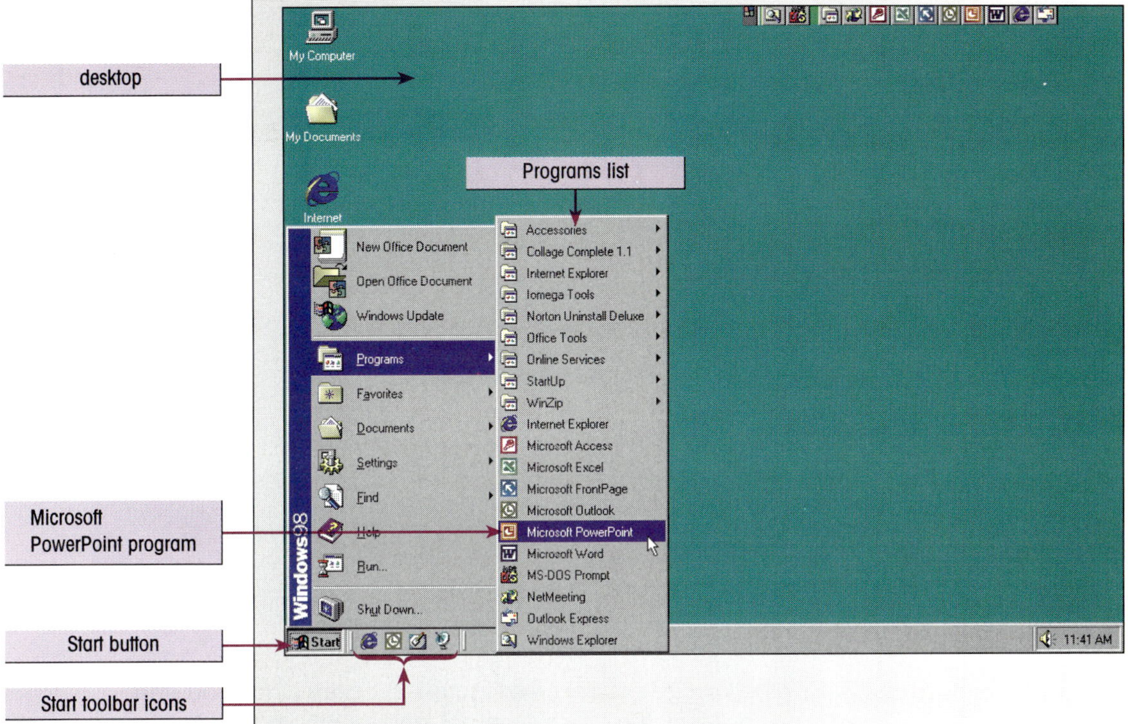

- desktop
- Programs list
- Microsoft PowerPoint program
- Start button
- Start toolbar icons

TROUBLE? If you don't see Microsoft PowerPoint on the Programs menu, ask your instructor or technical support person for help.

TROUBLE? If the Office Shortcut Bar, which appears along the top border of the desktop in Figure 1-1, looks different on your screen or does not appear at all, don't be concerned. Since the Office Shortcut Bar is not required to complete these tutorials, it has been omitted from the remaining figures in this text.

4. Click **Microsoft PowerPoint**. After a short pause PowerPoint opens, and the PowerPoint dialog box appears on the screen. If necessary, click the **Maximize** button so that the PowerPoint window fills the entire screen. See Figure 1-2.

Figure 1-2 THE POWERPOINT STARTUP DIALOG BOX

- dialog box on PowerPoint window
- select this
- select this
- Office Assistant "Clippit"

TROUBLE? If the Office Assistant (see Figure 1-2) opens when you start PowerPoint, right-click the Office Assistant, and then click Hide to close it; you'll learn more about the Office Assistant later in this tutorial.

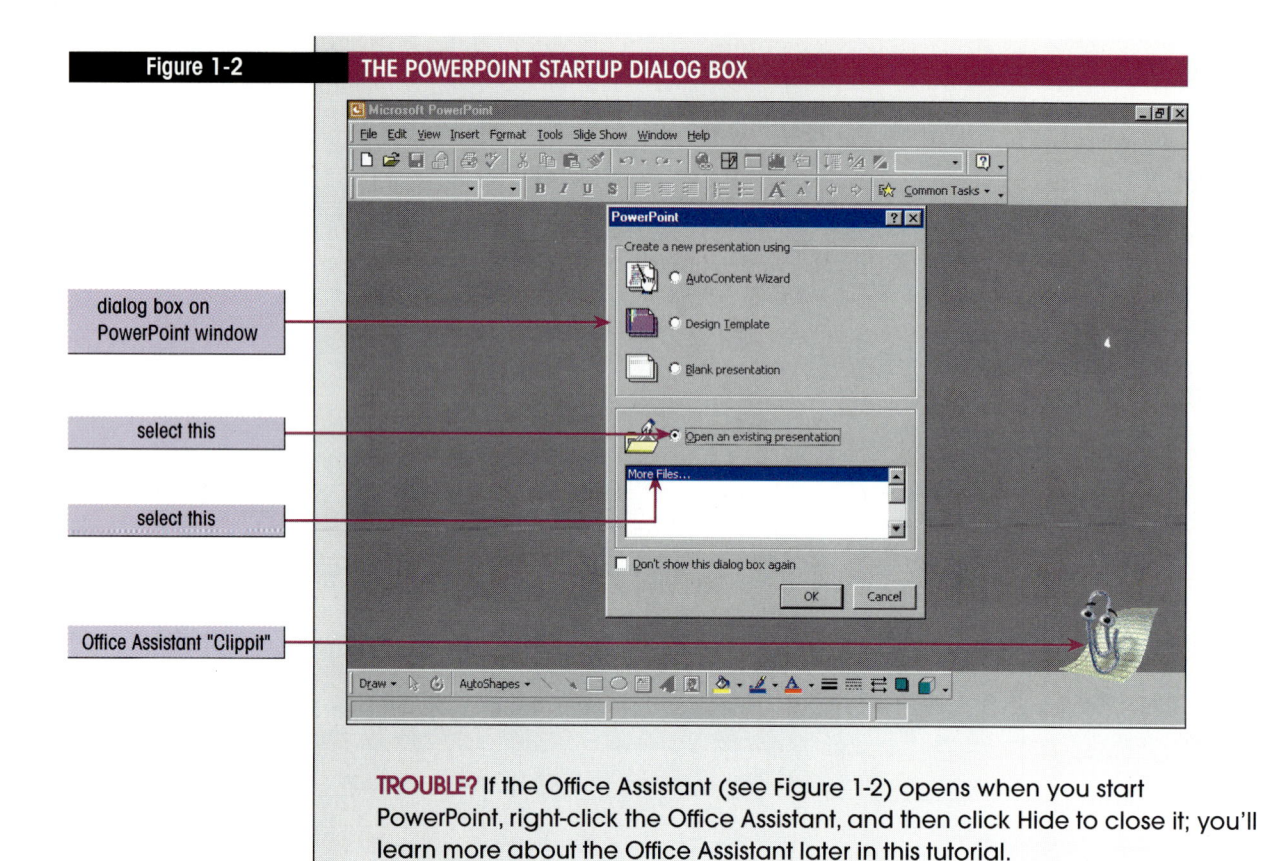

Now that you've started PowerPoint, you're ready to open Carl's existing presentation.

Opening an Existing PowerPoint Presentation

Before you prepare Carl's second presentation, Carl suggests that you view his first presentation as an example of PowerPoint features. He gives you a disk with a PowerPoint file so you can open and view it. You'll do that now.

To open an existing presentation:

1. Place your Data Disk in the appropriate drive.

   TROUBLE? If you don't have a Data Disk, you need to get one before you can proceed. Your instructor or technical support person will either give you one or ask you to make your own by following the instructions on the "Read This Before You Begin" page preceding this tutorial. See your instructor or technical support person for more information.

2. If necessary, click the **Open an existing presentation** option button to select it.

3. Make sure **More files** is selected in the list box below the Open an existing presentation option button (as shown in Figure 1-2), and then click the **OK** button. The Open dialog box appears on the screen.

4. Click the **Look in** list arrow to display the list of disk drives on your computer, and then click on the drive that contains your Data Disk.

TUTORIAL 1 USING POWERPOINT TO CREATE PRESENTATIONS   PPT   1.07   **POWERPOINT**

5. Double-click the **Tutorial.01** folder, double-click the **Tutorial** folder, click **Customer**, and then click the **Open** button to display Carl's presentation.

   TROUBLE? If you see filename extensions on your screen (such as ".ppt" appended to "Customer" in the filename), do not be concerned; they will not affect the accuracy of your work.

6. If necessary, click the **Maximize** button ▢ so the presentation window fills the screen, and then, if necessary, click the **Normal View** button ▢ near the lower-left corner of the screen. See Figure 1-3.

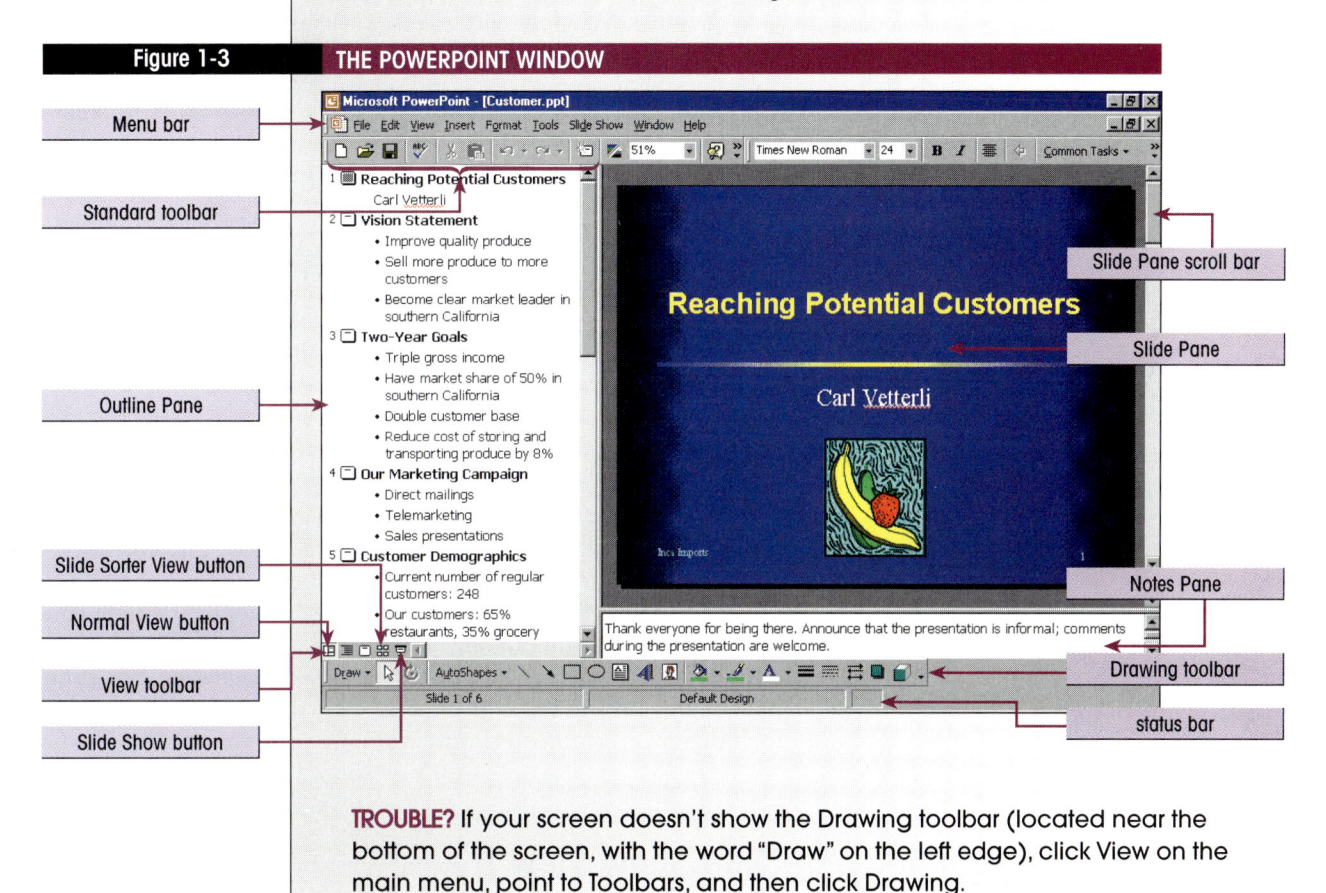

Figure 1-3   THE POWERPOINT WINDOW

[Screenshot of the PowerPoint window with labels pointing to: Menu bar, Standard toolbar, Outline Pane, Slide Sorter View button, Normal View button, View toolbar, Slide Show button, Slide Pane scroll bar, Slide Pane, Notes Pane, Drawing toolbar, status bar]

TROUBLE? If your screen doesn't show the Drawing toolbar (located near the bottom of the screen, with the word "Draw" on the left edge), click View on the main menu, point to Toolbars, and then click Drawing.

Now that you've opened Carl's presentation, you're ready to view some of the PowerPoint features. You'll begin by reviewing the PowerPoint window.

Understanding the PowerPoint Window

The PowerPoint window contains features common to all Windows programs, as well as features specific to PowerPoint, such as the options available on the toolbars.

Common Windows Elements

You'll recognize that several elements of the PowerPoint window are common to other Windows 98 programs. For example, as shown in Figure 1-3, the PowerPoint window has a title bar, menu bar, and window sizing buttons. These elements function the same way in PowerPoint as they do in other Windows programs. However, the PowerPoint window also includes items that are specific to PowerPoint, such as some of the toolbar buttons and the panes.

The Toolbars

Like many Windows programs, PowerPoint supplies several toolbars, as shown in Figure 1-3. Recall that a **toolbar** is a horizontal or vertical ribbon of icons that provides menu shortcuts. When you move the mouse pointer over one of the icons on the toolbar, the outline of the button appears, followed by a **ScreenTip**, which is a light yellow box containing the name of the button. Although many of the toolbar buttons accomplish the same tasks in PowerPoint as they do in other Windows programs, such as the Save button on the Standard toolbar, you'll also notice some differences. For example, the Drawing toolbar contains specific buttons for adding shapes, lines, and other graphic objects to the slides in your PowerPoint presentation.

Further, just above the Drawing toolbar on the left side of the screen is the View toolbar, which contains five buttons that allow you to change the way you view a slide presentation. You are currently in Normal View. Clicking the Outline View button allows you to see more of the outline and less of the slide, and clicking the Slide View button allows you to see more of the slide and less of the outline. Clicking the Slide Sorter View button changes the view to miniature images of all the slides at once and lets you reorder the slides or set special features for your slide show. Finally, to present your slide show, you click the Slide Show button.

The PowerPoint Panes

In Normal View, also called Tri-Pane View, the PowerPoint window contains three panes: the Outline Pane, the Slide Pane, and the Notes Pane (see Figure 1-3). The **Outline Pane** lists an outline of your presentation, including titles and text of each slide. The **Slide Pane** shows the slide as it will look during your slide show. You can use either the Outline Pane or the Slide Pane to add or edit text, but you can only use the Slide Pane to add or edit graphics. The **Notes Pane** contains any notes that you might prepare on each slide. For example, the Notes Pane might contain points to cover or phrases to say during the presentation.

Now that you're familiar with the PowerPoint window, you're ready to view Carl's presentation.

Viewing a Presentation in Slide Show View

You want to see how Carl's presentation will appear when he shows it in Slide Show View at Inca Imports' executive meeting. You'll then have a better understanding of how Carl used PowerPoint's features to make his presentation informative and interesting.

To view a presentation in Slide Show View:

1. Make sure Slide 1, "Reaching Potential Customers," appears in the Slide Pane. (If you would prefer to start the slide show on a different slide, use the Slide Pane scroll bar to move to the desired slide, and then start the slide show.)

    TROUBLE? If a different slide is in the Slide Pane, drag the scroll button in the vertical scroll bar (located on the right side of the Slide Pane) to the top of the scroll bar.

TUTORIAL 1 USING POWERPOINT TO CREATE PRESENTATIONS   PPT 1.09   **POWERPOINT**

2. Click the **Slide Show** button on the View toolbar (just below the Outline Pane). The slide show begins by filling the entire viewing area of the screen with Slide 1 of Carl's presentation. See Figure 1-4.

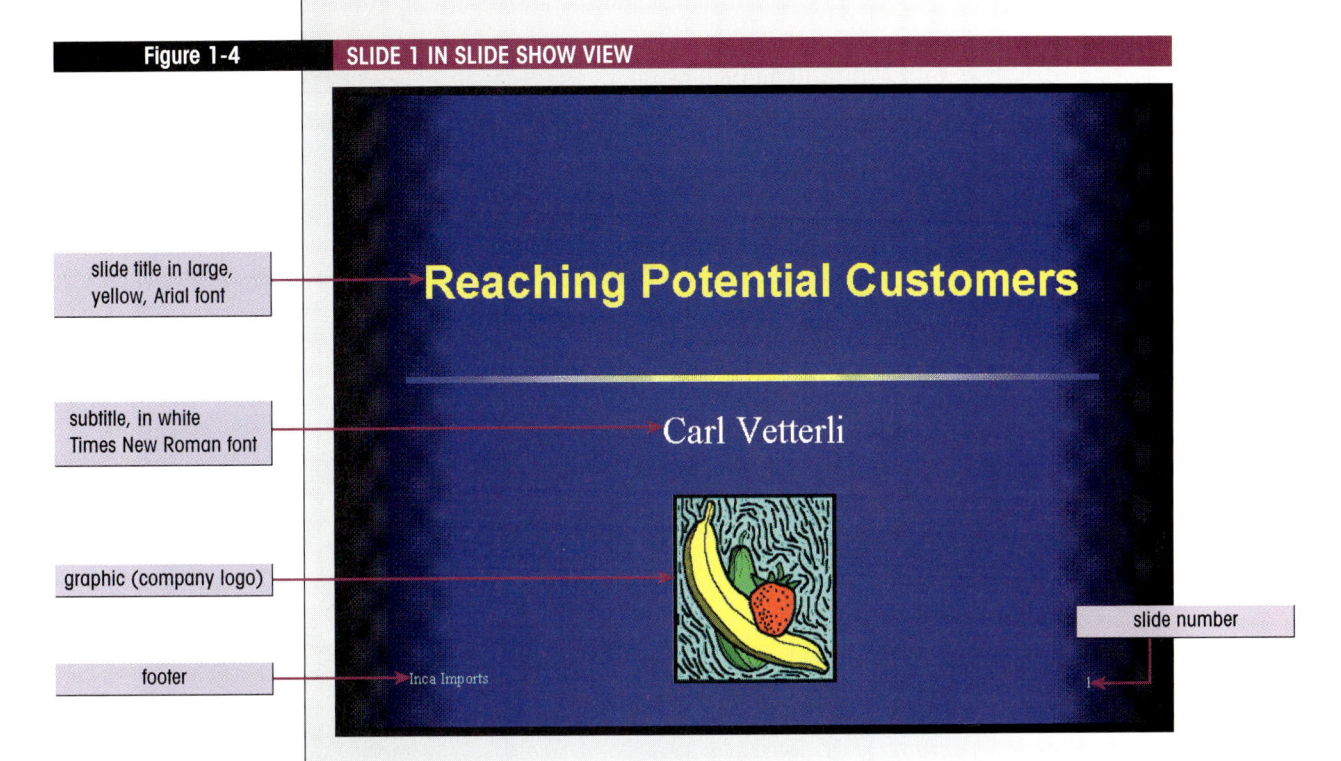

Figure 1-4   SLIDE 1 IN SLIDE SHOW VIEW

- slide title in large, yellow, Arial font → **Reaching Potential Customers**
- subtitle, in white Times New Roman font → Carl Vetterli
- graphic (company logo)
- footer → Inca Imports
- slide number → 1

As you view this first slide, you can already see some of the types of objects that PowerPoint allows you to place on a slide: text in different fonts, font sizes, and font colors (to differentiate between the slide title and subtitle); graphics (the Inca Imports' logo, to identify the company clearly); footers; slide numbers; and colored background with gradient fills. A **footer** is a word or phrase that appears at the bottom of each slide in the presentation (for example, "Inca Imports" in the lower-left corner of Figure 1-4). A **gradient fill** is a type of shading in which one color blends into another, which can help make the slide more eye-catching; for example, in Figure 1-4, black blends into blue and then back into black horizontally across the screen. Take a few minutes to study these elements, and then continue to the next slide.

3. Press the **Spacebar**. The slide show goes from Slide 1 to Slide 2. See Figure 1-5. You can also press the Right Arrow key or click the left mouse button to advance to the next slide.

Additionally, PowerPoint provides a method for jumping from a slide to any other slide in the presentation during the slide show: right-click anywhere on the screen, point to Go, and then click Slide Navigator. The **slide navigator** is a dialog box that displays a list of all the slides by their title. Simply click on a title, and then click the Go To button to go to that slide. You also can right-click on the screen during a slide show, and then click other options to view other slide features.

Notice that during the transition from Slide 1 to Slide 2, the presentation did three things: (1) played the sound of chimes, (2) displayed Slide 2 by splitting Slide 1 horizontally and scrolling the top and bottom of Slide 2 onto the screen (called a **slide transition**), and (3) shot three arrows at a target on the screen with an accompanying "whoosh" sound with each arrow (called **object animation**). These PowerPoint transition and animation effects are entertaining and reinforce the major points of information on the slide.

Figure 1-5   **SLIDE 2 WITH TITLE AND BULLETED LIST**

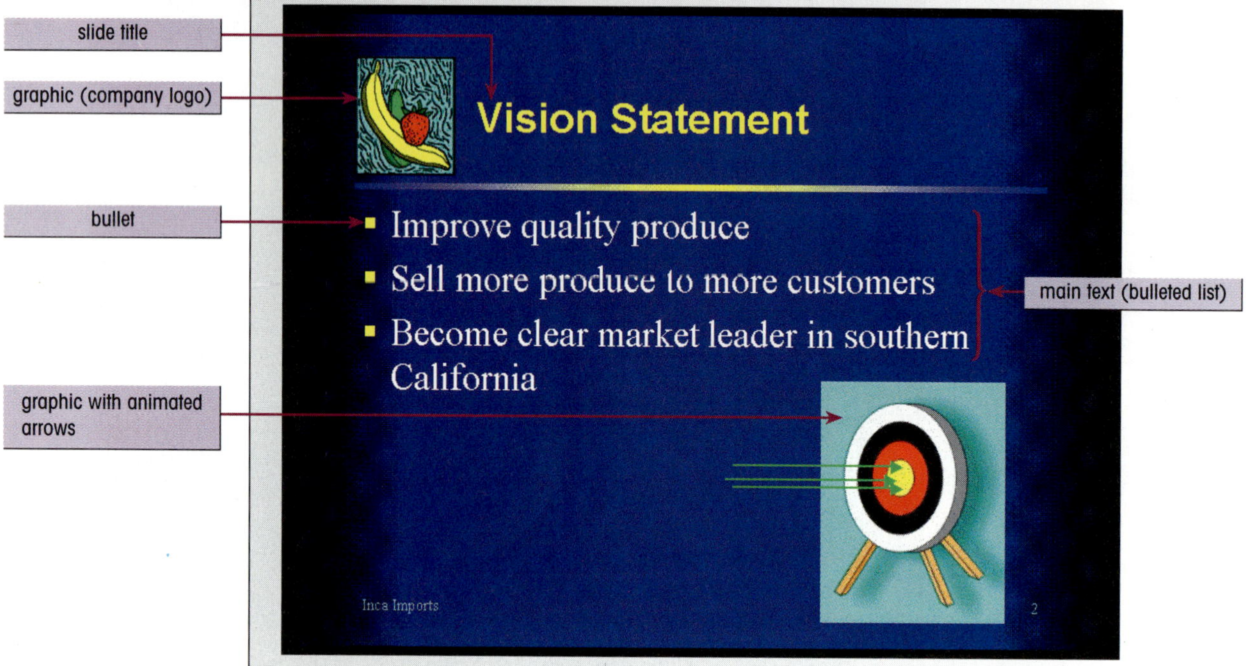

- slide title
- graphic (company logo)
- bullet
- main text (bulleted list)
- graphic with animated arrows

Vision Statement

- Improve quality produce
- Sell more produce to more customers
- Become clear market leader in southern California

Inca Imports

TROUBLE? If you missed some of the action during the transition from Slide 1 to Slide 2, or if you would like to see it again, press the Left Arrow key twice to redisplay Slide 1, and then press the Spacebar to go to Slide 2 again.

TROUBLE? If you didn't hear any sound as Slide 2 appeared on the screen, your computer may not have a sound card and speakers, or the computer sound may have been turned off. If you have questions about the sound on a laboratory computer, consult your technical support person.

Notice in Figure 1-5 that Slide 2 displays Inca Imports' logo, a title in a large yellow font, and a bulleted list, with yellow, square bullets and white text. A **bulleted list** is a list of paragraphs with a special character (dot, circle, box, star, or other character) to the left of each paragraph. A **bulleted item** is one paragraph in a bulleted list. Using bulleted lists reminds both the speaker and the audience of the slide's main points.

In addition to bulleted lists, PowerPoint also supports numbered lists. A **numbered list** is a list of paragraphs that are numbered consecutively within a main text box. To number a list automatically, select the text box, and then click the Numbering button on the Formatting toolbar.

4. Press the **Spacebar** to proceed to Slide 3. During the transition from Slide 2 to Slide 3, you again hear the sound and see the slide scroll onto the screen from the center. You also notice that the slide doesn't display a bulleted list. On this

slide, you'll display the bulleted items, as well as a chart, one at a time. This allows the speaker to keep the audience focused only on the item currently being discussed.

5. Press the **Spacebar** to display the chart "Projected Gross Income" onto Slide 3. You can easily create attractive and effective charts and graphs using PowerPoint. Now you're ready to display the first bulleted item on the slide.

6. Press the **Spacebar** to display the first bulleted paragraph, "Triple gross income."

7. Press the **Spacebar** again to display the next bulleted paragraph. Notice that as each new bulleted item appears in a white font with a yellow bullet, the previous item dims to a gray font and bullet. Again, this helps keep the audience focused.

8. Press the **Spacebar** twice more to display the final two items in the bulleted list in Slide 3. See Figure 1-6.

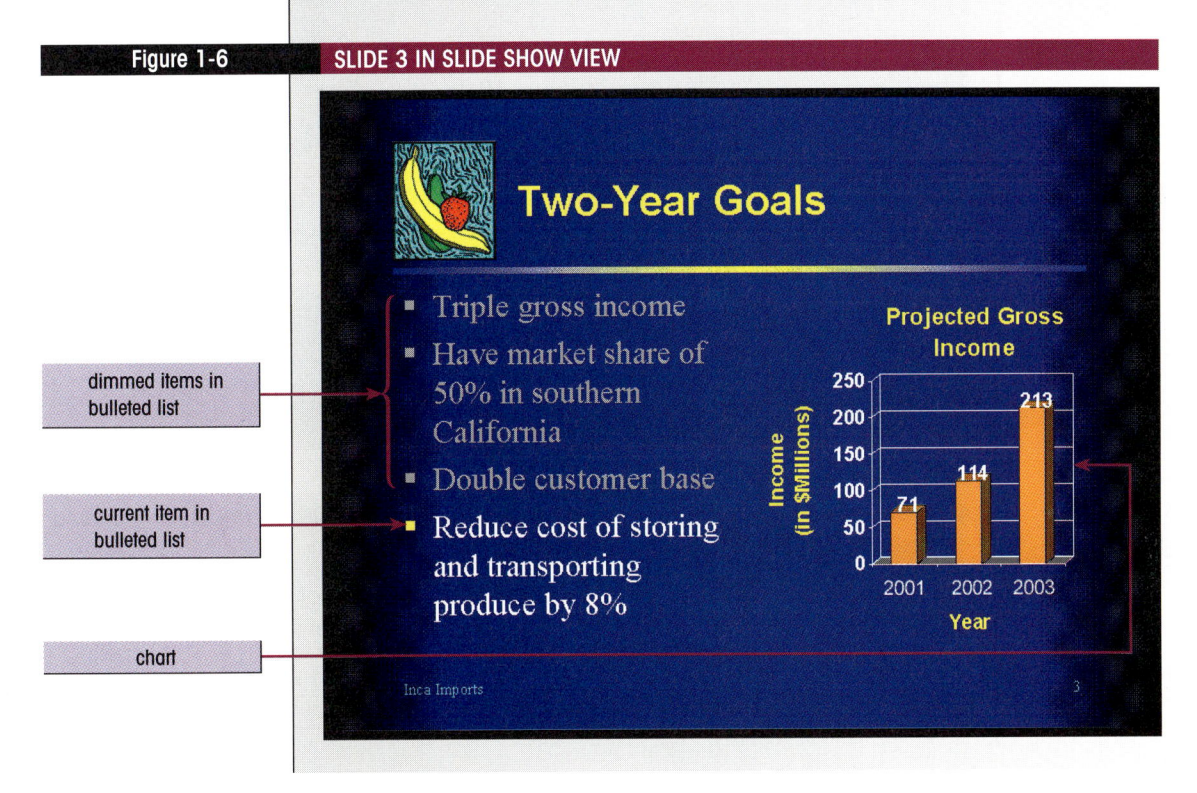

Figure 1-6 SLIDE 3 IN SLIDE SHOW VIEW

- dimmed items in bulleted list
- current item in bulleted list
- chart

In these first three slides, you saw many PowerPoint features that help make Carl's presentation informative and enjoyable. Next, you'll proceed to the other slides in Carl's presentation, where you'll see additional PowerPoint features.

To finish viewing the slide show:

1. Press the **Spacebar** to display Slide 4. Remember, you can see the slide number in the lower-right corner of the screen. This slide contains a clip-art image of a telephone. A **clip-art image** is a picture, often a drawing or cartoon, that you can get from the PowerPoint ClipArt Gallery. Using clip art visually emphasizes the main point of the slide.

2. Press the **Spacebar** to display the first bulleted item. This time the presentation makes a "laser" sound as the item appears on the screen.

3. Press the **Spacebar** as many times as necessary to see the rest of Slide 4, to move on to Slide 5 and view and read its contents, and then to display Slide 6. See Figure 1-7. As Slide 6 appears on the screen, instead of hearing chimes, you hear a drum roll. Using different sound effects can help keep your audience alert and entertained.

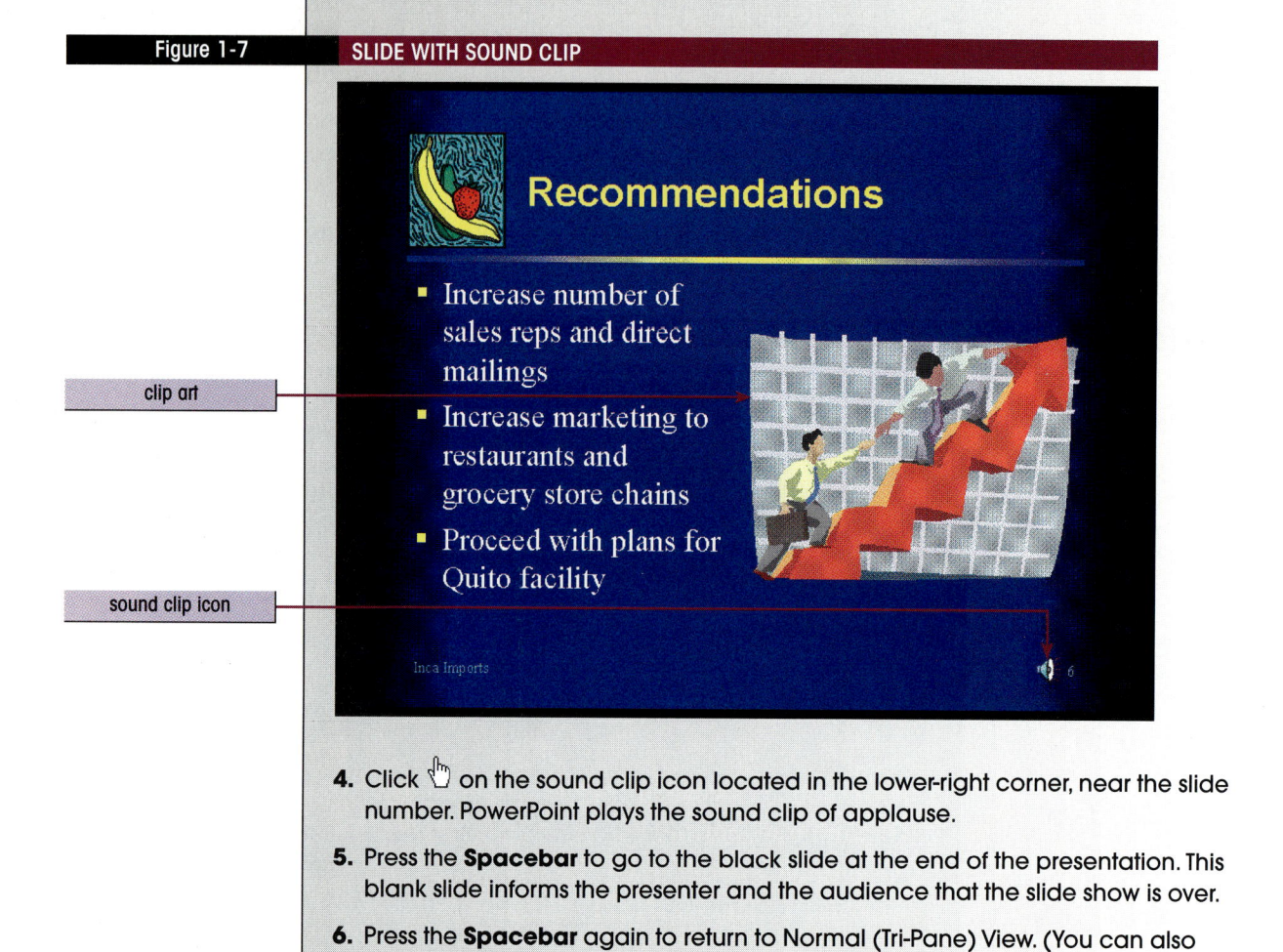

Figure 1-7   **SLIDE WITH SOUND CLIP**

clip art

sound clip icon

4. Click on the sound clip icon located in the lower-right corner, near the slide number. PowerPoint plays the sound clip of applause.

5. Press the **Spacebar** to go to the black slide at the end of the presentation. This blank slide informs the presenter and the audience that the slide show is over.

6. Press the **Spacebar** again to return to Normal (Tri-Pane) View. (You can also press the ESC key at any point during the slide show to return to Normal View.)

As you can see from this slide show, PowerPoint has many powerful features. You'll learn how to include many of these features in your own presentations as you work through these tutorials. Now that you've finished viewing Carl's presentation, you're ready to close it.

Closing a Presentation and Exiting PowerPoint

Once you've completed viewing a presentation, you can close it and exit PowerPoint. If you've created or edited a presentation, you should always save it first; you'll learn how later in this tutorial.

> **To close a presentation and exit PowerPoint:**
>
> 1. Click the **Close** button ⊠ on the right side of the menu bar. The presentation window closes but leaves the PowerPoint window on the screen.
>
>   **TROUBLE?** If you clicked the PowerPoint Close button in the extreme upper-right corner of the screen, the entire PowerPoint window closed. If this happened, just omit the next step.
>
> 2. Click the **Close** button ⊠ in the upper-right corner of the screen to exit PowerPoint. You should now be viewing your computer desktop on your screen (unless other programs are running).

You're now ready to create Carl's presentation for brainstorming on methods to help Inca Imports' sales representatives. Before you begin, however, you should plan the presentation.

Planning a Presentation

Planning a presentation before you create it improves the quality of your presentation, makes your presentation more effective and enjoyable, and, in the long run, saves you time and effort. As you plan your presentation, you should answer several questions: What is my purpose or objective for this presentation? What type of presentation is needed? Who is the audience? What information does that audience need? What is the physical location of my presentation? What is the best format for presenting the information contained in this presentation, given the location of the presentation?

In planning your presentation, you identify the following elements:

- **Purpose of the presentation**: To identify means of helping sales reps improve their sales
- **Type of presentation**: Brainstorming session
- **Audience for the presentation**: Patricia, Angelena, Enrique, and other key staff members in a weekly executive meeting
- **Audience needs**: To develop an environment conducive to developing new ideas
- **Location of the presentation**: Small boardroom
- **Format**: Oral presentation; electronic slide show of six to eight slides

Having carefully planned your presentation, you'll now use the PowerPoint AutoContent Wizard to create it.

Using the AutoContent Wizard

PowerPoint helps you quickly create effective presentations by using **Wizards**, which you'll recall ask you a series of questions about your tasks and then help you perform them. The **AutoContent Wizard** lets you choose a presentation category such as "Recommending a Strategy," "Generic," or "Brainstorming Session." After you've selected the type of presentation you want, the AutoContent Wizard creates a general outline for you to follow.

When you create a new presentation without using the AutoContent Wizard, you can start from an existing design template or existing PowerPoint presentation, or you can start with a blank presentation. A **design template** is a file that contains the colors and format of the background and the type style of the titles, accents, and other text. To create a new presentation from a design template, click File on the main menu, click New, and then select the desired template. To start with a blank presentation, simply click the New button on the Standard toolbar. Once you start creating a presentation with or without a design template, you can change to any other PowerPoint design template.

Because the presentation you'll create, a brainstorming session, is predefined, you'll use the AutoContent Wizard. The AutoContent Wizard will automatically create a title slide and standard outline, which you then can edit to fit Carl's needs.

To create a presentation with the AutoContent Wizard:

1. Start PowerPoint, click the **AutoContent Wizard** option button in the PowerPoint startup dialog box, and then click the **OK** button. The first of several AutoContent Wizard dialog boxes appears. See Figure 1-8.

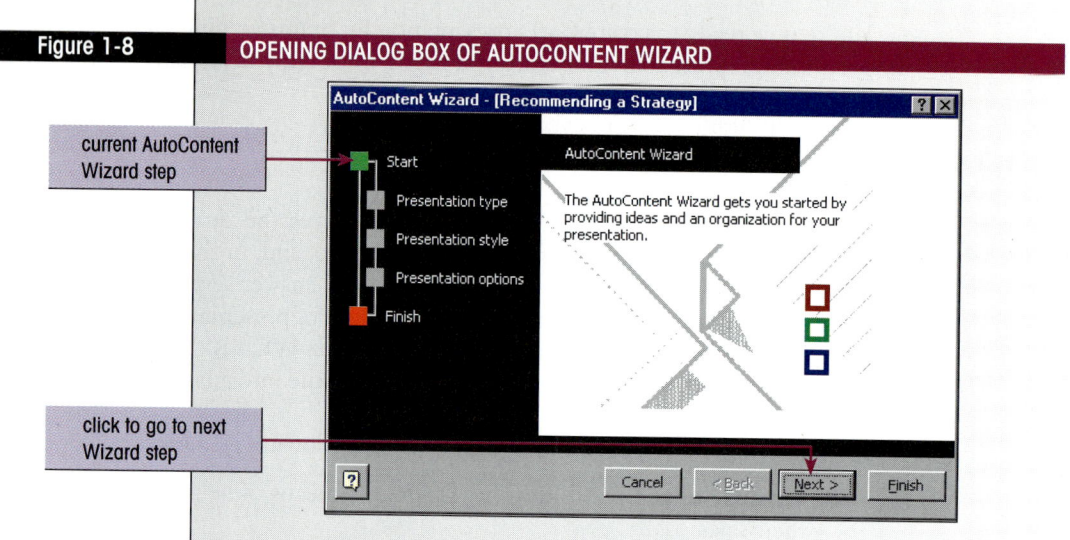

Figure 1-8 **OPENING DIALOG BOX OF AUTOCONTENT WIZARD**

current AutoContent Wizard step

click to go to next Wizard step

TROUBLE? If the PowerPoint startup dialog box doesn't appear on your screen, click File, and then click New. When the New Presentation dialog box opens, click the General tab, click the AutoContent Wizard button, and then click the OK button.

TROUBLE? If the Office Assistant opens, click the No, don't provide help now option button.

2. Read the information in the AutoContent Wizard dialog box, and then click the **Next** button to display the next dialog box of the AutoContent Wizard.

This dialog box allows you to select the type of presentation; you want to select the presentation on brainstorming.

3. In the list of types of presentation, click **Brainstorming Session**. See Figure 1-9.

TUTORIAL 1 USING POWERPOINT TO CREATE PRESENTATIONS   PPT 1.15

| Figure 1-9 | SELECTING TYPE OF PRESENTATION IN AUTOCONTENT WIZARD DIALOG BOX |

click to see list of desired presentation types

click to select this presentation type

TROUBLE? If you don't see Brainstorming Session in the AutoContent Wizard dialog box, click the General button, and then click Brainstorming Session.

TROUBLE? If a Microsoft PowerPoint dialog box appears with the message that PowerPoint can't find the template used in this document, insert the Office 2000 CD into your CD drive, and then click the Yes button. The desired template will then become installed on your computer. If you don't have an Office 2000 CD, consult your instructor or technical support person.

4. Click the **Next** button to display the dialog box with the question, "What type of output will you use?"

5. If necessary, click the **On-screen presentation** option button to select it, and then click the **Next** button. In this dialog box, you'll specify the title and footer (if any) of the presentation.

6. Click I in the Presentation title text box and type **Helping Our Sales Reps**, click I in the Footer text box and type **Helping Sales Reps**, and then click the **Date last updated** check box to deselect it. Leave the Slide Number box checked. The dialog box should now look like Figure 1-10.

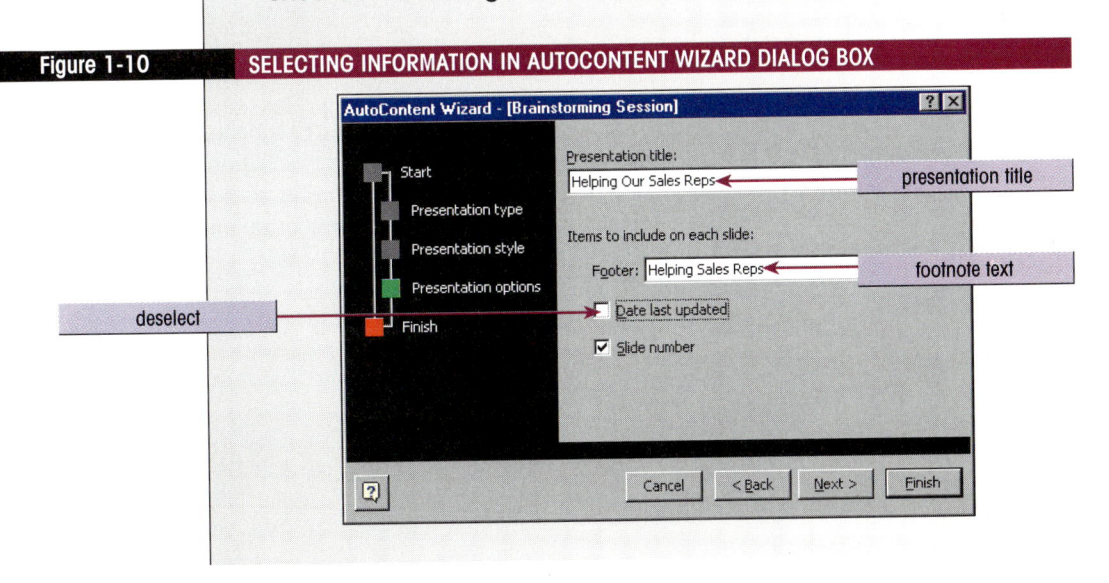

| Figure 1-10 | SELECTING INFORMATION IN AUTOCONTENT WIZARD DIALOG BOX |

presentation title

footnote text

deselect

7. Click the **Next** button. The final AutoContent Wizard dialog box appears, letting you know that you've completed the AutoContent Wizard.

8. Click the **Finish** button. PowerPoint now displays the AutoContent outline in the Outline Pane and the title slide (Slide 1) in the Slide Pane. See Figure 1-11.

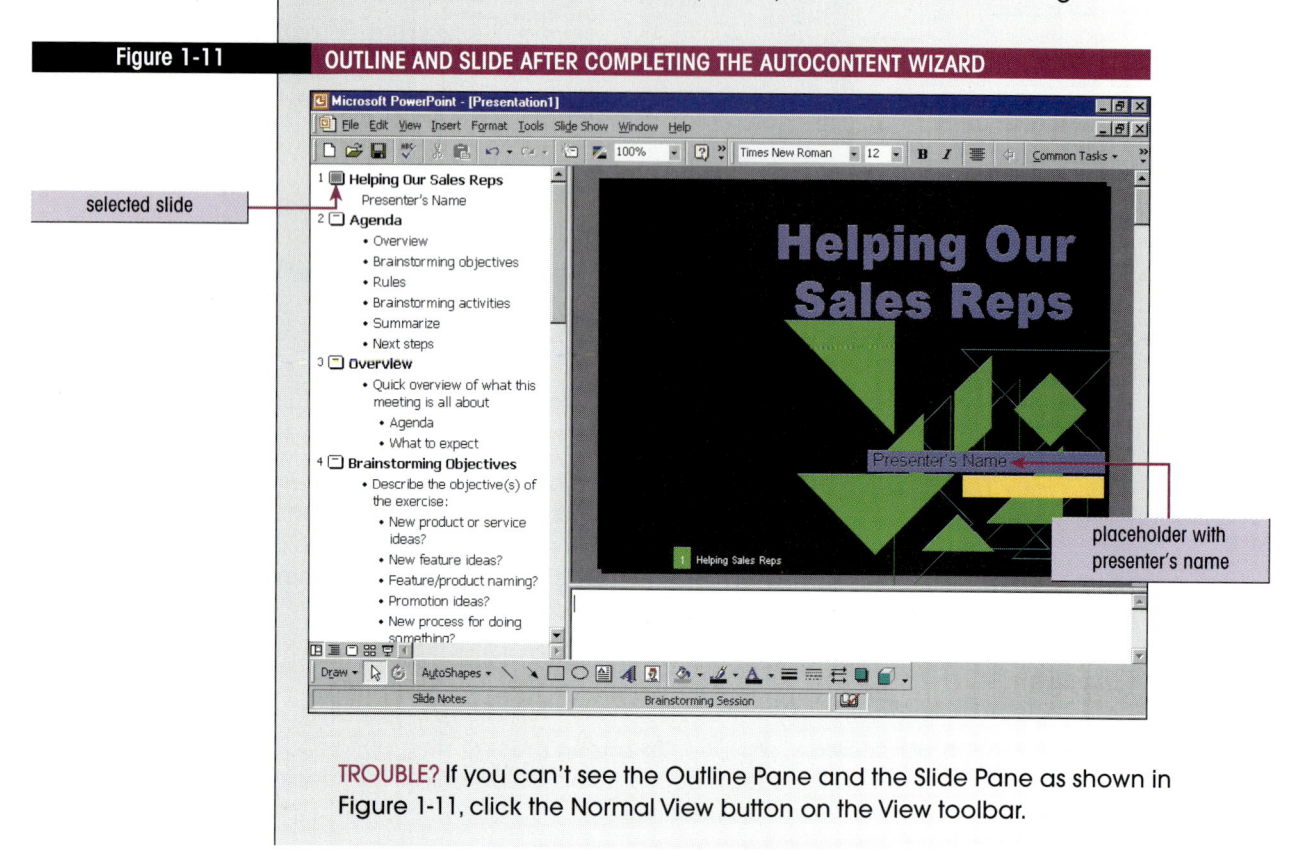

Figure 1-11   **OUTLINE AND SLIDE AFTER COMPLETING THE AUTOCONTENT WIZARD**

TROUBLE? If you can't see the Outline Pane and the Slide Pane as shown in Figure 1-11, click the Normal View button on the View toolbar.

Now that you've used the AutoContent Wizard, you're ready to edit its default outline to fit Carl's specific presentation needs.

Editing AutoContent Slides

The AutoContent Wizard automatically creates the title slide as well as other slides, with suggested text located in placeholders. A **placeholder** is a region of a slide or a location in an outline reserved for inserting text or graphics. To edit the AutoContent outline to fit Carl's needs, you must select the placeholders one at a time, and then replace them with other text.

TUTORIAL 1 USING POWERPOINT TO CREATE PRESENTATIONS   PPT 1.17   **POWERPOINT**

> **REFERENCE WINDOW** RW
>
> <u>Creating Effective Text Presentations</u>
> - Think of your text presentation as a visual map of your oral presentation. Show your organization by using overviews, making headings larger than subheadings, including bulleted lists to highlight key points, and numbering steps to show sequence.
> - Follow the 6 x 6 rule: Use six or fewer items per screen, and use phrases of six or fewer words. Omit unnecessary articles, pronouns, and adjectives.
> - Keep phrases parallel.
> - Make sure your text is appropriate for your purpose and audience.

You'll now begin to edit and replace the text to fit Carl's presentation. The first text you'll change is the presenter's name placeholder (which currently has your name or that of the person who owns the computer) with the actual presenter's name, Carl Vetterli. (If the scheduled presenter changes after creating the presentation, recall that you can use the Find command to locate Carl Vetterli's name and then replace it accordingly. Click Edit on the menu bar, click Replace, enter the text that you want replaced in the Find what text box, enter the replacement text in the Replace with text box, and then click either Replace or Replace All.)

To edit and replace text in a slide:

1. In the Outline Pane, drag I across the text of the presenter's name (currently your name or the computer owner's name) to select it. When the text becomes selected, it appears as white text on a black background.

2. Type **Carl Vetterli**, and then click anywhere else on the slide. As soon as you start to type, the placeholder disappears, and the typed text appears in its place.

   Notice that PowerPoint marks "Vetterli" with a red wavy underline to indicate that the word may be misspelled. This is a result of PowerPoint's **Spell Checker**, a feature that automatically marks any word not found in the PowerPoint dictionary. In this case, "Vetterli" is correctly spelled, but sometimes you might make typographical errors. If this happens, *right*-click on the red wavy underlined word to display a list of suggested spellings and then click the correct word, or simply edit the misspelled word. Instead of correcting the spelling, you'll tell PowerPoint to ignore the word "Vetterli" and not mark it as misspelled on this or any other slides.

3. Right-click I on the word **Vetterli** to display the shortcut menu, and then click **Ignore All**. See Figure 1-12.

Figure 1-12 SLIDE WITH PRESENTER'S NAME

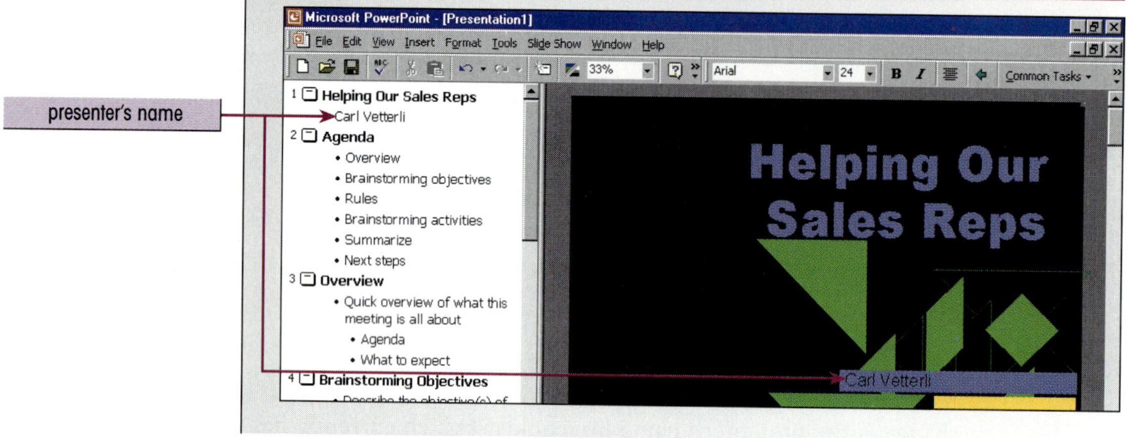

(presenter's name → Carl Vetterli)

Having made substantial progress in creating Carl's presentation, you'll now save the presentation. Then, because you realize you have to go to a meeting, you'll exit PowerPoint.

Saving a Presentation

As a general rule, you should save your PowerPoint work often, about every 15 minutes, so you won't lose your work.

To save a presentation for the first time:

1. If necessary, place your Data Disk into the appropriate drive.

2. Click the **Save** button on the Standard toolbar. The Save dialog box opens.

3. Click the **Save in** list arrow, and then click the drive that contains your Data Disk.

4. Double-click the **Tutorial.01** folder, and then double-click **Tutorial** to open that folder.

5. Drag across all or part of the current filename (probably **Helping Our Sales Reps**) in the File name text box to select it, type **Brainstorming for Sales Reps**, and then click the **Save** button. PowerPoint saves the presentation to the disk, using the filename Brainstorming for Sales Reps. That name now appears in the title bar of the PowerPoint window.

Having saved your work, you're now ready to exit PowerPoint.

6. Click **X** on the PowerPoint window to exit PowerPoint.

In addition to the Save command, PowerPoint also has a **Save As** command, which allows you to save the current presentation to a new file. For example, if you make modifications to an existing presentation but you want to keep the old version and save the new version to the disk, you would use the Save As command to save the modified presentation with a new filename.

When you return from your meeting, you'll continue to edit the text of Carl's presentation, as well as create notes.

Session 1.1 Quick Check

1. In one to three sentences, describe the purpose of the PowerPoint program and the components of a presentation that you can create with it.
2. Name and describe the PowerPoint panes.
3. Define or describe the following:
    a. gradient fill
    b. footer
    c. placeholder
    d. title (on a slide)
    e. bulleted list
4. Why should you plan a presentation before you create it? What are some of the presentation elements that should be considered?
5. Describe the purpose of the AutoContent Wizard.
6. What is the 6 × 6 rule?
7. What does a red wavy underline indicate?
8. Why is it important to save your work frequently?

SESSION 1.2

In this session, you'll learn how to move from one slide to the next, modify bulleted lists, add and delete slides, use the PowerPoint Help system, create notes, use the Style Checker, and preview and print a presentation.

Modifying a Presentation

While you were at your meeting, Carl looked over the presentation and has several suggestions for improving it. His first suggestion is to delete unnecessary slides.

Deleting Slides

When creating a presentation, you'll often delete slides. The AutoContent Wizard may create slides that you don't think are necessary, or you may create slides that you no longer want. For this presentation, Carl first asks you to delete Slide 3, titled "Overview," because he thinks that presenting the meeting agenda in Slide 2 provides sufficient overview.

To delete slides:

1. If you took a break after the previous session, make sure PowerPoint is running and Brainstorming for Sales Reps is open. If you're using the same computer as when you saved the presentation, you can click the **Open an existing presentation** option button, click **Brainstorming for Sales Reps** in the list of previously opened presentations, and then click the **OK** button.

2. Click ✥ in the Outline Pane on the slide icon ▭ for Slide 3. All the text of that slide becomes selected, and Slide 3 appears in the Slide Pane. See Figure 1-13.

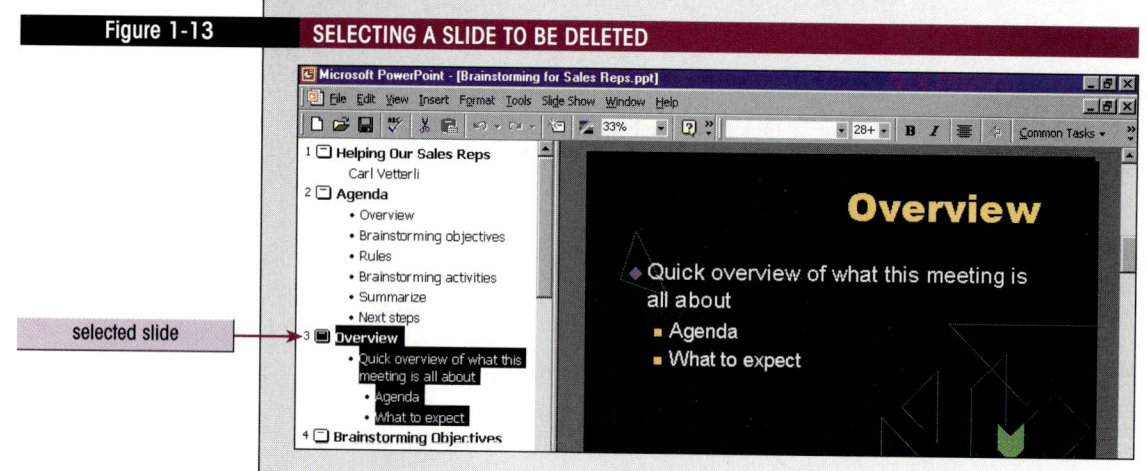

Figure 1-13 **SELECTING A SLIDE TO BE DELETED**

selected slide

3. Click **Edit** on the main menu, and then, if necessary, point to the double arrow to display the hidden menu items. PowerPoint, like other Office 2000 programs, initially displays the commands that are used most frequently on that computer. When you leave the menu open for a few seconds or click the double arrow, PowerPoint anticipates that you are looking for an item not currently displayed, and it expands the list of possible options. For the rest of these tutorials, click the double arrow if you do not see the option you are looking for.

4. Click **Delete Slide**. The entire slide is deleted from the presentation.

    Because you have deleted the Overview slide, you should now delete the "Overview" bulleted item in Slide 2. You'll do that next.

5. Move the mouse pointer to the bullet to the left of "Overview" in the text of Slide 2 in the Outline Pane, click ✥ on the bullet to select the text, and then press the **Delete** key. The word "Overview" disappears from the outline and from the slide in the Slide Pane.

    Next, you'll delete another slide from the presentation, Slide 8, because it doesn't contain any information. Because you've already learned how to delete slides in the Outline Pane, you'll delete this slide using the Slide Pane.

6. Click ▷ on the Slide Pane scroll bar, drag it until the scroll ScreenTip displays "Slide: 8 of 8" (see Figure 1-14), and then release the mouse button.

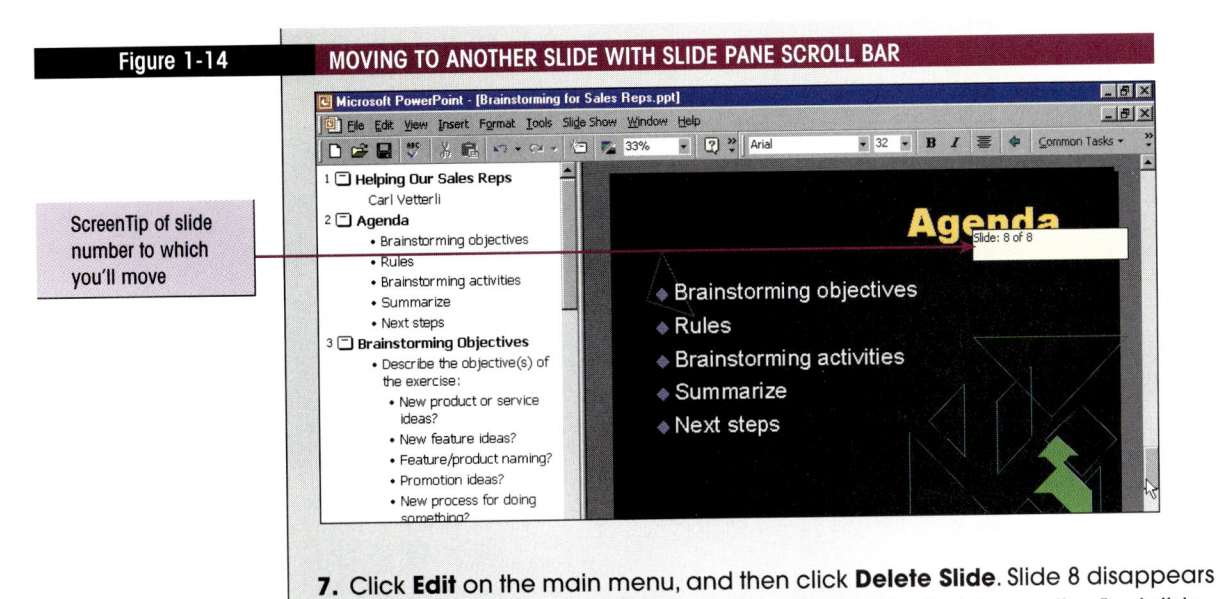

TUTORIAL 1 USING POWERPOINT TO CREATE PRESENTATIONS   PPT 1.21

| Figure 1-14 | **MOVING TO ANOTHER SLIDE WITH SLIDE PANE SCROLL BAR** |

ScreenTip of slide number to which you'll move

7. Click **Edit** on the main menu, and then click **Delete Slide**. Slide 8 disappears from the screen, and PowerPoint displays Slide 7, which is now the final slide.

Carl's next suggestion is to change both the order of some of the text on a slide, and the order of the slides in the presentation. You'll do so using the Outline Pane.

Moving Slides and Text in the Outline Pane

Carl would like you to move the current Slide 4, "Rules," ahead of the current Slide 3, "Brainstorming Objectives," because he would like to discuss brainstorming rules with the group before discussing the objectives. After that, you'll edit the order of the bulleted items in Slide 2, "Agenda," to reflect this change.

To move a slide and text using the Outline Pane:

1. If necessary, scroll up the Outline Pane so you can see Slide 4, and then click ✥ on the slide icon ▢ to select the entire Slide 4.

2. Drag the pointer up above Slide 3. As you drag up (moving the pointer while holding down the mouse button), the pointer becomes ↕, and the new position of the slide is represented by a horizontal line, as shown in Figure 1-15. When the horizontal line is above ▢ for Slide 3, release the mouse button. The slide titled "Rules" becomes Slide 3, and the slide titled "Brainstorming Objectives" becomes Slide 4. You also can rearrange slides using Slide Sorter View; you'll have a chance to use this method in the end-of-tutorial assignments.

Figure 1-15   **MOVING A SLIDE IN THE OUTLINE PANE**

- line to mark new position
- mouse pointer
- selected slide being moved

Now you'll have to change the order of the items on the agenda slide.

3. If necessary, scroll the Outline Pane so you can see all the text of Slide 2, and then click ✥ on the bullet to the left of "Brainstorming objectives" within the Outline Pane.

4. Drag the bulleted item down below "Rules" so that the Outline Pane and the Slide Pane appear as in Figure 1-16. (Note that you can also move text in the Slide Pane by selecting the text box, clicking ✥ on a bulleted item, and dragging it to a new location within that slide.)

Figure 1-16   **MOVING A BULLETED ITEM**

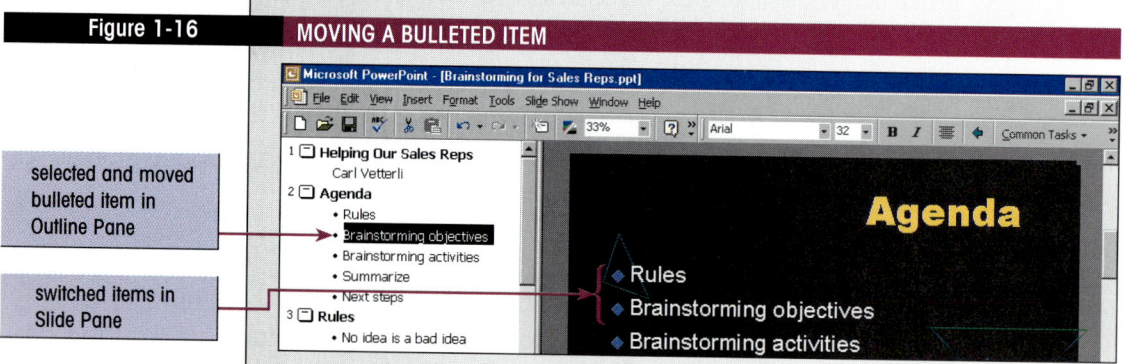

- selected and moved bulleted item in Outline Pane
- switched items in Slide Pane

As you can see, any time you want to move text from within a slide or from one slide to another, you can simply drag the text within the Outline Pane.

Carl is pleased with these changes, but decides that further editing is needed. He asks you to customize Slide 4, "Brainstorming Objectives," to fit the objectives of helping Inca Imports' sales representatives. You'll first replace and delete the current text, and then you'll promote some of the bulleted items.

Promoting and Demoting Outline Text

To **promote** an item means to increase the outline level of an item, for example, to change a bulleted item into a slide title. To **demote** an item means to decrease the outline level, for example, to change a slide title into a bulleted item within another slide. For Slide 4, your first task is to edit the current text.

To edit Slide 4:

1. Go to Slide 4 by clicking within the Slide 4 text in the Outline Pane or by dragging the scroll button in the Slide Pane.

2. Using the Outline Pane, delete the last bulleted item, "Define top requirements or restrictions."

   You could have made these deletions in the Slide Pane just as well. In the next step, you'll use the Slide Pane, just to see how you can use either pane for deleting or modifying text.

3. Make sure Slide 4 appears in the Slide Pane.

4. In the Slide Pane, drag I over the first sub-bulleted item, **New product or service ideas**, making sure you don't select the question mark, because you want to leave the question mark on the screen. See Figure 1-17.

   Notice that when you click within the bulleted list, or select text within the bulleted list, the text box containing the list becomes selected. A **text box** is a rectangular object that contains text. When it is selected, a box with hashed lines appears around it.

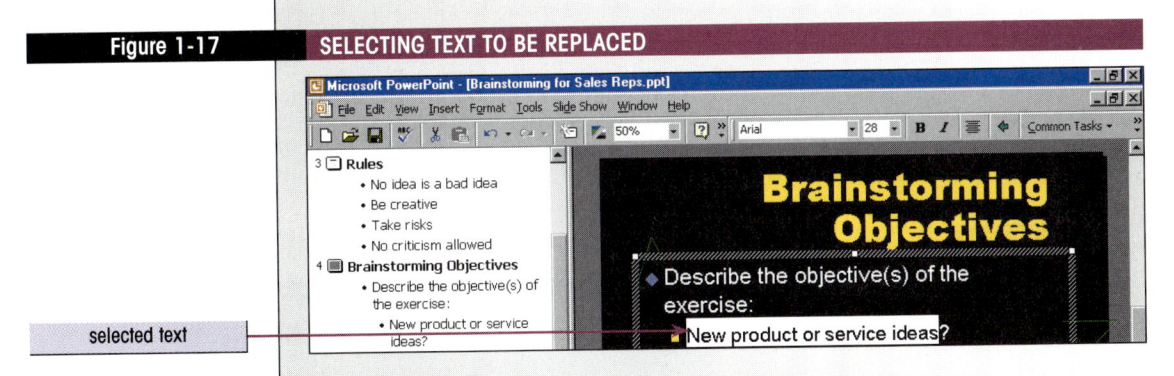

Figure 1-17   **SELECTING TEXT TO BE REPLACED**

selected text

5. Type **What are sales reps doing right**, select the next phrase, **New feature ideas** (but not the question mark), type **What are they doing wrong**, select the next phrase, **Feature/Product naming** (but not the question mark), type **What could they be doing better**, select the next phrase, **Promotion ideas** (but not the question mark), and then type **How can we reward them more for doing things better**.

6. Delete the entire final sub-bulleted item, "New process for doing something?" Your slide should now appear as in Figure 1-18.

Figure 1-18   **MODIFIED BULLETED LIST**

new text

Because these are important questions to consider, Carl asks you to promote all the second-level bulleted (or sub-bulleted) items (those with the yellow square bullets) to top-level bulleted items (those with blue diamond-shaped bullets).

To promote bulleted items:

1. Click on the yellow bullet to the left of "What are they doing right?" in the Slide Pane to select the text. (Note that you also could have clicked the bullet in the Outline Pane.)

2. Click the **Promote** button on the Formatting toolbar. The selected text moves to the left and increases in font size, and the bullet becomes a blue diamond.

3. Repeat this method to promote the other three second-level bulleted items.

4. Delete the first bulleted item, "Describe the objective(s) of the exercise", and then click in a blank area of the slide to deselect the text box. See Figure 1-19.

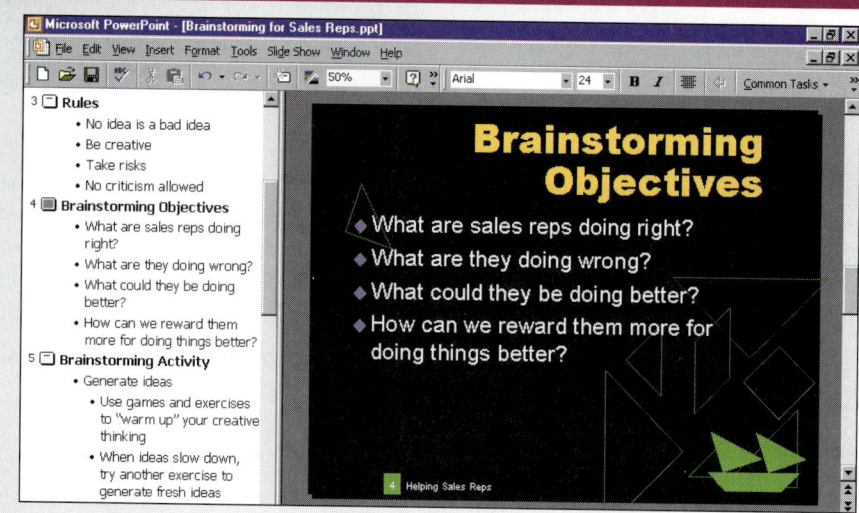

Figure 1-19   **COMPLETED SLIDE 4**

TUTORIAL 1 USING POWERPOINT TO CREATE PRESENTATIONS   PPT   1.25

You realize that you've worked for about 15 minutes since the last time you saved the presentation. You'll save your work now.

5. Click the **Save** button on the Standard toolbar to save the PowerPoint file. Because the presentation has been saved previously, PowerPoint automatically saves it using the current (default) filename.

You've now completed editing Slide 4. Next, you'll customize the presentation by promoting a bulleted item in the current Slide 5 so that it becomes a new slide.

To promote a bulleted item to a slide:

1. In the Outline Pane, scroll down so you can see all the text of Slide 5, and then click on the bullet to the left of the first bulleted item, "Generate ideas," to select this bulleted item and all its sub-bulleted items. (In the Slide Pane you can't promote a bulleted item to a slide, or sub-bulleted items into bulleted items in one step.)

2. Click so that the bulleted item becomes Slide 6. See Figure 1-20.

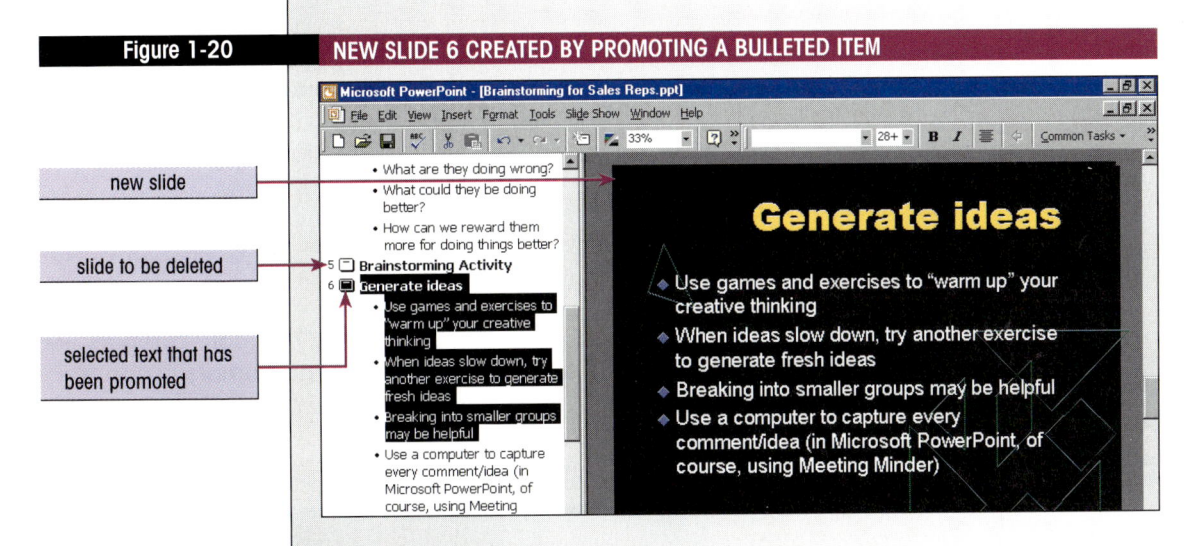

Figure 1-20   NEW SLIDE 6 CREATED BY PROMOTING A BULLETED ITEM

- new slide
- slide to be deleted
- selected text that has been promoted

TROUBLE? If PowerPoint displays a light bulb at the top of the screen, ignore it for now. It marks a problem with consistency or style in this slide and will be explained when the Style Checker is discussed.

Next, you'll delete the now unnecessary Slide 5 and then edit the newly created slide on generating ideas.

3. Delete Slide 5 using either method shown previously.

TROUBLE? If PowerPoint displays a warning that this will delete a slide and its notes page along with any graphics, click the OK button to perform the deletion.

4. Edit the new Slide 5 so that the outline and the slide appear as in Figure 1-21. Begin by changing the slide title from **Generate ideas** to **Generating ideas**, and then make the other indicated changes in the main text. Notice that as you add and delete text, the size of the font might increase or decrease so that all the text fits within the text box.

Figure 1-21   EDITED SLIDE 5

[Screenshot of PowerPoint showing Slide 5 "Generating ideas" with bulleted items:
- On paper, write down as many ideas as possible: 5 minutes
- Share each other's ideas: 10 minutes
- State new ideas or change current ones: 10 minutes
- Break into two- or three-person groups to generate new ideas: 10 minutes
- Share ideas of groups with everyone: 10 minutes]

TROUBLE? If, as you add bulleted items, the Office Assistant appears and tells you that PowerPoint will resize the font to fit within the text box, click the Office Assistant OK button.

TROUBLE? If you type a word that PowerPoint marks with a red wavy underline to indicate a misspelling, right-click on the marked word, and then click the correctly spelled word from the list of suggestions. If the correctly spelled word isn't among the list of suggestions, edit the word by deleting and adding letters in the appropriate places.

Because you've changed Slide 5, you'll need to edit Slide 2 ("Agenda") accordingly.

5. Edit Slide 2, "Agenda," so that the third bulleted item is "Generating ideas," not "Brainstorming activities."

6. Your last change is to edit Slide 7, "Next Steps." Edit Slide 7 so that it appears like Figure 1-22. Remember to use the Promote button ⬅ and Demote button ➡ as necessary.

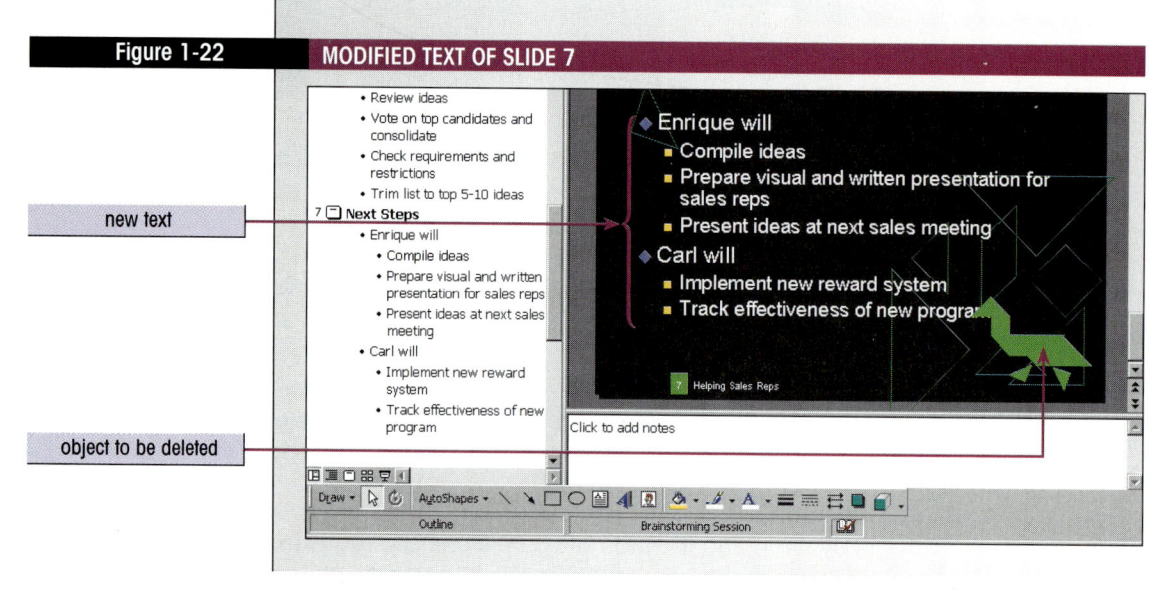

Figure 1-22   MODIFIED TEXT OF SLIDE 7

[Screenshot of PowerPoint showing Slide 7 "Next Steps" with outline pane and slide pane:
- Enrique will
  - Compile ideas
  - Prepare visual and written presentation for sales reps
  - Present ideas at next sales meeting
- Carl will
  - Implement new reward system
  - Track effectiveness of new program]

Callouts: "new text" and "object to be deleted"

As you can see, because a graphic (a green "duck") partially covers the word "program" of the last bulleted item of the slide, you'll need to remove this graphic.

7. Click ✥ on the graphic that you want to remove. The graphic becomes selected, as shown by the small squares surrounding it.

8. Press the **Delete** key to delete the graphic. Now you can read the entire text without difficulty.

9. Save the presentation using the default filename, "Brainstorming for Sales Reps."

This completes your first draft of the presentation for Carl. He looks over your work and is pleased with what he sees. However, he decides another slide is necessary, and asks you to create and add it to the presentation.

Adding a New Slide and Choosing a Layout

Carl would like the presentation to end with a slide that recognizes the outstanding service of the four members of the marketing team. You'll add the slide now.

To add a slide:

1. If necessary, go to the last slide (Slide 7) of the presentation. When you want to add a slide into a presentation, move to the slide after which you want the new one to appear.

2. Click the **New Slide** button on the Standard toolbar. PowerPoint displays the New Slide dialog box. See Figure 1-23.

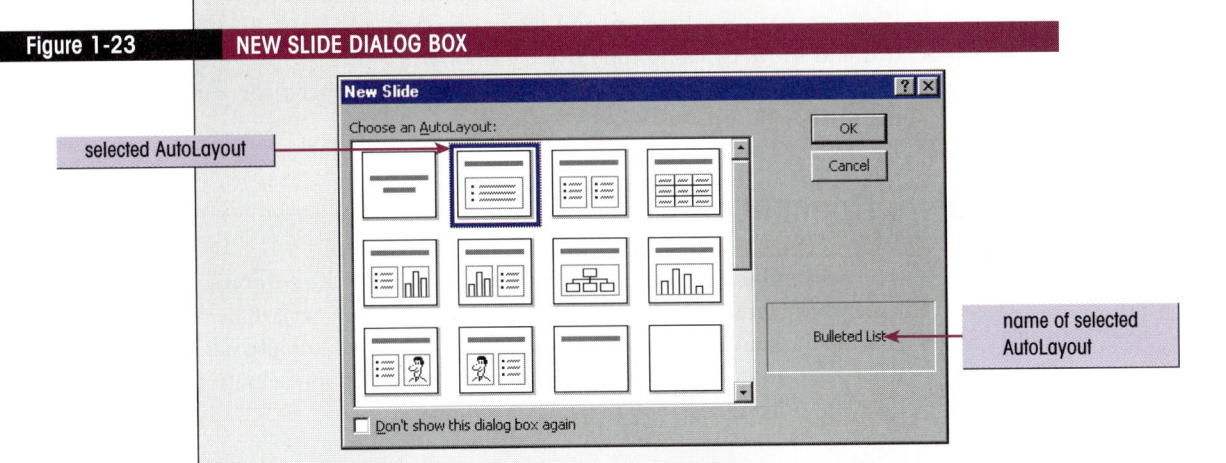

Figure 1-23   NEW SLIDE DIALOG BOX

Before adding a new slide, you must decide where you want the placeholders for titles, text, and graphics to go. PowerPoint lets you select a variety of **AutoLayout** slides, which are preformatted slides with placeholders already in them, as well as one with a blank layout. Carl wants the new slide to be a bulleted list.

3. If necessary, scroll up in the Choose an AutoLayout list box, and then click the **Bulleted List** layout (top row, second column), as shown in Figure 1-23.

4. Click the **OK** button. PowerPoint inserts a new slide containing a title placeholder and main text placeholder for the bulleted list.

5. Click the title placeholder (where the slide says "Click to add title"), and then type **Our Marketing Team**.

6. Click the main text placeholder, and then type the four bulleted items (names of the marketing team members) shown in Figure 1-24.

Figure 1-24   **COMPLETED NEW SLIDE 8**

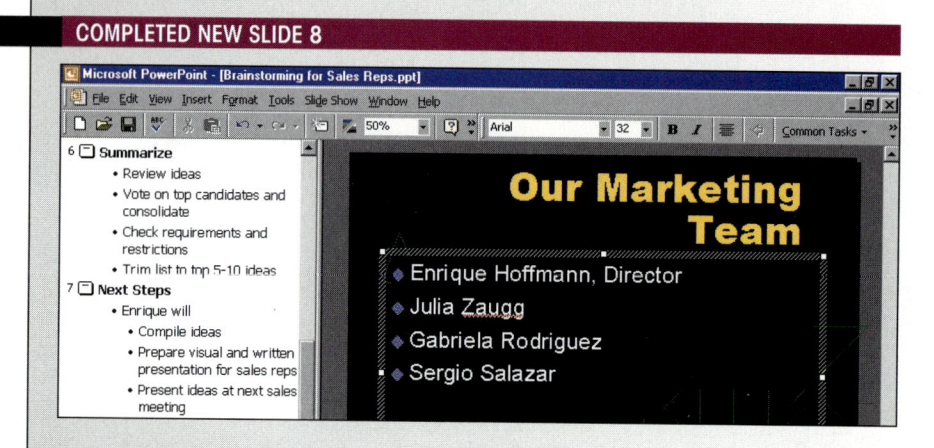

7. Click anywhere outside the text areas to deselect the text box.

You have now added a new slide, with a new layout, which completes the presentation. Note that you can also add (insert) slides into the current presentation from an existing presentation by clicking Insert on the main menu and then clicking Slides from Files. PowerPoint then lets you select the file that contains the other presentation, view the slides of that presentation, and insert the desired slides. Finally, you can also insert new text and slides by using the Office Clipboard.

Your next task is to use the Style Checker to check for consistency and style within your presentation.

Using the Style Checker

The **Style Checker** automatically checks your presentation for consistency and style, and marks problems on a slide with a light bulb. For the Style Checker to be active, the Office Assistant usually must appear on the screen. (PowerPoint also allows you to change the Style Checker options to meet the specific needs of your presentation.) For example, the Style Checker notes a potential problem on Slide 5.

To fix the problem marked by the Style Checker:

1. If the Office Assistant doesn't appear on your screen, click **Help** on the menu bar, and then click **Show Office Assistant**.

2. Go to Slide 5, which has the title "Generating ideas." A light bulb appears near the title of the slide because the capitalization is wrong. Often you won't know the style problem, but you can determine it by clicking the light bulb.

TUTORIAL 1 USING POWERPOINT TO CREATE PRESENTATIONS   PPT 1.29

3. Click the light bulb at the top of the screen. The Office Assistant displays the problem. See Figure 1-25. The Style Checker will automatically fix the problem if you click on the blue first option in the Office Assistant dialog box.

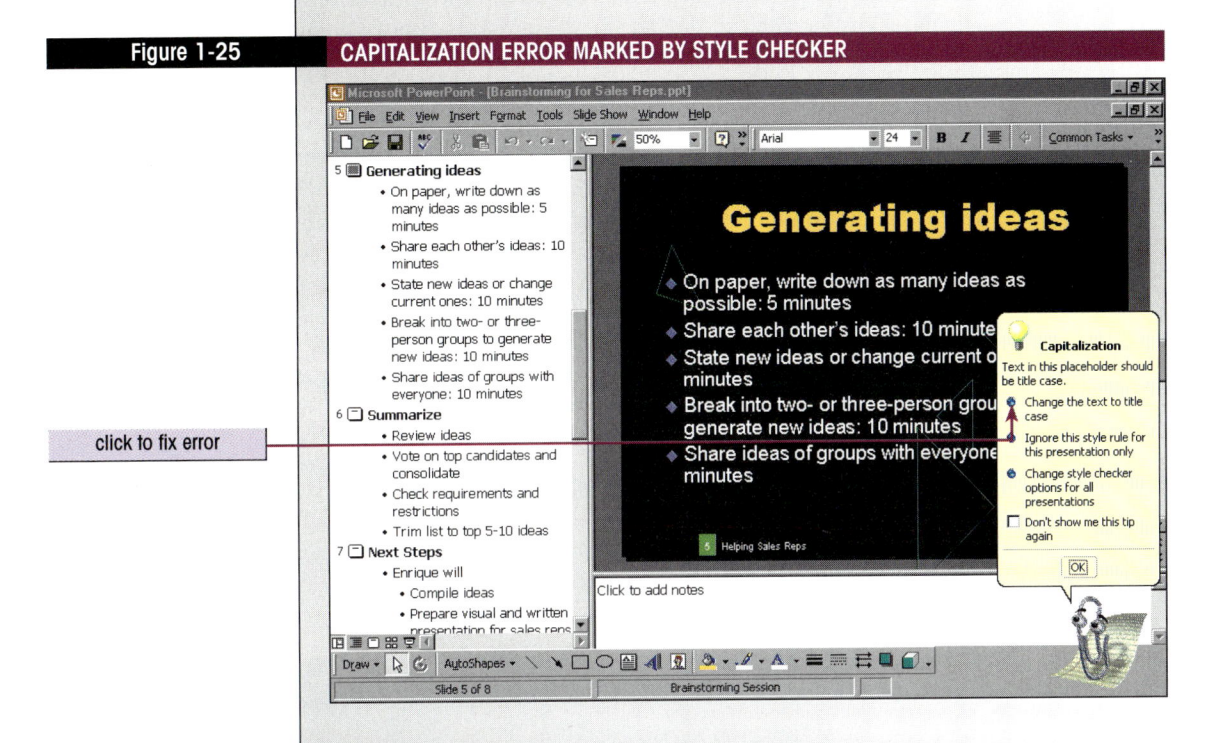

Figure 1-25   **CAPITALIZATION ERROR MARKED BY STYLE CHECKER**

click to fix error

4. Click the **Change the text to title case** option button. The title "Generating ideas" automatically becomes "Generating Ideas."

5. Go to Slide 8. A light bulb appears near the top of the bulleted list.

6. Click the light bulb to determine the problem and to list options for fixing or ignoring the problem. In this case, the Style Checker detects that the words are all capitalized, whereas normally in a bulleted list only the first word is capitalized. In this case, you want PowerPoint to ignore the problem for this slide only, which is not one of the options listed.

7. Click the **OK** button on the Office Assistant dialog box to close it and to ignore the problem in this slide. If a capitalization problem appears on any other slide, the light bulb will again appear.

As you create your own presentations, watch for the problems marked by the Style Checker. Of course, in some cases, you might want more than six bullets on a slide, or you might want the font size of the body text to be less than 20 points. In these cases, just ignore the light bulb, or click it and then click the OK button. It will not appear on the screen when you give your slide show, or when you print your presentation.

When you show the presentation to Carl, he is satisfied with it. You're now ready to prepare the other parts of Carl's presentation: the notes (also called speaker notes) and audience handouts (which are simply a printout of the slides). **Notes** are printed pages that contain a picture of and notes about each slide. They help the speaker remember what to say while a particular slide is displayed during the presentation. Because you aren't sure how to create notes, you consult the PowerPoint Help system.

Using Help

The PowerPoint online Help system provides the same options as the Help system in other Windows programs—asking for Help from the Office Assistant (such as Clippit), the What's This? command, the Help Contents, the Answer Wizard, and the Index. The What's This? command provides context-sensitive help information. When you choose this command from the Help menu, the pointer changes to the Help pointer, which you can then use to click any object or option on the screen to see a description of the object or option. You'll now use the Office Assistant to get help.

Getting Help with the Office Assistant

The Office Assistant is an interactive guide to finding information in the Help system. You can ask the Office Assistant a question, and it will look through the Help system to find an answer.

REFERENCE WINDOW

Using the Office Assistant

- Click the Microsoft PowerPoint Help button on the Standard toolbar or click the Office Assistant itself if it's on the screen (or choose Microsoft PowerPoint Help from the Help menu, or press the F1 key).
- Click in the text box, type your question, and then click the Search button.
- Choose a topic from the list of topics displayed by the Office Assistant. The Help Pane appears on the screen. Click additional topics as necessary.
- To access the Help Contents, Answer Wizard, or Index, click the Show button in the Help Pane, and then click the desired tab.
- When you're finished, close the Help window and, if desired, the Office Assistant.

Don't underestimate the power of the Office Assistant. If you type a question for which the Office Assistant has no answer or gives you an answer you don't want, try to rephrase your question. With the Office Assistant and other Help features, you can learn to use almost any of PowerPoint's features.

For example, you could use the Office Assistant to get help with creating notes in PowerPoint. When you click the Microsoft PowerPoint Help button to display the Office Assistant, you could type the question "How do I create notes?" The Office Assistant would then list options regarding notes, one of which is "Create notes." When you click that option, PowerPoint displays a Help Pane that explains how to create notes: You simply click the Notes Pane, and then type your notes for the current slide. With that information, you're ready to create notes in Carl's presentation.

TUTORIAL 1 USING POWERPOINT TO CREATE PRESENTATIONS   PPT   1.31   **POWERPOINT**

Creating Notes for Slides

You'll create notes for three of the slides in the presentation.

To create notes:

1. Go to Slide 1, and then click in the Notes Pane where the placeholder text "Click to add notes" is located. Carl wants to remember to introduce Inca Imports' employees who have joined the meeting for this part of the presentation.

2. Type **Introduce people who have joined meeting after break**. See Figure 1-26.

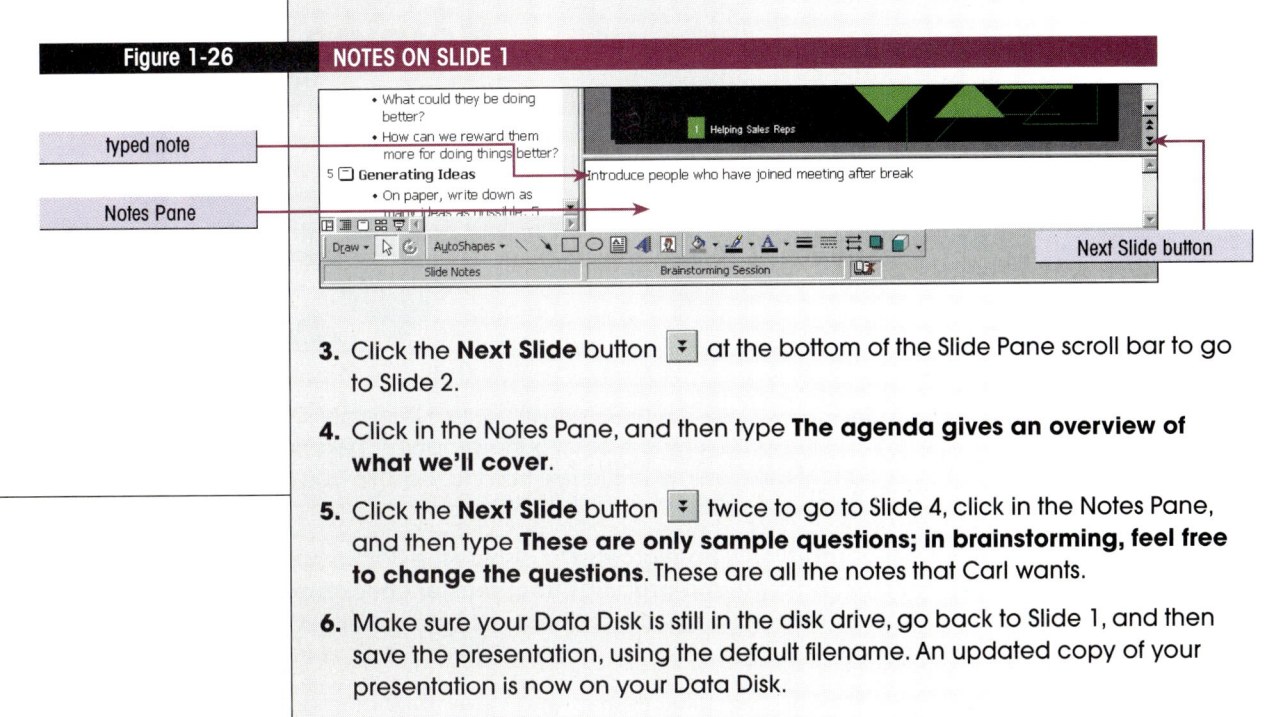

Figure 1-26   NOTES ON SLIDE 1

- typed note
- Notes Pane
- Next Slide button

3. Click the **Next Slide** button at the bottom of the Slide Pane scroll bar to go to Slide 2.

4. Click in the Notes Pane, and then type **The agenda gives an overview of what we'll cover**.

5. Click the **Next Slide** button twice to go to Slide 4, click in the Notes Pane, and then type **These are only sample questions; in brainstorming, feel free to change the questions**. These are all the notes that Carl wants.

6. Make sure your Data Disk is still in the disk drive, go back to Slide 1, and then save the presentation, using the default filename. An updated copy of your presentation is now on your Data Disk.

Before Carl gives his presentation, he'll print the Notes Pages of the presentation so he'll have the notes available during his presentation. Carl also might want the notes pages to include headers and footers. Similar to a footer, a **header** is a word or phrase that appears at the top of each page in the Notes Pages. You'll practice inserting a footer in an exercise at the end of the tutorial.

You can now view the completed presentation to make sure that it is accurate, informative, and visually pleasing. Click the Slide Show View button and then proceed through the slide show.

Previewing and Printing the Presentation

Before you print or present a slide show, you should always do a final spell check of all the slides and speaker notes by using the PowerPoint Spell Checker feature. You'll have a chance to use the spell checker in the Review Assignments and Case Problems at the end of this tutorial.

Before printing on your black-and-white printer, you should preview the presentation to make sure the text is legible in grayscale (shades of black and white).

POWERPOINT   PPT 1.32   TUTORIAL 1   USING POWERPOINT TO CREATE PRESENTATIONS

To preview the presentation in grayscale:

1. Make sure Slide 1 appears in the Slide Pane, and then click the **Grayscale Preview** button on the Standard toolbar. If necessary, drag the colored miniature out of the way so you can see the text in black and white. See Figure 1-27.

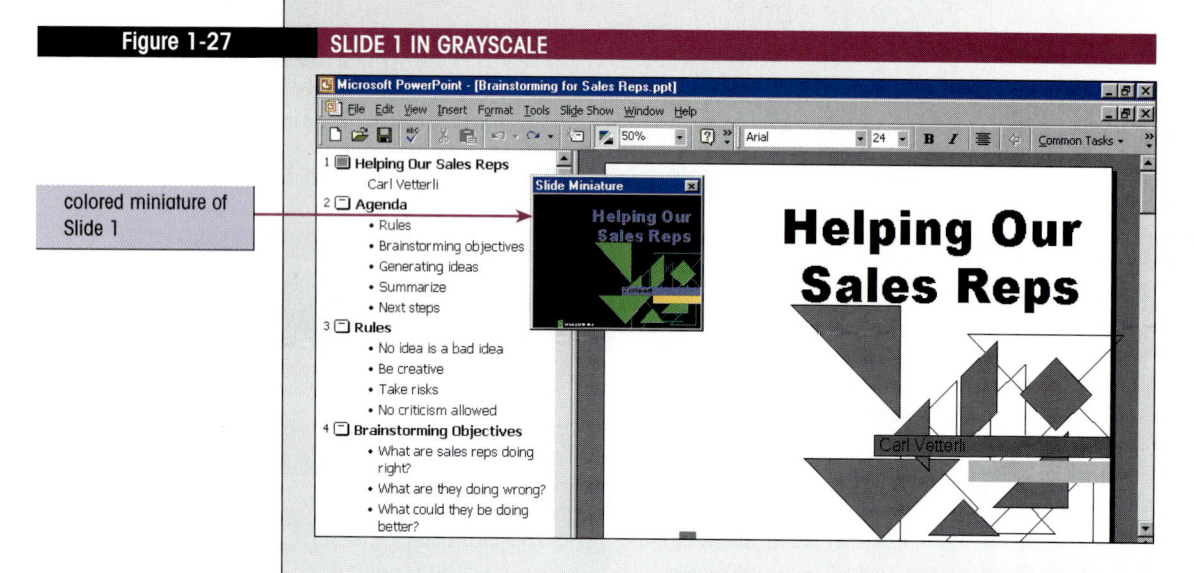

Figure 1-27   **SLIDE 1 IN GRAYSCALE**

colored miniature of Slide 1

2. Look at the text on each slide to make sure it is legible. Depending on your Windows printer driver, the background graphics (geometric shapes in this case) might make some of the text hard to read, so you might want to omit the graphics from the slides.

3. Click **Format**, click **Background** to display the Background dialog box, click the **Omit background graphics from master** check box, and then click the **Apply to All** button. The slide appears as before, but without the background graphics.

4. Click **File**, and then click **Print** to open the Print dialog box. Don't click the Print button on the Standard toolbar, or PowerPoint will immediately start printing without letting you change the print settings.

   PowerPoint allows you several printing options. For example, you can print the slides in color using a color printer, print in grayscale using a black-and-white printer, print handouts with 2, 3, 4, 6, or 9 slides per page, or print the notes pages (printed notes below a picture of the corresponding slide). You can also format and then print the presentation onto overhead transparency film (available in most office supply stores).

5. Click the **Print what** list arrow, select **Handouts**, and then in the Handouts section, click the **Slides per page** list arrow, and then click **4**. If you're using a black-and-white printer, make sure the **Grayscale** check box is selected. See Figure 1-28.

| Figure 1-28 | PRINT DIALOG BOX |

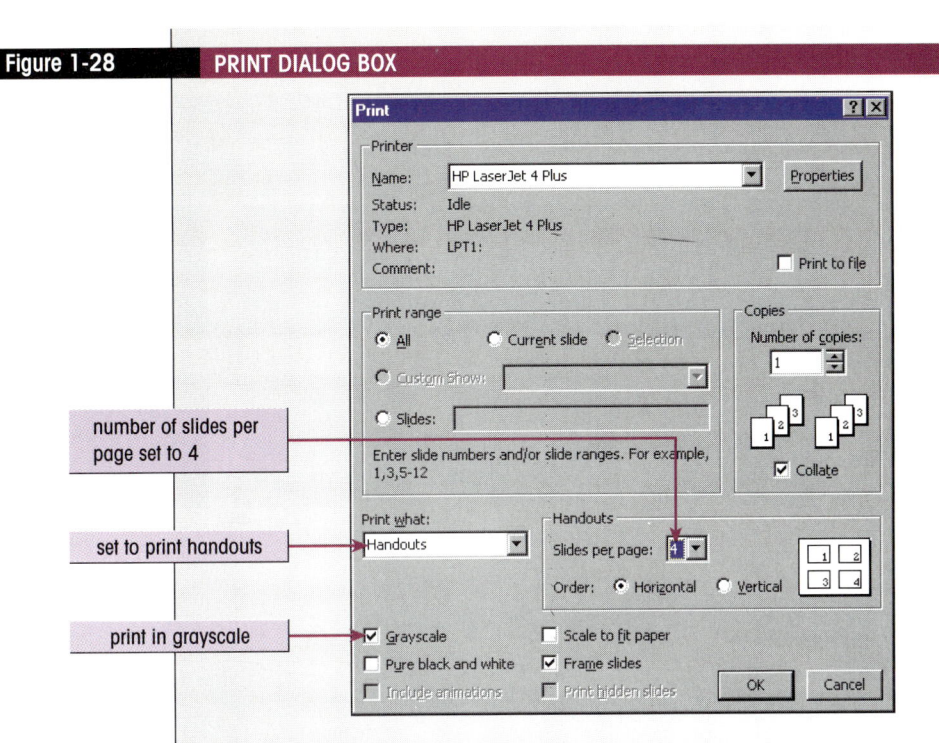

Callouts on figure:
- number of slides per page set to 4
- set to print handouts
- print in grayscale

6. Make sure all the other options are set as in Figure 1-28, and then click the **OK** button to print the handouts. Be patient. Graphics usually take a long time to print, even on a fast printer. You should have two handout pages, each containing four slides.

   You're now ready to print the notes.

7. Display the Print dialog box using the method above, click the **Print what** list arrow, click **Notes Pages**, and then click the **OK** button to print the notes.

8. To see how the slides look as a group, first click the **Grayscale View** button to return to color view, and then click the **Slide Sorter View** button on the View toolbar. Compare your handouts with the eight slides shown in Figure 1-29.

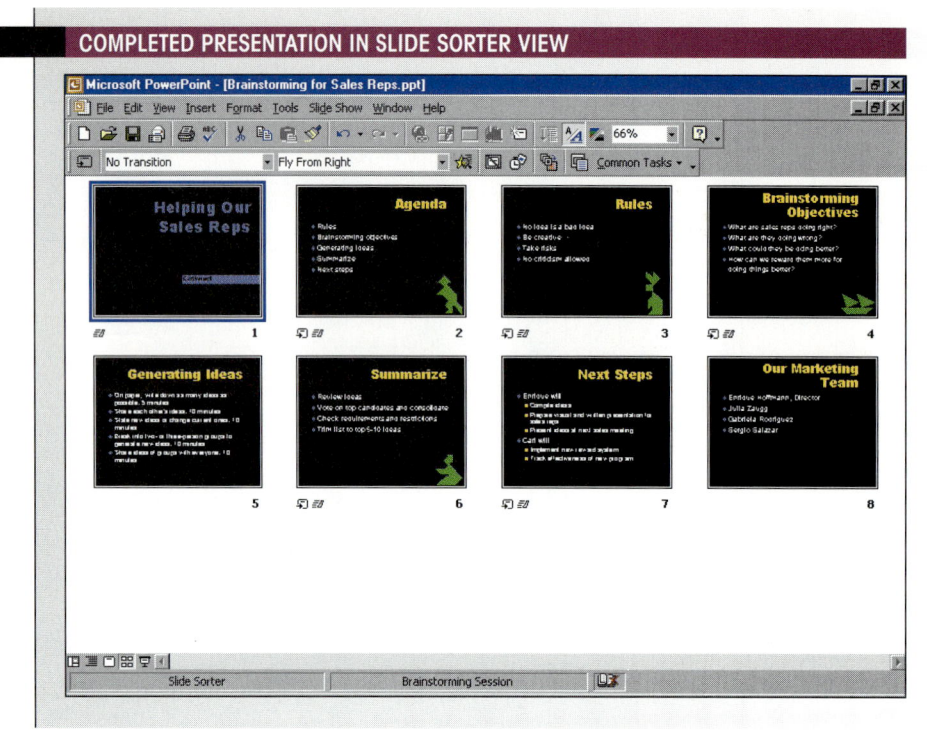

Figure 1-29 COMPLETED PRESENTATION IN SLIDE SORTER VIEW

In addition to delivering a presentation by an on-screen slide show or by printed pages, you can also send a presentation via e-mail or publish the presentation to the Web. To send a presentation via e-mail, click File on the main menu, point to Send To, and then click Mail Recipient (as Attachment) (which allows you to send the current slide as the e-mail message body), or Mail Recipient (which allows you to send the presentation as an attachment to an e-mail message). The first time you try to send the presentation via e-mail, PowerPoint will help you set up an e-mail account with your Internet Service Provider.

To publish a presentation to the Web, click File on the main menu, and then click Save as Web Page. You can then save the file in HTML format or publish it directly to a Web server.

Another option is to insert a hyperlink in your presentation that will connect to a file or Web page. To do this, click Insert on the main menu, click Hyperlink, and then complete the information in the Insert Hyperlink dialog box.

Now that you have created, edited, saved, and printed Carl's presentation, you can exit PowerPoint, but without saving the most recent changes, because you want the color slides to contain the background graphics that you just deleted.

To exit PowerPoint:

1. Click ⊠ in the upper-right corner of the PowerPoint window. Because you have made changes since the last time you saved the presentation, PowerPoint displays a dialog box with the message "Do you want to save the changes you made to Brainstorming for Sales Reps?"

2. Click the **No** button to exit PowerPoint without saving the current version of the presentation.

You have created a presentation using the AutoContent Wizard, edited it according to Carl's wishes, and created and printed notes and handouts. Carl thanks you for your help; he believes that your work will enable him to make an effective presentation.

Session 1.2 QUICK CHECK

1. Explain how to do the following in the Outline Pane:
   a. move text up
   b. delete a slide
   c. change placeholder text
   d. edit text

2. What does it mean to promote a bulleted item in the Outline Pane? To demote a bulleted item?

3. Explain a benefit of using the Outline Pane rather than the Slide Pane and a benefit of using the Slide Pane rather than the Outline Pane.

4. Explain how to add a slide to a presentation.

5. What is the Style Checker? What is an example of a consistency or style problem that it might mark?

6. How does the Office Assistant provide help?

7. What are notes? How do you create them?

8. Why is it beneficial to preview a presentation before printing it?

REVIEW ASSIGNMENTS

After Carl presents his market research and brainstorming presentations to his colleagues, Enrique Hoffman (Director of Marketing) accepts the assignment to prepare a presentation to the sales representatives on how to improve sales. Enrique asks you to finalize his slides by doing the following:

1. Start PowerPoint and make sure your Data Disk is in the disk drive.

Explore

2. Click the Open an existing file option button, open the file **Sales** in the Review folder of Tutorial.01 on your Data Disk, and then save the file as **New Marketing Campaign**. (*Hint*: To save a file with a different filename, click File and then click Save As.)

3. In the Outline Pane, delete unnecessary words, such as "a," "an," and "the," from each main text slide, to conform to the 6 × 6 rule.

4. In Slide 2, move the phrase "by telephone" so it immediately follows the phrase "Follow up" in the same item of the main text.

5. Move the second item in Slide 3, "Will develop slide presentation," down, so that it becomes the third (last) item in the main text.

6. In Slide 4, the third item of the main text is "Step #2. Establishing Contact with Potential Customers." Promote that item to become a slide title (new Slide 5).

7. In the new Slide 6, demote the second, third, and fourth bulleted items so they appear indented beneath the first item, "Organize data for our market advantage."

8. Edit the main text of Slide 8 so the phrase "Must hire" becomes simply "Hire."

Explore 9. In Slide Sorter View, move the entire Slide 9 ("Key Issues") up to become Slide 8, so that "Becoming More Effective" is the last slide. (*Hint*: Switch to Slide Sorter View, and then click and drag Slide 9 to the left until a gray line appears to the left of Slide 8.)

10. Add the following notes to the slides indicated. Slide 1: "For presentation to entire sales force." Slide 2: "Ask for suggestions of other goals." Slide 3: "Make assignments for who will do each of these tasks." Slide 8: "Ask what other key issues need to be addressed." Slide 9: "Assure sales staff that they are appreciated and are doing a great job. We just want to find ways to help them enjoy more success."

Explore 11. Add to the Notes and Handouts the header "Improving Sales" and the footer "Inca Imports." (*Hint*: Click View on the main menu, click Header and Footer, click the Notes and Handouts tab, click the Header check box, type the header in the appropriate input box, click the footer check box, type the footer in the appropriate input box, and then click the Apply to All button.)

Explore 12. Apply the Box Out transition effect to all the slides. (*Hint*: A transition effect is a method of moving one slide off the screen and bringing another slide onto the screen during a slide show. To apply the Box Out transition effect, go to Slide Sorter View, press Ctrl+A to select all the slides, click the Slide Transition Effects list arrow on the Formatting toolbar, and then click Box Out.)

13. Spell check the presentation by clicking Tools, and then clicking Spelling. Remember that if PowerPoint stops at a word that is spelled correctly but that it doesn't recognize, click the Ignore or Ignore All button.

14. Use the Style Checker.

15. View the entire presentation in Slide Show View.

Explore 16. View the presentation again in Slide Show View, only this time, begin with slide 5 and end with slide 8. (*Hint*: To begin with slide 5, go to slide 5 in the Slide Pane, and then start the slide show. To end with slide 8, move to slide 8, move to that slide in Slide Show View, and then press the Esc key.)

Explore 17. Again view the presentation in Slide Show View, except this time begin with slide 1, and then use the slide navigator to jump to slide 7, and view from slide 7 to the end. (*Hint*: To use the slide navigator, right-click anywhere on the screen, point to Go, and click Slide Navigator.)

18. Use the Save command to save the presentation to your Data Disk, using the default filename.

19. Use the Office Assistant to find out how to print the outline of the presentation, and then do so.

20. Print the notes of the presentation.

21. Close the file.

CASE PROBLEMS

Case 1. MailMinder, Inc. Tiana Wnuk works for MailMinder, Inc., a new franchise company that specializes in mail management and mail-order fulfillment service. MailMinder franchises contract with businesses to do their advanced inventory management, custom assembly, bulk mail services, and customer database management. Tiana's job is to provide training for new managers of MailMinder's fledgling franchises. She asks you to help her finalize a presentation, which she'll use to show the many services of MailMinder headquarters to franchise managers, by doing the following:

1. Open the file **Mailmndr** in the Cases folder of Tutorial.01 on your Data Disk, and save the file as **MailMinder Services**.

2. In Slide 1, change the presenter's name from "Tiana Wnuk" to your name.

Explore

3. Go to Slide 2. In the first bulleted item, use cut and paste to move the phrase "from 1998 to 2001" from the end of the bulleted paragraph to the beginning. Also, change "from" to "From" and "Gross" to "gross."

4. Also in Slide 2, demote the four bulleted items below "What accounts for the growth?" to make subparagraphs that answer this question.

5. In Slide 3, right-click on "MailMinder" and then click Ignore All so that PowerPoint won't mark the word as misspelled. Repeat this for "MailMinder's."

6. Right-click the misspelled "assistence," and then click the correct spelling.

7. Go to Slide 4. (Ignore for now the misspelled words in this and subsequent slides—you'll correct them all later.) Move the first bulleted item so that it becomes the second bulleted item, and then move the third bulleted item, "Setting up mail management systems with new clients," to the end of the bulleted list.

8. Go to Slide 5. Below the first main bulleted item, "Regional consultants," add a second and third sub-bulleted item, "Employee training," and "Help in generating quotations for potential clients." Move the last bulleted item, "Custom software," to become the first bulleted item.

9. Go to Slide 6. Promote the fourth bulleted item, "MailMinder's Other Asssistance Programs," to become the title of a new Slide 7.

10. Spell check the presentation, and then use the Style Checker.

11. View all the slides of the presentation in Slide Show View.

12. Preview the slides in Grayscale View. If some of the text is illegible, delete the background graphics.

13. Print handouts of all the slides (four slides per page) in black-and-white grayscale.

14. Save the file, using its default filename.

15. Close the file.

Case 2. Juica Juice Dawson Gappmeyer is seeking $180,000 in venture capital for his startup company, Juica Juice. Dawson hopes to expand his business, currently a one-store fast-food establishment in San Francisco, into a franchise. The store sells a wide variety of blended fruit juices, with standard and exotic flavors, along with other low-calorie and low-fat snack foods. Dawson has created a presentation to give to executives at the A. B. O'Dair & Company investment firm, and asks you to finalize the presentation by doing the following:

1. Open the file **Juica** in the Tutorial.01 Cases folder on your Data Disk and save the file as **Juica Juice Capital**.

Explore

2. Use the What's This? Help feature to learn how to increase the size of the title of Slide 1 from 44 to 54 points, and then do so. (*Hint*: Click Help on the menu bar, click What's This?, and then click the pointer on the Increase Font Size button on the Formatting toolbar.)

3. Right-click Juica and then select Ignore All so that PowerPoint won't mark this word as a misspelling.

4. Go to Slide 2. (Ignore the spelling errors on this and subsequent slides. You'll correct them all at once, later on.) Move the third bulleted item, "Capitalize on popularity...," to become the first bulleted item on this slide, and then add a bulleted item to the end of the list: "Expand to other locations."

5. Go to Slide 3. Edit as necessary to change "Exotic and standard" to "Standard and exotic."

6. Go to Slide 4. Demote the last three bulleted items so they appear as sub-bullets below "Other snacks."

7. Go to Slide 5. Following the 6 × 6 rule, simplify this slide by removing all the unnecessary words: "a," "an," "our," and "the." Further simplify by changing "by fourth year in operation" to "within 3 years" and delete the second ("This means you'll own...") and last ("Expansion to other...") bulleted items.

8. Go to Slide 6. Select the second main bulleted item, "Technical knowledge," along with its sub-bulleted items, by clicking the bullet to its left, and then move the selected text to become the first bulleted item on the slide.

9. Insert a new Slide 7 by clicking the New Slide button, and then selecting the Bulleted List AutoLayout. Type the title "Our Food Scientists." In the main text box, type the bulleted item "Dr. Sally M. Thursby," press the Enter key, and then press the Tab key. This causes the bulleted item to be demoted automatically. Type "Ph.D. in Food Science and Nutrition from Cornell University" and "13 years in developing commercial foods" as sub-bulleted items, and then press the Enter key. Now press the Shift + Tab keys to promote the next item. Type the bulleted item "Dr. Cecilia Goodman" and the two sub-bulleted items "Ph. D. in Food Science from Florida State University" and "8 years' experience in food industry."

10. Spell check the presentation, and then use the Style Checker.

Explore 11. Move Slide 5 to the end of the presentation. Switch to Slide Sorter View, click on Slide 5, press and hold the left mouse button, and then drag Slide 5 to the right of the last slide. When a line appears to the right of Slide 8, release the mouse button.

12. Return to Normal View, and then use the Slide Pane scroll bar to go to slide 1.

Explore 13. Change the design template from "Blueprint" (as shown in the center of the status bar at the bottom of the PowerPoint window) to "Nature." Use the Office Assistant to find the description of a design template and how to change it.

14. Save the file, using the default filename.

15. Preview the slides in grayscale to make sure they are all legible. If any text isn't legible, delete the background graphics from the slide.

16. Print the slides as handouts (four slides per page).

17. Close the file.

Case 3. PLI, Inc. Albert Bocanegra works for PLI, Inc., a national personal liability insurance company. Albert asks you to help him to prepare a presentation on the value of personal liability insurance, for the PLI sales representatives to use when they contact potential customers. Do the following:

1. Use the AutoContent Wizard to create an outline of the presentation. (If the startup PowerPoint dialog box isn't on the screen, click File, click New, click AutoContent Wizard, and then click the OK button.) Select "Selling a Product or Service" as the type of presentation from the Sales/Marketing group of presentation types, select On-screen presentation as the type of output, make the Presentation title "Personal Liability Insurance," make the footer "PLI, Inc.," and include the slide number on each slide, but not the date last updated. After finishing the AutoContent Wizard, make sure you're at Slide 1 in Normal View.

2. Click in the subtitle placeholder and then type "Why You? Why Now?"

3. Go to Slide 2. Change "Objective" to "Overview." Replace the current bulleted items (the placeholders) with these bulleted items:
   - Your liabilities in today's society
   - What can you be held liable for?
   - Financial effects of being sued
   - What is an umbrella liability insurance policy?
   - What does personal liability insurance cover?
   - How you can get this insurance for pennies a day?

Explore

4. Albert now informs you that he has created slides for each of these objectives, so you won't need the remainder of the slides in the current presentation. Delete Slides 3 through 8. (*Hint:* You can delete a range of slides all at once by clicking the slide icon in the Outline Pane on the first slide, and, while holding down the Shift key, clicking the slide icon on the last slide to be deleted, and then deleting all the slides at once just as you would delete one slide.)

Explore

5. Following Slide 2, insert all the slides from the file Insure located in the Tutorial.01 Cases folder on your Data Disk. (*Hint:* To insert slides, click Insert on the main menu, click Slides from Files, click the Browse button to find the desired presentation file, click the Display button to show the slides in that presentation, click the Insert All button, and then click the Close button.)

6. Save the presentation to your Data Disk, using the filename **Personal Liability Insurance**.

7. Go to Slide 3. Move the second bulleted item along with all its sub-bulleted items up above the first bulleted item.

8. Switch Slides 4 and 5, so that Slide 5 is "Financial Effects of Being Sued."

9. In Slide 5, move the last bulleted item, "You can owe thousands . . .," to make it the first bulleted item.

10. Go to Slide 6. Cut the first three bulleted items (which all begin with "Covers") so that the slide is left with only five bulleted items. Be sure to cut and not delete, because you'll paste the items into a new slide.

11. Use the New Slide button to insert a new slide after Slide 6. Select the Bulleted List AutoLayout.

12. On the new Slide 7, insert the title "Who Is Covered?"

13. Click in the main text placeholder, and then paste the text from the Clipboard.

14. Go to Slide 8. Demote the five bulleted items below "Protects against, for example." Note that you can demote the items together by selecting them all and then clicking the Demote button.

15. Spell check the presentation, and then use the Style Checker.

16. Save the presentation, using the default filename.

17. Preview the slides in grayscale, and then print them as handouts (three slides per page).

18. Close the file.

Explore

Case 4. Orienting Freshmen on College Social Life The chair of your college department has asked you to participate in an orientation for new freshmen. The chair has asked you to prepare and give a 20-minute presentation on the social life at your school. In other words, you need to give an overview on one area of "products and services" available to the incoming students. Prepare an on-screen presentation with the following features:

1. Use the AutoContent Wizard to begin developing an outline based on "Project/Services Overview" from the Sales/Marketing type of presentation. Make the presentation title "Social Opportunities at …" (with the name or abbreviation of your school, college, or university). Include a footer, "Social Life," the date last updated, and the slide number on each slide.

2. Use the Office Assistant to find out how to apply a different design template to a presentation, and then apply the "Blends" design.

3. Go to Slide 1, select and delete the large text box with the author's name, and then select and delete the placeholder for "Your Logo Here." (*Hint*: In both cases, click anywhere in the text box, click the edge of the box so that the entire object is selected, and then press the Delete key.) Insert the subtitle "Having Fun While Learning."

4. In Slide 2, create five or six bulleted items of the type of social activities that occur at your school. For example, you could include sororities and fraternities, clubs, service organizations, religious groups, and sporting events.

5. In Slide 3, delete "Features &," and leave only "Benefits" in the title. Delete the bulleted item placeholders and include a list of benefits of getting involved in the college social life. (If you can't think of any benefits, you're studying too hard.)

6. Delete all the remaining slides, from Slides 4 on. (*Hint*: You can delete a range of slides all at once by clicking the slide icon in the Outline Pane on the first slide to be deleted, and, while holding down the Shift key, clicking the slide icon on the last slide to be deleted, and then deleting all the slides at once just as you would delete one slide.)

7. Add a slide for each of the five or six items on your Slide 2. On each of these slides, list pertinent information, such as purpose or objectives of a social organization, examples of activities, time and place of selected events, or how to join an organization. Make sure each slide has three to six bulleted items.

8. Add a new final slide, "Summary," in which you summarize key points of your presentation.

9. Spell check the presentation, and then use the Style Checker.

10. Preview the presentation in Slide Show View.

11. Save the presentation as **Social Life at** on your Data Disk.

12. Use the Office Assistant to find out how to print the outline of your presentation, and then do so.

13. Save your presentation in HTML format on your Data Disk, in preparation for publication on the Web.

14. Close the file.

INTERNET ASSIGNMENTS

The purpose of the Internet Assignments is to challenge you to find information on the Internet that you can use to create effective documents. The actual assignments are updated and maintained on the Course Technology Web site. Log onto the Internet and use your Web browser to go to the Student Online Companion to accompany this text at **www.course.com/NewPerspectives/office2000**. Click the PowerPoint link, and then click the link for Tutorial 1.

Quick Check Answers

Session 1.1

1. PowerPoint provides everything you need to produce a presentation that consists of black-and-white or color overheads, 35 mm slides, or on-screen slides. The presentation component can consist of individual slides, speaker notes, an outline of the presentation, and audience handouts.

2. The Outline Pane lists an outline of your presentation, including titles and text of each slide. The Slide Pane shows the slide as it will look during your slide show. The Notes Pane contains any notes that you might prepare on each slide.

3. a. gradient fill: a type of shading in which one color blends into another

    b. footer: a word or phrase that appears at the bottom of each slide in the presentation

    c. placeholder: a region of a slide or a location in an outline reserved for inserting text or graphics

    d. bulleted list: a list of paragraphs with a special character (dot, circle, box, star, or other character) to the left of each paragraph

4. Planning improves the quality of your presentation, makes your presentation more effective and enjoyable, and saves you time and effort. You should answer several questions: What is my purpose or objective? What type of presentation is needed? What is the physical location of my presentation? What is the best format for presenting the information?

5. The AutoContent Wizard lets you choose a presentation category and then creates a general outline of the presentation for you.

6. Use six or fewer items per screen, and use phrases of six or fewer words.

7. a word that is not located in the PowerPoint dictionary, usually a misspelled word

8. so that you won't lose all your work if, for example, a power failure suddenly shuts down your computer

Session 1.2

1. a. Click on a slide or bullet icon, and drag the selected item up.

    b. Click Edit on the main menu, and then click Delete Slide.

    c. Select the text, and then type new text.

    d. Drag the I-beam pointer to select the text, and then delete or retype it.

2. Promote means to increase the level of an outline item; demote means to decrease the level of an outline item.

3. In the Outline Pane you can see the text of several slides at once, which makes it easier to work with text. In the Slide Pane you can see the design and layout of the slide.

4. Click the New Slide button on the Standard toolbar, select the desired layout from the New Slide dialog box, and then click the OK button.

5. The Style Checker automatically checks your presentation for consistency and style. For example, it will check for consistency in punctuation.

6. The Office Assistant provides help by looking through the Help system to find an answer to your question.

7. Notes are printed pages that contain a picture of and notes about each slide. Create them by typing text into the Notes Pane.

8. to make sure that the slides are satisfactory and that the presentation is legible in grayscale if you use a monochrome printer

LEVEL I

New Perspectives on

MICROSOFT®
OUTLOOK® 2000

TUTORIAL 1   OUT 1.03

Communicating with Outlook 2000
Sending and Receiving E-mail Messages for The Express Lane

Read This Before You Begin

To the Student

Data Disks
To complete the Outlook Tutorial, Review Assignments, and Case Problems in this book, you need one Data Disk. Your instructor will either provide you with the Data Disk or ask you to make your own.

If you are making your own Data Disk, you will need one blank, formatted high-density disk. You will need to copy a set of folders from a file server or standalone computer or the Web onto your disk. Your instructor will tell you which computer, drive letter, and folders contain the files you need. You could also download the files by going to www.course.com, clicking Data Disk Files, and following the instructions on the screen.

The following list shows you which folders go on your disk, so that you will have enough disk space to complete all the Tutorials, Review Assignments, and Case Problems:

Data Disk 1
Write this on the disk label:
Data Disk 1: Outlook Tutorial 1
Put these folders on the disk:
Tutorial.01

When you begin each tutorial, be sure you are using the correct Data Disk. See the inside front or inside back cover of this book for more information on Data Disk files, or ask your instructor or technical support person for assistance.

Course Lab
The Outlook tutorials in this book feature one interactive Course Lab to help you understand E-mail concepts. There is a Lab Assignment at the end of Tutorial 1 that relates to this Lab.

To start a Lab, click the **Start** button on the Windows taskbar, point to **Programs**, point to **Course Labs**, point to **New Perspectives Applications**, and click Databases.

Using Your Own Computer
If you are going to work through this book using your own computer, you need:

- **Computer System** Microsoft Office 2000 (including Outlook, Word, Excel, PowerPoint, and Access) and Windows 95 or higher must be installed on your computer. This book assumes a complete installation of Word 2000. Depending on your set-up you may need to install the Import/Export feature and the MailMerge feature on first use.

- **Data Disks** You will not be able to complete the tutorials or exercises in this book using your own computer until you have the Data Disk.

- **Course Lab** See your instructor or technical support person to obtain the Course Lab software for use on your own computer.

Visit Our World Wide Web Site
Additional materials designed especially for you are available on the World Wide Web. Go to http://www.course.com.

To the Instructor

The Data Files are available on the Instructor's Resource Kit for this title. Follow the instructions in the Help file on the CD-ROM to install the programs to your network or standalone computer. For information on creating Data Disks, see the "To the Student" section above.

You are granted a license to copy the Data Files to any computer or computer network used by students who have purchased this book.

TUTORIAL 1

OBJECTIVES

In this tutorial you will:

- Start and exit Outlook
- Explore the Outlook window
- Navigate between Outlook components
- Create and send e-mail messages
- Create and edit contact information
- Read and reply to e-mail messages
- Attach files to e-mail messages
- File, archive, sort, and filter messages
- Get help

LABS

E-mail

COMMUNICATING WITH OUTLOOK 2000

Sending and Receiving E-mail Messages for The Express Lane

CASE

The Express Lane

The Express Lane is a complete and affordable online grocery store in the San Francisco Bay Area, specializing in natural and organic foods. When Alan Gregory and Lora Shaw began The Express Lane in 1998, fewer than 200,000 U.S. households were using online services to purchase food and other household goods and services; by 2007, this number is expected to reach 15 to 20 million. These households span a wide demographic range and will spend approximately $85 billion a year on foods and other goods purchased online (Andersen Consulting, January 20, 1998).

People are drawn to online grocery shopping as a way to save time and simplify their lives. Customers span all income and educational levels, ages, and locations. The most common online grocery shoppers fall into one of four distinct categories: (1) they dislike grocery shopping; (2) they have limited ability to physically go to the store, whether from a disability, lack of transportation, and so on; (3) they enjoy using the latest technology; or (4) they want to free up time on their schedules. The Express Lane provides an easy shopping alternative for all of these groups.

Unlike traditional groceries, The Express Lane does not have a storefront where customers come to shop. Instead it stores both packaged goods and fresh produce in its warehouse. Customers place orders using fax, e-mail, or the company's Web site. The Express Lane staff then selects and packs the requested items, bills the customer's credit card for the cost of the groceries plus a $5 service fee, and delivers the groceries to the customer's front door within four to six hours. To coordinate these activities, The Express Lane relies on **Microsoft Outlook 2000**, an information management program that helps you perform a wide range of communication and organizational tasks, such as sending, receiving, and filing e-mail; organizing contacts; scheduling appointments, events, and meetings; creating a to-do list and delegating tasks; and writing notes.

OUT 1.03

To help manage their company's growth, Alan and Lora hired you to assist them. Alan focuses on the supplier end of the business, ensuring that the warehouse has the proper stock, locating new suppliers, and preparing budgets. Lora focuses on the customer end of the business, which includes finding new customers, responding to customer comments, and processing customer payments. In this tutorial, you'll use e-mail to send information about increasing an order to a supplier. You'll also set up contact information for suppliers and The Express Lane staff.

SESSION 1.1

In this session, you'll learn about the Outlook components. First, you'll start Outlook, view its window elements, and navigate between components. Then, you'll create and send an e-mail message. Finally, you'll create and organize a contact list.

Exploring Outlook

Outlook functions are organized into the six components listed in Figure 1-1. Each of these components generates a specific **item**, the basic element that holds information in Outlook (similar to a file in other programs). Items include e-mail messages, appointments, contacts, tasks, journal entries, and notes. These items are organized into **folders**.

Figure 1-1 OUTLOOK COMPONENTS

COMPONENT	DESCRIPTION
Mail	A messaging/communication tool for receiving, sending, storing, and managing e-mail. The **Inbox** folder stores messages you received and the **Outbox** folder stores outgoing messages you have written but not sent.
Calendar	A scheduling tool for planning your appointments, events, and meetings.
Contacts	An address book for compiling street addresses, phone numbers, e-mail and Web addresses, and other personal information about your contacts.
Tasks	A to-do list for organizing and tracking items you need to complete or delegate.
Journal	A diary for recording your activities, such as talking on the phone, sending an e-mail message, or working on a document.
Notes	A notepad for jotting down ideas and thoughts that you can group, sort, and categorize.

Starting Outlook

You can start Outlook in any of several ways. You can click the Outlook button on the Quick Launch toolbar, click the Outlook icon on your desktop, or use the Start menu.

To start Outlook:

1. Make sure that Windows is running on your computer and that the Windows desktop appears on your screen.

2. Click the **Start** button on the taskbar to display the Start menu, and then point to **Programs** to display the Programs menu.

3. Point to **Microsoft Outlook** on the Programs menu.

TUTORIAL 1 COMMUNICATING WITH OUTLOOK 2000   OUT 1.05

TROUBLE? If you don't see Microsoft Outlook on the Programs menu, point to Microsoft Office and then point to Microsoft Outlook. If you still can't find Microsoft Outlook, click the Outlook icon on the Quick Launch toolbar or on your desktop. If none of the above is available, ask your instructor or technical support person for help.

4. Click **Microsoft Outlook**. After a short pause, the Outlook program window, displaying the Inbox, appears.

   TROUBLE? If the Office Assistant or a dialog box appears, indicating that you need to configure Outlook 2000 or set up an account, enter the appropriate information in each dialog box and press the Next button. Click the Finish button to configure Outlook or set up the account. If you need more information, ask your instructor or technical support person for help.

   TROUBLE? If a dialog box opens, asking whether you want to import e-mail messages and addresses from Outlook Express or another e-mail program, click No.

   TROUBLE? If a dialog box opens, asking whether you want to make Outlook the default manager for Mail, News, and Contacts, click No.

5. If necessary, click the **Maximize** button ☐. Figure 1-2 shows the maximized Outlook window.

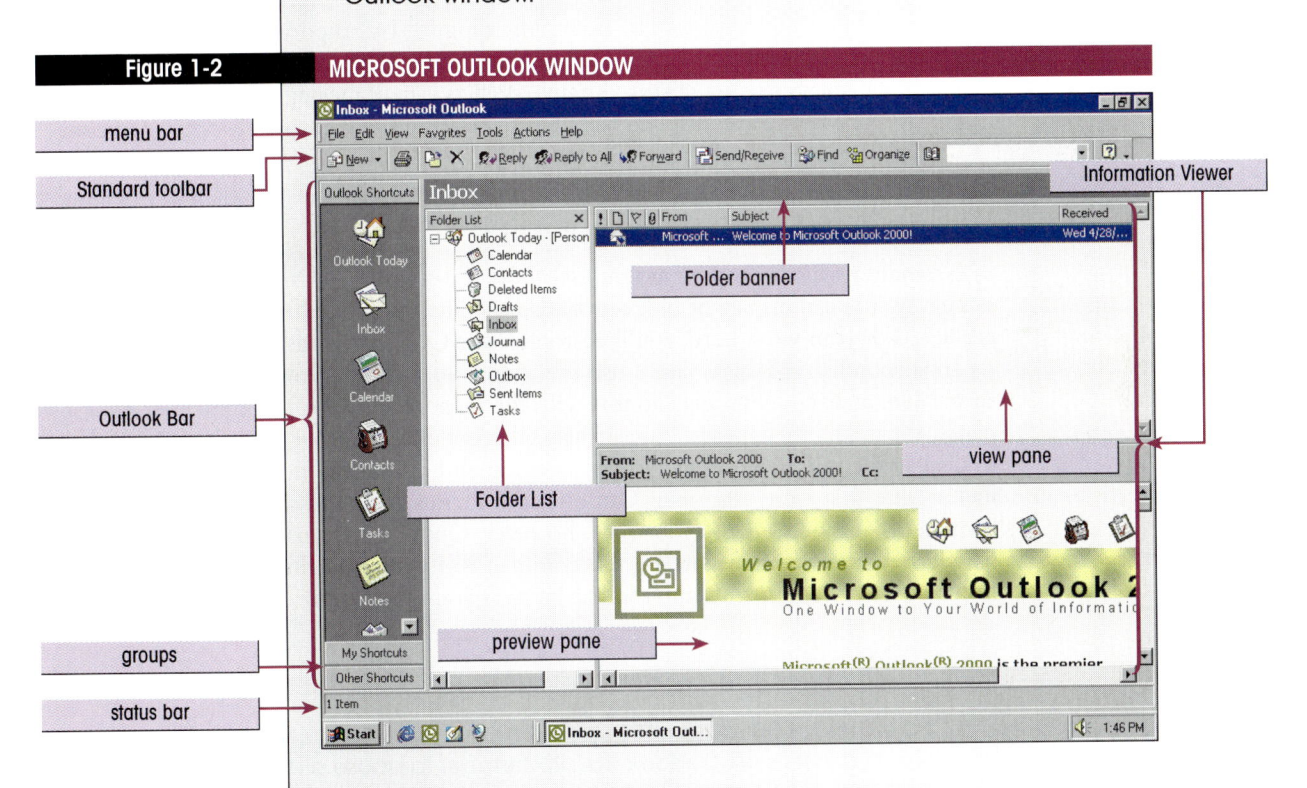

Figure 1-2   **MICROSOFT OUTLOOK WINDOW**

- menu bar
- Standard toolbar
- Information Viewer
- Folder banner
- Outlook Bar
- view pane
- Folder List
- preview pane
- groups
- status bar

TROUBLE? If your screen does not show the Outlook Bar, Folder List, status bar, or the Inbox, don't worry. You'll learn how to hide and display them next.

TROUBLE? If a dialog box appears, asking whether you want to AutoArchive your old items now, click the No button.

TROUBLE? Don't worry if your screen differs slightly from Figure 1-2. Although the figures in this book were created while running Windows 98 in its default settings, all Windows operating systems share the same basic user interface. Microsoft Outlook should run equally well using Windows 95, Windows 98 in Web style, Windows NT, or Windows 2000.

The Outlook window contains some elements that might be familiar to you from other programs, such as Word or Excel. Other elements are specific to Outlook. The Outlook window includes the following:

- **Menu bar**—groups of related commands that are organized into lists, called menus. You use the menu commands to perform tasks. Menu commands vary, depending on the displayed Outlook folder.
- **Standard toolbar**—a collection of shortcut icons to frequently used menu commands that you can click to quickly perform a task. The toolbar buttons vary, depending on the displayed Outlook folder.
- **Outlook Bar**—groups of shortcut icons that you can click to open frequently used folders. You can add more shortcut icons to quickly open other folders on your system or network.
- **Groups**—collections of related shortcuts. Click a group button to display its shortcuts.
- **Folder List**—a hierarchy of the Outlook folders that you use to store and organize items.
- **Folder banner**—displays the name of the open folder (Inbox in Figure 1-2). To display a list of all folders, click the folder name.
- **Information Viewer**—displays the items of the selected folder; may be divided into panes. For example, in Figure 1-2, the Information Viewer for the Inbox is divided into a view pane and a preview pane. The **view pane** displays the list of stored items, such as e-mail messages in the Inbox. The **preview pane** displays the item selected in the view pane, such as the contents of the selected e-mail message.
- **Status bar**—displays information about the current view, such as the number of items that appear in that view.

No matter which component you use, these features of the Outlook window work in the same way. You can display or hide any of these elements, depending on your needs and preferences. For your work here, you'll customize the Outlook window to match Figure 1-2.

To accomplish this task, you'll use the View menu. When you first display any menu, a short, personalized menu may appear with the most recently used commands. After a short pause, the full menu appears. You can also click the double arrow at the bottom of the menu to display the full menu. Once you use a command on the full menu, it moves to the short menu. The first time you open Outlook, the menus and toolbars display all of the basic commands and buttons. As you work, however, Outlook personalizes the menus and toolbars based on how often you use the commands. Eventually, the menus and toolbars will display only the commands and toolbar buttons you use most often.

To customize the Outlook window:

1. If the Outlook Bar does not appear on your screen, click **View** on the menu bar, and then click **Outlook Bar**. Remember to pause a moment or click the double arrow to display the full menu, if necessary.

2. If the preview pane does not appear, click **View** on the menu bar, and then click **Preview Pane**.

3. If the status bar does not appear, click **View** on the menu bar, and then click **Status Bar**.

4. If the Folder List does not appear, click **View** on the menu bar, and then click **Folder List**. Your screen should now look similar to Figure 1-2.

As you can see, the Folder List duplicates the information in the Outlook Bar. Next, you'll use both to navigate to the different Outlook folders. You'll then close the Outlook Bar, leaving more room for the Information Viewer.

Navigating Between Outlook Components

You can click any icon in the Outlook Bar to display its folder's contents in the Information Viewer. The Outlook Bar is split into three **groups,** collections of related components or folders. For example, the Outlook Shortcuts group shows all of the installed components—Outlook Today, Inbox, Calendar, Contacts, Tasks, Notes, and Deleted Items. You can add shortcuts to any group. You click a group bar to display its contents.

A second, perhaps simpler, way to navigate between folders is with the Folder List. There, you can click any folder icon to display its contents in the Information Viewer. You'll try both methods now.

To navigate between Outlook components:

1. Click the **Outlook Shortcuts** group bar to display its shortcuts.
2. Click **Calendar** on the Outlook Bar to switch to the Calendar. Notice the daily planner, current and next month calendar, and the TaskPad.
3. Click the **My Shortcuts** group bar to display its shortcuts.
4. Click **Journal** on the Outlook Bar to switch to the Journal. Notice that the Journal displays a timeline. If the Journal is turned on, you will see icons representing your e-mail messages, files, phone calls, tasks, and other items organized by date.

    TROUBLE? If a dialog box appears, asking whether you want to turn on the Journal, click the No button.

5. Click the **Outlook Shortcuts** group bar, and then click **Contacts**. Notice that the letter buttons will move you to contact cards beginning with that letter.
6. Click the **Calendar** icon in the Folder List.
7. Click the **Inbox** icon in the Folder List.
8. Click **View** on the menu bar, and then click **Outlook Bar**. Notice that the Outlook Bar disappears and the Information Viewer expands to fill the extra space.

You can switch quickly to any Outlook folder using either the Outlook Bar or the Folder List.

Creating and Sending E-mail Messages

E-mail, the electronic transfer of messages between computers, is a simple and inexpensive way to stay in touch with friends around the corner, family across the country, and colleagues in the same building or across the world. Not only can you send messages whenever you have time, but recipients can also read those messages at their convenience. The

Express Lane staff uses e-mail to correspond with its customers, suppliers, and each other. Staff members use e-mail for both internal and external communications because it is fast, convenient, and inexpensive, and it saves paper.

Before you can send and receive e-mail messages with Outlook, you must set up a mail account. To do so, you need an e-mail server or Internet service provider, an e-mail address, and a password. An **e-mail address** is a series of characters that you use to send and receive e-mail messages. It consists of a user ID and a host name separated by the @ symbol. A **user ID** (or **user name** or **account name**) is a unique name that identifies you to your mail server. The **host name** consists of the name of your Internet service provider's computer on the Internet plus its domain or level. For example, in the e-mail address "alan@theexpresslane.com", "alan" is the user ID and "theexpresslane.com" is the host name. Although many people might use the same host, each user ID is unique, enabling the host to distinguish one user from another. A **password** is a private code that you enter to access your account. (In this tutorial, you'll use your own e-mail address to send all messages.)

If you haven't already set up an Outlook mail account, complete the following steps.

To set up an Outlook mail account:

1. Click **Tools** on the menu bar, and then click **Accounts**.

2. Click the **Add** button, and then click **Mail**.

3. Type your name in the first Internet Connection Wizard dialog box, and then click the **Next** button.

4. Continue to enter the requested information in the Internet Connection Wizard dialog boxes. Click the **Next** button to move to the next dialog box.

    TROUBLE? If you are unsure of what information to enter, ask your instructor or technical support person.

5. Click the **Finish** button to have the Wizard set up your account based on the information you entered.

Choosing a Message Format

Outlook can send and receive messages in three formats: HTML, Outlook Rich Text, and plain text. Although you specify one of these formats as the default for your messages, you can always switch formats for an individual message. **HTML** provides the most formatting features and options (text formatting, numbering, bullets, alignment, horizontal lines, backgrounds, HTML styles, and Web pages). **Outlook Rich Text** provides some formatting options (text formatting, bullets, and alignment), but some recipients will not be able to see the formatting if you send messages over the Internet. **Plain text** messages include no formatting, and the recipient specifies which font is used for the message. When you reply to a message, Outlook uses the same format in which the message was created. For example, if you reply to a message sent to you in plain text, Outlook sends the response in plain text.

You'll set the message format to HTML so that you can customize your messages.

TUTORIAL 1 COMMUNICATING WITH OUTLOOK 2000 OUT 1.09

To choose a default message format:

1. Click **Tools** on the menu bar, and then click **Options**.
2. Click the **Mail Format** tab in the Options dialog box.
3. Select **HTML** in the Send in this message format box. See Figure 1-3.

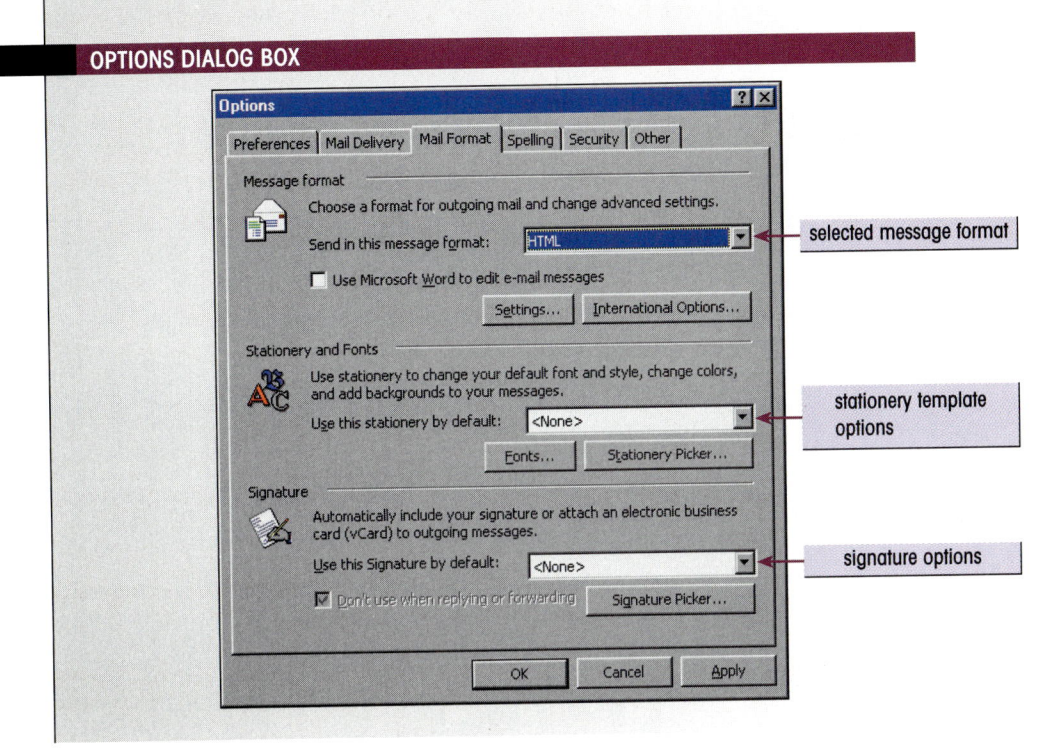

Figure 1-3 OPTIONS DIALOG BOX

[Screenshot of the Options dialog box with the Mail Format tab selected, showing the Message format section with "Send in this message format: HTML" (labeled "selected message format"), the Stationery and Fonts section (labeled "stationery template options"), and the Signature section (labeled "signature options").]

Because you selected HTML as your message format, you can customize your messages with a formatted signature. You'll do that before closing the Options dialog box.

Adding a Signature

A **signature** is text that is automatically added to every e-mail message you send. For example, you might create a signature with your name, job title, company name, and phone number. The Express Lane might create a signature containing a paragraph that describes how to order groceries. In addition, you can create more than one signature and then use the Signature button on the Standard toolbar to select which one you want to include in a particular message. Although you can attach a signature to a message in any format, the HTML and Outlook Rich Text formats enable you to apply font and paragraph formatting. For now, you'll create a simple signature with your name and the company name.

To create a signature:

1. Click the **Signature Picker** button, and then click the **New** button in the Signature Picker dialog box.
2. Type your name in the Enter a name for your new signature box, click the **Start with a blank signature** option button if necessary, and then click the **Next** button.

3. In the Signature text box, type your name, press the **Enter** key, and then type **The Express Lane**. See Figure 1-4.

Figure 1-4   **EDIT SIGNATURE DIALOG BOX**

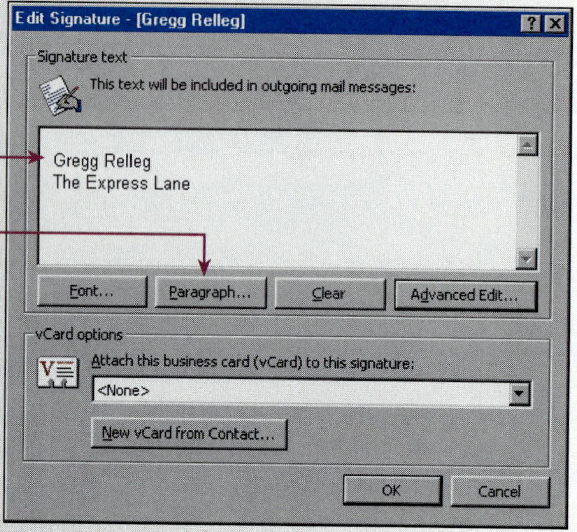

type signature text here

click to set formatting options

4. Select **The Express Lane**, click the **Font** button, change the font to 10-point, Bold italic, Arial, and then click **OK**.

5. Click the **Finish** button, preview your signature in the Signature Picker dialog box, and then click **OK** to return to the Options dialog box.

6. Make sure that the signature with your name appears in the Use this Signature by default list box.

7. If necessary, click the **Don't use when replying or forwarding** check box to insert a check mark.

8. Click **OK**.

Whenever you start a new e-mail message, your signature will appear at the end of the message.

Using Stationery

When you send e-mail, you can select a special look for your message, much as you would select special letterhead paper for your business correspondence. **Stationery templates** are HTML files that include complementary fonts, background colors, and images for your outgoing e-mail messages. To use one of the stationery templates that come with Outlook, which include announcements, invitations, greetings, and other designs, you click Actions on the menu bar, point to New Mail Message Using, and then click the stationery or the More Stationery option to open a dialog box with additional stationery options. You also can create your own stationery. Stationery is available only if you use HTML as your message format. Remember, too, that the recipient must be able to read HTML e-mail to view the special formatting. You'll work with stationery in the Case Problems.

Creating an E-mail Message

An e-mail message looks similar to a memo, with separate header lines for Date, To, From, Cc, and Subject followed by the body of the message. Outlook automatically fills in the Date line with the date on which you send the message and the From line with your name or e-mail address; these lines are not visible in the New Message window. You complete the other lines. The To line lists the e-mail addresses of one or more recipients. The Cc line lists the e-mail addresses of anyone who will receive a courtesy copy of the message. The Subject line provides a quick overview of the message topic, like a headline.

As you write and send e-mail messages, keep the following guidelines in mind:

- **Reread your messages.** Your name and e-mail address are attached to every message that you send. Also, employers can usually access their employees' e-mail messages.

- **Use uppercase and lowercase letters.** Excessive use of uppercase is considered shouting and exclusive use of lowercase is difficult to read.

- **Be concise.** The recipient should be able to read and understand your message quickly.

To create an e-mail message:

1. Click the **New Mail Message** button on the Standard toolbar. A new untitled message window opens. If necessary, maximize the window. Notice that your signature already appears in the message body.

    TROUBLE? If a dialog box appears and asks whether you want to use Word as your e-mail editor for all messages, click the No button.

2. Type your e-mail address in the To box. You could send the e-mail to multiple recipients by typing a semicolon between each address.

3. Press the **Tab** key twice to move to the Subject box. You skipped the Cc box because you aren't sending a courtesy copy of this e-mail to anyone.

4. Type **Asparagus Order** in the Subject box, and then press the **Tab** key to move to the message body, just above the signature.

5. Type **Your asparagus is a big hit with The Express Lane customers. Please double our order for the next three weeks.**, press the **Enter** key twice, and then type **Thank you,** (including the comma). See Figure 1-5.

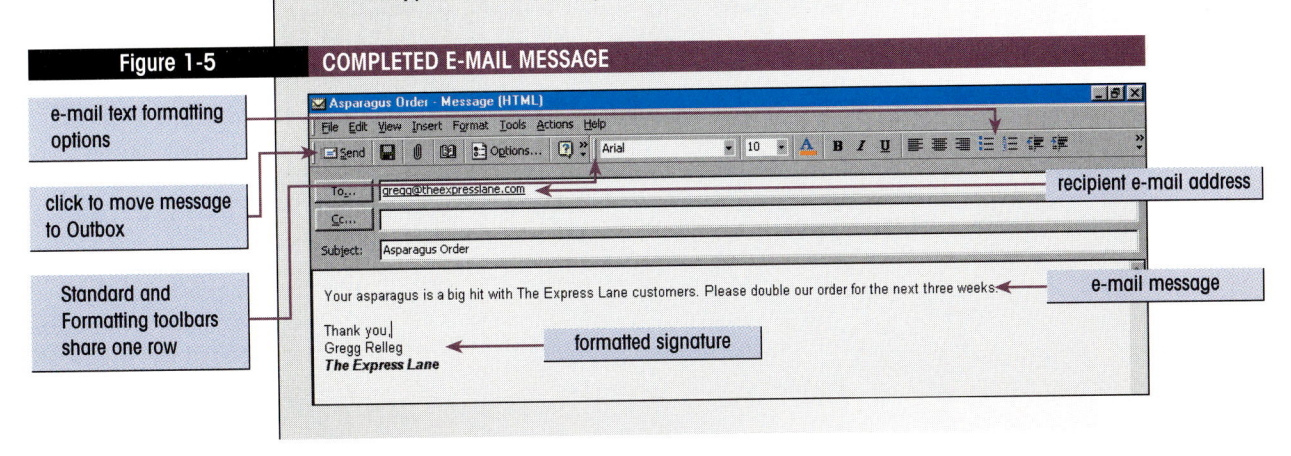

Figure 1-5 — COMPLETED E-MAIL MESSAGE

- e-mail text formatting options
- click to move message to Outbox
- Standard and Formatting toolbars share one row
- recipient e-mail address
- e-mail message
- formatted signature

To...: gregg@theexpresslane.com
Cc...:
Subject: Asparagus Order

Your asparagus is a big hit with The Express Lane customers. Please double our order for the next three weeks.

Thank you,
Gregg Relleg
The Express Lane

You don't need to type your name because you included it as part of the signature. Before sending your message, however, you want to add some text formatting. You can format e-mail text much as you would format text in a Word document. In fact, many of the buttons and commands are the same. For example, you can set bold, underline, and italics; change the font, font size, and font color; align and indent text; create a bulleted or numbered list; and even apply paragraph styles.

To format text in an e-mail message:

1. Select the text **a big hit** in the message body. You'll make this text bold and green.

2. Click the **Bold** button **B** on the Formatting toolbar.

    TROUBLE? If you don't see the Bold button, click the More Buttons list arrow, and then click the Bold button.

3. Click the **Font Color** button **A** on the Formatting toolbar, and then click the **Green** tile in the palette that opens.

    TROUBLE? If you don't see the Font Color button, click the More Buttons list arrow, and then click the Font Color button.

You could add more formatting, but a little goes a long way. Try to be judicious in your use of text formatting. Use it to enhance your message rather than overwhelm it.

Sending E-mail

After you finish creating your e-mail message, you can either send it immediately or move it to the **Outbox** (the outgoing message storage folder) to send later. If you have several messages to create or are working offline (not connected to your e-mail server), it is usually a more efficient practice to create all of your messages before you send them. You select how a messages are sent in the Options dialog box. You'll set these options now.

To change your message delivery options:

1. Click the **Inbox - Microsoft Outlook** button on the taskbar to return to the Inbox.

2. Click **Tools** on the menu bar, and then click **Options**.

3. Click the **Mail Delivery** tab.

4. In the Mail account options section, click the **Send messages immediately when connected** check box to remove the check mark. Now Outlook will move your completed messages into the Outbox until you choose to send them rather than immediately forwarding your completed message to your e-mail server.

5. Click the **Check for new messages every 10 minutes** check box to remove the check mark. If you leave this option selected, Outlook sends any messages in the Outbox and checks your e-mail server for new messages at the specified interval.

6. Click **OK**.

Now, when you click the Send button in the New Message window, the message moves to the Outbox. You must then click the Send/Receive button on the Standard toolbar to check for and deliver new messages.

To send a message to the Outbox:

1. Click the **Asparagus Order – Message (HTML)** button on the taskbar to return to your message.
2. Click the **Send button** on the Standard toolbar. The message moves to the Outbox.

Notice that the Outbox changes to boldface and is followed by (1), which indicates that there is one outgoing message. Although you can send and receive e-mail from the Inbox or the Outbox, you'll switch to the Outbox to deliver the message.

To switch to the Outbox and send the message:

1. Click **Outbox** in the Folder List. Notice that the message appears in the Information Viewer of the Outbox. See Figure 1-6.

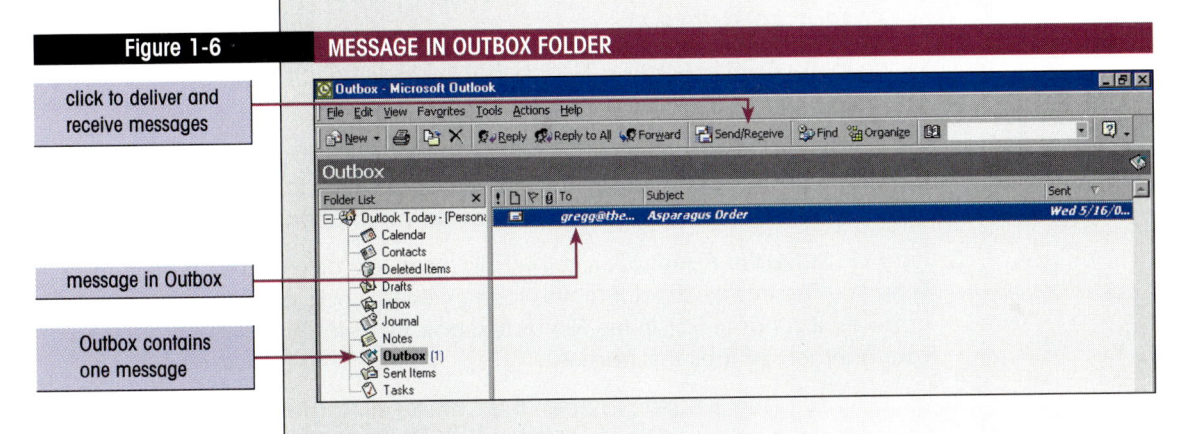

Figure 1-6   **MESSAGE IN OUTBOX FOLDER**

- click to deliver and receive messages
- message in Outbox
- Outbox contains one message

2. Click the **Send/Receive** button on the Standard toolbar to send the message. Notice that the Outbox is empty and that the boldface and (1) have disappeared.

   TROUBLE? If Outlook requests a password, you might need to enter your password before you can send and receive your messages. Type your password, and then click the OK button.

The time your e-mail takes to arrive at its destination will vary, depending on the size of the message, the speed of your Internet connection, and the number of other users on the Internet. When you send a message, your e-mail server identifies its final destination by the host name in the e-mail address. Rather than being sent directly to its final destination, your message passes from host to host until it arrives at the appropriate host. You may see a dialog box that shows the progress of the message to your mail server. While sending your outgoing messages, Outlook may check your mail server for incoming messages you have received since you last checked. These messages may be removed from your mail server and stored on the computer you are using.

Organizing Contact Information

The **Contacts** folder is an address book where you store information about the people and businesses with whom you communicate. Each person or organization is called a **contact**. You can store business-related information about each contact, including job titles, phone numbers, postal addresses, and e-mail addresses, as well as more personal information, such as notes, birthdays, anniversaries, and children's names.

Information you enter about a contact is split into individual units, called **fields**. For example, the contact name, Mr. Salvador F. Aiello, Jr., would be divided into a Title field, First field, Middle field, Last field, and Suffix field. Using fields allows you to sort, group, or look up contacts by any part of the name.

Creating Contacts

When you create a contact, you open a blank contact card and then enter all necessary information. The Express Lane stores information about its suppliers and customers in the Contacts folder. Alan asks you to create new contacts for several suppliers. You could start a new contact from any folder by clicking the New button list arrow and then clicking New Contact. Instead, you'll switch to the Contacts folder.

To create a contact:

1. Switch to the **Contacts** folder. Notice that the New button changes to reflect the most likely item you'll want to create from this folder.

2. Click the **New Contact** button on the Standard toolbar. A new, untitled Contact window opens, displaying text boxes in which to enter the contact information. The General tab stores the basic information about a contact.

3. Type **Mr. Salvador F. Aiello, Jr.** in the Full Name text box, and then press the **Enter** key. The insertion point moves to the next text box, and the contact name appears, last name first, in the File as text box. By default, Outlook organizes your contacts by their last names.

4. Click the **Full Name** button to open the Check Full Name dialog box. Although you entered the contact name in one text box, Outlook stores each part of the name as a separate field. See Figure 1-7.

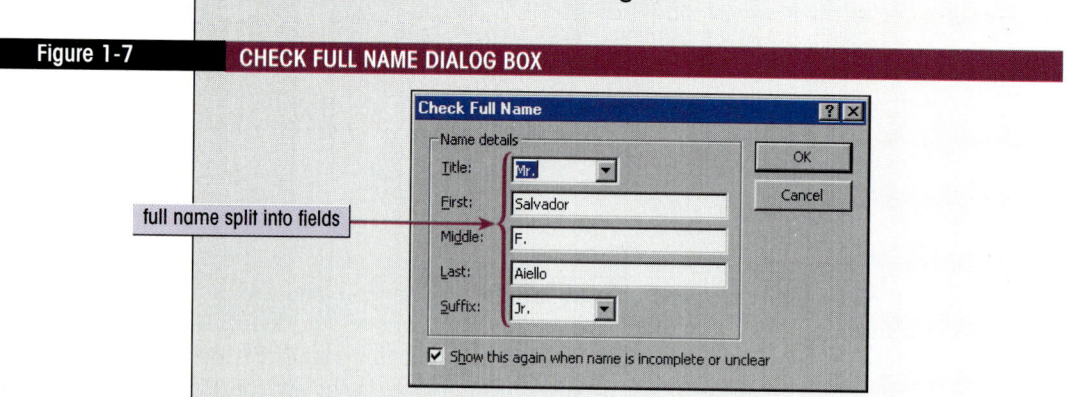

Figure 1-7   **CHECK FULL NAME DIALOG BOX**

full name split into fields

Title:	Mr.
First:	Salvador
Middle:	F.
Last:	Aiello
Suffix:	Jr.

☑ Show this again when name is incomplete or unclear

5. Click the **Cancel** button to close the dialog box without making any changes. If Outlook cannot tell how to distinguish part of a name, the Check Full Name dialog box will open so that you can correct the fields.

6. Click in the **Job title** text box, type **President**, press the **Tab** key, then type **Green Grocer Produce**.

7. Click in the **Business** text box, type **4155559753,** and then press the **Tab** key. Notice that Outlook formats the phone number with parentheses around the area code and a hyphen after the prefix, even though you didn't type them.

8. Click the **down arrow** button next to Home, click **Assistant** to change the field label, and then enter **4155559752** for the phone number of Salvador's assistant.

    Each of the down arrow buttons displays a list of options for that particular field. You can enter information for each option in the same text box.

9. Click the **Details** tab, and then enter **Antony Lopez** in the Assistant's name text box.

10. Click the **General** tab, and then enter **4155556441** as the Business Fax.

11. Click in the **Address** text box, type **12 Haymarket Blvd.**, press the **Enter** key, and then type **San Francisco, CA 94102**. You could verify that Outlook recorded the address in the correct fields by clicking the Address button, but you don't need to do so for a simple address. Notice that the This is the mailing address check box is checked. Outlook assumes that the first address you enter for a contact is the mailing address. You could enter additional addresses and specify any one of them as the mailing address.

12. Click in the **E-mail** text box and enter your own e-mail address. See Figure 1-8.

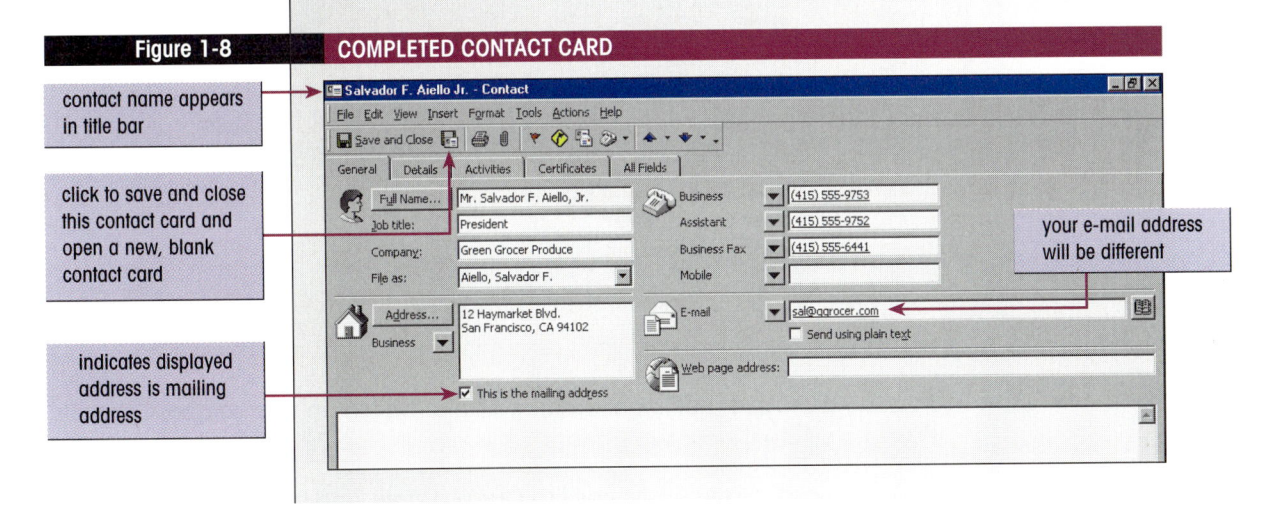

| Figure 1-8 | COMPLETED CONTACT CARD |

- contact name appears in title bar
- click to save and close this contact card and open a new, blank contact card
- indicates displayed address is mailing address
- your e-mail address will be different

In most cases, each contact would have a unique e-mail address to which you would send e-mail messages. For the purposes of this tutorial, you will use your own e-mail address and send all messages to yourself. So far, you have completed the contact information for Salvador. You can now close his contact card and open a new contact card in the same step.

To enter additional contacts:

1. Click the **Save and New** button on the Standard toolbar to save Salvador's contact information and open a new, blank contact card.

2. Enter the following information: **Julia Shang, Manager, Foods Naturally**, business phone **415-555-1224**, business fax **415-555-4331**, **19 Hillcrest Way, Novato, CA 94132**. Use your own e-mail address.

   Outlook detects that another contact already has the same e-mail address as this contact and opens the Duplicate Contact Detected dialog box.

3. Click the **Add this as a new contact anyway** option button, and then click **OK**.

4. Click , and then enter the following contact information: **Kelley Ming, Ming Nuts Company**, business phone **415-555-9797**, **2932 Post Street, San Francisco, CA 94110**. Use your own e-mail address.

5. Click , and then enter the following contact information: **Alan Gregory, The Express Lane**, your e-mail address, and add as a new contact anyway.

6. Click the **Save and Close** button on the Standard toolbar to save this contact information and return to the Contacts Information Viewer. See Figure 1-9.

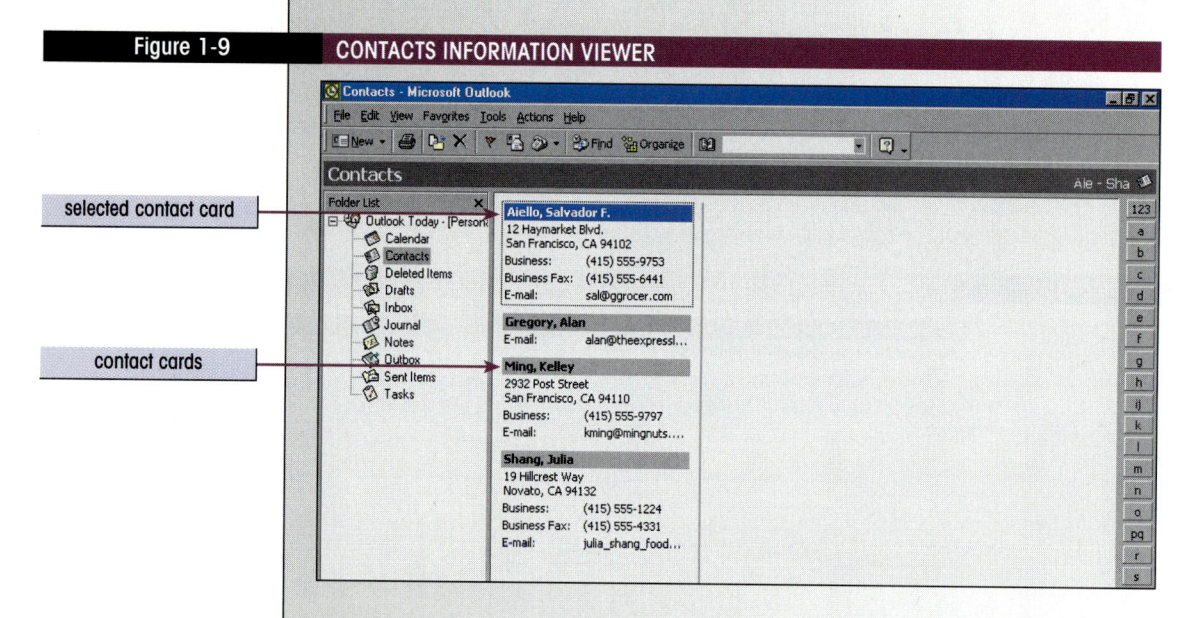

Figure 1-9   **CONTACTS INFORMATION VIEWER**

selected contact card

contact cards

TROUBLE? If you see a different amount of information on your screen, Contacts is set to a different view. You'll change this view in Step 7.

7. Click **View** on the menu bar, point to **Current View**, and then click **Detailed Address Cards**. The Information Viewer displays more contact information than the Address Cards view.

You just changed the view of the Contacts folder. **Views** organize information in a folder in different ways and control the details that are visible. For example, you just switched from Address Cards view, which displays names and addresses in blocks, to Detailed Address Cards view, which displays additional information in this same format. You could also choose other views, such as Phone List view, which arranges your contacts in columns of detailed information, such as job title, business phone, and other fields. Each Outlook folder has a set of standard views from which you can choose.

Notice that in the Detailed Address Cards view, Outlook organized your contacts in alphabetical order by last name as specified in the File as text box. When you have many contacts, you'll want to find the desired contact quickly. One way to do this is to click the letter button along the right side of the Information Viewer that corresponds to the first letter of a contact's last name. Then, use the scroll bar at the bottom of the window to display that contact.

Editing Contacts

Many aspects of a contact's information may change over time. People may move to a new street address, be assigned a new area code, or change jobs. Or, you may discover that you entered information incorrectly. Rather than starting over, you can update the existing contact card as needed by double-clicking in the contact to open the Contact window and edit the information much as you entered it originally. You also can make the change directly in the Contacts Information Viewer from the Address Card or Detailed Address Card view.

Alan tells you that the ZIP code for Foods Naturally is actually 94947. You'll make this correction directly in the Information Viewer.

To edit a contact:

1. If necessary, click the letter **S** along the right side of the Information Viewer, and use the scroll bars to display Julia Shang's contact information.
2. Click the address portion of the contact information to display the insertion point.
3. Use the arrow keys to move the insertion point between the 4 and 1 in the ZIP code.
4. Type **947**, and then press the **Delete** key three times to erase the incorrect digits.
5. Click anywhere outside Julia Shang's contact card. Outlook saves the changes.

QUICK CHECK

1. Describe the purposes of the Inbox and the Outbox.
2. Define e-mail and list two benefits of using it.
3. What is a signature?
4. What type of contact information can you store in Outlook?

SESSION 1.2

In this session, you'll receive, read, reply to, forward, and print e-mail messages. You'll work with adding and reading attachments to e-mail messages. You'll organize messages by filing, archiving, sorting, and filtering them. Finally, you'll learn how to get help in Outlook.

Receiving E-mail

You check for new e-mail messages by clicking the Send/Receive button on the Standard toolbar. Outlook connects to your e-mail server and downloads any messages that have arrived since you last checked. New messages are delivered into the Inbox. You'll switch to the Inbox and download the message you sent yourself earlier.

To receive e-mail:

1. Click **Inbox** in the Folder List.

2. Click the **Send/Receive** button on the Standard toolbar. If necessary, enter your password in the dialog box that opens.

3. Watch for the new message to appear in the Inbox. Notice that the number of new messages you receive appears within parentheses. See Figure 1-10. Your Inbox might contain additional e-mail messages.

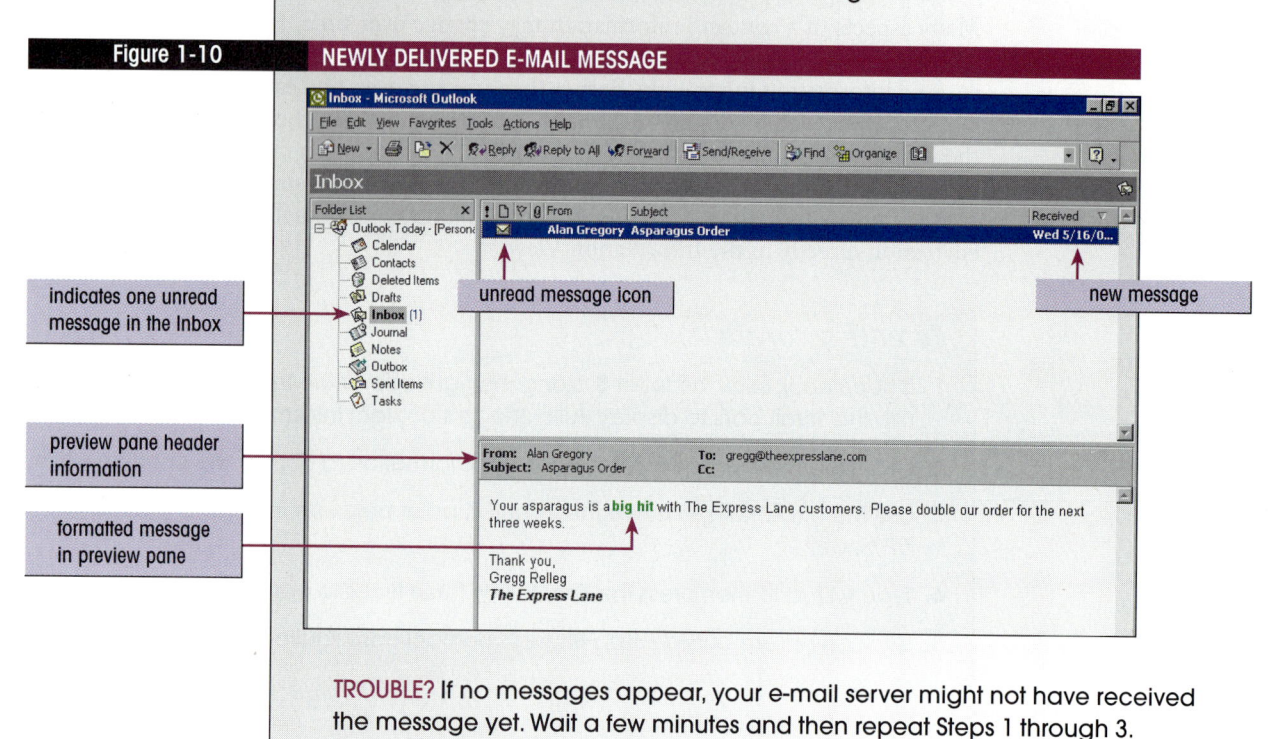

Figure 1-10 NEWLY DELIVERED E-MAIL MESSAGE

- indicates one unread message in the Inbox
- unread message icon
- new message
- preview pane header information
- formatted message in preview pane

TROUBLE? If no messages appear, your e-mail server might not have received the message yet. Wait a few minutes and then repeat Steps 1 through 3.

Reading Messages

The Inbox Information Viewer is divided into two panes. The upper pane displays a list of all e-mail messages that you have received, along with columns of information about the message. These columns include the sender's name, the message subject, and the date and time that the message was received, as well as icons that indicate the message's status. For example, the icons indicate the message's importance level and specify whether the message has been read. You can change any column width by dragging the border of any column header.

The lower preview pane displays the contents of the selected message. At the top of the preview pane is the message header, which indicates the sender, all recipients, and the subject. You can resize the panes by dragging the border above the message header up or down.

TUTORIAL 1 COMMUNICATING WITH OUTLOOK 2000   OUT 1.19

To read a message:

1. In the message list, click the **Asparagus Order** message to display its contents in the preview pane. In a moment, the mail icon changes from unread to read and the message no longer appears in boldface.

   TROUBLE? If the message header does not appear, right-click the top of the preview pane and then click Header Information in the shortcut menu.

2. Read the message. Because you can view HTML messages, the formatting you added to the message earlier is visible.

After you read a message, you have several options—you can leave the message in the Inbox and deal with it later, reply to the message, forward the message to others, archive the message, or delete it. As with paper mail you receive, it's best to organize and respond to messages as you receive them rather than letting them collect in your Inbox.

Replying to and Forwarding Mail

Many messages you receive require some sort of response—for example, confirmation you received the information, the answer to a question, or sending the message to another person. The quickest way to respond to messages is to use the Reply and Forward features. The **Reply** feature responds to the sender or to the sender and all recipients; Outlook inserts their e-mail addresses into the appropriate boxes. The **Forward** feature sends a copy of the message to one or more recipients you specify; you enter the e-mail addresses in the To or Cc box. With both the Reply and Forward features, the original message is included for reference, separated from your new message by the text "Original Message" and the original message header information.

You'll reply to the Asparagus Order message. In reality, you would respond to someone other than yourself.

To reply to a message:

1. Make sure that the Asparagus Order message is selected in the Inbox, and then click the **Reply** button on the Standard toolbar. A message window opens with the receiver's name or e-mail address in the To box (in this case, your name or address) and RE: (short for Regarding), inserted at the beginning of the Subject line.

2. Type **You will receive double shipments of asparagus for the next three weeks. Thank you for your order.** Press the **Enter** key twice, and then type your name. Notice that your reply message appears in blue type because you selected HTML format.

   TROUBLE? Depending on how your computer is configured, you might not see all HTML formatting.

3. Click the **Send** button on the Standard toolbar to move the message to the Outbox.

Next, you'll forward the message to Julia Shang, the manager at Foods Naturally. Because her contact information appears in the Contacts folder, you can address the message to her quickly.

To forward a message:

1. Make sure that the Asparagus Order message is selected in the Inbox, and then click the **Forward** button on the Standard toolbar. This time, the insertion point is in the empty To box and FW: (for Forward) precedes the Subject line.
2. Start typing **Julia Shang** and, when Julia Shang appears in the To box, press the **Tab** key. When Outlook recognizes the name as an item in the Contacts folder with a valid e-mail address, it underlines the Contact name.
3. Click at the top of the message body, and then type **Please update The Express Lane account**.
4. Click the **Send** button on the Standard toolbar.
5. Click the **Send/Receive** button on the Inbox Standard toolbar.

Printing Messages

Although e-mail eliminates the need for paper messages, sometimes you'll want a printed copy of a message to file or distribute. You can use the Print button on the Standard toolbar to print a selected message with the default settings, or you can use the Print command to verify and change settings before you print. All default print styles include the print date, user name, and page number in the footer. You'll verify the settings and then print the Asparagus Order message in your Inbox.

To verify settings and print a message:

1. If necessary, select the Asparagus Order message in the Inbox.
2. Click **File** on the menu bar, and then click **Print**. The Print dialog box opens, as shown in Figure 1-11.

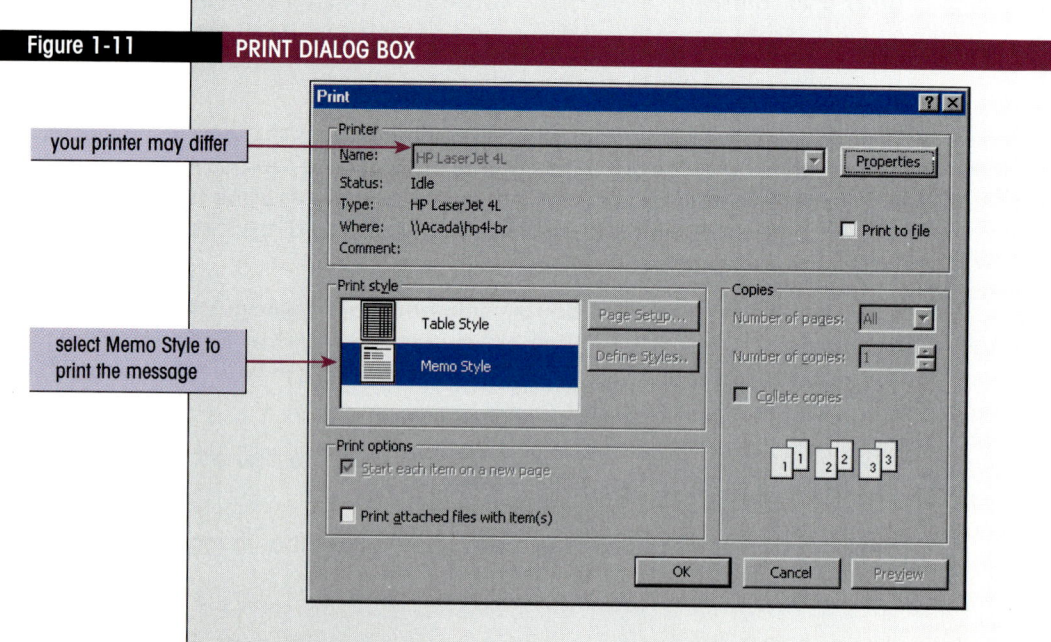

Figure 1-11   PRINT DIALOG BOX

your printer may differ

select Memo Style to print the message

3. Make sure that the correct printer appears in the Name list box.
4. If necessary, click **Memo Style** in the Print style section to select it. Memo style prints the contents of the selected item—in this case, the e-mail message. Table

TUTORIAL 1 COMMUNICATING WITH OUTLOOK 2000   OUT 1.21

Style prints the view of the selected folder—in this case, the Inbox folder. Other folders have different print style options.

5. Click **OK**. The message prints.

Working with Attachments

Attachments to e-mail are a great way to share information. An **attachment** is a program file (such as a Word document, Excel workbook, or PowerPoint slide presentation) that you send with an e-mail message; the recipients can then open and edit the file in the original program. For example, you might send an attachment containing The Express Lane's latest sales figures to Alan for his review.

To attach a file to an e-mail:

1. Click the **New Mail Message** button on the Standard toolbar in the Inbox.

2. Type **Alan Gregory** in the To box.

3. Type **Latest Sales** in the Subject box.

4. In the message area, type **The attached Excel workbook contains the latest sales figures. Looks like we're on track. Let me know if you have any comments.** Press the **Enter** key.

5. Click the **Insert File** button on the Standard toolbar. The Insert File dialog box appears and functions like the Open dialog box.

6. Change the Look in list box to the **Tutorial** folder within the **Tutorial.01** folder on your Data Disk.

7. Double-click the **Sales** document to insert it as an attachment to your e-mail message, as well as close the Insert File dialog box. See Figure 1-12. The message is ready to send.

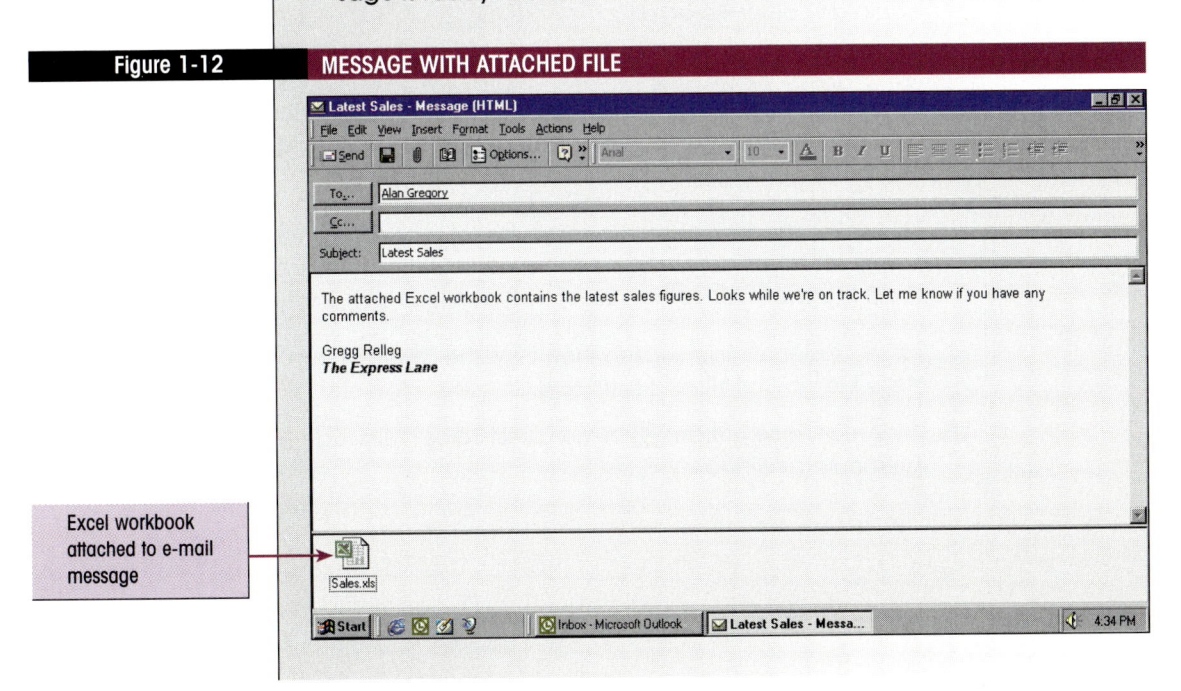

Figure 1-12   MESSAGE WITH ATTACHED FILE

Excel workbook attached to e-mail message

> **8.** Click the **Send** button 🖃 on the Standard toolbar, and then click the **Send/Receive** button 📨 on the Inbox Standard toolbar to send the message to your mail server.

A message with an attachment may take a bit longer to send because it's larger than an e-mail message without an attachment. Messages with attached files display a paper clip icon in the message list. If the appropriate program is installed on your computer, you can open the attached file from the message itself. You can also save the attachment to your computer and then open, edit, and move it like any other file on your computer. Although you can reply to or forward a message with an attachment, the attachment is included only in the forwarded message.

After you receive the message with the attachment, you'll save the attachment and then view it from within the message.

To save and view the message attachment:

1. Click the **Send/Receive** button 📨 on the Standard toolbar to download message. Again, it might take a bit longer than usual to download the message with the attachment.

2. Double-click the message in the message list to open the message in a new window. Notice that the attachment appears as an icon at the bottom of the window, similar to when you created the message.

3. Right-click the **Sales** icon, and then click **Save As** on the shortcut menu. The Save Attachment dialog box appears, allowing you to select the save location for the message.

4. Change the Save in list box to the **Tutorial** folder within the **Tutorial.01** folder on your Data Disk.

5. Change the filename to **Second Quarter Sales**, and then click the **Save** button to save the attached file to your Data Disk. You can work with this file just as you would any other file on disk.

   You can also view the attached file right from the message window.

6. Double-click the **Sales** icon to open Excel and display the attached file. You can read, edit, format, and save the file just as you would any other Excel workbook.

   TROUBLE? If the file opens in a spreadsheet program other than Excel, your computer might be configured to associate the file extension .xls with spreadsheet programs other than Excel. Just continue with Step 7.

7. Review the sales figures, and then click the **Close** button ✕ in the title bar to close the workbook and exit Excel.

8. Click the **Close** button ✕ in the Latest Sales - Message (HTML) title bar to close the message window.

TUTORIAL 1 COMMUNICATING WITH OUTLOOK 2000   OUT 1.23

Managing Messages

As you can readily see, messages can collect quickly in your Inbox. Even if you respond to each message as it arrives, all of the original messages will still remain in your Inbox. Some messages you'll want to delete. Others you'll want to file and store, just as you would file and store paper memos in a file cabinet. In fact, the Folder List acts like an electronic file cabinet. First, you create an organizational system; then, you label a series of folders in which to store your messages. For example, an employee of The Express Lane might create subfolders for Customers and Suppliers within the Inbox folder.

Creating a Folder

You can create folders at the same level as the default folders, such as Inbox, Outbox, and Sent Messages, or you can create subfolders within these main folders. For now, you'll create one subfolder in the Inbox folder, called Suppliers. Once you create a subfolder, the main folder is preceded by either a plus or minus sign. Which sign appears depends on whether the subfolders are displayed (minus sign) or hidden (plus sign).

To create a folder:

1. Right-click **Inbox** in the Folder List, and then click **New Folder**.

2. Type **Suppliers** in the Name text box.

3. Make sure that the Folder contains list box displays **Mail Items**. You can also create subfolders to store contacts, notes, tasks, and so on.

4. Click **Inbox** in the Select where to place the folder list. It is the location for your new folder. See Figure 1-13.

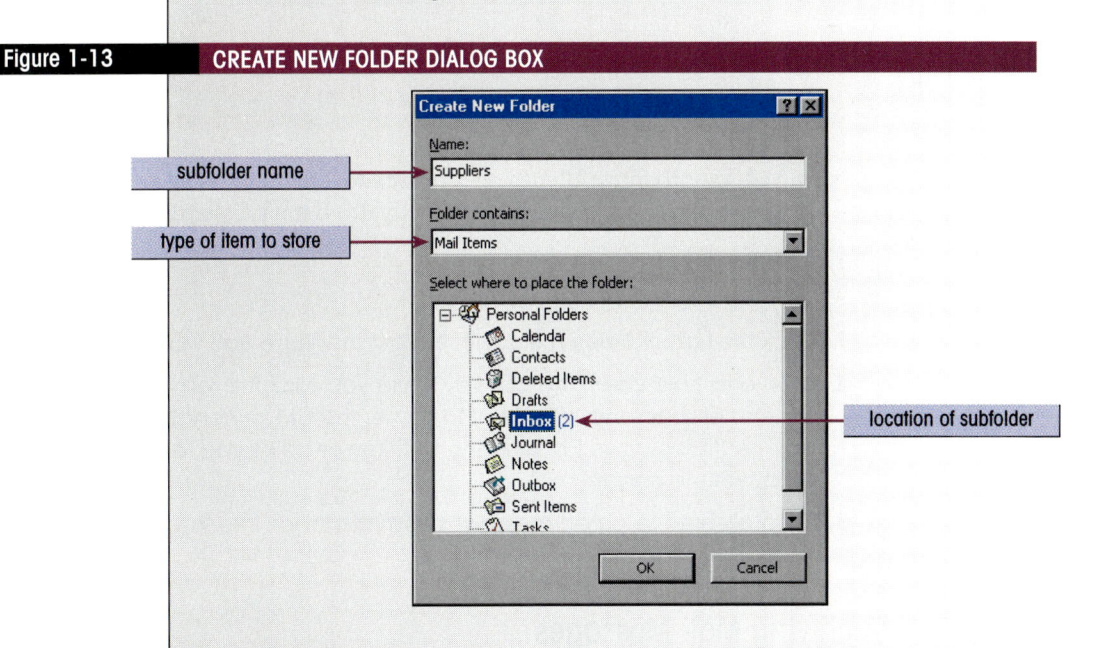

| Figure 1-13 | CREATE NEW FOLDER DIALOG BOX |

5. Click **OK**. The new folder appears in the Folder List.

   TROUBLE? If a dialog box appears, asking whether you want a shortcut to this folder displayed in the Outlook Bar, click the No button.

Now you can file any messages related to The Express Lane in the new folder.

Filing Messages

You can file any message in your Inbox at any time. The simplest way to file a message is to drag it from one folder to another.

To file messages:

1. If necessary click the **plus sign** next to the Inbox folder in the Folder List to display the Suppliers subfolder.
2. Select the **Asparagus Order** message in the Information Viewer. It is the first message that you will move.
3. Drag the **Asparagus Order** message to the **Suppliers** subfolder in the Folder List. See Figure 1-14.

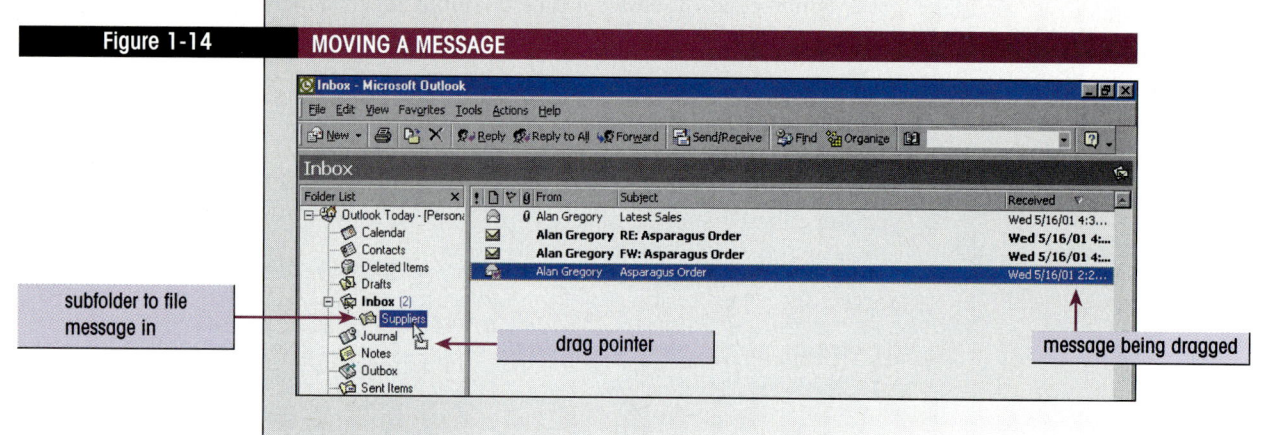

Figure 1-14   MOVING A MESSAGE

subfolder to file message in

drag pointer

message being dragged

4. Release the mouse button to move the message from the Inbox into the subfolder.

Next, you want to move all messages related to The Express Lane into the subfolder. You could continue to move each message individually, but it's faster to move all of them at once.

To file multiple messages:

1. Click the **Latest Sales** message, the first message you want to file.
2. Press and hold down the **Ctrl** key while you click the remaining two Asparagus Order messages that you want to move. The Ctrl key enables you to select non-adjacent messages. Pressing the Shift key enables you to select a range of adjacent messages.
3. Drag all three selected messages from the Inbox into the **Suppliers** subfolder.

Archiving Mail Messages

Eventually, even the messages in your subfolders will overflow. Rather than reviewing your filed messages and moving older ones to a storage file, you can archive your older messages. The **Archive** feature lets you manually transfer messages and other items stored in an e-mail folder (such as attachments) to a personal folder file when the items have reached the age you specify. A **personal folder file** is a special storage file with a .pst extension that contains folders, messages, forms, and files; it can be viewed only in Outlook. Outlook calculates the age of an e-mail message from the date the message was sent or received, whichever is later. Outlook also has an AutoArchive feature, which you can turn on to automatically archive aged messages each time you start Outlook. When you archive messages, your existing folder structure is recreated in your new archive file. If you want to archive a subfolder, the main folder is created in the archive file but none of its messages are archived. All folders remain in place after archiving—even empty ones. You'll archive messages in the Review Assignments.

Finding Messages

As your folder structure becomes more complex and the number of stored messages increases, it might become difficult to locate a message you filed. Rather than searching through multiple folders, you can have Outlook find the desired message. The Find command searches for text listed in the From or Subject box in a single folder. For searches of more than one criterion or multiple folders and subfolders, you must use the Advanced Find feature. You'll use the Find feature with the messages you filed in the Suppliers folder.

To find all messages related to asparagus:

1. Click the **Suppliers** subfolder in the Folder List to display its contents.

2. Click the **Find** button on the Standard toolbar. The Find pane appears.

3. Type **Asparagus** in the Look for text box.

4. Leave the **Search all text in the message** check box selected. This option tells Outlook to search for the text in the From box, the Subject box, and the message itself.

5. Click the **Find Now** button. After a moment, only the three messages that contain the word "asparagus" appear in the Information Viewer. See Figure 1-15.

Figure 1-15   RESULTS OF FIND

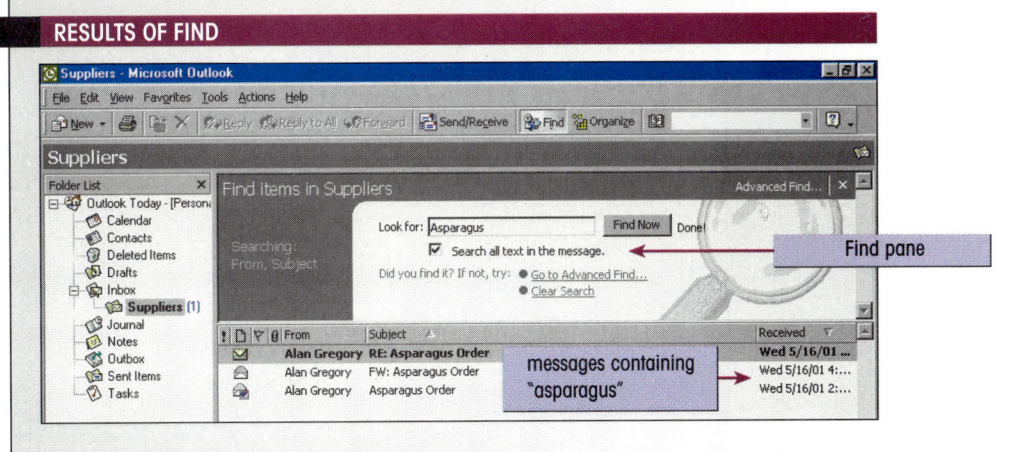

You could perform additional simple searches, but for now you're done.

6. Click again to close the Find pane.

Once you close the Find pane, all messages in that folder reappear. Another way to manage files is to sort them.

Sorting Messages

Sorting is a way to arrange items in a specific order—either ascending or descending. **Ascending** order arranges messages alphabetically from A to Z, chronologically from earliest to latest, or numerically from lowest to highest. **Descending** order arranges messages in reverse alphabetical, chronological, or numerical order. By default, all messages are sorted in descending order by their Receive date and time. You can, however, change the field by which messages are sorted; for example, you might sort e-mail messages alphabetically by sender. Alternatively, you can sort messages by multiple fields; for example, you might sort e-mail messages alphabetically by sender and then by subject. The simplest way to change the sort order is to click a column heading in the Information Viewer. You'll sort your messages first by subject, and then by date received within each subject.

To sort messages by subject:

1. Click the **Subject** column heading. The sort order changes to ascending by subject, as indicated by the up arrow icon in the Subject column heading.

   TROUBLE? If the arrow icon points down, then the sort order is descending. Click the Subject column heading again to sort messages in ascending order by subject.

   Next, you'll sort the messages within each subject in ascending order by the received date.

2. Press and hold the **Shift** key while you click the **Received** column heading until the arrow icon points up. See Figure 1-16.

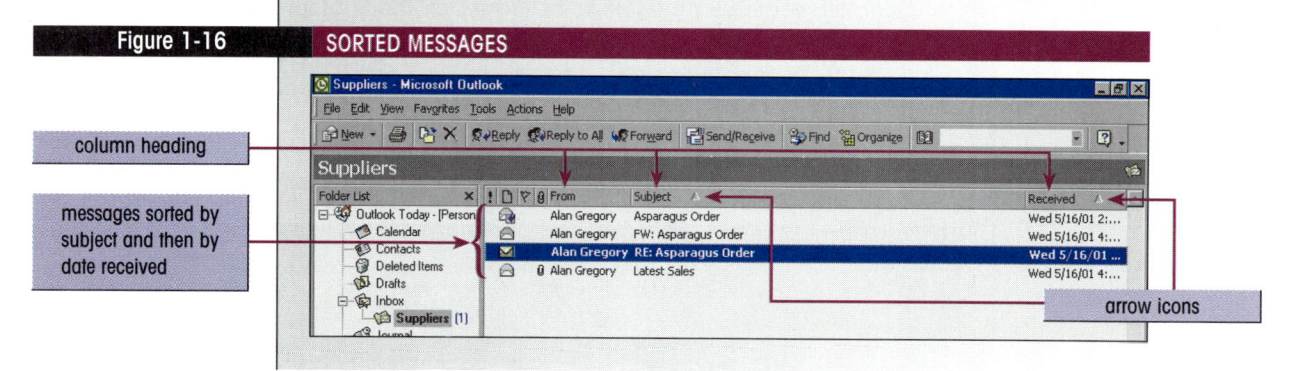

Figure 1-16 SORTED MESSAGES

- column heading
- messages sorted by subject and then by date received
- arrow icons

You can sort messages in any view except Message Timeline view. You'll switch between views now.

To switch views:

1. Click **View** on the menu bar, and then point to **Current View** to display the list of default views.

2. Click **By Conversation Topic**. The messages are rearranged according to the information in the Subject box. Each subject, or conversation topic, becomes a different group. The plus sign indicates that a group contains the number of messages indicated after the conversation topic.

3. Click the **plus sign** next to Asparagus Order. The messages in that group are displayed, and a minus sign precedes the conversation topic. See Figure 1-17. The other views arrange the e-mail messages in different ways.

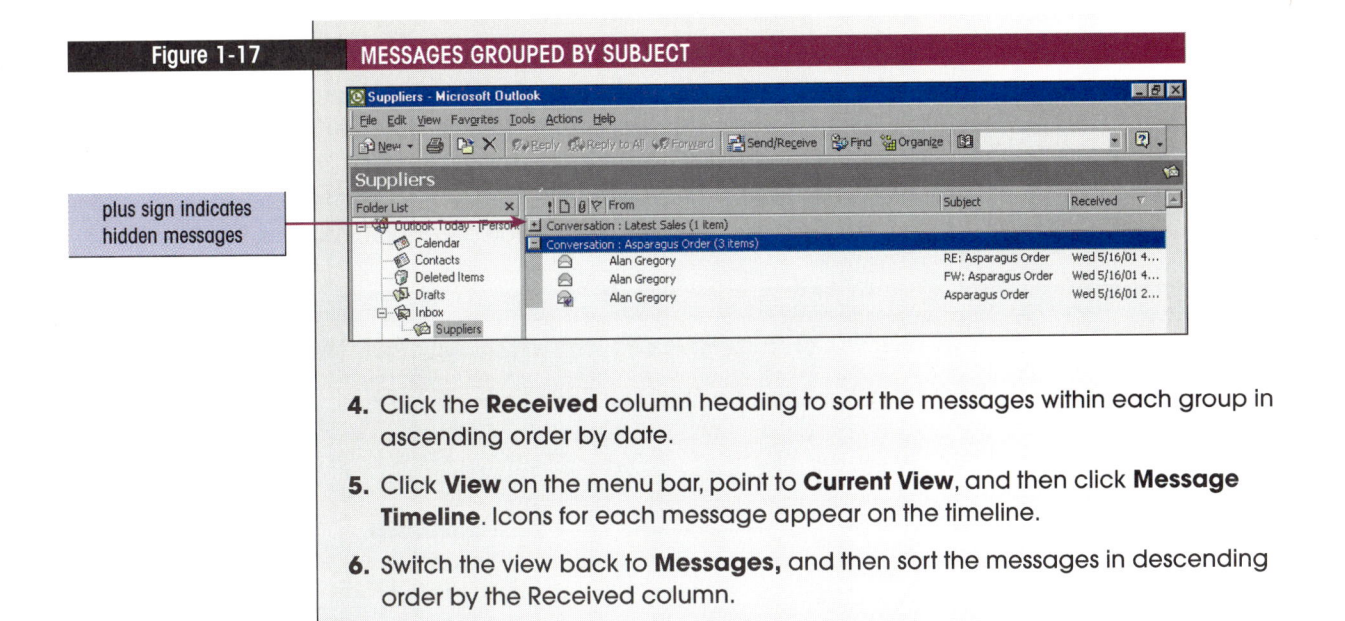

TUTORIAL 1   COMMUNICATING WITH OUTLOOK 2000   OUT   1.27

Figure 1-17   **MESSAGES GROUPED BY SUBJECT**

plus sign indicates hidden messages

4. Click the **Received** column heading to sort the messages within each group in ascending order by date.

5. Click **View** on the menu bar, point to **Current View**, and then click **Message Timeline**. Icons for each message appear on the timeline.

6. Switch the view back to **Messages,** and then sort the messages in descending order by the Received column.

You could further customize a view by removing some of the existing column headings and adding others. In addition, you could filter the view.

Filtering a View

A **filter** displays only those items in a folder that match certain criteria. For example, you could filter your messages to display only the ones from Alan Gregory. In this case, the other messages would remain in the folder but stay hidden until you remove the filter. To apply a filter, you display the appropriate folder, click View on the menu bar, point to Current View, and then click Customize Current View. Click the Filter button, and then enter the desired filter options in the Filter dialog box, such as the word for which to search or the sender's name. Click the OK button in both the Filter dialog box and the View Summary dialog box. Only the messages that match your filter will then appear in the folder. As a reminder, the words "Filter Applied" appear in the status bar until you remove the filter from the folder. To remove the filter, open the Filter dialog box again and click the Clear All button.

Getting Help

Like other Microsoft programs, Outlook has an extensive Help system. For quick reference, you can point to a button on a toolbar and see its name in a **ScreenTip**, a yellow box with the button's name. The **What's This?** command on the Help menu changes the pointer to ?. When you click this pointer on a menu command, dialog box option, or anything else on your screen, a brief description appears. If you need more in-depth help, you can turn to the **Office Assistant**, an animated character that acts as an interactive guide for finding information from the Outlook Help system. You simply type a question using everyday language, and the Office Assistant searches the Help system and supplies an answer in easy-to-understand language. The answer might consist of step-by-step instructions to guide you through a feature or a clear explanation of a particular concept.

Alan suggested that you customize the Outlook menus and toolbars to display only the items you use frequently. You decide to remove the Organize button from the Standard toolbar. Because you don't know how to perform this task, you'll ask the Office Assistant for help.

To use the Office Assistant and Outlook Help:

1. Click the **Microsoft Outlook Help** button on the Standard toolbar. The Office Assistant opens, offering help on topics related to the task you most recently performed.

2. Type **How do I customize toolbars?**, and then click the **Search** button. The Office Assistant balloon displays Help topics related to toolbar buttons. See Figure 1-18.

Figure 1-18 — OFFICE ASSISTANT

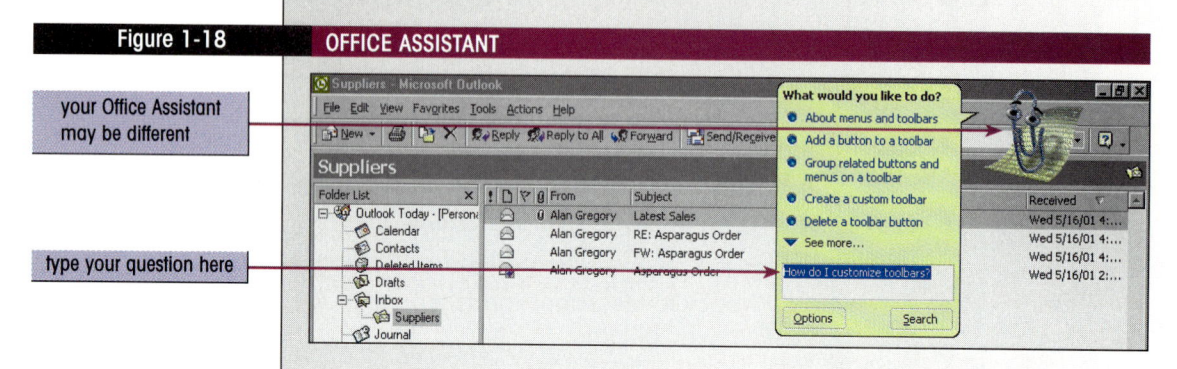

your Office Assistant may be different

type your question here

3. Click the **Delete a toolbar button** option. The Microsoft Outlook Help window opens, providing the steps and an explanation of how to customize a toolbar. Each underlined hyperlink connects to a related Help screen. The other hyperlinks provide definitions of the selected phrase.

4. Click the **Show** button. Additional Help window tabs appear, as shown in Figure 1-19.

Figure 1-19 — HELP WINDOW WITH TABS

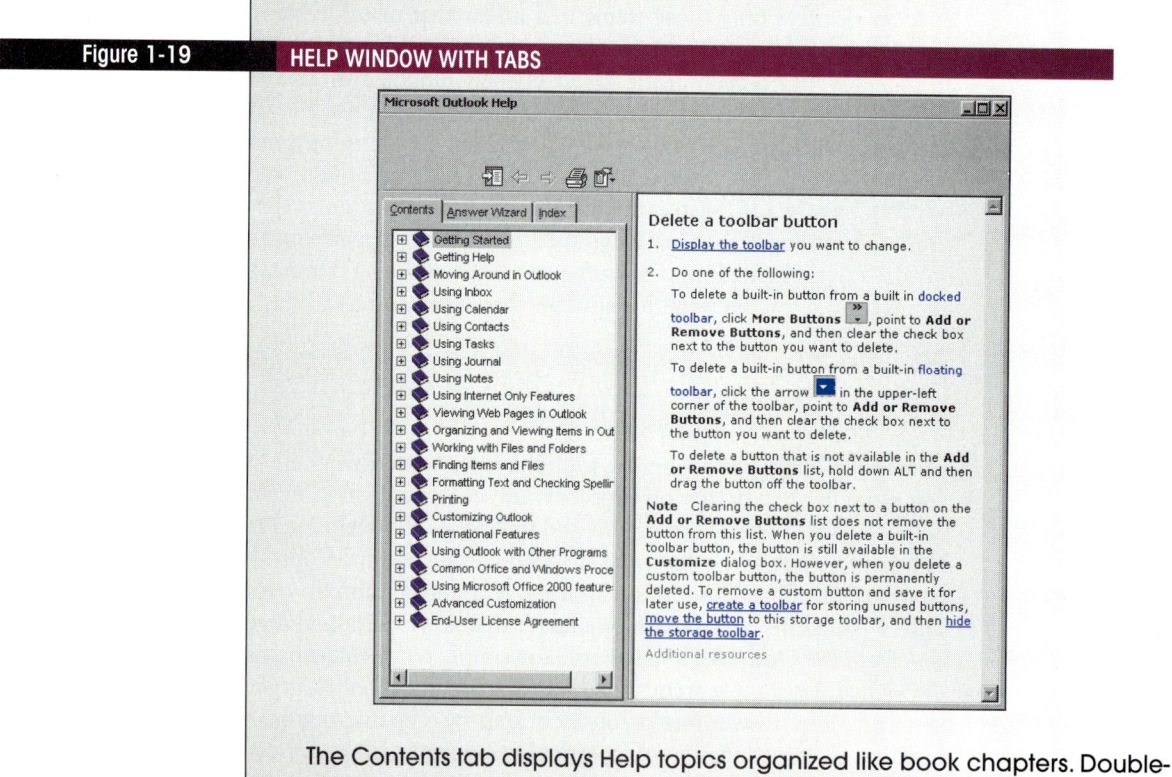

The Contents tab displays Help topics organized like book chapters. Double-click a book icon to display the Help topics, and then click a topic to display it. The Answer Wizard tab functions like the Office Assistant—type your question, click the Search button, and then select the appropriate topic. The Index tab lets you search the entire Help system by a keyword.

5. Click the **Hide** button to return the Help window to its original size.

6. Click the **Close** button on the Microsoft Outlook Help window. The window closes and Outlook fills the screen again.

7. Click **Help** on the menu bar, and then click **Hide the Office Assistant**. The animated character disappears.

   TROUBLE? If the Office Assistant asks whether you want to hide it permanently, click the No, just hide me option.

Exiting Outlook

When you finish using Outlook, you should **exit** (or close) the program. Unlike with other programs, you don't need to save or close any other files. Before you exit, however, you'll delete each of the items you created in this tutorial.

To delete items and exit Outlook:

1. Click the **Suppliers** folder in the Folder List.

2. Click the **Delete** button on the Standard toolbar, and then click the Yes button to confirm that the folder and all of its messages should be moved to the Deleted Items folder. This folder acts like the Recycle Bin. Items you delete stay in this folder until you empty it.

3. Switch to the **Contacts** folder, click the first contact you created, press and hold the **Ctrl** key as you click each additional contact you created, and then click . The contacts move to the Deleted Items folder. Next, you'll remove the signature you created.

4. Click **Tools** on the menu bar, click **Options**, and then click the **Mail Format** tab in the Options dialog box.

5. Click the **Signature Picker** button, click the name of your signature in the Signature box, and then click the **Remove** button.

6. Click **Yes** to confirm that you want to permanently remove this signature, and then click the **OK** button in each dialog box. Now you're ready to exit Outlook.

7. Click the **Close** button in the title bar to exit Outlook.

Alan thanks you for your help. The Express Lane can now fill all of its customers' orders for asparagus until the end of the season. A happy customer means a profitable business.

Quick Check

1. Explain the difference between the Reply button and the Reply to All button.
2. True or False: You can save a file attached to a message, but you cannot open it from Outlook.
3. How do you file an e-mail message in a subfolder?
4. What is the difference between a sort and a filter?

REVIEW ASSIGNMENTS

Lora Shaw asks you to help her with customer communication.

1. Start Outlook and, if necessary, set up an account. Make sure that the Outlook screen and settings match those in the tutorial.

2. Create a signature that uses your name and the title "Customer Service Representative."

3. Create an e-mail to yourself with the subject "Welcome New Customer" and the message "Welcome to The Express Lane. We're sure you'll find our grocery delivery service more convenient and cheaper than your local grocery store—not to mention more healthful, because all our foods are certified organic. If you have any questions or comments, feel free to e-mail us."

4. Format the text of your e-mail in 12-point Times New Roman.

5. Send the e-mail to the Outbox and then to your mail server.

6. Create a contact card for Alan Gregory, The Express Lane, at a fictional business mailing address and business phone number; use your own e-mail address.

Explore

7. Create a contact card for Lora based on Alan's contact card. Select Alan's contact card in the Contacts folder. Click Actions on the menu bar, and then click New Contact from Same Company. The new contact window opens with the company name, address, and phone number already entered. Type Lora Shaw in the Full Name text box. Type your own e-mail address in the E-mail text box.

8. Create contact cards for the following customers at their home addresses, using your e-mail address:
Elliot Zander, 384 Leavenworth Street, San Francisco, CA 94103, 415-555-1232
Mai Ching, 1938 Grant Avenue, San Francisco, CA 94110, 415-555-0907
Lester Newhoun, 2938 Golden Gate Avenue, San Francisco, CA 94124, 415-555-6497

9. Edit Mai Ching's contact card to change the address to 1938 Presidio Street.

Explore

10. You can create an e-mail message already addressed to a specific contact. From the Contacts folder, click the contact card for Lora Shaw, and then click the New Message to Contact button. Type "Tea health benefits?" as the subject. Type "I've heard that drinking tea has health benefits. Do you have any information about this?" as the message body.

11. Send the e-mail to the Outbox and then to your mail server.

12. Download your new messages. If the Tea health benefits? message hasn't arrived, wait a few minutes and try again.

13. Reply to the Tea health benefits? message with the text "In addition to being the world's second favorite drink to water, there is growing evidence of a link between tea and disease prevention, particularly cancer and heart disease. Check out our large selection of black, oolong, and green teas. The attached file has some information about teas. I hope this information is helpful."

14. Attach the **Tea** document located in the **Review** folder within the **Tutorial.01** folder on your Data Disk.

Explore

15. Because Lora plans to update the tea information sheet next week, she asks you to recall the message if the customer hasn't read it within one week. Click the Options button on the Standard toolbar, click the Expires after check box to insert a check mark, enter the date of one week from today, and then click the Close button. This option makes the message unavailable after the date you specified.

16. Send the message to the Outbox.
17. Forward the Tea health benefits? message to Alan Gregory with the message "Let's meet next week to talk about adding this information to our Web site."
18. Send the message to the Outbox and then to your mail server.
19. Create a subfolder called "Customers" in the Inbox.
20. Download your messages, and then file the Welcome New Customer message and the Tea health benefits? message in the new folder.
21. Sort the messages in the Customers folder in descending order by subject and then in descending order by date of receipt.
22. Find the messages in the Customers folder that contain the word "customer." Close the Find pane.
23. Save the attachment in the forwarded Tea health benefits? message as **Tea Health Benefits** to the **Review** folder within the **Tutorial.01** folder on your Data Disk.
24. Print the forwarded Tea health benefits? message and its attachment. (*Hint:* In the Print dialog box, select the Print attached files with item(s) check box.)

Explore
25. Archive all messages in the Customers folder. Click File on the menu bar, and then click Archive. Click the Archive this folder and all subfolders option button. Click the Customers subfolder in the Folder List. Click the Archive items older than list arrow, and then select tomorrow's date to ensure that you archive all items in the folder. Click the Browse button, change the Save in list box to the **Review** folder within the **Tutorial.01** folder on your Data Disk, leave the filename as **Archive** and the file type as .pst, and then click the OK button. Click the OK button in the Archive dialog box.
26. Delete each Outlook item you created, including all signatures, folders, messages, and contacts.

CASE PROBLEMS

Case 1. Answers Anytime Answers Anytime is a unique tutoring service. Students can e-mail specific questions and problem areas to subject experts and receive quick answers. The subject experts reply to students within two hours, either by e-mail message or e-mail message with an attachment.

1. Start Outlook and, if necessary, set up an account. Make sure that the Outlook screen and settings match those in the tutorial.
2. Create an e-mail message to your e-mail address with the subject "History questions" and the message "Please send information about the following: What was the Bill of Rights? When did women receive the right to vote? How does Rachel Carson fit into the environmental movement?" Press the Enter key after each question to place it on its own line, and then format the questions as a numbered list. Type your name at the end of the message. Send the message.
3. Create a contact card for Benji Tanago, Environmental History Expert, Answers Anytime, Pallas Road, Cincinnati, OH 45230, 513-555-6582, and your e-mail address.
4. Download your message.

5. Reply to the message using the following text formatted as a numbered list:
   1. See the attached document for information about the Bill of Rights.
   2. On August 26, 1920, Tennessee delivered the last needed vote and the Nineteenth Amendment was added to the Constitution. It stated that "the right of citizens of the United States to vote shall not be denied by the United States or by any State on account of sex."
   3. I've forwarded this question to Benji Tanago, our resident expert on the environmental movement.
6. Attach the **Amendments** document, which is located in the **Cases** folder within the **Tutorial.01** folder on your Data Disk, to the e-mail. Send the message to the Outbox.

Explore
7. Rather than retype Benji's information, you can send the contact card you created. Switch to the Contacts folder, click Benji's contact card to select it, click Actions on the menu bar, and then click Forward as vCard. A new message window opens with the contact card included as an attachment. Enter your e-mail address in the To box, and then send the message to the Outbox.

8. Forward the student's original message to Benji. Add the text "Hi Benji. Question 3 is yours. Thanks."

Explore
9. Add a flag to the message. Flags mark a message or contact so as to remind you or the recipient to follow up. You can also set a reminder. When you send a message with a flag, the recipient sees a comment with the purpose of the flag at the top of the message. If you set a reminder, a date will appear as well. Click the Flag for Follow Up button on the Standard toolbar. You can choose flag text from the Flag to list or type your own in the box. Make sure that "Follow up" appears in the Flag to box. Click the Due by list arrow, and then click the Today button. Click OK. Notice that the flag message banner appears near the top of the message window.

10. Send the message to the Outbox, and then send all messages to your mail server.
11. Create a subfolder named "Answers" in the Inbox.
12. Download your messages. Notice the red flag that appears in the Flag column of the message list next to the message you forwarded to Benji.

Explore
13. Use the Office Assistant to find out more about flags and the process of changing a flag to complete. Follow the steps in the Office Assistant to change the flag to complete.

14. Find all messages in the Inbox related to the subject "History questions," and then file them in the Answers folder.
15. File the message with the vCard in the Answers folder.

Explore
16. Save each message in the Answers subfolder as a file in the **Cases** folder within the **Tutorial.01** folder on your Data Disk. Select the first message in the message list, click File on the menu bar, and then click Save As. Change the Save in location to your Data Disk, but leave the subject as the filename and the file type as HTML. If you wanted to read the messages in Word or WordPad, you would change the file type to .txt. Click the Save button.

17. Delete the Answers folder, messages, and contact card you created in Outlook by clicking each item and then clicking the Delete button on the Standard toolbar.

Case 2. Party Planners Jace Moran plans events ranging from company picnics to children's birthday parties to weddings. Right now, she is working on a graduation party. The client has given Jace the e-mail addresses for the entire guest list so that Jace can send the invitations using Outlook.

1. Start Outlook and, if necessary, set up an account. Make sure that the Outlook screen and settings match those in the tutorial.

Explore
2. Send an e-mail message to yourself using an Excel worksheet as the message body. From the Inbox, click Actions on the menu bar, point to New Mail Message Using, point to Microsoft Office, and then click Microsoft Excel Worksheet. In column A,

enter a list of foods for the party. In column B, enter the probable cost for the food. Total the Cost column. Send the e-mail to the Outbox and then to your mail server.

3. Create contact cards for at least five guests. Include their names, addresses, phone numbers, and e-mail addresses. Enter your own e-mail address for each contact.

Explore 4. Edit each contact to include one item of personal information, such as a birthday or spouse's name.

Explore 5. Use stationery to create the party invitation. From the Inbox, click Actions on the menu bar, point to New Mail Message Using, and then click More Stationery. Click Balloon Party Invitation in the Stationery box, and then click OK.

Explore 6. Send the invitation to each of the contacts you created. Remember to type a semicolon between the names in the To box. Type an appropriate subject.

Explore 7. Fill in the Day, Time, and Place. (*Hint:* Click after the text heading and then enter the appropriate information.) Experiment by modifying the format of the stationery; try changing the font of existing text or moving the balloons.

8. Send the message to the Outbox and then to your mail server.

9. Read and print the food cost e-mail.

10. Switch to the Contacts folder, and then change the view to Detailed Address Cards.

Explore 11. Print the contact cards you created. If other contact cards exist in addition to the ones you created, press and hold the Ctrl key as you click the contact name for each card you created. Open the Print dialog box. Use Card Style as the Print style and, if you selected contact cards, click the Only selected items option button in the Print range. Click the OK button.

12. Create a subfolder in the Contacts folder called "Guests" and move the contact cards you created into it.

Explore 13. Export your contact list. Click File on the menu bar, and then click Import and Export. Click Export to a file, and then click the Next button. Click Microsoft Access, and then click the Next button. If necessary, click the plus sign next to Contacts to display the Guests subfolder, select the subfolder, and then click the Next button. Use the Browse button to save the file as **Guest List** to the **Cases** folder within the **Tutorial.01** folder on your Data Disk. Click the Next button, and then click the Finish button. The contact list is exported as an Access database to your Data Disk. You'll need this file to complete Case 2 in the next Outlook tutorial.

14. Download your messages. Print one message, and save one message to the **Cases** folder within the **Tutorial.01** folder on your Data Disk.

15. Delete the subfolder, contacts, and messages you created in Outlook by clicking each item and then clicking the Delete button on the Standard toolbar.

LAB ASSIGNMENTS

E-mail that originates on a local area network with a mail gateway can travel all over the world. That's why it is so important to learn how to use it. In this Lab you use an e-mail simulator, so even if your school computers don't provide you with e-mail service, you will know the basics of reading, sending, and replying to electronic mail.

1. Click the Steps button to learn how to work with e-mail. As you proceed through the Steps, answer all of the Quick Check questions that appear. After you complete the Steps, you will see a Quick Check Summary Report. Follow the instructions on the screen to print this report.

2. Click the Explore button. Write a message to re@films.org. The subject of the message is "Picks and Pans." In the body of your message, describe a movie you have recently seen. Include the name of the movie, briefly summarize the plot, and give it a thumbs up or a thumbs down. Print the message before you send it.

3. In Explore, look in your In Box for a message from jb@music.org. Read the message, then compose a reply indicating that you will attend. Carbon copy mciccone@music.org. Print your reply, including the text of JB's original message before you send it.

4. In Explore, look in your In Box for a message from leo@sports.org. Reply to the message by adding your rating to the text of the original message as follows:

Equipment:	Your Rating:
Rollerblades	2
Skis	3
Bicycle	1
Scuba gear	4
Snowmobile	5

Print your reply before you send it.

Quick Check Answers

Session 1.1

1. The Inbox stores e-mail messages you have received. The Outbox stores e-mail messages you have written but not yet sent.
2. E-mail is the electronic transfer of messages between computers on the Internet. It's inexpensive for communicating with others who are nearby or far away. You can send and read messages at your convenience.
3. Text that is automatically added to every e-mail message you send, such as your name, job title, and company name
4. In addition to the usual contact name, job title, company name and address, phone and fax numbers, you can store personal information such as birthdays, anniversaries, and children's names.

Session 1.2

1. Reply responds to only the sender of the e-mail message; Reply to All responds to the sender and any other recipients of the e-mail message.
2. False
3. Drag the message from the message list to the subfolder in the Folder List.
4. A sort changes the order in which messages are displayed in a view. A filter displays only messages that match certain criteria.

INDEX

Special Characters
(number sign), EX 3.08–09
* (asterisk), EX 1.16, EX 2.07
+ (plus sign), EX 1.16, EX 2.07
     EX 1.16, EX 2.07,
= (equal sign), EX 2.07
@ (at sign), OUT 1.08
$ (dollar sign), EX 2.12, EX 3.05–07
←, ↑, →, ↓ (arrows), EX 3.28–29,
     EX 3.29–30,
/ (slash), EX 1.16, EX 2.07
^ (caret), EX 1.16, EX 2.07

A

absolute references, copying
     formulas, EX 2.10–12
Access, AC 1.03
     exiting, AC 1.13, AC 2.33
     merging data with Word documents.
          See merging Access data with
          Word documents
     starting, AC 1.07–08
Access window, AC 1.08, AC 1.10
Accessories
     locating information about in Help,
          WIN 98 1.28
account names, OUT 1.08
Accounting format, EX 3.05–07
activating
     toolbars, EX 3.24–25
active cell, EX 1.06, EX 1.07
active program, WIN 98 1.13
addition operator (+), EX 1.16,
     EX 2.07
addresses
     e-mail, OUT 1.08
Address toolbar
     display options, WIN 98 2.17–18
aggregate functions, AC 3.34–36
aligning
     cell contents, EX 3.11
     controls. *See* aligning controls
     text, WD 2.22–23
anchoring
     toolbars, EX 3.24

AND function, EX 2.16
And logical operator, AC 3.26,
     AC 3.27–28
Archive feature, OUT 1.24–25
archiving e-mail messages,
     OUT 1.24–25
arguments, functions, EX 2.16
arithmetic mean, calculating,
     EX 2.16–18
arithmetic operations, order of
     precedence, EX 2.07–08
arithmetic operators, EX 1.16
arrow(s) (**)
     adding using Drawing toolbar,
          EX 3.28–29
     moving in worksheets, EX 3.29–30
arrow(s), scroll. *See* scroll arrows
arrow keys, moving insertion point,
     WD 2.07–08
ascending order, OUT 1.26
at sign (@), e-mail addresses,
     OUT 1.08
attachments, e-mail messages,
     OUT 1.21–22
AutoComplete feature, WD 1.14–15
AutoContent Wizard, PPT 1.13–17
     creating presentations, PPT 1.13–16
     editing slides, PPT 1.16–17
AutoContent Wizard dialog box,
     PPT 1.14, PPT 1.15
AutoCorrect feature, WD 1.22–24
AutoFormat feature, EX 2.26–27
AutoForm Wizard, AC 1.17–18
AutoLayout slides, PPT 1.27–28
AutoNumber data type, AC 2.05
     assigning sizes, AC 2.05–06
AutoReport Wizard, AC 1.23–24
AutoSum button, EX 2.06–07
average, calculating, EX 2.16–18
AVERAGE function, EX 2.16–18
Avg aggregate function, AC 3.34

B

Back button
     in Help, WIN 98 1.30
     on Standard toolbar, WIN 98 2.23
backing up databases, AC 1.27
Backspace key, WIN 98 2.4
backup copies
     importance of, WIN 98 2.26
Backup program, WIN 98 2.26
blocks of text. See also text
     selecting, WIN 98 2.5–6
bolding text, WD 2.29–30
borders
     worksheets, EX 3.19–22
**Borders button, Formatting toolbar,
     EX 3.20**
**Border tab, Format Cells dialog box,
     EX 3.20**
browsers. *See* Internet Explorer;
     Netscape Navigator; Web
     browsers
bulleted items, PPT 1.10
     moving, PPT 1.22
     promoting, PPT 1.25–27
**bulleted lists, PPT 1.10,
     WD 2.25–26**

C

calculated fields, AC 3.30–37
     adding to queries, AC 3.32–34
     aggregate functions, AC 3.34–36
     record group calculations,
          AC 3.36–37
Calendar, OUT 1.04,
cascade deletes option, AC 3.08,
     AC 3.10
cascade updates option, AC 3.08,
     AC 3.10
cell comments, EX 2.34–35
cell contents, EX 1.06
     aligning, EX 3.11
     clearing, EX 1.29–30

copying using copy-and-paste method, EX 2.13–14
cell ranges, EX 1.18–19
   moving, EX 2.25–26
   nonadjacent, selecting to create charts,
cell references, EX 1.07
   absolute, EX 2.10–12
   mixed, EX 2.12
   relative, EX 2.10, EX 2.12
center alignment, WD 2.22
centering
   column titles within cells, EX 3.11
   text across cells, EX 3.12–13
   worksheet printouts, EX 2.29–30, EX 3.33
CD Player
   locating information about in Help, WIN 98 1.28, WIN 98 1.30
changing. *See* **modifying**
Channel Bar, WIN 98 2.13
characters
   inserting, WIN 98 2.6
check boxes
   in dialog boxes, WIN 98 1.26
Check Full Name dialog box, OUT 1.14–15
checklist for Word screen settings, WD 1.11
check marks
   in menus, WIN 98 1.22–23
Classic style, WIN 98 2.12
   opening disk A in, WIN 98 2.16
clearing. *See also* **deleting; removing**
   cell contents, EX 1.29–30
   formats from cells, EX 3.17
clicking
   defined, WIN 98 1.7
   right-clicking, WIN 98 1.9–10, WIN 98 2.21–22
   selecting with, WIN 98 1.8–9
clip art, PPT 1.11
Clipboard
   moving text, WD 2.13–15
   Office, AC 2.29–30
   Windows, AC 2.29

Close button,
   Access window, AC 1.08
   dialog boxes, AC 1.08
   document, WD 1.06, WD 1.07
   Print Preview window, EX 2.29
   program, WD 1.06, WD 1.07
Close button, WIN 98 1.19
closing. *See also* **exiting**
   forms, AC 1.19
   presentations, PPT 1.12–13
   reports, AC 1.25,
   workbooks, EX 1.33–34
Closing Outlook, OUT 1.29
color(s)
   worksheets, EX 3.22–23
column(s)
   datasheets, changing size, AC 3.23–24
   newspaper. *See* desktop publishing columns
   tables. *See* table columns
   worksheets. *See* worksheet column(s)
column selector, AC 1.12
commands
   selecting from menus, WIN 98 1.21–23
comments
   adding to cells, EX 2.34–35
common fields, AC 1.05, AC 2.03
compacting databases, AC 1.25–26
   automatically, AC 1.26
comparison operators, AC 3.20, AC 3.24–26
composite keys, AC 2.03
CONCATENATE function, EX 2.16
conditions, AC 3.20.
contact(s)
   creating, OUT 1.14–17
Contacts feature, OUT 1.04
Contacts folder, OUT 1.14–17
   creating contacts, OUT 1.14–17
   editing contacts, OUT 1.17
Contents tab
   in Help, WIN 98 1.27–28
Control menu buttons, WD 1.07
copy-and-paste method, EX 2.13–14

Copy Disk command, WIN 98 2.26
copying
   cell contents, using copy-and-paste method, EX 2.13–14
   entire floppy disk, WIN 98 2.25–26
   files, WIN 98 2.22–23
   formats using Format Painter button, EX 3.08
   paragraph formatting, WD 2.24–25
   verifying, WIN 98 2.22–23
copying formulas
   absolute references, EX 2.10–12
   copy-and-paste method, EX 2.13–14
   fill handle, EX 2.08–10
   relative references, EX 2.10, EX 2.12
copying records between databases, AC 2.27–30
   Office Clipboard, AC 2.29–30
Count aggregate function, AC 3.34
COUNT function, EX 2.16
Creat New Folder dialog box, OUT 1.23
creating forms, AC 1.17–18
currency data type, AC 2.05
Currency format, EX 3.05
current record symbol, AC 1.12
customizing, Outlook window, OUT 1.06–07
cut and paste method, WD 2.13–15

D

database(s), AC 1.04–07, AC 2.01–33
   backing up, AC 1.27
   components, AC 1.04
   copying records between, AC 2.27–30
   design guidelines, AC 2.02–04
   opening, AC 1.09–10
   relational, AC 1.05–07
   repairing, AC 1.25
   restoring, AC 1.27
   saving, AC 2.20
database management systems (DBMSs), AC 1.06–07
Database window, AC 1.10
data redundancy, avoiding, AC 2.03

datasheets, AC 1.12
  changing font size and column size, AC 3.23–24
  navigating, AC 1.12–13
  opening, AC 2.25–26
Datasheet view, AC 1.12
data types, assigning to fields, AC 2.04–05
date(s), inserting using AutoComplete tip, WD 1.15
Date button, EX 2.31
Date format, EX 3.05
date format(s), AC 2.12
Date/Time control, WIN 98 1.5
date/time data type, AC 2.05
  defining fields, AC 2.11–13
Date/Time list box, WIN 98 1.24–25
decimal points, EX 3.05–07
  Number format, EX 3.09–10
  Percentage format, EX 3.10
default settings, WIN 98 1.4
  Word screen, WD 1.07
Delete dialog box, EX 3.18
Delete key, WIN 98 2.4
deleting. *See also* **clearing; removing**
  cell contents, EX 1.29–30
  cells from worksheets, EX 3.18
  fields from table structure, AC 2.21–22
  files, WIN 98 2.24
  files from floppy drives, WIN 98 2.24
  folders, WIN 98 2.24
  icons, WIN 98 2.22, WIN 98 2.24
  records. *See* deleting records
  rows and columns in worksheets, EX 2.23–24
  slides, PPT 1.19–21
  text, WD 2.09–10
deleting records
  databases, AC 2.30–31
demoting outline text, PPT 1.23–27
descending order, OUT 1.26
design grid, AC 2.08, AC 3.04
Design view
  creating queries, AC 3.02–04, AC 3.22
  creating tables, AC 2.08
  sorting multiple fields, AC 3.14–17

desktop
  accessing with Quick Launch toolbar, WIN 98 1.14–15
  components, WIN 98 1.5
  customized, WIN 98 1.4–5
  default, WIN 98 1.4
  defined, WIN 98 1.4, WIN 98 1.5
  locating information about in Help, WIN 98 1.28
  returning to, WIN 98 1.14
Desktop Style settings, WIN 98 2.12–14
  Classic style, WIN 98 2.12
  Web style, WIN 98 2.12–14
Details view, WIN 98 2.19–20
dialog box controls, WIN 98 1.25–26
dialog boxes
  defined, WIN 98 1.23
  Close button, AC 1.08
  panes in, WIN 98 1.25
Dial-Up Networking folder, WIN 98 2.15
directories, WIN 98 2.20–21
  copying files into, WIN 98 2.22–23
  moving files between, WIN 98 2.21–22
  root (top-level), WIN 98 2.20
disk drives
  inserting disk into, WIN 98 2.2
disks
  copying entire, WIN 98 2.25–26
  deleting files from, WIN 98 2.24
  formatting, WIN 98 2.2–3
  inserting into disk drive, WIN 98 2.2
distance education, WIN 98 2.1
displaying. *See also* **previewing; previewing documents; viewing; viewing presentations**
  Drawing toolbar, EX 3.25
  formulas, EX 2.35–36
  gridlines in worksheets, EX 3.30–31
  Help system features, AC 1.22
  nonprinting characters, WD 1.10–11
  ruler, WD 1.09
  toolbars, WD 1.08

  worksheet rows and columns, EX 3.34, EX 3.35
displaying. *See* **viewing**
division operator (/), EX 1.16, EX 2.07
.doc extension, WIN 98 2.7
document-centric computing, WIN 98 2.8–9
document Close button, WD 1.06, WD 1.07
document view buttons, WD 1.06, WD 1.07
document window, WD 1.07
documenting workbooks, EX 2.33
documents. *See also* **files**
  defined, WIN 98 2.1
  file and folder icons, WIN 98 2.19
  opening in Documents list, WIN 98 2.8–9
  opening in My Computer window, WIN 98 2.8–9
  opening in Web style, WIN 98 2.14
  opening in WordPad, WIN 98 2.9–10
  previewing, WIN 98 2.10
  printing, WIN 98 2.10–11
  printing selected pages of, WIN 98 2.11
Documents list
  selecting files from, WIN 98 2.8–9
dollar signs ($)
  absolute references, EX 2.12
  Currency format, EX 3.05–07
double spacing, WD 2.20
drag-and-drop method, WD 2.12–13
  moving cell ranges, EX 2.25–26
dragging
  files between directories, WIN 98 2.21–22
  windows, WIN 98 1.20–21
Drawing toolbar, EX 3.24–30, PPT 1.07
  activating, EX 3.24–25
  adding arrows, EX 3.28–29
  adding text boxes, EX 3.25–28
  displaying, EX 3.25
  removing, EX 3.30

drive A
   in My Computer window, WIN 98 2.16–17

drive C
   in My Computer window, WIN 98 2.16

drives
   selecting for saving, WIN 98 2.7–8

E

Edit Relationships dialog box, AC 3.09–10

Edit Signature dialog box, OUT 1.10

editing, WD 1.04. *See also* **modifying entries**
   properties page contents, WD 1.18
   slides, PPT 1.16–17

editing contacts, OUT 1.17

editing mode, AC 2.31–32

ellipsis
   in menus, WIN 98 1.22–23

e-mail, OUT 1.07–13, OUT 1.17–27
   attachments, OUT 1.21–22
   creating messages, OUT 1.11–12
   forwarding messages, OUT 1.19, OUT 1.20
   managing messages. *See* managing e-mail messages
   message formats, OUT 1.07–08
   printing messages, OUT 1.20–21
   reading messages, OUT 1.18–19
   receiving messages, OUT 1.17–18
   replying to messages, OUT 1.19
   sending messages, OUT 1.12–13
   signatures, OUT 1.09–10
   sorting messages. *See* sorting e-mail messages
   stationery, OUT 1.10

e-mail addresses, OUT 1.08

end of file mark, WD 1.06, WD 1.07

entering.
   data in worksheets, EX 2.05–06
   functions, EX 2.17–18
   values, EX 1.16

   worksheet labels, EX 2.04–05
   worksheet titles, EX 2.03–04

entering formulas, EX 1.17–18, EX 2.07–08
   using functions, EX 1.19–20

entering text, WD 1.16–17
   column heading labels, EX 1.14–15

entity integrity, AC 2.15

envelopes, printing, WD 1.28–30

equal sign (=), formulas, EX 2.07

error correction, EX 1.25–26, WD 1.22–24
   AutoCorrect, WD 1.22–24
   Spelling and Grammar checker, WD 2.05–07
   spelling errors, EX 2.20–21
   Style Checker, PPT 1.28–29
   Undo button, EX 2.23–24

error values, EX 2.11

exact matches, AC 3.20–22

Excel,
   description, EX 1.04
   exiting, EX 1.34
   starting, EX 1.04–06

Excel window, EX 1.06–07

exiting. *See also* **closing**
   Outlook, OUT 1.29

exiting programs,
   Access, AC 1.13, AC 2.33
   Excel, EX 1.34
   PowerPoint, PPT 1.13, PPT 1.34
   Word, WD 1.30–31

Explorer windows
   defined, WIN 98 2.23
   navigating, WIN 98 2.23

exponentiation operator (^), EX 1.16, EX 2.07

expression(s), AC 3.30

Expression Builder, AC 3.30–31

extensions, WIN 98 2.7
   hiding, WIN 98 2.20
   renaming files and, WIN 98 2.24

extreme values, EX 2.20

F

field(s), AC 1.04
   adding to table structure, AC 2.23–24
   assigning data types, AC 2.04–05
   assigning sizes, AC 2.05–06
   calculated. *See* calculated fields
   common, AC 1.05, AC 2.03
   contacts, OUT 1.14
   defining, AC 2.08–14
   deleting from table structure, AC 2.21–22
   grouping, AC 2.02
   identifying for database design, AC 2.02
   moving in table structure, AC 2.22–23
   multiple, sorting in Design view, AC 3.14–17
   naming, AC 2.04
   properties, AC 2.24–25
   selecting for queries, AC 3.05

field list, AC 3.04

field properties
   changing, AC 2.24–25
   determining, AC 2.04

field selector, AC 1.12

field values, AC 1.04

file icons, WIN 98 2.19

File menu
   selecting Print Preview menu option from, WIN 98 1.22

filenames
   extensions, WIN 98 2.7, WIN 98 2.20, WIN 98 2.24
   long, WIN 98 2.7
   selecting, WIN 98 2.7

filename(s), WD 1.17
   renaming documents, WD 2.05
   renaming worksheets, EX 2.14
   saving workbooks, EX 1.21–23, EX 3.03

Filename button, EX 2.31

filename extensions, OUT 1.24–25

files. *See also* **documents**
   backup copies of, WIN 98 2.26
   copying, WIN 98 2.22–23

defined, WIN 98 2.1
deleting, WIN 98 2.24
details view, WIN 98 2.19–20
editing name of, WIN 98 2.24
large icon view, WIN 98 2.19–20
moving, WIN 98 2.21–22
naming, WIN 98 2.7
opening, WIN 98 2.8–10
opening in Web style, WIN 98 2.14
opening in WordPad, WIN 98 2.9–10
printing, WIN 98 2.10–11
renaming, WIN 98 2.24
saving, WIN 98 2.7–8
selecting files from Documents list, WIN 98 2.8–9
selecting from My Computer Window, WIN 98 2.8–9

filing e-mail messages, OUT 1.24

fill handle, copying formulas, EX 2.08–10

filter(s), OUT 2.22–23

Filter By Form, AC 3.17

Filter By Selection, AC 3.17, AC 3.18–19

filtering views, OUT 1.27

filtering data, AC 3.17–19

Find and Replace dialog box, WD 2.17

finding e-mail messages, OUT 1.25

finding
text, WD 2.15–18

F2 key, AC 2.31

floating toolbars, EX 3.24

floppy disks. *See* **disks**

folder banner, Outlook window, OUT 1.06

folder list, Outlook window, OUT 1.06

folder icons, WIN 98 2.19

Folder Options dialog box, WIN 98 2.12–13

folder(s), OUT 1.04
creating, OUT 1.23

folders, WIN 98 2.20–21
creating, WIN 98 2.21
defined, WIN 98 2.21
deleting, WIN 98 2.24

font(s)
changing, WD 2.27–28
setting, WD 1.09–10
worksheets, EX 3.14, EX 3.15–16

Font button, EX 2.31

font size
changing, WD 2.27–29
datasheets, changing, AC 3.23
setting, WD 1.09–10
worksheets, EX 3.15–16

Font Size list box, WIN 98 1.25

font styles
changing, WD 2.29–31
worksheets, EX 3.14–15, EX 3.16

footers, forms. *See* **Form Headers and Form Footers**

footers, PPT 1.09
worksheets, EX 2.30–32, EX 3.33

foreign keys, AC 1.06

form(s), AC 1.17–19
closing, AC 1.19
printing, AC 1.19
saving, AC 1.19

format(s)
e-mail messages, OUT 1.08–09

format(s), WD 1.10
dates, AC 2.12
paragraphs, copying, WD 2.24–25

Format Cells dialog box, EX 3.20, EX 3.22–23

Format dialog box, WIN 98 2.3

Format Painter, WD 2.24–25

Format Painter button, EX 3.08

Format Results dialog box, WIN 98 2.3

formatting, WD 1.04
charts. *See* formatting charts
defined, WIN 98 2.2
disks, WIN 98 2.2–3
Full option, WIN 98 2.3
numbers, EX 3.05–10

presentations. *See* formatting presentations
tables. *See* formatting tables
text. *See* formatting text
worksheets. *See* formatting worksheets

Formatting toolbar, EX 1.06, EX 3.04, WD 1.06, WD 1.07
aligning text, WD 2.22–23

formatting worksheets, EX 3.04–19
aligning cell contents, EX 3.11
AutoFormat feature, EX 2.26–27
centering text across cells, EX 3.12–13
clearing formats from cells, EX 3.17
copying formats using Format Painter button, EX 3.08
deleting cells, EX 3.18
fonts, font styles, and font sizes, EX 3.14–26
headers and footers, EX 2.30–32
indenting text in cells, EX 3.13
number formats, EX 3.05–10
number symbol replacement, EX 3.08–09
Percentage format, EX 3.10
styles, EX 3.17
wrapping text in cells, EX 3.11–12

formula(s), EX 1.16–18
arithmetic operators, EX 1.16
copying. *See* copying formulas
displaying, EX 2.35–36
entering. *See* entering formulas
pointing method for building, EX 2.19–20
recalculating, EX 1.23–25

formula bar, EX 1.06

Form Wizard(s), AC 1.17
creating forms, AC 1.17–18

Forward button
on Standard toolbar, WIN 98 2.23

Forward feature, OUT 1.19

forwarding e-mail, OUT 1.19, OUT 1.20

functions, EX 1.18–20, EX 2.15–20
aggregate, AC 3.34–36
arguments, EX 2.16
entering, EX 2.17–18
entering formulas using, EX 1.19–20
syntax, EX 2.15

FV function, EX 2.16

G

General format, EX 3.04, EX 3.05
General tab, Options dialog box, AC 1.26
gradient fills, PPT 1.09
grammatical errors, correcting, WD 2.05–07
graphical user interface (GUI), WIN 98 1.3
graphic image documents
   file and folder icons, WIN 98 2.19
grayed-out options
   in menus, WIN 98 1.22–23
grayscale, previewing presentations, PPT 1.32–34
   display in worksheets, EX 3.30–31
groups, Outlook window, OUT 1.06
Group bar, AC 1.10
Group By operator, AC 3.36–37
GUI, WIN 98 1.3

H

hanging indents, WD 2.23
hard drive
   deleting files from, WIN 98 2.24
hardware
   My Computer window and, WIN 98 2.15–16
headers,
   Notes Pages, PPT 1.31
   worksheets, EX 2.30–32, EX 3.33
Help, WIN 98 1.27–30
   Contents tab, WIN 98 1.27–28
   defined, WIN 98 1.27
   Index tab, WIN 98 1.27, WIN 98 1.28–29
   returning to previous topic, WIN 98 1.30

   Search tab, WIN 98 1.27, WIN 98 1.30
   selecting topics from index, WIN 98 1.28–30
   starting, WIN 98 1.27
   viewing topics from Contents tab, WIN 98 1.27–28
Help button, Print Preview window, EX 2.29
Help pointer, WD 1.28
Help system, AC 1.19–22, EX 1.26–29, OUT 1.27–29 PPT 1.30, WD 1.28–30
   displaying features, AC 1.22
   Office Assistant, AC 1.19–20, EX 1.26–29, PPT 1.30, WD 1.06, WD 1.16–17, WD 1.28–30
   What's This? command, AC 1.19
Help window, OUT 1.28–29
hiding
   file extensions, WIN 98 2.20
   gridlines in worksheets, EX 3.30–31
   worksheet rows and columns, EX 3.34–35
hiding toolbars, WD 1.08
highlighting, WIN 98 1.8
horizontal ruler, WD 1.06, WD 1.07
hovering, WIN 98 2.13–14
hyperlink data type, AC 2.05
Hypertext Markup Language (HTML), *See also* **HTML** *entries*
HTML, e-mail messages, OUT 1.08–09

I

I-beam pointer, WIN 98 2.4–5
icons
   changing display of, WIN 98 2.19–20
   defined, WIN 98 1.5
   deleting, WIN 98 2.22, WIN 98 2.24
   moving, WIN 98 2.22
   selecting in Web style, WIN 98 2.13–14
IF function, EX 2.16

importance weights, EX 1.13
   changing, EX 1.25
inactive programs, WIN 98 1.14
Increase Indent button, WD 2.23–24
indenting
   paragraphs, WD 2.23–24
   text in cells, EX 3.13
Index tab
   in Help, WIN 98 1.27, WIN 98 1.28–29
INDIRECT function, EX 2.16
Information Viewer, Outlook window, OUT 1.06
inserting. *See also* **entering; entering formulas; entering text**
   cell comments, EX 2.34–35
   dates using AutoComplete tip, WD 1.15
   headers and footers in worksheets, EX 2.31–32
   headers in Word documents, WD 2.10–12
   page breaks in tables, WD 2.15
   rows in tables, WD 2.21, WD 2.22
   rows in worksheets, EX 2.22–24
   section breaks, WD 2.06–07
insertion point, WD 1.06, WD 1.07
   defined, WIN 98 2.4
   I-beam pointer *vs.*, WIN 98 2.4–5
   moving, WIN 98 2.5
   moving around documents, WD 2.07–08
insert mode, WIN 98 2.6
Internet, WIN 98 1.3, WIN 98 2.1
italicizing text, WD 2.30–31
items, OUT 1.04

J

joins, AC 3.06–07
justified alignment, WD 2.22
Journal, OUT 1.04

K

key(s)
  foreign, AC 1.06
  primary. *See* primary keys
  primary sort keys, AC 3.14
  secondary sort keys, AC 3.14
keyboard, navigating in worksheets, EX 1.07–08
keyboard shortcuts
  in menus, WIN 98 1.22–23

L

labels
  worksheets, EX 2.03–05
landscape orientation, EX 3.32–33
Large Icons view, WIN 98 2.19–20
layout
  presentations, PPT 1.27–28
  workbooks, EX 1.12
  worksheets, EX 2.21–28
left alignment, WD 2.22
LEFT function, EX 2.16
line(s), selecting, WD 2.09
line spacing, WD 2.20–21
list arrows, WIN 98 1.25
list boxes, WIN 98 1.24–25
lists
  bulleted, PPT 1.10, WD 2.25–26
  numbered, PPT 1.10, WD 2.26–27
logical operators, AC 3.26–30
Log Off option, WIN 98 1.15
long filenames, WIN 98 2.7
Lookup Wizard data type, AC 2.05

M

Mail feature, OUT 1.04
mail merges. *See* merging Access data with Word documentsMail
managing e-mail messages, OUT 1.23–27
  archiving messages, OUT 1.24–25
  creating folders, OUT 1.23
  filing messages, OUT 1.24
  filtering views, OUT 1.27
  finding messages, OUT 1.25
  sorting messages, OUT 1.26–27
margins, setting, WD 2.18–20
Margins button, Print Preview window, EX 2.29
Max aggregate function, AC 3.34
MAX function, EX 2.19
Maximize button,
  Table window, AC 2.08,
  WIN 98 1.19–20
mean, arithmetic, calculating, EX 2.16–18
memo data type, AC 2.05
menu bar, Outlook window, OUT 1.06
menu bar, WIN 98 1.17, WIN 98 1.18
menu bars, WD 1.06, WD 1.07
  Database window, AC 1.10
  PowerPoint window, PPT 1.07–08
  Table window, AC 2.08
menus, WIN 98 1.21–23
  conventions, WIN 98 1.22–23
  defined, WIN 98 1.7
  selecting commands from, WIN 98 1.21–23
  selecting options on, WIN 98 1.8–9
merge(s). *See* merging Access data with Word documents
Min aggregate function, AC 3.34
MIN function, EX 2.19
Minimize button, WIN 98 1.18–19
mixed references, EX 2.12
modifying presentations, PPT 1.19–28
  adding slides, PPT 1.27–28
  deleting slides, PPT 1.19–21
  layout, PPT 1.27–28
  moving slides and text in Outline Pane, PPT 1.21–22
  promoting and demoting outline text, PPT 1.23–27
modifying table structure, AC 2.21–27
  adding fields, AC 2.23–24
  adding records, AC 2.26–27
  changing field properties, AC 2.24–25
  deleting fields, AC 2.21–22
  moving fields, AC 2.22–23
  saving modified structure, AC 2.25
mouse. *See also* pointing devices
  clicking with, WIN 98 1.7
  defined, WIN 98 1.5
  dragging windows with, WIN 98 1.20–21
  moving cell ranges, EX 2.25–26
  moving files with right mouse button, WIN 98 2.21–22
  navigating in worksheets, EX 1.07–09
  pointing with, WIN 98 1.6–7
  right-clicking, WIN 98 1.9–10, WIN 98 2.21–22
  selecting objects with, WIN 98 1.8–9
  using, WIN 98 1.5–10
  wheels on, WIN 98 1.6
mouse pad, WIN 98 1.6
mouse pointer (I-beam), EX 1.06, EX 1.07, WD 1.06, WD 1.07
moving. *See also* navigating
  arrows in worksheets, EX 3.29–30
  bulleted items, PPT 1.22
  cell ranges, EX 2.25–26
  e-mail messages, OUT 1.24
  fields in table structure, AC 2.22–23
  files, WIN 98 2.21–22
  insertion point, WD 2.07–08
  slides in Outline Pane, PPT 1.21–22
  toolbars, WD 1.09
  windows, WIN 98 1.20–21
moving text
  within documents, WD 2.12–15
  Outline Pane, PPT 1.21–22
multiple programs
  running, WIN 98 1.12–13
  switching between, WIN 98 1.13–14
multiplication operator (*), EX 1.16, EX 2.07

multitasking, WIN 98 1.12
My Computer icon, WIN 98 2.15
   selecting in Web style, WIN 98 2.13–14
My Computer window, WIN 98 2.15–20
   changing icon display in, WIN 98 2.19–20
   changing toolbar display options in, WIN 98 2.17–18
   computer hardware and, WIN 98 2.15–16
   contents, WIN 98 2.15–16
   defined, WIN 98 2.2
   hiding file extensions in, WIN 98 2.20
   selecting files from, WIN 98 2.8–9
   viewing in Web view, WIN 98 2.18–19
   view options, WIN 98 2.17–20
   Windows 98 Format command, WIN 98 2.2–3

N

name(s)
   filename extensions, OUT 1.24–25
name box, EX 1.06
naming
   editing file names, WIN 98 2.24
   files, WIN 98 2.7
   renaming files, WIN 98 2.24
naming documents, WD 2.05
naming fields and objects, AC 2.04
navigating
   datasheets, AC 1.12–13
   between Outlook components, OUT 1.07
   between worksheets, EX 1.12
   within worksheets, EX 1.07–09
navigation
   of Explorer windows, WIN 98 2.23
navigation buttons, AC 1.12
navigation mode, AC 2.31–32
navigational buttons, WIN 98 2.23

new documents, WD 1.13–14
New Form dialog box, AC 1.18
New Query dialog box, AC 3.03
New Table dialog box, AC 2.07
Next button, Print Preview window, EX 2.29
nonprinting characters, displaying, WD 1.10–11
nonunique sort fields, AC 3.14–17
normal view, WD 1.08
   panes, PPT 1.08
Normal View button, WD 1.06
notes, PPT 1.29, PPT 1.31
Notes Feature, OUT 1.04
Notes Pages, PPT 1.31
Notes Pane, PPT 1.07, PPT 1.08
null value, AC 2.15
number(s)
   entering in worksheets, EX 1.16, EX 2.05–06
   formatting, EX 3.05–10
   argest, finding, EX 2.19
   smallest, finding, EX 2.19
   too long to fit in cells, EX 3.08–09
number data type, AC 2.05
numbered lists, PPT 1.10, WD 2.26–27
Number format, EX 3.05, EX 3.09–10
number sign (#)
   numbers too wide for cells, EX 3.08–09

O

object(s),
   naming, AC 2.04
object animation, PPT 1.10
objects
   right-clicking, WIN 98 1.10
   selecting, WIN 98 1.8–9
Objects bar, AC 1.10
Office Assistant, AC 1.19–20, EX 1.26–29, OUT 1.27–29, PPT 1.30, WD 1.06, WD 1.16–17, WD 1.28–30
Office Clipboard, AC 2.29–30

OLE object data type, AC 2.05
1.5 line spacing, WD 2.20
one-to-many relationships, AC 3.07–11
   defining, AC 3.08–11
Open dialog box, WD 2.03–04
opening
   datasheets, AC 2.25–26
   documents. *See* opening documents
   existing databases, AC 1.09–10
   existing presentations, PPT 1.06–07
   Query window, AC 3.02–03
   tables, AC 1.11–12
   workbooks, EX 1.10–11, EX 3.02–03
opening documents,
   existing documents, WD 2.02–04
operating systems, WIN 98 1.3
option buttons
   in dialog boxes, WIN 98 1.26
options
   selecting from menus, WIN 98 1.21–23
Options dialog box, General tab, AC 1.26
Options dialog box, OUT 1.09
order of precedence for arithmetic operations, EX 2.07–08
organizing documents, WD 1.04
Or logical operator, AC 3.26, AC 3.28–30
orphaned records, AC 3.07
Outbox, OUT 1.12–13
Outline Pane
   moving slides and text, PPT 1.21–22
   PowerPoint window, PPT 1.07, PPT 1.08
outline text, promoting and demoting, PPT 1.23–27
outline view, WD 1.07
Outlook 2000
   components, OUT 1.04
   exiting, OUT 1.29
   navigating between components, OUT 1.07
   starting, OUT 1.04–07
Outlook Bar, OUT 1.06

Outlook Rich Text, e-mail messages, OUT 1.08

Outlook window, OUT 1.05–07
customizing, OUT 1.06–07

P

Page Break Preview button, Print Preview window, EX 2.29

page numbers, adding to reports, EX 2.31

Page Setup dialog box, EX 2.29–30

Page Setup settings, saving, EX 2.32, EX 3.34

Paint
closing, WIN 98 1.15
mouse pointer in, WIN 98 1.13
running at same time as WordPad, WIN 98 1.12–13

panes, WIN 98 1.25

paper orientation, EX 3.32–33

paragraph(s), WD 2.22
copying formatting, WD 2.24–25
indenting, WD 2.23–24
selecting, WD 2.09

paragraph mark, WD 1.10, WD 2.22

passwords, e-mail, OUT 1.08

Paste Function button, entering functions, EX 2.17–18

pasting, WD 2.13–15. *See also* copy-and-paste method
records into tables, AC 2.28–29

Patterns tab, Format Cells dialog box, EX 3.22–23

Percentage format, EX 3.05, EX 3.10

personal folder files, OUT 1.24–25

placeholders, PPT 1.16

Plain text, e-mail messages, OUT 1.08

planning
presentations, PPT 1.13
worksheets, EX 2.02–03

PMT function, EX 2.16

pointer, EX 1.06, EX 1.07

pointers
defined, WIN 98 1.5, WIN 98 1.17, WIN 98 1.18
I-beam, WIN 98 2.4–5
in Paint, WIN 98 1.13

pointing, WIN 98 1.6–7
selecting with, WIN 98 1.8–9

pointing devices. *See also* mouse
defined, WIN 98 1.5
types of, WIN 98 1.6
using, WIN 98 1.5–10

pointing method for building formulas, EX 2.19–20

portrait orientation, EX 3.32–33

pound sign (#)
numbers too wide for cells, EX 3.08–09

PowerPoint
checking for consistency and style, PPT 1.28–29
closing, PPT 1.12–13
creating using AutoContent Wizard, PPT 1.13–17
description, PPT 1.04
existing, opening, PPT 1.06–07
exiting, PPT 1.13, PPT 1.34
formatting. *See* formatting presentations
notes, PPT 1.29, PPT 1.31
planning, PPT 1.13, PPT 2.02
previewing, PPT 1.31–34
printing, PPT 1.34, PPT 2.25
publishing to Web, PPT 1.34
saving, PPT 1.18
selecting type, PPT 1.15
starting, PPT 1.04–06

PowerPoint window, PPT 1.07

practice folder
creating, WIN 98 2.21

previewing
presentations, PPT 1.31–34
worksheets, EX 2.28–29, EX 3.31–32

preview pane, Outlook window, OUT 1.06

previewing documents, WD 1.26–27, WD 2.31

Previous button, Print Preview window, EX 2.29

primary keys, AC 3.14
determining, AC 2.02–03
specifying, AC 2.14–16

primary sort keys, AC 3.14

primary table, AC 3.07

Print button
Print Preview window, EX 2.29

Print command, EX 1.31, EX 1.32–33

Print dialog box, OUT 1.20, WIN 98 2.10–11

print layout view, WD 1.07–08

Print Preview button, WIN 98 1.24, WIN 98 2.10

Print Preview command, EX 1.31

Print Preview menu option
selecting, WIN 98 1.22

Print Preview window, WD 1.26
buttons, EX 2.29
previewing worksheets, EX 2.28–29, EX 3.31–32

printing, WD 1.04
documents, WD 1.27–28, WD 2.31
e-mail messages, OUT 1.20–21
envelopes, WD 1.28–30
files, WIN 98 2.10–11
forms, AC 1.19
presentations, PPT 1.34
query results, AC 1.17
reports, AC 1.25
selected pages of documents, WIN 98 2.11
table data, AC 2.33
tables, AC 1.13, AC 2.20

printing worksheets, EX 1.31–33, EX 2.32–33, EX 3.31–35
centering printouts, EX 2.29–30
displaying formulas, EX 2.36
headers and footers, EX 2.30–32, EX 3.33
hiding and unhiding rows and columns, EX 3.34–35
paper orientation, EX 3.32–33
saving Page Setup settings, EX 3.34
setting print area, EX 2.33

program button, WIN 98 1.12
defined, WIN 98 1.17, WIN 98 1.18

program Close button, WD 1.06, WD 1.07
program icons, WIN 98 2.19
program menus, WIN 98 1.21–23
programs
    active, WIN 98 1.13
    closing, WIN 98 1.12
    closing inactive programs from taskbar, WIN 98 1.14–15
    file and folder icons, WIN 98 2.19
    inactive, WIN 98 1.14
    multiple, running, WIN 98 1.12–13
    running, WIN 98 1.12
    starting, WIN 98 1.11–12
    switching between, WIN 98 1.13–14
promoting outline text, PPT 1.23–27
proofreading documents, WD 2.07
properties
    adding to documents, WD 1.19–20
    fields. *See* field properties
properties page, WD 1.19–20
    editing contents, WD 1.20
    viewing, WD 1.19–20
Property dialog box, EX 2.33
.pst filename extension, OUT 1.24–25

Q

queries, AC 1.14–17, AC 3.01–37
    calculated fields. *See* calculated fields
    creating, AC 1.14–16, AC 3.02–05, AC 3.11, AC 3.20–22, AC 3.25–26
    filtering data, AC 3.17–19
    printing results, AC 1.17
    record selection criteria. *See* record selection criteria
    running, AC 3.04, AC 3.05–06, AC 3.11–12, AC 3.22
    saving, AC 3.12
    select, AC 3.02
    sorting results, AC 1.16–17
    table relationships. *See* table relationships
    technical, AC 3.02
query by example (QBE), AC 3.02
Query Design toolbar, AC 3.04
Query Type button, AC 3.04
Query window, AC 3.02–04
    opening, AC 3.02–03
Query Wizards, AC 1.14–16, AC 1.15–16, AC 3.02, AC 3.20–22
    starting, AC 1.14–15
Quick Launch toolbar, WIN 98 1.14–15

R

ragged alignment, WD 2.22
RAND function, EX 2.16
reading e-mail messages, OUT 1.18–19
recalculation, what-if analysis, EX 1.23–25
receiving e-mail messages, OUT 1.17–18
records, AC 1.04
    adding to tables, AC 2.17–20, AC 2.26–27
    calculations for groups of records, AC 3.36–37
    modifying, AC 2.31–33
    orphaned, AC 3.07
record selection criteria, AC 3.20–30
    comparison operators, AC 3.20, AC 3.24–26
    entering, AC 3.22
    exact matches, AC 3.20–22
    multiple, AC 3.26–30
record selector, AC 1.12
Recycle Bin, WIN 98 2.24
redisplaying windows, WIN 98 1.20
Redo button, WD 2.10–11
referential integrity, AC 3.08
related table, AC 3.07
relational database(s), AC 1.05–07
relational database management systems, AC 1.06–07
Relationships window, AC 3.08
relative references, copying formulas, EX 2.10, EX 2.12
removing. *See also* clearing; deleting
    display of gridlines in worksheets, EX 3.30–31
    toolbars, EX 3.24, EX 3.30
Rename option, WIN 98 2.24
renaming files, WIN 98 2.24
repairing databases, AC 1.25
replacing text, WD 2.15–18
Reply feature, OUT 1.19
reports, AC 1.23–25
    closing, AC 1.25
    creating, AC 1.23–24
    printing, AC 1.25
    selected pages of documents, WIN 98 2.11
responding
    to e-mail messages, OUT 1.19
Restore button, WIN 98 1.19–20
restoring
    databases, AC 1.27
right alignment, WD 2.22
right-clicking, WIN 98 1.9–10
    accessing shortcut menus with, WIN 98 1.9–10
    moving files with, WIN 98 2.21–22
right indents, WD 2.23
root directory, WIN 98 2.20
ROUND function, EX 2.16
rounding, Accounting format, EX 3.07
row headings, EX 1.06
row selector, AC 1.12
ruler, displaying, WD 1.09
running programs, WIN 98 1.12
running queries, AC 3.04, AC 3.05–06, AC 3.11–12, AC 3.22

S

Save As command, EX 1.21–23, EX 2.14–15, PPT 1.18
Save As dialog box, WD 1.18 WIN 98 2.7–8
Save button, WIN 98 2.7

Save command, EX 1.21, EX 1.22, PPT 1.18
saving
   databases, AC 2.20
   e-mail attachments, OUT 1.22
   files, WIN 98 2.7–8
   forms, AC 1.19
   Page Setup settings, EX 2.32, EX 3.34
   presentations, PPT 1.18
   queries, AC 3.12
   selecting drive for, WIN 98 2.7–8
   table structures, AC 2.16–17, AC 2.25
saving Word documents, WD 1.25–26, WD 2.31
   first time, WD 1.17–18
   new name, WD 2.05
saving workbooks, EX 1.21–23, EX 2.14–15
   new name, EX 1.21–23
Scheduled Tasks folder, WIN 98 2.15
ScreenTips, PPT 1.08, WD 1.07
ScreenTips, OUT 1.27
scroll bars, WD 1.06, WD 1.07, WD 1.25 WIN 98 1.24–25
scroll box, WD 1.06, WD 1.07
scrolling
   documents, WD 1.21–22, WD 1.25
   worksheets, EX 1.20–21
Search tab
   in Help, WIN 98 1.27, WIN 98 1.30
secondary sort keys, AC 3.14
"select, then do" feature, WD 2.09
Select Browse Object button, WD 1.06, WD 1.07
selecting
   by pointing and clicking, WIN 98 1.8–9
   fields for queries, AC 3.05
   record selection criteria. *See* record selection criteria
   slides, PPT 1.20
   text, WD 2.09
   text, WIN 98 2.5–6
selection bar, WD 2.09
select queries, AC 3.02

Select Query window, AC 3.03–04
sending e-mail, OUT 1.12–13
sentences, selecting, WD 2.09
Setup button, Print Preview window, EX 2.29
shadow, adding to text boxes, EX 3.27–28
Sheet name button, EX 2.31
sheet tabs, EX 1.07
sheet tab scroll buttons, EX 1.06, EX 1.07, EX 1.10
shortcut menus
   opening, WIN 98 1.9–10
Show Desktop button, WIN 98 1.14
Show Table dialog box, AC 3.09
Shut Down option, WIN 98 1.15–16
signatures, e-mail messages, OUT 1.09–10
Simple format, EX 2.26–27
Simple Query dialog box, AC 1.15
Simple Query Wizard dialog box, AC 3.21
single spacing, WD 2.20
size, AutoNumber fields, AC 2.05–06
sizing
   text boxes, EX 3.27
   windows, WIN 98 1.21
sizing buttons, WIN 98 1.17
sizing handles, WIN 98 1.21
slide(s)
   adding to presentations, PPT 1.27–28
   AutoLayout, PPT 1.27–28
   deleting from presentations, PPT 1.19–21
   editing, PPT 1.16–17
   moving in Outline Pane, PPT 1.21–22
   selecting, PPT 1.20
slide navigator, PPT 1.09
Slide Pane, PPT 1.07, PPT 1.08
Slide Pane scroll bar, PPT 1.07
Slide Show button, PPT 1.07
Slide Show View, viewing presentations, PPT 1.08–12
slide sorter view, PPT 1.33–34

Slide Sorter View button, PPT 1.07
slide titles, PPT 1.10
slide transitions, PPT 1.09–10
Sort Ascending button, AC 3.13–14
Sort Descending button, AC 3.14
sorting e-mail messages, OUT 1.26–27
sorting query results, AC 1.16–17, AC 3.12–17
   toolbar buttons, AC 3.13–14
   unique and nonunique sort keys, AC 3.14–17
sort keys, AC 3.14
spacing lines, WD 2.20–21
Specific Record box, AC 1.12
spell checking presentations,
spell checking worksheets, EX 2.20–21
Spelling and Grammar checker, WD 2.05–07
Spelling and Grammar dialog box, WD 2.06
spelling errors, correcting, WD 1.22–24, WD 2.05–07
spin boxes
   in dialog boxes, WIN 98 1.26
spreadsheets, EX 1.04. *See also* worksheet(s)
Standard toolbar
   display options, WIN 98 2.17–18
   navigation buttons on, WIN 98 2.23
Standard toolbar, EX 1.06, PPT 1.07, WD 1.06, WD 1.07
Standard tuberculosis, Outlook window, OUT 1.06
Start button, WD 1.06, WD 1.07
Start menu
   defined, WIN 98 1.7
   opening, WIN 98 1.7
starting
   Access, AC 1.07–08
   Excel, EX 1.04–06
   Outlook, OUT 1.04–07
   PowerPoint, PPT 1.04–06
   Query Wizard, AC 1.14–15
   Word, WD 1.05–06

stationery, e-mail, OUT 1.10

stationery templates, OUT 1.10

status bar Outlook window,
OUT 1.06 AC 1.08, EX 1.06,
PPT 1.07, WD 1.06, WD 1.07
WIN 98 1.17, WIN 98 1.18

STDEV function, EX 2.16

Student Disk
   adding practice files to, WIN 98 2.15
   copying, WIN 98 2.25–26
   creating, WIN 98 2.15
   exploring contents of,
     WIN 98 2.16–17

Style Checker, PPT 1.28–29

styles, EX 3.17

subfolders, WIN 98 2.21

submenus
   selecting options on, WIN 98 1.8–9

subtraction operator (-), EX 1.16,
EX 2.07

Sum aggregate function, AC 3.34

SUM function, EX 2.06–07, EX 2.16

switching views, OUT 1.26–27

syntax, functions, EX 2.15

T

tabs
   in dialog boxes, WIN 98 1.26

table(s), AC 1.04, AC 2.06–20
   adding records, AC 2.17–20,
     AC 2.26–27
   copying records from, AC 2.27–28
   creating, AC 2.07–08
   defining fields, AC 2.08–14
   opening, AC 1.11–12
   pasting records into, AC 2.28–29
   primary, AC 3.07
   printing, AC 1.13, AC 2.20
   printing data, AC 2.33
   related, AC 3.07
   specifying primary key, AC 2.14–16

Table Design toolbar, AC 2.08

table relationships, AC 3.06–12
   joins, AC 3.06–07
   one-to-many, AC 3.07–11

   referential integrity, AC 3.08
   between two tables, defining,
     AC 3.08–11

table structure
   saving, AC 2.16–17

Table window, AC 2.08

taskbar, WD 1.06, WD 1.07
   closing inactive programs from,
     WIN 98 1.14–15
   location information about in Help,
     WIN 98 1.29

Tasks feature, OUT 1.04

technical queries, AC 3.02

templates, stationery, OUT 1.10

testing worksheets, EX 2.20

test values, EX 2.20

text, EX 1.14–15. *See also* **Word**
documents
   aligning, WD 2.22–23
   bolding, WD 2.29–30
   centering across cells, EX 3.12–13
   deleting, WD 2.09–10
   editing and replacing in slides,
     PPT 1.17
   entering in column heading labels,
     EX 1.14–15
   finding and replacing, WD 2.15–18
   highlighting, WIN 98 2.6
   indenting in cells, EX 3.13
   italicizing, WD 2.30–31
   outline, promoting and demoting,
     PPT 1.23–27
   selecting, WIN 98 2.5–6 WD 2.09
   typing in, WIN 98 2.4
   underlining, WD 2.30
   working with, WIN 98 2.4–6

text blocks, selecting, WD 2.09

text box(es)
   in dialog boxes, WIN 98 1.26

text boxes, EX 3.24, PPT 1.23
   adding shadow, EX 3.27–28
   adding using Drawing toolbar,
     EX 3.25–28
   sizing, EX 3.27

text data type, AC 2.05
   defining fields, AC 2.09–11,
     AC 2.13–14

text documents
   file and folder icons, WIN 98 2.19

Text Labels option,
WIN 98 2.17–18

Time button, EX 2.31

title(s)
   worksheets, entering, EX 2.03–04

title bar, EX 1.06, WD 1.06, WD 1.07
WIN 98 1.17
   Database window, AC 1.10

toolbar buttons
   defined, WIN 98 1.8
   determining function of,
     WIN 98 1.23
   selecting, WIN 98 1.24

toolbars, EX 1.06, PPT 1.07,
PPT 1.08. *See also* **specific**
toolbars
   Access window, AC 1.08
   activating, EX 3.24–25
   anchoring, EX 3.24
   database window, AC 1.10
   defined, WIN 98 1.14, WIN 98 1.17,
     WIN 98 1.18
   displaying and hiding, WD 1.08
   display options, WIN 98 2.17–18
   floating, EX 3.24
   moving, WD 1.09
   personal. *See* personal toolbars
   removing, EX 3.24, EX 3.30
   using, WIN 98 1.23–24

Toolbars submenu,
WIN 98 2.17–18

ToolTips, WIN 98 1.23
   defined, WIN 98 1.6
   viewing, WIN 98 1.7

top-level directory
   defined, WIN 98 2.20

total(s), calculation using AutoSum
button, EX 2.06–07

Total pages button, EX 2.31

trackballs, WIN 98 1.6

triangular arrows
   in menus, WIN 98 1.22–23

Tri-Pane View, PPT 1.08

U

underlining
   text, WD 2.30
   worksheet column titles, EX 3.20
Undo button, EX 2.23–24, WD 2.10–11
unique sort fields, AC 3.14–17
Up button
   on Standard toolbar, WIN 98 2.23
updating databases, AC 2.30–33
   changing records, AC 2.31–33
   deleting records, AC 2.30–31
user IDs (user names), OUT 1.08

V

values, EX 1.15–16. *See also* **number(s)**
   error, EX 2.11
   extreme, EX 2.20
   field, AC 1.04
   matching range using comparison operator, AC 3.20, AC 3.24–26
   null, AC 2.15
   test, EX 2.20
verification
   of copying, WIN 98 2.22–23
view(s)
   Contacts folder, OUT 1.16–17
   filtering, OUT 1.27
   switching, OUT 1.26–27
View toolbar, PPT 1.07
view pane, Outlook window, OUT 1.06
view(s), setting, WD 1.07–08
viewing
   e-mail attachments, OUT 1.22
viewing. *See also* **displaying; previewing**
   e-mail attachments, OUT 1.22
viewing. *See also* **displaying; previewing; previewing documents**
   properties page, WD 1.19–20
   Word screen, WD 1.06–07

viewing presentations
   Slide Show View, PPT 1.08–12
VLOOKUP function, EX 2.16

W

Web
   publishing presentations, PPT 1.34
Web, WIN 98 2.1
Web layout view, WD 1.07 7.27–29
Web style, WIN 98 2.12–14
   defined, WIN 98 2.12
   opening files in, WIN 98 2.14
   selecting icon in, WIN 98 2.13–14
   switching to, WIN 98 2.12–13
Web view, WIN 98 2.3, WIN 98 2.17
   defined, WIN 98 2.18
   disabling, WIN 98 2.18–19
what-if analysis, EX 1.23–25
What's This? command, AC 1.19, PPT 1.30, WD 1.28
What's This? command, OUT 1.27
wheels
   on mouse, WIN 98 1.6
window controls, WIN 98 1.17–18
window titles, WIN 98 1.17
windows
   changing size of, WIN 98 1.21
   defined, WIN 98 1.17
   dragging to new location, WIN 98 1.20–21
   location information about in Help, WIN 98 1.29
   manipulating, WIN 98 1.18–21
   maximizing, WIN 98 1.19–20
   minimizing, WIN 98 1.18–19
   moving, WIN 98 1.20–21
   redisplaying, WIN 98 1.20
   restoring, WIN 98 1.19–20
Windows 98
   defined, WIN 98 1.3

shutting down, WIN 98 1.15–16
   starting, WIN 98 1.4
Windows 98 applications, WIN 98 2.1
Windows 98 Format command, WIN 98 2.2–3
Windows 98 Help. *See* **Help**
Windows Clipboard, AC 2.29
wizards, PPT 1.13. *See also specific types of wizards*
   exiting, WD 1.30–31
   integrating with Excel. *See* integrating
   starting, WD 1.05–06
word(s), selecting, WD 2.09
Word documents
   adding properties, WD 1.19–20
   converting to HTML. *See* converting documents to HTML
   moving insertion point around, WD 2.07–08
   moving text, WD 2.12–15
   opening. *See* opening documents
   previewing, WD 1.26–27, WD 2.31
   printing, WD 1.27–28, WD 2.31
   proofreading, WD 2.07
   renaming, WD 2.05
   saving. *See* saving Word documents
   scrolling, WD 1.21–22, WD 1.25
   selecting, WD 2.09
WordPad
   changing window size, WIN 98 1.21
   closing, WIN 98 1.15, WIN 98 1.19
   Date/Time list box, WIN 98 1.24–25
   exiting, WIN 98 1.12
   Font Size list box, WIN 98 1.25
   maximizing windows, WIN 98 1.19–20
   minimizing windows, WIN 98 1.18–19
   moving windows, WIN 98 1.20–21
   opening documents, WIN 98 2.9–10
   redisplaying windows, WIN 98 1.20
   restoring windows, WIN 98 1.19–20

running at same time as Paint, WIN 98 1.12–13
selecting Print Preview option from File menu, WIN 98 1.22
starting, WIN 98 1.11–12
typing text in, WIN 98 2.4

word-processed documents
file and folder icons, WIN 98 2.19

Word screen, WD 1.05–12
checklist for settings, WD 1.11
default settings, WD 1.07
displaying nonprinting characters, WD 1.10–11
displaying toolbars and ruler, WD 1.08–09
document view setting, WD 1.07–08
font and font size settings, WD 1.09–10
viewing, WD 1.06–07

word wrap, WD 1.21

word wrap, WIN 98 2.4, WIN 98 2.6

workbooks, EX 1.04
closing, EX 1.33–34
documenting, EX 2.33
layout, EX 1.12
opening, EX 1.10–11, EX 3.02–03

workbook window, EX 1.07

worksheet(s). *See also* **list(s)**

worksheet(s), EX 1.04
AutoSum button, EX 2.06–07
borders, EX 3.19–22
cells. *See* cell contents; cell ranges; cell references; worksheet cells
color, EX 3.22–23
columns. *See* worksheet column(s)

developing, EX 2.02
Drawing toolbar. *See* Drawing toolbar
entering, EX 2.07–08
entering data, EX 2.05–06
entering titles, EX 2.03–04
footers, EX 2.30–32, EX 3.33
formulas. *See* formula(s)
gridline display, EX 3.30–31
headers, EX 2.30–32, EX 3.33
layout, EX 2.21–28
navigating between, EX 1.12
navigating within, EX 1.07–09
planning, EX 2.02–03
previewing, EX 2.28–29, EX 3.31–32
printing. *See* printing worksheets
renaming, EX 2.14
rows. *See* worksheet rows
scrolling, EX 1.20–21
spell checking, EX 2.20–21
testing, EX 2.20

worksheet cells, EX 1.07
active, EX 1.06, EX 1.07
centering column titles, EX 3.11
centering text across, EX 3.12–13
clearing formats, EX 3.17
contents. *See* cell contents
deleting from worksheets, EX 3.18
indenting text in, EX 3.13
numbers too long to fit, EX 3.08–09
ranges. *See* cell ranges
references. *See* cell references
wrapping text in, EX 3.11–12

worksheet column(s)
centering text across, EX 3.13
centering titles, EX 3.11
changing width, EX 2.21–22, EX 3.24
deleting, EX 2.23–24

entering labels for headings, EX 2.04
hiding and unhiding, EX 3.34–35
increasing width, EX 3.09
titles. *See* worksheet column titles
underlining titles, EX 3.20

worksheet column titles
centering, EX 3.11
underlining, EX 3.20

worksheet labels, entering, EX 2.03–05

worksheet rows
deleting, EX 2.23–24
hiding and unhiding, EX 3.34–35
inserting, EX 2.22–24

worksheet window, EX 1.07

workspace, WIN 98 1.17, WIN 98 1.18

World Wide Web, WIN 98 2.1

wrapping text
text in cells, EX 3.11–12
worksheet cells, EX 3.11–12

WWW. *See* **Web entries; World Wide Web (WWW)**

Y

YEAR function, EX 2.16

yes/no data type, AC 2.05

Z

Zoom box, AC 3.30

Zoom button, Print Preview window, EX 2.29

TASK REFERENCE

TASK	PAGE #	RECOMMENDED METHOD
Access, exit	AC 1.13	Click ☒ on the program window
Access, start	AC 1.07	Click Start, point to Programs, click Microsoft Access
Action, redo	WD 2.11	Click ↻
Action, undo	WD 2.11	Click ↺
Aggregate functions, use	AC 3.34	Display the query in Design view, click Σ
Attachment, add to e-mail	OUT 1.21	Create e-mail message, click 📎, switch Look in list box to file location, double-click filename
Attachment, save	OUT 1.22	Double-click message in message list, right-click attachment icon, click Save As, change Save in list box to desired location, type filename, click Save
Attachment, view	OUT 1.23	Double-click message in message list, double-click attachment icon, click ☒
AutoComplete, use	EX 1.15	To accept Excel's suggestion, press Enter. Otherwise, continue typing a new label.
AutoContent Wizard, run	PPT 1.14	Click AutoContent Wizard on PowerPoint startup dialog box and click OK, or click File, click New, click the General tab, click AutoContent Wizard, click OK
AutoFormat, use	EX 2.28	Select the range to format, click Format, then click AutoFormat. Select desired format from Table Format list, then click OK.
AutoSum button, use	EX 2.07	Click the cell where you want sum to appear. Click Σ. Make sure the range address in the formula is the same as the range you want to sum.
Background graphic, remove	PPT 1.32	Click Format, click Background, click Omit background graphic from master, click Apply or Apply to All
Border, apply	EX 3.21	See Reference Window: Adding a Border
Bullets, add to paragraphs	WD 2.25	Select paragraphs, click ☰
Calculated field, add to a query	AC 3.31	See Reference Window: Using Expression Builder
Cancel action	EX 2.26	Press Esc, or click Undo ↺.
Cell contents, clear	EX 1.29	Select the cells you want to clear, then press Delete.
Cell contents, copy using Copy command	EX 2.10	Select the cell or range you want to copy, then click 📋.
Cell contents, copy using fill handle	EX 2.10	Click cell(s) with data or label to copy, then click and drag the fill handle to outline the cell(s) to which the data is to be copied.
Cell reference types, edit	EX 2.14	Double-click cell containing formula to be edited. Move insertion point to part of cell reference to be changed, then press F4 until reference type is correct, then press Enter.
Character, insert	WIN 98 2.6	Click where you want to insert the text, type the text
Clipboard, erase contents of	WD 2.15	Click ✂

TASK REFERENCE

TASK	PAGE #	RECOMMENDED METHOD
Clipboard contents, paste into range	EX 2.15	Click .
Colors, apply to a range of cells	EX 3.24	See Reference Window: Applying Patterns and Color
Column, adjust width of	AC 3.23	Double-click the right border of the column heading
Column width, change	EX 2.23	See Reference Window: Changing Column Width
Contacts, create	OUT 1.14	In Contacts folder, click , enter contact information, click or click
Contacts, edit	OUT 1.17	Click in contact card, make necessary corrections using keyboard, click outside contact card
Copy formula, use copy-and-paste method	EX 2.14	Select the cell with the formula to be copied, click , click the cell you want the formula copied to, then click .
Database, compact and repair	AC 1.25	Click Tools on the menu bar, point to Database Utilities, click Compact and Repair Database
Database, compact on close	AC 1.26	Click Tools on the menu bar, click Options, click the General tab, click Compact on Close, click OK
Datasheet view, switch to	AC 2.17	Click
Design view, switch to	AC 2.22	Click
Desktop, access	WIN 98 1.14	Click on the Quick Launch toolbar
Disk, copy	WIN 98 2.25	See Reference Window: Copying a Disk
Disk, format	WIN 98 2.2	Open My Computer, right-click 3½ Floppy (A:), click Format, click Start
Document, close	WD 1.30	If more than one document is open, click on title bar; if only one document is open, click on menu bar
Document, create new	WD 1.13	Click
Document, open	WD 2.02	Click , select drive and folder, click the filename, click OK
Document, preview	WD 1.26	Click
Document, print	WD 1.27	Click , or click File, click Print, specify pages or number of copies, click OK
Document, save	WD 1.17	Click
Document, save with new name	WD 2.05	Click File, click Save As, select drive and folder, enter new filename, click Save
E-mail messages, create and send to Inbox	OUT 1.11	Click , type recipient's e-mail address, topic, and message, click Send
E-mail messages, format	OUT 1.12	Select text in message body, click desired formatting buttons
E-mail messages, forward	OUT 1.20	Select message in Inbox, click , type recipient's e-mail address, type message, click
E-mail messages, print	OUT 1.20	Select message, click File, click Print, verify printer and print style, click OK

TASK REFERENCE

TASK	PAGE #	RECOMMENDED METHOD
E-mail messages, read	OUT 1.19	Click message in message list, read in preview pane
E-mail messages, receive	OUT 1.18	In Inbox or Outbox, click 📧, enter password if necessary
E-mail messages, reply to	OUT 1.19	Select message in Inbox, click 📧, type reply, click Send
E-mail messages, send from Outbox	OUT 1.13	In Inbox or Outbox, click 📧, enter password if necessary
Envelope, print	WD 1.29	Click Tools, click Envelopes and Labels, click Envelopes tab, type delivery and return addresses, click Print
Excel, exit	EX 1.34	Click File, then click Exit, or click the Excel Close button.
Excel, start	EX 1.05	Click the Start button, point to Programs, if necessary click Microsoft Office, and then click Microsoft Excel.
Explorer windows, navigate	WIN 98 2.23	Click ⇦, ⇨, or ⬆
Field, add	AC 2.23	See Reference Window: Adding a Field Between Two Existing Fields
Field, define	AC 2.08	See Reference Window: Defining a Field in a Table
Field, delete	AC 2.21	Display the table in Design view, right-click the field's row selector, click Delete Rows
Field, move	AC 2.22	Display the table in Design view, click the field's row selector, drag the field with the pointer
File, copy	WIN 98 2.22	See Reference Window: Copying a File
File, delete	WIN 98 2.24	Right-click the file, click Delete
File, move	WIN 98 2.21	See Reference Window: Moving a File
File, open from My Computer	WIN 98 2.9	Open My Computer, open the window containing the file; in Web style, click the file; in Classic style, click the file then press Enter
File, print	WIN 98 2.10	Click 🖨
File, rename	WIN 98 2.24	See Reference Window: Renaming a File
File, save	WIN 98 2.7	Click 💾
File extensions, hide	WIN 98 2.20	Open My Computer click View, click Folder Options, click View tab, make sure the Hide file extensions for known file types check box is checked, click OK
File Properties, add	WD 1.19	Click File, click Properties, click Summary tab, add desired information, click OK
Filter By Selection, activate	AC 3.18	See Reference Window: Using Filter By Selection
Folder, create	OUT 1.23	Right-click appropriate folder in Folder List, click New Folder, type folder name, verify item type, select folder location, click OK
Folder, create	WIN 98 2.21	See Reference Window: Creating a New Folder
Font, change	WD 2.27	Select text, click Font list arrow, click new font

TASK REFERENCE

TASK	PAGE #	RECOMMENDED METHOD
Font, select	EX 3.17	Select the cell or range you want to format. Click Format, click Cells, and then click the Font tab. Select the desired font from the Font List box.
Font, select size	EX 3.16	Select the cell or range you want to format. Click Format, click Cells, and then click the Font tab. Click the Font Size list arrow, then click the desired font size.
Font size, change	WD 2.27	Select text, click Font Size list arrow, click new font size
Font style, change	WD 2.29	Select text, click **B**, *I*, or U
Footer, add	EX 2.32	In the Print Preview window, click Setup, then click the Header/Footer tab in the Page Setup dialog box. Click Custom Footer and edit the existing footer in the Footer dialog box.
Footer, insert	WD 3.10	Click View, click Header and Footer, click [icon], type footer text, click Close
Format, bold	EX 3.16	Select the cell or range you want to format, then click **B**, which toggles on and off.
Format, center in cell	EX 3.12	Select the cell or range you want to format. Click [icon], which toggles on and off.
Format, center text across columns	EX 3.14	Select the cell or range with text to center. Click Format, click Cells, then click the Alignment tab. Click the Horizontal Text alignment arrow and select Center Across Selection.
Format, comma	EX 3.11	Select the cell or range of cells you want to format, then click [,].
Format, copy	EX 3.09	Select the cell or range of cells with the format you want to copy. Click [icon], then select the cell or range of cells you want to format.
Format, currency	EX 3.06	Select the cell or range of cells you want to format. Click Format, then click cells. Click the Number tab, click Currency in the Category box, then click the desired options.
Format, font		Select the cell or range you want to format. Click the Font arrow and select the desired font.
Format, indent text	EX 3.15	Select the cell or range you want to indent. Click [icon].
Format, italic	EX 3.18	Select the cell or range you want to format, then click *I*, which toggles on and off.
Format, percent	EX 3.11	Select the cell or range of cells you want to format, then click [%].
Format, wrap text	EX 3.13	Select the cell or cells you want to format. Click Format, click Cells, then click the Alignment tab. Click the Wrap text check box.
Format Painter, use	WD 2.24	Select text with desired format, double-click [icon], click paragraphs you want to format, click [icon]
Formula, enter	EX 2.08	Click the cell in which you want the result to appear. Type = and then type the rest of the formula. For formulas that include cell references, type the cell reference or select each cell using the mouse or arrow keys. When the formula is complete, press Enter.

TASK REFERENCE

TASK	PAGE #	RECOMMENDED METHOD
Formulas, display	EX 2.37	Click Tools, then click Options. Click the View tab, then click the Formulas check box.
Function, enter	EX 1.18	Type = to begin the function. Type the name of the function in either uppercase or lowercase letters, followed by an opening parenthesis. Type the range of cells you want to calculate using the function, separating the first and last cells in the range with a colon, as in B9:B15, or drag the pointer to outline the cells you want to calculate. *See also* Paste Function button, activate.
Grayscale, view	PPT 1.32	Click
Gridlines, add or remove	EX 3.32	Click Tools, click Options, then click View. Click the Gridlines check box.
Header, add	EX 2.32	In the Print Preview window, click Setup, then click Header/Footer tab in the Page Setup dialog box. Click the Custom Header button to add a header in the Header dialog box.
Help, activate	EX 1.26	*See* Reference Window: Using the Office Assistant, and Figure 1-23
Help, display topic from Contents tab	WIN 98 1.28	From Help, click the Contents tab, click until you see the topic you want, click to display topic
Help, display topic from Index tab	WIN 98 1.28	From Help, click the Index tab, scroll to locate topic, click topic, click Display
Help, get from Office Assistant	OUT 1.28	Click , type question, click Search, click topic, click
Help, get	WD 1.28	Click and type a question, click Search, click topic
Help, return to previous Help topic	WIN 98 1.30	Click
Help, start	WIN 98 1.27	Click Start , click Help
Help, use the Office Assistant to get	PPT 1.30	Click Office Assistant, click in the text box, type question, click Search, click topic, click additional help topics as necessary
Insertion point, move	WIN 98 2.5	Click the location in the document to which you want to move
Items, delete	OUT 1.30	Click item, click , click Yes
Labels, enter	EX 1.14	Select cell, then type text you want in cell.
Line spacing, change	WD 2.20	Select the text you want to change, then press CTRL+1 for single spacing, CTRL+5 for 1.5 line spacing, or CTRL+2 for double spacing
List box, change option	WIN 98 1.24	Click , then click option you want in list that appears
Mail account, set up	OUT 1.08	Click Tools, click Accounts, click Add, click Mail, in each dialog box enter information and click Next, click Finish
Margins, change	WD 2.18	Click File, click Page Setup, click Margins tab, enter margin values, click OK
Menu option, select	WIN 98 1.8	Click the menu option, or, if it is a submenu, point to it

TASK REFERENCE

TASK	PAGE #	RECOMMENDED METHOD
Message delivery options, change	OUT 1.12	Click Tools, click Options, click Mail Delivery tab, select options, click OK
Message format, choose	OUT 1.08	Click Tools, click Options, click Mail Format tab, select HTML, click OK
Messages, archive	OUT 1.25	Click File, click Archive, select desired options and folder, click Browse button, change Save in list box to appropriate location, type filename, click OK twice
Messages, file multiple	OUT 1.25	Click message in message list, hold Ctrl and click other messages, drag selected messages to desired folder in Folder List
Messages, file one	OUT 1.24	Drag message from message list to desired folder in Folder List
Messages, find	OUT 1.26	Switch to folder to search, click [icon], type search text, click Find Now
Messages, sort by multiple fields	OUT 1.27	Click desired column heading in Information Viewer, hold Shift and click other column headings
Messages, sort by one field	OUT 1.27	Click desired column heading in Information Viewer
My Computer, open	WIN 98 2.14	In Web style, click My Computer on the desktop; in Classic style, click My Computer on the desktop then press Enter
Next slide, go to	PPT 1.31	In Slide View, click [icon]
Nonprinting characters	WD 1.10	Click [¶]
Normal view, change to	WD 1.07	Click [icon]
Notes, create	PPT 1.31	Click in Notes Pane, type notes
Numbering, add to paragraphs	WD 2.25	Select paragraphs, click [icon]
Numbers, enter	EX 1.15	Select the cell, then type the number.
Office Assistant, close	WD 1.28	Click Help, click Hide Office Assistant
Office Assistant, hide	OUT 1.30	Click Help, click Hide the Office Assistant
Office Assistant, hide	PPT 1.06	Right-click Office Assistant, click Hide
Office Assistant, open	OUT 1.28	Click [icon]
Office Assistant, open	WD 1.28	Click [icon]
Office Assistant, use to get Help	AC 1.20	See Reference Window: Using the Office Assistant
Outline text, demote	PPT 1.26	In Outline Pane, place insertion point in paragraph, click [→] or press Tab
Outline text, move	PPT 1.21	In Outline Pane, click [icon] or click a bullet, drag selection up or down
Outline text, promote	PPT 1.24	In Outline Pane, place insertion point in paragraph, click [←] or press Shift + Tab
Outlook, exit	OUT 1.30	Click [X] on title bar
Outlook, start	OUT 1.04	Click Start, point to Programs, click Microsoft Outlook

TASK REFERENCE

TASK	PAGE #	RECOMMENDED METHOD
Paragraph, change indent	WD 2.23	Select paragraph, drag left or first-line indent marker on ruler; click [icon] or [icon]
Paste Function button, activate	EX 2.19	See Reference Window: Using the Paste Function button
Patterns, apply to a range of cells	EX 3.24	See Reference Window: Applying Patterns and Color
Presentation, open	PPT 1.06	Click [icon], select disk and folder, click filename, click Open
Presentation, print	PPT 1.32	Click File, click Print
Presentation, save	PPT 1.18	Click [icon]. If necessary, select disk and folder, type filename
Presentation, send via e-mail	PPT 1.34	Click File, point to Send To, click Mail Recipient
Primary key, specify	AC 2.15	See Reference Window: Specifying a Primary Key for a Table
Print Preview window, open	EX 2.30	Click [icon]
Printout, center	EX 2.31	In the Print Preview dialog box, click the Setup button. Click the Margins tab, then click the Horizontally and/or Vertically check boxes.
Printout, landscape orientation	EX 3.34	In the Print Preview window, click the Setup button. Then click the Page tab in the Page Setup dialog box, then click the Landscape option button in the Orientation box.
Program, close	WIN 98 1.12	Click [icon]
Program, close inactive	WIN 98 1.15	Right-click program button then click Close
Program, start	WIN 98 1.11	See Reference Window: Starting a Program
Program, switch to another	WIN 98 1.14	Click the program button on the taskbar that contains the name of the program to which you want to switch
Query, define	AC 3.03	Click Queries in the Objects bar, click New, click Design View, click OK
Query, run	AC 3.05	Click [icon]
Query results, sort	AC 3.15	See Reference Window: Sorting a Query Datasheet
Range, highlight	EX 1.30	Position pointer on the first cell of the range. Press and hold the mouse button and drag the mouse through the cells you want, then release the mouse button.
Range, move	EX 2.27	Select the cell or range of cells you want to move. Place the mouse pointer over any edge of the selected range until the pointer changes to an arrow. Click and drag the outline of the range to the new worksheet location.
Range, select	EX 1.30	See Range, highlight
Record, add a new one	AC 2.17	Click [icon]

TASK REFERENCE

TASK	PAGE #	RECOMMENDED METHOD
Record, delete	AC 2.30	Right-click the record's row selector, click Delete Record, click Yes
Record, move to first	AC 1.12	Click
Record, move to last	AC 1.12	Click
Record, move to next	AC 1.12	Click
Record, move to previous	AC 1.12	Click
Record, move to a specific one	AC 1.12	Type the record number in the Specific Record box, press Enter
Records, redisplay all after filter	AC 3.19	Click
Relationship, define between two tables	AC 3.08	Click
Row or column, delete	EX 2.26	Click the heading(s) of the row(s) or column(s) you want to delete, click Edit, then click Delete.
Row or column, insert	EX 2.24	Click any cell in the row/column above which you want to insert the new row/column. Click Insert and then click Rows/Columns for every row/column in the highlighted range.
Ruler, display	WD 1.09	Click View, click Ruler
Sheet, activate	EX 1.10	Click the sheet tab for the desired sheet.
Sheet tab, rename	EX 2.15	Double-click the sheet tab for the desired sheet.
Shortcut menu, activate	EX 3.10	Select the cells or objects to which you want to apply the command, click the right mouse button, then select the command you want.
Signature, create	OUT 1.09	Click Tools, click Options, click Mail Format tab, click Signature Picker, click New button, type signature name, click Start with a blank signature option, click Next, type and format signature, click OK three times
Slide, add new	PPT 1.27	Click
Slide, delete	PPT 1.20	In Outline Pane, click, press Delete. In Slide Pane, click Edit, click Delete Slide
Slide Show, exit	PPT 1.12	Press Esc
Slide Show, view	PPT 1.09	Click ; press Spacebar or click left mouse button to advance; press Backspace or right-click to go back
Slide Sorter View, switch to	PPT 1.33	Click
Sort, specify ascending	AC 3.13	Click
Sort, specify descending	AC 3.13	Click
Spell check	EX 2.22	Click Tools, click Spelling.
Spelling, correct	WD 1.23	Right-click misspelled word (as indicated by red wavy underline), click correctly spelled word

TASK REFERENCE

TASK	PAGE #	RECOMMENDED METHOD
Spelling and grammar, correct	WD 2.05	Click at the beginning of the document, click [ABC], review any errors, accept suggestions or ignore errors as desired; to type corrections directly in the document, click outside the Spelling and Grammar dialog box, make the desired correction, and then click Resume in the Spelling and Grammar dialog box
Start menu, open	WIN 98 1.7	Click [Start] or press Ctrl-Esc
Stationery, use	OUT 1.10	Click Actions, point to New Mail Message Using, click stationery name (or click More Stationery, click stationery name, click OK)
Student Disk, create	WIN 98 2.15	Click [Start], point to Programs, point to NP on Microsoft Windows 98 – Level I, click Disk 1, click OK
Style Checker, fix style problem	PPT 1.35	Click light bulb on slide, click option to fix style problem
Table, create	AC 2.07	Click Tables in the Objects bar, click New, click Design View, click OK
Table, open	AC 1.11	Click Tables in the Objects bar, click the table name, click Open
Table, print	AC 1.13	Click [printer icon]
Table structure, save	AC 2.16	See Reference Window: Saving a Table Structure
Text, align	WD 2.22	Select text, click [≡], [≡], [≡], or [≡]
Text, copy by copy and paste	WD 2.13	Select text, click [copy], move pointer to target location; then either click [paste] or, if Clipboard opens, click item to paste in Clipboard
Text, copy by drag and drop	WD 2.12	Select text, press and hold down Ctrl and drag pointer to target location, release mouse button and Ctrl key
Text, delete	WD 2.09	Press Backspace key to delete character to left of insertion point; press the Delete key to delete character to right; press Ctrl + Backspace to delete to beginning of word; press Ctrl + Delete to delete to end of word
Text, find	WD 2.15	Click [○], click [binoculars], type search text, click Find Next
Text, find and replace	WD 2.15	Click [○], click [binoculars], click Replace tab, type search text, press Tab, type replacement text, click Find Next
Text, format	WD 2.29	See "Font Style, change"
Text, move by cut and paste	WD 2.13	Select text, click [scissors], move to target location, click [paste]
Text, move by drag and drop	WD 2.12	Select text, drag pointer to target location, release mouse button
Text, select	WIN 98 2.6	Drag the pointer over the text
Text, select a block of	WD 2.09	Click at beginning of block, press and hold down Shift and click at end of block
Text, select a paragraph of	WD 2.09	Double-click in selection bar next to paragraph

TASK REFERENCE

TASK	PAGE #	RECOMMENDED METHOD
Text, select a sentence of	WD 2.09	Press Ctrl and click within sentence
Text, select entire document of	WD 2.09	Press Ctrl and click in selection bar
Text, select multiple lines of	WD 2.09	Click and drag in selection bar
Text, select multiple paragraphs of	WD 2.09	Double-click and drag in selection bar
Text box, add	EX 3.27	Click [icon] on the Drawing toolbar. Position pointer where text box is to appear, then click and drag to outline desired size and shape. Type comment in box.
Toolbar, add or remove	EX 3.26	Click any toolbar with right mouse button. Click the name of the toolbar you want to use/remove from the shortcut menu.
Toolbar, display	WD 1.08	Right-click any visible toolbar, click name of desired toolbar
Toolbar button, select	WIN 98 1.24	Click the toolbar button
Toolbars, control display	WIN 98 2.17	Click View, point to Toolbars, then select the toolbar options you want
ToolTip, view	WIN 98 1.7	Position the pointer over the tool
Undo button, activate	EX 2.26	Click [icon]
View, change	WIN 98 2.18	Click View then click the view option you want
View, switch	OUT 1.16	Click View, point to Current View, click desired view
Web style, switch to	WIN 98 2.12	Click [Start], point to Settings, click Folder Options, click Web style, click OK
Web view, switch to	WIN 98 2.18	Open My Computer, click View then click as Web Page
Window, maximize	WIN 98 1.20	Click [icon]
Window, minimize	WIN 98 1.18	Click [icon]
Window, move	WIN 98 1.21	Drag the title bar
Window, redisplay	WIN 98 1.20	Click the program button on the taskbar
Window, resize	WIN 98 1.21	Drag [icon]
Window, restore	WIN 98 1.20	Click [icon]
Windows 98, shut down	WIN 98 1.15	Click [Start], click Shut Down, click the Shut Down option button, click OK
Windows 98, start	WIN 98 1.4	Turn on the computer
Word, exit	WD 1.30	Close all open documents, then click [X] on the title bar
Word, start	WD 1.05	Click Start, point to Programs, click Microsoft Word

TASK REFERENCE

TASK	PAGE #	RECOMMENDED METHOD
Workbook, open	EX 1.10	Click 📂 (or click File, then click Open). Make sure the Look in box displays the name of the folder containing the workbook you want to open, then click Open.
Workbook, save with a new name	EX 1.21	Click File, then click Save As. Change the workbook name as necessary. Specify the folder in which to save workbook in the Save in box. Click Save.
Workbook, save with same name	EX 1.21	Click 💾
Worksheet, close	EX 1.33	Click File, then click Close, or click the worksheet Close button.
Worksheet, print	EX 1.31	Click 🖨 to print without adjusting any print options. Use the Print command on the File menu to adjust options.

Windows 98 Level I File Finder

Location in Tutorial	Name and Location of Data File	Student Saves File As...	Student Creates New File
WINDOWS 98 LEVEL I, DISK 1 & 2			
Tutorial 2			
Session 2.1			Practice Text.doc
Session 2.2 *Note:* Students copy the contents of Disk 1 onto Disk 2 in this session.	Agenda.doc Budget98.wks Budget99.wks Exterior.bmp Interior.bmp Logo.bmp Members.wdb Minutes.wps Newlogo.bmp Opus27.mid Parkcost.wks Proposal.doc Resume.doc Sales.wks Sample Text.doc Tools.wks Travel.wps Practice Text.doc *(Saved from Session 2.1)*		
Tutorial Assignments	*Note:* Students continue to use the Student disks they used in the Tutorial. For certain Assignments, they will need a 3rd blank disk.	Resume 2.doc *(saved from Resume.doc)*	Letter.doc Song.doc

Note: The "NP on Microsoft Windows 98-Level I" Make Student Disk Program must be installed to obtain the student files for the Windows 98 tutorials.

Word Level I File Finder

Location in Tutorial	Name and Location of Data File	Student Saves File As...	Student Creates File
WORD LEVEL I, DISK 1			
Tutorial 1			
Session 1.2			Tutorial.01\Tutorial\Tacoma Job Fair Letter.doc
Review Assignments			Tutorial.01\Review\Job Fair Reminder.doc
Case Problem 1			Tutorial.01\Cases\Confirmation Letter.doc
Case Problem 2			Tutorial.01\Cases\Rock Climbing Request Letter.doc
Case Problem 3			Tutorial.01\Cases\Awards Memo.doc
Case Problem 4			Tutorial.01\Cases\My Template Letter.doc

Word Level I File Finder

Location in Tutorial	Name and Location of Data File	Student Saves File As...	Student Creates File
WORD LEVEL I, DISK 1			
Tutorial 2			
Session 2.1	Tutorial.02\Tutorial\Annuity.doc	Tutorial.02\Tutorial\RHS Annuity Plan.doc	
Session 2.2	Tutorial.02\Tutorial\RHS Annuity Plan.doc *(Saved from Session 2.1)*	Tutorial.02\Tutorial\RHS Annuity Plan Copy 2.doc Tutorial.02\Tutorial\RHS Annuity Plan Final Copy.doc	
Review Assignments	Tutorial.02\Review\RHSQuart.doc Tutorial.02\Review\RHSPort.doc	Tutorial.02\Review\RHSQuarterly Report.doc Tutorial.02\Review\RHS Portfolio Changes	
Case Problem 1	Tutorial.02\Cases\Store.doc	Tutorial.02\Cases\Store-It-All Policies.doc	
Case Problem 2	Tutorial.02\Cases\UpTime.doc	Tutorial.02\Cases\UpTime Training Summary.doc	
Case Problem 3	Tutorial.02\Cases\Ridge	Tutorial.02\Cases\Ridge Top Guide.doc	
Case Problem 4			Tutorial.02\Cases\Restaurant Review.doc Tutorial.02\Cases\Edited Restaurant Review.doc

Excel Level I File Finder

Location in Tutorial	Name and Location of Data File	Student Saves File As...	Files the Student Creates from Scratch
EXCEL LEVEL I, DISK 1			
Tutorial 1			
Session 1.1	Tutorial.01\Tutorial\Inwood.xls		
Session 1.2	Tutorial.01\Tutorial\Inwood.xls	Tutorial.01\Tutorial\Inwood 2.xls	
Review Assignments	Tutorial.01\Review\Inwood 3.xls	Tutorial.01\Review\Inwood 4.xls	
Case Problem 1	Tutorial.01\Cases\Enroll.xls	Tutorial.01\Cases\Enrollment.xls	
Case Problem 2	Tutorial.01\Cases\Budget.xls	Tutorial.01\Cases\BudgetSol.xls	
Case Problem 3	Tutorial.01\Cases\Medical.xls	Tutorial.01\Cases\Medical 2.xls	
Case Problem 4			Tutorial.01\Cases\CashCounter.xls
Tutorial 2			
Session 2.1			Tutorial.02\Tutorial\MSI Sales Report.xls
Session 2.2	Tutorial.02\Tutorial\MSI Sales Report.xls *(Saved from Session 2.1)*	Tutorial.02\Tutorial\MSI Sales Report.xls	
Review Assignments	Tutorial.02\Review\MSI 1.xls	Tutorial.02\Review\MSI Sales Report 2.xls	
Case Problem 1			Tutorial.02\Cases\MJ Income.xls
Case Problem 2			Tutorial.02\Cases\Arline.xls
Case Problem 3	Tutorial.02\Cases\Fresh.xls	Tutorial.02\Cases\Fresh Air Sales Incentives.xls	
Case Problem 4			Tutorial.02\Cases\Portfolio.xls

Excel Level I File Finder

Location in Tutorial	Name and Location of Data File	Student Saves File As...	Files the Student Creates from Scratch
EXCEL LEVEL I, DISK 1			
Tutorial 3			
Tutorial, Session 3.1	Tutorial.03\Tutorial\Pronto.xls	Tutorial.03\Tutorial\Pronto Salsa Company.xls	
Tutorial, Session 3.2	Tutorial.03\Tutorial\Pronto Salsa Company.xls *(Saved from Session 3.1)*	Tutorial.03\Tutorial\Pronto Salsa Company.xls	
Review Assignments	Tutorial.03\Review\Pronto 2.xls Tutorial.03\Review\Explore3.xls	Tutorial.03\Review\Pronto 3.xls Tutorial.03\Review\Pronto 4.xls Tutorial.03\Review\Explore3 Solution.xls	
Case Problem 1	Tutorial.03\Cases\Running.xls	Tutorial.03\Cases\Running2.xls	
Case Problem 2	Tutorial.03\Cases\Recycle.xls	Tutorial.03\Cases\Recycle2.xls Tutorial.03\Cases\Recycle Data.xls Tutorial.03\Cases\Recycle3.xls	
Case Problem 3	Tutorial.03\Cases\StateGov.xls	Tutorial.03\Cases\State Government.xls	
Case Problem 4			Tutorial.03\Cases\Payroll.xls

Access Level I File Finder

Location in Tutorial	Name and Location of Data File	Student Creates New File
Tutorial 1		
Session 1.1	Disk1\Tutorial\Restaurant.mdb	
Session 1.2	Disk1\Tutorial\Restaurant.mdb	
Review Assignments	Disk2\Review\Customer.mdb	
Case Problem 1	Disk3\Cases\MallJobs.mdb	
Case Problem 2	Disk4\Cases\Payments.mdb	
Case Problem 3	Disk5\Cases\Walks.mdb	
Case Problem 4	Disk6\Cases\Lexus.mdb	
Tutorial 2		
Session 2.1	Disk1\Tutorial\Restaurant.mdb *(continued from Session 1.2)*	
Session 2.2	Disk1\Tutorial\Restaurant.mdb *(continued from Session 2.1)* Disk1\Tutorial\Valle.mdb	
Review Assignments	Disk2\Review\Barbara.mdb Disk2\Review\Coffee.dbf	Disk2\Review\Valle Products.mdb
Case Problem 1	Disk3\Cases\MallJobs.mdb *(continued from Tutorial 1)* Disk3\Cases\Openings.mdb	
Case Problem 2	Disk4\Cases\Payments.mdb *(continued from Tutorial 1)* Disk4\Cases\PlusPays.mdb	
Case Problem 3	Disk5\Cases\Walks.mdb *(continued from Tutorial 1)* Disk5\Cases\Pledge.db	
Case Problem 4	Disk6\Cases\Lexus.mdb *(continued from Tutorial 1)* Disk6\Cases\Lopez.xls	
Tutorial 3		
Session 3.1	Disk1\Tutorial\Restaurant.mdb *(continued from Session 2.2)*	
Session 3.2	Disk1\Tutorial\Restaurant.mdb *(continued from Session 3.1)*	
Review Assignments	Disk2\Review\Valle Products.mdb *(continued from Tutorial 2)*	
Case Problem 1	Disk3\Cases\MallJobs.mdb *(continued from Tutorial 2)*	
Case Problem 2	Disk4\Cases\Payments.mdb *(continued from Tutorial 2)*	
Case Problem 3	Disk5\Cases\Walks.mdb *(continued from Tutorial 2)*	
Case Problem 4	Disk6\Cases\Lexus.mdb *(continued from Tutorial 2)*	

PowerPoint Level I File Finder

Location in Tutorial	Name and Location of Data File	Student Saves File As...	Files from Scratch
Tutorial 1			
Session 1.1	Tutorial.01\Tutorial\Customer.ppt	Customer.ppt	
Session 1.2			Brainstorming for Sales Reps.ppt
Review Assignment	Tutorial.01\Review\Sales.ppt	New Marketing Campaign.ppt	
Case Problem 1	Tutorial.01\Cases\Mailmndr.ppt	MailMinder.ppt	
Case Problem 2	Tutorial.01\Cases\Juica.ppt	Juica Juice Capital.ppt	
Case Problem 3			Personal Liability Insurance.ppt

Outlook File Finder

Location in Tutorial	Name and Location of Data File	Student Saves File As...	Student Creates New File
OUTLOOK			
Tutorial 1	Tutorial.01\Tutorial\Sales.xls	Tutorial.01\Tutorial\Second Quarter Sales.xls	
Review Assignment	Tutorial.01\Review\Tea.doc	Tutorial.01\Review\Tea Health Benefits.doc	Tutorial.01\Review\Archive.pst
Case Problem 1	Tutorial.01\Cases\Amendments.doc		Tutorial.01\Cases\ (Each message in Answers subfolder).htm
Case Problem 2			Tutorial.01\Cases\Guest List.doc Tutorial.01\Cases\(message).htm